The Monster Book of Canadian Monsters

The
Monster Book of
Canadian Monsters

JOHN ROBERT COLOMBO

2004

Book Design · David Shaw

Images: (Top left) Matt Fox, Wendigo (detail), *Famous Fantastic Mysteries*, June 1944. / (Top right) B. Kroup, Lake Utopia Monster (detail), *Canadian Illustrated News*, 30 Nov. 1872. / (Bottom left) The Golden Eagle (mirrored), Thomas Boreman, editor, *A Description of Three Hundred Animals* ... (1786) / (Bottom right) Untitled surrealist collage (detail), André Breton's *La Femme 100 Têtes* (Paris: Editions du Carrefour, 1929). / (Frontispiece) Untitled illustration, Henri de Graffigny's *Voyage de cinq Américains dans les planètes* (Paris, 1925) / Sources: The Toronto Public Library, The Osborne Collection of Early Children's Books / The Toronto Public Library, The Merril Collection of Science Fiction, Speculation and Fantasy.

National Library of Canada Cataloguing in Publication

Colombo, John Robert, 1936-
  The monster book of Canadian monsters / John Robert Colombo.

Includes bibliographical references and index.
ISBN 1-55246-565-9

  1. Monsters. I. Title.

QL89.C64 2004   001.944   C2003-907413-7

Printed in Canada
First Printing June 2004

All Inquiries and Orders;
George A. Vanderburgh, *Publisher*
THE BATTERED SILICON DISPATCH BOX™
Fax: (519) 925-3482 * *e-Mail:* gav@bmts.com

P. O. Box 204
Shelburne, Ontario
CANADA L0N 1S0

P. O. Box 122
Sauk City, Wisconsin
U.S.A. 53583-0122

We are as ignorant of the meaning of the dragon
as we are of the meaning of the universe.

Jorge Luis Borges

Contents

Preface · *9*
Acknowledgements · *13*

PART THREE · **CREATURES OF AIR**
(Atmosphere, plasma, ether, sky)

PART FOUR · **CREATURES OF FIRE**
(Flames, intelligences, aliens, dimensions)

Preface

THE MONSTER BOOK OF CANADIAN MONSTERS, plausibly the wildest and weirdest book ever published in this country, seems certainly the most monstrous. It is a big book, 962,035 characters in length, 212,845 words long, and the bulk of it consists of 200-odd accounts of encounters with monsters and other mysterious beings, entities, and energies. The encounters were recorded at irregular intervals over the last four centuries by men and women who were often as baffled by these events and experiences as are readers of the present-day. The episodes took place in Canada, or early Canada, or they occurred to Canadians. In large part the witnesses themselves describe their own experiences, though some second-hand and third-hand accounts have been included. As records of events and experiences, the first-person accounts are told as true.

So the narratives that comprise this tome are weird in deed and in nature, using the word *weird* to refer to the terrific and the horrific. Readers are advised to clutch the margins of these pages because the words on them describe monsters, menaces, and mysteries, both beings and non-beings: cryptids (species unknown to science and society), supernatural forces (spirits, spectres, poltergeists), alien entities (humanoid creatures), jinxes (fireships, hoodoo vessels), visions (hallucinations), etc. All are to greater or lesser degrees held to be monstrous.

The monsters that appear in these pages are beings or non-beings in their own right. They are not literary creations that flow from the pens of writers of imaginative fiction. While it is true that one does not need to be a writer of imaginative fiction to tell tall tales, each episode is taken to be a record of an objective event or subjective experience. (There is no way to prove their nature one way or the other.) In point of fact, each account is a *memorate*, to use the folklorist's term for a first-person story of an occurrence that is meant to "fix" an experience by sharing it with a small circle of relatives, friends, or associates. Its aim is to "fix," not to convince. The reader may wish to relegate these narratives to the contested middle ground between folklore and reportage, the no-man's-land or the state of *liminality* or *imaginality*, between what we know we believe and what we believe we know.

These accounts are taken from a great variety of sources that have appeared since the 16th century, and they include the journals and records of explorers and adventurers, traders and pioneers, settlers and travellers, country folk and urban dwellers, scholars and scientists. Some of the accounts are straight-forward enough; others are couched in words of qualification. Not a few require that readers of today keep in mind Coleridge's famous statement about "the willing suspension of disbelief." (The words come from Samuel Taylor Coleridge's *Biographia Literaria* [1817], Chapter 14, where the poet writes about "that willing suspension of disbelief for the moment, which constitutes poetic faith." Indeed, the message of Coleridge's words may be usefully inverted: From time to time readers should be willing to suspend not *disbelief* but *belief*.) All of these accounts are highly readable, yet each one of them is remarkable in its own particular way, being part of its own darkness, yet shedding rays of light on the dark areas of the reader's inner life. While they may bask in our ignorance of the things of the night, they may also question boundaries, the *liminal* state, the *teremos*, or the *imaginal* realm, where our knowledge ends and human ignorance begins.

In the pages that follow, the monsters are grouped according to the four traditional elements of Earth, Water, Air, and Fire.

Creatures of Earth, like Sasquatch or Bigfoot, the Werewolf and the Windigo, are those that live off the land, fields, prairies, foothills, woods, forests, mountains, taiga, tundra, etc.

Creatures of Water, like sea serpents and lake monsters, Sedna and Misshipisshu, mermaids and mermen, survive in the country's streams, ponds, marshes, lakes, rivers, seas, oceans, and beneath thick ice.

Creatures of Air, like ghosts and spirits, the Wynyard crisis apparition, the revenant of Mackenzie King, the spectres and wraiths, seem to infect the very air we breath and haunt the ambience and the atmosphere if not the ether that is said to connect and be common to all things living and non-living.

Creatures of Fire, like fire-starters of the past and alien beings of the future, Jennie Bramwell and the alien craft of the Falcon Lake Encounter, dwell in the heart of combustion and in conflagration and in space, creatures from other solar planets or other solar systems or forces from dimensions unknown to reason yet apparently accessible to experience.

The reader may well ask, "Why an anthology of Canadian monsters?"

"Why not?" the anthologist may ask in response. "Monsters are part of mankind's past and man's psyche. They make surprising appearances in accounts of Canada's history, heritage, society, and culture. If only to be well informed — and well frightened! — we should know more about them!"

The time and the place were appropriate for the compilation of this work. Inspiration struck me on the eve of Halloween 2002, while I was browsing among the books at the Leaside Public Library in Toronto. I was staring at the titles in the section devoted to folklore of the supernatural variety. The word "Canadian" on the spine of one book caught my attention, then the word "Monsters" on the spine of another book. I felt a *frisson* of fear, appropriate for October 31st and for categories 001 and 133 of the Dewey Decimal System classification! The book was born that moment. I hope readers will share that conception and that fright with me.

From the first I resolved that I would collect descriptions of encounters with *real* monsters, not imagined ones. I would sidestep the creatures described in *belles-lettres* and make my way through the thicket of Canadian non-fiction, memoirs, documentaries, and news stories, blazing a trail of real-life adventures. I succeeded in doing that in short order because for four decades I have been collecting anomalistic materials — Canadian references to the supernatural, the paranormal, the mysterious, and the occult. (These key words refer to accounts of custom, behaviour, emotion, and thought.) During the forty years I wrote or edited some two dozen books devoted to the supernatural and the paranormal in Canadian history and lore. (I also edited a number of anthologies of fantastic literature — tales of fantasy fiction, science fiction, and weird fiction, Canadian "firsts.")

Many of the accounts that appear in these pages made early appearances in some earlier books, though their earliest appearances were in old tomes, journals, magazines, and the columns of newspapers, some centuries old. Through it all I came to appreciate the fact that the grim and the grotesque are not strangers to Canadians but companions, even "kissing cousins." There is a grotesque or gothic element or dimension to the country's official iconography, its heraldic imagery. Gargoyles stare down on visitors to Parliament Hill. Fantastic beasts are emblazoned on the Dominion's Coat of Arms, including griffins, unicorns, hippogriphs, and fire-spewing dragons. Canada Post has issued stamps to honour the country's monsters and its superheroes. (The four monsters so honoured in 1990 were Ogopogo, Sasquatch, the Kraken, and the Loup-garou / Werewolf. In a similar vein, four superheroes were commemorated in 1996: Superman, Nelvana of the Northern Lights, Johnny Canuck, Captain Canuck, and Fleur de Lys.) These accounts, images, and activities reflect the fact that monsters dwell in the corridors of our collective imagination.

After you read these descriptions of events and experiences, perhaps you will agree with me that we share the land, the sea, the air, and symbolically the fires of energy, with beings and creatures we barely recognize or identify with the Dominion of Canada. We have read about them in the literatures of Greece and Rome. They are familiar to us from accounts of life and thought in the Middle Ages of Europe. They live in myths, legends, folklore, and urban lore. They permeate our everyday lives. We read about them in thrillers by Stephen King and Tim Wynne-Jones, and watch them in major motion pictures and in television series–notably the horror films of the director David Cronenberg (a.k.a. "Dave Deprave").

Is there a child among us who has not been "frightened to death" by the Goblin, the Sandman, or the Bogey Man? I am sure that I was not alone when, as a youngster, I was petrified by thoughts of "the creature that lurks under the bed," and dared not dangle my arms over the edges of the bed lest my hands be seized and I be pulled off the bed and under it! As youths at summer camps, we felt thrills and chills when the counsellors told us tales about the crazy hermit (or escaped killer) who lurked in the woods and peered into the windows and rattled the doors of our cabins. As adults, from time to time, we have experienced fear and fright if not the shock of terror on dark city streets at night. We wonder about what we will encounter at the moment of death..and maybe beyond that moment. We are lucky. Not many of us will find ourselves caught in the clutches of creatures or critters of the sort recalled in these pages, yet all of us are able to *imagine* what it would be like. We are able to *recall* some deeply disturbing experiences from the past, or we may know a friend (what urban folklorists like to call a FOAF, a friend of a friend) who

Two separate sets of stamps were issued by Canada Post to honour the country's monsters and superheroes. Ogopogo, Sasquatch, Kraken, and Loup-garou/Werewolf appeared in October 1990. Six years later — in the nick of time! — came Nelvana, Captain Canuck, Fleur de Lys, Johnny Canuck, and Superman.

has an eerie episode to relate that would be quite "at home" in this collection.

Each episode, whether an event or an experience, is unique. Yet the objects — if not the subjects — of these encounters have some characteristics in common. Here are a number of the distinguishing features of the monsters whose exploits are recalled in these pages.

In the first place, each monster has to constitute a menace, a malevolence, a malignancy, a potential threat to our lives or our well-being — to our bodies, to our emotions, to our states of mind, to our states of souls, even to "the order of things" or "the world as we know it." I have interpreted "menace" most broadly to include some experiences that are religious in nature that might seem appealing to pious believers (but certainly oppressive to confirmed sceptics!).

In the second place, there had to be a vivid description of creature or encounter that would grip and enthrall present-day readers. The authors of these accounts are not poets or dramatic writers, so they devote hardly any time to setting the stage, describing the cast of characters, articulating the themes, or anticipating the reactions of readers or listeners. Yet their descriptions, bare-bones as many of them are, seem humanly riveting.

In the third place, variety was a requirement, as the reader does not expect to meet essentially the same beast or being page after page. Indeed, it would have been a simple task to fill the book to overflowing with descriptions of the Windigo, or the Sasquatch, and while it might have added to the reader's understanding of the constitutions and habits of those creatures, nothing would have been added to the variety or the appeal of the menagerie of menace.

In the fourth place, on purpose there is no definition of the elusive word *monster*, which is assumed to refer to a being or a non-being that is a menace to mankind and the world because of its size, its shape, its power, its energy, or its motive force. Monster is often equated with size. A virus magnified many times would be monstrous; also monstrous would be a human being who was miniaturized, a micro-man, micro-woman, or micro-baby. As well, a monster may be corporeal or incorporeal, a substance or a shadow. He, she, or it may be categorized as animal, vegetable, human, or even mineral (as in a strange meteorite, a totemic object, or a radioactive substance). It is easier to think of a monster as demonic than as angelic, to be sure; yet the appearance of a host of angels in a public square would wreak havoc in the world as we know it. As well, the notion of the monster includes the propensity for devastation and evil.

In the fifth place, while the witnesses describe their reactions to what they experienced, they do not necessarily believe in the existence of spirits, werewolves, fire-ships, etc. One or other of my guiding maxims may prove to be useful here: "Ghosts belong to the category of experience, not to the category of existence." "We do not have to believe in ghosts to believe in ghost stories." Witnesses know how they reacted but not necessarily what caused those responses — those sensations, feelings, or thoughts. This may seem to be paradoxical, but inconsistency seems to be characteristic of human beings and the order of things. We willingly discuss entities which may or may not exist (unicorns, griffins, ghosts, spirits, gods, auras, values, to name a few) if only to engage in debates about their properties and whether existence is included among them.

In the sixth place, here are beings "whose powers are not ours." The creatures are inferior to mankind. They exist on a lower level than does man, yet they possess some ability, talent, mastery, priority, superiority, power, or energy that is lacking in us. The creature, then, is superior in one respect and may overpower and immobilize us, dehumanize or destroy us. Face to face with these critters, we learn to appreciate our strengths and our weaknesses in the face of the unknown. They represent the elements of shock and surprise and cathartic change.

In the seventh place, from reading these accounts, we may observe how people before us have remembered, recorded, and communicated their basic fears of the unknown, whether their images are those of beings who lurk in the cellars or the attics of our homes or on the landings of haunted houses or in the niches of our psychies or in the depths of the Earth or in the far reaches of outer space. Their histories are intriguing. The earliest descriptions are best regarded as fanciful expressions, and these are followed by interpretations that verge on the supernatural, and these in turn are followed by explanations of impressions that veer to the naturalistic or verge on the realistic. Thereafter there appear psychical and parapsychological accounts couched in semi-scientific vocabularies that are all their own. Finally, there are the psychological descriptions of our own time, which are perhaps the most compelling of all, at least for readers of the present day.

In the eighth place, reading these descriptions of dreadful encounters, the reader may wish to categorize them. There are two categories that are readily apparent. There is the threat of physical destruction — think in terms of the Frankenstein monster, which is the basis of *horror*. Then there is the threat of psychological assault — think in terms of Count Dracula, which is the basis of *terror*. The assault is on the body and brain or on the mind and spirit. The present collection offers both types — threats and assaults of physical horror and psychological terror.

In the ninth place, we should realize that in our heart of hearts we yearn to experience the *frisson* of fear. It is human to admit fear, to be scared, to be frightened, to feel goose-bumps, to shiver with dread, to sweat it out! Entrepreneurs in the entertainment industry have grown rich meeting this basic human need. (Many a swimming pool in Hollywood would not be in operation but for the Creature from the Black Lagoon.) Fear is big business because it plays an important role in our lives and hence in our psyches. These are creatures or constructions that are part of us and that call for recognition; the beings are part of our being. We may doubt that they exist in the "real" world, but in the final analysis the wisest among us would not wish to begrudge them the benefit of a doubt. We may or may not be willing to admit to a belief in their objective existences, yet undeniable are the effects of their subjective existences. (There may even be a domain that singles the doubles: the liminal state, the imaginal realm.) I expect that the level-headed and generous of heart among us will exclaim, "Okay, so what if ... ?"

In the tenth place, I have striven to represent the various kinds or breeds of monsters that propagate in this country or that reside in the minds of its inhabitants. I have tried to do justice to its most celebrated creatures, yet there are so many of them. They are legion. All I have been able to do is scratch the surface. Innumerable books and articles in magazines and journals are devoted to such creatures as Ogopogo, Sasquatch, and Windigo, so I have under-represented the country's most terrible trio. I have done less than justice to some other creatures or beings that deserve to join the threesome. Among these, in Eskimo or Inuit traditions, are Sedna, the goddess of the sea and the guardian of the seals, as well as the Skraelings (dwarfish people) and the Tunnit (giant people) of the past. Among the traditions of the Indians or First Nations traditions, will be encountered a wealth of super-beings, including transformer / trickster figures like Nanabush and Coyote, and aquatic or submarine beings like Misshipisshu, the spirit of the waters, and all of these could qualify for inclusion. I cannot conjure up first-hand descriptions of encounters with these beings, yet I am sometimes able to draw attention to the shadows they cast and to their existence here.

Do such monsters really exist — these animals, beasts, brutes, beings, creatures, demons, devils, entities, fiends, monstrosities, ogres?

Of course not. Certainly not in Canada today!

And yet ... and yet ... responsible, sober-sided citizens have testified to sensing, seeing, hearing, feeling, touching, smelling, and in some instances tasting these creepy creations. Perhaps they are living legacies of the past.

The Swiss psychologist Carl Jung addressed the question of the veridicality of creatures like these in different ways at different times. The young analytical psychologist, influenced by his mentor Sigmund Freud, observed that we project onto the world around us our highest hopes and our deepest fears. These are "transferences" or "projections." The elder sage, influenced by the I Ching and alchemy, inched toward the notion that the dynamic, especially when allied with what he called the "the uncanny," may produce "transferences" or "projections" that are more than private; they are public "exteriorizations." The latter exhibit characteristics that are both objective and subjective, material and immaterial. He referred to flying saucers as "mandalas" but also as "things seen in the sky." He interestingly compared the unseen world with the seen world to an airplane propeller. At low speeds, the propeller is visible; at high speeds, it is invisible. Are we dealing here with low-speed and high-speed worlds?

Some years ago the literary critic Tzvetan Todorov observed that the hallmark of the fantastic in art and in reality is a temporal one: that moment of "hesitation" when it suddenly strikes us "that such things may be." So, set the ontological status of these creatures to one side. Sit down in an easy chair, before a roaring fire in the fireplace. Glance to the left, glance to the right, look above, look below, peer behind, squint ahead ... then open this weird book at random and begin to read....

ACKNOWLEDGEMENTS

Accompanying me on this expedition into the interior of a continent, a country, and a consciousness were trusted companions, researcher Alice Neal and librarian Philip Singer. They were able to make use of the holdings of the Toronto Reference Library and the Toronto Public Library system, where members of the staff were unfailingly courteous and helpful and where library interloans were arranged through the kind offices of Norman McMullen.

My attention was drawn to numerous accounts that would otherwise have gone unseen and unnoted by fellow researchers Dwight Whalen of Niagara Falls, Ont., Chris Rutkowski of Winnipeg, Man., and W. Ritchie Benedict of Calgary, Alta.

I wish to acknowledge the assistance and support of my wife Ruth, whose preference for rational beings over irrational ones is one of long standing.

Publication was made possible by George A. Vanderburgh of The Battered Silicon Dispatch Box, to whom I wish to express my gratitude.

Let me add that because the text is an assembly of documents and not a single-authored work, on display are numerous variations in style, spelling, punctuation, usage, reference, etc. Except for the correction of typographical errors, the documents are reproduced in the main as they were originally printed or published. The epigraph has been adapted from a sentence that appears in *The Book of Imaginary Beings* (New York, 1957) written by Jorge Luis Borges with Margaritta Guerro and translated by Norman Thomas di Giovanni.

PART ONE

Creatures of Earth

IN THIS section appear depictions and descriptions of the monstrous creatures that are identified with the planet Earth. These are beings that may dwell on the surface of the earth or make their habitation beneath the ground, spawning in its dank caves or in the dank caverns to be found in the interior of the earth. These creatures may take refuge from the preying eyes of man in woodlands, the foothills, or the mountains. The accounts go back a bit in time. The earliest dates from the year 1691, the latest the year 1981.

We like to think of the planet Earth as the home of our race, of mankind, of *Homo sapiens*, and it is our homeland. But over the geological ages, it has also been held to be the domain of legions of other creatures and beings, both great and small, both known and unknown.

"There were giants in the earth in those days; and also after that...." (Genesis 6:4) There were also minute life forms of great weirdness. The Burgess Shale of British Columbia, formed 530 million years ago, is today a site of immense geological interest, what with the remains of an ancient sea wherein swam strange creatures, including Opabinia, a sea-being with five eyes, and Pikaia, the first known chordate or creature with a backbone. Stephen Jay Gould devoted a book *Wonderful Life: The Burgess Shale and the Nature of History* (1989) to these pre-Cambrian creatures.

Who knows what other manner of creature roamed the Earth in prehuman or prehistoric times? Fossil-hunters have some answers to that question, for their finds prove the existence of giant creatures like dinosaurs and pterodactyls that once walked the face of the earth and flew its heavy skies.

In the ancient past, classical scholars inform us, the bards recited the genealogies of the gods, and the poets recounted the tales of the demi-gods, the Titans, the Olympians, and the races of giants. Then there are the legends and tales that delight collectors of folklore, old and urban, that tell about giants and dwarfish creatures.

Five hundred years ago, imaginative cartographers added flourishes to their maps of the polar regions of the globe, delineating unicorns, serpents, and unipeds to add to our fauna. Closer to our own time, imaginative writers populated the caverns, crevices, fissures, and pits of the Earth with forms of life that are hostile to our own kind. Contemporary accounts bear witness to the present-day appearances of creatures who may wander our woodlands or inhabit the foothills of our mountainous regions. Are memories or descendants of these creatures to be found lurking under the eaves of dusty attics and in the dank corners of the basements of our homes ... in closets ... under beds....

If so, watch out for them!

ON ORIGINS

Chrestien LeClercq (1641-*c.* 1700), a Recollect missionary from France, arrived in Quebec in 1675 and conducted an itinerant mission which extended from the Gaspé to the Miramichi River, sometimes going as far as the Sainte-Croix River in present-day Maine. In Paris in 1691, he published an account of his observations, travels, and missionary work among the Gaspesiens (the Micmacs, now the Mi'Kmaq), for whom he devised a system of hieroglyphics. The text of his book preserves some of the intriguing traditions of the Micmacs. It was translated for the Champlain Society by William F. Ganong as *New Relation of Gaspesia with the Customs and Religion of the Gaspesian Indians* (1910).

Among the traditions of the Micmacs that LeClercq records is the legend of the arrival by sea of pre-Columbian white colonists who suffered a shipwreck and lost all their possessions except for their Christian faith and their fishing and hunting skills. The tradition is interesting in light of the work of investigator and researcher Michael Bradley who in his intriguing book *Holy Grail Across the Atlantic* (1988) suggested that rubble on a farm outside New Ross, N.S., is all that remains of a "crusader castle" that once, for a brief time, housed the Holy Grail.

LeClercq, alluding only to "the sacred mysteries of our holy Religion," records the basic legend in Chapter II, "On the Origin of the Gaspesians," which is reprinted here.

The origin of these peoples, and the manner in which this new world has become inhabited by an almost infinite multitude of peoples of many different nations, seems to us so obscure that, even after the most careful and most exact researches which have been made into the subject up to the present time, every one must admit and frankly confess it to be impossible to have any exact and trustworthy knowledge about it.

It seems as if this secret must be reserved solely to the Indians, and that from them alone one ought to learn all the truth about it, seeing that, indeed, there has been a time among ourselves when it was unknown that there was a North America, which even the most learned made no difficulty in assigning to the extra-mundane regions, since they were unable to locate it within the compass of their minds; and it is not yet two hundred years since the first discovery of it was made. Our Gaspesians, however, can teach us nothing certain upon this subject, perhaps because they have no knowledge of letters, which could give them information as to their ancestors and their origin. They have, indeed, if you will, some dim and fabulous notion of the creation of the world, and of the deluge. They say that when the sun, which they have always recognized and worshipped as their God, created all this great universe, he divided the earth immediately into several parts, wholly separated one from the other by great lakes: that in each part he caused to be born one man and one woman, and

they multiplied and lived a very long time: but that having become wicked along with their children, who killed one another, the sun wept with grief thereat, and the rain fell from the heaven in such great abundance that the waters mounted even to the summit of the rocks, and of the highest and most lofty mountains. This flood, which, say they, was general all over the earth, compelled them to set sail in their bark canoes, in order to save themselves from the raging depths of this general deluge. But it was in vain, for they all perished miserably through a violent wind which overturned them, and overwhelmed them in this horrible abyss, with the exception, however, of certain old men and of certain women, who had been the most virtuous and the best of all the Indians. God came then to console them for the death of their relatives and their friends, after which he let them live upon the earth in a great and happy tranquillity, granting them therewith all the skill and ingenuity necessary for capturing beavers and moose in as great number as were needed for their subsistence. They add also certain other wholly ridiculous circumstances, which I purposely omit, because they do not bear at all upon a secret which is unknown to men, and reserved to God alone.

Others hold that this new world has been peopled by certain individuals who, having embarked upon the sea for the purpose of establishing a colony in foreign parts, were surprised by storm and tempest, which threw them upon the coasts of North America. Here they were unfortunately shipwrecked, and, with their ships, they lost everything which they must have had with them of property, and of the things which they valued most in the world. Affairs were such that this shipwreck having left them wholly without hope of ever returning into their own country, they resolved to set to work in earnest at the preservation of their lives by applying themselves to fishing and hunting, which have always been very good in those parts, while, in default of their clothes, necessity, which is the mother of inventions, gave them the ingenuity to clothe themselves with skins of beaver, of moose, and of other animals which they killed in hunting. They hold, further, that it could well have been a fact that these individuals were instructed in the sacred mysteries of our holy Religion, and that they had even a knowledge of the use of letters, since, in the establishment of colonies, it is customary to send there men who are alike learned and pious, in order that they may teach to the peoples, along with purely human knowledge, the most solid maxims of Christian wisdom and piety. Nobody, however, having followed them in these glorious employments, the knowledge which they had of the true God, of letters, and of their origin, was thus gradually lost and effaced from the minds of their unfortunate posterity by the lapse of time.

However this may be, the ancient worship and religious use of the Cross, which still in our own day is held in admiration among the Indians of the River of Mizamichis — a place we have honoured with the august title of the river of Sainte-Croix — might well persuade us that, in some manner or other these people had received in times past a knowledge of the Gospel and of Christianity, which they have finally lost through the negligence and the licentiousness of their ancestors. It is very like something we read in the life of Saint François Xavier, who found in one of his missions a fine Cross, which the Apostle Saint Thomas had planted there, among a people who no longer had anything more than a faint idea, or almost none, of the true religion which this illustrious disciple of JESUS had preached to them with so much of zeal at the expense of his life and his blood. I will give a particular discussion of this matter when I come to speak of the religion of the Gaspesians, of which the origin is altogether unknown to us. They observe, however, and embody in their conduct, a number of maxims of our first fathers, like how they are clothed, lodged and fed. Nor have they even any other arms, whether for war or for hunting, than those which were first in use among our ancestors after the creation of the world.

THE LOUP-GAROU

Cryptozoology is the name given the study of strange or secret animals, animals like the Yeti (the wild mountain man of Nepal) and Nessie (the fabulous creature said to make its home in Scotland's Loch Ness). The Canadian equivalents of the Yeti and Nessi are the Sasquatch and Ogopogo, respectively a land creature and a lake monster that are frequently sighted in British Columbia. There is no shortage of such creatures in Canada and in the literature of cryptozoology.

References to the werewolf appear in the lore and literature of Quebec, where the werewolf is known as the *loup-garou*. Indeed, there are intriguing references to the werewolf in the history and literature of the *Ancien Régime*. Here is one reference which is mentioned from time to time in books about strange creatures prepared by writers who have yet to see a *loup-garou*, none the less the printed reference to it! The reference, but one paragraph in length, appeared under the heading "*Intelligence Extraordinaire*" in a general column in the issue dated 16 July 1767 of the newspaper *La Gazette de Québec*.

Apparently this *loup-garou* was seen in October and November of 1766 in the vicinity of Kamouraska on the Shore of the St. Lawrence River. It appears to have been some wild creature or other, a rather weak and retiring one at that, unlike the champion shape-shifter, the half-man, half-wolf played by Lon Chaney, Jr., in the Republic movies of the 1940s. The passage has been translated by Annie Bergeron from the French.

Extraordinary Intelligence

From Kamouraska, 2 December. We learn that a certain Werewolf, that has lurked in this province for several years, and that has done much damage in the district of Quebec, has suffered several considerable assaults in the month of October last, on various animals who have been unleashed against this monster, and notably the following 3rd of November, that he received such a furious blow from a little lean animal, that the people believed that they were entirely delivered from that fatal animal in view of the fact that it remained for some time having withdrawn to its lair, to the great pleasure of the public. But they came to learn, by the most mournful of misfortunes, that, to the contrary, it had reappeared, more violent than ever, and it created terrible carnage wherever it went.

Distrust, then, all the tricks of this evil beast, and be very careful not to get caught between its paws.

MAN EATERS

The great surveyor and explorer David Thompson (1770-1857) captured the anxieties of the Cree who feared the Windigo (or Wendigo), the spirit of cannibalism and covetousness found among the Algonkian-speaking Indians of North America. There are two extracts here. The first relates to the Nahathaways in "the great Stoney Region" of today's Saskatchewan, August 1796; the second, to the Indians between Rainy River and Lake of the Woods, March 1799. Both passages appear in *David Thompson's Narrative: 1784-1812* (Toronto, 1962) edited by Richard Glover. The texts retain the characteristics of Thompson's irregular punctuation.

Wiskaho was naturally a cheerful, good natured, careless man, but hard times had changed him. He was a good Beaver worker and trapper, but an indifferent Moose Hunter, now and then killed one by chance, he had been twice so reduced by hunger, as to be twice on the point of eating one of his children to save the others, when he was fortunately found and relieved by the other Natives; these sufferings had, at times, unhinged his mind, and made him dread being alone, he had for about a month, been working Beaver and had now jointed Tapappahtum; and their Tents were together; he came to trade, and brought some meat and the other had sent. It is unusual when the Natives come to trade to give them a pint of grog; a liquor which I always used very sparingly; it was a bad custom, but could not be broken off: Wiskahoo as soon as he got it, and while drinking of it, used to say in a thoughtful mood "Nee weet to go" "I must be a Man eater." This word seemed to imply "I am possessed of an evil spirit to eat human flesh"; "Wee tee go" is the evil Spirit, that devours humankind. When he had said this a few times, one of the Men used to tie him slightly, and he soon became quiet; these sad thoughts at times came upon him, from the dreadful distress he had suffered; and at times took him in his tent, when he always allowed himself to be tied during this sad mood, which did not last long.

Three years afterwards this sad mood came upon him so often, that the Natives got alarmed. They shot him, and burnt his body to ashes, to prevent his ghost remaining in this world.

I called to Mr Cadotte's attention a sad affair that had taken place a few months past on the shores of the Lake of the Woods. About twenty families were together for hunting and fishing. One morning a young man of about twenty two years of age on getting up, said he felt a strong inclination to eat his Sister; as he was a steady young man, and a promising hunter, no notice was taken of this expression; the next morning he said the same and repeated the same several times in the day for a few days. His Parents attempted to reason him out of this horrid inclination; he was silent and gave them no answer; his Sister and her Husband became alarmed, left the place, and went to another Camp. He became aware of it; and then said he must have human flesh to eat, and would have it; in other respects, his behaviour was cool, calm and quiet. His father and relations were much grieved; argument had no effect on him, and he made them no answer to their questions. The Camp became alarmed, for it was doubtful who would be his victim. His Father called the Men to a Council, where the state of the young man was discussed, and their decision was, that an evil Spirit had entered into him, and was in full possession of him to make him become a Man Eater (a Weetego). The father was found fault with for not having called to his assistance a Medicine Man, who by sweating and his Songs to the tambour and rattle might have driven away the evil spirit, before it was too late. Sentence of death was passed on him, which was to be done by his Father. The young man was called, and told to sit down in the middle, there was no fire, which he did, he was then informed of the resolution taken, to which he said "I am willing to die"; The unhappy Father arose, and placing a cord about his neck strangled him, to which he was quite passive; after about two hours, the body was carried to a large fire, and burned to Ashes, not the least bit of bone remaining. This was carefully done to prevent his soul and the evil spirit which possessed him from returning to this world; and appearing at his grave; which they believe the soul of those who are buried can, and may do, as having a claim to the bones of their bodies. It may be though the Council acted a cruel part in ordering the father to put his Son to death, when they could have ordered it by the hands of another person. This was done, to prevent the law of retaliation; which had it been done by the hands of any other person, might have been made a pretext of revenge by those who were not the friends of the person who put him to death. Such is the state of Society where there are no positive laws to direct mankind....

The word Weetego is one of the names of the Evil Spirit and when he gets possession of any Man, (Women are wholly exempt from it) he becomes a Man Eater, and if he succeeds; he no longer keeps company with his relations and friends, but roams all alone through the Forests, a powerful wicked Man, preying upon whom he can, and as such is dreaded by the Natives. Tradition says, such evil Men were more frequent than at present, probably from famine. I have known a few instances of this deplorable turn of mind, and not one instance could plead hunger, much less famine as an excuse, or cause of it. There is yet a dark chapter to be written on this aberration of the human mind on this head.

THE MAMMOTH

Races of humanoid beings are said to have roamed the face of the earth well before the arrival of *Homo sapiens*, our own species. One early race was a that of rapacious giants, and apparently one lone member of that early hominid group survived well into our own period. This at least is the burden of "The Mammoth" which appeared in *Canadian Courant*, 15 Feb. 1808.

The Mammoth · An Indian Tradition

Ten thousand moons ago when nought but gloomy forests covered this land of the sleeping Sun; long before the pale men, with thunder and fire at their command, rushed on the wings of the wind to ruin this garden of nature. — When nought but the untamed wonders of the wilderness and men as unrestrained as they, were lords of the soil — a race of animals existed, huge as the frowning precipice, cruel as the bloody panther, swift as the descending eagle and terrible as the Angel of night. The pines crashed beneath his feet, and the lake shrunk when he slaked his thirst: the forceful javelin in vain was hurled, the barbed arrow fell harmless from their side. Forests were laid waste at a meal — the groans of expiring animals were every where heard! and whole village inhabited by man were destroyed in a moment. The cry of universal distress extended even to the region of peace in the west, and the good Spirit interposed to save the unhappy. The forked lightning gleamed all around, and loudest thunder rocked the globe. — The bolts of Heaven were hurled upon the cruel destroyers alone, and the mountains echoed with the bellowing of death. All were killed except ONE male, the fiercest of the race, and him even the artillery of the skies assailed in vain. He ascended the bluest summit which shades the source of the Monogaheli, and roaring aloud, bid defiance to every vengeance. The red lightning scorched the lofty firs, and rived the knotted oaks, but only glanced upon the enraged monster. At length maddened with fury, he leaped over the waves of the West at a bound, and this moment reigns the uncontrolled monarch of the wilderness, in despite of Omnipotence itself.

MASTODON OR MAMMOTH

The explorer David Thompson (1770-1857) recorded in the narrative of his explorations references to the existence of gigantic beasts.

In the first instance, he noted the fact that the Peigan Indians believed that such beasts lived among them. He heard about the traditional beliefs from members of the tribes on the bank of the Athabaska River in the vicinity of the Rocky Mountains in present-day Alberta. He recorded the tradition in the entry in his narrative for 5 January 1811, where he referred to the gigantic animal in question as "the Mammoth." The passage appears, in the explorer's characteristic style, in David Thompson's *Narrative of His Exploration in Western America, 1784-1812* (Toronto: Champlain Society, 1916) edited by J.B. Tyrrell.

In the second instance, Thompson was traveling in the vicinity of present-day Jasper on 7 January 1811, when he and his guides came upon an extraordinary set of giant footprints. The explorer described the discovery in detail in his journal. The prints were very much on his mind when he returned to the site later that year. There he saw not only the tracks but the beast itself, as he noted in his journal on October 5, 1811. The two excerpts reproduced here are taken from *Travels in Western North America, 1784-1812* (1971) edited by Victor G. Hopwood. It is interesting to add in this context that Thompson's celebrated journal went unpublished until 1916.

Thompson was omnivorously curious about the natural world and possessed great powers of observation. He felt impelled to keep in check his penchant for the exotic. In this regard, as in his work generally, he succeeded admirably. Elsewhere he explained that as a child in Scotland he doted on highly imaginative writing, mentioning specifically two books, the *Arabian Nights* and *Gulliver's Travels*.

As an adult Thompson was aware that throughout Northern Europe and North America there were peoples, both European and Aboriginal, who claimed that they had seen mammoth beasts roaming the wilds at large and at will. Today these beasts might be called "prehistoric creatures," but the words would have meant little or nothing to Thompson. The concept of "prehistory" had yet to evolve, and the first fossils of life forms that had lived in earlier geological periods and eras were yet to be systematically studied. Thompson would have equated descriptions of mammoth beasts with Job's account of the rhinoceros-like Behemoth.

The great mammals of the past are the Mastodons. A Mastodon is any one of a number of prehistoric mammals of the extant genus *Mammul*, from which it is believed the modern elephant developed. During the Miocene era, Mastodons rose in the Old World and spread to the New. They died out at the end of that era in the Old World, but in the New they survived well into the late Pleistocene or Ice Age.

One Mastodon which roamed the Northern Hemisphere was the Siberian Mammoth or Woolly Mammoth. This large, prehistoric, elephant-like creature stood nine feet tall, wore a coat of long shaggy hair, and thrust its upward-curving tusks. Its appearance is familiar today through the cave paintings of Cro-Magnon man. Its ivory tusks are commonly found in Siberia, but from time to time the carcass of a Woolly Mammoth is recovered from the permafrost of the polar regions. There are even instances of these carcasses being thawed out and eaten —

once on site by starving peasants; once by scientists at a learned conference in Europe. The species is now extinct. It is generally held that the Woolly Mammoth has been extinct throughout the whole of the historical period, but sightings reported by native and non-native observers would tend to question that belief.

... Strange to say, here is a strong belief that the haunt of the Mammoth, is about this defile, I questioned several, none could positively say, they have seen him, but their belief I found firm and not to be shaken. I remarked to them, that such an enormous heavy Animal must leave indelible marks of his feet, and his feeding. This they all acknowledged, and that they had never seen any marks of him and therefore could show me none. All I could say did not shake their belief in his existence....

Continuing our journey in the afternoon we came on the track of a large animal, the snow about six inches deep on the ice; I measured it; four large toes each of four inches in length to each a short claw; the ball of the foot sunk three inches lower than the toes, the hinder part of the foot did not mark well, the length fourteen inches, by eight inches in breadth, walking from north to south, and having passed about six hours. We were in no humour to follow him: the Men and Indians would have it to be a young mammoth and I held it to be the track of a large old grizzled Bear; yet the shortness of the nails, the fall of the foot, and it's great size was not that of a Bear, otherwise that of a very large old Bear, his claws worn away; this the Indians would not allow. Saw several tracks of Moose Deer.

I now recur to what I have already noticed in the early part of last winter, when proceeding up the Athabasca River to cross the Mountains, in company with ... Men and four hunters, on one of the channels of the River we came to the track of a large animal, which measured fourteen inches in length by eight inches in breadth by a tape line. As the snow was about six inches in depth the track was well defined, and we could see it for a full one hundred years from us, this animal was proceeding from north to south. We did not attempt to follow it, we had no time for it, and the Hunters, eager as they are to follow and shoot every animal made no attempt to follow this beast, for what could the balls of our fowling guns do against such an animal. Report from old times had made the head branches of this River, and the Mountains in the vicinity the abode of one, or more, very large animals, to which I never appeared to give credence; for these reports appeared to arise from that fondness for the marvellous so common to mankind; but the sight of the track of that large beast staggered me, and I often thought of it, yet never could bring myself to believe such an animal existed, but thought it might be the track of some monster Bear.

AN INFERIOR ANIMAL

In pioneering societies the appearance of a feral or "wild child" was not uncommonly reported. It was still a noteworthy if somewhat frightening occurrence. Foundlings or abandoned children were frequently encountered in rural areas in the 19th century. "A Wild Man" appeared in the *Niagara Mail*, 26 July 1847. It describes the appearance of a "wild child" in Cape Breton, N.S.

A Wild Man. — The Halifax (N.S.) Herald of the 7th inst., contains the following singular narrative. "Considerable interest has been created within the last few days past, by the arrival in this city on Thursday last of a wild man who had been discovered in the woods at Cape Breton, in the state of nudity. For a short time this strange individual has been in the Poor's Asylum. He has received numerous visits and although in a condition of complete barbarism begins to afford encouragement that attempts to civilize him may not be altogether hopeless. He is both deaf and dumb and his

appearance is extremely haggard. He remains generally, whether awake or asleep, in a sitting position. His skin is considerably shrivelled from constant exposure to the weather, and his whole deportment resembles more of an inferior animal than a human being. When food is offered him he seizes it and pressing it to his mouth with both hands, devours it ravenously. He is remarkably fond of salt, which he eats in large quantities. The first steps toward civilization have been partially successful; he having learned the use of a spoon, and to a limited extent allowed his body to be covered with light wearing apparel. It is said that the parents of this singular character emigrated some years ago to Sydney, from Scotland: and having permitted him in his juvenile days to range the woods at pleasure, he acquired a habit of leaving his parent's residence for a number of days at a time, until compelled, for want of food, to return home, and on the death of his parents he took up his abode in the forest altogether, until the time of his capture."

AN ENORMOUS OURANG-OUTANG

In the following account, the writer goes without identification and the locale goes without being specified. Brevity may be the soul of wit but it impedes scholarly inquiry! "A Strange Visitor" appeared in the *St. Catharines Journal*, 18 July 1850.

A Strange Visitor

A Strange Visitor. — I had been sitting in the verandah reading and went away for a few minutes to speak to my wife. When I came back my chair was occupied. There, sitting as quietly as possible, was an enormous ourang-outang, or monkey of some sort. When I first caught sight of him he had my book in his hands, and was to all appearances reading. It happened, however, to be rather a stupid book, and he threw it down. He then placed his hands upon his knees, and sat perfectly still, just as if he had been meditating on what he had been reading. I should say, as nearly as I could judge, that he must have been about five feet in height, supposing him to stand erect. — He sat as upright as any man. After watching him for a minute or two, and observing that the calves of his legs were thicker and more like those of a man than monkeys' legs usually are, I stepped quietly back and called my wife. All this time I had not seen his face. However, as she came one of the parrots screamed, and the old gentleman turned his head. His face was very dark, with large whiskers and beard, and all perfectly white, his body a high brown, and his hands peculiarly large. Yet soon as he saw me he half rose, laid both hands on the below of the chair, and began to grin and show his teeth and spit at me. I did not quite like it, as I was afraid he might make a spring in my direction; I knew my voice would at once frighten him away, if I raised the horrid unearthly yell used by the natives to scare wild beasts and which even the tiger would hardly resist, unless much pressed by hunger. Still I felt more inclined to watch him. Once I thought of going round the other way, and getting my gun, and really he looked so much like a man, that I could not have shot him. He continued to grin and spit till I turned away, hoping he would resume his former sedate position. As soon, however, as he thought my eye was off him, he rose leisurely from the chair, stepped slowly out of the verandah, caught hold of a branch of the banyan tree, and swung himself up into it. While he did that I saw he had a long tail, so that he could not, I believe, have been an ourang-outang. Indeed, I never heard of them coming into this little island, nor I think, into the district. I went into my study, and immediately afterwards heard him scuttling away over the roof of the house.

EXTRAORDINARY, IF TRUE

There were giants in those days. How else to explain deposits of the gigantic bones of early men and women? "Extraordinary, If True" appeared in the *Nova Scotian* (Halifax, N.S.), 26 Nov. 1860.

Extraordinary, If True. — An correspondent of the Mira michi *Colonial Times* writing from Youghal, N.B., Oct. 28, relates the following extraordinary circumstance. He says that one night last spring he had a peculiar dream, repeated several times during the night, of digging up a large quantity of money at a certain locality called Tinker Point. On visiting the spot in the morning, he was so impressed with the accuracy with which the locality had been described in his dream, that he resolved to test the truth of the nocturnal revelation still further, and, furnishing himself with pick and spade, commenced digging. He says:—

"After working for a time, and almost going to give it up for a bad job, my spade struck upon some wooden substance which proved to be a coffin, in which was the remains of a human body, of extraordinary length and size, measuring 8 feet 6 inches, which apparently has been buried some years ago. There was no appearance of flesh or clothing, and when the coffin was opened there was no difficulty in discerning the outlines of a huge well-developed body, but immediately after the air coming in contact with it, the body seemed to dissolve leaving nothing but the immense skeleton and a quantity of dust. In the coffin was found some old rusted implements of warfare. In a small earthenware vessel singularly sealed, I found an old manuscript written on parchment in some foreign language, but not being able to decipher or translate the contents of the same, I some time ago deposited it with Mr. End of this place, but having not since had any conversation with that gentleman on the subject.

"The skeleton I have had conveyed to Dr. Nicholson's office, where the curious have an opportunity of feasting their eyes on this giant!"

THE SIM-MOQUI

Here is an account of a race of humanoids unknown to modern man.

"An Indian Tradition" appeared in the *Daily Colonist* (Victoria, B.C.), 6 Oct. 1860. The identity of the correspondent, whose initials are J.D., is unknown. The Sim-moqui seem to be "wild men of the woods" but not hairy Sasquatches.

An Indian Tradition · The Sim-moqui

Having a little leisure time, one fine evening in the spring of 1853, I started out for a few hours' ramble on the banks of the Camas-sau (the Indian name for the Victoria arm or slough). As I walked along, I met a Cowichan Indian, and understanding the language perfectly, I entered into conversation with him. He commenced telling a heap of stories about hob-goblins, ghosts, etc., and after I had listened some time, he asked if I had ever heard of the Sim-moquis? I replied I never had. "Well," said he, "sit down a bit, and I'll tell you a story about them."

I obeyed and, sitting down, listened to his tale, which ran very much as follows:

"By the side of a lake amongst the highest mountains of this Island, where the crack of a rifle has never yet been heard and the deer and bears roam all unacquainted with the smell of the deadly gunpowder, lives the terrible Sim-moquis. From these mountains the daring hunter, who ventures to pursue the game to their fastnesses, seldom returns to tell the tale of his wanderings. No berries in the whole world are so large, or so sweet, or so nourishing, as the berries in the Sim-moquis country; yet who dare gather them besides their terrible owners?

"The Sim-moquis are a tall, strong, athletic race, with heavy black whiskers and matted hair. They are totally without knee or elbow-joints, and depend upon staffs to assist them in rising from recumbent attitudes, or in sitting down. They never rise but leap with the aid of their staffs to a great distance. Like the deer, whose wide-spread antlers would seem to be a hindrance to its rapid progress through the forests and thickets, the Sim-moqui never miscalculates the distance he has to spring, or the space allowed him in which to leap. His eyes are large and red, and shine like a torch; his teeth are black; his hands and feet are webbed like a water-fowl. They have canoes and hunt with bows and arrows made from the bones of dead Sim-moquis.

"The unfortunates, who chance to visit their country, are immediately seized upon and led into captivity. If they happen to be men, they perform all the drudgery; if women, they take them to wife, to try if they cannot introduce the fashion of knee and elbow-joints into the race."

"Did you ever see any of those strange people?" I asked my companion.

"No," he replied; "but my father did. It was one time when some of the Nanimooch (Nanaimo) Indian women went out berrying, and wandered far up the side of a very high mountain. The farther they went, the larger and the better the berries became, and as they gathered them into their baskets, they wondered at their size and excellence. Higher and higher they went, alternately filling their baskets and pouring them out upon the ground, only to fill them again with still finer *olallies*. At last they reached the top of the mountain, and there their wondering eyes gazed upon a sight which caused them to cry aloud. Berries grew everywhere as large as their baskets; the air was filled with the fragrance from the many-coloured flowers that adorned the green carpet at their feet. The trees, too, were mighty, and their tops were lost to view among a few fleecy clouds that were wafted by a gentle breeze through the air high above them.

"As they stood and wondered at the strange sights above and around them, the sun suddenly sank to rest behind a still higher mountain in the west, and then they felt their danger. The 'Sim-moquis!' burst from their pallid lips, and they seized their baskets and swiftly prepared to descend. But, alas! they had not bent the twigs of the saplings as they came along, and they had no mark by which to guide them back to their homes. They sought for a Sim-moquis trail; but those people leave no trail. As I said before, they leap, by aid of their staffs, over the closest thickets and through the densest forests. After searching for a long, long time in vain for the way down, the poor women threw themselves upon the ground and wept bitterly. Tears dropped like rain, and the ground at their feet was moistened by the crystal drops that fell from their eyes. They thought of their homes and of their little ones, and bemoaned their sad lots in accents of grief and despair.

"Suddenly, while they were seated thus, they saw two lights in the distance, and heard a rushing sound through the air (as of a limb of a tree falling to the ground). The poor creatures started to their feet and essayed to run; but, too late! A Sim-moqui leaped with the swiftness of an arrow shot from a bow into their midst, and motioned them to stay. The affrighted maidens obeyed, and examined the stranger critically. He was tall and straight; his hair was blacker than the features of the blackest raven, and it was neatly combed too. His features were regular and handsome, and half concealed by the flowing whiskers and moustaches that adorned his face; but his colour was much darker than that of any Indian ever before seen. His limbs — who shall describe them? — were straight and appeared strong,

but were thin as that sappling (our friend here pointed to a young fir-tree about six inches in circumference). "His arms, too, were straight like sticks, and as he extended his hand as a token of friendship towards the unfortunate girls, they saw that the stories which their grandparents had often told them of the absence of knee and elbow-joints among the Sim-moquis were indeed true. His red eyes glistened and shone in the dark like a lantern, and were the lights which had first attracted the women's attention. After they had sat some little time in silence — for the Sim-moqui language was strange to them — their visitor rose, by means of his staff, and placing his hand to his chin, opened his mouth, and uttered a loud, piercing cry. In an instant a commotion was heard in the bushes, and in a few seconds lights glanced in all directions, and soon huge, unwashed, unjointed Sim-moquis leaped into the open space in which the captives stood. The light from their flaming eyes fell upon the maidens, and objects in the immediate vicinity became as clear as noon-day. No need for torches where the Sim-moquis live," continued the narrator. "Every Sim-moqui is provided with two torches — that is, his eyes. If a fire be needed, dry sticks of matches are not required — his eyes start the wood into a blaze; if his hands be cold, he raises them to a level with his natural torches and warms them.

"The newcomers held a short consultation with the Sim-moqui who had first joined the unhappy women, and then, at the word of command, six stalwart youths approached, and each seizing a woman threw her over his shoulder and commenced leaping through the air, on their way up the mountain. The rest of the party followed, singing a war-song, and so they went on during the night, toiling up the mountainside, until the first dawn of day. Then they sat down by the side of a running brook, prepared a hasty meal of dried venison, and coiling themselves up like hedgehogs, went to sleep, after binding their captives securely. I might here remark that the Sim-moqui never travels in the daytime, as he is as blind as a bat while the sun is shining.

"When the night came, and the women did not return, the lodges of the Nanimooches were in a state of excitement, and a solemn council was held. The unanimous opinion was that the Sim-moquis had carried their females off. For some time, no one ventured to go forth and attempt their rescue, such was the dread in which the mountain savages were held by the coast Indians. At last my father, who was a chief, addressed them in tones of eloquence — pictured the distress which the poor creatures must feel, and the horrible treatment they would receive. At the conclusion of his speech a dozen braves started up, seized their rifles, and prepared to follow my father in search of the lost ones. It was midnight when they commenced to travel up the mountain side, but they walked briskly, and by daylight reached the top of the mountain, the beauties of which had so charmed their countrywomen the evening before. They were so astonished, and wished to remain a short time to feast their eyes upon the wonders of nature. But my father urged them to continue their search, and after a brief rest, they commenced to climb another high mountain — the same over which the Sim-moquis had passed with their captives a few hours before. Night was coming on apace when the pursuers reached the summit, and throwing themselves upon the ground, after a hasty meal, sought repose.

"My father, however, could not sleep, but lay wrapped in his blankets for a short time musing upon the lost ones and the probabilities of rescuing them. At last, he rose from his couch, and was walking up and down in front of the camp, when his eyes suddenly detected the glimmer of a light at some distance to the north. Awakening his companions, they stole, gun in hand, towards the light, and soon came upon the band of Sim-moquis, who had encamped for the night on a grassy knoll. They were all asleep; and to the utter amazement of my father, he discovered that the light he had seen came from the eye of a sentry, perched upon a high rock. Levelling his gun at this sentinel, my father directed his followers each to pick his man. This having been done, a dozen rifles cracked at once, and a dozen Sim-moquis bit the dust. The rest, owing to the absence of joints, were slaughtered before they could rise to their feet. The captives were unloosened, and they threw themselves sobbing upon the breasts of their rescuers. My father, before he left the spot, examined the body of the sentry, and discovered that one of his red eyes was still open; the other was closed tightly. The party, after securing all the valuables they could find, started down the mountain and reached home the next day."

"And are there any Sim-moquis now-a-days?" I asked the narrator, as he turned to leave.

"Oh, yes," said he as he walked away; "lots of them. They live by the side of a lake on a big mountain, and the shores of the lake are covered with gold."

I walked home in the dark, Mr. Editor, musing on what I had heard, and after seven years' lapse have committed it to paper for your especial benefit. If you believe it, publish it; but if you are at all sceptical on the subject, commit the document to the flames.

AN UNKNOWN RACE OF GIANTS

There are traditions that our ancestors, far from being short Neanderthals or stocky Cro-Magnons, were veritable giants. There are references to such beings in the Old Testament.

"An Unknown Race of Giants" appeared in the *St. John's Daily Mercury* (St. John's, Nfld.), 31 Aug. 1871. Apparently the story, which consists of two dispatches, is reprinted from the *Toronto Telegraph*.

Men of Gigantic Stature
The Discovery of a Great Charnel House
Under Trees of Centuries Growth —
Who First Inhabited America?
(Correspondence of the Toronto Telegraph)

Cayuga, Aug. 21. — On Wednesday last the Rev. Nathaniel Wardell, Messrs. Orin Wardell (of Toronto) and Daniel Fridenburg, were digging on the farm of the latter gentleman, which is on the banks of the Grand River, in the township of Cayuga. When they got to five or six feet below the surface, a strange sight met them. Piled in layers, one upon top of the other, were some 200 skeletons of human beings nearly perfect — around the neck of each one being a string of beads. There were also deposited in this pit a number of axes and skimmers made of stone. In the jaws of several of the skeletons were large stone pipes, one of which Mr. O. Wardell took with him to Toronto a day or two after this Golgotha was unearthed.

The skeletons are those of men of gigantic stature, some of them measuring nine feet, very few of them being less than seven feet. Some of the thigh bones were found to be at least half a foot longer than those at present known, and one of the skulls, being examined, completely covered the head of an ordinary person. These skeletons are supposed to belong to those of a race of people anterior to the Indians. Some three years ago the bones of a mastodon were found embedded in the earth about six miles from this spot. The pit and its ghastly occupants are now open to the view of any who may wish to make a visit there.

* * *

Dunnville, August 28. There is not the slightest doubt that the remains of a lost city are on this farm. At various times within the past years the remains of mud houses with their chimneys had been found; and there are dozens of pits of a similar kind to that just unearthed, though much smaller, in the place which has been discovered before, though the fact has not been made public hitherto. The remains of a blacksmith's shop, containing two tons of charcoal and various implements, were turned up a few months ago. The farm, which consists of 150 acres, has been cultivated for nearly a century, and was covered with a thick growth of pine, so that it must have been ages ago since the remains were deposited there. The skulls of the skeletons are of an enormous size, and of all manner of shapes, about half as large again as are now to be seen. The teeth in most of them are still in an almost perfect state of preservation, though they soon fell out when exposed to the air. It is supposed that there is gold or silver in large quantities to be found in the premises, as mineral rods have invariably, when tested, pointed to a certain spot and a few yards from where the last batch of skeletons was found directly under the apple tree.

Some large shells, supposed to have been used for holding water, which were also found in the pit, were almost petrified. There is no doubt that were a scheme of exploration carried on thoroughly the result would be highly interesting. A good deal of excitement exists in the neighborhood, and many visitors call at the farm daily. The skulls and bones of the giants are fast disappearing, being taken away by curiosity hunters. It is the intention of Mr. Fridenburg to cover the pit up very soon. The pit is ghastly in the extreme. The farm is skirted on the north by the Grand River. The pit is close to the banks, but marks are there to show where the gold or silver treasure is supposed to be under.

From the appearance of the skulls it would seem that their possessors died a violent death, as many of them were broken and dented. The axes are shaped like tomahawks, small, but keen, instruments. The beads are all of stone, and of all sizes and shapes. The pipes are not unlike in shape the cutty pipe, and several of them are engraved with dog's heads. They have not lost their virtue for smoking. Some people profess to believe that the locality of Fridenburg Farm was formerly an Indian burial place, but the enormous stature of the skeletons and the fact that pine trees of centuries' growth covered the spot go far to disprove this idea.

THE MAN-WOLF

This account reveals the appalling treatment of a mad man or an insane person in Ontario in the latter half of the 19th century. "The Man-Wolf" appeared in the *Toronto Telegraph*, 14 April 1871. It is apparently reprinted from the columns of the *Detroit Free Press*.

The Man-Wolf · Who He Is, and What He Is

Detroit Free Press.

Early last winter, parties living several miles from Windsor discovered in the woods, huddled up against a log in a vain effort to get warm, a curious kind of beast or man, one can scarcely tell which. The "it" is fearfully deformed, his hand covered with long, coarse hair, face grown full of rank whiskers, eyes looking like those of a wolf, and his present captors are said to treat him more like a dog than a poor unfortunate lunatic. After being on exhibition in Windsor for a few days, the "Man-Wolf," as he is named, was brought over here, and is at present on Michigan avenue in charge of parties who intend to travel with him as a "show" this summer. It is the general opinion that the strange being is the man who escaped from the lunatic asylum at Malden last fall, but this is an error. The fugitive was a strong, tall man, standing very stiff and erect, whereas this specimen is badly deformed, and would not have been capable of making the stout resistance and the rapid flight made by the lunatic in question. But how the being came in the vicinity of Windsor no one is able to tell or at least has not yet informed the public. A man named Seth Narmore, from Sarnia, was at the Central Station yesterday, and, after paying a visit to the keeping place of the strange creature, returned and reported that he believed he knew its history. Some years since, a man named Rosscommon, living about twelve miles from Sarnia, received in charge from his brother at Montreal, a lunatic, supposed by outsiders to be some relative of the family, although Rosscommon was not communicative of facts.

The lunatic was at first confined in a chamber of the house, but he attracted so much attention from the passers by, and so disturbed the inmates of the house, that a small building was soon built for his special keeping. Very few people ever saw the unfortunate, but hundreds of farmers passing by, used to hear him scream and beat the walls of his prison. At length one night he made his escape, and Rosscommon was compelled to ask the assistance of his neighbors to secure him. They found him in a swamp eating bark and roots, but he exhibited the utmost ferocity when an attempt was made to catch him, finally leaving the swamp when a couple of dogs were sent in after him, and one of the scars on his face was received while the men were binding him. Mr. Narmore was one of the pursuers, and he is quite positive that this "man-wolf" is the identical lunatic, as that one did finally make good his escape, and no one was able to hunt him down. It is asserted, and it has been reported to the Superintendent of Police, that the "owners" of this stranger do not treat him as they should. He is kept chained a good share of the time, and the rough boys of the neighborhood are allowed to tease and vex him. If there is good reason for believing that he has escaped from any lunatic asylum, there ought to be an investigation made by the police, or some proper official. Without doubt, he is crazy, as well as fierce and ravenous, and it would be only human and decent for him to be taken from his present owners and sent to the county house of the insane asylum.

A WILD BOY IN THE WOODS

Here is another "wild child." Such abandoned children made a strong impression on members of close-knit pioneering families. "A Wild Boy in the Woods" appeared in the *St. Catharines Journal*, 27 June 1871. It is apparently reprinted from the *London Free Press*.

A Wild Boy in the Woods
Strange Sensation in the Gore of London
The Boy Lives on Roots and Herbs, and Flees from Men
An Unsuccessful Chase

Periodically we are startled by a Wild Man of the Wood who appears in the press of the United States, to horrify the world with his fantastic tricks; and now we have nearer home, not a wild man, but a wild boy, treading the forest recesses of the Gore, albeit they are not so deep as in days of old, to the uneasiness of men and the awe of maids. He was first seen about two weeks ago, on the edge of a forest extending about a mile and a half, and situated about four miles from the city. Five residents of the neighborhood, passing by the bush, saw him wandering aimlessly about, and made an effort to enter into conversation. But he no sooner saw them than he appeared to be very much frightened, and bounded off into the woods with the fleetness of a deer. He wore a peculiarly wild and haggard aspect, with nothing to cover him but a pair of dark pantaloons and a white shirt, both of which are torn and hanging in shreds to his person; one sleeve of the shirt was entirely gone. His hair all matted and awry lent him a lost and savage look. He has been seen on several occasions, but has always eluded his watchers, perhaps too timid to pursue him, and escaped from their sight into the depths of the wood. How he manages to subsist may be imagined from the fact that one day in the latter part of last week, an old resident whose name is in our possession, suddenly surprised him reclining on a knoll, and, Nebuchadnezzar-like, plucking the grass and herbs around him to eat. The old gentleman in question hallooed to attract his attention, when the unfortunate demented being hastily arouse, uttered a howl of dismay and rambled off as fast as he could into his shadowy retreat. On Friday evening a party of ten men went in pursuit, and scoured the bush thoroughly, but no trace of the wild boy could be found. It is supposed that he inhabits a cave which he has burrowed in some lonely place, and to which only his own instinct attracts him. On Saturday night a still larger party was to have been formed for the purpose, if possible, of ferreting out this strange being, and bringing him back to the walks of civilized life. The result, up to the hour of going to press, we have not learned, but as his conduct has created a strange sensation in the locality, and there seems a deep determination to hunt him down, and curtail his wild pranks, no doubt he will soon be captured. No one knows who he is, where he came from, or by what strange hallucination he has been prompted to run wild in the woods. — *London Free Press.*

ODDLY EXPRESSIVE EYES

"A Mysterious Family History" appeared in *Daily British Colonist* (Victoria, B.C.), 27 Nov. 1874. The feral-child story is apparently reprinted from the *Spectator* (Hamilton, Ont.). If a subsequent "sketch of their history" was published, it has not been located.

A Mysterious Family History
Three Children Taken Wild off an Island in Lake Huron

One morning about a month ago a man "of strange, wild mien," and not very respectable dress nor intelligent appearance, came to the Orphan's House in connection with the Sisters of St. Joseph, and knocked at the door. One of the Sisters came and opened it, and the man presented three children to be taken care of. The children bore a much stranger aspect than himself, and the group excited the surprise and wonder of the sisters. They consisted of a girl and two boys. The boys were clad in loose plaids and were attired altogether with a neatness and respectability which contrasted singularly with their deportment and looks. The girl was about fourteen years old, and was the eldest of the three. She was dressed in a plain and rustic style, but had an expression of much more intelligence than her younger brothers. All of them were small in stature, but the boys especially so, and still they were not dwarfish. They were not deformed, but there was an unnatural and inhuman appearance about them which could be suggested by scarcely any other word than deformity. Their oddly expressive eyes, their apish features, their thin, bony, fang-like hands, their slender limbs and attenuated forms, their strange apathy to what was said by their father, their general inattention, their peculiar way of crouching in the corners of the passage-way, made them an object of curiosity and pitying interest. They were led in by one of the Sisters, who also invited the father — for such he announced himself in disjointed sentences to be — to partake of something to eat. But he refused in a hurried manner, saying that he had something in his pocket, and seemed fidgety to get away. As soon as the children were in, the man left with the same wild, unintelligible stare which he wore throughout the short interview, and did not make any sign of parting or say a farewell word to his children, or indeed to any one. But as he passed out of the entrance he turned round and furtively looked in through the side lights of the door. Then he ran off hastily and was soon out of reach and out of sight. The children were taken into the Home and had food offered them. About two o'clock in the afternoon the wild-looking father was seen to steal softly up to the convent and again entered the gate and peered inquisitively into the side lights. His offspring were not there, however, and the moment he saw he was observed, again fled and was seen no more. The youngest would not taste any food that was offered them, though they were as emaciated and exhausted as could be. Their hands resembled bird's claws more than anything else and their feet were but a cluster of bones. On talking to them it was found that they could not speak, albeit they possessed the natural capacity for articulation, having a full set of teeth, perfectly formed roof of the mouth, and tongue capable of every movement. Neither did they pay attention any words or kind of noise. They have been kept and kindly cared for by the sisters ever since their advent. But it was discovered that the boys were afflicted with a desperate cough, and though every kindness has been bestowed upon them and every mode of treatment adopted, it is not thought likely they will survive long. However, they appeared to be gaining strength for some time after being introduced. Their stay in the house has shown them to have lived in the wildest manner and to have been totally unacquainted with the habits of civilized people. They can utter no articulate sound, as was said, but at various times they have been heard to give vent to a weird cry, entirely unlike any human utterance, but somewhat resembling the low wail of some wild animal. This is the sole expression the boys have been known to make, but the girl seems much more intelligent, and can speak common words, though she knows nothing of the ways of civilized life. The boys have a constant habit of crouching in corners, and one of them sits with his shoulder "hunched up," as if by malformation. They prefer raw edibles to cooked food, and have only lately taken to eating at the table. At first they greedily devoured raw cabbage, leaves of turnips, and even have been known to gulp up the swill that stood in the pail. Of the commonest acts of decency they at first had no idea (showing their former habits of life), but they have latterly improved in many respects. They sleep mostly in the day-time, and at night wander around the rooms, one of them being found one night in a dangerous position on a staircase in the middle of the night. As to their former history only this is known, that they were found by Father Chenier, of Owen Sound R.C. Mission, on a lonely isle in Lake Huron, where the father lived with these strange children and would allow no one but themselves to live there. The Father seeing their condition obtained the father's permission at last to have them taken to a refuge and cared for. The parent came with them voluntarily and brought them here. The parents of these singular beings were not married but are said to have been nearly related. The mother has been dead for years. A letter is expected here giving a sketch of their history.

THE BLOOD OF THE INSANE

The West Coast has a rich tradition of sightings of wild creatures, whether they are sea serpents, lake monsters, ape-like creatures, or human foundlings. "A Wild Man in British Columbia" appeared in the *Ottawa Times*, 4 Dec. 1875. Apparently the account was reprinted from the *Victoria Colonist*.

A Wild Man in British Columbia

The Victoria *Colonist* of the 9th November, has the following extract from a private letter received from Clinton. The person alluded to was an axe man in the employ of a C.P.R. survey party in 1871, and suddenly went mad while on Thompson River, and plunged into the woods. From the extract there would seem to be no doubt that he is still living in a state of wildness: —

"You may perhaps remember Martin, a German, who had a store on Kanaka road, Victoria. He left a C.P.R. survey party and was occasionally seen for that season on the mountains, last winter in the coldest time he was also seen by Indians after he had crossed the Thompson river on ice. It is wonderful how he managed to exist during the intense cold. A few days ago he came to the sheep-run of Peter Frazer, on Stump Lake, between Kamloops and Nicola. He carries his rifle which was very rusty; he had as clothing a strip of what appeared to be a piece of old trousers, around his neck, and not another rag or hat; his hair is gray and matted, and hangs down on his shoulders, and his body has become thickly covered with hair like an animal of the gorilla species. He asked the shepherd for something to eat and he gave him the remnants of his dinner. The shepherd asked many questions, but received no answer, the wild man appearing to be deaf. After he had finished eating he said, "That is the first bread I have eaten in five years." Whilst eating he stood leaning on his rifle. The shepherd offered him clothes, but he seemed unconscious of anything said, and walked away. From carrying his rusty rifle his right shoulder is a little dropped. He carries it in his hand and walks slowly and erect. The reason he has not been seen more frequently is that he keeps to the high benches, and does not appear to want to leave them. He headed towards Nicola Valley. When he first took to the woods he got into the mountains at the back of Cornwall's, and was frequently seen there, but would run away and hide. It seems impossible to live without freezing, with the mercury at 50 deg. below zero, and the inference is that the blood of the insane has a cold resisting power much greater than that of sane people."

BADGE OF GENERAL MONKEYHOOD

Gorillas? In Canada? In the Interior of British Columbia? Who knows ... ! "A Singular Animal" appeared in the *Daily Patriot*, Charlottetown, P.E.I., 28 June 1881. It apparently is reprinted from the columns of the *Advance*, Chatham, N.B.

A Singular Animal
(Chatham Advance)

Quite a sensation was caused last week in the vicinity of Redbank, Northesk, by the appearance of a strange and terrifying animal, which those who have seen it describe as a gorilla. It was first seen on Tuesday 14th instant, about three miles from Redbank, on the South side of the Little Southwest River, by Messrs. Benj. Hubbard, of Redbank, Thomas Mews, of Nelson, and another man whose name we have not learned. It was seen again on last Thursday near the same place by Mr. James Powers, Blacksmith, of Redbank, whose horse took fright of it. Mr. Hubbard was quite near to the creature and shouted at it, whereupon it turned about in an ungainly kind of way and ran off on all fours. It is described as being about seven feet long with arms and legs, but running on all fours. The head is a dark color and the face has features resembling those of a human being. The body is of lighter color and covered with hair. When Mr. Hubbard shouted at the animal it threw one of its hind feet forward with a kind of latter motion, overlapping the foreleg or arm and then twisted the body after it and went off in a slouching manner. It was observed that the creature had no tail, a fact which gives color to the supposition that it is an animal of the gorilla family. Prof. Grote, describing the gorilla, says it has no more tail than a professor, while the knowledge that monkeys have tails, and the idea that these external appendages are a badge of general monkeyhood are deeply rooted in the popular mind. But the apes are as tailless as man and no more so.

THE BEAR-MAN

"A New 'What Is It'" appeared in the *Daily Sun* (Saint John, N.B.), 7 Oct. 1882. It was credited to the New York *Correspondence*. The reference in the second sentence to "Quilp" is obscure.

A New "What Is It"
From the Woods of Northern New Brunswick

The transition may be somewhat sudden, but I saw the "Bear-Man" at Brighton the same day. He reminded me of Quilp, only he was less intelligent and consequently not as capable of being a villain. A sort of a lair is partitioned off in one corner of the museum for him, where he is concealed from view except when the spectators are allowed to pass through and look at him. When we went in he was sitting quietly on a raised platform which was carpeted and railed in. This was a special privilege given by his keeper, a weak-looking man with a long brown beard. On seeing us the wild man sprang forward and snapped his jaws like a dog. His head is abnormally large, and is covered with long, curly brown hair. His eyes are gray, very small and shaped something like those of the Japanese. From his broad forehead his face tapers to a pointed chin, on which there is a tuft of fine hair. There is a suggestion of the pig in his lips, when they are extended as they are when he snaps. The neck is thick and strong; the chest and shoulders broad in proportion to his height, (or rather length, as he does not walk erect), and his arms are thick and muscular between the shoulder and elbow. The muscles of his arms are at the back instead of on the anterior surface. His forearms are smaller in proportion than the upper arms, but his hands are large and fat. Each hand has a double thumb and six fingers. They are stubby and callous on the palm, like the paws of an animal. His knees have the appearance of being double-jointed, and his legs below the knees are without the usual muscular development. There are six toes to each foot, which is broad and flat like the hands.

While he was being inspected, "Heddy," as his keeper called him, sat with his legs drawn up, much as a tailor sits when at work on his bench, playing with a string of beads. Occasionally he picked a few loose beads from a box and added them to the string.

"He is always doing something," said the keeper, "just like a bear. He can't keep still."

"I must do something," said Heddy, looking up.

This remark was a revelation to us, as we had been informed that the bear-man could understand a few words, but could not talk.

One of the doors swung part way open.

"Shut that door, Jack," said the man-bear, addressing the giant.

The monster kept up his snapping at intervals. Once he snapped at me and made me jump back involuntarily, striking my elbow against the iron railing. When he perceived that I suffered pain he appeared to be very sorry for me.

"You made me do that," said I sharply.

"No, I didn't," he replied, as if he meant he didn't intend anything of the kind.

When several spectators came into the small enclosure, Heddy jumped down upon the floor and made at them. He hopped along upon his hands and feet after the manner of a toad. The crowd retreated perceptibly. A man whom he seized by the leg shook him off and slammed the door shut.

The keeper said that he captured the bear-man in the woods in the northern part of New Brunswick. He was in the nude state then, and lived on what he could pick up around lumber camps. His mother was an intelligent woman, but the monster was supposed to have received the physical formation of the bear, from the fact that the mother was frightened by a bear before his birth. The man-bear, he said, had a tail, which was not a prolongation of the spinal column, but a tail like that of an animal. This was his story, and he looked like a man who was lying. Of course he was.

When the time came to admit the crowd, a wisp of rope was tied around Heddy's belt loosely. A chain, which was fastened to the wall, was snapped into this, and the wild man was fast. As each person passed before him, he jumped at them as a chained bull-dog would, grinding his teeth and growling. Women screamed and shrank from him, and almost went into hysterics. The very nervous persons were warned against going in. The man-bear knew enough not to jump too hard. If he had he would have broken the rope.

This creature, divested of all humbug, is a queer animal and makes one feel a trifle uncertain about one's ancestry.

WILD MAN

Lucknow is a village on the CN line between Wingham and Kincardine, Ont. Its cedar swamp was the habitat of a "wild man." This article about the deranged person appeared in the *London Advertiser* (London, Ont.), July 28, 1883.

Lucknow's Sensation
A Monster Running Wild in a Bruce Swamp

The *Lucknow Sentinel* tells the following story: "For some three weeks past considerable excitement has been created to the people living near the cedar swamp, just north of the village, by the appearance of a "wild man," as they affirm, running naked in the woods. At one time it was thought to be some evil disposed person living in the village, who only made his appearance to women, but lately the monster has been seen at different times by several, and all agree that he is a heinous looking creature. He is described as a man about six feet in height, raw-boned and very active, and possessing the double advantage of being able to travel at a rapid rate on his hands and feet, the latter being his favourite mode of travel when pursued or going up hill. On Monday last, when a son of Mr. Thomas Lawrence was going to the pasture field for the cows, he saw the man standing at the edge of the swamp, near the road, and when within a short distance of him the brute gave utterance to a frightful screech and chased the young lad some distance down the road. A lady living in the neighbourhood also saw him that morning holding a cow, which he was trying to milk. In the afternoon a number of citizens went in pursuit of the green-eyed monster, but as yet nothing definite is known as to who or what the creature is. A number of young girls who were picking berries in a patch about a mile northeast of the village report having seen a crazy man running through the patch a short distance from them quite nude, and having a parcel of clothing under his arm. Since that time, however, he has not been seen or heard of, but in our opinion the authorities should take the matter in hand and have the mystery cleared up."

JACKO

Jacko is the name of a gorilla-like creature and the subject of this correspondent's report which appeared in the *Daily Colonist* (Victoria, B.C.), 4 July 1884. The account has been widely discussed. Is it the first record of the elusive Bigfoot? Does it constitute the first appearance, in print at least, of the fugitive Sasquatch? What should be made of this account of the capture of a "half man and half beast" in the wilds of British Columbia?

Connoisseurs of the weird are inclined to accept the report as a news story, whereas cryptozoologists are happy to dismiss it as a tall tale or a hoax, an entertaining one to be sure, as did researchers Loren Coleman and Jerome Clark, writing in *Cryptozoology A to Z* (1999): "A young Sasquatch? Alas, no. Historically minded Bigfoot researchers have reluctantly concluded that this is just another tall tale cooked up by a local newspaper."

If the account is true, why are there no "follow-up" stories about Jacko in later issues of the *Daily Colonist* or in the province's other newspapers? Then there is the oddity of the dating of the event. Why was the story two years old upon publication? Finally, there is the curious matter of the correspondent making no attempt to determine whether the smallish creature is a hairy animal or a hirsuite human being.

The reader may make up his or her mind about these matters. In the meantime, it makes intriguing reading....

A Strange Creature Captured above Yale
A British Columbia Gorilla
(Correspondent of The Colonist)
Yale, B.C., July 3, 1882.

In the immediate vicinity of No. 4 tunnel, situated some twenty miles about this village, are bluffs of rock which have hitherto been unsurmountable, but on Monday morning last were successfully scaled by Mr. Onderonk's employees on the regular train from Lytton. Assisted by Mr. Costerton, the British Columbia Express Company's messenger, and a number of gentlemen from Lytton and points east of that place who, after considerable trouble and perilous climbing, succeeded in capturing a creature which may truly be called half man and half beast. "Jacko," as the creature has been called by his capturers, is something of the gorilla type standing about four feet seven inches in height and weighing 127 pounds. He has long, black, strong hair and resembles a human being with one exception, his entire body, excepting his hands, (or paws) and feet are covered with glossy hair about one inch long. His fore arm is much longer than a man's fore arm, and he possesses extraordinary strength, as he will take hold of a stick and break it by wrenching or twisting it, which no man living could break in the same way. Since his capture he is very reticent, only occasionally uttering a noise which is half bark and half growl. He is, however, becoming daily more attached to his keeper, Mr. George Tilbury, of this place, who proposes shortly starting for London, England, to exhibit him. His favourite food so far is berries, and he drinks fresh milk with evident relish. By advice of Dr. Hannington raw meats have been withheld from Jacko, as the doctor thinks it would have a tendency to make him savage. The mode of capture was as follows: Ned Austin, the engineer, on coming in sight of the bluff at the eastern end of No. 4 tunnel, saw what he supposed to be a man lying asleep in close proximity to the track, and as quick as thought blew the signal to apply the brakes. The brakes were instantly applied, and in a few seconds the train was brought to a standstill. At this moment the supposed man sprang up, and uttering a sharp quick bark began to climb the steep bluff. Conductor R.J. Craig and Express Messenger Costerton, followed by the baggageman and brakesman, jumped from the train and knowing they were some twenty minutes ahead of time immediately gave chase. After five minutes of perilous climbing the then supposed demented Indian was corralled on a projecting shelf of rock where he could neither ascend nor descend. The query now was how to capture him alive, which was quickly decided by Mr. Craig, who crawled on his hands and knees until he was about forty feet above the creature. Taking a small piece of loose rock he let it fall and it had the desired effect of rendering poor Jacko incapable of resistance for a time at least. The bell rope was then brought up and Jacko was now lowered to terra firma. After firmly binding him and placing him in the baggage car "off brakes" was sounded and the train started for Yale. At the station a large crowd who had heard of the capture by telephone from Spuzzum Flat were assembled, each one anxious to have the first look at the monstrosity, but they were disappointed, as Jacko had been taken off at the machine shops and placed in charge of his present keeper.

The question naturally arises, how came the creature where it was first seen by Mr. Austin? From bruises about its head and body, and apparent soreness since its capture, it is supposed that Jacko ventured too near the edge of the bluff, slipped, fell and lay where found until the sound of the rushing train aroused him. Mr. Thos. White and Mr. Gouin, C.E., as well as Mr. Major, who kept a small store about half a mile west of the tunnel during the past two years, have mentioned having seen a curious creature at different points between Camps 13 and 17, but no attention was paid to their remarks as people came to the conclusion that they had either seen a bear or stray Indian dog. Who can unravel the mystery that now surrounds Jacko? Does he belong to a species hitherto unknown in this part of the continent, or is he really what the train men first thought he was, a crazy Indian?

THEY ARE ALL DEAD NOW

Here is a "lost-race" story with a Canadian locale. The style is such as to convey a semblance of verisimilitude. It probably delighted its readers in Manitoba at the time of its republication. "A Subterranean Story" appeared in the columns of the *Manitoba Daily Free Press* (Winnipeg), 22 April 1890. It was written by one Charles Howard Sinn and was reprinted from the *Washington Critic*.

This tale bears some resemblances to James de Mille's *A Strange Manuscript Found in a Copper Cylinder*, which was published in 1888. But Sinn's tale will never rival De Mille's for drama or imagination. There are possible references to the Columbia River and to Mount Assiniboine, the highest mountain in the Rocky Mountain chain, which is situated on the Continental Divide between the present-day Trans-Canada Highway and U.S. border.

A Subterranean Story

Last Summer the schooner William Haley, of Galveston, trading among the West Indies, was becalmed near the Gulf Stream. The second day the captain's curiosity was aroused by a strange floating mass, and he ordered the mate to take a boat and examine it. The mate returned towing a log, from which the men had cut away the marine growth which had made it seem at a distance like a sea monster. The captain ordered it to be hoisted to the deck, declaring that in forty years spent at sea he had never found anything like it.

When laid on the deck it was seen to be about twenty feet long and two feet in diameter. It was of some very hard, dark colored wood, like palm, charred in places, and worn and broken, cut and torn, as if it had been whirled through torrents and maelstroms for hundreds of years. The ends were pointed, and five bands of dark metal, like bronze, were sunk in the wood, and the whole bore evidence of having passed through intense heat. On closer examination the log was seen to consist of two parts, and these bands were to bind it together. The captain had the bands cut, and in the exact center, fitted into a cavity, was a round stone eighteen inches in diameter. The rest of the wood was solid.

The captain, more disappointed at this result than he cared to confess, picked up the stone wand and was greatly astonished at its lightness. Examining it more closely, he remembered that when a boy on the old New Hampshire farm he used to find hollow stones with crystals in them — geodes, as he afterwards heard them called. This was probably a geode, placed in this strange receptacle for some unknown purpose. He carried it to his cabin and put it into his chest.

Two months later the old captain returned to his cottage on Galveston bay and placed among his curiosities the geode he had so strangely found in the Gulf stream. One day he studied it again, and the sunlight chanced to fall upon a narrow, irregular line.

"I declare," said the old man, "it looks like as if this stone had been patched together!"

He struck it with a hammer and it fell apart and proved to be filled with small pieces of yellowish brown wood. The shell of the stone was about an inch thick, studded over inside with thousands of garnet crystals. It had been broken into three parts and fastened together again with some sort of cement which showed plainly on the inside.

The old captain poured the pieces of wood on the table. They were perfectly dry and hard. They seemed like strips of bamboo and were numbered and covered with writing, made by pricking marks with some sharp instrument like an awl. He found the first piece of wood and began to read, for it was in English. The work of deciphering the tiny dents on the bits of wood soon became the captain's chief occupation. He copied each sentence off in his old log book as fast as it was made out. Five or six sentences were about all his eyes would stand without a rest, so that it was a long time before the narrative was at all complete. The narrative runs as follows:

Hearts of the Rockies,
About Sept. 17, 1886.

I am an American, Timothy Parsons, of Machias, Me. I have no living relatives. I write this in a vast vaulted chamber, hewn from the solid granite by some prehistoric race. I have been for months a wanderer in these subterranean spaces, and now I have contrived a way to send my message out to the world that I shall probably never see again. If some miner, tunneling in the Rockies, comes upon a vaulted chamber, with heaps of ancient weapons of bronze, bars of gold and precious stones that no man may number, let him give Christian burial to the poor human bones that lie in this horrible treasure house. He will find all that is left of my mortal frame near the great ever burning lamp, under the dome of the central hall. That lamp is fed from some reservoir of natural gas. It was lighted when I came, months ago. For all I know otherwise, it has burned there for thousands of years.

The entrance to this sub-montane river is in the Assinnaboine mountains, north of the United States lines. I was a prospector there for several years, and I heard stories among the older Indians that a river greater than the Columbus had once flown where the Rocky mountains now are; that the Great Spirit had piled the mountains over it and buried it deep underground. At last a medicine man, whose life I had once saved, told me that he knew how to get to the river, and he took me into a cavern in a deep gorge. Here we lived for a week, exploring by means of pine torches, and at last found a passage which ran steadily downward. This, the Indian told me, was the path by which his ancestors, who once lived in the middle of the earth, had found their way to the light of day.

I think we were about three thousand feet below the entrance of the cave, when we began to hear the sound of roaring waters. The sound increased until we stood by an underground river, of whose width and depth we could form no ideas. The light of our torches did not even reveal the height of the roof overhead. My guide told me that this was the mother of all the rivers of the world. No other person except himself knew of its existence. It flowed from the end of the north to the extreme south. It grew even warmer and warmer. There was a time when the people lived along its channel, and there were houses and cities of the dead there and many strange things. It was full of fish without eyes and they were good to eat. If I could help him build a raft he would float with me down this river. The old, old stories said that no one could go upon it for many miles. It ran down a hollow under the mountains.

We built and equipped our raft and launched it on the most foolhardy adventure, I do believe, that ever occupied the attention of men. We lit torches and set them in sockets on the raft, and we were well armed. For two weeks we moved down the high archway at a steady rate of only about three miles an hour. The average width of the stream was about 500 feet, but at times it widened out to almost twice that. It swarmed with many kinds of fish, and they were very easy to secure. The rock walls and roof seemed to be of solid granite. We were below the latter formations.

As nearly as I can calculate we were about a thousand miles from where our voyage began, and nothing had yet happened to disturb its monotony, when we began to find traces of ancient work and workers. An angle in the wall was hewn into a Titanic figure; at another point there seemed to be regular windows, and a dwelling was perched far up in the granite dome.

The Indian told me more of the traditions of his race as we drifted past these things. "They were very great people who lived here. They had many things; they knew more than the white men. They are all dead now." And I gathered from his chance remarks that he thought they had left secrets in their cave dwellings which would make him the biggest Indian on the continent if he could discover them.

Suddenly we found that the river was flowing much faster, and we failed to check our raft. We went over a waterfall, perhaps seventy feet high, and were thrown on a shelf of rock at the side of the river below. I was unhurt, but my companion was so badly injured that he died in a few hours. I repaired the raft after a fashion and continued the voyage, finding it impossible to contrive any way to scale the sides of the waterfall and attempt a return. All our torches were lost, and the attempt to proceed further seemed but the last act of despair. A few hours later I saw a light gleam over the river in a very remarkable way, shining clear across, as if from the headlight of a locomotive high up on the wall. This aroused me somewhat from my stupor and misery. I sat up on the raft and steered it close to the edge of the river to see what wonderful thing had happened.

As I came nearer I saw that an irregular hole was in the wall a thousand feet above the water, and the light shone out through it. It was a cheerful thing to look at, and I hung to the granite and shouted, but to no effect. Then I saw a broken place in the wall a little further down, and let the raft drift along to the base of a broad though much worn and broken flight of steps winding up the cliff. That brought me at last to the place of the light, a domed hall overlooking the river, hewn out of the rock and having in its centre a metal basin with a jet of natural gas. I have had to cut off a part of this metal basin since, but I have not harmed the inscriptions. There are many gas jets, but in the other chambers I have had to light them.

I have lived here for months, and I have explored all the chambers of the place. There is no escape, so far as I can see. The river, twenty miles below, plunges down vaster descents, and the water gets so hot that I should be boiled alive if I tried the voyage. I have discovered a log of tropic wood like palm and a geode in which I can send a message to the world of sunlight. Perhaps this will get through the fires and float to the surface somewhere. I am convinced that the river which brought me here flows on into the Gulf of Mexico, and that sooner or later my log will be picked up. Perhaps this river is really the source of the Gulf stream.

I will not write down my discoveries, not in their order, but as a whole. My story must be brief, or this scant means of record will fail me.

This place seems to have been approached only by the river. It consists of six large, domed halls, connected with a seventh, in which the light burns. There are swords of bronze, spearheads and other weapons stored in one chamber. There have been costly fabrics also, but they have perished, and only a few fragments are left. In another hall are many treasures accumulated.

One hall is especially the hall of pictures and of writing. I spend many hours there. I see the history of this race — their wars, their heroes, their mythology.

The most wonderful chamber of all is the hall to the north. That is the chamber of death and silence. When first I entered this hall I lighted all the gas jets. Around the walls were high cases of drawers and on the front of each was a portrait. I examined them for hours before I felt any desire to do more. Among them I observed a very beautiful face — that of a young girl just entering womanhood. This wonderful race possessed the highest artistic skill and delicacy of expression. The face of this girl, except that the colors had faded, might have been the admired masterpiece of the Paris Salon. I felt a sudden interest in the face and caught the drawer handles and pulled it out. In the wide, deep space into which I looked lay, robed in white, her hands folded, the form of the girl whose picture was outside. How beautiful she was. She lay as if only asleep. Then slowly, as I looked, the whole figure melted down and faded away to a pile of dust. I closed the shrine and touched no more of them, but I often go and look at the faded painting and think how lovely the girl was.

The paintings on the walls of this mural chamber show that the people had two systems of disposing of their dead. The great mass were consigned to the river, but the bodies of all those who were famous for beauty, wisdom or any good quality were preserved by a process of embalming, which they evidently thought would make them endure for ages. There are probably 12,000 separate bodies here, and they represent more than twenty successive generations, if I rightly understand the system of family grouping. If people lived as long as they do now, there was an average of about fifteen additions each year to this great Westminster Abbey of the past. From a sort of map painted on one of the walls I obtain the idea of many and thickly populated communities which used this place as the sepulchre of their chosen few.

Evidently that was before volcanic outbursts made the channel of the river like a cauldron boiling over endless fires. All along the course are towns marked, groups of rock hewn rooms on the cliffs, populated lands on the river, promontories from whose sides fountains of light seemed to spring. Did thousands of people once live and find happiness in these vast vaults of death? Things must have been very different then from now. They must have had many reservoirs of natural gas. The animal life in the river must have been much more varied. Indeed, there are pictures in the Hall of War, as I have named it, that show two things plainly — that there were thousands of caverns extending over hundreds of miles, and peopled by animals with which the heroes fought, and that the river was swarming with existence.

Moreover, I find everywhere, chief of the symbols of life, in the most sacred places, a food root like a water nut, from which grew white leaves and seeds. There must have been some electric principle evolved here, by the vast warm lakes of the river, lit with soft light everywhere at certain seasons. For now I come to the strangest fact of all that I gather from the records of the race; these people had two kinds of light; one they found and lit — that they knew as the lesser God of Life; the other, coming from north to south, twice each year, filled for many weeks the whole channel of the river, from depth to dome, making the very water translucent. The water root and its grain ripened and were harvested in the last days of the light. Two crops a year they gathered, and held their days of the feasts of the great God of Life.

I have tried to put together all I can of their picture writings and their paintings, so as to understand what sort of men and women they were. I confess that I have learned to admire them greatly. They were a strong, brave, loving and beautiful people. I am sorry they are all gone. I never cared half as much about the dead Etruscans or Carthaginians. The earliest chapter in their history, so far as I discover, is a picture of a line of men and women descending into a cave and a dragon pursuing them. This seems to point to a former residence on the face of the earth, and to some disaster — war, flood, pestilence or some fierce monster — which drove the survivors into the depths of the earth for shelter.

But all these thoughts are vain and foolish. I have explored the cliffs of the river and the walls of the mighty halls which shelter me. I have attempted to cut a tunnel upward past the waterfall, using the ancient weapons which lie in such numbers on the floor. The bronze wears out fast, but if I live long enough something may be done. I will close my record and launch it down the river. Then I may try to cut my way out to the sunlight.

Here the story closed. Some day, perhaps, an old man, white haired and pale as one from the lowest dungeon of a bastille, will climb slowly out of some canyon of the Rockies to tell the world more about his discovery of a lost race. — Charles Howard Sinn in *Washington Critic.*

CASE OF PETRIFICATION

Petrification is the process of living matter hardening into stone. When an animal or human bone is petrified, it becomes a fossil. It is one of nature's eerie processes and for it to occur it requires the right circumstances and the passage of considerable time. Anything petrified has an odd, time-defying look. It is preservation at the cost of death.

"Remarkable Transformation" appeared in the *Mail* (Brandon, Man.), 8 July 1886. The account is apparently reprinted from the *Argus* (St. Mary's, Ont.).

Remarkable Transformation
Details of an Interesting Case of Petrification
A Resurrected Body that Weighed over Half a Ton

The St. Mary's *Argus* says: — A well-developed case of petrification has recently been discovered at Sault Ste. Marie, in the following interesting manner: — Several years ago there dwelt on Sugar Island a family by the name of Chappel. Mrs. Chappel who, though rather a corpulent person, weighing up to the time of her death, over 200 pounds, was, nevertheless, very handsome, energetic, intelligent, and beautiful, and, though still possessed of many beautiful traits of Christian character, also retained some very peculiar notions. Amongst these latter might be recorded her earnest desire to be buried in a lovely, sequestered nook on the farm; that her coffin be made of tamarack and her shroud of black satin. It is needless to say that these wishes, with many other minor details, were faithfully and affectionately fulfilled by her sorrowing husband and children. Two years later the husband was laid beside his beloved consort, P.M. Chappel, merchant, Sault Ste. Marie, and W.W. Chappel, proprietor of the Summer Resort, Horse Shoe Harbor, Drummond Island, sons of the deceased, resolved to have the family burying ground, in the beautiful cemetery at Sault Ste. Marie. Having given directions to have the remains conveyed up the river, they, in company with a number of friends, proceeded to the wharf, where a great surprise awaited them. As it required the united efforts of half-a-dozen men to remove the coffins from the boat, it was thought advisable to remove the lids, and an examination of the contents revealed a more than ordinary transformation, for instead of earth and ashes, two stone bodies lay before them, that of Mrs. Chappel being pronounced perfectly petrified, and weighing about eleven hundred pounds. The grave clothes had not changed, and even the tints of the artificial flowers that composed the wreath and motto, "Safe in the arms of Jesus," which lay on her breast, were as fresh and beautiful as when placed there ten years before by loving hands.

For three days previous to their reinterment, the bodies lay at the grave's mouth, and were inspected by hundreds of people, including the resident doctors and army surgeon of that place.

NEITHER A MAN NOR A BRUTE

Before the principles of genetics were well understood, the popular view was that the forests were full of hybrids of man and beast, just as there are combinations of animals that produced the hippogriphs or the syrinx. Even though the principles of genetics are now accepted and reasonably well understood, there are folk who believe that alien beings have interbred with human beings and produced a race of half-alien, half-human hybrids.

"A Human Bear" appeared in the *Daily Colonist* (Victoria, B.C.), 21 Sept. 1887.

A Human Bear
It Looks like a Bear, Crawls like a Bear,
and Acts like a Bear

A large party of Clayoquot Indians, says the Seattle *P.-I.*, from British Columbia, appeared in this city yesterday on their way to the hop fields. Accompanying them is probably as curious a specimen of unfortunate humanity as ever was born. It is neither a man nor a brute, but appears to be on the line dividing the one from the other. Considered as a human being, the being is a man; considered as a brute, it is a bear. It looks but little more like a man than a monkey does, except that the features are a little more distinct and there is not a coat of hair on his body. It cannot talk or walk upright. It crawls along on its hands and feet with the peculiar swinging motion of the bear. Its feet are at a very acute angle with the front of the leg, and when crawling the hands move with an inward swing like the front feet of a bear. The expression is almost that of a bear. There is a peculiarly wild look about it, and the eyes are restless and sharp. Everybody instinctively called it an "Indian Bear."

The Indians said they seldom take it along with them anywhere, but this time there was no one to stay with it. They say it is 20 years old. But little attention appears to be paid to it by the Indians, and it wobbles around with about the aimlessness of an old dog, seeking a warm place, and eyeing suspiciously the approach of anyone not familiar with it. The Indians say that a short time before it was born, its mother was frightened by a bear.

CHASED BY A WILD MAN

The motif of the Wild Man of the Woods is a staple of folklore and is encountered in most if not all of the world's cultures. In Europe the legend took the form of the Feral Child who is denied the benefits of human affection, discourse, and civilization. The "wild child" is sometimes a foundling or an orphan, perhaps a dauphin in disguise or a figure like Kaspar Hauser whose parentage becomes the concern of the "crowned heads" of Europe. In the summer camp tales of Ontario, it takes the form of the Hermit in the Bush. In Western Canada, the characteristic figure is the hairy wild man, the Sasquatch.

"Chased by a Wild Man — The Weird Adventure of Two Manitoba College Students" appeared in the *Winnipeg Free Press* (Winnipeg, Man.), 8 Oct. 1887. The account is apparently reprinted from the *Brandon Sun* (Brandon, Man.).

About a week since two young gentlemen, Messrs. McEwen and Mulvey, who are teaching school some distance southwest of this city, were on their way to Brandon to attend the convention of teachers. They left the place at which they were staying very late in the evening, and were accompanied part of the distance by some young friends, who had a dog with them. Taking leave of their friends they started northward. They had not gone far before they entered a wheat field, and were somewhat surprised to see an apparition in the shape of a man spring from behind the shocks, and run towards them. They were not frightened at first, thinking it was one of the party they had left playing pranks upon them. The figure approaching nearer, though, gave them a close and better view, and they discovered that it was a man with nothing upon him but a breech cloth, his hair, long and dishevelled, flying in the wind, and was foaming at the mouth. The man was coming towards them at a rapid gait, and they ordered him to stand back. At this he commenced to bark, and the young men to run. It was a test of fleetness. There is no question that the wild man, for there is no doubt that the man was fairly wild, would have caught them. His bounds are described as being leaps such as they had never seen a man take. His barking caused the dog that was with the young men to bark, and hearing this, he immediately turned and ran in the direction of the noise. In a few minutes he caught up to them; but the dog giving him chase he ran, and ran so swiftly that he soon outfooted the dog, and was soon lost in the distance. The time was about one o'clock in the morning, and the night well lighted by the moon. The neighbours turned out to follow, but he had either hidden himself or got far away before they turned out. No one else in the district has ever seen him that we have heard of, and his appearance is shrouded in the mysterious.

CANNIBALS

What to make of this tale of cannibalism among the Indians of the Northwest Coast of British Columbia? Tall or true? Embellished in the telling or sticking to the facts? Whatever, the account seems innocent of details about locale, customs, dress, etc.

"A Night with Cannibals" originally appeared in Seattle's *Post-Intelligencer*, but is reprinted from *The Globe and Mail* (Toronto), 10 May 1890.

A Night with Cannibals
The Feasts of British Columbian Man-Eaters Described
(Seattle Post-Intelligencer)

Gen. Lyman Banks and John Hutcheson, two citizens of Seattle, have just returned from a two-months' cruise of the northern coast of British Columbia, and they tell some thrilling stories of sights they have seen and dangerous adventures they experienced during their cruise.

The old Hudson Bay Company's trappers all unite in calling the past winter the worst that has been known in that part of the country in the last forty years, and a leaf or two from their log-books show that the cruisers found that fact to be only too true.

A reporter happened to meet Gen. Banks on the street, and at his request the General recited the story of his most exciting and interesting cruise. The story is interesting and it is given below in the language of Gen. Banks himself. He began his narrative as follows: —

"We started out full of great expectations and pleasant anticipations, and we did not realize for a moment what trials we would have to go through, and I tell you at times it required a great deal of western grit and push to get ahead. Those who are acquainted with the difficulties of traversing in summer a coast forest, with its thousands of uprooted trees and still worse upheaved foundations, can perhaps readily imagine how much greater a hardship it was for us to travel over three feet of snow on a level and occasionally strike drifts much deeper and a great too much tangle of sallal bush for snow shoes. But, to add to all our difficulties, our Halfbreed guide and the Indian packers refused to go on with us as soon as we had penetrated a short distance inland. We had just sighted some hills which they said we could never pass over, and they alleged that no human being had ever succeeded in the attempt.

"They strongly urged and prayed us not to proceed any further, but we had started out with a determination to accomplish a work and we were not to be baffled so easily in the beginning of our journey. So we packed up a couple of weeks' rations and an axe in our blankets and shouldering our Winchesters, we pushed on alone. Oh, what a journey it was! I shall never forget it as long as I live.

"Where the snow was too soft and deep we managed to make progress by crawling on our hands and knees, and at times we were obliged to lay down and roll to get out of the snow. It was hard struggling by day, but the snow made a soft bed at night. We canoed over three hundred miles of our journey, and some of it was over very rough waters. But the most startling experience we had, and the one that would interest you most, happened one day just as we were running into a cave to avoid a storm. We got into the cave all right enough, but imagine our horror and disgust when we found ourselves in the midst of the Nahwitti Indian tribe at their cannibal orgies. Cannibalism is prohibited by the Dominion Government, but there being only a monthly visit from vessels, and the nearest port being miles away, they carry on the horrible practice with impunity.

"We watched the heathens during the day at long range, but, under assurance of safety, we ventured after a while into their circle at night and watched them. I can only describe the sight this way: — There was a high fire of logs in the centre of the circle, which was constantly attended by two men, and occasionally there was an extra hiss and flash as some uneaten fat was thrown on. The entire tribe encircled the fire, dressed in blankets of many brilliant hues. There were naked dancers, and a dozen or more lusty savages with clubs in their hands beating an accompaniment to their wild songs and dances, and the whole sight made a weird sense that is not soon forgotten. Their beast consisted of the bodies of their dead. They seldom kill strangers to furnish food for these horrible orgies, as they were all the time quarrelling between themselves and generally had enough dead bodies of braves to satisfy their appetites.

"I had been told in Victoria of the possibility of this, and was warned that when wild with the dance the braves rush out and bite a piece out of the first person they come to. Now I have no objection to being eaten after I am dead, but to be bitten by ones of those wild fellows would be as undesirable as the bite of a mad dog, and lest in their excitement they might forget their promise of immunity I held my hand under my overcoat and grasped a 44-calibre revolver that would have furnished rations fitting the occasion.

"Our sense of security was not increased by one of them making a speech, noticing our presence and berating the white man's Government for trying to deprive the poor Indian of the pleasure of being a cannibal occasionally, especially if he only fed upon his own dead.

"The boys crawled behind the older people and hid, men were bitten or simulated it, and I was afterward shown scars where they claimed to have been bitten. But we were not molested. One brave, however, probably to test us, made a dash in our direction, but others caught him and turned him another way. It was an "all night session," no one was allowed to leave till through, which was 6 o'clock the next morning. We had seen enough, though, and were glad to leave. We proceeded on our journey and came back again without any more exciting adventures, arriving in Seattle only a short time ago. But I never in all my life put in such a night as I did the time of those frightful orgies, and I candidly confess I don't want to soon again."

It Makes Me Shudder Even Now

Here is a scary tale about a creature all the more frightening for being unseen. "The Swamp Horror" appeared in the *Calgary Herald* on 18 Jan. 1890. Its editors reprinted it from the *Winnipeg Free Press*. It seems the reminiscence was written by someone named Luke Sharp for the *Free Press* (Detroit, Michigan).

The Swamp Horror

I spoke in the previous article of the dismal swamp that stood on the eastern limits of the village of Bruceville. Some time or other, probably before the village had been settled, there had come through the forest a tornado, and it had lashed the trees down in all sorts of shapes over the partly submerged land. Then at some other period a fire had swept through this, and had left it one of the most desolate, forlorn-looking, tangled mazes of half-burnt wood that could be imagined. Years had passed since that time, and repeated rains had washed most of the black off the wood and left the white, gaunt limbs sticking up in the air, like spectral arms, and made the ghostly place to us boys a region of terror and a first-rate place to avoid. Nobody, as far as I have been able to learn, had penetrated into the innermost recesses of that swamp. No boy that I ever knew dared to enter the swamp even in the brightest sunlight, while the thought of that swamp at night! — whew — it makes me shudder even now.

Nobody was more afraid of that swamp than I was, yet I think I may claim to have been the first boy that ever explored it, and that is the reason that my hair today is gray. I may say that about this time a great mystery shook the village from its circumference to its centre. The mystery was the strange disappearance of three cows that belonged to three of our villagers. Nearly every one of the villagers kept a cow, and these cows grazed on the commons that adjoined the village.

One day three of the most valuable cows were missing, and a search all over the country for them was unsuccessful. This mysterious disappearance caused more talk and gossip in that village than the murder of three men would have done in a larger town. Everybody had a theory as to how the cows had disappeared. I remember that a lot of wandering gypsies came along at that time, and one of the owners of the cows consulted a gypsy as to their whereabouts. After paying the fee the gypsy told him, somewhat vaguely, that he would hear of the cow, but that she feared he would not take as much interest in the animal after she was found as he had done before. This turned out, however, to be strictly accurate.

About this time someone introduced in the village a strange contrivance which was known as a kite. Improbable as it may seem, this invention would sail in the upper skies without the aid of gas, which is used to elevate a balloon. The way it was made was thus:

A hoop of a barrel was taken and was cut so that it made a semi-circle; then a piece of lath was fastened to the centre of that semi-circular hoop, and a piece of string was tied to the end of the hoop and down to the bottom of the lath. A cross piece of lath was also made to strengthen the affair, and then we cut a newspaper into shape and pasted it over the string and lath and hoop ends. A long tail was attached to the end of the lath, made of string, to which was tied little bits of paper, somewhat after the forms of curl papers used by ladies in those days to keep their hair in curl. Then a long string was attached to this kite, and if the breeze was good and you held on one end of the string, the affair rose gracefully in the heavens.

There was great competition among us boys in kite flying, and the wild desire to own the kite that would fly the highest caused bitter rivalry. I succeeded in getting a very good kite, and bankrupted myself in buying a lot of string as an attachment. After purchasing that ball of twine, I was poor in this world's goods, with the exception of that kite, which proudly floated away above its fellows. We used to tie our kite string to the fences, and leave the kites floating up all day, and I have seen as many as ten or fifteen kites hovering away above the village.

One day, when the wind was blowing from the village over the swamp, some envious villain, whose identity I have not been able to discover to this day, cut the string of my kite at the fence. If I had found out who the boy was at the time, I venture to say that there would have been the biggest fight that the village of Bruceville ever saw. I was in another part of the village when the disaster happened, and I saw with horror that my kite, which floated so high above the rest, suddenly began to waver and then floated off towards the east, wobbling to one side and then to the other in a drunken, stupid sort of fashion, and finally fluttered down to the ground somewhere on the other side of the swamp. In doing this it trailed the long line of valuable string clear across the dismal swamp.

It was hard to believe that there could exist in the world such desperate villainy as would prompt a boy to the awful deed. I passed through the village weeping loudly over the disaster, but this attracted very little attention; it was merely thought that I had got one of my usual thrashings, and there seemed to be a belief in the village that whenever that interesting episode occurred, it was richly deserved. I found the end of the string near the edge of the swamp, and I got a stick and began to wind it and save as much as possible of the string. I don't suppose any less consideration would have induced me to brave the terrors of that swamp, but through the wild entanglement I went, winding up the string, which was stretched over bush and bramble, and now and then stuck on the gaunt branches of some of the dead trees.

When I got about half way through the swamp, I began to realize that I was going to present a very picturesque sight when I got to the other side of it. My clothes were all in rags. I had fallen into the mud three or four times and my face and hands were scratched and bleeding with the brambles, but I saw that if I kept on I was going to save all the string and ultimately get the kite.

Just beyond the middle of the swamp there appeared to be an open place, and when I broke through the bushes I found there a little lake and in the centre a dry and grassy island. The dead stillness of the spot, although it was so near the village, began to make an impression on my sensitive nerves, and I wondered whether, after all, the string was worth the fearful price I was paying for it. I began to fear ghosts, spooks, bears, lions, tigers and one thing and another, when a sight more horrible than all of those together burst upon me as I cleared the brambles and stood in this green place. There, huddled together, lay the three cows. Their bulging, sightless eyeballs stared at me. Their throats were cut so that their heads were nearly half off. Their bodies were bloated and swollen out of all semblance to the original cows.

Thousands of years of life could not bring to me a moment of greater horror than that was. It would not have been so bad if I had been on the road, where I could have run at the top of my speed for the village. But here I was, hemmed in by an almost impassable swamp, that had taken me already an hour of hard wear and tear to get through. With a yell that pierced the heavens and must have startled the villagers, if any of them had been listening, I dropped the coveted string and dashed madly through the wilderness. How I ever got out to dry land again I never knew. It was a fearful struggle of unprecedented horror. I dared not look around. The hot breath of the cows was on the back of my neck. I felt that their ghosts were following. Those awful eyeballs peered from every dark recess of the swamp.

When I tore through the outer edge of the swamp, I had still strength enough to rush across the commons and dash madly down the main street of the village, all tattered and torn and bleeding, the light of insanity in my eye and the strength of insanity in my limbs, yelling at the top of my voice, calling: "The cows! The cows! They are in the middle of the big swamp with their throats cut!" and when I reached my own door, stumbled and fell into the entrance, to the consternation of my relatives, and, either from the excitement of the fearful episode or the fall, lay there insensible.

A body of men, although they seemed to doubt my story, penetrated in to the green island of the swamp, where they found the cows and buried them, but no one ever knew how the animals got in there or who committed the dastardly deed that led to their death.

THE FORMATION OF THE SKULL

In the early days the planet was populated by a race of giants. At least myth and legend accept this as a fact. But accounts of giants generally go hand-in-hand with accounts of pygmies or dwarfs.

This article makes clear that the West Coast of Canada was the home of a race of dwarfs. Inuit legends seem to make the same claim. "Unearthed Remains of a Dwarf Race" appeared in the *Toronto News*, 2 Jan. 1891. It is apparently reprinted from the *San Francisco Chronicle*.

Unearthed Remains of a Dwarf Race
San Francisco Chronicle

Capt. J.S. Prescott, who recently returned here from Victoria, B.C., describes an interesting experience which he had while north. He was in Victoria at the time when considerable excitement had been caused by the discovery of ancient human remains in some mounds. The little hillocks were dug into and skeletons were brought to sight by the shovel and pickaxes. The discovery was made at a place called Macaulay's Point. A workman clearing away what he thought was a natural rise in the ground touched a hard metallic substance with his pick. On digging further the object came to view. It was an iron war weapon shaped like a harpoon, only much shorter and stouter. Curious characters were etched in it, and their lines had survived through centuries.

One of the mounds was excavated and a flat stone was exposed. It had been designed as a door to a sepulchre, for on being raised a grave, walled on all sides by tightly cemented stones, was seen. In it was a dwarfed body doubled up in a sitting position, a custom followed by the ancient Indian tribes along the entire Pacific coast. The formation of the skull was like that of a Chinese. The body, though small, was that of an adult dwarf. Several other graves were opened and the occupants of all of them were similar in anatomical construction and size. In many of the graves rough hewn utensils, evidently used for cooking, were found, together with arrow heads known to have been used by coast tribes extinct for centuries.

At Cadboro Bay similar mounds were excavated with like result.

WINDAGOOS! CANNIBALS!

The Windigo, the spirit of cannibalism and covetousness among the Algonkian-speaking Indians, is a creature of the woods or a condition of the human spirit, or both or neither. In recent years the Windigo (or Windego or Windagoo) has been compared and confused with a cannibalistic fiend, a Sasquatch or a Bigfoot, a mindless malignancy, and even the acquisitiveness of capitalism and corporate concentration. Plainly the Windigo is as free as the wind and not one thing but many things.

Fear is coupled with whimsy in this passage about the beliefs of the Saulteaux (or Ojibwa) at Norway House, north of Lake Winnipeg, in today's Manitoba, between 1868 and 1888. Egerton Ryerson Young (1840-1909) was a Methodist missionary and the author of *Stories from Indian Wigwams and Northern Camp-Fires* (London, 1893) in which this true account first appeared.

Young mentions maps. For an outline of the frightful head of the Windigo, invert the map of James Bay and behold the figure of a hooded terrorist. Terrorist? It is the head and shoulders of the dreaded Windigo; its eye, Akimsk Island, glares through its balaklava-like cape.

[That] these Indians should have in many of the tribes a most remarkable tradition of a great deluge, in which the world was overwhelmed, and the whole human race perished except one family who escaped either in a big canoe or on a great raft, is very suggestive and instructive. Among the many errors and superstitions into which they have fallen is the belief in the existence of windagoos, or gigantic creatures half satanic and half human, whom they represent as being of great size and dwelling in the dark, dreary forests. They describe them as being so powerful that when they march along they can brush aside the great pine-trees as an ordinary man does the grass of the prairies as he strides along through it. We found the Saulteaux Indians especially living in dread of these imaginary monsters. At many a camp-fire they used to tell us with bated breath that these windagoos were terrible cannibals, and that whenever they caught a lonely hunter far away from his home they soon devoured him. When I tried to disabuse their minds of these fears they proceeded to tell me of this one and that one who had been seized and devoured. The instances they brought before me were of hunters who had gone away on long journeys down dangerous rivers and treacherous rapids. On my expressing my opinion that the poor fellows had been drowned or had met with some other accident the Indians refused to be convined. They will never admit that an accident could happen to any of their great hunters, and so the one theory always before them is that those who mysteriously disappear have been caught and devoured by the windagoos.

Of the power and grip this superstition had on these Saulteaux I had a startling and somewhat amusing illustration shortly after I had gone to their first missionary to live among them. Very cordially were we received, and much encouraged were we by the attention given to our words and the really sincere desire manifested to improve their circumstances socially as well as religiously. As there were many of their countrymen still without missionaries they used to frequently ask why it was that more missionaries with the great book were not sent among them. So one Sunday afternoon I held a kind of a missionary meeting with them. I took into the church my large maps of the world, with a number of pictures of heathens of many lands. I explained the map to them and showed them their own country, and told them that while we had a great land as regards size, yet there were many single cities with more people in them than all the Indians in our land put together. Then I showed them pictures of the cannibals of the isles of the Pacific, and described others of the wild, wicked nations of the earth, and told them that good white people were sending missionaries to a great many of these lands, and they must not expect to have them all come to them. "For," said I, "as bad as you and your forefathers were, some of these other people were much worse;" And then I particularized by describing some of the vilest and most degraded of the sinful races. I dwelt on cannibalism especially, and told of the man-eaters of the Pacific islands, who did not even object to a roasted missionary and some of his people cooked up with him. They were intensely interested, and also became very much excited before I finished, especially at what I had said about the cannibals.

The service closed and the people quickly returned to their little houses and wigwams at the Indian village, which was a little distance from the mission-house and church. The next morning, bright and early, I was up, and after breakfast and prayers started off to continue the work in which I had been engaged, namely, acting the part of a surveyor and helping the men run the dividing-lines between their little fields. To my great surprise, when I reached the first home I found that every body was away, and stick tied across the door was the sign that they did not soon expect to return. On to the next and the next houses I went, and thus on through the whole village, and found, to my amazement, that I was literally a shepherd without a flock, a missionary without his people. Not a man, woman, child, dog, or canoe was to be found. After about an hour of aimless wandering around the wondering what had happened I returned to my home and told my good wife of the loss of our flock. Like myself she was perplexed, and neither of us could make out what it meant.

The Indians had often, in large numbers, gone away on their great hunting excursions, but they never all went at the same time, and never without telling us of their going. So we were indeed perplexed. Toward evening I saw a solitary Indian coming from a distant island in his canoe. I quickly hurried down to the shore, and as he stopped paddling a few hundred feet from the beach I shouted to him to come to land. He immediately came in, and when at the shore I said to him:

"Where are the Indians?"

"Out there far away on that island in Lake Winnipeg," he replied.

"Why are they there?" I asked.

"Very much afraid," he said.

"Very much afraid! Of what are they afraid?" I asked.

"Windagoos! Cannibals!" he answered.

"Did any of you see any windagoos?" I asked.

"No, I don't think we did, but what you said about them in your address in the church made our hearts melt like water, and then the winds began to blow, and there from the dark forests, with the sighing winds we seemed to hear strange sounds, and some said, 'Windagoos! windagoos!' and that was enough, so we all got so alarmed that we launched our canoes, and, taking our families and dogs, away we paddled out to that distant island, and there the people all are now."

I confess I was amused as well as annoyed at the startling effect of my *moving* speech, and picking up a paddle I sprang into the canoe, and telling the Indian to show me what he could do as a canoe-man I struck in with him, and in less than an hour we had traversed the distance of several miles that lay between the mainland and that island. The Indians crowded down to the shore to meet us, and seemed delighted to see me. They wanted to shake hands and make a great fuss over me, but I repelled all their advances and would not shake hands with one of them. At this they were very much crestfallen and surprised.

"Why did you leave us in this way?" I asked the principal ones.

"Windagoos, windagoos!" they fairly shouted. "When you told us about those windagoos who used to eat the missionaries and their people you made us very much afraid, and our hearts got like water, and the more we talked the worse we got, and so we all hurried over here."

"Did I not tell you that those windagoos were more than a hundred days' journey away, even with your best canoes?" I asked.

"O, yes, you did, missionary," they said; "but we did not know but some of them might have started many days ago to come and catch us, and so we hurried out here."

"And you left your missionary and his wife and their little ones, whom you profess so to love, behind to be eaten by the windagoos, did you? And yet you say you so love us and are so thankful we have come to live among you and teach you the good way. Why, I am ashamed of you. Suppose the windagoos had come and no stalwart men had been there to help the missionary fight them off. What would he have thought of your love when he heard you had all, like a lot of old grandmothers, run away?"

Heartily ashamed of themselves, they speedily launched their canoes and returned with me to their village, and very little did we hear after that about the windagoos.

GIGANTIC FOOTPRINTS

Giants abounded in the past and make their appearances in the Bible and other sacred scriptures. They are rarely reported in the present. Perhaps their race has died out with the passing of the years, the decades, the centuries, or the millennia. "A Prehistoric Man" appeared in the *Herald* (Calgary, Alta.), 26 Dec. 1896.

Prehistoric Man
Discovery of an Ancient Giant's Footprints in British Columbia
Is He the Ancestor of the American Race?
The Finder of the footprints, and an Ethnologist's Calculations
Heights of All the Giants We Know Of

Dispatches from Victoria, British Columbia, announce the discovery of a series of gigantic footprints in that province. They are apparently made by a human being, and if so, it is prima facie evidence of the existence of a race of prehistoric giants on the Pacific coast.

The footprints were found on the Island of Victoria, near the town of Quatsino, on the west coast. Their discoverer was John L. Leason, a storekeeper of the town, and a man of intelligence. He reported his find to Captain Foot, of the steamer *Mischief*, who repeated his account to the members of the Provincial History Society. They were satisfied of its interest and importance and a party was sent out to make an investigation.

It appears that Leason was walking at some distance from the town when his curiosity was aroused by a strange depression in a large flat rock that lay before him. He was at the time at the foot of a mountain.

The depression at once suggested a human foot, but it was of enormous size. There was a well-marked hollow where the heel would have been, and a very faint depression indicated the arch of the foot. The ball of the big toe and the rest of the forward part of the foot were plainly to be seen. It is to be remembered that no other animal has an arched foot, like that of man.

Leason immediately proceeded to measure the print, and found that it was twenty-nine inches in length. Its greatest depth was four inches. Fascinated by his discovery, he carefully examined the vicinity. At first he saw nothing which he could connect with the print, but after a few minutes he came upon another, almost identical. It was nine feet away from the first. This apparently was the length of the stride, which the giant had been in the habit of taking.

Following the direction indicated by these two prints,

Leason found a number of others. They came to an end abruptly, which was not surprising for their surroundings must have undergone tremendous changes since they were made. The mountain itself may have come into existence in that time.

It is not surprising that footprints should have been preserved for so many ages. They may have been made in soft mud, which subsequently hardened and was then buried in the earth by volcanic action, and there turned into stone and preserved from injury until another volcanic disturbance brought them to daylight again. A large part of the knowledge of animals of early geological periods has been obtained from imprints left by them in this way.

Leason, it is said, has already set to work to chisel out the first footprint which he found. He intends to ensure public recognition as its discoverer.

Here is a table which gives the names of all the giants, ancient and modern, whom we know of, going back to the period B.C. 1063, when Goliath of Gath lived:

ANCIENT

Name	Birthplace	Height — feet
Goliath	Palestine	11.0
Galbara	Rome	10.0
Funnam	Scotland	11.5
De Vallemont	Rouen	17.0
Count Buchart	Dauphiny	22.6
Theotbochus	Dauphiny	25.5
Unknown	Palermo	30.0
John Middleton	England	9.3

MODERN

Name	Birthplace	Height — feet
Frederic's Swede	Sweden	8.4
Cujanus	Finland	7.9
Gilly	Tyrol	8.1
Patrick Cotter	Cork	8.7
Chang Gow	Pekin	7.8

Dr. S.A. Binion, the New York ethnologist, in speaking of this find, tells how to build the prehistoric man pictured alongside Chang given herewith. Says the learned gentleman:

It is easy to reconstruct from the footprint of this prehistoric man his entire form, according to the proportions of a modern man. An ordinary man six feet high has a foot about twelve inches in length. A man with a foot twenty-nine inches long would be about two and a half times as tall or between seventeen and eighteen feet high.

To the man six feet high a weight of 200 pounds may be allowed. Two and a half times that would be 500 pounds. Add to this one-third for a proportionate increase in all directions and you have a total of 660 pounds. That would be the approximate weight of our prehistoric man.

According to the same system of reckoning he would have a brain weighing 125 ounces. That would give him large thinking powers.

He would be about one hundred inches round the chest, and would have biceps eighteen inches in circumference. Corbett and Sullivan would be ridiculous pigmies compared to him.

THE BODY OF A PETRIFIED MAN

This body-snatching story appeared with the heading "A Curious Case" in *The Gazette*, Macleod, Canada West, the future Province of Alberta, 31 June 1896.

After reading about the proceedings, the contemporary reader with an interest in such matters might ponder the resolution of the case before the Winnipeg court, and also might wonder about the nature of the process of petrifaction.

A Curious Case

A curious case is now occupying the attention of the police court in Winnipeg, two men being charged with stealing the body of a petrified man from a farm in Minnesota. The story in connection with this petrified man is decidedly romantic. The body was discovered on June 8th last by two farm laborers who were putting in a culvert, buried in a bed of white alkali clay, three feet below the surface. The body was then sold to a third party for $1000. In the meantime the owner of the farm where the body was discovered heard of the incident, claimed the body and replevied it. A compromise was effected by a company being formed and the body was taken on exhibition through several towns. New claimants then appeared on the scene in the persons of two old gentlemen named Lecount, who state that the petrified remains were those of their father. The company, however, got the body by furnishing a bond, and took it to the Winnipeg fair, where the Lecounts followed them and swore out warrants against them. The Lecounts claim their father, Antoine Lecount, a French half-breed guide, was conducting a party of English tourists from Fort Garry to Fort Snelling. He was accompanied by his wife and two sons— the prosecutors— who were then 10 and 11 years of age. This was 58 years ago. One of the English gentlemen was insane and one morning seized a rifle and shot their father in the breast. The mother and her two sons buried the body in the spot in which the petrified corpse was found. Their only desire, they state, is to give their father's remains Christian burial.

THE WILD MAN

Abandoned babies? Foundlings? Dauphins in the New World? Kaspar Hausers of the wilderness?

From the "wild child" to the "wild man" is but a small step for man. "They Caught a Wild Man" appeared in the *Moose Jaw Times*, 26 Feb. 1897.

They Caught a Wild Man A Strange Being
Who Has Been Terrorizing Farmers
Lived in Huts in the Woods and Subsisted on Game
and the Results of Raiding Hen-Houses —
Knows Nothing of His Past Life

The Wild Man of the Woods, who has been terrifying the people about Red Creek, N.Y., for several months, has been captured. His capture was effected Thursday night. Since that time efforts have been made to learn something about him and his residence, but so far they have been unsuccessful.

The Wild Man was first seen six months ago near Lake Ontario. When sighted he invariably ran into the woods and was soon lost to sight. It was a hunter who first saw him in a secluded spot with no residence near. Afterwards the Wild Man was seen by farmers while at work or passing along a road. Occasionally the strange creature approached the farm-houses and was seen in the clearings, but on seeing that he was observed he hurries into the woods.

The country around the shore of Lake Ontario is rough and heavily wooded. Ravines cut it up and the woods offer a splendid retreat for game. Cold winds sweep across the waters and the autumns are cold and disagreeable. When seen at as close range as he ever permitted the Wild Man did not appear to be warmly clad, and how he had endured some of the cold weather and chilling blasts of the fall is a mystery. It was supposed that he lived on game, although numerous farmers lost chickens and a few found that their meat-houses had been entered, and they charged the lost eatables to the account of the Wild Man.

Although the Wild Man committed no hostile act and appeared to be anxious to avoid an encounter with civilized people as they were to avoid him, his presence terrorized the residents of the vicinity. Women and children were afraid to venture out either day or night, and even the men were alarmed at the sight of the axe which the Wild Man usually carried over his shoulder. So it was resolved to capture him, and on Thursday a posse started under the leadership of Mr. Flint. Traces of the creature were easily found and various huts that he had constructed for temporary use were discovered. It was finally concluded that it would be advisable to wait until night and that was done.

After dark the search was resumed and towards midnight the Wild Man was found asleep in a bark hut in the dense woods. His capture was effected without much trouble. At first the man was restless and he made endeavors to escape, but finally he quieted down and became passive. But he refused to answer questions and what talking he did was an almost unintelligible gibberish.

After he was brought to Red Creek the Wild Man became reconciled to his capture and submitted to confinement with better grace. He objected, however, to having his picture taken, and it required the efforts of several men to hold him while the photographer focused his camera. All efforts to learn anything of the man or his former place of abode failed.

He talked, but his talk was full of visionary schemes. From his senseless prattle it was learned that he had a scheme to dig a canal that will parallel the Erie canal, but his waterway was to be an improvement as it was to be lined with iron. Then he talked about a railroad that he was to construct and which was to pass through numerous large cities which he intended to build. When questioned about his name he became silent and sullen and refused to talk.

EXORCISM OF A WENDIGO

Wehtiko, Wendigo, Windigo ... the spellings are legion.

"Exorcism Tried in Vain, Axe Supplanted Medicine" appeared in the *Standard* (Regina, Sask.), 20 Sept. 1899. The account seems to be based on one that appeared in the *Post* (Edmonton). The condescension of the editorial writer is lamentable, yet his compassion is considerable.

Exorcism Tried in Vain, Axe Supplanted Medicine
Trial of Indians for Slaying a Wehtiko or Wendigo

The Edmonton *Post* contains a report of the trial of the Indians charged with killing a Wendigo or Wehtiko. It is as follows:

The very interesting trial of the Indians charged with killing Louison Moostoos ended on Saturday last by the conviction of Napaysoosis and the acquittal of Payoo. The former, as he had been in prison since March last, was sentenced to only two months' hard labour. Although it was confidently expected both Indians would have been acquitted, this verdict and sentence are satisfactory, inasmuch as they will teach the northern tribes respect for the majesty of the law, and prove a salutary lesson.

The whole story of the killing is an interesting example of one of the deep-rooted beliefs and superstittons of these unfortunate people, and better than a whole volume shows up the devil worship and sorcery of the Wood Crees, to which tribe both the prisoners belong.

The history of the crime, if crime there were, may be best learned from the words of Napaysoosis himself, as taken down from his own lips by Mr. George W. Gairdner, who was retained by the Crown as interpreter for the accused and was in constant attendance at the trial. Mr. Gairdner, having spent many years in the north country as a factor in the Hudson's Bay Company, is proficient in Cree and other Indian dialects, and well versed in Indian lore, and readers of the *Post* may expect from his pen a series of sketches of life in this country in the early days which promise to be most interesting.

Last winter a band of us, thirty-two in number, counting women and children, were living at the Bald Hills, some 75 miles west of Lesser Slave Lake. We lived in two shacks and two teepees. Entominahoo, our Chief, along with Kunuksoos and myself and our families, lived in one shack, Moostoos and his family, with some others, lived in the other shack, and the other Indians in the two teepees. We were all on the best of terms with one another and Moostoos was especially well liked by all of us.

Some months before he was killed Moostoos told several of us that he was afraid an evil spirit was getting the better of him and that he would turn Sehtiko (Cannibal), adding, "If I ever go wrong you had better kill me, as I do not wish to destroy my children." The time passed on, however, till about the 23rd of March.

At that time some sickness was affecting the Indians, and two of them — Napaysis and the "little old man" — were being treated by Entominahoo, in his own shack, which might be termed the hospital, as all the sick were taken there to be doctored. Entominahoo was chief medicine man. The third day before he was killed Moostoos also went there to join in the medicine-making and sorceries, which were being practised with a view to curing the sick men.

During the last day and night I saw Moostoos was not looking as usual. His eyes were rolling and glittering, and he seemed afraid to look anyone in the face, and he was all the time muttering to himself. On one occasion he said: "I look on these children as young moose, and long to eat them." I was absent from the shack part of the day, and when I came back towards evening, Moostoos looked wilder and more dangerous than ever, and it was clear to all present that he was becoming a Wehtiko.

Ordinary incantations were tried, but without result, and as a last resort the "medicine lodge" was erected in the shack, and the whole skill and power of all our sorceries was enlisted in the attempt to bring Moostoos back to reason. It was certain from his appearance, words and actions, that he had no bodily complaint, but that he was possessed with a devil. Our usual ceremonies were begun. The singing of medicine songs, drumming and dancing were carried on from sundown till about midnight, and as Moostoos was lying, covered with two blankets, comparatively quiet, the medicine seemed to have a good effect.

There were in the house at that time Entominahoo and his wife, Eliza, the wife of "Redhead," Felix's wife, "Redhead," Kunuksoos and his wife, Napaysis, and "the little old man"; as I said before, these last were lying sick. All but the sick men and Kunuksoos, who was taking care of them, were grouped round Moostoos, striving, by medicine songs and other means at our command, to drive the evil spirit out of him. Entominahoo, our chief "doctor," was inside the "medicine" circle, having his wand, and using all his science and skill toward the same end.

Suddenly Moostoos called out, "This night you will all die," and commenced twitching his limbs and rolling his eyes. Two of us, Chuckachuck and myself, went and sat on each side of him at his shoulders, prepared to hold him down if he became violent, while the two young women, Eliza and Felix's wife, sat at his feet. At this juncture, "Redhead," sick with fright, left the shack. Moostoos began throwing his arms about, and tried to get up, saying again, "If I get up I will kill you all tonight." The four of us laid hold of his arms and legs and held him down, while Entominahoo continued his "medicine," using the most powerful songs and incantations at his command.

Moostoos now became unmanageable, flung us off, rose to his feet, and sprang into the air, exclaiming, "I will kill you all; I will not leave one alive." Fear, intense, blind fear, took hold of us. We jumped up and, in spite of his gigantic struggles, we managed to pull him down and cover him with blankets. Entominahoo left his medicine lodge and sat down close to Moostoos, saying, "It's no use; I can do no more; do your best to hold him."

Moostoos struggled fearfully, throwing his head about and grinding his teeth, and twice he tried to bite me, tearing my coat. At that time I was holding his right arm, Chuckachuck his left, while the two women held his feet. I covered his face after he tried to bite me. The noise of the drumming and singing had been going on all the time.

By this time we were crazy with fear, and what followed is like a dream. Eliza sprang to her feet holding in her right hand a medicine belt and in her left an axe. Her hair was flying loose, and she was dancing and singing. All of a sudden she ran around and thrashed Moostoos over the face and breast with this medicine help several times.

"Did she strike him with the axe?"

I cannot say as my head was bent low over Moostoos, say, but I saw blood outside the blanket after she thrashed him, and I only knew of two cuts on the head, while the policeman found three. She then handed the axe to Chuckachuck (which I saw) and said, "Here, brother-in-law." Chuckachuck struck him with the axe and split his skull.

That blow killed Moostoos. Chuckachuck then handed me the axe and a knife which I refused at first, till Chuckachuck called me a coward, and said I wanted them all killed. I then drove the knife into his belly, and stuck the axe into his body over the heart, leaving both weapons in the wounds.

"Did Moostoos breath after he got the first blow?"

Yes, a little; but he had stopped breathing before I struck him. At that moment Payoo, the other prisoner, alarmed by the screams of fear from the women and the calls of the men, entered the shack. He was handed an axe, and very reluctantly, and actually without looking where he was striking, struck the corpse on the head with the axe.

"What did we do that night?"

Why, we sat around the body till daylight, by the light of the fire.

"What for?"

We expected him to rise from the dead, and we wanted to kill him again if he tried to get up.

"What do you think was the matter with Moostoos?"

He was a Wehtiko, and I know he had a lump of ice in his body causing the malady. Why, we made strong tea and poured it boiling hot into the axe hole and the breast to thaw that ice, but first Dayoo and I drove a stake into the ground; then we pulled out the stake and poured in the hot tea. After that towards morning, Entominahoo's wife and I tied his legs with chains to two pickets driven into the ground.

"Why did you do this?"

So that if he came to life again he could not get up and run after us. And last of all, next day I cut his head off with an axe.

"What was that for?"

To be sure he was dead, and in order that even if he got up he could not eat us. Then we left him in the shack, tied up the door and left the place.

"What is a Wehtiko?"

A Wehtiko is a person, man or woman, into whose body enters a most malignant evil spirit, which incites him to kill and eat his fellow men. He is possessed of superhuman strength and cunning, and the only thing that saves the Indians is that a Wehtiko generally warns them of his coming state some time beforehand. It has always been our custom to kill these people. It was the only way to protect our lives from their violence.

This story was not taken from the lips of a raving maniac, nor was it copied from some old black-letter history of the ninth or tenth century. The atrocity occurred not five months ago, within three hundred miles of this town, and, above all, the details were sworn to in open court. The pitiful story, shocking in its hideous circumstance, must excite detestation on account of its depravity, but at the same time it must arouse compassion for these debased beings who can be so remorselessly moved by their superstitions.

WE FOUND THE SARCOPHAGUS

This newspaper story makes entertaining reading. One wonders just how much of it is based on fact. No contemporary archaeologist, anthropologist, or ethnologist would make the statements that are reported here!
"The Mummy of Harrison Lake" appeared in the *Daily Colonist*, 16 Sept. 1899.

The Mummy of Harrison Lake
Harlan Smith's Contribution to Archaeological Lore of This Province
His Ancient [Mummy] Sent to New York Museum as Ruler of Northwest Indians

From our Own Correspondent.

Vancouver, Sept. 14. — Prof. Harlan L. Smith, of New York, who recently made the discovery of an Indian mummy near Harrison Lake a few days ago, shipped it to New York. Professor Smith thinks, and local archaeologists agree with him, that the mummy is probably hundreds of years old.

It is the most remarkable find of a two years' search for native relics, pursued by Professor Smith on this Coast.

A couple of years ago a well-known New York millionaire, whose interests were, particularly at that time, in the Klondike, subscribed a large amount of money to the National Museum of New York, as an endowment for the purpose of carrying on anthropological research on the Pacific Coast.

Professor Smith and his staff are now about finishing their work here, and the find that they made the other day is by far the most interesting of any discoveries ever made west of the Rockies.

Professor Smith had been scouring the district around Harrison Lake for two months. The section is a well-known mining district, and the formation of a limestone character, in which relics of soft material have been easily preserved. The mummy was found in a cave immediately alongside a trail leading up the mountain. Smith and his men had passed the place dozens of time, without ever thinking of the possibility of the existence of a cave in the vicinity. A great mass of white limestone and granite formed the "hog's back" of the mountainside, and where the cave was found was somewhat moss grown and weather beaten. Big boulders, which scores of years ago had fallen from the mountain, were piled up several feet in front of the cave. One day in passing by Professor Smith noticed the smooth stones which blockaded the entrance to the cave, and he immediately proceeded to investigate.

The face of the rock was covered with strange hiero-glyphics, much defaced. Professor Smith says:

"After using a pick a short time we had practically to blast the face of the rock away, as the cave had been hermetically sealed. The reason for this was apparent from what we found later. We lighted ourselves into the cave, which was perhaps 20 feet square, and high enough for convenient standing room. I do not think that there had ever been any mineral found in the cave, but as the sunlight streamed in at the newly made opening, the walls fairly blazed with crystal reflections. Around the sides of the cave were shelves hewn out of the rock, and in one of these we found the sarcophagus which contained the mummy which has been shipped to New York. The other shelves had evidently been intended for like receptacles, but for some reason the cave had been sealed up with only one body in the vault.

"The sarcophagus was simply a stone coffin, and without any top covering. Anyone who has ever opened an Egyptian mummy case, no matter how many thousand years the subject has been disposed of in this way, will always afterward recognize the peculiar odour, which was the same which emanated from the sarcophagus we found.

"The wrappings were of peculiar texture. From the neck downwards there was fully a dozen folds of a thick cloth composed half of hair and half of stringy bark. I have seen the same sort of matting used by the Indians in Alaska. The face looks very similar to the ordinary Egyptian mummy, and was preserved as well as any of the mummies I have seen. The particular feature of the ancient's head was his high forehead, which makes me think that he was of the tribes who must have lived before the flat-faced, squat-headed Siwash Indians of the present day.

"We unwrapped one hand, which was shrivelled up to mere skin and bone, some of the nails having already disappeared. The mummy had been a tall man of large proportions, another indication of his being of a race different from the Pacific Coast Indians, who are short, and do not average 5 feet. The mummy, by actual measurement, was over 6 feet tall.

"Around the ankles and wrists were bands of silver, alloyed with some other metal, which went to show, with the other trappings and the sarcophagus, that the man must have been a ruler of his people.

"I think he must have been a member of the tribes living in the Northwest before the forbears of the present race arrived — as is generally conceded — from the Eastern Asiatic coast.

"The texture of the wrappings, as I have already mentioned, bore some evidences of a civilization at least a few degrees above the standard of savages."

Professor Smith's statements are verified by parties living in the district, who have examined the cave and have seen the mummy.

Professor Smith is now in Secum, Ore., looking up the particulars of some important discoveries there. He will return to New York in October.

THE EVIL SPIRIT OF THEIR CHIEF

Is it permissible to slay a person possessed of the Wendigo?

The Wendigo or Windigo is the spirit of cannibalism and the personification of greed among the Algonkian-speaking Indians who comprise about two-thirds of Canada's Indian population. But it is also (in this instance, at least) a person.

"Killed a Wendigo: Two Cat Lake Indians to Be Tried in Winnipeg for Murdering Their Chief" appeared in the *Medicine Hat Weekly News* (Medicine Hat, Alta.), 2 Nov. 1899. The Dominion Police was founded as a security force and intelligence unit in 1868; in 1920 it was incorporated into the Royal Canadian Mounted Police. Rat Portage is the old name of Kenora, Ont.

Killed a Wendigo:
Two Cat Lake Indians to Be Tried in Winnipeg
for Murdering Their Chief

RAT PORTAGE, Oct. 29. — R.G. Chamberlain, of the Dominion police, Ottawa, and A.B.J. Bannatyre, Indian agent at Lac Seul, are in town with three Indians in their custody. Two of the Indians are charged with shooting their chief last winter at Cat Lake, about 350 miles northeast of Dinorwie. The story told by the two prisoners is essentially as follows: The chief of the Cat Lake Indians called Abw-ah-sa keh-mig, became a wendigo, or insane, and ordered the prisoners to shoot him. A council of the tribe was called and they discussed the matter for two days, when they arrived at the conclusion that the chief's orders would have to be obeyed. The wendigo lay down in his wigwam and indicated with his hand where they were to shoot him. After he was dead, wood was heaped upon his body and the fire kept going for two days, thereby, according to the belief of the Indians, thoroughly destroying the evil spirit of their chief.

The matter was reported to Mr. Bannatyre, but as the Cat Lake tribe are non-treaty Indians, special legislation was passed last July to cover the case. Constable Chamberlain went to Lac Seul, where Mr. Bannatyre and two guides joined him, and they made the 700 mile journey in twenty days. The arrest of the two Indians was effected without trouble and when seen by a correspondent yesterday smoking their pipes at the Russel house they appeared to rather enjoy their captivity. The third Indian was brought along as a witness. Two of them had never seen a railroad or train before and only one of them had ever seen horses or cows. They are magnificent specimens of the red man and are above the average of their race in intelligence.

They are being held here for an order to take them to Winnipeg for trial, as the assizes are over here. The greatest wonder of the prisoners since their arrival here has been how the white man gets his living. They say everyone seems to be walking about doing nothing. By doing something their idea is hunting or fishing. Messrs. Bannatyre and Chamberlain say they are under great obligations to J.W. Anderson and Robt. Arnett of the Hudson Bay posts at Lac Seul and Cat Lake respectively, for assistance on the trip.

THE NEW RACE OF PEOPLE

Lost Races abound in the polar regions of the world, at least in imaginative novels of fantasy and science fiction.

Here is a traveller's tale — in part a survivor's tale — of a journey made to an otherwise inaccessible locale where there are wonders to behold.

"Saw North Pole" appeared in the *St. John Daily Sun* (Saint John, N.B.), 28 March 1900. The French Canadian's name is spelled "Le Joie" in the subheading and "La Joie" in the news story itself. The story presumably originally appeared in the *New York Herald*, a once-popular newspaper like a tabloid that was widely read because it carried bizarre tales and inventive stories.

Saw North Pole Strange Story of a Trapper —
Joseph Z. Le Joie a French Canadian,
Excites Interest of Scientists by Claim
That He Visited "Farthest North" and Found New Race

New York, March 18. — Joseph Zotique La Joie says that he discovered the north pole and a new race of people. He is a French-Canadian hunter and trapper, who has spent many years in the Arctic regions. His story is a marvellous one. By the request of the New York Herald, and accompanied by one of the New York Herald's reporters, he went on Wednesday last to Washington. He courted scientific investigation of his stories, and they are now being scientifically investigated.

At the Hotel Raleigh in Washington on Wednesday last Mr. La Joie met General A.W. Greely, chief of the signal service and an Arctic explorer of great fame; Admiral George W. Melville of the United States navy (retired), of whom Melville Island is named and who is recognized as one of the greatest living authorities on Arctic matters. Professor J.W. McGee of the Smithsonian Institution, of world wide celebrity as an ethnologist, and other great scientists. Not one of these scientists is willing to unqualifiedly endorse the statements made by M. La Joie. All have found in his explanations some apparent inconsistencies, but all have also found in them much accuracy concerning matters with which they are well acquainted.

On the whole, it seems that there is probably considerable truth in the strange stories told by M. La

Joie. That the man penetrated far into the Arctic is certain. He claims to be able to substantiate all of his amazing statements by producing relics of the new race of people which he found in the "farthest north," and even by showing the bodies of two natives of this strange tribe, which he says are cached within comparatively easy access.

In December, 1886, according to his narrative, La Joie and his father started from Montreal for Battleford, Northwest Territory. After three years' hunting through British Columbia and Alaska he arrived at Great Bear Lake in the fall of 1889. Game having grown scarce, he determined to push further north with a partner, a man named George White. Toward the spring of 1892 they found themselves near Cape Brianard. Hunting in this vicinity, they learned from the natives of an iron post left by some explorer. On this they found the following marks: "82 degrees latitude north, 83 degrees longitude west."

To the north of this a few miles they made their camp in May, 1892. This camp was established at the junction of two immense icebergs, and White proposed that they separate and each take a ten days' journey on three diverging points of ice to find the best hunting ground. La Joie, while returning, felt on the seventh day a tremendous shock like an earthquake. It meant that the ice had parted and that he was adrift. Admiral Melville, the other day in Washington, agreed that La Joie's description of the phenomenon was accurate. The berg drifted to the north. For three days he lived on fish, hoping against hope that a wind that had sprung up from the south would drive him back to the main land. For a period of thirty-six days he was adrift, he says, amid terrible storms of snow, hail and sleet. Land was sighted on several occasions, but he was unable to get ashore. On the morning of the thirty-seventh day, hav-ing eaten six of his dogs and suffered many torments, La Joie found that the berg on which he had drifted had touched land. He got ashore with his remaining dogs. He says that the farther north the berg drifted the milder became the climate.

That night La Joie was awakened by the barking of his dogs. He jumped to his feet and found that he was surrounded by a tribe of copper colored natives, who were shooting at him with bows and arrows. La Joie was armed only with a knife and a club, but his double suit of skin protected him from the arrows. The next day they were willing to treat for peace.

He describes the men whom he joined as belonging to a strange race, speaking a tongue entirely unlike that of the other natives whom he had met in his travels. Their complexion, he states, was of a reddish-brown hue, and their eyes and hair were either black or brown. The men were very large, averaging more than 6 feet in height. Their clothes were made of skins and shaped after a strange fashion. He remained in the camp five months. The party, having concluded the hunt in which they were engaged, took La Joie with them to their principal settlement, a five days' journey across a rocky country. They came finally to the entrance to a great cave. The sub-chief in charge of the party summoned to the mouth of the cave the great chief of all the tribes which inhabit that country. The leader scrutinized the stranger for a period of five minutes, and then said something to his people in their native language. The stranger, thinking that they were about to kill him, turned and ran until out of the range of arrows, then, stopping, he took from his pocket a flint a steel. With these he struck fire. La Joie gathered some twigs and built a fire. For a few minutes the natives watched him, and then approached, threw down their bows and arrows, and indicated that they wished to be friends. They had known nothing of fire previously.

La Joie states that he soon came to live with the natives on terms of the most friendly intercourse. Owing to the reverence in which he was held, they made him, he says, the chief and ruler of the tribe, a position he held for two years. Since his arrival on the island La Joie's attention had been repeatedly attracted by a strange and apparently volcanic light. This shone forth steadily at all times, casting an effulgent glowing over the surrounding country. La Joie determined to investigate. He finally set forth with a party of natives and came within full view of the great mountain from which the light seemed to come. Here he discovered what he firmly believes to be the north pole.

THE KNIGHTS OF THE THROTTLE

Lonely stretches of railroad track are said to be haunted. There are innumerable reports of haunted stations and even round-houses. But this story is a rarity: the account of a haunted locomotive engine. This news story appeared in the *St. John's Daily News*, St. John's, Nfld., 9 Dec. 1904.

A Haunted Locomotive on the Intercolonial
Engine 239, — The Man Killer —
Said to Be Infested with a Ghostly Visitor —
Several Engineers Have Been Killed on Her — Has Unenviable Record

Has the I.C.R. a haunted engine?

This question is agitating the minds of the public generally, and particularly the knights of the throttle and their assistants in the cab who are employed on the government railway.

Is 239 haunted?

Is this ill-fated engine hooded?

The general opinion of I.C.R. men is that she is, and this particular locomotive is now looked upon with fear and trembling.

Superstition has its devotees in every calling of life. At the cradle the anxious mother will be heard saying, "The goblins will catch you if you don't watch out." Time goes on and as one enters the state of manhood he has his misgiving, his forebodings, governed by his superstitious make-up; the sailors at sea, the soldier in the battlefield, the ordinary individual in every day life — each has his problems in this respect.

Probably no calling has more cause for superstition than that of the man in front, or in other words, the man who handles the throttle and lever, and to whose exactness, wisdom and foresight is intrusted the lives of the travelling public.

Coming back to the direct basis of these few preliminary remarks, no doubt the past history of engine No. 392 will be read with interest.

It is said, and on good authority, that since the construction of this locomotive for the I.C.R. several fatalities are recorded. Trainmen, and the public generally remember the disaster at Belmont when Sam Trider, who for thirty-odd years ran an engine between Moncton and Truro, met his death. The train on this occasion was running by Belmont station. Suddenly there was a smash and a general mix-up. No. 239 had left the rails. From what cause is as yet a mystery. She swayed to and fro and suddenly lunged to the right, toppling over. Fireman Harry Campbell was thrown through the cab window and landed in a pile of snow dazed but uninjured, while Sam Trider, the engineer, met death at his post.

Again, 239 was in the wreck at Windsor Jct. In this, Driver Wall, an old and trusted I.C.R. man, lost his life. It was late in the evening and a C.P.R. train driven by Wall, and the freight from Halifax with Driver Mel. Copeland, were to cross at the junction. Copeland passed the semaphore and danger signals, and the crash came. Four persons including Driver Wall were killed and several more or less injured. Upwards of 70 cars were derailed, many being dashed over the embankment and smashed into kindling wood.

On another occasion, No. 239 jumped the rail at Humphrey's mills and the driver and firemen miraculously escaped death or at least serious injury. Again, north of Moncton, she met with a serious mishap.

After each accident she was sent to the Moncton shops and repaired, and the query was frequently voiced by I.C.R. men, "Who will be her next victim?"

At all events, even the I.C.R. round house cleaners at Moncton have a great aversion to working on 239. A story of a somewhat ghostly character is told.

It is reported that not long ago a cleaner while doing some work around a locomotive, casually glanced into the cab, says that he saw a man standing at the throttle. Not having seen any one enter the cab he hailed the supposed driver, and receiving no reply, again looked in, but the man had vanished. He made immediate enquiries, but nearby workmen had not seen anyone entering or leaving the cab.

The cleaner in question is positive that he saw a man

there, and no argument can alter his opinion.

At all events the general opinion among the men is that 239 should now be consigned to the scrap heap.

Repairs and renovations to this locomotive during her career on the I.C.R. have gone to prove her a veritable white elephant.

The engine has been in the service of the I.C.R. for some two years and her record is an unenviable one. — *St. John Times.*

ASTONISHING AGILITY

Mowgli is the familiar name of the wild boy of Rudyard Kipling's *The Jungle Books* (1894-95). The so-called Jungle Books are works of fiction, albeit popular and influential ones. (I have long suspected that they were eagerly read by the young Edgar Rice Burroughs and hence were an influence on his memorable creation Tarzan of the Apes.) Here is an account, albeit a brief one, of a real-life Mowgli.

"Alberni Has a Wild Man" appeared in the *Yukon World*, 24 Aug. 1906. It is possible that the woods in the vicinity of Dawson City, Y.T., were full of wild men, or at least full of exhibitionists. For instance, the following item appeared in the same newspaper, 21 July 1907:

Wild Man Not Yet Captured
Police Are Still Hunting in the Mountain for the Man without Clothes

"Two policemen were out on the hill back of Dawson all yesterday afternoon, looking for the wild man who shed his clothes and scared the berry pickers.

"The two men were on horseback so as to make more rapid progress. They went over the whole of the summit back to the next dome, but failed to discover any trace of the missing man."

But back to the original tale....

Alberni Has a Wild Man
Vancouver Island Mowgli Said to Be No Myth
Seen by a Prospector Recently

Vancouver, B.C., Aug. 5. — The famous Vancouver Island mowgli is no myth. A prospector is now in Vancouver who says he saw the wild man at Alberni a few days ago. He will not allow his name to be used, asserting that he is "not looking for notoriety." He says:

"A few days ago myself and another prospector dropped right onto the wild man on the shores of Horn Lake, Alberni. The mowgli was clothed in sunshine and a smile, except that his body was covered with a growth of hair much like the salmon berry-eating bears that infest the region. The wild man ran with astonishing agility as soon as he saw us.

"We found the wickieup in which he had been sheltering and also many traces of where he had been gathering roots along the lake bank for sustenance. That wild man is no figment of the imagination. You can take my word for that."

WILD WOMAN

Although only two paragraphs long, this news story sparks the imagination! Who is this woman of the woods? Who is Prof. McAuley, and why does he remember seeing her? How come he knows so much about her and her way of life?

"Wild Woman in Gatineau Woods" is reprinted from the *Bulletin* (Edmonton, Alta.), Aug. 28, 1907.

Wild Woman in Gatineau Woods Harvard Professor Tells Story of Woman Who Hunts like Diana and Dresses like Eve

Ottawa, Aug. 17. — Prof. McAuley, of Harvard University, Cambridge, Mass., is in town, having spent a few weeks in the country surrounding the Gatineau, and he brings down with him a strange story of a wild woman. While hunting one day in the woods, a scurry in the undergrowth caused him to turn his loaded rifle in the hope that game was near.

Reverts to Fig Leaves

To his surprise, however, a face peered at him from the shadows. It was a wild face, tanned to a dark brown by the sun, but she seemed to be dressed in nothing but leaves. The poor creature has not a companion, save a number of dogs, who help her in procuring food. She lives mostly on the fruits of her hunting excursions. It appears that owing to some injury done the woman some years ago, she has shunned human company since.

THE FACE OF THE RELIC

This article describes an "interesting Indian relic" that seems to have appeared and then disappeared. One wonders where it is today. In 2003 it will not be found among the holdings of the Library of the Saskatchewan Legislature.

"Mound Dwellers Sun God in Stone" is reprinted from the *Regina Leader-Post*, Sask., 21 Nov. 1907.

Mound Dwellers Sun God in Stone An Interesting Indian Relic from File Hills sent to Regina

A curious stone is to be seen at the Government library, Regina. It was dug up in the File Hills district between Fort Qu'Appelle and the Beaver Hills on Christmas eve, 1905, by Mr. Chas. Noddings, an English gentleman who has resided for many years in the province.

We have been favored with the manuscript of a letter from Mr. Victor Noddings, son of the above named, which contains some interesting particulars. Mr. Victor Noddings, writing from File Hills, under the date of April 27, 1906, before the stone had been forwarded to Regina, says:

"I must tell you about a wonderful prehistoric stone carving we have in our possession. It was found by a young fellow on top of a steep hill near here. Carved upon it is the representation of a face, a setting sun, and other marks. The people here did not take much notice of it. We, however, thought it was of some value so one day we (father and son) went with a friend to take a sketch of it. We took with us, besides pencil and paper, a pick and shovel, intending to dig some of the earth from around it in order to discover if possible any other marks there might be.

"The ground was frozen, so it took us longer than we had expected, and as there was no time to complete the drawing then, we were obliged to bring it home.

"My father wrote to several scientific societies, among others the Smithsonian Institute, who informed us that it was the opinion of the Chief of the American Ethnological Bureau that the stone was a petroglyph, common in southern countries, and had probably been the site of the altar, during the time of the Mound Dwellers. We could not help connecting this stone in our minds with Hultzilopochtle, the Mexican Sun God. The place where we found it was weird and desolate being an abrupt hill overlooking a great plain. One rather dramatic incident in connection with the stone I cannot refrain from mentioning. It was Christmas Eve and we had been working hard at the frozen ground for three hours and had almost given up in despair as darkness would soon be upon us.

"Suddenly we succeeded in loosening the stone, and at that moment the sun, which had been sinking behind a bank of clouds, burst out and bathed the stone for the last time in a flood of light. We stood silently watching till the last rays had disappeared and I thought of how many sunsets our old Sun God had witnessed, and wondered if he might not also have taken his silent part in many a terrible sacrifice. The stone will be sent to Regina, and will be the first specimen of the future Provincial Museum of Saskatchewan. The Museum of Toronto tried hard to get possession of it, but my father thought it right to offer it to our own province first."

The face of the relic is about two feet by two feet three. Perhaps some of our readers may have information relating to other Indian stones of this description.

A WILD MAN

This is a surprisingly gripping account of a deranged man's descent into the state of barbarity. The reader can only feel sorry for the man, whose name is given as Beck, and wish him well.

The story is reproduced from the columns of the *Capital* (Edmonton, Alta.), 21 Feb. 1911. Some minor changes have been made in punctuation. As well, in the first sentence, the word "incredible" has been changed to the more likely "incredible." Indeed, this news story is among the most *creditable* of the stories in this collection.

Wild Man of the Woods Capture
Lived Near Kenora like Animal for Four Years
Threatened to Kill All Who Came Near

Toronto, Feb. 21. — An almost incredible tale of the existence in the northern woods of a wild man, who for four years lived like a beast, threatening to kill everyone with whom he came in contact, reached Toronto this morning with the news of the arrest near Kenora of a man named Beck. The "wild man" was arrested in his rocky cave in the woods and is now in Regina jail waiting to be sent to an asylum.

Beck is forty years old and his career as a wild man dates back to 1907 when his hand was blown off while he was dynamiting for fish. The accident apparently unhinged his mind for, upon his discharge from the hospital, he took to the bush.

For two or three years he roamed the woods, living upon fish, rabbits and other animals, which he killed with his naked hand and devoured raw. All this time his presence was unknown to the lumbermen and trappers. Some lumbermen, who saw a figure flitting through the woods at dusk, thought he was the ghost of some murdered prospector, while superstitious men refused to venture forth from their shanties at night.

During the past year or so, he has been seen on a number of occasions, and the bushmen decided that he was no ghost, but a lunatic. To some lumbermen with whom he talked, he declared that he was a timber baron and owned all the timber in the woods where he lived. He threatened to kill any man who trespassed upon his domain and several times tried to burn the woods.

The amazing endurance of the man was indicated by his appearance of a district 26 miles square, and he appeared to be constantly on the move.

The matter finally was taken up by the provincial authorities, and Constable Grassick of Ignace received instructions to capture the wild man and take him to Kenora. A few days ago he secured the assistance of two C.P.R. constables and set out for the cave in the woods where Beck was supposed to live.

When taken to Kenora jail he presented a most pitiable sight and looked more like a gorilla than a human being. The hair on his head and face was fifteen inches long and matted hair and grime obscured his features. His clothing was the skins of sheep he had killed bound together with fragments of wire. The provincial authorities, it is understood, will have him sent to an asylum.

I STOOD STILL WONDERING

This most interesting statutory declaration was made in September of 1957 by Charles Flood of New Westminster, B.C.

Flood, an old-timer at the time, was a one-time prospector, and in his declaration he recalled a most unusual event that had happened to him more than four decades earlier. At the time he was prospecting in the Chilliwack Lake area of British Columbia with two of his friends. Did they espy the Sasquatch, the hairy wild man of the rugged B.C. Interior?

Flood's declaration appeared in full in Ivan T. Sanderson's book *Abominable Snowmen: Legend Come to Life* (New York: Jove/HBJ Book, 1977).

I, Charles Flood of New Westminster (formerly of Hope), declare the following story to be true:

I am 75 years of age and spent most of my life prospecting in the local mountains to the south of Hope, towards the American boundary and in the Chilliwack Lake area.

In 1915, Donald McCrae and Green Hicks of Agassiz, B.C., and myself, explored an area over an unknown divide, on the way back to Hope, near the Holy Cross Mountains.

Green Hicks, a half-breed Indian, told McCrae and me a story, he claimed he had seen alligators at what he called Alligator Lake, and wild humans at what he called Cougar Lake. Out of curiosity we went with him; he had been there a week previous looking for a fur trap line. Sure enough, we saw his alligators, but they were black, twice the size of lizards in a small mud lake.

Awhile further up was Cougar Lake. Several years before a fire swept over many square miles of mountains which resulted in large areas of mountain huckleberry growth. Green Hicks suddenly stopped us and drew our attention to a large, light brown creature about eight feet high, standing on its hind legs (standing upright) pulling the berry bushes with one hand or paw toward him and putting berries in his mouth with the other hand, or paw.

I stood still wondering, and McRae and Green Hicks were arguing. Hicks said, "It is a wild man," and McCrae said, "It is a bear." As far as I am concerned the strange creature looked more like a human being. We had seen several black and brown bear on the trip, but that thing looked altogether different.

Huge brown bear are known to be in Alaska, but have never been seen in southern British Columbia.

THE PHANTOM FORM DISAPPEARED

Mammoths are part of the fossil record. These elephant-like creatures roamed the polar world during the Pleistocene Epoch (which lasted 2.5 million years and ended 10,000 years ago). Reliable reports have been published of the carcasses of woolly mammoths being accidentally exposed and thawed out and then consumed by dogs. Indeed, the Russian chronicler Alexander Solzhenitsyn describes prisoners in the Gulag uncovering and then hungrily consuming the once-frozen flesh of a mammoth.

"Dawson Prospector Says He Has Found Ancient Mammoth" appeared in the *Dawson Daily News*, 22 July 1915. R.A. Fox's tale may very well be a tall tale. Perhaps the "mammoth steak" was asbestos fiber.

Dawson Prospector Says He Has Found Ancient Mammoth

"Waitah, bring me a mammoth steak!"

Such may be the cry in Dawson within a few days if R.A. Fox has just what he thinks he has. Fox blew into town today from up the Yukon with a gunnysack filled with what he declares is the steak of a prehistoric mammoth.

"Have I got it? Well, I should say I have," declared Fox today.

"Just wait a few minutes," continued Fox, "and I will bring you some of the mammoth with the fat clinging to the sides of the meat.

Fox was gone a short while, and returned to the News office with several slabs wrapped in a gunnysack. Unwrapping it in the presence of several who had not been informed what the material was supposed to be, Fox said:

"Now, see here, what is it?"

A sourdough miner stepped up and looked through his glasses carefully as he turned over the strange substance.

"Why," exclaimed the sourdough, "that's asbestos. Sure thing. I've seen it in the raw state, and I've seen the finished product."

A veteran "print" who had called on the News dropped in and asked what it was.

"Feeling the material carefully," he declared, "why asbestos, of course. Wish I had plenty of that for future use."

In ambled a third man, who was shown a piece, and asked his verdict. "Well, it looks like wood fibre," declared he cautiously.

A cheechaco from Tacoma walked in and was shown the samples.

"What does she look like, Mr. Cheechaco?" said the discoverer.

"You don't get me on that," said the cheechaco. "I've visited Seattle in my day, and I have nothing to say."

"Well, now just let me tell you fellows what it is you are looking at," said Fox. "That long, white, stringy, slabby stuff is nothing more or less than the flesh of a prehistoric mammoth reduced to fibre. That whiter portion, which is less marked by strings, is the residue of the fat. The real grease evaporated."

"Where did you shoot that mammoth?" piped a fellow in the crowd.

"Well, may be you boys think you have it on me," rejoined Fox, "but let me tell you I did shoot him, and I shot him on the Yukon river bank above Dawson, and the carcass is now there."

All the fellows opened their mouths with astonishment. Everyone was from Missouri.

"But it's the way," said Fox. "I shot him while he was lying compressed under a million tons of rock, and where he had been resting for two hundred million years.

"As I was coming down the Yukon river in the canoe the other day, I put over to the right limit of the river below the mouth of the Sixty-mile river.

"In a secluded bend in the river, where it was almost a cove, I observed in a cliff about thirty feet high a singular whitish object projecting a foot or so from the regular face of the rock. I got closer to it, and on inspection found it was the end of a mammoth tusk. I took a shot at it with my rifle and brought down a part of the ivory. That confirmed my first suspicions. I had done ivory carving in Dawson for years, and I know mammoth ivory from mastodon ivory quite well. The mastodon ivory is checked like a crocodile hide, and yellow-ish, while that of the mammoth is whitish and has a long grain.

"After securing the sample of the tusk, I got several sticks of dynamite, and placed them in the face of the bluff just beneath the point where the tusk protruded. There is where I shot the mammoth. Those several shots of dynamite disturbed enough of his prehistoric majesty to afford me these samples. The dynamite explosions freed a cap of rock along the face of the bluff so that the mammoth remains were exposed. The strata is two feet thick and twenty feet along the exposed edge. I did not have time to drift in on the proposition, but I feel assured the bones are there unless absorbed or done away by leaching of the water and the chemical action in the rocks.

"Now, it is only a matter of recovering the rest of the fibre. I believe that the mammoth was caught under the heavy rock from above, which crushed him against the other rock beneath, and, being encased hermetically, the fibre was preserved. I threw some of the white fibre to my cats, and they gnawed on it. Since it did not hurt them, I have eaten some, and I think mammoth steak is all right. Of course it is a little drier than jerked beef, and lacks the salt, but we can get plenty of salt.

"Dr. Alfred Brooks, the American geologist, will be here tomorrow on the Dawson, and I shall call the mammoth discovery to his attention, and get his views on the matter. When Dr. Cairnes, the Canadian geologist, arrives here later this season, I shall ask him to go up and examine the find, and he may tell me just now to remove the big fellow."

Mr. Fox has samples of the mammoth at Nick's place, on Queen street. Mr. Fox has been prospecting and following other pursuits in Yukon several years.

Several years ago he had a thrilling experience in a cabin on Quartz creek, where a miner who had been killed by an accident, reappeared at night in the corner of the cabin and operated a rocker and held a conversation with Fox. At the end of the conversation the phantom form disappeared suddenly.

ABDUCTED BY THE SASQUATCHES

Here is an astonishing tale, a "classic case" of an abduction by a sasquatch. It is also an amazingly readable narrative. The characteristics that set it apart from other accounts of chance encounters between human beings and those hairy, ape-like creatures that are believed by some observers to inhabit the wild interior of British Columbia are its detail, its sweep, its drama, and its verisimilitude.

Albert Ostman, a Canadian prospector with a Scandinavian background, was sixty-four years old in 1957 and living near Fort Langley, B.C. In longhand in a scribbler, he wrote out the account of his 1924 abduction. Before a Justice of the Peace on August 20, 1957, he sword as follows: "And I make this solemn Declaration conscientiously believing it to be true, and knowing that it is of the same force and effect as if made under oath and by virtue of the Canada Evidence Act."

There is a description of Ostman in the process of writing out his experiences by journalist John Green in his publication *On the Track of the Sasquatch* (1968):

When he was asked to recall all he could of his encounter with the Sasquatch back in 1924, he went about it by gathering whatever he could on hand from that period, including, among other things, a shopping list used in getting ready for one of his prospecting trips. Then he set about rebuilding the experience in detail, including his own actions prior to and following the actual encounter, in an attempt to re-enter, as much as possible, the scene of events that took place more than 30 years ago.

When he was later asked if he would swear to the accuracy of the account, he made it clear that he could do so only as to the main elements of the story, not the surrounding detail. Here is the story that he wrote. Here is his account. It is in the hands of the reader to decide what to make of it.

I have always followed logging and construction work. This time I had worked over one year on a construction job, and thought a good vacation was in order. B.C. is famous for lost gold mines. One is supposed to be at the head of Toba Inlet — why not look for this mine and have a vacation at the same time? I took the Union Steamship boat to Lund, B.C. From there I hired an old Indian to take me to the head of Toba Inlet.

This old Indian was a very talkative old gentleman. He told me stories about gold brought out by a white man from this lost mine. This white man was a very heavy drinker — spent his money freely in saloons. But he had no trouble in getting more money. He would be away a few days, then come back with a bag of gold. But one time he went to his mine and never came back. Some people say a Sasquatch killed him.

At that time I had never heard of Sasquatch. So I asked what kind of animal he called a Sasquatch. The Indian said: "They have hair all over their bodies, but they are not animals. They are people. Big people living in the mountains. My uncle saw the tracks of one that were two feet long. One old Indian saw one over eight feet tall."

I told the Indian I didn't believe in their old fables about mountain giants. It might have been some thousands of years ago, but not nowadays.

The Indian said: "There may not be many, but they still exist."

We arrived at the head of the inlet about 4:00 p.m. I made camp at the mouth of a creek. The Indian was in no hurry — he had to wait for high tide to go back. That would be about 7:00 p.m. I tried to catch some trout in the creek — but no luck. The Indian had supper with me, and I told him to look out for me in about three weeks. I would be camping at the same spot when I came back. He promised to tell his friend to look out for me too.

Next morning I took my rifle with me, but left my equipment at the camp. I decided to look around for some deer trail to lead me up in the mountains. On the way up the inlet I had seen a pass in the mountain that I wanted to go through, so see what was on the other side.

I spent most of the forenoon looking for a trail but found none, except for a hog back running down to within about a hundred feet of the beach. So I swamped out a trail from there, got back to my camp about 3:00 p.m. that afternoon, and made up my pack to be ready in the morning. My equipment consisted of one 30-30 Winchester rifle. I had a special home-made prospecting pick, axe on one hand, and pick on the other. I had a leather case for this pick which fastened to my belt, also my sheath knife.

The storekeeper at Lund was co-operative. He gave me some cans for my sugar, salt and matches to keep them dry. My grub consisted mostly of canned stuff, except for a side of bacon, a bag of beans, four pounds of pancake flour and six packets Rye King hard tack, three rolls of snuff, one quarter sealer of butter and two one-pound cans of milk. I had two boxes of shells for my rifle.

The storekeepers gave me a biscuit tin. I put a few things in that and cached it under a windfall, so I would have it when I came back here waiting for a boat to bring me out. My sleeping bag I rolled up and tied on top of my packsack — together with my ground sheet, small frying pan, and one aluminum pot that held about a gallon. As my canned food was used, I would get plenty of empty cans to cook with.

The following morning I had an early breakfast, made up my pack, and started out up this hog back. My pack must have been at least eighty pounds, besides my rifle. After one hour, I had to rest. I kept resting and climbing all that morning. About 2:00 p.m. I came to a flat place below a rock bluff. There was a bunch of willow in one place. I made a wooden spade and started digging for water. About a foot down I got seepings of water, so I decided to camp here for the night, and scout around for the best way to get on from here.

I must have been up to near a thousand feet. There was a most beautiful view over the islands and the Strait — tug boats with log booms, and fishing boats going in all directions. A lovely spot. I spent the following day prospecting around. But no signs of minerals. I found a deer trail leading towards this pass that I had seen on my way up the inlet.

The following morning I started out early, while it was cool. It was steep climbing with my heavy pack. After a three hours climb, I was tired and stopped to rest. On the other side of a ravine from where I was resting was a yellow spot below some small trees. I moved over there and started digging for water.

I found a small spring and made a small trough from cedar bark and got a small amount of water, had my lunch and rested here till evening. That was not a good camping site, and I wanted to get over the pass. I saved all the water I got from this spring, as I might not find water on the other side of this pass. However, I made it over the pass late that night.

Now I had downhill and good going, but I was hungry and tired, so I camped at the first bunch of trees I came to. I had about a gallon of water so I was good for one day. Of course, I could see rough country ahead of me, and I was trying to size up the terrain — what direction would I take from here. Towards west would lead to low land and some other inlet, so I decided to go in a northeast direction, but I had to find a good way to get down.

I left my pack and went east along a ledge, but came to an abrupt end — was two or three hundred feet straight down. I came back, found a place only about 50 feet down to a ledge that looked like good going for as far as I could see. I got down on this ledge all right and had good going and slight down hill all day — I must have made 10 miles when I came to a small spring and a big black hemlock tree.

This was a lovely campsite. I spent two days here just resting and prospecting. There were some minerals but nothing interesting. The first night here I shot a small deer (buck) so I had plenty of good meat, and good water. The weather was very hot in the daytime, so I was in no hurry, as I had plenty of meat. When I finally left this camp, I got into plenty of trouble. First I got into a box canyon, and had to come back to almost where I started this morning, when I found a deer trail down to another ledge, and had about two miles of good going. Then I came to another canyon, on the other side was a yellow patch of grass that meant water. I made it down into this canyon, and up on the other side, but it was tough climbing. I was tired and when I finally got there I dug a pit for water and got plenty for my needs. I only stayed here one night, it was not a good camping site. Next day I had hard going. I made it over a well-timbered ridge into another canyon. This canyon was not so steep on the west side, but the east side was almost plumb. I would have to go down hill to find a way out. I was not well below timber line.

I found a fair campsite that night, but moved on next morning. It was a very hot day, not a breath of wind.

Late that day I found an exceptionally good campsite. It was tow good-sized cypress trees growing close together and near a rock wall with a nice spring just below these trees. I intended to make this my permanent camp. I cut lots of brush for my bed between these trees. I rigged up a pole from this rock wall to hang my packsack on, and I arranged some flat rocks for my fireplace for cooking. I had a really classy setup. I shot a grouse just before I came to this place.

Too late to roast that tonight — I would do that tomorrow.

And that is when things began to happen.

I am a heavy sleeper, not much disturbs me after I go to sleep, especially on a good bed like I had now.

Next morning I noticed things had been disturbed during the night. But nothing missing that I could see. I roasted my grouse on a stick for my breakfast — about 9:00 a.m. I started out prospecting. I always carried my rifle with me. Your rifle is your most important equipment.

I started out in a southwest direction below the way I had come in the night before. There were some signs (minerals) but nothing important. I shot a squirrel in the afternoon, and got back to camp at 7:00 p.m. I fried the squirrel on a stick, opened a can of peas and carrots for my supper, and gathered up dry branches from trees. There are always dead branches of fir and hemlock under trees, near the ground. They make good fuel and good heat.

That night I filled up the magazine of my rifle. I still had one full box of 20 shells in my coat pocket. That night I laid my rifle under the edge of my sleeping bag. I thought a porcupine had visited me the night before and porkies like leather, so I put my shoes in the bottom of my sleeping bag.

Next morning my packsack had been emptied out. Some one had turned the sack upside down. It was still hanging on the pole from the shoulder straps as I had hung it up. Then I noticed one half-pound package of prunes was missing. Also most of my pancake flour was missing, but my salt bag was not touched. Porkies always look for salt, so I decided it must be something else than porkies. I looked for tracks but found none. I did not think it was a bear, they always tear up and make a mess of things. I kept close to camp these days in case this visitor would come back.

I climbed up on a big rock where I had a good view of the camp, but nothing showed up. I was hoping it would be a porky, so I would get a good porky stew. These visits had now been going on for three nights.

I intended to make a new campsite the following day, but I hated to leave this place. I had fixed it up so nicely, and these two cypress trees were bushy. It would have to be a heavy rain before I would get wet, and I had good spring water and that is hard to find.

This night it was cloudy and looked like it might rain. I took specially notice of how everything was arranged.

I closed my packsack, I did not undress, I only took off my shoes, put them in the bottom of my sleeping bag. I drove my prospecting stick into one of the cypress trees so I could reach it from my bed. I also put the rifle alongside me, inside my sleeping bag. I fully intended to stay awake all night to find out who my visitor was, but I must have fallen asleep.

I was awakened by something picking me up. I was half asleep and at first I did not remember where I was. As I began to get my wits together, I remembered I was on this prospecting trip, and in my sleeping bag.

My first thought was — it must be a snow slide, but there was no snow around my camp. Then it felt like I was tossed on horseback, but I could feel whoever it was, was walking.

I tried to reason out what kind of animal this could be. I tried to get at my sheath knife, and cut my way out, but I was in an almost sitting position, and the knife was under me. I could not get hold of it, but the rifle was in front of me, I had a good hold of that, and had no intention to let go of it. At times I could feel my packsack touching me, and I could feel the cans in the sack touching my back.

After what seemed like an hour, I could feel we were going up a steep hill. I could feel myself rise for every step. What was carrying me was breathing hard and sometimes gave a slight cough. Now, I knew this must be one of the mountain Sasquatch giants the Indians told me about.

I was in a very uncomfortable position — unable to move. I was sitting on my feet, and one of the boots in the bottom of the bag was crossways with the hobnail sole up across my foot. It hurt me terribly, but I could not move.

It was very hot inside. It was lucky for me this fellow's hand was not big enough to close up the whole bag when he picked me up — there was a small opening at the top, otherwise I would have choked to death.

Now he was going downhill. I could feel myself touching the ground at times and at one time he dragged me behind him and I could feel [what] was below me. Then he seemed to get on level ground and was going at a trot for a long time. By this time, I had cramps in my legs, the pain was terrible. I was wishing he would get to his destination soon. I cold not stand this type of transportation much longer.

Now he was going up hill again. It did not hurt me so bad. I tried to estimate distance and directions. As near as I could guess we were about three hours travelling. I

had no idea when he started as I was asleep when he picked me up.

Finally he stopped and let me down. Then he dropped my packsack, I could hear the cans rattle. Then I heard chatter — some kind of talk I did not understand. The ground was sloping so when he let go of my sleeping bag, I rolled head first downhill. I got my head out, and got some air. I tried to straighten my legs and crawl out, but my legs were numb.

It was still dark, I could not see what my captors looked like. I tried to massage my legs to get some life in them, and get my shoes on. I could hear now it was at least four of them. They were standing around me, and continuously chattering. I had never heard of Sasquatch before the Indian told me about them. But I knew I was right among them.

But how to get away from them, that was another question. I got to see the outline of them now, as it began to get lighter though the sky was cloudy, and it looked like rain, in fact there was a slight sprinkle.

I now had circulation in my legs, but my left foot was very sore on top where it had been resting on my hobnail boots. I got my boots out from the sleeping bag and tried to stand up. I was wobbly on my feet but had a good hold of my rifle.

I asked, "What you fellows want from me?"

Only some more chatter.

It was getting lighter now, and I could see them quite clearly. I could make out forms of four people. Two big and two little ones. They were all covered with hair and no clothes on at all.

I could now make out mountains all around me. I looked at my watch. It was 4:25 a.m. It was getting lighter now and I could see the people clearly.

They look like a family, old man, old lady and two young ones, a boy and a girl. The boy and the girl seem to be scared of me. The old lady did not seem too pleased about what the old man dragged home. But the old man was waving his arms and telling them all what he had in mind. They all left me then.

I had my compass and my prospecting glass on strings around my neck. The compass in my left-hand shirt pocket and my glass in my right-hand pocket. I tried to reason our location, and where I was. I could see now that I was in a small valley or basin about eight or ten acres, surrounded by high mountains, on the southeast side there was a V-shaped opening about eight feet wide at the bottom and about twenty feet high at the highest point — that must be the way I came in. But how will I get out? The old man was now sitting near this opening.

I moved my belongings up close to the west wall. There were two small cypress trees there, and this will do for a shelter for the time being. Until I find out what these people want with me, and how to get away from here. I emptied out my packsack to see what I had left in the line of food. All my canned meat and vegetables were intact and I had one can of coffee. Also three small cans of milk — two packages of Rye King hard tack and my butter sealer half full of butter. But my prunes and macaroni were missing. Also my full box of shells for my rifle. I only had six shells beside what I had in the magazine of my rifle. I had my sheath knife but my prospecting pick was missing and my can of matches. I only had my safety box full and that held only about a dozen matches. That did not worry me — I can always start a fire with my prospecting glass when the sun is shining, if I got dry wood. I wanted hot coffee, but I had no wood, also nothing around here that looked like wood. I had a good look over the valley from where I was — but the boy and the girl were always watching me from behind some juniper bush. I decided there must be some water around here. The ground was leaning towards the opening in the wall. There must be water at the upper end of this valley, there is green grass and moss along the bottom.

All my utensils were left behind. I opened my coffee tin and emptied the coffee in a dishtowel and tied it with the metal strip from the can. I took my rifle and the can and went looking for water. Right at the head under a cliff there was a lovely spring that disappeared underground. I got a drink, and a full can of water. When I got back the young boy was looking over my belonging, but did not touch anything. On my way back I noticed where these people were sleeping. On the east side wall of this valley was a shelf in the mountain side, with overhanging rock, looking something like a bit undercut in a big tree about 10 feet deep and 30 feet wide. The floor was covered with lots of dry moss, and they had some kind of blankets woven of narrow strips of cedar back, packed with dry moss. They looked very practical and warm — with no need of washing.

The first day not much happened. I had to eat my food cold. The young fellow was coming nearer me, and seemed curious about me. My one snuff box was empty, so I rolled it towards him. When he saw it coming, he sprang up quick as a cat, and grabbed it. He went over to his sister and showed her. They found out how to

open and close it — they spent a long time playing with it — then he trotted over to the old man and showed him. They had a long chatter.

Next morning, I made up my mind to leave this place — if I had to shoot my way out. I could not stay much longer, I had only enough grub to last me till I got back to Toba Inlet. I did not know the direction but I would go down hill and I would come out near my packsack — packed the few cans I had — swung the sack on my back, injected shell in the barrel of my rifle and started for the opening in the wall. The old man got up, held up his hands as though he would push me back.

I pointed to the opening, I wanted to go out. But he stood there pushing towards me — and said something that sounded like "Soka, soka." Again I pointed outside. He only kept pushing with his hands saying "Soka, soka." I backed up to about sixty feet. I did not want to be too close, I thought, if I had to shoot my way out. A 30-30 might not have much effect on this fellow, it might make him mad. I only had six shells so I decided to wait. There must be a better way than killing him, in order to get out of here. I went back to my campsite to figure out some other way to get out.

If I could make friends with the young fellow or the girl, they might help me. If I only could talk to them. Then I thought of a fellow who saved himself from a mad bull by blinding him with snuff in his eyes. But how will I get near enough to this fellow to put the snuff in his eyes? So I decided next time to give the young fellow my snuff box to leave a few grains of snuff in it. He might give the old man a taste of it.

But the question is, in what direction will I go, if I should get out? I must have been near 25 miles northeast of Toba Inlet when I was kidnapped. This fellow must have travelled at least 25 miles in the three hours he carried me. If he went west we would be near salt water — same thing if he went south — therefore he must have gone northeast. If I then kept going south and over two mountains, I must hit salt water someplace between Lund and Vancouver.

The following day I did not see the old lady till about 4:00 p.m. She came home with her arms full of grass and twigs of all kinds from spruce and hemlock as well as some kind of nuts that grow in the ground. I have seen lots of them on Vancouver Island. The young fellow went up the mountain to the east every day, he could climb better than a mountain goat. He picked some kind of grass with long sweet roots. He gave me some one day — they tasted very sweet. I gave him another snuff box with about a teaspoon of snuff in it. He tasted it, then went to the old man-he licked it with his tongue. They had a long chat. I made a dipper from a milk can. I made many dippers — you can use them for pots too — you cut two slits near the top of any can — then cut a limb from any small tree — cut down on the limb — down the stem of the tree — then taper the part you cut from the stem. Then cut a hole in the tapered part, slide the tapered part in the slit you made in the can, and you have a good handle on your can. I threw one over to the young fellow that was playing near my camp, he picked it up and looked at it, then he went to the old man and showed it to him. They had a long chatter. Then he came to me, pointed at the dipper then at his sister. I could see that he wanted one for her too. I had other peas and carrots, so I made one for his sister. He was standing only eight feet away from me. When I had made the dipper, I dipped it in water and drank from it, he was very pleased, almost smiled at me. Then I took a chew of snuff, smacked my lips, said that's good.

The young fellow pointed to the old man, said something that sounded like "Ook." I got the idea that the old man liked snuff, and the young fellow wanted a box for the old man. I shook my head. I motioned with my hands for the old man to come to me. I do not think the young fellow understood what I meant. He went to his sister and gave her the dipper I made for her. They did not come near me again that day. I had now been here six days, but I was sure I was making progess. If only I could get the old man to come over to me, get him to eat a full box of snuff that would kill him for sure, and that way kill himself, I wouldn't be guilty of murder.

The old lady was a meek old thing. The young fellow was by this time quite friendly. The girl would not hurt anybody. Her chest was flat like a boy — no development like young ladies. I am sure if I could get the old man out of the way, I could easily have brought this girl out with me to civilization. But what good would that have been? I would have to keep her in a cage for public display. I don't think we have any right to force our way of life on other people, and I don't think they would like it. (The noise and racket in a modern city they would not like any more than I do.)

The young fellow might have been between 11-18 years old, about seven feet tall and might weigh about 300 lbs. His chest would be 50-55 inches, his waist about 36-38 inches. He had wide jaws, narrow forehead,

that slanted upward round at the back about four or five inches higher than the forehead. The hair on their heads was about six inches long. The hair on the rest of their body was short and thick in places. The women's hair was a bit longer on their heads and the hair on the forehead had an upward turn like some women have — they call it bangs, among women's hair-do's. Nowadays the old lady could have been anything between 40-70 years old. She was over seven feet tall. She would be about 500-600 pounds.

She had very wide hips, and a goose-like walk. She was not built for beauty or speed. Some of those lovable brassieres and uplifts would have been a great improvement on her looks and her figure. The man's eye teeth were longer than the rest of the teeth, but not long enough to be called tusks. The old man must have been near eight feet tall. Big barrel chest and big hump on his back — powerful shoulders, his biceps on upper arm were enormous and tapered down to his elbows. His forearms were longer than common people have, but well proportioned. His hands were wide, the palm was long and broad, and hollow like a scoop. His fingers were short in proportion to the rest of his hand. His fingernails were like chisels. The only place they had no hair was inside their hands and the soles of their feet and upper part of the nose and eyelids. I never did see their ears, they were covered with hair hanging over them.

If the old man were to wear a collar it would have to be at least 30 inches. I have no idea what size shoes they would need. I was watching the young fellow's foot one day when he was sitting down. The soles of his feet seemed to be padded like a dog's foot, and the big toe was longer than the rest and very strong. In mountain climbing all he needed was footing for his big toe. They were very agile. To sit down they turned their knees out and came straight down. To rise they came straight up without help of their hands and arms. I don't think this valley was their permanent home. I think they move from place to place, as food is available in different localities. They might eat meat, but I never saw them eat meat, or do any cooking.

I think this was probably a stopover place and the plants with sweet roots on the mountain side might have been in season this time of year. They seemed to be most interested in them. The roots have a very sweet and satisfying taste. They always seem to do everything for a reason, wasting no time on anything they did not need. When they were not looking for food, the old man and the old lady were resting, but the boy and the girl were always climbing something or some other exercise. His favourite position was to take hold of his feet with his hands and balance his rump, then bounce forward. The idea seems to be to see how far he could go without his feet or hands touching the ground. Sometimes he made 20 feet.

But what do they want with me? They must understand I cannot stay here indefinitely. I will soon be out of grub, and so far I have seen no deer or other game. I will soon have to make a break for freedom. Not that I was mistreated in any way. One consolation was that the old man was coming closer each day, and was very interested in my snuff. Watching me when I take a pinch of snuff, he seems to think it useless to only put it inside my lips. One morning after I had my breakfast both the old man and the boy came and sat down only ten feet away from me. This morning I made coffee. I had saved up all dry branches I found and I had some dry moss and I used all the labels from cans to get a fire.

I got my coffee pot boiling and it was strong coffee too, and the aroma from boiling coffee was what brought them over. I was sitting eating hard-tack with plenty of butter on, and sipping coffee. And it sure tasted good. I was smacking my lips pretending it was better than it really was. I set the can down that was about half full. I intended to warm it up later. I pulled out a full box of snuff, took a big chew. Before I had time to close the box the old man reached for it. I was afraid he would waste it, and only had two more boxes. So I held on to the box intending him to take a pinch like I had just done. Instead he grabbed the box and emptied it in his mouth. Swallowed it in one gulp. Then he licked the box inside with his tongue.

After a few minutes his eyes began to roll over in his head, he was looking straight up. I could see he was sick. Then he grabbed my coffee can that was quite cold by this time, he emptied that in his mouth, grounds and all. That did no good. He stuck his head between his legs and rolled forwards a few times away from me. Then he began to squeal like a stuck pig. I grabbed my rifle. I said to myself, "This is it. If he comes for me I will shoot him plumb between his eyes." But he started for the spring, he wanted water. I packed my sleeping bag in my packsack with the few cans I had left. The young fellow ran over to his mother. Then she began to squeal. I started for the opening in the wall — and I just made it. The old lady was right behind me. I fired one shot at the rock over her head.

I guess she had never seen a rifle fired before. She turned and ran inside the wall. I injected another shell in the barrel of my rifle and started downhill, looking back over my shoulder every so often to see if they were coming. I was in a canyon, and good travelling and I made fast time. Must have made three miles in some world record time. I came to a turn in the canyon and I had the sun on my left, that meant I was going south, and the canyon turned west. I decided to climb the ridge ahead of me. I knew I must have two mountain ridges between me and salt water and by climbing this ridge I would have a good view of this canyon, so I could see if the Sasquatch were coming after me. I had a light pack and was soon making good time up this hill. I stopped soon after to look back to where I came from, but nobody followed me. As I came over the ridge I could see Mt. Baker, then I knew I was going in the right direction.

I was hungry and tired. I opened my packsack to see what I had to eat. I decided to rest here for a while. I had a good view of the mountain side, and if the old man was coming I had the advantage because I was up and above him. To get me he would have to come up a steep hill. And that might not be so easy after stopping a few 30-30 bullets. I had made up my mind this was my last chance, and this would be a fight to the finish. I ate some hard tack and I opened my last can of corned beef. I had no butter, I forgot to pick up my butter sealer I had buried near my camp to keep it cold. I did not dared to make a fire. I rested here for two hours. It was 3:00 p.m. when I started down the mountain side. It was nice going, not too steep, and not too much underbrush.

When I got near the bottom, I shot a big blue grouse. She was sitting on a windfall, looking right at me, only a few hundred feet away. I shot her neck right off.

I made it down the creek at the bottom of this canyon. I felt I was safe now. I made a fire between two big boulders, roasted the grouse, made some coffee and opened my can of milk. My first good meal for days. I spread out my sleeping bag under a big spruce tree and went to sleep. Next morning I woke up, I was feeling terrible. My feet were sore from dirty socks. My legs were sore, my stomach was upset from that grouse that I ate the night before. I was not too sure I was going to make it up that mountain. It was a cloudy day, no sun, but after some coffee and hard tack I felt a bit better. I started up the mountain side but had no energy. I only wanted to rest. My legs were shaking. I had to rest every hundred feet. I finally made the top, but it took me six hours to get there. It was cloudy, visibility about a mile.

I knew I had to go down hill. After about two hours I got down to the heavy timber and sat down to rest. I could hear a motor running hard at times, then stop. I listened to this for a while and decided the sound was from a gas donkey. Someone was logging in the neighbourhood. I made for this sound, for if only I can get to that donkey, I will be safe. After a while I heard someone holler "Timber" and a tree go down. Now I knew I was safe. When I came up to the fellows, I guess I was a sorry sight. I hadn't had a shave since I left Toba Inlet, and no good wash for days. When I came up out of the bushes, they kept staring at me. I asked where the place was and how far to the nearest town. The men said, "You look like a wild man, where did you come from?"

I told them I was a prospector and was lost. I had not had much to eat the last few weeks. I got sick from eating a grouse last night, and I am all in. The bucker called to his partner, "Pete, come over here a minute." Pete came over and looked at me and said this man is sick. We had better help him down to the landing, put him on a logging truck and send him down to the beach. I did not like to tell them I had been kidnapped by a Sasquatch, as if I had told them they would probably have said, he is crazy too. They were very helpful and they talked to the truck driver to give him a ride down to the beach. Pete helped me up into the truck cab, and said the first aid man will fix you up at the camp. The first aid man brought me to the cook and asked, "Have you a bowl of soup for this man?" The cook came and looked me over. He asked, "When did you eat last, and where did you come from?" I told him I had been lost in the wood. I ate a grouse last night and it made me sick.

After the cook had given me a first class meal, the first aid man took me to the first aid house. I asked, "Can you get me a clean suit of underwear and a pair of socks? I would like a bath, too." He said, "Sure thing, you take a rest and I will fix all that. I'll arrange for you to go down to Schelt when the timekeeper goes down for mail." After a session in the bathroom the first aid man gave me a shave and a hair trim, and I was back to my normal self. The Bull of the Woods told me I was welcome to stay for a day and rest up if I liked. I told him I accepted his hospitality as I was not feeling any too good yet. I told him about my prospecting but nothing about being kidnapped by a Sasquatch.

The following day I went down from this camp on Salmon Arm Branch of Sechelt Inlet. From there I got the Union Boat back to Vancouver. That was my last prospecting trip, and my only experience with what is known as Sasquatches. I know that in 1924 there were four Sasquatches living, it might be only two now. The old man and the old lady might be dead by this time.\

THE PETRIFIED BODY

"The Petrified Woman of Mud Island" tells or retells a "tall tale" set in the Maritimes in a style that was more characteristic of the last half of the 19th century than it is of the first half of the 20th century.

The news story was written by a journalist named Bonnycastle Dale and it appeared in the *Herald* (Calgary, Alta.), 23 Nov. 1929.

The Petrified Woman of Mud Island

While we call Sable Island, 150 miles seaward, "The Graveyard of the Atlantic," we call the reefs and submerged islands — past the "Devil's Limb" and "Limb's Limb" westward to the "Noddy," twenty miles out — "The Hospital." On the jagged spears of these foam-streaked rocks, many's the stout bark, the tall creaking ship, the wallowing, smoke-spurting tug and collier have crashed — all now rusted, sea-wracked, torn and riven hulls, some that we ourselves saw wrecked, others for half a century back, others like the unknown bottom that struck on Mud Island (Big Mud) sometimes in the dim past, so long ago that only this odd story survives it for three-score years and ten.

As you go westward around Cape Sable, Nova Scotia, past "Seal" and "Noddy," you come to the far outlying Mud Island. It is in the twenty-five-fathom line and subject to the mighty tides that sweep and scour the Bay of Fundy. (Imagine, my mid-continental readers, the great Lake Ontario — twice — filled and twice emptied every twenty-four hours, and then you can glimpse the power and fury of the fifty-six-foot tide which sweeps on and up to the end of "The Bay.")

The distressed vessel with its human burden was swept thus far up the great bay and struck on "Big Mud," and the next tides the pitiful bodies of Negroes and whites were swept ashore on the flood. The great bay was not girdled by lighthouses as it is today, and the story spread but slowly. We know that the boat was a packet — steam and sail — and that not all the bodies which came ashore were dead; in one, a white girl, life still lingered. But, notwithstanding all the few lobster-fishermen gathered there could do (so my informant, the lighthouse-keeper, told me), she died, and was given Christian burial.

Big Mud Island was then used mainly for summer shanties for the lobstermen of the Mud Island Lobster Company, and soon the wreck and the few lonely graves lay unnoticed, a nine-days' wonder passed by. The lobster pots were set, drawn, the season passed, and the island lay almost deserted. Year after year, every March, these lobstermen, and at times their families, too, returned for the short spring season, and one day, in an idle moment, a visitor with that fiendish lust for curiosities dug down into the shallow grave of the shipwrecked girl. The spot where it had been buried was right in the seepage run of a tiny creek, full only in the early spring melting time.

Soon the rude shelf which enclosed the body was reached and torn asunder and the digging tool struck something which sounded like stone. The visitor sent out a call for assistance, and soon the petrified body of the poor drowned girl was exposed to the glare of the spring sun. It was as hard and as unyielding as marble. The lime contents of the underground seepage had thoroughly filled each cavity and vein and artery, soaking in and replacing its natural contents with the filmy deposits which, once they dried out as the summers advanced, were stone-like in their formation.

This story, sent abroad by word of mouth in the early seventies, spread like wildfire, and the result was that visitors poured in daily to see the strange sight of a body marble-like in its consistency but faithful still to its human form in every line, shrunken though some of the once fuller parts were. Merciful people reburied the poor body, but the next few hours saw fresh visitors feverishly digging up what should by all our precepts be hallowed ground. Nor were the ghoulish excavators careful.

The fingers of the petrified body were especially brittle and were broken off and some were carried away to the great scandal of this most peaceful people, for, though the waters of Fundy writhe and tear along, sixty feet deep of continual ebb and flow, and the winds thrash the seas, and these Acadians and Nova Scotians, French and British, all good neighbours now, daily snatch a living from this confused sea, they are a most simple hospitable people.

The priests and the clergy and the councils took up the tale, and orders were sent to Big Mud Island to bury the body deeply and put up a headboard. This, too, was thrown over and the body again exhumed. Now the real governors of the island, the Mud Island Lobster Company, took a hand, and they wrote to the man who lived there all the year, shepherding the half-wild sheep (which also snatched a living from the sea, a precarious living on dulce and laver and kelp), ordering him to take the poor abused body and secretly and at night convey it into the woods and hide it and to bury it deeply.

They also bade him make a sketch of the exact spot where the body lay. So at last the harried remains rested securely hidden from the clutching fingers of the ghouls. So well did the island shepherd do his work that not a trace of the body can be found today.

You can get this tale from the mouths of the older people all along that shore. Go by motor-boat, from Wedgeport via Calf Island, Bald and Inner Bald direct to Mud Island. See Gannet Rock, if you pass outside Spectacle Island. If ever the body comes to light again, I trust that a fund will be raised for cement block interment and a suitable headstone erected.

I thoroughly believe the story, as it was told to me by a man so faithful in his work, so trustworthy, so hospitable to us during the two years when we dwelt in the little cabin by "The Light," and we also heard it repeated by many mouths for miles along Fundy's rude shores.

SASQUATCH

There is an entry for "Sasquatch" in *The Canadian Encyclopedia* (1988) and its contributor explains that the word *sasquatch* means "wild man" or "hairy man" in the language of the Salish Indians of British Columbia. The contributor explains that it is "the name of the mysterious, ape-like creature said to inhabit the remoter regions of the Pacific Northwest. In northern California the giant creature is called 'Big Foot.' Evidence for the existence of the Sasquatch in British Columbia and Alberta is based on references in Indian legend and myth, in passages from journals kept by early travellers and on modern sightings."

Credit for the first use of the word is accorded the Indian agent and writer J.W. Burns in an article that he wrote for *Maclean's* (when the publication was known as *MacLean's Magazine*). The article was titled "Introducing B.C.'s Hairy Giants" and it appeared in the issue of April 1, 1929. Sceptics have noted that the contribution was published on April Fool's Day, yet Burns is anything but a practical joker and the article is anything but foolish. The writer took pains to establish that the sasquatch is a race of hairy mountain men and not apes or bogey men. He went on to ask the following question, "Are the vast mountain solitudes of British Columbia, of which but very few have been so far explored, populated by a hairy race of giants — men — not ape-like men?" He answers the question in the affirmative.

For the next thirty years the mysterious creature of the remote interior has been known as the "hairy wild man of the mountains" or the Sasquatch. The term Bigfoot (or Big Foot) did not appear in print until October 5, 1958, when it was coined by Andrew Genzoli, editor of the *Humbolt Times*, who used it to describe the plaster cast of a large hominid footprint found in the mud of Bluff Creek Valley, California. The American media immediately adopted the new name.

It was one year later, in 1959, that the term *cryptozoology* was coined to refer to "the scientific study of hidden animals, i.e., of still unknown animal forms about which only testimonial and circumstantial evidence is available, or material evidence considered insufficient by some." This is the definition of the Belgian-born researcher, investigator, and theorist Bernard Heuvelmans, who was recognized as the world's leading cryptozoologist with the publication of two trend-setting books: *On the Track of Unknown Animals* (1958) and *In the Wake of the Sea-Serpents* (1968).

What follow are narrative excerpts from J.W. Burns's landmark article from *Maclean's*. It will be appreciated that the Sasquatches described by Burns resemble supersized, muscle-bound, hirsute human beings who were known to the Indian population, but these are quite distinct from the ape-like aspects of creatures that one associates with Genzoli's word Bigfoot. In other words, the Canadian creatures are humans, the American creatures animals.

Peter's Encounter with the Giant

Peter Williams lives on the Chehalis Reserve. I believe that he is a reliable as well as an intelligent Indian. He gave me the following thrilling account of his experience with these people.

"One evening in the month of May twenty years ago," he said, "I was walking along the foot of the mountain about a mile from the Chehalis reserve. I thought I heard a noise something like a grunt nearby. Looking in the direction in which it came, I was startled to see what I took at first sight to be a huge bear crouched upon a boulder twenty or thirty feet away. I raised my rifle to shoot it, but, as I did, the creature stood up and let out a piercing yell. It ws a man — a giant, no less than six and one-half feet in height, and covered with hair. He was in a rage and jumped from the boulder to the ground. I fled, but not before I felt his breath upon my cheek.

"I never ran so fast before or since — through bush and undergrowth toward the Statloo, or Chehalis River, where my dugout was moored. From time to time, I looked back over my shoulder. The giant was fast overtaking me — a hundred feet separated us; another look and the distance measured less than fifty — then the Chehalis and in a moment the dugout shot across the stream to the opposite bank. The swift river, however, did not in the least daunt the giant, for he began to wade it immediately.

"I arrived home almost worn out from running and I felt sick. Taking an anxious look around the house, I was relieved to find the wife and children inside. I bolted the door and barricaded it with everything at hand. Then with my rifle ready, I stood near the door and awaited his coming."

Peter added that if he had not been so much excited he could easily have shot the giant when he began to wade the river.

"After an anxious waiting of twenty minutes," resumed the Indian, "I heard a noise approaching the trampling of a horse. I looked through a crack in the old wall. It was the giant. Darkness had not yet set in and I had a good look at him. Except that he was covered with hair and twice the bulk of the average man, there was nothing to distinguish him from the rest of us. He pushed against the wall of the old house with such force that it shook back and forth. The old cedar shook and timbers creaked and groaned so much under the strain that I was afraid it would fall down and kill us. I whispered to the old woman to take the children under the bed."

Peter pointed out what remained of the old house in which he lived at the time, explaining that the giant treated it so roughly that it had to be abandoned the following winter.

"After prowling and grunting like an animal around the house," continued Peter, "he went away. We were glad, for the children and the wife were uncomfortable under the old bedstead. Next morning I found his tracks in the mud around the house, the biggest of either man or beast I had ever seen. The tracks measured twenty-two inches in length, but narrow in proportion to their length."

The following winter while shooting wild duck on that part of the reserve Indians call the "prairie," which is on the north side of the Harrison River and about two miles from the Chehalis village, Peter once more came face to face with the same hairy giant. The Indian ran for dear life, followed by the wild man, but after pursuing him for three or four hundred years the giant gave up the chase.

Old village Indians, who called upon Peter to hear of his second encounter, nodded their heads sagely, shrugged their shoulders, and for some reason not quite clear, seemed not to wish the story to gain further publicity.

On the afternoon of the same day another Indian by the name of Paul was chased from the creek, where he was fishing for salmon, by the same individual. Paul was in a state of terror, for unlike Peter he had no gun. A short distance from his shack the giant suddenly quit and walked into the bush. Paul, exhausted from running, fell in the snow and had to be carried home by his mother and others of the family.

"The first and second time," went on Peter, "I was all alone when I met this strange mountain creature. Then, early in the spring of the following year, another man and myself were bear hunting near the place where I first met him. On this occasion we ran into two of these giants. They were sitting on the ground. At first we thought they were old tree stumps, but when we were within fifty feet or so, they suddenly stood up and we came to an immediate stop. Both were nude. We were close enough to know that they were man and woman. The woman was the smaller of the two, but neither of them as big or fierce-looking as the gent that chased me. We ran home, but they did not follow us."

One morning, some few weeks after this, Peter and his wife were fishing in a canoe on the Harrison River, near Harrison Bay. Paddling round a neck of land they saw, on the beach within a hundred feet of them, the giant Peter had met the previous year.

"We stood for a long time looking at him," said the Indian, "but he took no notice of us — that was the last time," concluded Peter, "I saw him."

Peter remarked that his father and numbers of old Indians knew that wild men lived in caves in the mountains — had often seen them. He wished to make it clear that these creatures were in no wise related to the Indian. He believes there are a few of them living at present in the mountains near Agassiz.

Charley Victor's Story

Charley Victor belongs to the Skwah Reserve near Chilliwack. In his younger days he was known as one of the best hunters in the province and had many thrilling adventures in his time.

Did he know anything about the hairy ape-like men who were supposed to inhabit the distant mountains? Charley smiled, and answered that he had had a slight acquaintance with them. He had been in what he thought was one of their houses. "And that is not all," said he. "I met and spoke to one of their women, and I shot...." But let Charley tell the story himself.

"The strange people, of whom there are but few now — rarely seen and seldom met — " said the old hunter, "are known by the name of Sasquatch, or, 'the hairy mountain men.'

"The first time I came to know about these people," continued the old man, "I did not see anybody. Three young men and myself were picking salmon berries on a rocky mountain slope some five or six miles from the old town of Yale. In our search for berries we suddenly stumbled upon a large opening in the side of the mountain. This discovery greatly surprised all of us, for we knew every foot of the mountain, and never knew nor heard there was a cave in the vicinity.

"Outside the mouth of the cave there was an enormous boulder. We peered into the cavity but couldn't see anything.

"We gathered some pitch wood, lighted it and began to explore. But before we got very far from the entrance of the cave, we came upon a sort of stone house or enclosure; it was a crude affair. We couldn't make a thorough examination, for our pitch wood kept going out. We left, intending to return in a couple of days and go on exploring. Old Indians, to whom we told the story of our discovery, warned us not to venture near the cave again, as it was surely occupied by the Sasquatch. That was the first time I heard about the hairy men that inhabit the mountains. We, however, disregarded the advice of the old men and sneaked off to explore the cave, but to our great disappointment found the boulder rolled back into its mouth and fitting so nicely that you might suppose it had been made for that purpose."

Charley intimated that he hoped to have enough money some day to buy sufficient dynamite to blow open the cave of the Sasquatch and see how far it extends through the mountain.

The Indian then took up the thread of his story and told of his first meeting with one of these men. A number of other Indians and himself were bathing in a small lake near Yale. He was dressing, when suddenly out from behind a rock, only a few feet away, stepped a nude hairy man. "Oh! he was a big, big man!" continued the old hunter. "He looked at me for a moment, hs eyes were so kind-looking that I was about speak to him, when he turned about and walked into the forest."

At the same place two weeks later, Charley, together with several of his companions, saw the giant, but this time he ran toward the mountain. This was twenty years after the discovery of the cave.

Charley Shoots a Sasquatch Boy

"I don't know if I should tell you or not about the awful experience I had with these wicked people about fifteen years ago in the mountains near Hatzie."

The old man rubbed his knee, and said he disliked recalling that disagreeable meeting — it was a tragedy from which he had not yet fully recovered.

"I was hunting in the mountains near Hatzie," he resumed. "I had my dog with me. I came out on a plateau where there were several big cedar trees. The dog stood before one of the trees and began to growl and bark at it. On looking up to see what excited him, I noticed a large hole in the tree seven feet from the ground. The dog pawed and leaped upon the trunk, and looked at me to raise him up, which I did, and he went into the hole. The next moment a muffled cry came from the hole. I said to myself, 'The dog is tearing into a bear,' and with my rifle ready, I urged the dog to drive him out, and out came something I took for a bear. I shot and it fell with a thud to the ground. 'Murder! Oh my!' I spoke to myself in surprise and alarm, for the thing I had shot looked at me like a white boy. He was nude. He was about twelve or fourteen years of age."

In his description of the boy, Charley said that his hair was black and woolly.

"Wounded and bleeding, the poor fellow sprawled upon the ground, but when I drew close to examine the extent of his injury, he let out a wild yell, or rather a call as if he were appealing for help. From across the mountain a long way off rolled a booming voice. Near and more near came the voice and every now and again the boy would return an answer as if directing the owner of the voice. Less than a half-hour, out from the depths of the forest came the strangest and wildest creature one could possibly see.

"I raised my rifle, not to shoot, but in case I would have to defend myself. The hairy creature, for that was what it was, walked toward me without the slightest fear. The wild person was a woman. Her face was almost negro black and her long straight hair fell to her waist. In height she would be about six feet, but her chest and shoulders were well above the average in breadth."

Charley remarked that he had met several wild people in his time, but had never seen anyone half so savage in appearance as this woman. The old brave confessed he was really afraid of her.

"In my time," said the old man, "and this is no boast, I have in more than one emergency strangled bear with my hands, but I'm sure if that wild woman laid hands on me, she'd break every bone in my body.

"She cast a hasty glance at the boy. Her face took on a demoniacal expression when she saw he was bleeding. She turned upon me savagely, and in the Douglas tongue said:

"'You have shot my friend.'

"I explained in the same language — for I'm part Douglas myself — that I had mistaken the boy for a bear and that I was sorry. She did not reply, but began a sort of wild frisk or dance around the boy, chanting in a loud voice for a minute or two, and, as if in answer to her, from the distant woods came the same sort of chanting troll. In her hand she carried something like a snake, about six feet in length, but thinking over the matter since, I believe it was the intestine of some animal. But whatever it was, she constantly struck the ground with it. She picked up the boy with one hairy hand, and as much ease as if he had been a wax doll."

At this point of the story, Charley began to make pictures in the sand with his maple stick, and paused or reflected so long that he thought he had come to the end of his narrative, when he suddenly looked up, and said with a grin: "Perhaps I better tell you the rest of it, although I know you'll not believe it. There was challenge of defiance in her black eyes and dark looks," went on Charley, "as she faced and spoke to me a second time and the dreadful words she used set me shaking."

"You remember them?" I asked.

"Remember them," he repeated, "they will ring round my old ears like the echo of a thunder-storm. She pointed the snake-like thing at me and said:

"'Siwash, you'll never kill another bear.'"

The old hunter's eyes moistened when he admitted that he had not shot a bear or anything else since that fatal day.

"Her words, expression, and the savage avenging glint in her dark, fiery eyes filled me with fear," confessed the Indian, "and I felt so exhausted from her unwavering gaze that I was no longer able to keep her covered with my rifle. I let it drop."

Charley had been paralyzed for the last eight years, and he is inclined to think that the words of the wild woman had something to do with it.

The old man told how his "brave dog, that never turned from any bear nor cougar," lay whimpering and shivering at his feet while the Sasquatch woman was speaking, "just," said Charley, "as if he understood the meaning of her words."

The old man said that she spoke the words "Yahoo, yahoo" frequently in a loud voice, and always received a similar reply from the mountain.

The old hunter felt sure that the woman looked somewhat like the wild man he had seen at Yale many years before, although the woman was the darker of the two. He did not think the boy belonged to the Sasquatch people, "because he was white and she called him her friend," reasoned Charley. "They must have stolen him or run across him in some other way," he added.

"Indians," said Charley, "have always known that wild men lived in the distant mountains, within sixty and one hundred miles east of Vancouver, and of course they may live in other places throughout the province, but I have never heard of it. It is my own opinion since I met that wild woman fifteen years ago that because she spoke the Douglas tongue these creatures must be related to the Indians."

The Wild Man of Agassiz

At Agassiz, near the close of September, 1927, Indian hop-pickers were having their annual picnic. A few of the younger people volunteered to pick a mess of berries on a wooded hillside, a short way from the picnic grounds. They had only started to pick, when out of the bush stepped a naked hairy giant. He was first noticed by a girl of the party, who was so badly frightened that she fell unconscious to the ground. The girl's sudden collapse was seen by an Indian named Point, of Vancouver, and as he ran to her assistance, was astonished to see a giant a few feet away, who continued to walk with an easy gait across the wooded slope in the direction of the Canadian Pacific railway tracks.

Since the foregoing paragraph was written, Mr. Point, replying to an enquiry, has kindly forwarded the following letter to the writer, in which he tells of his experience with the hairy giant:

"Dear Sir: I have your letter asking is it true or not that I saw a hairy giant-man at Agassiz last September, while picking hops there. It is true and the facts are as follows: This happened at the close of September (1927) when we were having a feast. Adaline August and myself walked to her father's orchard, which is about four miles from the hop fields. We were walking on the railroad track and within a short distance of the orchard, when the girl noticed something walking along the track coming toward us. I looked up but paid no attention to it, as I thought it was some person on his way to Agassiz. But as he came closer we noticed that his appearance was very odd, and on coming still closer we stood still and were astonished — seeing that the creature was naked and covered with hair like an animal. We were almost paralyzed from fear. I picked up two stones with which I intended to hit him if he attempted to molest us, but within fifty feet or so he stood up and looked at us.

"He was twice as big as the average man, with hands so long that they almost touched the ground. It seemed to me that the eyes were very large and the lower part of his nose was wide and spread over the greater part of his face, which gave the creature such a frightful appearance that I ran away as fast as I could. After a minute or two I looked back and saw that he resumed his journey. The girl had fled before I left, and she ran so fast that I did not overtake her until I was close to Agassiz, where we told the story of our adventure to the Indians who were still enjoying themselves. Old Indians who were present said: the wild man was no doubt a 'Sasquatch,' a tribe of hairy people whom they claim have always lived in the mountains — in tunnels and caves."

Do hairy giants inhabit the mountain solitudes of British Columbia? Many Indians, besides those quoted, are sincerely convinced that the "Sasquatch," a few of them at least, still live in the little-known interior of the province.

MEDICINE MAN VS. SASQUATCH MAN

Here is an account which may very well be unique. It records an encounter between an Indian medicine man and a Sasquatch. The medicine man is Frank Dan; the Sasquatch is nameless.

The author is J.W. Burns, a teacher and agent who lived on the Chehalis Indian Reserve in the interior of British Columbia. Burns is credited with popularizing the word Sasquatch for Big Foot, or Bigfoot, the North American Yeti. (He did so in an article in *Maclean's* published on April 1, 1929.) The word Sasquatch is variously translated but is generally said to mean "hairy wild man" in the language of the Salish Indians.)

Burns's account refers to an incident that he described as occurring in July 1936 along Morris Creek, a small tributary of the Harrison River which lies generally north of Chilliwack, B.C. It is not without its charm. It is reproduced from Ivan T. Sanderson's *Abominable Snowmen: Legend Come to Life* (New York: Jove/HBJ Book, 1977).

It was a lovely day, the clear waters of the creek shimmered in the bright sunshine and reflected the wild surroundings of cliff, trees, and vagrant cloud. A languid breeze wafted across the rocky gullies. Frank's canoe was gliding like a happy vision along the mountain stream. The Indian was busy hooking one fish after another hungry fish that had been liberated only a few days before from some hatchery. But the Indian was happy as he pulled them in and sang his medicine song. Then, without warning, a rock was hurled from the shelving slope above, falling with a fearful splash within a few feet of his canoe, almost swamping the frial craft. Startled out of his skin, Frank glanced upward, and to his amazement beheld a weird looking creature, covered with hair, leaping from rock to rock down the wild declivity with the agility of a mountain goat. Frank recognized the hairy creature instantly. It was a Sasquatch. He knew it was one of the giants — he had met them on several occasions in past years, once on his own doorstep. But those were a timid sort and not unruly like the gent he was now facing.

Frank called upon his medicine powers, sula, and similar spirits to protect him. There was an immediate response to his appeal. The air throbbed and some huge boulders slid down the rocky mountain side, making a noise like the crack of doom. This was to frighten away the Sasquatch. But the giant was not to be frightened by falling rocks. Instead he hurried down the declivity carrying a great stone, probably weighing a ton or more, under his great hairy arm, which Frank guessed — just a rough guess — was at least two yards in length. Reaching a point of vantage a jutting ledge that hung far out over the water — he hurled it with all his might, this time missing the canoe by a narrow margin, filling it with water and drenching the poor frightened occupant with a cloud of spray.

Some idea of the size of the boulder may be gained from the fact that its huge bulk blocked the channel.

Later it was dredged out by Jack Penny on the authority of the department of hinterland navigation. It may now be seen on the tenth floor of the Vancouver Public Museum in the department of "Curious Rocks"....

The giant now posed upon the other ledge in an attitude of wild majesty as if he were monarch of these foreboding haunts, shaking a colossal fist at the "great medicine man" who sat awe-struck and shuddering in the canoe, which he was trying to bail out with his shoe. The Indian saw the Sasquatch was in a towering rage, a passion that caused the great man to exude a repugnant odour, which was carried down to the canoe by a wisp of wind. The smell made Frank dizzy and his eyes began to smart and pop. Frank never smelt anything in his whole medicine career like it. It was more repelling than the stench of moccasin oil gone rotten. Indeed, it was so nasty that the fish quitted the pools and nooks and headed in schools for the Harrison River. The Indian, believing the giant was about to dive into the water and attack him, cast off his fishing lines and paddled away as fast as he was able.

MAYBE THIS WAS A SASQUATCH

Not much is known of William Roe except that he was a hunter and trapper and also a roadworker on the highway near Tête Jaune Cache, B.C. One day in Oct. 1955, he climbed Mica Mountain in the Monashee range, close to the Alberta border, to explore the site of an odd deserted mine. Instead of exploring the mine, he made a much, much more interesting discovery....

Roe felt it was necessary to prepare a sworn statement that he was telling the truth. So, two years later, on Aug. 26, 1957, before a Commissioner of Oaths in Edmonton, he attested to the truth of this account of his strange encounter.

Roe's report of this encounter is reproduced here in its entirety, as it appeared in the publication *On the Track of the Sasquatch* (1968) by John Green. Green corresponded with Roe and from him gained the following additional information about the creature:

"The nails were not like a bear's, but short and heavy like a man's finger nails are. Its eyes were not light and large but small and black like a bear's. You couldn't see any knotted corded muscles. This animal seemed almost round. It was as deep through as it was wide, and I believe if this animal should have been seven feet tall, it would have weighed close to 500 pounds.

"We have to get away form the idea of comparing it to a human being as we know them."

Ever since I was a small boy back in the forest of Michigan, I have studied the lives and habits of wild animals. Later, when I supported my family in Northern Alberta by hunting and trapping, I spent many hours just observing the wild things. They fascinated me. But the most incredible experience I ever had with a wild creature occurred near a little town called Tête Jaune Cache, British Columbia, almost eighty miles west of

Jasper, Alberta.

I had been working on the highway near Tête Jaune Cache for about two years. In October 1955, I decided to climb five miles up Mica Mountain to an old deserted mine, just for something to do. I came in sight of the mine about three o'clock in the afternoon after an easy climb. I had just come out of a patch of low brush into a clearing, when I saw what I thought was a grizzly bear, in the brush on the other side. I had shot a grizzly near that spot the year before. This one was only about seventy-five yards away, but I didn't want to shoot it, for I had no way of getting it out. So I sat down on a small rock and watched, my rifle in my hands.

I could just see part of the animal's head and the top of one shoulder. A moment later it raised up and stepped out into the opening. Then I saw it was not a bear.

This, to the best of my recollection, is what the creature looked like and how it acted as it came across the clearing directly toward me. My first impression was of a huge man, about six feet tall, almost three feet wide, and probably weighting somewhere near three hundred pounds. It was covered form head to foot with dark brown silver-tipped hair. But as it came closer I saw by its breasts that it was female.

And yet, its torso was not curved like a female's. Its broad frame was straight from shoulder to hip. Its arms were much thicker than a man's arms, and longer, reaching almost to its knees. Its feet were broader proportionately than a man's, about five inches wide at the front and tapering to much thinner heels. When it walked it placed the heel of its foot down first, and I could see the grey-brown skin or hide on the soles of its feet.

It came to the edge of the bush I was hiding in, within thirty feet of me, and squatted down on its haunches. Reaching out its hands it pulled the branches of bushes toward it and stripped the leaves with its teeth. Its lips curled flexibly around the leaves as it ate. I was close enough to see that its teeth were white and even.

The shape of this creature's head somewhat resembled a Negro's. The head was higher at the back than at the front. The nose was broad and flat. The lips and chin protruded farther than its nose. But the hair that covered it, leaving bare only the arts of its face around the mouth, nose and ears, made it resemble an animal as much as a human. None of this hair, even on the back of its head, was longer than an inch, and that on its face much shorter. Its ears were shaped like a human's ears. But its eyes were small and black like a bear's. And its neck also was unhuman. Thicker and shorter than any man's I had ever seen.

As I watched this creature, I wondered if some movie company was making a film at this place and that what I saw was an actor, made up to look partly human and partly animal. But as I observed it more, I decided it would be impossible to fake such a specimen. Anyway, I learned later there was no such company near that area. Nor, in fact, did anyone live up Mica Mountain, according to the people who lived in Tête Jaune Cache.

Finally, the wild thing must have got my scent, for it looked directly at me through an opening in the brush. A look of amazement crossed its face. It looked so comical at the moment I had to grin. Still in a crouched position, it backed up three or four short steps, then straightened up to its full height and started to walk rapidly back the way it had come. For a moment it watched me over its shoulder as it went, not exactly afraid, but as though it wanted no contact with anything strange.

The thought came to me that if I shot it, I would possibly have a specimen of great interest to scientists the world over. I had heard stories about the Sasquatch, the giant hairy Indians that live in the legends of British Columbia Indians and also, many claim, are still in fact alive today. Maybe this was a Sasquatch, I told myself.

I levelled my rifle. The creature was still walking rapidly away, again turning its head to look in my direction. Although I have called the creature "it," I felt now that it was a human being and I knew I would never forgive myself if I killed it.

Just as it came to the other patch of brush it threw its head back and made a peculiar noise that seemed to be half laugh and half language, and which I can only describe as a kind of a whinny. Then it walked from the small brush into a stand of lodge-pole pine.

I stepped out into the opening and looked across a small ridge just beyond the pine to see if I could see it again. It came out on the ridge a couple of hundred yards away from me, tipped its head back again, and again emitted the only sound I had heard it make, but what this half-laugh, half-language was meant to convey, I do not know. It disappeared then, and I never saw it again.

I wanted to find out if it lived on vegetation entirely or ate meat as well, so I went down and looked for signs. I found it in five different places, and although I examined it thoroughly, could find no hair or shells or bugs or insects. So I believe it was strictly a vegetarian.

I found one place where it had slept for a couple of nights under a tree. Now, the nights were cool up the mountain, at that time of year especially, and yet it had not used a fire. I found no sign that it possessed even the simplest of tools. Nor a single companion while in this place.

Whether this creature was a Sasquatch I do not know. It will always remain a mystery to me, unless another one is found.

I hereby declare the above statement to be in every part true, to the best of my powers of observation and recollection.

I'M A SASQUATCH

By and large the reader will find the contributions to this collection to be scary, eerie, or weird. That is as it should be, but from time to time the reader might appreciate a touch of humour; certainly the compiler does! It is seldom amiss, especially when fabulous creatures like Sasquatchs abound.

As far as I know, this is the first time the following verse has been reprinted. "I'm a Sasquatch" appeared in the columns of *Innisfail Province* (Alta.), 11 Feb. 1975, and it issued forth from the pen of Percy Maddux. I know nothing about Mr. Maddux, except that as a versifier he has a deft touch.

I'm a Sasquatch

I'm a big, rough, tough Sasquatch from back of beyond,
I'm not a monster from a prehistoric pond,
I'm a semi-human being, and surely it's no crime
If I want to leave my footprints on the sands of time.
Many people have seen me vanish in the woods,
And they maintain I was absconding with stolen goods,
But all I did was steal away, get out of sight:

At the approach of man, I took to the hills in flight.
I'm a big, rough, tough Sasquatch, I am indeed,
And I can disappear with most uncanny speed.
So whenever people say that they've seen me around,
The only proof they can show is footprints on the ground.

EVOLUTIONARY PRECURSOR

Don Hepworth and I met on the set of *The Shirley Show*, CTV's popular daily talk show that is now a happy memory. Shirley Solomon, the vivacious host of the show, had invited us to be among the guests on the program devoted to the intriguing subject of "Canadian Monsters." When it came my turn to speak, I discussed about various monsters, including "the Monster of Meech Lake," Brian Mulroney!

On camera, Hepworth recounted for the studio and television audiences an experience that had taken place ten years earlier and had lasted all of eleven seconds. But that was long enough for him to see two creatures which could, for lack of a better name, be called Sasquatches.

As much as his event intrigued me, what impressed me even more was Don Hepworth himself. He is a no-nonsense kind of person, an accomplished man, and a highly credible witness. He was born and raised in the Calder Valley of West Yorkshire, England. At the age of seventeen he enlisted in the British Army. He is a former member of the élite Special Branch. He also served with British Military Intelligence and the Metropolitan Police of London. After a stint with the British High Commission in Canada, he served as Chief Inspector for the Ontario Humane Society from 1973 to 1981. He resides in Mount Albert, Ont., and trains horses and riders for dressage and eventing. He is the author of *Gorilla in the Garage ... and Other Stories* (1987).

Hepworth and I chatted following the taping of the program. I encouraged him to prepare a written account of his experience and to send it to me, along with a photocopy of the drawing that he had prepared of the creature he had seen. Both the account and the photocopy arrived on 30 Jan. 1991.

As he explained in the covering letter, "The phenomenon I encountered may be more common in other places and parts of the world than we thought. Although I don't believe we are overrun by primitive beings, I do think they are found in North and South America, Asia, Russia and Africa, Malaya and some of the Pacific Islands (Sumatra for instance)."

This is a Rare Evolutionary Precursor

It was early evening, on Monday, April 7th, 1980, as I drove southwest on U.S. Highway 95. I was heading towards the Idaho-Oregon border and, I hoped, accommodation for the night in the small town of Weiser.

With my wife Vickey, I spent the day in a leisurely drive through Moscow, the Salmon River Valley, and into the wild Snake River uplands. We had marvelled at the steep grades of the roadways, with their "runaway safety exits." Indeed, we had actually seen one large truck run away, its failed braking system smoking profusely, before coming to a halt on a boggy stretch of flat median.

We stopped to ascertain if all was well with the driver. (My wife is a registered nurse.) He assured us he was fine, but his elderly vehicle less so. It would require towing. He had summoned help on his CB radio. We chatted with him in the interval. We inquired if he knew of a motor inn nearby. "Oh, yes, New Meadows, some ten miles away, has a motel." The heavy-duty tow truck could be seen approaching, so we said farewell to our driver friend and drove on to New Meadows.

It may be we came in from the wrong direction or didn't explore the hamlet thoroughly, but in any event the only motel we saw looked well-used; battered would perhaps be a more appropriate description. We elected to drive on to Weiser, forty-odd miles distant.

The road wound its way through the Payett National Forest, climbing steadily upwards to semi-open range land, past the little village of Council and the hamlet of Mesa. Meanwhile, the sun was setting behind the Seven Devils Mountains west of Hell's Canyon, 7,900 feet deep. Wild country! Yes, you could say that.

As I drove along, I reflected on the events of the past week. I had completed a short seminar at Washington State University Veterinary College at Pullman. The subject had been Freeze Branding and Livestock Fraud. The week before that had found me in Vancouver, on loan to the Canadian Animal Welfare Association, completing a survey of slaughter-houses in B.C. I was at that time employed as the Chief Inspector of the Ontario Humane Society and was possibly the most experienced Humane Inspector in the whole of Canada.

Having completed my employer's business, I had taken time to study at Pullman, although initially I had decided to attend the course of study there on my own time and at my own expense. However, on learning my intention to visit the Pacific Northwest on leave, my employers asked me to advance my plans a week to assist the Animal Welfare Foundation. Since it would be a saving for me, I had agreed. My wife had joined me at the weekend. All was now completed. So now we were free to spend a few days exploring the wild areas of Idaho, Oregon, and Washington.

As I drove along at a steady sixty to seventy kilometres an hour, I was observing passing terrain. My wife dozed in the passenger seat beside me. Since she leads a high-pressure working life, she usually dozes off after thirty or so minutes on the road.

I suppose I was approaching the highest point of land on that stretch of highway, somewhere in the region of 2,000 feet above sea level. The surrounding mountains loomed several thousand feet higher at their respective peaks. But that is when I noticed two figures walking towards the road-edge on my left. They were black in colour. My first thought was, "Two Negro kids from a nearby ranch, not as yet visible." Then I reflected that I hadn't seen any Negro persons all day. Only Nez Perce Indians and Caucasians like myself. And not too many of the latter.

The two dark forms seemed indifferent to my oncoming car lights. I slowed to a crawl, but drove closer so as to get the best possible illumination of the pair. I was aghast. At a distance of eight to ten yards, I could see they were both covered with short black hair, something like a Labrador retriever.

The smaller of the two walked one or two steps in front of the other. It was clearly female and appeared to be clutching something to its left upper torso. The one behind was a few inches taller than the female and more bulky. I guess it would be about five-foot-seven or eight in height. I estimated it would weigh between two hundred and two hundred and thirty pounds.

As the male crossed the road, it turned to look at the car. As its neck was extremely short, it had to turn from the waist. I saw the flash of white in its right eye, the bulge of its male genitalia. I noticed the hands on the loose-swinging arms. They were thick, elongated, and powerful. Their heads were low-set. The skulls were flat, back-sloping from heavy brow ridges to a top-knot, almost like the start of the sagittal crest of a young gorilla.

They walked bent forward slightly from the hips with feet and arms moving diagonally and arms swinging loosely. To the right of the road was a grass-covered bank about six feet high. The smaller creature paused on reaching the foot of this incline, flexing its legs and body. Then it sprang easily to the top and out of sight. The larger creature put its left foot flat against the slope and simply stepped up. I don't know anyone or anything that could duplicate this instance of locomotion.

"See that?" I exclaimed to my wife. She grunted, stirred, and said, "What is it?" She had missed seeing one of the most extraordinary sights of my life. I was too excited to explain.

About half an hour later, sitting in the warmth and comfort of a motel room in Weiser, I took a sheet of paper from my briefcase and tried to sketch what I had seen....

I am convinced that what I saw were young "teenagers" of this particular species of animal. I checked height later, by having my wife, who is five foot, five inches, stand roughly the same distance from the car as the creatures. She matched the height of the small one. So my estimate of height was correct.

What exactly were they? I don't know. I can't claim to be a scientist. But during nine years of service with the Ontario Humane Society in the position of Chief Inspector, I have physically handled many species of exotic animals. Amongst them were black, brown, cinnamon, and grizzly bears.

I may well be the only Humane Official in North America, perhaps in the whole world, who has actually seized a male mountain gorilla. Oh, yes. He was five feet, eight inches, covered with black hair, and weighed four hundred pounds. So I know that the creatures I saw weren't gorillas. Nor would a pair of chimpanzees be suitable candidates. Their walk would not coincide with the walk of this primate.

For now, the matter rests. But one day, one day, I'm going back to the Pacific Northwest, to take my time and make a better effort at securing some really tangible evidence of this creature's existence. Perhaps I will find some hair, teeth, bones. They might turn up in some winter den where old age and general debility have caught up with an older specimen. Maybe the smaller forest scavengers have left something inedible to show the passing of this rare evolutionary precursor of ourselves.

I hope so. Shooting one would be out of the question.

THE HAIRY MAN

I am indebted to a correspondent, Fred Habermehl of Niagara Falls, Ont., for the following account of the sighting of a ghostly man. He mailed it to me on 28 May 1996.

The account was written by his daughter Cathy Craig who with her husband Stuart and their children then lived (and may still live) in a duplex on Briarwood Avenue, south of Thorold Stone Road and west of Dorchester Road, Niagara Falls.

Do they share their duplex with the "hairy man"? It is true that children are known to acknowledge the presence of "imaginary playmates." Is the "hairy man" an "imaginary playmate"? Or is it the ghost of some real person?

In 1981, we moved into a duplex on Briarwood Avenue, next to Meadowvale Park, in Niagara Falls. Almost immediately, our eight-month-old daughter, Tabitha, started seeing something. I would pass it off as just my imagination, a glimpse of something passing down the hall, a presence in the room when you knew you were alone, or a baby laughing at someone behind you, when there was no one there.

When she was old enough to talk, Tabitha and I were in the north end of the basement, when she began to have a conversation with something in the dark laundry room at the south end of the house. I asked her who she was talking to. She replied, "The man."

"What man?" I asked, to which she replied, "The big, hairy man."

I immediately dropped the conversation, picked her up, and went upstairs. I kept all the lights and the TV on. I always knew there was something there and that she sensed it too. Her blunt response, as if I should have been able to see him too, was too much. Since we were usually home alone and I tend to hear things that go bump in the night, I never told anyone. I didn't want them to think I was nuts. That was the most obvious and haunting incident with Tabitha, and eventually the hairy man faded away.

In 1984, Deidre was born and the hauntings returned. The "hairy man" frightened her one day in the upstairs hall, when I sat within eyesight in the living-room reading the paper. Deidre was playing quietly in front of the hall mirror. I glanced at her just as she jumped up with a look of terror on her face. She ran right up over my paper and onto my lap, screaming that the man was scaring her and he was going to get her.

Deidre's other memorable encounter was in the laundry-room. I was putting clothes in the washer, as she stood beside my leg facing the opposite way. She was talking to someone and I asked, "Who are you talking to?"

She answered, "The big, hairy man."

I looked to where she was pointing and asked her what he looked like, but she just lowered her head and stopped talking. I kept asking questions, trying to be calm and chatty, but she didn't speak of him again. I knew he was always around and she was aware of him. As with my first child, he seemed to appear less and less often as she got older.

In 1988, Michael was born and the man returned. By the time he was two, he had verbalized his sightings to his father and we discussed openly what I had known for years. On one occasion, at about age three, he had gone downstairs to sleep in our bedroom next to the laundry room. He wasn't down there long, before he came racing up the stairs, saying, "Daddy, the hairy man wants to talk to you." His father, refusing to play this silly game, told Michael to tell the man to come upstairs if he wanted to talk to him. Seriously, as if the man was truly downstairs, Michael leaned over the rail and bellowed, "My father says to come up if you want to talk to him." That night, because his son's reaction was so convincing, his father became a believer.

Two years after Michael's birth, our neighbours in the adjoining house, Chris and Roger, had a baby Alyssa. Within the year, they had seen enough to speak openly to me about this presence. They had stories of their own. Roger was vacuuming the recreation-room one day, when he felt someone enter behind him. He began chatting with his wife. When she didn't answer, he turned around to see that no one was there. He later questioned his wife, who said she had not even been downstairs.

On another occasion, Chris was in the shower, when she sensed someone else in the room. She struck up a conversation with Roger. When he didn't answer, she pulled back the curtain and found she was alone. Later, he confirmed he had never entered the bathroom. As with me, they knew their baby could see someone else in the house. They also felt something moving about. As Alyssa got older, the man faded.

In 1992, Chris and Roger moved to the house on the other side of us. Since then they have had twins, but the man has never appeared to them in that house, even though there are only ten feet between the two houses. The hairy man seems to be only in the two homes of the duplex and only when there are young children present.

THE GIANT RABBIT

I have never met Debbie Ridpath Ohi, but I know that she lives in Toronto and that she is the author of this memoir. It was written in 1995 and reads like fiction. By that I mean it reads so smoothly it feels more like fiction than it does fact. But it is a memoir.

In her account, Ms. Ohi asks a question. I wonder what the answer to it is. Indeed, I wonder whether or not she will ever be able to answer her own question.

When I was six years old, my babysitter and her friend told me about the giant rabbit who lived in the forest near our house.

"It eats children," Rebecca told me solemnly.

I was horrified, of course. My parents had never warned me of the monstrous predator in our vicinity, and had even taken me for walks on the trail. Perhaps they didn't know.

"Everyone knows about it," added Rebecca. "Three kids have been eaten, just this year. All that were left were their bones and their hair."

My lower lip trembled. "I don't believe you," I said, even though I did.

The next day Rebecca and her best friend Genevieve took me for a walk.

"What are those for?" I asked, apprehension stirring. Both Rebecca and Genevieve had a carrot in their hands.

"In case we run into the rabbit," Rebecca said matter-of-factly. "So he'll eat the carrots instead of us. I would have brought you a carrot except my mom only had two."

"Anyway, you said you don't believe there's a rabbit," added Genevieve. I didn't like Genevieve very much.

She was right, though; I had expressed disbelief in the existence of their giant child-munching rabbit. So I didn't say anything and pretended not to be scared to death as we started on the trail.

The trees rustled with the wind as we moved deeper into the forest, and I struggled to keep my eyes on the trail, away from the shadows beneath the trees.

"What was that?" Rebecca gasped.

"I don't know. Maybe it's following us," Genevieve spoke in a whisper.

Panicked, I strained to hear. "What? What?"

"Ssshhh," whispered Rebecca, and we kept walking. I was numb with fear, and I kept looking around the forest behind us.

The giant rabbit knew I was here! I pictured its huge pink nose twitching malevolently as it caught my scent. I wondered how long it had been since it had eaten.

A few minutes later, Rebecca and her friend stopped. I was not happy about this, of course. All my instincts were screaming at me to run home as fast as my little legs could carry me.

"We've got something to show you," said Rebecca mysteriously.

They knelt, and motioned for me to come closer. I did, and glanced down at where they were pointing.

It was a giant rabbit footprint.

I gasped and took a step back.

"See?" said Genevieve. "Rebecca told you it was real. You didn't believe her."

Panic-stricken, I started looking around us, my head turning in jerks. "I wanna go home." It was here, I could sense it. Somewhere in that shadowy forest lurked an evil child-devouring monster with a twitching nose and pink-rimmed eyes.

Then I screamed.

To this day I swear I saw something, behind a clump of trees. What exactly, I cannot say. It was more a fleeting glimpse, a flash of raggedy fur perhaps, a single twitch of a giant whiskered nose. Whatever it was, the glimpse galvanized me into action.

Without waiting to consult Rebecca or Genevieve, I ran down the path towards home, screaming at the top of my little lungs all the way.

Rebecca managed to catch up with me two-thirds of the way back. The incident must have unnerved her, because she immediately took me to the ice cream store and bought me a cone (pralines and cream, my favourite) with some of her baby-sitting money, warning me not to tell my parents about what had happened just in case it scared them, too.

Years later I still go over the entire event in my mind and wonder. The rabbit footprint could easily have been created by Rebecca and her friend, as "proof" to me that the creature existed.

But what did I see in the forest that day?

A VERY STRANGE EXPERIENCE

From time to time, for some people, the sense of the reality of the world seems to wax and wane. It recedes from their senses and memories. It does not always return. Familiar things take on a curiously unfamiliar aspect; unfamiliar things assume a surprisingly familiar form. Such experiences are quite striking and unsettling and make a strong impression.

Psychiatrists, observing elements of dissociation, speak of the condition they called *derealization* (and of its companion *depersonalization*). Psychologists, noting the ability of memory to knit the factual and the fictitious into a seamless whole, refer to *confabulation*. Parapsychologists are free to talk about altered states of consciousness (ASCs) and other dimensions of reality.

Here is one account of the familiar becoming the unfamiliar — or the unfamiliar becoming the familiar. It was prepared for me by "Margaret Fyfe" and when it was originally published in one of my earlier books of mysteries, it appeared as by "Margaret Fyfe." I am now able to identify the writer. The pen name was assumed by the well-known folklorist, the late Edith Fowke, a good friend, fellow researcher, and companion on the pathways of folklore. Her reminiscence was written in October 1989 and it refers to an event that she had experienced that had taken place in England two months earlier, in August of that year. She could never explain it and was deeply puzzled by it.

A Very Strange Experience

Last summer I had a very strange experience. I was going to a festival in England, and needed to reserve a room before I left Canada. The festival was being held in the seaside town of Sidmouth which is quite small and very popular so hotels tend to fill up early.

I phoned the festival office and asked them to see if they could find a room for me, saying I would phone again the next day. When I called the second time I was told that the Devoran Hotel had a cancellation and that I should phone Mrs. Clifford at Sidmouth 3151. I said that was fine because I'd stayed at the Devoran the year before and had liked it. Accordingly I phoned the number and booked for the week. When I mentioned that I had stayed there for a few days the previous summer, Mrs. Clifford said I hadn't, because she booked only by the week.

When I got to London I took a train from Paddington to Honiton, the railway station closest to Sidmouth, and got a taxi there, telling the driver to take me to the Devoran Hotel. When we reached Sidmouth I remembered the hotel's location and directed the driver to it. When we got there, it look just as I remembered it. However, when I went in I didn't recognize Mrs. Clifford. Thinking that the hotel might have changed hands, I asked how long she had been there and she told

me fifteen years. I then noticed some differences to what I remembered. The desk was placed at right angles to the front door while I remembered it as being parallel last year. The dining room was on the opposite side of the front hall to what I remembered. However, the location was just as I remembered, and when I started going to the various festival programs I knew exactly how to reach them from the Devoran. The whole block was familiar to me, and there was no other hotel in it that looked enough like the Devoran for me to think that that was where I had stayed.

Another strange point was that the previous year the festival office had given me a phone number to book a room, saying it was for the Elizabeth Hotel. I had called and made my booking, but when, on reaching the town, I went to the Elizabeth Hotel, which was at the corner of a block, they had no record of my booking. I showed the clerk the phone number I had been given and he said it might be for the Devoran, which was right next door. I went into the Devoran, and they had my reservation. The confusion over the phone number and hotel name apparently resulted from the fact that the Devoran and the Elizabeth were together on the festival office's alphabetical listing. If my memory was wrong on this point, it might have been the Elizabeth Hotel I stayed at the previous year. However, it was considerably larger than the Devoran: I remembered it, but it didn't seem to me that I had stayed there.

This confusion naturally puzzled me, and during the week I was there I tried to think of some explanation. I looked at all the hotels in the block where I knew I had stayed, and none except the Devoran looked familiar. When I came home I looked to see if I had kept my receipt from the previous year, but I hadn't. Thus this experience remains a mystery to me.

GLIMPSING THE BUSHMAN

John Bernard Bourne, the author of this thoughtful and moving memoir, summers in Holland Landing, Ont., where he was born, but he spends the rest of the year in Gameti, N.W.T.

"Glimpsing the Bushman" originally appeared in *Maclean's,* March 3, 2003. It captures the essence of the contradictory thoughts and feelings that accompany a "glimpse" of an order of creation that is unexpected, undocumented, unreasonable, and inhuman.

I moved to Rae Lakes, this small, isolated community in the Northwest Territories, almost three years ago. In the parlance of the local population, I was a white man from Ontario coming to live amongst the Aboriginals. In this case it was a group of Aboriginals I had never heard of before — the Dogribs. At the time, I looked at myself as an anthropologist going to observe a unique and isolated culture.

When I first arrived, I was inundated with cultural orientation. I listened to the stories of the elders and observed some of the local customs. In those early days the story that stuck out to me the most was the one about the Bushman.

According to the Dogrib people there exists a creature known as the Bushman. It is tall and hairy and lurks in the bush ready to abduct anyone travelling alone. Those who have been taken by the Bushman are usually never seen again, and if they are, they are found mute and mentally deranged. As an outsider, this story sounded a lot like a cross between B.C.'s sasquatch and eastern Canada's windigo; but for the Dogribs it is something to be taken very seriously.

The Bushman story aside, I tried to leap into life in this Aboriginal community by embracing all of the rituals of their culture. I went on the caribou hunt, I attended the community feasts and I went every time there was a drum dance. Participating in the rituals was easy enough and I took it in as one would take in the symbols of any unique community and tradition. Although I felt detached and out of place most of the time, I still found it interesting.

The difficult part was adjusting to the challenges of everyday life. Many of the people in my village can only speak their native language, so the linguistic hurdle is the first one you have to overcome. Issues of illiteracy and substance abuse would also raise its ugly head and become an obstacle in trying to live and work with the people. There were many times when I would forget that I was still in Canada because I felt like such a foreigner. I had previously lived in South Korea for a couple of years, and I found that there was less culture shock living in that far away Asian nation than there was in the far north of the country I called home.

And then there is the darkness. Long and indescribable, the lack of sunlight creeps up on you at the end of October and stays until March. The phenomenon is fascinating at first, but the novelty soon wears off and you begin counting down the days until spring and the endless daylight that it brings.

It was when the daylight was beginning to reappear that I saw the Bushman. It was the middle of March and I was driving with my wife and a friend on the winter road (the ice road that is open about six weeks every year to bring in food and supplies). We were caught in a blizzard and our visibility had deteriorated to nothing. We were stuck on the frozen, endless white of Faber Lake, halfway between Gameti and Rae-Edzo (which means in the middle of nowhere). It was just a flash. In fact, I would have thought it was an illusion brought on by the snow, but the two other people with me saw it as well.

It was tall and hairy, running on its two hind legs. The hair was long and hung from its body in an unkempt and wild manner. It was gone before we could say anything. My friend who was driving shouted, "What was that?" But we all knew. We tried to push our original instinct away and rationalize it as something else. But we couldn't.

When I told my friends and family in Ontario about the experience, they thought I was making it up. Or worse, they tried to logically explain it ("It was probably a bear coming out of hibernation"). It was only the Dogrib people who did not treat the story with any type of condescension. They nodded solemnly and understood the story for what it was.

Shortly after, things began to make more sense to me in the community. The drum dance, which I initially perceived as being primitive and unsophisticated, became full of new meaning. I learned to drum. The hunt, which I had always thought was a little atavistic and barbaric, seemed almost spiritual. I became familiar with the various uses of the caribou, including the consumption of the unborn fetus by the elders because it is soft and easy to chew when you have no teeth.

This past fall, a story began circulating around our village. The wise ones were giving everybody fair warning — they had a premonition that the Bushman would be abducting somebody this year. We were warned to be careful and not to go walking by ourselves into the bush. I was surprised by how I reacted. Three years ago I would have laughed and made fun of it. Now, I just accepted the warning and kept it at the back of my mind.

Logically, I know there is no Bushman. It makes no sense and defies any type of scientific evidence. I know it is symbolic of other things, like the loneliness and darkness one feels when living in isolation in the Far North. It is a parable to understand a unique and distinct culture in the world.

But I did see something on that winter road.

Winter is here again, and the long darkness gives you time to think. Tales of the Bushman do not really pervade your thoughts during the times of daylight. But now, it almost seems plausible.

Every night, when I put my baby daughter to bed, I lie beside her, singing songs and telling stories. When she falls asleep, I used to creep out quietly and sit with my wife in the other room. Lately, however, I find myself staying longer, well after she has fallen into a deep slumber. I feel this subconscious urge to guard and watch over her, and protect her from the Bushman.

Just in case.

PART TWO
Creatures of Water

WE have misnamed the planet Earth. It should be called planet Water. Two-thirds of its surface is covered by liquid. Covering the remaining one-third of its surface is often moist, irrigated earth.

It is sometimes argued that its life forms originated not on the planet itself but in the realm of space, the source being other planets in our solar system or the stars of outer space. This is the theory of "panspermia" and it is identified with Sir Fred Hoyle, the astronomer, scientist, and science-fiction writer. He held that cosmic spores or sperm from the space "infected" Earth through falls of meteorites.

That is one theory. Another theory is the marine-basis for the origin of life. Fauna emerged from the depths of the seas. The theory may account for the fact that man is strangely "at home" with water — oceans and seas, lakes and lochs, rivers and streams, creeks and brooks, bayous and ponds, springs and fountains.

Whatever the origin of life forms, strange creatures inhabit the country's storm-tossed waters. Among the earliest of creatures is Sedna, whose domain is the frigid waters of the Arctic, and Misshipisshu, the sea creature whose churning accounts for the ripples and waves that appear on the surface of the Great Lakes.

The traditions of the Native Peoples about their monstrous beings lead readers today to the tall tales told by mariners about encounters with strange, ambiguous creatures of the sea, mermen and mermaids, but also to the stories told by sailors of the lengths they went to avoid boarding "jinxed" ships or sailing "hoodoo" vessels as well as visions of ghostly "fire ships" scudding across the horizon at sunset. In our own day there are landlubbers' accounts of sightings of lake monsters creatures like Ogopogo and Memphré.

Descriptions of most (if not all) of these awe-inspiring (if not these frightening) creatures of the waters of the planet are to be found here.

Just when you thought it was safe to go near the water...!

ISLE OF DEMONS

Should there be a more appropriate domain or habitat for marine monsters and sea creatures than the Isle of Demons set amid the waters of the Gulf of the St. Lawrence River, I am unaware of its geographical coordinates in the the world as we know it or on charts and maps as we imagine it.

We have a description of the domain known as the Isle of Demons in a single if extended sentence from an antique document *Le Grand Insulaire* composed in French by the cosmographer André Thevet (1502-1590). But rather than simply quote that sentence and leave it at that, here is some background information, in the words of the modern historian John George Bourinot (1837-1902), describing the fabled Isle of Demons in his article "Canadian Historic Names," *The Canadian Monthly and National Review*, Vol. 7, No. 4, April 1875. Bourinot's description is followed by Thevet's single sentence.

The Island of Anticosti is very little known to the world, except as a bleak waste, to be avoided by the sailor in stormy weather. A considerable degree of mystery, for many years, naturally hung about an island of which so few persons had a definite knowledge. Even Lever, in one of his novels, chose it as the appropriate scene of an exciting episode in the life of one of his heroes, Con Cregan, who was cast upon its sterile shores. But now-a-days it is the resort of fishermen, and it has even been proposed to make it the arena of industrial enterprise on an extended scale. The derivation of the name is not difficult to seek. Cartier first discovered it in 1534, and called it L'Ile de l'Ascension. Thevet, in his *Universal Cosmography*, names it Ile de l'Assomption. The same authority, however, says in his Grand Insulaire, "that the savages of the country call it Naticousti," which the French changed into Anticosti, the meaning of which I cannot find in any authority.

It will not be remembered, except by the ardent student of Canadian geography, that the islands of Belle-Isle and Quirpon — at least these are generally believed to be the places in question — once bore the startling title of the Isles of Demons. The sailors, in old times, passed those isles with feelings of awe, and more than one credulous voyager could hear at night the shouts of the demons as the wind swept through the rigging and the waves dashed over the bulwarks. André Thevet, in his famous old book, *Le Grand Insulaire*, tells some wondrous stories of these demons."

* * *

True it is, I myself have heard it, not from one, but from a great number of the sailors and pilots with whom I have made many voyages, that, when they passed this way, they heard in the air, on the tops and about the masts, a great clamour of men's voices, confused and inarticulate, such as you may hear from the crowd at a fair or market-place; whereupon they well knew that the Isle of Demons was not far off.

SEA CREATURE

The early explorers of the Atlantic seaboard reported seeing all manner of marine life, some comfortably familiar, some uncomfortably unfamiliar. Sir Humphrey Gilbert (1539-1583), the English explorer, is one of these explorers and adventurers. On his second voyage to the New World, made in the Summer of 1583, he took possession of Newfoundland, establishing the first of England's overseas colonies. He also reported seeing a "spectacle."

It was while on the return voyage, on 31 August 1583, that Gilbert spotted a strange creature disporting in the waves of the Grand Banks off Cape Race. He likened the unfamiliar site to "a lion in the ocean sea, or fish in shape of a lion." The sea creature was spotted by Gilbert, aboard the *Squirrel*, and witnessed by four captains under his command, including his next-in-command, the captain of the *Golden Hind*.

Perhaps the strange creature took a scunner to Gilbert or to the *Squirrel*. Nine days later the *Squirrel*, encountering rough weather and icebergs, sank; all hands were lost. Over the tumult and the shouting the captain of the *Golden Hind* reported hearing the voice of Gilbert repeatedly calling out, as if to comfort his crew, "We are as near to heaven by sea as by land!"

Gilbert's narrative of the voyage was first published by the marine historian Richard Hakluyt in 1589. The text reproduced here derives from *Selected Narratives from the Principal Navigations of Hakluyt* (Oxford: Clarendon Press, 1909) edited by Edward John Payne.

So upon Saturday in the afternoon, the 31. of August, we changed our course, and returned back for England. At which very instant, even in winding about, there passed along between us and towards the land which we now forsook a very lion to our seeming, in shape, hair, and colour, not swimming after the manner of a beast by moving on his feet, but rather sliding upon the water with his whole body, excepting the legs, in sight, neither yet diving under, and again rising above the water, as the manner is of whales, dolphins, tunnies, porpoises, and all other fish: but confidently showing himself above water without hiding: notwithstanding, we presented ourselves in open view and gesture to amaze him, as all creatures will be commonly at a sudden gaze and sight of men. Thus he passed along turning his head to and fro, yawning and gaping wide, with ugly demonstration of long teeth, and glaring eyes; and to bid us a farewell, coming right against the Hind, he sent forth a horrible voice, roaring or bellowing as doth a lion, which spectacle we all beheld so far as we were able to discern the same, as men prone to wonder at every strange thing, as this doubtless was, to see a lion in the ocean sea, or fish in shape of a lion. What opinion others had thereof, and chiefly the General himself, I forbear to deliver: but he took it for *bonum omen*, rejoicing that he was to war against such an enemy, if it were the devil. The wind was large for *England* at our return, but very high, and the sea rough, insomuch as the frigate, wherein the General went, was almost swallowed up.

SAW A MERMAID

During the 17th century in England, it was believed that marvels were to be found in the East, that the way to the East lay across the Western seas, and that the surfaces and the depths of these seas teemed with marvels and wonders all their own. Among these surprises were believed to be fabulous creatures like mermaids.

The English navigator and explorer Henry Hudson (d. 1611), a sober and sometimes somber captain, reported that two members of his crew aboard the *Half Moon* spotted a mermaid. The account appears in his log titled "Henry Hudson's Voyages" which was included by Samuel Purchas in his collection of travel literature, *Purchas His Pilgrims* (1625).

Here is Hudson's description from "Chapter 15: Sea Colours, Sights and Descriptions of a Mermaide" as included in Part III of "Voyages" for 15 June 1610. The text is reproduced as it appears in the original, with archaic spelling and puncutation, but without the antique letterforms.

What did Hudson himself make of the sighting? It is hard to tell, for the Master Mariner is matter-of-fact about the matter. It is likely that he reported what he heard, just as his crewmen Thomas Holles and Robert Rayner reported to him what they saw or think they saw in the choppy waters. Perhaps the two sailors projected onto the sea a scene that they wished to see, an object of their desires.

Mermaide seene, and described.

The fifteenth, all day and night cleere sun-shine; the wind at East, the latitude at noone 75 degrees 7 minutes. We held Westward by our account 13 leagues. In the after-noone the Sea was asswaged; and the wind being at East we set sayle, and stood South and by East, and South South-east as we could. This morning, one of our companie looking overboord saw a Mermaid, and calling up some of the companie to see her, one more came up, and by that time shee was come close to the ships side, looking earnestly on the men: a little after, a Sea came and overturned her: from the Navill upward, her backe and breasts were like a womans, (as they say that saw her) her body as big as one of us; her skin very white; and long haire hanging downe behind, of colour blacke: in her going downe they saw her tayle, which was like the tayle of a Porposse, and speckled like a Macrell. Their names that saw her, were *Thomas Holles* and *Robert Rayner*.

SOME THING OF A STRANGE CREATURE

I am not aware of any contemporary descriptions of mermaids cavorting in Canadian waters, but innumerable reports of their disporting were made in the past. Perhaps the reason for this is that mariners of previous centuries expected to see these female creatures of the sea, whereas no mariner of the 20th or 21st century expects to behold a denizen of the deep with a woman's head, long hair to hide her two breasts, and fish-scales to cover her form from navel to fins!

Sir Richard Whitbourne (1579-1626), the English sea captain and commissioner, was a colonist who felt that Newfoundland's new communities offered English colonists unparalleled opportunities for enrichment and advancement. To further the cause of immigration, he wrote a book with a noteworthy title: *A Discovrse and Discovery of New-found-land, with many reasons to prooue how worthy and beneficiall a Plantation may there be made, after a far better manner than now is* (1620). The archbishops of Canterbury and York were directed by King James I of England to take up collections in their parish churches to assist in the costs of the book's publication and distribution. It ends with a description of the mermaid, perhaps an exotic lure in itself!

Sir Richard's report of a "Maremaide" in St. John's harbour in 1610 is vivid and detailed, and the creature is "so beautifull" that readers since then have crossed their fingers that it really was a mermaid that Sir Richard espied and described and that such a race of creatures exists or at least existed some four centuries ago. The account comes from a facsimile of the original edition of his book printed by Da Capo Press in 1971. The passage is reproduced from that edition, complete with its archaic spelling.

A conclusion to the Reader, containing a particular Description, and relation of some things omitted in the former discourse.

Now also I will not omit to relate some thing of a strange Creature that I first saw there in the yeere 1610. in a morning early as I was standing by the water side, in the Harbour of Saint Johns; which I espyed very swiftly to come swimming towards me, looking cheerefully, as it had been a woman, by the Face, Eyes, Nose, Mouth, Chin, Eares, Necke and Forehead: It seemed to be a so beautifull, and in those parts so well proportioned, hauing round about vpon the head, all blew strakes, resembling hayre, dovvne to the Necke (but certainly it vvas no haire:) for I beheld it long, and another of my Company also, yet liuing, that vvas not then farre from me; and seeing the same comming so svviftly tovvards me, I stepped backe, for it vvas come vvithin the length of a long Pike. Which vvhen this strange Creature savv, that I vvent from it, it presently thereupon diued a little vnder vvater, and did swim tovvards the place where before I landed; whereby I beheld the shoulders and backe dovvne to the middle, to be as square, vvhite and smooth as the backe of a man, and from the middle to the hinder part, poynting in proportion like a broad hooked Arrow; how it was proportioned in the forepart, from the necke and shoulders, I know not; but the same came shortly after vnto a Boate, wherein one *William Hawkridge*, then my seruant, was, that hath bin since a Captaine in a ship of the *East Indies*, and is lately thre imployed againe by Sir *Thomas Smith*, in the like Voyage; and the same Creature did put both his hands vpon the side of the Boate, and did striue to come in to him and others then in the said Boate: whereat they were afraide; and one of them strooke it a full blow on the Head; whereby it fell off form them: and afterwards it came to two other Boats in the said Harbour; the men in them, for feare fled to land: This (I suppose) was a Maremaide. Now because diuers haue written much of Mermaids, I haue presumed to relate, what is most certaine of such a strange Creature that was seene at *New-found-land*: whether it were a Maremaid or no, I know not; I leaue it to others to iudge, &c.

THAT MONSTER OF A MERMAN

Nicolas Denys (1598-1688), born in Tours, France, was a colonist and promoter of the fisheries and the fur trade throughout Acadia. He worked as a merchant at La Rochelle from 1632 and died at his Acadian trading post at Nepisiguit Acadia. He is the narrator of the account of the sighting of "a Merman."

Denys' account appears in his book *The Description and Natural History of the Coasts of North America (Acadia)*, translated into English from the original edition published in Paris in 1672 and edited for the Champlain Society by W.F. Ganong in 1908. The passage that is of cryptozoological interest appears in the "Collateral Documents" section of Ganong's edition; it first appeared, not in the original French edition, but as an interpolation into the Dutch translation of Denys' book, first published in 1688.

Did the mariners of Acadia of the 1650s believe in the existence of a race of mer-beings, creatures that are half-human and half-fish? Whether or not they did, they reported seeing at least one such creature.

I must here make a little digression in order to relate a matter which deserves special notice and of which there have been eye-witnesses enough so as not to bring the truth of the same into doubt. While in the year 1656 three ships were lying on this coast for the sake of catching cod, the men of Captain *Pierre Rouleau*, lying farthest away from the shore, noticed some distance away in the sea a peculiar commotion that was not caused by anything which had the form of any known fish. They stared at it for some time without knowing what to make of it. Since the opinions about it were very much divided, as it usually is among men who have little knowledge, they rowed in the boats to the ship to get a telescope. Then they saw clearly that this fish, or to say better, this monster, which still retained the same appearance, seemed to take pleasure in the beams of the sun (for it was about 2 P.M. and very clear and fine weather); it seemed to play in the gently undulating water, and looked somewhat like a human being. This caused general astonishment and likewise great curiosity to see this strange creature near by, and, if possible, to catch it. Upon the order of the Captain they therefore kept very quiet, in order not to drive it away by any noise, and descended quickly into the boats with ropes and other things, by means of which they thought they could most easily get the monster alive into their hands. But while the men of the Captain named were thus engaged, those also of the other two ships, although they had lain farther away, had caught sight of the same object, and being extremely curious to get a nearer acquaintance, had betaken themselves to their boats and had taken the oars in hand. Captain

Rouleau, who was himself in one of his boats, rightly understanding that in this way they would by no means attain their end, but, on the contrary, would by untimely noise drive away the monster, beckoned all these vessels together and gave command to row out a long way on both sides, in order thus unforeseen to fall upon it from behind. This was done in all quietness, but it came to pass that one of the sailors, or the fishermen, throwing out overboard away from the boat, cast a rope over the head of the Merman (for it was in fact a Merman), but since he did not quickly enough draw it shut, he shot down through the loop and away under water, presenting in his lowest part, which became of the quick movement could not well be made out, the appearance of a great beast. At once all the boats gathered round in order to catch him in case he should come up once more, each one holding himself ready for that purpose with ropes and cords. But instead of showing himself there again above water, he came to view farther out to sea, and with his hands, whereof the fingers (if indeed the things were fingers that stood in the place of fingers) were firmly bound to each other with membranes just as those of swans' feet or geese feet, he brushed out of his eyes his mossy hair, and which he also seemed to be covered over the whole body as far as it was seen above water, in some places more, in others less. The fishermen distributed themselves again, and went a long way around, in order to make another attempt; but the Merman, apparently noticing that they had designs on him, shot under water, and after that did not show himself again, to the great dejection of the fishermen, who many a time went there to be on the lookout, and incessantly racked their brains to invent stratagems to catch him.

I am sure this digression has not been unpleasant to the reader, yet one might have wished that the trouble of the fishers had had better success, and that they might have gotten that monster of a Merman into their power. Now let us take up again the broken thread of our story.

SOME GREAT WHITE THING

Theories about other dimensions of human and extra-human experience are quite popular these days. Such theories hold that the world as we know it is but one of an infinite number of worlds, each one with its own causal chain, every one slightly different from its neighbours. The information in the paragraph that follows about "some great white thing" in Hudson Bay in the 1670s or so may well be true in a world other than our own.

The French explorer Pierre-Esprit Radisson (1640-1710) is the author of the account that appear below. In it he recalls the description of a strange ship or mysterious being of pre-Columbian times given him by a native informant from the native's own point of view. The source that is generally given is Radisson's book of travel titled *Being an Account of His Travels and Experiences among the North American Indians, from 1652 to 1684* (1885).

That may very well be true. But close perusal of the pages of that volume and of other accounts of Radisson's life and travels have failed to locate the passage in question. Yet it reads like Radisson's prose. (Perhaps it exists in a world of its own and is to be found in some other dimension.)

Being about the great sea, we conversed with people that dwelleth about the salt water namely, Hudson's Bay, who told us that they saw some great white thing sometimes upon the water, and came towards the shore, and men in the top of it, and made a noise like a company of swans; which made me believe that they were mistaken, for I could not imagine what it could be, except the Spaniard; and the reason is that we found a barill broken as they use in Spaine.

A SEA-MONSTER

This is a very short but nonetheless vivid account of a "sea-monster" that resembled an "allegator" or alligator that was caught and brought ashore at "Hallifax, in Nova-Scotia." The description appeared as the first item in "The Monthly Chronicle" column of *London Magazine*, August 1752.

Hallifax, in Nova-Scotia, May 28. A few days since was taken, within a month of our harbour, and brought to town, a sea-monster, a female of the kind, whose body was about the bigness of that of a large ox, and something resembling one, covered with short hair, of a brownish colour; the skin near one inch and a half thick, very loose and rough; the neck thick and short, resembling that of a bull; the head small in proportion to the body, and very like an alligator; in the upper jaws were two teeth of about nine or ten inches long, and crooked downwards; the legs very short and thick, ending with fins and claws, like those of a sea-turtle; the flesh and inwards have been opened, and resemble those of an ox or horse.

HER FACE HUMAN

Here is a vividly and vigorously written description of a mermaid who was captured by sturdy sailors and survived for fifteen years in captivity before languishing and succumbing to some unimaginable condition or disease.

The description appeared as "Account of a Mermaid" in the columns of *The Gazette* (Halifax, N.S.), 5 Dec. 1765. The account is seemingly set in the days of the Dutch occupancy of Manhattan Island.

Account of a Mermaid. — Some Years ago, as the Milk maids of *Campen*, (a Port-Town in the United Provinces) were crossing a Lake in order to come at their Flocks, they espied a human Head above Water, but believed their eyes deceived them, till the repeated Sight confirmed their Assurance, whereupon they resolved one Night, to watch her, and saw that she repaired to a slaggy Place, where it was Ebb, and near the Side; whereupon, early in the Morning they got a great many Boats, and invironed the Place in the form of a half Moon, and disturbed her, but she attempting to get under the Boats, and finding her Way stopt up by Staves and other Things on purpose flattened, began to flounce and make an hideous deafening Noise, and with her Hands and Tail sunk a Boat or two, but at last was tired out and taken; the Maids used her kindly, and cleansed the Sea Mess and Shells from off her, and offered her Water, Fish, Milk, Bread, &c. which she refused, but with good Usage in a Day or two, they got her to eat and drink, though she endeavoured to make her Escape again to Sea; her Hair was long and black, her Face human, her Teeth very strong, her Breasts and Belly to her Navel were perfect; the lower Parts of her Body ended in a strong Fish Tail; the Magistrates of *Harlem*, commanded her to be sent to them, for that the Place where she was caught, was in their Jurisdiction: When she was bro't thither, she was put into the Town-house, and had a Dame to attend on her and to teach her. She learnt to Spin and show Devotion at Prayer, she would laugh, and when Women came into the Town-house to spin with her for Diversion, she would signify by Signs she knew their Meaning, though she could never be taught to speak. She would wear no Cloaths in Summer; Part of her Hair was filleted up in a Dutch Dress, and Part hang'd long naturally. She would have her Tail in Water, and accordingly had a Tub of Water under her Chair made on purpose for her. She eat Milk, Water, Bread, Butter and Fish; she lived thus out of her Element (except her Tail) fifteen Years: Her Picture was painted on a Board with Oil, and hangs now in the Town-house of *Harlem*. When she died the Magistrates suffered a Place in the Church-yard for her Interment.

MERMAID?

Venant St. Germain was a trader with the North West Company and then the Seigneur of Repentigy in Lower Canada. Researchers of remarkable occurrences recall him as "the man who saw a mermaid." That description is inexact because it was not a "mermaid" that St. Germain saw in the waters of Lake Superior on May 3, 1782, nor was it a "merman." There is no word in French or English to apply to the creature or being that he saw and later described.

He prepared an account of his experience in Montreal on Nov. 13, 1812. It took the form of an English-language affidavit which he swore before two judges of the Court of King's Bench. Nowhere does the affidavit refer to a "mermaid." That word was introduced by whoever it was who contributed the preface to the account which was printed as "A Mermaid in Lake Superior" in the May 1824 issue of *The Canadian Magazine*.

Whatever it is that St. Germain saw, it is worth taking the time to read his description and then to ponder the nature of the "mer-creature" that so impressed him on that occasion.

A Mermaid in Lake Superior

The following relation of some particulars of an animal resembling the human form, which was seen in Lake Superior many years ago, is given, if not as a proof of the existence of the mermaid, as an undeniable testimony that even in these lake, as well as in the ocean, there are inhabitants with which our philosophers are not yet acquainted. This account is given in the form of a deposition before two of the Judges of the Court of King's Bench, and, as appears from his character, the relator was entitled to belief: although the opinion he had formed of the narrative being liable to be doubted, induced him to give it under the solemnity of an oath.

Appeared before us, Judges of the Court of King's Bench for the District of Montreal, Venant St. Germain, Esquire, of Repentigny, Merchant and Voyageur, who being sworn on the Holy Evangelists, sayeth: —

That in the year 1782, on the 3d of May, when on his return to Michilimackinac from the Grand Portage, he arrived at the south end of the Isle Paté, where he formed his encampment to stop for the night. That a little before sunset, the evening being clear and serene, deponent was returning from setting his nets, and reached his encampment a short time before the sun went down. That on disembarking, the deponent happened to turn towards the lake, where he observed, about an acre or three quarters of an acre distant from the bank where he stood, an animal in the water, which appeared to him to have the upper part of its body, above the waist, formed exactly like that of a human being. It had the half of its body out of the water, and the novelty of so extraordinary a spectacles, excited his attention, and led him to examine it carefully. That the body of an animal seemed to him about the size of that of a child of seven or eight years of age, with one of its arms extended and elevated in the air. The hand appeared to be composed of fingers exactly similar to those of a man; and the right arm was kept in an elevated position, while the left seemed to rest upon the hip, but the deponent did not see the latter, it being kept under the water. The deponent distinctly saw the features of the countenance, which bore an exact resemblance to those of the human face. The eyes were extremely brilliant; the nose small but handsomely shaped; the mouth proportionate to the rest of the face;

the complexion of a brownish hue, somewhat similar to that of a young negro; the ears well formed, and corresponding to the other parts of the figure. He did not discover that the animal had any hair, but in the place of it he observed that woolly substance about an inch long, on the top of the head, somewhat similar to that which grows on the heads of negroes. The animal looked the deponent in the face, with an aspect indicating uneasiness, but at the same time with a mixture of curiosity; and the deponent, along with other three men who were with him at the time, and an old Indian woman to whom he had given a passage in his canoe, attentively examined the animal for the space of three or four minutes.

The deponent formed the design of getting possession of the animal if possible, and for this purpose endeavoured to get hold of his gun, which was loaded at the time, with the intention of shooting it; but the Indian woman, who was near at the time, ran up to the deponent, and, seizing him by the clothes, by her violent struggles, prevented his taking aim. During the time which he was occupied in this, the animal sunk under water without changing its attitude, and, disappearing, was seen no more.

The woman appeared highly indignant at the audacity of the deponent in offering to fire upon what she termed the God of the Waters and Lakes; and vented her anger in bitter reproaches, saying that they would all infallibly perish, for the God of the Waters would raise such a tempest as would dash them to pieces upon the rocks; saying, that "for her own part, she would fly the danger," and proceeded to ascend the bank, which happened to be steep in that part. The deponent, despising her threats, remained quietly where he had fixed his encampment. That at about 10 or 11 o'clock at night, they heard the dashing of the waves, accompanied with such a violent gale of wind, so as to render it necessary for them to drag their canoe higher upon the beach; and the deponent, accompanied by his men, was obliged to seek shelter from the violence of the storm, which continued for three days, unabated.

That is in the knowledge of the deponent, that there exists a general belief diffused among the Indians who inhabit the country around this island, that it is the residence of the God of the Waters and of the Lakes, whom in their language they call *Manitou Nibe Nabais*, and that he had often heard that this belief was peculiar to the Sauteux Indians. He farther learned from another voyageur, that an animal exactly similar to that which deponent described, had been seen by him on another occasion when passing the Paté to Tonnerre, and deponent thinks the frequent appearance of this extraordinary animal in this spot had given rise to the superstitious belief among the Indians, that the God of the Waters had fixed upon this for his residence.

That the deponent, in speaking of the storm which followed the threats of the Indian woman, merely remarked it as a strange circumstance which coincided with the time, without attributing it to any other cause than what naturally produces such an effect, and which is a well known occurrence to voyageurs: that fish in general appear most numerous near the surface, and are most apt to show themselves above water on the approach of a storm.

And further the deponent saith not.

Signed, *Venant St. Germain.*

Sworn before us, 13th November, 1812.
Signed, P.L. Panet, J.K.B.
J. Ogden, J.K.B.

A MYSTERY OF THE GULF

The Gulf of St. Lawrence has taken its toll of ships and men. It presents pilots and navigators with peculiar sailing difficulties and atmospheric anomalies.

One particular anomaly is the appearance at unpredictable times of "phenomenal lights." Were such "mystery lights" responsible for the wreck of the fleet above the ramparts of Quebec? Are such lights the cause of the "burning ships" seen in Maritime waters?

"A Mystery of the Gulf," appeared in the *London Daily Advertiser* (London, U.C., later Ontario), Sept. 1828.

A Mystery of the Gulf What the Phenomenal Lights Seen in the Lower St. Lawrence Portend to the Canadian Fishers

Miramichi, N.B., August 27: — The mysterious lights in the Gulf and the Lower St. Lawrence, those sure precursors of a tempestuous fall with grievous shipwrecks, have been unusually brilliant this season. The light off the Cape Maria Cascapediac has blazed almost every night since May 15. In the Baie des Chaleurs, the Point Mizuenette light has been seen nightly by hundreds of people from the settlements of New Bandon, Grand Anse, Caraquette and Salmon Beach. The *habitant* says they are supernatural manifestations marking scenes of wreck and murder, or warning the sailor of great tempests; while the English settlers think they are the Will-o'-the-wisps of the ocean. Whatever they may be, it is a fact established by the experience of a century that when they blaze brightly in the summer nights the fall is invariably marked by great storms. One would think on looking at these mysteries from the shore that a ship was on fire. The heavens behind are bright and the clouds above silvered by the reflection. The sea for half a mile is covered with a sheen as of phosphorous. The fire itself seems to consist of blue and yellow flames, now dancing high above the water, and then flickering, paling and dying out only to spring up again with fresh brilliancy. If a boat approaches it flits away, moving further out, and the bold visitor pursues in vain. At the first streak of daylight it vanishes in the form of a mist, and is seen no more until darkness again sets in. These lights are brightest when there is a heavy dew, and are plainly visible from the shore from midnight until two in the morning. They appear to come in from the sea shoreward, and at dawn retire gradually and are lost in the morning fog.

Paradis, the French pilot who took charge of the British fleet under Admiral Sir Hovenden Walker when it sailed up the St. Lawrence from Boston to seize Quebec in 1711, declared he saw one of these lights just before the armada was shattered on the 22nd of August; in fact, he said it danced before his vessel, the Neptune, all the way up the Gulf. Walker's squadron comprised the flagship Edgar, 70 guns; the Windsor, 60 guns; the Montague, 60 guns; the Swiftshire, 70 guns; the Monmouth, 70 guns; the Dunkirk, 60 guns; the Humber, 80 guns; the Sunderland, 60 guns; the Devonshire, 80 guns; the Enterprise, 40 guns; the Sapphire, 40 guns; the Kingston, 60 guns; the Leonard, 54 guns, and the Chester 50 guns; with no less than seventy transports, of which the Despatch, Four Friends, Francis, John and Hannah, Henrietta, Blessing, Antelope, Hanna and Elizabeth, Friend's Adventure, Rebecca, Martha and Hanna, Johannah, Unity and Newcastle were from New England ports. On leaving Boston Sir Hovenden drew from Governor Dudley rations for 9,385 Englishmen, seamen and soldiers, and 1,786 colonists on board the fleet. On the 20th August when they lay off Egg Island, on the north shore of the St. Lawrence, having just cleared Gaspé Bay, a dense fog fell upon them. The Admiral ordered the vessels to keep together, and soundings were taken every half hour, but the land gave no bottom. On the night of the 22nd Paradis lost his head and signalled for the fleet to close upon the shore. While they were moving slowly a dreadful gale arose and as Sir Hovenden said in his journal which was published in London in 1720: "We soon found ourselves amongst rocks and small islands, fifteen leagues further than the log gave, when the whole fleet had like to have been lost." "But by God's good providence," he goes on, "all the men-of-war, though with extreme hazard and difficulty, escaped. Eight transports were cast away and had I not made the signals as I did, but continued sailing, it is a great question whether any ship or men had been saved." After the wreck the roster showed only 8,878 survivors. The Labrador shore, says the historian Charlevoix, was strewn with the bodies of at least a thousand soldiers, including two complete companies of the Royal Guards and many more of Marlborough's veterans, whose corpses were easily distinguishable by their scarlet coats. It was suspected that Paradis had willfully cast the fleet away. In his defence, as found in the writings of Mère Juchereau, he pleaded that he saw the moving lights when they first made Gaspé Bay and told some of the high officers that heaven had ordained a terrible catastrophe, "so clearly and with such vividness did the celestial fires burn not only by night but often when there was a fog throughout the day." The disaster saved Canada to France for the time being, and the pious colonists reared many churches in gratitude to Notre Dame des Victoires. The court of Queen Anne went into mourning, and Sir Hovenden exiled himself to South Carolina, where, as a French writer quaintly said, "he wrote humorous apologies for the disaster with which God had been pleased to visit the English fleet." The flagship Elgar, with 470 men, blew up at Portsmouth on her return from the Gulf, which was "further evidence of God's displeasure at the invasion of New France."

Every great wreck that has taken place since Sir Hovenden's calamity has been preceded, if tradition is to be believed, by these mysterious lights; or rather they have warned the mariner of the fatal storm. When the Gulf gives up its dead there will be a vast muster. In 1797 the French warship La Tribune was lost, with 300 souls. In 1805 the British transport Nacas went down, with 800. In 1831 the emigrant ship Lady Sherbrooke, from Derry to Quebec, was lost, only 32 out of 273 passengers being saved. In 1847 nearly 200 Irish emigrants were lost with the big Carrick, and 240 more on the Exmouth. Two hundred and twenty-five souls perished in the wreck of the Hungarian on the 19th February, 1860; 35 on Canadian on the 4th of June, 1861, and 237 when the Anglo-Saxon was lost in a fog off Cape Race on the 27th April, 1863. How many fishing boats and coasters have gone down with all hands, leaving no sign, it is not safe even to guess. This fall, if the lights are to be believed — and the Gulf fishermen say they cannot lie — storms of unexampled fierceness will rage from the autumnal equinox until the winter is past. Should this augury be fulfilled perhaps it may be worth while for meteorologists and seafaring men to inquire into the source and origin of these strange watchmen of the deep.

TRUE AND VERITABLE SEA-SERPENT

Here is an account of a sighting of a sea-serpent off the south-east coast of Nova Scotia not far from St. Margaret's Bay and Mahone Bay. The account was written by one of the witnesses, Henry Ince, Ordnance storekeeper, a native of Halifax, N.S. The incident took place in 1833 but was only published in *The Zoologist* in the year 1847.

On the 1st May, 1833, a party, consisting of Captain Sullivan, Lieutenants Maclachlan and Malcolm of the Rifle Brigade, Lieutenant Lyster of the Artillery, and Mr. Ince of the Ordnance, started from Halifax in a small yacht for Mahone Bay, some forty miles to the westward, on a fishing excursion. The morning was cloudy, and the wind at S.S.E., and apparently rising.

We had run about half the distance, as we supposed, and were enjoying ourselves on deck, when we were surprised by the sight of an immense shoal of grampuses, which appeared in an unusual state of excitement, and which, in their gambols, approached so close to our little craft, that some of the party amused themselves by firing at them with rifles....

Our attention was presently diverted from the whales and "such small deer" by an exclamation from Dowling, our man-of-war's man, who was sitting to leeward, of "Oh, sir, look here!" We were startled into a ready compliance, and saw an object which banished all other thoughts save wonder and surprise.

At the distance of from 150 to 200 yards on our starboard b~w, we saw the head and neck of some denizen of the deep, precisely like those of a common snake, in the act of swimming, the head so far elevated and thrown forward by the curve of the neck as to enable us to see the water under and beyond it.

The creature rapidly passed, leaving a regular wake, from the commencement of which, to the fore part, which was out of water, we judged its length to be about eighty feet; and this within rather than beyond the mark.

There could be no mistake, no delusion, and we were all perfectly satisfied that we had been favoured with a view of the "true and veritable sea-serpent," which had been generally considered to have existed only in the brain of some Yankee skipper, and treated as a tale not much entitled to belief It is most difficult to give correctly the dimensions of any object in the water. The head of the creature we set down at about six feet in length, and that portion of the neck which we saw, at the same; the extreme length, as before stated, as between eighty and one hundred feet. The neck in thickness equalled the bole of a moderate-sized tree. The head and neck of a dark brown or nearly black colour, streaked with white in irregular streaks. I do not recollect seeing any part of the body.

Such is the rough account of the sea-serpent, and all the party who saw it are still in the land of the living- Lyster in England, Malcolm in New South Wales, with his regiment, and the remainder still vegetating in Halifax.

Signed by:

> W. SULLIVAN, Captain, Rifle Brigade.
> A. MACLACHLAN, Lieutenant, Rifle Brigade.
> G.P. MALCOLM, Ensign, Rifle Brigade.
> B. O'NBAL LYSTER, Lieutenant, Artillery.
> HENRY INCE, Ordnance Storekeeper at Halifax.

SEA SERPENT ALIVE

Sir Charles Lyell was one of the most distinguished natural scientists of the 19th century. Sir Charles made two scientific excursions to North America where he was shown the natural wonders of the New World by fellow scientists who treated him like the celebrity he was. Like all great scientists of his day and ours, Lyell displayed a boundless curiosity about all aspects of the natural world. Nothing was foreign to his intelligence; nothing resisted for very long his need to describe and categorize all aspects of the world of nature.

In Chapter VIII of *A Second Visit to the United States of North America* (London: John Murray, two volumes, 1849), he wrote about a "pretended fossil sea serpent" reported from Alabama. This led him to the sighting of "a sea serpent" in the Gulf of St. Lawrence and then to a comparable sighting off the coast of Norway. Sir Charles personally examined the "pretended fossil" but he had to make do with reports of sightings of the "sea serpents." The descriptions of the Maritime monster were supplied to him by the distinguished Nova Scotian geologist Sir John William Dawson who would later, in 1855, be appointed Principal of McGill University.

This Appearance of the Monster
Sir Charles Lyell

During the first part of my stay in Boston, October, 1845, we one day saw the walls in the principal streets covered with placards, in which the words SEA SERPENT ALIVE figured conspicuously. On approaching near enough to read the smaller type of this advertisement, I found that Mr. Koch was about to exhibit to the Bostonians the fossil skeleton of "that colossal and terrible reptile the sea serpent, which, when alive, measured thirty feet in circumference." The public were also informed that this hydrachos, or water king, was the leviathan of the Book of Job, chapter xli. I shall have occasion in the sequel, when describing my expedition in Alabama to the exact site from whence these fossil remains were disinterred by Mr. Koch, of showing that they belong to the zeuglodon, first made out by Mr. Owen to be an extinct cetacean of truly vast dimensions, and which I ascertained to be referable geologically to the Eocene period.

In the opinion of the best comparative anatomists, there is no reason to believe that this fossil whale bore any resemblance in form, when alive, to a snake, although the bones of the vertebral column, having been made to form a continuous series, more than 100 feet in length, by the union of vertebrae derived from more than one individual, were ingeniously arranged by Mr. Koch in a serpentine form, so as to convey the impression that motion was produced by vertical flexures of the body.

At the very time when I had every day to give an answer to the question whether I really believed the great fossil skeleton from Alabama to be that of the sea serpent formerly seen on the coast near Boston, I received news of the reappearance of the same serpent in a letter from my friend Mr. J.W. Dawson, of Pictou, in Nova Scotia. This geologist, with whom I explored Nova Scotia in 1842, said he was collecting evidence for me of the appearance, in the month of August, 1845, at Merigomish, in the Gulf of St. Lawrence, of a maritime monster, about 100 feet long, seen by two intelligent observers, nearly aground in calm water, within 200 feet of the beach, where it remained in sight about half an hour, and then got off with difficulty. One of the witnesses went up a bank in order to look down upon it. They said it sometimes raised its head (which

resembled that of a seal) partially out of the water. Along its back were a number of humps or protuberances, which, in the opinion of the observer on the beach, were true humps, while the other thought they were produced by vertical flexures of the body. Between the head and the first protuberance there was a straight part of the back of considerable length, and this part was generally above water. The color appeared black, and the skin had a rough appearance. The animal was seen to bend its body almost into a circle, and again to unbend it with rapidity. It was slender in proportion to its length. After it had disappeared in deep water, its wake was visible for some time. There were no indications of paddles seen. Some other persons who saw it compared the creature to a long string of fishing-net buoys moving rapidly about. In the course of the summer, the fishermen on the eastern shore of Prince Edward's Island, in the Gulf of St. Lawrence, had been terrified by this sea monster, and the year before, October, 1844, a similar creature swam slowly past the pier at Arisaig, near the east end of Nova Scotia, and, there being only a slight breeze at the time, was attentively observed by Mr. Barry, a millwright of Pictou, who told Mr. Dawson he was within 120 feet of it, and estimated its length at sixty feet, and the thickness of its body at three feet. It had humps on the back, which seemed too small and close together to be bends of the body.

The body appeared also to move in *long undulations*, including many of the smaller humps. In consequence of this motion the head and tail were sometimes both out of sight and sometimes both above water, as represented in the annexed outline, given from memory.

*Drawing from memory of a sea serpent
seen at Arisaig, Nova Scotia, Oct. 1844.*

The head, *a*, was rounded and obtuse in front, and was never elevated more than a foot above the surface. The tail was pointed, appearing like half of a mackerel's tail. The color of the part seen was black.

It was suggested by Mr. Dawson that a swell in the

sea might give the deceptive appearance of an undulating movement, as it is well known "that a stick held horizontally at the surface of water when there is a ripple seems to have an uneven outline." But Mr. Barry replied that he observed the animal very attentively, having read accounts of the sea serpent, and feels confident that the undulations were not those of the water.

This reappearance of the monster, commonly called the sea serpent, was not confined to the Gulf of St. Lawrence; for, two months after I left Boston, a letter from one Captain Lawson went the round of the American papers, dated February, 1846, giving a description of a marine creature seen by him from his schooner, when off the coast of Virginia, between Capes Henry and Charles — body about 100 feet long, with *pointed* projections (query, dorsal fins?) on the back; head small in proportion to its length.

Precisely in the same years, in July, 1845, and August, 1846, contemporaneous, and evidently independent accounts were collected in Norway, and published in their papers, of a marine animal, of "a rare and singular kind," seen by fishermen and others, the evidence being taken down by clergymen, surgeons, and lawyers, whose names are given....

THE SPECTRE BRIG

The most famous brigantine of all time was the *Mary Celeste*, the Nova Scotia-built "hoodoo ship" that was encountered crewless and drifting in the Atlantic Ocean near the Azores on June 10, 1861. Why had it been abandoned by its crew, its cargo intact, during calm weather? This unsolved mystery of the sea attracted the attention of Sir Arthur Conan Doyle, who wrote a lively short story about its fate, and Bela Lugosi, who starred in a Hollywood movie based on the treachery behind its abandonment on the high seas. The *Mary Celeste* was a twin-masted ship of sail with a terrible reputation, the type of vessel avoided whenever possible by experienced sailors.

This first-person account of life aboard a brigantine appeared as "The Spectre Brig" in *The Examiner* (Charlottetown, P.E.I.), 26 January 1863. Its authorship is attributed to Frank R. Ross.

The Spectre Brig. — The fall of 1853 saw me on board the bark *Swordfish*, bound from New York to Yarmouth, Nova Scotia, thence to Liverpool and a market. I cannot imagine what odd freak decided the owners of the bark to give her a name so inappropriate, for the swordfish is known to be of uncommon symmetry, and moves with the quickness of light, while its ungainly namesake was tub-built, blunt-bowed, short-sparred, requiring four men at the wheel in a gale of wind to keep her within six points of the compass, and then she would make more lee-way than a Dutch galliot.

However, she proved to be a tolerable sailor, despite her unpromising appearance, and the fifth day out, we made the Seal Islands, in the Bay of Fundy, and a few hours later were moored alongside the wharf at Yarmouth.

Here we were informed that our cargo would not be in readiness for several days, and as but little remained to be attended to aboard the vessel, I concluded to take a cruise over the city and surrounding country.

The city has a gloomy and antique appearance, looking as though the blight of ages had fallen upon her buildings in a night. The houses are of a style and architecture in vogue half a century ago, being built still earlier by Tory refugees, who fled from the Colonies during the Revolutionary war.

Many of these were offshoots of noble families in England, and clinging to their sovereign with fanatical blindness, they fled to this and adjacent provinces, where their descendants have managed to keep up a dingy show of gentility in their old tumble-down tenements.

Their hatred of republicanism, a hatred gathered and intensified through many generations, until it has become almost a passion, is only equalled by their love and veneration for their sovereign. The poorer class, mostly Irish and Scotch, are ardent admirers of republican institutions, and are outspoken in their sentiments.

Between them and their more aristocratic neighbours exists a bitter feeling partizan hostility which increases in intensity with each succeeding year, and must, ere long, break forth in a rougher shape than a mere war of words.

The Home Government is fully alive to this and accordingly grants every indulgence consistent with its dignity. But still the people are dissatisfied. They feel that there is a lack, a moral blight that deadens their enemies and clouds their prospects.

They know their country to be rich in mineral wealth, yet it remains undeveloped. Rich in its fisheries, yet they are unprofitable.

One day, while taking a stroll on the high ground bordering the bay, and watching the tide as it came in from the sea, rolling in the solid wall thirty feet in height that reared and rumbled like distant thunder, I chanced to hear some remarks made by a group of persons near me, that drew my attention. Not wishing to play the part of listener, I was turning from the spot when the foremost speaker of the party exclaimed:

"I tell you, gentlemen, it is no illusion! There is not a person for miles around who has not heard or seen the 'Spectre Brig.' Furthermore, if you will remain a few days longer, you can satisfy yourselves of the truth of my statement, as it is nearly time for her annual visitation."

Being interested by these strange remarks, I turned and joined them. During the conversation that followed, I referred to the above and requested to be enlightened as to its meaning, addressing myself to the person who had attracted my attention. He looked at me as though surprised at the request, but seeing I was a stranger, he replied:

"Certainly, sir; with pleasure if it will be of any interest to you."

Seating ourselves, he then proceeded to relate the story, as nearly as I can recollect as follows:

"Fifty years ago, the brig *Yarmouth*, commanded by Capt. Bruce, and manned by a crew from this neighborhood, sailed from this port to the West Indies. Days and weeks went by, and the time for her return came and passed. Apprehensions began to be felt for her safety as the days went by, and daily an anxious crowd of women and children might have been seen gathered on the headlands that overlooked the bay, straining their eyes seaward in the faint hope of catching a glimpse of the missing vessel that had borne away a husband, a brother, a father, or son. Each night only witnessed a deeper disappointment, and at last apprehension had become almost certainty, and people began to speak of her as a thing of the past.

"A year had just passed away, when one night as the watchman was going his rounds among the wharves, he chanced to look seaward, and was surprised to see a vessel covered with canvass from truck to kelson, standing boldly into the harbour, although it was blowing a living gale sufficient to swamp the strongest craft with half the amount of sail. On she came, plowing before the blast like a thing of life until she had reached within a cable's length of the shore; when suddenly her main topsail was backed, her anchor dropped into the water with a splash, followed by the rattling of the chains as it ran out through the hawse-hole. At the same instant her tacks and sheets were let go, her sails clowed up and furled, and in less time than it takes me to narrate it she had swung round with the current and was riding quietly at a single anchor.

"As she swung broadside to the wharf the astonished watchman recognized her, and started up town with a tearing rate. 'The *Yarmouth* has come.' The glad cry ran from house to house and street to street, and in a few minutes a crowd of people had gathered upon the wharf making the air ring with their cheers, while wives, mothers and sisters were kneeling and with streaming eyes returned thanks for the wanderer's return.

"As yet not a sound had been heard or an object seen aboard the brig to denote that a soul was near her. Every one recognized her as she lay silent and dark, rising and settling with every wave.

"Finding their efforts to arouse the crew to be of no avail, they procured boats, and in spite of the violence of the wind, put out to board her. Bending stoutly to the oars with a hearty good will they soon found themselves within a few yards of her, when they were surprised to hear a hoarse voice exclaim, 'Keep off! Keep off!' Hardly believing their senses, they returned to the shore, which they had scarcely reached before a thick black fog, peculiar in that land of fogs, swept in from the sea and enveloped everything in an impenetrable veil. Surprised and terrified at what they had seen, the people returned to await the morning, hoping, yet scarcely daring to believe that with daylight everything would be explained. The gale still continued, and as morning broke, the vapor raised for a few moments, but not a vestige of the vessel of the preceding night was to be seen.

"Another year went by and the phantom vessel again appeared under nearly the same circumstances, and all attempts to board her resulted as before.

"'Thus,' continued my narrator, 'nearly fifty years have gone by, and still she makes her annual visit at just such a period of each succeeding year. Of late no attention is paid to her whatever, her arrival being hardly noticed, as she comes in invariably at midnight, and disappears within an hour.'"

Here the story concluded, and thanking my informant for his kindness, I arose, bid the party good-bye, and returned to my vessel and retired to my berth, as it was getting late.

I felt feverish and restless, and lay tossing about for several hours. Not being able to rest, I got up, dressed myself and went on deck, where the night air soon cooled my heated blood, and I was about to go to my state-room again, when my attention was arrested by hearing a loud splash in the water, followed by the rattle of a chain as it was rapidly paid out. Looking out into the harbor, I saw to my astonishment, a large, old-fashioned full-rigged brig laying quietly at anchor, with sails snugly furled and everything in ship-shape style. I was at first considerably startled, as I knew it would be impossible for any sailing vessel to come in and anchor when not a breath of wind was stirring. Not believing in anything of a supernatural character, whether it be ghost or ghoul, hobgoblin or witch, I resolved to pay the strange craft a visit, feeling confident it was the "spectre brig," whose history I had heard a few hours before.

Going to the forecastle, I turned out two of the men, and ordered them to lower away the boat, throw out a pair of oars, and jump in, which they promptly did. I followed them over the side, and taking the tiller, sat down to wait the result.

In a few minutes we were within a dozen yards of the stranger, and rising in the boat I hailed:

"Brig, ahoy!"

No answer.

"Brig, ahoy!" I again shouted, with all the force of my lungs, but still no answer.

The third hail resulted as before.

There she lay, grim and dark, her sides covered with barnacles and clothed with seaweed. Not a sound could be heard, not even the creaking of a block, or the rattling of a rope.

Determined to board her at all hazards, I directed the men to pull with all their strength, and lay the boat alongside, while I grappled the rigging.

Bending themselves to the oars they sent the light boat seething through the water like a dart; but when, apparently with an oar's length of her side, the stranger craft began to grow indistinct, like a vapor. A moment her outline could be plainly seen, stamped against the sky, and the next she had vanished wholly, without a sound, without a sigh.

A thick fog soon set in from the bay, and we were compelled to grope our way to the shore as best we could, feeling awed and perplexed at what we had seen.

In vain I have tried to explain this phenomenon, but without success, and at last I am forced to the conclusion that it must remain one of those secrets that must continue until the Last Great Day, when the "heavens shall roll away like a scroll, and the mysteries of the universe stand revealed!"

A HUGE MONSTER OF THE SERPENT KIND

Visitors from around the world are attracted to the picturesque Eastern Townships of Quebec, and many of them linger in the city of Magog which lies along the shores of Lake Memphremagog. A few, curious visitors may gaze across the waters of the lake and wonder if they will be privileged to see ... Memphré.

Memphré? That is the name of the creature that is said to inhabit the waters of Lake Memphremagog. The name may be fairly new, but references to the presence of a monster in this lake turn up in the historical record. Sightings go back to 1816, at least, when the hilly region, which lies southeast of Montreal, was first being settled.

Often seen, sometimes reported, the creature was first named Memphré in the 20th century by Jacques Boisvert, long-time Magog resident, former realtor, and active scuba-diver. He is a tireless promoter of local traditions and one of the two founding spirits of the Société internationale de dracontologie du lac Mémphremagog.

Boisvert is the guardian of the flame. He collects accounts of the creature's appearance and has computerized them. In Sept. 1995 he had over 180 references or descriptions of sightings. The earliest known reference to Memphré comes from a diary kept by a resident of the area. That reference may not constitute an eye-witness account, but it does inaugurate a series of sightings and descriptions that span more than one and a half centuries.

The incidents recounted here took place in the year 1816. The passage comes from the diary kept by Ralph Merry IV, scion of the well-respected Merry family of settlers. The extract, reproduced here in a slightly edited form, but replete with misspellings, comes from Merry's Diary No. 11, extract of 17 Sept. 1854. The original diaries are part of the permanent collection of the Stanstead Historical Society, Stanstead, Que.

Put up at night with brother Henry Wadleigh, he told me the following as near as memory serves me. Within a few years he saw one of the great serpents of Magog opposite of his farm and Wadleigh being on high land and the sun shining he had a good opportunity to view him.

The serpent appeared to be about 30 rods from the west shore (it is said that when one is seen a great part of the tail end is under water) what he saw of the forward part was as long as a skiff and as large as a good sized mill log, his head was large enough to take in a man and he held it out of water about 2 feet. The wind blew down the lake and he saw it swimming in an indirect course towards the easterly shore (that is it swam somewhat north easterly) it went as swift as men would row a skiff and seemed but a few minutes in crossing nearly to the east side when it arrived there it dropped its head and immediately disappeared.

W. is a man in whom I can rely; I have not the least reason to doubt his having seen the monster. Elder Rider and his son saw one and thought it was a mill log at first till they saw it move. They had a plain view of the animal and its motion.

Steward Channel and his wife and Uriah Jewet all saw one of them at once at Georgeville. It is said that some have seen about 25 or 30 feet of one above water and the neck bowed and the head and neck looked like a horse's. B. Merry and his wife before they were married were crossing the lake and near the northend saw a huge monster of the serpent kind in a fair day 50 rods from west shore the water perhaps 10 feet deep one end partly out of water and the body slaunted towards the bottom of the lake it had 12 or 15 pair of legs about a foot apart the legs were the size of a boys arms 12 years old and a foot long the feet were as large as a boys hands 14 years old with the fingers cut off at the knuckles and the claws were spread apart. He saw 15 feet of its length but did not see the whole; the body was two thirds as large as a man's and the colour of a white sheep's skin with the wool off they were within a rod of it and both young had good eye sight and a fair view of it and the lake was calm and the weather fair. She was frightened; he set her on shore and returned with 2 men to find it made considerable search for a considerable time but did not see it again.

I heared them tell the story at that time and now he tells me the same. They saw the above about 38 years ago about 54 years since soon after I came to Canada. I heared it said that indians would not go into this lake because they said there were great serpents or aligators in it.

THE GREAT SEA-SERPENT

"The Great Sea-Serpent" is the title of the account of a sighting of a lake monster somewhere in Nova Scotia. The account appeared in *The Huron Expositer* (Seaforth, Ont.), 21 May 1869. The account makes for good reading, but it falls short on specifics: where, when, who, what, why, etc.

The name of the fishing village in Nova Scotia where the events described are said to have occurred is unknown. The account is related in the first person, so it would be nice to know who wrote it, but the writer is not identified. The nameless narrator's "two rough sketches," mentioned in the text of the story, were not reproduced in the newspaper. It is likely the account is reprinted from a Maritime or Montreal newspaper which did reproduce the sketches. Despite these shortcomings, the account makes good reading.

The Great Sea-Serpent. — In the year 1855 I had occasion to visit the neighbouring province of Nova Scotia, and was compelled, from the nature of my business, to remain there several months. I heard, while there, many curious stories related by persons well educated and intelligent, as well as by ignorant fishermen, which were so remarkable that I took the trouble of ma[r]king the circumstances in the hope that time might give me an opportunity to unravel the mystery, and among these was the report of repeated appearances in the harbours of the Province, of the veritable sea-serpent.

The shores of the peninsula, both in the Atlantic and the Bay of Fundy coast, are deeply indented with numerous capacious harbours, which on the western side, are subject to remarkable tides, or periodical currents, so powerful as to divert vessels crossing the mouth of the Bay from their course to the extent of many miles.

It was on the afternoon of a warm quiet day in the month of August, when I arrived. I drove up the one single street of the village and inquired for the house of Tom Larkin, whose acquaintance I had made on my trip from Boston. I found it without difficulty, a one-story cottage of wood, unpainted, and protected with an embankment of rock wood or kelp that reached almost to the windowsill. Great heaps of wood, in lengths of from eight and twenty feet, rose behind the cottage almost to the ridge pole, and a barn of modest dimensions stood at the edge of the hill at the foot of which the cottage was built. In front, across the rarely used road, stretched a slope of grass and gray rock, while beyond was the smooth waters of the harbour and the boundless sea, whose restless surges beat upon the beach across the narrow strip which separated the cove from the Atlantic.

Larkin, I ascertained, was not at home. He and his two boys were outside the harbour in their little sloop, making a catch. His daughter, a stout, rosy maid of fourteen, led my horse to the barn and fed him. At her invitation, I partook of some cold salmon and barley bread and we walked over to the "Pint," where half the women and children of the village were gathered. As we ascended the slope, which overhung the mouth of the harbour, I noticed a great agitation among the women,

some throwing up their hands, some running towards the village, giving utterance to the screams of terror. "Something's happened to the boats," said Jenny, "or one of the children has fell in." We sped up the hill, inquiring of the screaming fugitives what was the matter. The only reply I understood was, "The snake! The snake!" Jenny uttered an exclamation of alarm but we went on. A fleet of fishing boats were pulling rapidly in for the mouth of the harbour with every appearance of apprehension. The men, we could see, were straining every muscle to gain shelter.

It was an improvised race, each boat seemingly determined to outstrip the others. They did not appear to be a musket-shot from us as we looked down upon them from the cliff. I could see the agonized exertions of the men, and hear plainly the swift and regular strokes of their oars. But nothing to cause the alarm was visible.

"It is a sheer panic," said I, aloud.

"It's the snake, and that's what it is," answered Jenny.

"Can you see it?"

"No. He's sounded, may hap." Then with a shriek, she exclaimed, "There he comes! My God!" and she covered her eyes with her apron and pointed with her hand at the last lagging boat.

I looked, and sure enough, there was a monster apparently within a stone's throw of the two-masted white boat, whose crew of one man and two boys was making every effort to escape. Ah, never can I forget that sight! It was terrible! Slowly and majestically moved that hideous length of undulating terror but fast enough to keep pace with the boats. Near what might be a head, rose a hump of crest, crowded with a waving mass of long, pendulous hair like a mane, while behind, for forty or fifty feet, slowly moved, or rolled, the spirals of his immense snake-like body. The movement was in vertical curves, the contortions of the back alternately rising and falling from the head to the tail, leaving behind a wake, like that of a screw-steamer upon the glassy surface of the ocean.

The noise of the yells on the shore and the rattle of the oars in the row locks did not seem to disturb him, but on he came and was now so near, as he followed the boats through the channel into the harbour, that I believe I could have shot him from where I stood. In a moment he raised his head, from which the water poured in showers, and opening the horrid jaws he gave utterance to a noise resembling nothing so much as the hissing sound of steam from the escape-pipe of a boiler. In spite of the knowledge of the security of my position, I shuddered as I gazed and heard.

He turned his head and displayed the inside of the jaws, armed with rows of glistening teeth, while from the lower section depended a long tuft of hair like a goat's beard. The deep-sunk evil eye was defended by a projectile that gave it a most sinister expression. The head and upper portion of the body was of a dark, dingy blue, fading to yellowish white on the belly. Under the mane as it floated about the neck, I could see the scales which defended the hide glistening in the sun. The head appeared to be of a smooth, horny texture and perhaps five or six feet long from the muzzle to the neck. I could see nothing like a fin or gills. I am thus particular in describing the monster, as I had a remarkably good opportunity to observe his appearance at a very moderate distance.

After the boats arrived at the shore, the monster turned slowly around and moved towards the sea, remaining at least ten minutes in full view, so that I had ample time to make two rough sketches of him. Before reaching the open sea, and while abreast of the cliff on which I stood, he slowly sunk while he moved ocean ward, and I supposed I had seen the last of him. But I was mistaken, as will be seen.

The little village was in a state of unusual excitement that night. Knots of men gathered about the two little stores, and in hoarse whispers talked of the cause of their panic. The great regret seemed to be that for a while, at least, their fishing operations must be suspended, none having the hardihood to venture out while the presence of the snake was suspected. I was anxious, notwithstanding the alarming indications, to have a day's fishing on the morrow, but could not find anyone to go with me. Larkin told me he "wouldn't go for the best catch of the season." One of the boys, however, a fine manly fellow of seventeen, offered to go if he could prevail on Sam Hethcote to accompany us. Sam was found and promised.

Next morning was foggy, so that it was near noon before we had a clear sky. Then the fog dissipated, and we started down the harbour, two at the oars, amid the warnings of old, grave-looking fishermen, and the evil prophecies of the women. Just outside the harbour we anchored and prepared to fish. The water was of that transparent hue which, at times, allows the eye to pierce twenty or thirty feet below the surface. For more than an hour we enjoyed excellent success when the fish refused to bite. After long silence in the hope of a nibb[l]er, Hethcote remarked that "the snake must have come again, or we'd do better," and proposing baiting for him. I, tired of the dullness, stretched myself athwart, and with my head over the gunwale, gazed down into the clear green depths. By using my hands as a tube to concentrate my sight, it seemed as though I could pierce at least fifty feet. Thus silently musing on the wonders of the unknown depths of Neptune's dark empire, and particularly of that monstrous denizen who yesterday showed his huge proportions, I became aware of some immense, moving mass in the line of my sight. First it was confused and indistinct, but presently, as it assumed form and I became aware of its character, the cold perspiration of fear started out from my face. It was the snake.

Fear paralyzed my voice. I dared not speak. I gazed in entranced horror at the object of terror. There he lay directly under my face. It seemed that I could touch him with an oar. Supposing, seeing the shadow of the boat, he should rise and crush it with his powerful jaws?

The though was agony [but] still I gazed silently. The tide was "making," and the serpent lay head to the current, which was flowing into the harbour, keeping up an undulatory movement just sufficient to retain his position. The shell-like head was just abaft the stern of the boat, and the immense mane flowing wavingly, either by the motion of the current or the convulsions of the body. To my affrighted sight, that portion of the body in the line of my clearest vision appeared to be six or seven feet in diameter. It may have been, yet I think not.

The instinct of self-preservation nerved me at last. I turned to my companions who were as listless as I had been, and placing my fingers on my lips, motioned them to look over the side. As they did so, one after the other, the ghastly appearance of terror struck their faces [and] showed that they comprehended the situation.

Hethcote moved silently to the stern and cut the rope that held the killick, and we drifted quietly with the tide into the harbour. At what was deemed a safe distance, we put out the oars and pulled steadily forward. I watched the spot we left as I pulled the after oar, when I was startled by a "breach," and the convulsions of the snake could be seen sculling his huge carcass seaward.

SPIRIT LAKE

Many of the powerful myths and legends of the native peoples have been recorded by Europeans, but when they are repeated by Europeans they are treated as little more than stories for children. Imagine the effect on the reader and the howls of protests from social historians and literary critics if the mythologies of Europe were reduced to "Jack and the Beanstock," "Little Red Riding Hood," and such superstitious rhymes as "Sun at night, sailor's delight; / Sun in the morning, sailors take warning." The native traditions are embedded in a world view and a narrative cycle that is adult and neither childish nor primitive or savage. It pays to ponder the native tales, both Indian and Eskimo, for the purposes of the tale-telling: cautionary, explanatory, anticipatory, etc.

The tales included in the column "Spirit Lake," reprinted from the *Quebec Morning Chronicle*, 28 May 1847, were randomly collected and selected. As the Aborigines of Australia had their "songlines," which told the traditional tales of the features of the landscape and revealed the inner natures of the forces that met there, so the Indians of Canada had their tales of the lakes and rivers, mounds and hollows, of the land.

The writer of the article suggests that these "idle legends" give us "an insight into the Indian mind." What he should say is that they give us insights into human minds and into mindsets quite unlike our own.

It is not known what lake the writer was describing, but he might have meant "Mille Lac" rather than "Mill Lac." For some reason quotation marks introduce the second and subsequent paragraphs. As there is no indication of the source of the copy, if it is indeed quoted, these are not reproduced.

Spirit Lake. — This lake, which the French have named Mill Lac, and certain ignorant Yankees, Rum Lake, was originally called by the Chippeways, Minsisagai-goming, which signifies the dwelling place of the Mysterious Spirit. In form it is almost round, and about twenty across in the widest part. The shores are rather low, but covered with a luxuriant growth of oak, hard maple and tamarack. It is shallow, but clear and cold: has a sandy bottom, and yields a variety of fish; and contains only three islands, which are small and rocky.

The Mysterious Spirit alluded to above has acquired a great notoriety on account of his frequently taking away into the spirit land certain people whom he loved.

A little boy was once lost upon the margin of this lake. The only trace of him that ever could be discovered, was one of his arrows found lodged in a tree. And the Indians believe, too, that the aged mother of Hole-in-the-day (the great chief) was also carried away by the Mysterious Spirit. One thing is certain, say they, she disappeared in the twinkling of an eye from the party with whom she was travelling many years ago. These are indeed idle legends, but give us an insight into the Indian mind.

The ruling chief of Spirit Lake, at the present time, is Naguanabic, or Outside Feather. A son of this old Indian, while hunting once pursued a deer to a very great distance, which he finally captured. Out of revenge for the *improper* conduct of the animal, the cruel Indian tortured it in a variety of ways, and came home boasting of what he had done. At the feast usually given on such occasions, the old chief addressed his son in the following words: "We are thankful to the Great Spirit for furnishing us with food. But my son has acted wrong in torturing that animal, and if the laws of the Great Spirit are not changed from what they were in times past, that boy shall not be privileged to kill another deer during the whole winter." And I was told that he did not, and that no cruel-hearted man ever can, under similar circumstances.

It was from the lips of this aged Indian that I obtained the following legend:

"A thousand winters ago, the Great Spirit caused the sun to be fastened in the heavens, for the purpose of destroying the world on account of an enormous sin which had been committed. The men of that time assembled together in council, but could devise no means to avert the calamity. The animals of the earth also held a council, and they were about to give up all hopes of a release, when a small animal stept forth and avowed its intention of gnawing off the string that held the sun. He entered the earth, and after travelling a long time, finally reached the desired planet and accomplished his purpose. The heat of the sun, however, was so great, that the sight of the heroic little animal was impaired, and it returned to the earth — a poor blind mole."

A New Sea Monster

The title of this news story is "A New Sea Monster" and from it one may glean the fact that sightings of sea serpents and lake monsters were quite common in Canada in the middle of the nineteenth century.

The article appeared in the *Gleaner* (Fredericton, N.B.), 1 Oct. 1859. The item is apparently a reprint from another newspaper. At the time there were neither newspaper chains nor news services of any consequence, but there were informal "exchanges" among the editors of some daily and most weekly papers, exchanges of interesting news stories — like reports of lake monsters.

A New Sea Monster. — The following account of a new Monster of the Deep, we clip from a late exchange:

"Capt. John Dunn, of the schooner *Rover*, on a trip from Quebec to Belle Isle, reports as follows: — On Saturday, 20th August, in lat. 59.14 N., long. 59.10 W., at 4:00 o'clock A.M., weather fine — saw something like a vessel bottom up, S.E., about 3 miles distant — bore down to ascertain what it was, and on approaching close to it could discern something like the bow of a clinker built vessel bottom up, showing the rows of planks apparently the same. About what seemed to be the head, noticed a great deal of red. Bowsprit apparently under or in a wash with the water. On nearing the larboard side saw something snow white on the centre of the body. Brought the schooner close alongside, and to our great astonishment found it to be a living monster. The large part of the body or shell was about 50 feet long and 16 feet high, conical shape and sharpening to the fore part, with a long neck and jaws about 14 feet from the body. At the junction of the neck with the body was a large horn. It had large white fins something like the wings of a bird under the middle of the shell. We were scarcely 30 feet distant when we saw the head come above water and turn towards our boat; we hauled off, tacked, and stood in on the other side for a further survey. The right fin was more under water than the left, and the horn we could see distinctly. It was very long and blood red. The neck and head again moved towards the boat, when we got somewhat alarmed, and made all sail from this floating monster. We counted the strakes from the centre of the back to the water 15 of a side, and the top of the shell or back was partly covered with birds' dung. The shell was of a dark colour and came down in wash with the water. Under the shell we could plainly see a curve, and then a second projection. The hind part very much the shape of a Turtle, but the fore part was sharper. At 5:30 A.M., soon after we hauled off, saw an American schooner passing very close to it."

A MERMAID IN THE GULF

Sailors have been seeing mermaids and sirens in the waters of the world's Seven Seas since time immemorial. Now and then landlubbers report the unexpected sight of these creatures. The creatures themselves are usually as surprised to see humans as humans are to see them.

Neither the newspaperman who penned this story nor a certain Mr. Graham who reported seeing this "mythological marine animal" attempted to relate the description to any known species of marine animal. Instead the creature is related to previous sightings by natives and to their belief systems.

"A Mermaid in the Gulf" is reprinted from the columns of the *Victoria Daily Colonist*, 1 July 1863.

A Mermaid in the Gulf — Mr. Graham, who is erecting a saw mill on Burrard Inlet, has just given us an interesting description of one of these mythological marine animals which he saw on Monday week in the Gulf of Georgia, about midway between the Inlet and the mouth of the Fraser. It was about 6 o'clock P.M., when he saw it gradually rise above the surface of the water within about 30 yards of where he was, showing the entire bust, in which position it remained for the space of five minutes looking in the direction of the boat in which he and two Indians were sitting, when it slowly sank into its native element. The Indians evinced considerable alarm at the strange phenomenon. Mr. Graham describes it as having the appearance of a female with long hair of a yellowish-brown tinge drooping over its shoulders, the color of the skin being a dark olive. The Indians have a legend that if this animal is seen and not killed, those by whom it is seen will pine away and die, and relate an instance of the kind as having occurred amongst the Squamish tribe. Hence the alarm of these Indians at the sight of the one alluded to. They also state that many years ago one was killed on Squamish river by an aged Indian. — *British Columbian*.

A GREAT LAKE SERPENT

Serpents regularly rise to the surface in Canadian lakes and rivers. Indeed, there has never been any shortage of them in the St. Lawrence River and in the waters of the Bay of Quinte. One lake monster was spotted in September 1864 by a couple at Trenton, Canadian East, today's Ontario. This serpent made "a dreadful noise," a novel touch. The journalist's appeal to the trustworthiness of the couple is characteristic of a good many reports of anomalies and curiosities.

"A Great Lake Serpent" appeared in the *Montreal Witness*, 17 Sept. 1864. It was apparently reprinted from the *Belleville Intelligencer* published in Belleville, C.W., later Ontario.

A Great Lake Serpent. — The Trenton people are just now considerably agitated about a great serpent which has been seen in the bay by a number of the inhabitants of the village. There have been a good many reports about the existence of such a serpent for some time past, but as they could not be definitely traced, very little credence was attached to them. However, the matter has at length been settled beyond any question for the "sea monster" has been seen by a resident of the village, a Mr. Julius Baker, who is said to be perfectly reliable. Not many days ago, while he and his wife were in a boat near the Indian Island, they were suddenly startled by a great splashing in the water and looking around discovered within about ten rods of the boat, the head and neck of a great serpent, about two feet out of water. Mr. Baker describes the head to be in appearance like a bull-dog, and says the neck was about "three feet through." Both were very much frightened, and immediately pulled for shore. Before reaching land the snake was seen three times, once only six yards from the boat, and again after they had landed only a few feet off. Mr. Baker said it followed him to shore, and made at times a dreadful noise. We may remark that the story is believed by some of the most respectable inhabitants to be strictly true, they having the utmost confidence in the statements of Mr. and Mrs. Baker. — *Belleville Intelligencer.*

THE MONSTER OF LAKE UTOPIA

The lakes and rivers of the Maritimes are the domain of innumerable "monsters." Of these the Lake Utopia Monster is probably the best known, if only because it bears the best and most memorable name! Who would not wish to boast that he or she had seen the Lake Utopia Monster?

"The Monster of Lake Utopia" appeared in the *Summerside Progress* of Sunnyside, P.E.I., 19 Aug. 1867. It was contributed by the correspondent of the *St. John Globe* of Saint John, N.B.

A correspondent of the St. John, N.B., *Globe*, writing from "St. George, Aug. 6," gives the following account of a monster in Utopia Lake, in addition to that which he contributed some time ago to the same paper, and which we then transferred to our columns:

Agreeably to my promise that should any further be developed respecting the strange monster in Lake Utopia, I would write you, I now beg to say that it has been seen by a number of persons since, in different parts of the lake, and on Wednesday, July 24th, by thirteen persons, some of whom are of the most reliable character. I would have written you sooner, but being rather sceptical about it myself, I waited to get the correct accounts from the lips of the individuals themselves; and I now have no hesitation in saying that some huge animal of fearful aspect exists in the waters of Utopia. To the north and east of lake Utopia, there is a small lake well known to the sporting fraternity, which connects with the larger waters by a stream, perhaps 400 yards in length. About midway on this stream, between the two lakes, Messrs. H. & J. Ludgate have a saw mill in operation. The deals when sawn are floated down the stream to the deep water in Utopia, where they are made into rafts to float down to St. George. On the day before alluded to, a number of men engaged in rafting, had their attention drawn to a violent agitation of the water, about 100 yards distant out in the lake, which continued for a time, and then, there appeared distinctly above the water a huge bulky object, variously estimated from 20 to 40 feet in length, and from 4 to 10 feet across the widest part. The men describe the skin as presenting a shaggy appearance, not unlike a buffalo robe, and of a reddish brown color. It created a great quantity of foam which drifted up to the shore in huge flakes. At no time could they see the head of it; but at a distance of 20 or 25 feet in rear of the large mass, could be seen what they supposed to be a tail from the movements. The man called H. Ludgate, Esq., who was at the mill, and he and his son, together with others, ran down and witnessed the evolutions of this strange creature. Mr. Ludgate told me himself that it agitated the water to a perfect boiling, seething state, and threw up in its course edgings and mud from the bottom, occasionally rising itself to the top; a dark cumbrous body — not unlike a large stick of timber — disappearing again almost instantly. It finally moved off, and they could trace its course down the lake by the foam it created long after it went below the surface. Later in the day Mr. Thomas White, his two sons, and a hired man haying in the field, saw it *seven different times*, and Mr. White says it came up at the outer end of the raft, quite close to it; the men at work at the inner end being turned away did not observe their acquaintance of the morning.

Mr. White's description of it is about the same. He being farther off could not describe the skin of the animal, but says that when most exposed it resembled a large rock left bare of the tide, 10 feet across; and he further states that he can safely swear he saw 30 feet in length of it. His statement is corroborated by his sons, and by all of the thirteen persons who saw it the same day. Now, Mr. Editor, heretofore I could scarcely believe in the existence of such an animal and unprecedented inhabitant of our lake; but when I heard men of the character of H. Ludgate, Esq., Charles Ludgate, Charles Mealy, Thomas White, Robert White and many others say *positively* that they saw it as described, and when I take into consideration the destruction of fish which must take place in Utopia every year — otherwise it would teem with splendid trout, perch, cusk and smelt, and together with these the tradition of forty years, — I must say that in common with the majority of our citizens, I firmly believe that a monster of vast dimensions and formidable appearance is located in the lake. Two of our most enterprising citizens, Mr. H.A. Smith, and W.W. Shaw, have had hooks made and attached to lines buoyed in the lake for some time, but so far without any satisfactory result. It is the opinion of many that a large net will be required to capture the creature, and I understand that a movement is on foot quietly, to make the attempt, which I hope will succeed. The people living in the vicinity of the lake are really afraid to cross it in boats; and if you could only hear some of the oldest settlers who saw this "thing" tell the story with fear and trembling, you would be fully impressed with the truth of their assertions, and consider them justified in their fears.

A LAKE SUPERIOR LEGEND

Creation myths and "just so" stories abound in the oral traditions of the native peoples of the country. Here is one such creation story. "A Lake Superior Legend" appeared in *The Nor'Wester* (Winnipeg, Red River Settlement, now Manitoba), 24 Aug. 1869.

In the summer of 1864, while in the Lake Superior country, I took a notion one day to have a swim. So, donning a light bathing dress, I dropped into the water. The plunge almost took my breath away. I had anticipated coldness, but I had not anticipated such icy coldness as this. The Lake Superior Indians never bathe; the reason they assign is, that the water of the Lake is never warm.

A great many years ago the waters of the mighty lake were warm in the summer season. The Indians were the sole inhabitants of the land in those days. Manabozho was a great manitou (good spirit), and the Lake Superior tribes were his favourite children. But sometimes Manabozho used to put on his Seven League Boots, and stride away over the mountains on a visit to his mighty brother of the setting sun. He had gone on such a journey one melting day in July, and the Indians lay in their forests, dreaming dreams about the fairy lands of the East.

There was a bad spirit who hated the Indians fiercely. This bad spirit was a monstrous snake. He was very much afraid of the good manitou, Manabozho, and when Manabozho was at home the bad spirit stayed in his fiery lake, away back into the forest.

But now Manabozho was gone on a journey, so the bad spirit resolved to take advantage of his absence to destroy the tribes whom he hated. He had a large number of demons in his service, who were ready for any work he might set them. He despatched an army of these demons to annihilate the Indians. For his part he set himself to watch for Manabozho, in case that good manitou should return unexpectedly.

The Indians saw the army of demons coming, and knowing that in the absence of their chief they were powerless to fight against them, they gathered their women and children together, and paddled away in their canoes across the lake. The demons could not swim, and had taken a great dislike to the water, and when they saw the Indians paddling away, they howled in their rage, and belched forth great clouds of flame and smoke.

But as soon as the Indians had safely reached an island, a thick covering of ice suddenly overspread the lake, and the demons yelling with joy rushed upon it. When they were all safely upon the ice bridge, it parted as suddenly as it had appeared, and became an ice-craft, and floated hither and thither. The demons were in great distress, being unable to get to either shore. And now the form of Manabozho rose to view. Manabozho understood the situation at once, and stretching out his mighty arm, larger than a pine tree, roared with a voice louder than thunder, "Sink, sink, and rise no more!"

And the raft sunk, and the demons perished, and the Indians came back and worshipped Manabozho. And this is why the waters of Lake Superior are so cold.

A NEW ANIMAL ON THIS CONTINENT

A "new animal" was captured apparently while it was swimming in the Mackenzie River of the Great Northwest. "A New Animal on This Continent" appeared in the *Ottawa Times*, 22 Nov. 1870.

A gentleman who came down on the Farragut from Fort Burford, says the Sioux City *Daily Times*, gives us the following information regarding a species of animal hitherto unknown on this continent:

"Sir John E. Packenham, an officer in the English army, who has been spending the last year in her Majesty's northern provinces, arrived at Fort Buford with an animal of rare beauty, and never before caught on this continent, nor has it been known till late years that the specie existed in this country. It is of the same family as the giraffe, or cameleopard, of Africa, and is known to naturalists as the tygomelia. They are known to inhabit the high table lands of Cashmere and Hindoo Kush, but are more frequently seen on the high peaks of the Himalaya Mountains. The animal was taken when quite young, and is thoroughly domesticated, and follows its keeper like a dog. It is only four months old, and ordinarily stands about five feet high, but is capable of raising its head two feet, which makes the animal seven feet when standing erect. It is of a dark brown mouse color, large projecting eyes, with slight indications of horns growing out. This wonderful animal was caught north of Lake Athabasca, on the water of McKenzie's river. It has a craw similar to the pelican, by which means it can carry subsistence for several days. It was very fleet, being able to outfoot the fastest horse in the country. The black dapper spots on the rich brown color make it one of the most beautiful animals in existence, more beautiful than the leopard of the Chinese jungle. Sir John did not consider it safe to transport this pet by water down the Mississippi river, fearing the uncertain navigation and the great change of climate from the Manitoba to the sunny south. He has, therefore, wisely concluded to go by way of St. Paul, Minn. The commander of Fort Buford furnishes him with an escort for the trip. He will then proceed through Canada to Montreal, where he will ship his cargo to England.

A GREEN-EYED MONSTER

Not all marine monstrosities are imaginary yet the language used to describe these menaces in action is often fanciful in the extreme. This thrilling article is replete with exaggeration and rhetorical devices; still, it moves along briskly and offers details of great specificity. "A Green-Eyed Monster" appeared in the *Citizen* (Halifax, N.S.), 15 Nov. 1873.

The writer is The Rev. M. Harvey. He wrote, "'Fact is often stranger than fiction.' The wildest dreams of the novelist are often surpassed by realities." Indeed they are!

Harvey met the public's fascination with such marine creatures by returning to the subject on at least two occasions. His second and third articles appear hereinafter.

A Green-Eyed Monster
The Devil Fish Seen off the Coast of Newfoundland
Amputation of an Arm of the Monster
Narrow Escape of Two Firemen from a Gigantic Cuttle-Fish
Nineteen Feet of One of the Tentacles Cut Off and Brought Ashore
(Correspondence New York World)

St. John's, N.F. Oct. 29. — The readers of Victor Hugo cannot fail to remember this thrilling account of the devil-fish, in his "Toilers of the Sea." Perhaps a majority of those who have read that splendid tale have the impression that the monster who wound its slimy arms, covered with suckers, which enabled it to take a death-like grip around the body of Gilliat, was merely a creation of the imagination, and that no such frightful thing as the kraken or devil-fish is to be found in the world of waters. Many critics found fault with Victor Hugo for having transcended the bounds of possibility in the scene which he has painted in such vivid colours. But an event has occurred here which leads me to think that there is no exaggeration whatever in the picture he has drawn, and that [within] the caverns of the deep are to be found monsters even more gigantic and powerful than that which figures on Hugo's canvas.

Two days ago two of our fishermen were out in a small boat in Conception Bay, a short distance from Portugal Cove, plying their avocation. Suddenly they discovered a dark, shapeless mass floating on the surface of the water a short distance from them. On approaching it the men concluded that it was a huge bale of goods, perhaps part of the cargo of some wrecked vessel, and that they had found a valuable prize. One of them struck the object with his boat hook, when suddenly the dark heap became animated, opened out like a huge umbrella without a handle, and the horror-stricken fishermen beheld a face full of intelligence but also of ferocity, and a pair of ghastly green eyes glaring at them, its large parrot-like beak seeming to open with a savage and malignant purpose.

The men were petrified with terror, and for a moment so fascinated with the horrible sight that they were powerless. The eyes of the monster were peculiarly large and prominent, bright and apparently gleaming with rage. Before the fishermen could make any effort to escape, the creature, now but a few feet from the boat, appeared to open out, and suddenly there shot out from around its face several arms of corpse-like fleshiness, grappling for the boat and seeking to develop it in their livid folds. Had these little, slimy arms, with their death-like adhesive powers, once fastened themselves on the boat or the men, nothing could have saved them from destruction; for when the suckers with which they are furnished have taken hold nothing can tear them away. They would have been brought in a moment within reach of the powerful beak, which was ready to dart upon them.

Only one of the longer tentacula reached the boat, and owing to its length, went completely over and beyond it. Quick as lightning one of the men seized his tomahawk, and at one blow severed the corpse-like arms which was flung over the boat to drag it to destruction. The green-eyed monster uttered no cry of pain, but disappeared beneath the waters, and the fishermen who had thus escaped from a horrible death found themselves in possession of the amputated arm — an unprecedented trophy, for I believe no parallel occurrence is on record.

The portion of the kraken's arm amputated by this rude surgical operation has been forwarded to St. John's. I have just returned from a careful examination of it. It measures nineteen feet in length, and is tough and fibrous, but not thicker than a man's wrist. The fisherman who acted as surgeon declares that there must have been at least six feet of the arm left behind attached to the monster's body. Indeed, I am inclined to think from the description that the devil-fish must have still ten feet of its arm remaining, making its entire length twenty-nine feet. He could well spare a few feet, though he will probably feel awkward for a time in grappling for his prey, owing to the want of his forearm. Perhaps, like the lobster, he can grow a new limb. But the question remains, what size is the body of the monster?

I am unable to answer that question with any approach to accuracy; but I am heartless enough to hope that this devil-fish may die soon of the wound inflicted by the tomahawk, and that the body may float ashore in Conception Bay. The account of the fishermen in regard to the size of the fish is hardly reliable, as they were sorely frightened, but they describe it as forty feet in length. This, I consider, is an exaggeration, as the body of the cuttle-fish is small. The amputated arm is livid in colour, pointed at the extremity, where it is covered with rows of suckers, which are cartilaginous, horny, and about the size of a quarter dollar. I have suggested some measures for its preservation in spirits, and it will be placed in our museum. If we could only get the body what a keen competition there would be for it between the Smithsonian Institution, Agassiz and Barnum!

It seems to me that the arms of this gigantic cuttle which we now possess is one of the two long tentacula which in certain species extend in the midst of the shorter arms, and which, like them, are furnished with disks or suckers. There are eight antennae in all, two of them being much longer than the others; by means of these it can either anchor itself to a rock or grasp its prey almost as quick as lightning at the distance of at least thirty feet. It is evident that this is a far more gigantic monster than even that which Victor Hugo describes. His devil-fish, with outstretched arms, was only "four or five feet in diameter," and had no snake-like appendages reaching out thirty feet. The body, too, was nothing in comparison with that of our kraken. "Fact is often stranger than fiction." The wildest dreams of the novelist are often surpassed by realities.

What a horrible thing to be entwined in the embrace of those clammy corpse-like arms, and to feel their folds creeping and gliding around you, and the disks, with their cold adhesive touch, glueing themselves to you with a grasp that nothing could relax. The monster darts them out with a snake-like, undulating motion; swiftly they glide around their victim, with a pressure like a tightening cord, the suckers feeling like so many mouths devouring him at the same time. Slowly the horrible arms, supple as leather, strong as steel, cold as death, draw their prey under the terrible beak, and press it against the glutinous mass which forms the body. The cold, slimy grasp paralyzes the victim with terror as the powerful mandibles rend and devour.

Each of the eight arms carries fifty sucking disks, according to Victor Hugo, or 400 in all. Probably the monster I have been describing has many more. These suckers act on the principle of a cupping-glass. Each of them consists of a firm, fleshy, cartilaginous ring, across which a disk of muscular membrane is stretched, with a circular aperture in the centre. A cone-shaped mass of flesh fills the aperture, like a prison, capable of being drawn backward. The membranous disk itself can also be drawn in. The moment one of the sucking disks of a tentacle touches the prey the devil-fish feels the contact, and with the speed of lightning retracts the fleshy piston. A vacuum is thus created, and the edges of the disk are pressed against the surface of the water that is above it, added to the weight [of the] victim with a force equal to the weight of the atmosphere.

If need be — as when the victim makes strenuous efforts to escape — the vacuum, and consequently the adhesion, is increased by the withdrawal of the membranous disk. The more the victim writhes, it comes in contact with more and more of the disks in succession, which of which adheres, and other arms soon encircle it and drag it to the central mouth. When we take into account the size of some of these cuttles, and their tremendous power, we do not wonder at the tales told in Oriental legends, and created once by our old-fashioned naturalists, of some of them of sufficiently colossal dimensions to throw their arms over a ship's hull and drag her under water. There may be a touch of exaggeration in this, but certain it is that this monster met with in Conception Bay was a mighty "ugly customer," and could have made short work with any small craft had he set his mind on it.

I am not aware that any cuttle so large has been seen in cold latitudes. It is in the tropical seas that large cuttles are usually found. Three others of gigantic size were reported to have been seen at various times in our bays, but we were incredulous regarding their size till now.

Rev. M. Harvey

GIGANTIC CUTTLE-FISH

Marine wonders were the marvel of sailors and fishermen in the 19th century and provided work and subject for speculation in the hands of naturalists and anatomists. Size was the factor that determined whether or not a marine creature was to be described as a "monster." Gigantic creatures were "monstrosities" of size. If they were sufficiently monstrous and dangerous looking, they were described collectively as "devil fish."

Here are two reports of "devil fish." The reports are related and appeared side-by-side in the *St. John Morning Chronicle* (St. John's, Nfld.), Dec. 6, 1873. The first report is titled "Gigantic Cuttle-Fishes in Newfoundland"; the second, "The Devil Fish."

These reports describe marine monstrosities (even if they are only "gigantic cuttle-fishes" — the words make they sound even cuddly!). But they are certainly outsized, and one is said to have "ten arms," which is unusual to say the least.

What is most "monstrous" about these reports is perhaps the combination of earnestness and awe that they strike in the hearts of their observers.

Gigantic Cuttle-Fishes in Newfoundland

At the last meeting of the Natural History Society, held Nov. 24th, the President, Principal Dawson, read the following communication from [the] Rev. M. Harvey, of St. John's, Newfoundland: —

He (the President) stated that, in addition to many ancient accounts, some of them evidently exaggerated, Prof. Steenstrup, Dr. Morch and Prof. Allman had recorded the appearance of similar gigantic cuttle-fishes on the coasts of Denmark and Scotland. — Steenstrup has described two specimens under the names of Architew — the monachus, and A. dux, and it seems not improbable that the specimens spoken of by Mr. Harvey may be referred to one of these. One of the Danish specimens is stated to have had arms 18 feet long, and the body 21 feet, so that it may have been as large as the Newfoundland specimens. Dr. Packard has directed attention to these monsters in the February number of the "American Naturalist" and has described a specimen found by a Gloucester fisherman on the Grand Bank of Newfoundland. Mr. Harvey's communication gives us the clearest evidence of the occurrence of these creatures on the shores of Newfoundland.

His letter runs as follows: —

"St. John's., Nfld., Nov. 12, 1873.
"My Dear Doctor,

"I take the liberty of bringing under your notice some account of a gigantic cuttle-fish which was seen a few days ago in Conception Bay. The circumstances under which it was seen were as follows: —

"Two fishermen were out in a small punt, on Oct. 26th, off Portugal Cove, Conception Bay, about 9 miles from St. John's. Observing some object floating on the water at a short distance, they rowed towards it, supposing it to be a large sail or the debris of a wreck. On reaching it, one of the men struck it with his 'gaff,' when immediately it showed signs of life, reared a parrot-like beak, which they declare was 'as big as a six gallon keg,' with which it struck the bottom of the boat violently. It then shot out from about its head two huge livid arms and began to twine them round the boat. One of the men seized a small axe and severed both arms as they lay over the gunwale of the boat; whereupon the fish moved off and ejected an immense quantity of inky fluid, which darkened the water for two or three hundred yards. The men saw it for a short time afterwards, and observed its tail in the air, whch they declare was ten feet across. They estimate the body to have been sixty feet in length, five feet in diameter, of the same shape and colour as the common squid; and they observed that it moved in the same way as the squid, both backwards and forwards.

"One of the arms which they brought ashore was unfortunately destroyed, as they were ignorant of its importance; but the clergyman of the village assures me it was ten inches in diameter and six feet in length. The other arm was brought to St. John's, but not before six feet of it were destroyed. Fortunately I heard of it, and took measures to have it preserved. Mr. Murray, of the Geological Survey, and I, afterwards, examined it carefully, had it photographed, and immersed in alcohol; it is now in our Museum. It measured nineteen feet, is of a pale pink color, entirely cartilaginous, tough and pliant as leather, and very strong. It is but three inches and a half in circumference, except towards the extremity where it broadens like an oar to six inches in circumference, and then tapers to a pretty fine point. The under surface of the extremity is covered with suckers to the very point. At the extreme end there is a cluster of small suckers, with fine sharp teeth round their edges, and having a membrane stretched across each. Of these there are about seventy. Then come two rows of very large suckers, the movable disk of each an inch and a quarter in diameter, the cartilaginous ring, not being denticulated. These are twenty-four in number. After these there is another group of suckers, with denticulated edges (similar to the first), and about fifty in number. Along the under surface about forty more small suckers are distributed at intervals, making in all about 180 suckers on the arm.

"The men estimate that they left about ten feet of the arm attached to the body of the fish, so that its original length must have been thirty-five feet.

"A clergyman here assures me that when he resided at Lamaline, on the Southern Coast, in the winter of 1870, the bodies of two cuttles were cast ashore, measuring 40 and 45 feet respectively.

"More than once we have had accounts of gigantic cuttles cast ashore in different localities; but not until now have any portions of them been preserved.

"By this mail I send you a photograph of the arm, it is one fourth the original in size. You will readily see the suckers at the extremity of the arm. The disks of several of the larger ones have been torn off by carelessness on the part of the captors. A few of them, however, are perfect, and the smaller ones are not injured. I shall send you also, by this mail, three or four of these suckers which I cut off, the smallest being from the very tip of the extremity and not much larger than a pin's head.

"I shall be glad to hear your opinion of this fish at your earliest convenience.

"It is a great pity one arm was destroyed, and it is still more to be regretted that we did not get the head of the monster.

"Yours very sincerely,
"M. HARVEY."

The photograph and specimens of the suckers of the creature, both forwarded by Mr. Harvey, were exhibited at the meeting. The Kraken, of Scandinavian superstition, is an exaggerated representation of one of these colossal cuttles. Its existence was gravely alleged by Pontopiddan as the cause of the occasional disappearance of islands. Denys de Montfort, who evidently disbelieved in their existence, having represented as "kraken octopod" in the act of scuttling a three master (by way of caricature), told Mr. Defrance that if this were "swallowed," he would, in his next edition, represent the monster embracing the Straits of Gibraltar, or capsizing a whole squadron of ships. Truth is, however, at all times, stranger than fiction, as any one may see, in the present instance, who takes the trouble to compare Victor Hugo's fanciful and inaccurate description of the "devil fish," in Les Travailleurs de Mer, with the careful notes on a member of the same group of animals, as given above by Mr. Harvey. The cuttle-fishes are by far the most highly organized member of the great division Mollusca. By many writers they are considered as forming almost a link, as it were, between the vertebrate and invertebrate

animals. The glassy internal pon of the squid, and the calcareous internal "bone" of the true cuttles, are held to foreshadow the spinal column of the higher animals. The eyes of the cuttles are large, brilliant, and more complicated in their structure than are those of some fishes. The late Mrs. Barret[t] Browning, probably unconscious of this circumstance, whoever, commences a short poem, entitled Lord Walter's Wife, with the following couplet:

"But why do you go? said the lady, while both sat under the yew;
And her eyes were alive in their depth, as the kraken beneath the sea blue."

The Devil Fish

To the Editor Morning Chronicle:

Sir, —

The descriptions of the gigantic cuttle-fish, seen in Conception Bay, has awakened very great interest in the United States and Canada. The Natural History Society of Montreal have had a discussion on the subject, the matter having been brought before them by the President, Dr. Dawson; and in other quarters much interest and curiosity regarding this marine monster, the existence of which was not credited previously, has been expressed. It is to be hoped, therefore, that should any specimens of these giants of the deep be captured in future by our fishermen, every effort will be made to preserve them entire; or should it be found impossible to preserve the body, the head with the arms attached, beak, &c., could be readily placed in a large cask, and immersed in strong brine and forwarded to St. John's. It would be well for our outport "planters" to make known the importance of this matter among the fishermen.

Since the appearance of the large cuttle in Conception Bay, I have been fortunate enough to obtain possession of a perfect specimen, though far inferior in size to the monster whose arms were amputated. It was taken in a net near Logy Bay. The body is upwards of seven feet in length, and about five feet in circumference. From the head ten arms radiate, two of them being each twenty-four feet in length, and armed at the extremities with a cluster of sucking disks, some of them an inch and a quarter in diameter, and furnished with small sharp teeth round their edges. Eight of the arms are each six feet in length, and nine inches in circumference at the junction with the head. They are completely covered, on the inner surface, with rows of large denticulated suckers. The beak is in the middle of the central nucleus from which the arms radiate; and the large eyes, which unfortunately have been destroyed, were on each side of this central mass. The remains of one of the eye-lids shows that the eyes were four inches in diameter. They are dark and beautiful, but when the creature is enraged assume an expression of intense ferocity. The beak is sharp and powerful. The fishermen were compelled to kill it by cutting off its head before it could be landed, and it was with great difficulty that three men dispatched it.

Messrs. McKenny and Parsons have succeeded in obtaining admirable photographs of this specimen, which will shortly be for sale at their rooms, and probably in all the book stores. One of these photographs shows the head and surrounding arms, with the beak in the centre. The head is supported on a stand, and the arms hang down with the rows of suckers displayed, and taper to a fine point. The two long tentacles are coiled in short lengths, and hang from the ends of the rail, on the right and left of the larger arms. They are but three inches in circumference; and the rows of splendid suckers at their extremities are very distinct in the photograph. The body had to be photographed separately. The formation of the tail is very striking. Altogether this is one of the most extraordinary creatures found in the great deep. No specimen at all to be compared with this is to be found in any museum in Europe or America. In the Acquaria of Brighton in England and Hamburgh in Germany there are two living specimens, but they are not more than two or three feet between the extremities of the extended arms. This one is 48 feet between the extremities of the larger arms and nearly 14 feet from tip to tip of two of the shorter arms.

Yours truly,
M. HARVEY.

THEIR WORD FOR THE DEVIL

It was customary in the past to refer to the native people who occupy the polar regions of Canada as the Eskimo (or the Esquimaux). In the 1960s, as if to mark the coming to political power of these hardy people, the word Eskimo was dropped in favour of the word Inuit (which means "people" in Inuktitut, their language). The word Eskimo is retained here since these newspaper accounts predate the 1960s by almost one century.

"Spiritism among the Esquimaux" appeared in the *Sarnia Observer*, 4 Dec. 1874. It must have represented a novelty to the readers of that paper. Nothing is immediately known of its source, which is the publication that is named in the last line.

The religion of the Esquimaux is of all curious systems of theology, the most curious. Nevertheless they are not polytheists, demon worshippers, not even idolaters, in the common acceptance of that term. They believe in one supreme deity, whom they call Toongarsoon, their word for the devil, who is of the feminine gender, but whose proper name, if she has one, I could never ascertain. Their god is supposed to reside in a handsome dwelling situated somewhere in the sea. His occupation, according to their notion, is a very benevolent one, for he is said to keep large herds of seals, sea-horses, etc., for the express purpose of providing entertainment for the souls of the good men, which are transported immediately after death to the apartments assigned for him in the marine palace where his godship resides. A large apartment of this place, is said to be fitted up with cooking apparatus, on the most extensive scale; pots and kettles of such dimensions that walruses, sea unicorns, seals, etc., in large numbers are boiled or baked therein every day to furnish a perpetual feast for the happy spirits of deceased Esquimaux hunters, or such of them as behaved themselves with tolerable propriety while in the flesh. Hence it will appear that the Esquimaux heaven consists of a never ending feast of fat things, an eternity of well cooked walrus meat and seal's blubber.

The devil (a female one, remember) is supposed to be an unworthy sister of the divine, Toongarsoon. She resides at some distance from her brother's palace, on an island, where she takes charge of deceased sinners, who, under her domestic management, fare worse if possible than the inmates of some of the cheap boarding-houses in New York. In fact, these delinquent spirits suffer the pangs of starvation, and their cries and shrieks of agony are often heard above the howling of the arctic gales and the angry war of the mountain torrents. — Prof. Sountage's *Narrative*, etc.

MUST HAVE BEEN A SEA-SERPENT

Here is a splendid account of the sighting of a "sea-serpent" off the Grand Banks of Newfoundland. The account appeared as "The Sea-Serpent Shows Himself" in the *New York Times*, New York, N.Y., 11 Nov. 1879.

The Sea-Serpent Shows Himself Mr. Rowell's Story —
A Water-Snake 400 Feet Long, with a Bed Head

Fourth Officer F.G. Rowell, of the steam-ship Anchoria, of the Anchor Line, which arrived at this port from Glasgow late Sunday evening, says that on Thursday last, while on the Newfoundland Banks, he saw a sea-serpent which he estimates to have been fully as long as the steam-ship. According to "Lloyd's Shipping Record," the Anchoria is 408 feet long. Mr. Rowell was walking the bridge at four bells in the afternoon watch, when he noticed a disturbance in the water about a mile distant on the port beam. At first he thought the common was caused by a school of porpoises, but, on closer observation, he changed his mind. When he looked through a pair of strong glasses he saw the head and a portion of the body of the sea-serpent rising above the water. Portions of the back of the creature could be seen rising out of the sea at intervals as it propelled itself along on the top of the water. Its motions were similar to those of the land-snake as it moves along on the ground. The water in the wake of the creature had been lashed into foam by its tail. Its head was large and contained an enormous mouth, which opened frequently and spat out large quantities of water. Its tongue, which was extremely long, could be seen at times, but no teeth or fangs were observed. The body of the serpent was round, and its color was black. It was moving in the same direction as the steam-ship, and at a greater rate of speed. When the creature had got a little ahead of the vessel it sank down into the water and disappeared.

Several passengers were on deck at the time. Observing the commotion on the sea, they asked Mr. Baxter, the second officer, what the thing moving in the water could be. He was able to take only a hurried glance, before he was called to the other side of the vessel in the performance of his duties. When he returned with his glasses the creature was not in sight. Mr. Baxter says he thinks that it must have been a sea-serpent, and he places implicit reliance on the fourth officer's statement. Mr. Rowell has made marine animals the subject of study, and has always believed in the existence of sea-serpents; but his desire to see one of these animals had never before been gratified.

A BIG SEA WORM

"A Big Sea Worm" appeared in the *Daily Sun* (Saint John, N.B.), 23 Dec. 1880. It is apparently reprinted from the *News* (London, England).

Although the great sea snake has not deigned to put in an appearance during the past year, yet it will interest our readers to know of the recent capture of a gigantic sea worm by some long-distance fishermen, among some sea wrack, on one of their cod hooks off Dunrobin Castle, Golspie, N.B. This worm, whose existence is known to scientific naturalists, is but very seldom seen or heard of by the general public. This specimen, now alive in the aquarium in the Duke of Sutherland's museum at Dunrobin Castle, is only about five feet long, but it is probable that he has not uncoiled himself to his full length. In shape he is flat, like a ribbon, and only five or six lines in width, of a brown, violet colour, smooth, and shining like varnished leather. When full grown, this remarkable worm is stated, on excellent authority, to attain the length of from 40 to 90 feet. Fishermen not infrequently haul in as much as 30 fathoms in length, but it is very rare to see him extended his full dimensions, as his habit is to coil himself up into a heap of knots, and when in this ball shape to take up his habitation under stones in the hollows of rocks.

In this position he attracts notice by the continual tightening and loosening of his complicated, knotted body. When he wishes to shift his quarters, he has the power of unknotting himself and gliding in a graceful manner through the water, propelled by ciliae which run the length of the body. As regards his food and habits, nothing whatever is known for certain. It is, in fact, a sea form of the freshwater "hair-worm" found in stagnant ponds and ditches, viz.: — the *Gordius aquaticus*, and which our ancestors used to say were horse-hairs in the process of transformation into eels. The scientific name of this curious sea worm is Leneus marinuslongissimus.

SEA SPIDER

Sea Spider? Apparently this was — or perhaps is — nautical slang for an octopus.

This thrilling narrative begins in a light and chatty way but quickly turns dark and heavy, and it presents the octopus as enormous and dangerous. It has rather more human than horror interest, if the two categories are distinct ones.

The account appeared as "Fisherman and Octopus" in *The Bay Pilot* (Vancouver, B.C.), March 16, 1882.

Fisherman and Octopus · A Combat in the Pacific Near Vancouver's Island

"Here's a delicacy," a Fulton Market, New York fish dealer said, pointing to a long spider-like animal hanging from a hook. The creature's body was about the size of a man's fist, of a mottled brown color. From it extended eight long feelers, lined with suckers, and as the base two black, horny bills protruded. "It's an octopus, or sea spider. I have a standing order from a Chinaman up town to get them whenever I can, and once in a great while one is sent north or from California, and I buy it and let him know. For some museum? Bless you, no. He eats them, and by the price he pays, they must be extra nice. I reckon there'll be a grand spread over this one. It measures three feet across, which is about the ordinary size, although I have seen them nearly three times as big. I'd rather meet half a dozen sharks than one octopus. In almost any market in San Francisco you will find them from ten to twelve feet long. They are sold by the pound to the Chinese, and sometimes to Frenchmen and Italians. I kept a stall there once, and I have sold hundreds of them. The Chinese call them Chang Kwei Yu, and they are very fond of them. Italians and Frenchmen always wanted them cleaned, but Chinamen wouldn't buy them unless they were whole. I didn't understand this until one day when I sold about fifty of them to an old Chinaman, who was so particular about their having bills and suckers on that I sent a boy to follow him. He traced him to a Chinese doctor, who paid the old chap more for the suckers and bills than he had paid me for the entire lot. It seems that these parts were very valuable to them as medicine; so after that I made just double on my sales. They taste something like frogs, but are too soft and jelly-like to suit me. Angel Island is a great place for them, and any pleasant day you can see Chinamen hunting among the rocks at low tide, or hauling long nets for them.

"The largest one I ever saw alive had a spread of about twenty-two feet. It was a good many years ago. I was knocking about 'Frisco, where I met a friend who had got together a party to go up the coast somewhere near Vancouver's Island, and hunt for a rich wreck, and I shipped. We discovered the old hulk in about four fathoms. In the crew were two halfbreeds from Mexico, who could stay under water, it seemed to me, about ten minutes. They were pearl divers from the Panama Coast, and when they went down they carried a heavy stone to sink them, and a rope to make fast to anything they could find. When the oldest diver slipped over we could follow him on the bottom by the air bubbles. His mate held a small line that he signalled by. In about four minutes the signal came, and we hauled away. He came aboard with a jump, and said that he had hooked on to a cask or a box, and that as soon as he moved it a cloud of mud or sand rose, as if some big fish had moved, and, thinking of sharks, he had come up for his knife, which he generally took down at first. He seemed somewhat winded, and the other man said he would go. Taking a sharp knife in his mouth, he was lowered down and was soon out of sight. After he had been down about five minutes there came a pull on the life line that nearly jerked the skipper overboard. We pulled and pulled, until it was evident something was wrong, and we all gave way hard, and by the way it came we thought the whole wreck was afoul. In half a minute we had Pedro's head out of water, but the sight of it almost made us drop the line. The poor fellow seemed almost covered with a mass of snakes that twisted all over him. The arms and legs of the animal writhed about, some around his neck, others around his body, while fastened to his breast was a big bag-like body with a pair of eyes like a cat's, with the same green light you see in them in the dark. The skipper and the other diver knew what it was, and sung out for knives. They couldn't get it on deck, because three or four of its arms were slung below the bow cable. The diver lowered himself, and putting his knife in under the animal he slit it in two. The skipper in the meantime was at work in the fore chains, and he cut off the arms. Then with a jerk we had the man on deck. He was half dead and we had to cut the octopus from him piece by piece, and even after it was cut up the two claws clung to his chest and had to be cut out. It took us half an hour to clean him, as each sucker — and there were hundreds of them — brought blood when it was torn off. We filled two barrels with the pieces that we took from him, and the whole animal must have weighed 260 pounds, and probably more. We put it together afterward on the deck, and it measured from the tip of one arm to the tip of the opposite one twenty-two feet.

"It seems that the first man down started the thing, and when the next one reached the bottom he was tied up in a knot. For a minute he couldn't use his knife, and when he did make a cut at the animal it let go its hold on the bottom and sprang at him, and in that way we hauled him up."

A Peculiar Looking Object

"A Sea Monster" appeared in the *Star* (Montreal, Que.), 26 Nov. 1881. Buzzard's Bay is the early name of a bay of the St. Lawrence River in the Province of Quebec.

A Sea Monster. — Considerable excitement exists at Buzzard's Bay, especially among that class who "go down to the sea in ships," regarding the exciting story related by Henry H. Smith, an old sea-dog, who for years has plowed the surging billows in every clime. "Never," said he, "was I so frightened as yesterday just off Wing's Neck Light. I had been sailing on and off, skipping here and there about all day for fish. The sun was just sinking below the western horizon when I bore away for Monument Beach, off which place I have my moorage. When about one-half mile from the light I observed distinctly a peculiar-looking object just about two points off the port bow, and I should say one-eighth of a mile away, and making right for my frail little craft. It stood out of the water about six or more feet. The head resembled somewhat that of a full-bodied bulldog, although from each side of its head protruded horns, and away in the rear I could see part of his body or tail, as it propelled along at a frightful rate of speed through the smooth waters of the bay. The serpent, or whatever it was, came within twenty-five feet of my craft — near enough for me to plainly distinguish its colour, which somewhat resembled that of our native seal, a sort of a very dark brown, mingled with light spots, as it apparently appeared from the boat. When nearly opposite my craft he made a terrific breach out of the water, when I could see over twenty feet of his slim body, as with a hissing sound he quickly descended into the depths again, when all of this mystery of the sea was lost to view.

LAST MARINE MONSTER

"Canada Captures the Sea Serpent and Ends His Life" appeared in the *Daily Colonist* (Victoria, B.C.), 30 July 1882. Apparently the news story was originally published in the *Chronicle* (Arnprior, Ont.).

Canada Captures the Sea Serpent and Ends His Life
The Very Last Marine Monster Story (Arnprior Chronicle)

Sea serpent stories have been given the go-by by newspaper paragraphs of late, owing to the incredible yarns of persons who profess to have seen the "rale ould divil himself." Many people are said to have seen these monsters in various parts of the country, but as no one had ever been known to capture one, the public received the tall yarns related *cum grano salis*.

It is but a few years since Mr. Robert Young, one of our most worthy and respected citizens, caught a glimpse of an aquatic monster in Chats Lake, which he describes as being of enormous size and proportions. Captain Brown, of the steamer *Alliance*, also got a view of one of these monsters in the same waters the summer before last, and various other people claim to have seen large specimens at different times and at divers places. But this week we are in a position to announce the capture of what is probably one of the progeny of the real original old Chats Lake serpent, which has often struck terror to the hearts of superstitious river men. While coming down from the Snow Rapids with a tow last Monday morning, and while off Blackwell's I., the crew of the *Levi Young* noticed a huge serpent swimming ahead of the boat. Mr. John Dungan, chief engineer, and a deck hand named Shaw, jumped into a boat and started in pursuit of the reptile. They succeeded in getting within striking distance of the serpent, when Mr. Dungan struck it a blow over the head with his oar. The beast then turned and made for the occupants of the boat, literally churning the water with his tail in his fury. Another powerful and well-directed blow with an oar on the neck of the serpent laid it out dead, when it was taken in tow and brought aboard the steamer. The crew of the boat stretched it out on the rail, and measured it with a rule. Its total length was eleven feet, while the body was thirteen inches in circumference. Its jaws were pried open and a pair of compasses inserted, which were opened out to a distance of 6 inches. The description given of this reptile is the same as that given by Mr. Young and Capt. Brown, so that it is possible that the one just killed is a lineal descendant of the old king snake who has sported himself in Chats Lake for years past.

ITS EYES WERE SMALL

Sea serpents and lake monsters are interchangeable except for their locale. Sea serpents are associated with the coastal waters of the Atlantic and the Pacific. Lake monsters are identified with the inland lakes and rivers.

Although Toronto is spread for dozens and dozens of miles along the north shore of Lake Ontario, sightings of lake monsters are few and far between. Here is a verbatim description of the city's very own creature of the deep, its Metro saurus, from the columns of a leading newspaper of the day: "A Marine Monster," *The Daily Mail* (Toronto), 22 Aug. 1882.

A Marine Monster
Which Some of the Markers Saw at the Ranges Yesterday
Another Edition of the Sea Serpent

The sea serpent is not dead by any means, and the only thing to be wondered at (apart from its existence) now is that it is able to appear at widely separated points within comparatively short intervals. A few months ago it was seen (!) in the Indian ocean by a jovial party of pleasure seekers. It next turned up in the Mediterranean, but was frightened off by the prospect of a collision with one of the ironclads. It was again heard of in a creek in the vicinity of Hog[g]'s Hollow, and yesterday morning turned up in the lake in the neighbourhood of the Garrison common. The monster appears to have the power of altering its size to suit circumstances also. Sometimes if any faith is to be placed in the veracity of those who profess to have seen it — it is of brobdingnagian proportions. The locality also seems to have an effect on its size. In the Mediterranean and other warm latitudes it swells out, while further north it dwindles down from the size of an ordinary saw-log to a ship's hawser. This may be attributed to the witnesses, as the tropical heat of low latitudes has such a magnifying effect on some brains that they see everything "double." Further north this is not so apparent, and hence the size of the monster diminshes.

Yesterday morning was cool, and perhaps this was the reason why some of the workmen engaged at the targets on the Garrison ranges say the serpent they saw was not more than fifty feet long, and the size of a man's body. The story as told by one of them is in substance as follows: — Between eight and nine o'clock, while placing the targets in position on No. 1

range, a boy rushed up saying that there was a queer thing floating near the shore. Some of the men were curious enough to leave their work and hasten down to the shore. There sure enough was a large, blueish-grey mass floating lazily near shore. It had ever appearance of being asleep, as its body yielded to every ripple. Part was submerged, but the upper portion of the head floated just above the water. That part which was visible was covered with short stiff bristles in front, which increased in length towards the sides, and extended for a distance of about ten feet on each side. The back, or at least that portion of it which appeared above the water, was lighter-coloured than the head. A good view was had of the monster for upwards of three minutes, when suddenly raising its head out of the water, it gave a swish with its tail and started directly south in the direction of one of the steamers. Its head, as it raised it above the water, was very much like that of an eel, with the exception of the long trailing hair or whiskers. Its eyes were small, and as he thought he heard it give a short, sharp bark. A line of foam marked its progress out into the lake for about half a mile, when, turning sharp around, it dashed towards the Exhbition wharf, and again out into the lake, where they soon lost sight of it.

The men did not appear at all anxious to speak of the matter, as they feared their veracity would be questioned. As it is, their story is given for what it is worth, but surely the word of three men who saw it is worth that of thirty who did not see it.

HALF TERROR, HALF MADNESS

Here is a grizzly account of "one of the most frightful apparitions ever seen by mortal," to quote the words of old Captain Jones, as cited by an unnamed writer, probably in the employ of the *Cleveland Leader*, where this story originated. It was reprinted as "An Apparition" in the *Winnipeg Free Press*, December 14, 1882.

An Apparition
What an Old Sailor Saw Some Years Ago on Lake Ontario

Cleveland Leader.

"Talking about ghosts," said old Captain Jones last evening, as he cast a wary eye over the dark and stormy bosom of Lake Erie, while making a header against the storm down Bank street, "I hain't exactly superstitious, you know, but the dismal roar of that treacherous water and the sullen gloom of those storm clouds hanging over it remind me of a similar night long since past, when I was knocking about in an old-fashioned schooner on Lake Ontario. You see I have been a sailor man pretty much all my life," said he, as he tenderly shifted a very large chew of navy plug into the other cheek, "and I have had some mighty tough times of it, you may calculate. Well, as I was going to say:

"One Fall I shipped on board an old schooner from a port on Lake Ontario. We were engaged in the lumber trade. I had heard from some of the older sailors about the port that the vessel was haunted, but I was young, and not being a believer in ghosts paid but very little attention to the rumor. We made two or three trips and everything went smoothly, but one afternoon, while pounding down the north shore of the lake, we detected signs of a storm coming up from the nor'west. We made all preparation for a night of it, and if ever a crew underwent a tough one we did. The wind rose as the night came on, and the old lake was lashed into a perfect fury, while the darkness was fairly suffocating in its intensity. Of course all hands were on deck and each man had plenty to do. Suddenly the man at the wheel started from his post, and with a wild and terrified exclamation said: 'Look up there!' All eyes were instantly turned aloft, and the sight which met my gaze was seared and burned into my memory for all time. Standing erect in the cross tree of the old hulk was one of the most frightful apparitions ever seen by mortal. It was the figure of a man posing as silently as the rock of Gibraltar. A dim, unearthly light surrounded the motionless form and shed a pallor of death over it. Its right arm was raised and the fingers pointed steadily into the very teeth of the storm. The face was white as marble, and a look, half terror, half madness, gave it an expression of indescribable horror. Its hair was long and wild, and the furious winds that shrieked through the rigging tossed it in confusion around the head and shoulders. We were fairly benumbed with fright as you can imagine, and every man aboard the vessels stood looking spellbound at the awful visitor. I can't say how long it remained there, but after what seemed an age, the light surrounding it grew fainter, and finally the ghastly specter melted into storm and clouds and was lost to sight. After the first sense of terror had left us, a grizzled old sailor remarked to me that the ship was doomed as sure as fate, and he was right, for we went ashore that night, and all but two of us were swallowed up in the frenzied lake. The schooner was battered all to pieces, and with her cargo proved a total wreck.

"I learned afterward that a sailor had lost his life by falling overboard from the vessel some years previous to her destruction.

"Do I think it was his ghost? Well, if it wasn't no man ever saw one."

OF AN ENORMOUS SIZE

This is a lively and detailed account of the appearance off the Gaspé coast of a super-sized eel (perhaps). The sight of the marine creature (whatever its nature) may result in a "conversion experience" like the one described here. The "old salt" who beholds the creature is converted from criticism to acceptance, from scepticism to belief. "The Sea Serpent" is reprinted from the *Free Press* (Winnipeg, Man.), 21 Aug. 1884.

The Sea Serpent In Canadian Waters
A Huge Monster Passed off the Gaspé Coast
Not Only Seen but Heard

The much-vexed sea serpent question is at last brought home to Canadians by the appearance of one of those monsters off the Gaspé coast. The creature was seen from the steamship *Silksworth*, of Sunderland, which arrived in port the day before yesterday from Pictou, N.S., with a cargo of coal consigned to Wm. Muir & Sons. A *Star* reporter visited the vessel this morning at her berth in the new canal basin, and the chief officer, a gentleman of wide experience, very readily gave the particulars of the appearance of the monster. He stated that the point where the creature had been sighted was about mid-way between West Point, in Prince Edward Island, and Cape Gaspé, in the Province of Quebec. It was seen on Saturday morning between three and four o'clock. He was in charge of the deck for the middle watch and was passing up and down the bridge when the lookout on the forecastle called out, "There's a queer-looking thing on the starboard beam." He immediately looked in the direction indicated, and saw something about a quarter of a mile off. It was a remarkably clear moonlight night and the sea was calm, and he could easily see what, in the momentary glance he took, looked like a sail. Without giving any particular attention to it, he thought it must be a vessel, but jokingly replied to the hail of the lookout that it was probably the sea-serpent. He assured the reporter that previous to this he looked upon sea-serpent yarns as the sheerest nonsense. A second glance at the object, however, showed him that there was something remarkable about it. This prompted him to take up the night glasses, and he brought them to bear on it. The result was a perfect surprise to him, for there undeniably was the much doubted sea-serpent. It rose between twenty and thirty feet from the water there at least. It appeared to rise perpendicularly from the sea by a movement which resembled more the opening of a telescope than anything else he could name. As it appeared above the water its body seemed to expand as if inflated with the air, and the body tapered off from the surface of the water towards the head. At the water, as near as he could judge, the diameter of the body must have been between 3 and 4 feet. The whole appearance of the creature was that of a huge conger eel, the head, which was of an enormous size, resembling that of this species of fish in every particular. The head was the most prominent part of the creature and principally attracted his attention. The body of the beast appeared to be striped like a mackerel, with black and light coloured bars running round the body mingled in black at the back and silver gray at the belly. After looking at the creature through the glass sufficiently long to comprehend what it was, he ran aft to notify the captain and a couple of passengers they had aboard. By the time they had hurried into their clothes and got on deck, however, the serpent had disappeared. It appeared suddenly to sight the ship and sank beneath the water with the same steady telescopic movement with which it had elevated itself, although quicker. The part of the brute which appears particularly to have impressed itself upon his memory was the mouth, which much resembled that of a shark. About two feet below the head two tremendous fins stuck out from the body, extending for several feet on either side. Fortunately the creature rose to the surface again and was seen by Captain Read and the passengers, or the serpent might have been set down as the fruit of the imagination of himself, the lookout and the wheel man. As a matter of fact, he remarked that even with so many reliable witnesses as to the genuineness of the serpent he would not have believed in it. He had, he said, given the matter serious consideration since seeing the serpent, and he is now unable to account for his previous scepticism on the subject of sea serpents, as it is easy to suppose that sea eels are capable of attaining a giant size. The serpent on the second occasion of rising was about half a mile distant from the ship and well within range of the night glass. It rose in the same quiet manner as before, and was exposed to view altogether about three minutes. Before sinking below the surface it opened its mouth to its fullest extent, as if gulping in a supply of air, and closing its jaws gave vent to a loud bellow resembling both a dog's bark and the lowing of a cow. The noise was one of the most horrifying things imaginable, and involuntarily all on the deck of the *Silksworth* trembled when they heard it.

The lookout and the other members of the steamship's crew who saw the creature corroborate the chief officer's statement in every particular, and the affair is regularly entered in the log. The lookout states that he first saw it when its head had risen above the surface, and his attention was directed to it as the only object in sight.

An Extraordinary Object

There is a long history of reports that say that serpents dwell in the depths of Lake Cowichan in the interior of British Columbia. This account was titled "Snaix!" and appeared in the columns of the *Daily Colonist* (Victoria, B.C.), 17 Nov. 1885.

"SNAIX!"
An Extraordinary Appearance in Cowichan Lake

A short time ago Mr. Charles Morrow, accompanied by an Indian man and woman, was paddling in a canoe through Cowichan Lake. He was suddenly transfixed with astonishment and terror at the appearance of an extraordinary object which quickly lifted its head out of the water, and continued to raise it until it was some 20 feet above the surface. The head was eel-like in shape and the part of the body that appeared above the water resembled that of a gigantic snake, being of a reddish brown hue on the back and a dull white star on the belly. The monster, Mr. Morrow says, was "as big around as the *Amelia*'s smokestack." After surveying the party in the canoe for a few moments the serpent (for such it appeared to be) took a "header" and disappeared, leaving the water as greatly agitated as were the occupants of the canoe. In conversation with some old Indians afterwards, Mr. Morrow was told that there was a tribal tradition that many years ago several huge water snakes were often seen in the lake and that the forefathers of the Indians now living were in the habit of shooting arrows into them. If the presence of a veritable serpent in Cowichan Lake should be demonstrated, what an attraction for tourists the lake would become; and a price would probably be set on the head of any man who should offer to harm one of the remarkable creatures.

A Mirage of Some Sort

The Maritimes are fabled for their "fire-ships" and "phantom ships." Allow me to distinguish between these two groups of marine mirages or illusions. Fire-ships appear on the horizon and look like ships that are aflame. They used to strike terror in the hearts of all good Maritime seamen. Phantom ships are ghostly galleons manned by spectre crews. They too strike terror, though there are fewer sightings of phantom ships than there are of fire-ships.

Over the centuries fisherfolk and seafarers on the Bay of Chaleur have reported seeing fire-ships in their waters. They regard such sightings as forbearers or harbingers of bad luck.

In the account offered here, there is a reference to the Intercolonial Railway which linked Halifax and Montreal. "Bay Chaleur's Phantom Ship" appeared in the *Halifax Morning Herald*, 17 July 1885.

Bay Chaleur's Phantom Ship
(Special Correspondence Halifax Herald)

Chatham, Dec. 16. — The reports in regard to the phantom ships seen in the Bay Chaleur have been revived. Operators at Jaquet River and Charles stations on the northern division of the Intercolonial, report that the phantom, which is said to be an exact likeness of a full-rigged ship on fire, was plainly seen for miles along the Bay shore on Monday night. Various legends more or less ancient are current concerning the apparition or whatever it may be. The story is that long ago a mutiny occurred on a ship in the Bay Chaleur, and that so fierce was the conflict that the only person to escape barely survived to reach the shore and tell the terrible story of the conflict. Another story, still more improbable, is to the effect that during the continuance of the apparition a good many years ago, a boat put off from the shore with several men to see the strange thing, neither boat nor men being heard from afterwards. The phantom ship does not appear at very regular intervals, and had not been seen before Monday night for about two years. It appears to come quite close to the shore at times, and is probably a mirage of some object in the surrounding country similar to a ship.

CELEBRATED PHANTOM SHIP

Here is a thoughtful report of a mysterious vessel that rides the waves and tides of the Bay of Chaleur. "New Brunswick's Phantom Ship" appeared in *Newfoundland Evening Telegram* (St. John's, Nfld.), 18 Jan. 1886. Apparently the account is reprinted from the *Herald* (Halifax, N.S.).

New Brunswick's Phantom Ship
A Queer Tradition Lingering about the Bay of Chaleur

Annapolis, Dec. 18. — Some years ago, while on a visit to the Bay de Chaleur, I had an opportunity of learning a little about the celebrated phantom ship spoken of in the *Herald* of the 17th inst. A man named Harper, living at Little Shippegan, informed me that the phantom ship generally appeared on the Bay about the 22nd or 23rd of November, and stated that he had seen it several times. Some years ago, he said, a vessel belonging to the firm of Robin & Company, doing business at Paspebiac, on the opposite side of the bay, was given up as lost. One hazy afternoon, after all hopes of ever seeing the vessel again were abandoned, the fishermen living in the vicinity of Point Miscow were surprised to see the vessel (a small brigantine) enter the bay and cast anchor between the point and Shippegan. The news spread like wild fire, and soon the beach was alive with a joyous throng, assembled to give a welcome to the supposed lost ones. A boat was soon launched and five men got on board and rowed off to the vessel. The people on the shore watched them eagerly as they climbed on the brigt.'s side. Now the vessel was enveloped in a heavy mist or fog and the watchers patiently waited for the mist to clear away. The mist, however, hung on till near 5:00 o'clock, and when it raised nothing was to be seen of the vessel or boat.

This is the story as given by an English resident and one who firmly believes it to be true. The French seem to be a little mixed as to the origin of the delusion. A Frenchman at Port Daniel said that it was the Devil's ship coming after the fish, and the French in general believe that the summer following the visit of the Phantom Ship will be an unlucky one and consequently they do not exert themselves, as they do not believe in wasting energies. As far as I can learn the story of the ship coming into the bay, and the men beaching her, is quite correct. But that it was Robin's vessel is another matter.

A man named Campbell, a magistrate at Shippegan Gully, said he believed the vessel was looking for men and sailed away with the visitors on board. It was his idea that she was a pirate. Nearly every "old inhabitant" of the Bay has seen the Phantom Ship. It is very often seen near Gaspé Rock. During the equinoctial gales the French keep a regular watch, and someone generally manages to work up his superstition to such a pitch that he imagines he sees the ship, and exclaims: "Grand Dieu! I see the ship!" The report then spreads that the vessel has been seen, and nearly everybody believes it.
— *Halifax Herald.*

WONDERFUL SERPENT OF THE OCEAN

This is a long but lively narrative about the exciting escape of sailors and fishermen from the clutches of a creature of the depths that was "considered mythical." The story smacks of the sea. It was told by Thomas Grant of St. John's, owner of the schooner *Augusta*, whose account appeared as "Monster of the Deep" in two successive issues of the *Newfoundland Evening Telegram*, Aug. 25 and 27, 1888.

Monster of the Deep
"The Sea-Serpent Without Doubt!"
A Dory Hotly Pursued
Terrible Experience of the Crew
Captain Chidley's Narrative
Mr. Grant Vouches for Its Correctness

The following extraordinary narrative, left at this office by Mr. Thomas Grant of this city, owner of the banking schooner *Augusta*, is vouched for as being true in every particular by himself, the captain of the banker, named Chidley, and the fishermen who were chased by the sea-monster. The statement speaks for itself; the forcible sincerity with which the terror-stricken men afterwards told their impressions, and the detailed particulars which they give of the animal's appearance and size, establish the veracity of their assertions.

The existence of the sea-serpent has heretofore been considered mythical, yet it keeps on cropping up so persistently that it looks as if he were determined to force on a skeptical public the recognition of his *locus standi*. The creature, though rarely seen, has yet at some of those long intervals been viewed so close at hand and his shape and proportions have been so closely discerned as to resolve away the doubts of many unbelievers and to convince them that the sea-serpent is a veritable being and no mistake about it.

The evidence of Captain Chidley and his fishermen tallies with the description of some previous observers of this strange inhabitant of the deep, and would seem to place the question of its existence beyond dispute. The cuttle-fish had also a fabled life till the capture of a specimen of the tribe set the subject forever at rest.

It only now remains for our hardy "toilers of the sea," when next they come up with the animal, to capture it. The sea-serpent, on view in the museums of New York, London and the capitals of the world generally, would draw millions to see it, and would be worth more to its captors than all they would make at the Grand Bank fishery for years. It's only a question of time, with the crowded navigation of the seas increasing year by year, when a specimen of the monster shall be taken, and it would be a feather in the cap of Terra Nova if the honor and profit — which latter is more to the point — fell to the credit of her hardy sons, who man such vessels as the *Augusta*.

As respects the attack upon them by the sea-serpent, they state that while on Saturday, August 11th, a dory's crew (two men) of their number were setting out their trawls, they saw the monster following in their wake. So startling and threatening was its appearance that they were overcome with fright, threw away their trawls, and with the instinct of self-preservation, rowed with all their might for their vessel. For a moment, they thought 'twas a school of squid hounds, so many parts of the creature appeared above the surface. When it got close to the dory, one of the men threw a bait-tub at its head, upon which it turned its head and sniffed the tub, then turned again quickly and looked after the dory, its head being stretched up fifteen to twenty feet over the water. In shape the head was square and about twelve feet across. It then laid its head flat on the water, straightened out and pursued the boat. Now ensued a life-and-death struggle. The two men threw the strength of despair into the oars. For the best part of a mile their boat tore though the water with incredible velocity; but the monster-fish kept even pace, its head close to dory's quarter. At times it would gain upon its prey and would try to secure them by flinging a coil of its tail upon the boat; but the speed with which it was propelled baffled these manoeuvres. These attempts were made repeatedly, but each time the two fishermen were fortunate in eluding them. The monster seemed to make these attempts at the expense of speed, for each time that it did so it fell behind the boat. At one of these moments of danger the men flung the second bait-tub at it to lure it from the trail. It again turned its head and inspected the floating decoy, but at once plunged after the fleeing craft with greater fury than ever.

The two men, James Furlong and Richard Grant, pulled their oars with the force of desperation, their dory must have sped at the rate of, at least, eight or ten knots an hour; so overmastering were their efforts that they barked the skin of their fingers. The monster raised its long neck and head sheer above the water, looked down threateningly into the boat and threw immense coils of its tail at the starboard bow, its head being on the part quarter. The speed of the dory carried it safely through the impending danger; the monster's coils fell short of their aim, and struck the water in the boat's wake. This second escape invigorated the two seamen with hopes of safety, but they were still a long distance from their vessel, and their enemy, against laying his length along the surface, continued the chase. The race was still a stern one, but the beast had no further chance of scuttling the boat and devouring its occupants, by striking the frail craft with its tail. It pursued the dory to within a cable's length of the *Augusta*, and then sank in the sea, and for the time was seen no more. As nearly as the fishermen could judge, the creature was from eighty

to one hundred feet long, and above twenty feet across the middle of the body, in which part it bore a fin about two feet in length. Its eyes were full and wide, each about a foot or a foot and a half in diameter, and its head was shaped like that of a sculpin. Its tail was tapering, and resembled an eel's. Altogether, it was a formidable monster — a "hard ticket," as the fishermen term it — one that adds an additional danger to the fishermen's calling on the Grand Bank. About two hours afterwards all the crew manned their several dories and started off to their trawls again, assuming that by this time all danger of being molested by their ugly acquaintance had passed away. Five dories escaped it going out, but the sixth met it half way between the vessel and the buoy, at the end of the trawls, and at once the two oarsmen ceased rowing. The monster perceived his prey and in a few minutes was alongside the boat, and, as he stretched up his head, the two looked over the side and saw the glare of its fierce, threatening eyes just beneath them, and close astern they saw its tail in three or four heavy coils. The appalling sight and fear of instance and frightful death terrified them, and one of them gave a fearful screech, which was heard by the captain afar off on the vessel. Seeing the boat, he supposed there was a man overboard, and he fired a gun to direct the attention of the other dories to the danger. The imperilled fishermen recovered from the fright which had paralysed their faculties in time to put one stroke on their boat and escape the descent of the monstrous tail, which was lifted aloft to annihilate them. The huge blow fell in the water only one or two feet clear of the boat's stern. Again occurred a similar life-and-death struggle as ensued a few hours before. The two fishermen put forth superhuman efforts to save themselves, and eventually were successful; but the monster pursued up to the last moment, darting heavily through the water after them. The speed of each was about the same; the boat gained nothing on its would-be destroyer, and barely maintained a lead. At last, as they neared the vessel, the monster again raised its neck and head high above the surface and, bending toward the boat, gazed into it, when just at that instant the captain discharged a heavily-loaded firearm, upon which the brute fish dropped its head down upon the water and was lost to view. The men got aboard in safety, but were severely prostrated by the shock. In color they described their enemy as being of brown, and striped across its body. From the preceding narrative, it would seem as if this wringling monstrosity of the deep was reluctant to strike at its victims on either occasion when he looked at them from above the boat, with its head, in which respect it differs widely from the instinct of its namesake of the land. It may be that its head is its vulnerable point, and, with the proverbial wisdom of the serpent, kept it at a safe distance from the oars of the fishermen, and that its nature is to kill by strokes of its tail. However that may be, certain it is that these perilous adventures of the *Augusta's* fishermen have placed the world in possession of many new facts about the wonderful serpent of the sea.

A CURIOUS ADVENTURE

Here, indeed, is a curious adventure. It was titled "A Sea Serpent Story" for its appearance in the *Daily Colonist* (Victoria, B.C.), 18 July 1890.

A Sea Serpent Story
The Curious Adventure that Befell a Party of Vancouverites
While Crossing Howe Sound in Row Boat

The Vancouver *News-Advertiser* says: On Tuesday night Mr. S.M. Stewart arrived in the city from his logging camp, where he has been for some weeks. Yesterday, in conversation with some of his friends, Mr. Stewart recited an interesting adventure he and the companions with whom he came from the camp had on their way down.

They were crossing the mouth of Howe Sound about sundown on Tuesday night, rowing leisurely, when Mr. Stewart drew attention to a peculiar-looking log about two hundred feet away from them on their right hand. The log was a deep black colour, straight from end to end as an arrow and about 75 feet long. They rested on their oars for a moment, looking at it in a languid sort of way, and then concluded to row to it and see what kind of wood it was. They headed their boat straight for it and when within about 30 feet it sank in the water like a stone without the slightest noise and disappeared from sight.

The boat's crew were deeply astonished at this unexpected turn of affairs and were somewhat alarmed. They paused once more, half expecting to see it rise again, and dreading lest it would rise under and capsize the boat. After about three minutes of this expectancy they concluded, as nothing resulted, to continue their course. They accordingly headed their boat for home and started. They had not gone very far, however, when they again beheld the same object, this time on their left and a little nearer. They were now determined to see what it was, and directed their course once more toward it. When they got within about fifteen yards of it, the object again sank, but almost immediately reappeared, blowing a stream of water at the boat's crew and drenching them. This at once convinced the men that it was not a log they had encountered, and when the animal began lashing the water with its tail, which it did in such a manner as almost to swamp the boat, each man came to the conclusion that it was the sea serpent they had run across. They turned their boat and made off as rapidly as possible, but the animal seemed to think it was its turn to assume the offensive, and it pursued them, keeping at about ten yards distance, and lashing the water unremittingly. This flight and pursuit continued for about a mile, when the animal left as suddenly as it came. Mr. Stewart avers that the animal, whatever it was, was not a whale, and while he does not claim that it was the traditional sea serpent on a cruise in northern waters, he contends that it was an inhabitant of the sea not very often met with, and a very undesirable companion on a voyage in a small boat.

THE FLYING DUTCHMAN

This rare, real-life account describes an encounter in the sea-lanes of the New World the legendary Captain Vanderdecken, the master of the *Flying Dutchman*. Richard Wagner was inspired by the figure of the homeless captain, whose brigantine is doomed to ride the Seven Seas until the Day of Judgement, to compose his haunting opera on the theme of endless wandering and unrequited love. James Mason and Ava Gardner appeared in a popular 1950s movie titled *Pandora and the Flying Dutchman* loosely based on this lugubrious legend.

"A Spectre of the Sea" appeared in the *Herald* (Calgary, Alta.), 16 Jan. 1890. The article is apparently reprinted from the *Examiner* (San Francisco, California).

A Spectre of the Sea
The Bark that Sails by the Shores of the Unshapen Land
Canvas Set, but No Time at the Helm
Skirting the Crushing Pack and Dodging the Crumbling Bergs
How John Hansen Was Shocked

Stout John Hansen, wrapped up in furs, stood at the wheel of the bark *Reindeer*, a whaler of the Arctic seas. It was night, and the vessel was working along the ice pack with Cape Smythe just looming in the distance. The biting wind twirled about Hansen's feet, catching up the light snow and sending it swirling across the darkling water. There was a brisk breeze and the night was too cold for comfort by reason of the proximity of the floe; but Hansen cared little and cheerily whistled the tune of a folklore song he learned while a child sporting on the shore of a Norwegian fjord. He seemed as strong and fearless as one of his Viking ancestors when they faced the unknown Atlantic until "cloud-like they saw the American shore stretching to leeward."

Suddenly, right out of the pack came another bark, bow on. Her mizzen was gone and she veered and yawed strangely, but her sails were set and she was making fair headway. Hansen could hear the swish of the wind in her shrouds and the swash as she munched the bone in her mouth. In an instant she tacked and bore away. Then, before going 100 yards, she came about and made straight for the *Reindeer* again.

Hansen hailed her. There was no answering hail. His voice rang hollow and strange as the wind took it up and seemed to make of it a mocking echo. Then he hailed again. No return.

Hansen's lips grew white. His knees shook. He put his helm hard over and made for the open sea. Then he muttered a prayer which had not come to him since a ship burned under his feet in the Southern ocean way back in the 60s.

He had seen the spectral ship, the *Flying Dutchman* of the frozen ocean. The phantom came so near that he could see the glisten of the salt spume frozen on her rigging and the icicles which hung from her spars. There was ice upon her deck, and upon her wheel, and upon her battered hatches — ice, and nothing more.

Her decks gave back no echo of footsteps. Her sailing lights were out. She was so low in the water that she seemed almost awash — but she kept on into the darkness, reeling, staggering, unsteady, but on and on and out of sight.

John Hansen came into port. Death sat watching by his bedside. He chattered and gibbered, and stared with straining eyeballs. For no man may look upon the phantom ship and live.

But what John Hansen saw in the depths of that July night was not a spectre of the seas; nor was it the grim vision of a fever-stricken brain. It was something far more dangerous than an airy phantom — a derelict of the deep. It was the wreck of the *Young Phoenix*, which since the 5th of Aug., 1888, has been sailing through ice and gale, breasting the crushing pack, dodging the toppling bergs, guided by an unseen hand, and sailing for no known port. No one may say she has not touched the northern pole. No man may tell where she will be seen again.

On Aug. 8 of that year the whaling fleet was riding

between Point Barrow and Cape Smythe, waiting for the ice pack to clear, when down came the southwest gale, beating the sea into ridges and tossing the stout ships like the paper argosies of children. Down went the bark *Fleetwing* that had outlived many an Arctic storm. The *Mary and Susan* strained, plunged and foundered. The sea's great maw took in the schooners *Ino* and *Jane Gray*.

Things were lively on the *Young Phoenix* then. Both anchors were let go and the men were ordered to the pumps. She was leaking badly and the heavy seas swept clear over her. With the night the wind shifted to the west and came in stronger gusts. One after the other the cables parted and the bark drifted. Then an effort was made to get to sea, but the vessel fouled the *Triton* when trying to get over the bar. Her rudder, stern post and jib boom were carried away and the leaks were started freer.

The crew of thirty-seven men stuck by the bark until Aug. 6. By that time the water was at her lower deck. Her mizzenmast had been cut away. It was not thought that she could float more than an hour or two longer. The sails on the fore and main masts were set or partially furled when Capt. Millard ordered the men to the boats, and the *Young Phoenix* sailed away, rudderless and undirected, to meet whatever fate might come.

She was not seen again that year, and it was supposed she had foundered or been squeezed between the floes. But she kept on her erratic course, buffeted by the winds, caught by the currents, lonely and forlorn.

On May 5, 1889, she was seen again and boarded by Mr. Leavitt, manager of the whaling station on Cape Smythe. She was then close to shore, some sixty miles from where she had been abandoned. A few relics were taken from her, and the next morning she was gone again. She was little changed, and though water-logged, made good headway.

This abandoned craft is probably the phantom whose ice-sheathed shrouds and silent decks loomed upon the startled vision of big John Hansen that chilly night in July, and gave him that shock from which he may never recover. For nearly a year she had roamed the chartless sea, touching at no port, piloted by no hand, answering no hail, purposeless, silent and alone. — *San Francisco Examiner*.

A HUGE LOBSTER

This is a rivetting account of a struggle with a creature of the sea intent on destruction.

"Deep Sea Monsters" appeared in the *Herald* (Calgary, Alta.), 9 Sept. 1893. The account originated with a newspaper published in Saint John, N.B.

Deep Sea Monsters Experience of a Diver Off Newfoundland
A Lobster Like Thing, Eight Feet Long, Tries to Claw Him to Pieces

The correspondent at St. John, N.B., writes:

Sailors are said to be superstitious, and perhaps they are, yet who is the land lubber who has not read Jules Verne of Victor Hugo's *Toilers of the Sea*? The monster described was identical with the octopus or giant squid. Once in a while newspapers contain articles about sea monsters and their doings. So, too, Newfoundland men and men living on the coast of Maine report that living in the deep and silent caves of the sea is a huge lobster resembling the smaller fish in structure, but being very voracious. It is said that he seldom comes near the shore but that enormous lobster shells are sometimes found thrown up on land after a gale. All northern fishermen have heard of the monster, and I have seen them shiver in the cuddles of their fishing smacks as someone described the size and appearance of the fish. Never having seen it myself, I do not know how far the general impression is correct, but I have no doubt that it exists, and I will relate the story as it was told me by a Newfoundland diver.

"When the *Anglo Saxon*, a ship laden with costly merchandise, as many will remember, ran into Chance Grove, on the Newfoundland coast, striking a reef and sinking, the government at once took steps to have all that the unfortunate vessel contained removed. There was over a hundred person on board, but not a single one escaped.

"As soon as possible divers were brought to the spot, but it was difficult to go down. The first day we got below we could do little but lay out the plan of operations. The ship was on her side, the stumps of the masts turned toward land. I had never gone down before in water so far north, and the place was so wild that I was timid. Lines were attached to our bodies, and the ends fastened in the skiff above, so that if any diver pulled his line he was at once drawn to the surface. We walked around the bottom and around the ship with our feet weighted to keep us from rising. The water was a pale green, and I could notice objects quite plainly for many yards distant. There was a huge break, in the bottom of the ship, while her stem was staved in and so was her stern.

"One afternoon while my town men remained above repairing their diving apparatus I went down alone. We were now removing the bales from the after compartment of the break in the stern. The method of raising the goods was to lower down heavy hooks, which could be fastened into the bales after they were pushed outside. Some of these bales or cases would float and some would rest lightly on the bottom. I had selected a large case which I was about to move when, happening to turn my eyes, I saw outside a huge creature moving toward the vessel. I had never seen anything like it before. Its body seemed to be several feet high and about eight feet long and it had on each side an enormous arm.

"There seemed to be an unlimited number of legs attached to the hideous beast. Its colour was a dull brown mottled over with dark spots. Two round, shining black eyes were in its forehead and two supple horns, each resembling an enormous whip, likewise came out of his head. All this I noticed in one glance. A numb terror seized me, and involuntarily I moved for the outlet from the ship. But, as if knowing what I intended, this brute, looking straight at me with its frightful, motionless eyes, walked or rather crawled directly toward me. I hurried in the hope of being able to seize the hanging hook, now my only means of signalling the skiff, but I had hardly put my foot upon a gray rock outside when the two writhing horns of the detestable monster were twining about me and again untwining. Then he would touch me with those and sweep them up and down as if feeling what kind of prey I was.

"In my hand I held a crowbar, which I used to loosen the cargo. In my belt I carried a heavy sheath-knife. These were my only weapons. Suddenly and without any warning the monster threw out one of its arms and seized me below the shoulder. I felt as if my bones were being crushed. The more I resisted the more terrible was the pain. I still had the crowbar in my right hand, but it was of no use to me. So I let it drop. The monster's arm terminated in a claw, which opened and shut convulsively. This horrible mouth-shaped thing had two rows of shining white teeth as seen often on the inside of the two fingers of the lobster's claw. Several of these were piercing my arm almost to the bone. Some distance above the mouth-like hand I observed a joint, and then I drew my knife. But alas! The heavy shell so overlapped the flesh tissue that I could not injure my captor.

"For the first time I saw those terrifying eyes move and turn upon me. The whip-like arms again began to move and curl about my body. His head was not only about a foot from my body, and drawing my life once more I plunged it into the eye near me, turning the blade round and round. I saw that I had destroyed the eye, for an inky fluid issued out of the socket, darkening the water above the head. This checked the aggressive movements of the animal, but it did not seem to hurt it. I waited until its head turned, so I supposed, that he might be able to see his prey with the other eye.

"This was what I wanted, and with a swift thrust I sent my knife into the other eye down to the hilt. The creature reeled and the grip on my arm slightly relaxed, but though totally blind my captor did not release me.

"The agony of my arm soon grew unbearable. Then the light went out of my eyes and I remembered nothing more.

"When I recovered my senses I was in the skiff and learned how the divers, alarmed at my long silence below, had come down. They saw my plight, and after a time succeeded in severing my arm from the body of the fish, which they both declared was the awful deep sea lobster."

A MIGHTY SEA GOD

Here is a fictionalized retelling of a West Coast legend. Such retellings of native stories were a common feature of Canadian newspapers a century ago.

"Tribal Romance" appeared in the columns of *The Globe* (Toronto), 8 Dec. 1894.

Tribal Romance
Totem Story of Gi-a-wak, the Bird God
The Sea God's Command
Adventures of a Disobedient Kit-Kat-La Youth
Curiosity Satisfied
Saved by a Beautiful Maiden
As in Modern Romances the Course of Their Love
Does Not Run Smoothly —
A Typical Legend from the West Coast
(Special Correspondence of the Globe)

Victoria, B.C., Dec. 1 — Away back in the misty past a mighty sea god dominated the inlet which penetrates the territory of the Kit-Kat-La tribe on the west coast. On one occasion he issued an order forbidding, under pain of his extreme displeasure, anyone throwing clam shells into the water. The chief of the tribe was the unhappy possessor of two sons, who were continually in trouble because they refused to listen to the advice of their elders, and who were a source of great anxiety to their parents. One fine day as they sat upon the shore of the inlet they decided for lack of other diversion to stir up the sea god and find out what manner of deity he might be. Procuring a canoe they loaded it with clam shells, and the elder of the lads paddled to the middle of the inlet, while the younger took his position in the bow of the little craft and awaited developments. The big brother then proceeded to throw his cargo of shells overboard, but the first handful had scarcely touched the water when a tremendous commotion took place. The canoe was overturned, and the youth who had so wantonly offended the sea god was overwhelmed and sank to the bottom of the inlet. After a time he recovered consciousness, and when he opened his eyes he found bending over him a tall and beautiful maiden, who regarded him with tender compassion for a moment, and then in gentle tones asked him why he had allowed himself to commit such an indiscretion as that which had placed him in the position in which she had

found him. The gentleness of her speech served to allay his fears, and when he had recovered his self-possession she told him that she was the sea god's daughter, and that the only reason that his life had been spared was that her father was absent attending a great potlatch amongst the minor celebrities of that part of the world. When she had heard the commotion which had been the result of the foolish young man's disobedience she hastened forth to ascertain the cause. She took him by the hand and led him away across the bottom of the inlet, where he was enabled to live by the magic power of the nok-nok.

They came to an immense stone house. In front of it was a tremendous totem pole, on which were carved a crest and story that no mortal man would dare to attempt to interpret. They entered the house and found that during the absence of the daughter the sea god had returned. Before the fire he sat, an old man, with penetrating eyes and an expression of indescribable ferocity on his wrinkled countenance. As he turned his head in the direction of the newcomers the poor young man's blood froze in his veins. Not a word was spoken. The girl placed the young man near the fire and brought him food. When he had partaken of it he fell into a profound slumber. He awoke, only to have his fears excited by the terrible visage of the old man, who sat silently as before. The maiden again brought him food, and again he slept. Four times did he sleep and awake, and to him it appeared that four days had thus been consumed. Finally the sea god spoke. Addressing himself to the young man he said: —

"Your disobedience of my command merits death, but my daughter has pleaded for you because she loves you. There is one way that you may be spared your life and restored to your home and friends, and that is by making her your wife. Bear in mind that she is not to be treated as a being of earthly origin, but as the child of the sea god. Fail not to honor, to respect, and to love her, for if there be any lack of fidelity or affection it will result not only in her loss, but in the visitation of vengeance upon you."

The sea god, having thus delivered himself, relapsed into silence, and the young man again slept. When he awoke he found himself on the shore of the inlet at the exact spot where he and his brother had planned the adventure. Beside him was the sea god's daughter. He was unable to recognize the surroundings, for since his departure to the realm of the sea god a great change had come over the land. The maiden explained to him that each of the seeming days that he had slept had in reality been a period of ten years, and that forty years had passed away since he had disappeared beneath the waters of the inlet.

Together they proceeded to the home of his tribe, where the young man, for his was a perennial youth, told of his strange adventure. He was received with great rejoicing, and elevated to the chieftainship. Time went on, and the pair settled down to the enjoyment of domestic life. He fished and hunted and discharged the duties of his chieftainship, while she twisted his fish lines, made his nets, built the fires, and prepared the food.

But there was one thing that she refused to do. She never would bring the water from the spring. Every day the husband brought home a bucket of water, and on its arrival the wife stirred it with her forefinger. He questioned her as to the reason of this proceeding, but every time he introduced the subject she gave him a look that reminded him of the sea god, and he finally dropped it. He was a handsome fellow, as the maiden of the sea had long ago discovered, and he fell a prey to

feminine charms other than those of his wife. On the day that he had forgotten the charge of the sea god he took the water from the spring as usual to his home. His wife stirred it with her finger; but no sooner had she touched it than it turned an inky black.

"Time will dull the keenest weapon; the sea god's warning has been blotted out." Thus spoke the sea god's daughter. Then she darted towards the shore of the inlet. He called to her to come back, and ran after her, but she sped on with the fleetness of the gazelle, and upon reaching the water leaped in and disappeared from view. He tried to follow her, but the waves dashed him back upon the shore and left him in helpless despair. Now that she was gone he discovered that he loved her more than any of the Kit-Kat-La maidens, whose seductive smiles had lulled his recollection of the sea god's admonition, and he felt that he was the most wretched man in the world.

He launched his canoe and paddled out upon the inlet, calling and calling to his wife, but the echo of his voice was his only answer. Finally, when he was about to give up the search a large bird flew down to the edge of the canoe and made inquiry of the poor man as to the cause of his trouble. When he had related his story the bird said: —

"I have need of a servant in my house, and if you will serve me faithfully and perform the task I have for you I will restore your wife to you."

At the end of the period of the man's service he reminded the bird of its promise and called for a fulfilment of the obligation. When the bird, by many questions, had assured himself that his love for his lost wife had remained true despite his troubles, it revealed itself, and the husband was astonished and overjoyed to find that he had been serving his wife, who had taken on the form of Gi-a-Wak, the bird-god. Together they returned home, lived happily and founded the family of Gi-a-Wak.

This is the tale related by Mr. J.F. Bledsoe, now of Victoria, upon whom was conferred the honor of the family name and the totem story by the Kit-Kaw-La tribe of Indians, among whom he sojourned for a time.

A MONSTER FISH

"A Mysterious Serpent" appeared in the *Calgary Herald* (Calgary, Alta.), 7 Jan. 1896. The account, slightly reedited, is apparently reprinted from the *Montreal Star* (Montreal, Que.). Louis Cyr, who is mentioned in passing, was Quebec's well-loved "strong man."

A Monster Fish.—A monster fish, or something of that sort, has been seen in Black Lake, and people are wondering what it is. According to the tales told, on unimpeachable authority, there is a strange "something" in the lake resembling a gigantic serpent.

Years ago some strange animal, or fish, or serpent, or something of the kind, was seen at various times by different individuals, notably one Macfarlane, who for years trapped in the forest surrounding the lake, and who would take oath that many times he had seen a monster rearing its head out of the water and exposing a body from twenty to thirty feet in length. Occasionally since, the same animal has been seen by fishermen and others. In the summer of 1894, it was said to have been seen by many here, but the statements were discredited.

Now there is every reason to believe them to have been true, as within the last week or ten days it has been visible to many.

On July 19, Mr. Louis Cyr, with some other men, were crossing the lake, when suddenly there appeared on the surface of the water, about one hundred feet from their boat, what appeared to be a gigantic snake. It reared its head and showed from ten to fifteen feet of body, which in size was about the diameter of an ordinary stove pipe. It floated for quite a while, in fact they lost sight of it in the distance, as immediately it appeared they had business on shore.

On Thursday of last week, it had been seen by men working in the iron mines, some two hundred or more feet above the lake. Mr. J. B. Clearihew, one of our best-known residents, described it as "like a serpent showing a body the size of a man's head, and in length, visible, from fifteen to twenty feet. It lashed the water, and crossed the lake above the island in three minutes, making apparently for the mouth of the white stream, where it was lost to view." These people have since seen it: Fred Lamontagne, Louis Gagné, Joseph Vanbon, Francis Marron and Joseph Cloutier. The view was afforded while returning from the mines to the village from the railway track, and as late as July 25, and all agreed in regard to its length and appearance. If possible it will be captured, as all the available boats on the lake are kept in readiness for a chase.

IT WAS A SMALL PLESIOSAURUS

Generally newspaper articles about marine creatures published in the last century went unsigned. This article is an exception for it bears a signature.

Maybe its author E. Stone Wiggins should be addressed as Professor Wiggins, but it is uncertain what he professed or even where he professed it. Probably he was a natural scientist. Whatever his identity, he was certainly the author of record of "Monsters of the Great Lakes," this long and interesting newspaper article in the *Ottawa Evening Journal*, 26 Feb. 1898.

The rest of the heading pretty well outlines the contents of Professor Wiggins's article. Here is a small part of it, his own account of an encounter with a sea serpent along with a few particulars of related sightings.

Monsters of the Great Lakes
Sea Serpents and All Sorts of Living Things.
Prof. Wiggins Tells What He Has Himself Seen.
Of the Strange Inhabitants of the Fresh Waters of Canada.
Captains of Lake Steamers Add Their Testimony
to the Existence of These Creatures.
Their Stories Re-told

I had seen many stories in the newspaper regarding monsters in Canadian lakes, but took no interest in them till 1876. During the summer of that year I was spending my holidays on the Grand Lake, New Brunswick, a large deep water, twenty miles long and with an average breadth of four miles, connected to the sea by the outlet into the River St. John. During a gale I saw distinctly a large massive animal passing me in the teeth of the storm, about two hundred yards away, and though the waves were high the body did not rise and fall with them. In the trough of the sea I could now and then see its body which could not have been less than four or five feet in thickness and ten or fifteen feet long. It may have been and probably was twice that length. Its head, which greatly resembled that of a horse, was at least four feet above the level of the water. It moved with great swiftness — I should judge twelve miles an hour.

The following year it was seen by a number of persons, in one case but one hundred feet distant, and by the description they gave me I concluded that it was a small plesiosaurus which had come up the St. John River from the sea. The white bass, which frequently weighs thirty pounds, had been plentiful in the lake since the times of the Loyalists, many of whom settled along this lake. None of these fish have been hooked since the appearance of this monster. Two serpents were seen in this lake by Indians in 1824 and though Indians were numerous till 1850, not one of them would ever cross the lake.

A monster similar to this was seen in Skiff Lake near Woodstock, N.B., in 1887. Another, answering the same description, was seen at different times and by responsible persons, in Machias Chain Lake, Maine, in 1881, and was minutely described by the *St. Croix Courier*. It was fifty feet in length and two feet across the head. In September, 1886, a monster twenty feet in length was seen in Lake Ainslie, N.H., and in McQueen's Lake, N.S., one of much greater proportions in 1889.

THE PHANTOM RE-APPEARS

Phantom ships plough the Seven Seas.

The archetypal phantom ship has to be the one that was — or still is — captained by the Flying Dutchman, Captain Vanderdecken. When he cursed the Almighty as foul weather made it impossible for him to "round the Cape," the Almighty in turn cursed him to live and sail the Seven Seas till the end of days. His spectral ship, complete with its ghostly crew, is spotted from time to time, especially during stormy weather, and it will continue to be ... until he is redeemed through the love of a woman who is "pure in heart."

The coastal and inland waters of Canada have been visited by phantom vessels. "The Phantom Re-Appears" appears in the *Victoria Daily Colonist*, 6 Sept. 1899. The account has been slightly re-edited, and the list of the passengers of the *Willapa* has been dropped.

The Phantom Re-Appears —
Mysterious Barkentine Now Reported from Hesquoit —
Away for Dawson

Somewhat after the fashion of another famous ghost, that of the late Mr. Banquo, that phantom barkentine reported several times recently from points along the West Coast, resolutely refuses to be laid. It was thought that the last had been heard of it when Mr. Thomas Earle's manager at Clayoquot gave the denial to the previous reports to the effect that there was no sign of life on board. He said that he had seen men walking about the deck, and it was then concluded that the mysterious craft had only got a little closer inshore than safety would warrant, and had at the first opportunity stood out again. The *Willapa*, returning from the Coast yesterday, brings another report, however, which would indicate something serious amiss, if not on this same barkentine, upon some other and very similar craft afloat in the waters skirting the Vancouver Island coastline. This time the news comes from Hesquoit, considerably farther up the Coast than Clayoquot. John Goltz, a prospector, giving the information that he saw a barkentine, or at all events a three-masted vessel appearing to be barkentine rig, on the afternoon of August 20 for a week later than the vision had appeared out of the fog to the Clayoquot folks. At this time the weather was clear, and the unidentified craft rode within two miles of the shore, with sails partially set, and unpleasantly close to Sunday rock. Goltz distinctly made out a flag in the rigging and apparently reversed — in any event a signal of distress, and he would have gone out to learn more of the ship and her people but for the fact that the water was too rough to think of venturing on it in a small boat. He could not see any movement of people on board, nor recognize the nationality indicated by the distress flag. It seemed, however, darker than an American flag would be. The winds since the 20th ultimo have been westerly, which would carry the ship to the southward in the event of her rudder being carried away, which is supposed to be the case. Aside from this supplementary news of the phantom barkentine, the *Willapa* brought little specially interesting information from the Coast.

FIGHT WITH A SEA SERPENT

Here is an engaging article, with a depiction of some action and an affidavit that attests to the truth of the experience. "Was Not a Sea Serpent" appeared in the *Leader Post* (Regina, Sask.), 9 Nov. 1899.

Was Not a Sea Serpent
Eight Feet Long, and Looks like a Wolf Fish
Affidavits Made to the Fact of the Capture
Description of the Creature

Has the sea serpent at last been captured? That is the question residents of Victoria, British Columbia, are asking. Three thousand persons have seen the monster. Not one has been able to recognize it as belonging to any known species of fish or reptile family.

The man who captured it, when he saw it in the water, thought it must be at least twenty feet long. Great was his surprise when actual measurement proved that it was less than eight feet long. Pictures and descriptions of the monster seem to indicate that it is a variety of the ferocious wolf fish, a common article of diet among the natives of Iceland. Not that the residents of Victoria are ready to believe this. So firmly convinced are they that a new monster of the deep has been captured that affidavits have been taken of the method in which the fish or serpent was taken in the Euklatat Rapids, on the southern coast of British Columbia.

The following is a true copy of the sworn statement regarding the capture:

"These are the facts as to the fight with the sea

serpent, or wolf fish, or whatever it may be: — Three of us were in a fifteen-foot Indian canoe, anchored in the rapids, which run about twenty miles an hour in the spot where we were located. We were engaged in fishing for codfish. The man in the bow, named "White-Frenchman," who has been fishing the rapids for nine years, and who hasn't any other name in these parts, was just in the act of hauling in a cod on the line when the sea serpent poked its head above the water and made after the cod to devour it.

"As the monster was coming direct for the boat, 'White-Frenchman' thought he would take no chances, and, poising his gaff, thrust it into the serpent's side two feet from its head. After being landed in the boat, the animal or fish made a desperate fight for liberty and attacked the Frenchman who had wounded him. The old fisherman thereupon seized the canoe paddle and struck at the monster's head.

"In a half-stunned condition, the creature then seized the paddle between its jaws and crushed it in two, but afterward lay quiet.

"The serpent was then taken quickly to land and thrown into a salt water tank to keep it alive. The creature was afterward shipped to Vancouver, British Columbia, where it was on exhibition for four days alive in a tank, but finally died from its wounds.

"When alive it came to the surface of the water constantly for air, but was for the most time underneath the surface. Three thousand persons have seen the animal up to the present, and not one of them has ventured to give the creature a name or classify it.

"Sworn before me this 18th day of September, 1899.
    "A.A. ANDERSON,

"Notary Public.
    "SIMON RYAN,
    "D.H. FORBES."

This baby sea serpent, although only eight feet long and ten inches through the thickest part of its snake body, possessed enormous strength, and in fighting used its two sets of teeth, its flippers as claws, and its muscular body snake-fashion.

The snake had a gray mottled body, almost round, and had a mane composed of a hairy substance, which will stretch out over eight inches. The body is some inches over seven feet long. It has two flippers near the head, which look like reversed claws more than a fish's fins.

The head of the creature is the most remarkable part. It has an enormous jaw, and a long tongue, which when the animal was alive, was constantly darting in and out like the forks of a venomous snake. It is asserted that this tongue contains poison. The tongue is pointed, but not forked.

The creature had a large, clear eye, much like the eyes of a fur seal, but black and vicious looking. The jaw is heavy and of great strength, and encloses two sets of teeth. The front set are pointed much like cats' teeth and are strong set in the mouth. The top set, five in number, protrude, and when the jaw is closed lap into the lower set, which retreat from the mouth. Behind this set is another combination of molars, upper and lower, massed together in circular form. Evidently after the prey was torn by the front teeth it was masticated on the crunchers behind.

The monster will be sold to the British Columbia Museum of Curiosities at Victoria.

SEMI-AQUATIC CREATURE?

"Scientists Make a Discovery" appeared in the *Daily Colonist* (Victoria, B.C.), 12 Sept. 1899. Although the account is presented as a news story, it has many of the earmarks of a tall tale or a hoax.

Scientists Make a Discovery
Specimen of the Melanerpes-Eryphrocephalus Secured at Sooke
Thrilling Adventure with the Monster which Reaches Victoria Today

Those of British Columbia or the West whose residence extends over a period of ten years will recall without difficulty the circumstances in connection with the finding of the famous fossil human giant in the Happy

Valley section of West Sooke.

They will doubtless remember with interest also the notable discoveries of petrified remains of animals and birds of prehistoric immensity reported by Dr. Franz Boas and other equally eminent scientists, from the neighbourhood of Sooke River, some five years later.

Yet while these facts are entirely sufficient to invest the country lying between the city and the entrance to Sooke harbour with a peculiar interest to savants, and while the world of science must regard with especial attention any investigations intelligently conducted in this old feeding and fighting ground of the might sauranodontidae, it would seem that discovery as well as invention has still some things left wherewith to astonish the world.

The realm of studious research was rejoiced less than six months ago to learn that the perfect skeleton of a mastodon had been rescued from the icy preservation of an ancient Klondike creek bed, and great incidental discoveries were anticipated.

What, then, will science say when it becomes generally known that while the last members of the massive saurian family were supposed to have disappeared from the earth centuries upon centuries ago, it has remained for a party of Victoria scientists to discover in the heart of a little cup-like valley, hemmed in by majestic hills and not more than 30 miles from British Columbia's capital, an existent specimen of the Melanerpes-Eryphrocephalus — a specimen which until the culmination of the efforts of the party to capture it WAS A LIVING BREATHING ACTUALITY?

The party to whose endeavours science owes this great discovery started out from Victoria about ten days ago, establishing their temporary headquarters at the M. & L. Young ranch, at the farther end of the West Sooke road. They include among their number Mr. H. Wille, like Professor Boas, a scholar of German birth and education, for many years resident in Cincinnati, Ohio; Mr. C. Jameson Harrison, whose investigations have been directed chiefly to aboriginal life and lore; Mr. George Denny, whose interesting hand-book on the co-relation of Sanskrit and Chinook has attracted much attention; and Mr. E. Wardale Bradley, the name-giver and first explorer of Typewriter Island in the Maguire chain.

The scene of their discovery is not many miles from a small sheet of water known as Kemp Lake, yet so circumscribed and tightly walled in a spot — a veritable well within mountainsides — that it is not to be wondered at that its abrupt, precipitous sides have defied exploration throughout past centuries, and the heart of the mysterious treasury of ancient days might for another thousand years have remained undreamed of had not accident revealed the subterranean entrance way.

The discovery is due to Mr. Bradley primarily, for it was through his having lost his Virgil and retracing his walk of the previous day in the hope of recovering his treasure, that he quite literally stumbled upon the key to the great secret.

Passing through the darkness and swimming a narrow but black and forbidding subterranean waterway, he gained the closed-in nook in the mountains and soon noted the strange footprints in the blackish water.

They seemed to him to be clearly those of the Mela-nerpes-Eryphrocephalus, but scarce daring to trust his own unendorsed conclusions in so grave a subject, he braved the difficulties of return in order that Professor Denny might himself pronounce upon the pedal formations that had so attracted his attention.

There could be no doubt upon the subject, and having satisfied themselves conclusively as to the genuineness of the track, it became merely a matter of systematic trailing and organized attack.

The battle ensuing must indeed have been fierce and horrible, for Mr. Bradley learned unhappily and to his cost the danger of venturing too near to the scissor-like jaws of the savage creature.

His life was not endangered, but his beard and moustache were irretrievably ruined.

Eventually the Melanerpes-Eryphrocephalus was despatched, and the party regained their temporary home.

The steamer *Bessie* has been chartered to convey the remains to this city, and for this purpose goes out to Sooke today in charge of Captain James Fletcher.

The scientists report the country in which their explorations have been prosecuted as simply alive with game.

SAW SMALL SEA SERPENT

This news story appeared in the Toronto *World*, 19 July 1901. The journalist takes a jaundiced view of the whole affair. Woodbine refers to a race track that once stood near the Beaches area in the East End of the city of Toronto.

Saw Small Sea Serpent
First of the Season Scared Bathers
on Wednesday at the Foot of Woodbine Avenue
They Threw Stones at Him
Long, Dark and Sinuous, He Moved
Beneath the Surface and Departed Hence

Campers and cottagers who are trying to keep cool by spending these hot days along the lake shore in the vicinity of the Woodbine are more enterprising than any of the sea-side watering places, and beg to report the first sea-serpent of the season. That is, they say it was a sea-serpent; and altho they do not claim it was a hundred feet long and as big round as a barrel, they do aver with all solemnity and sincerity that it was the real thing. And it was seen not by one person alone, but by many, whose testimony cannot in the least be impugned by alleging hot weather potations as a cause for visionary trouble, why should others doubt?

The plain tale of fact has it that on Wednesday evening bathers and other persons on the beach, near the Woodbine, observed a long ripple on the water, which deserved more than a passing thought and glance, and got it. After watching it closely, they saw the ripple was caused by something long, dark and sinuous moving beneath the surface of the water. Whatever it was, it was apparently about 10 feet in length and approached close enough to the shore to be plainly seen. Tho a man might easily have waded out to it, there was no person sufficiently interested to take any chances by mixing it up with the stranger. Still, it made a good target for many stones, large and small, but they seemingly had no effect beyond causing it to turn out into the lake again and disappear.

Had a boat been handy the tale of the sea-serpent, as related by those who saw it, might have been substantiated beyond question by its capture and exhibition, but failing this unimpeachable evidence no doubt the campers will cheerfully show anyone who disbelieves the story the exact spot in Lake Ontario where the first real live, genuine sea-serpent of the season disported itself within their view.

WHAT THE MERMAID SAW

The words "comic relief" best describe the story that follows.

It might well be regarded as an early instance of an "infomercial." The story leads the unsuspecting reader from editorial content to advertising matter, seamlessly, in the manner of a news item. It appeared in the *Saint John Daily Sun*, N.B., 20 Dec. 1902.

What the Mermaid Saw in the Canadian Lakes
A Message to Canadian Women

Being a Mermaid of the Canadian Lakes, I only know Canadian women as they can be seen from my watery bed in the vast depths. I often wonder if up there in the sunlight you have pretty dells, mountains, and sandy wastes, such as we have in dear old water-land. I don't know about your mountains and your dells, but I do know you must have wastes; for every day, and particularly on one day of the week, you send down to us more waste than you know of. When your soap suds flow into our pure water, we have the power of sight to divide in the water the true from the false; and we find that in your soap suds there is a mixture that you cannot see, a mixture of silicates, ground glass, and adulterations that never dissolve in water, and consequently must be useless for washing purposes. You must waste money in buying such concoctions, you waste time in using them, you waste your clothes in rubbing them in. Alas! there is a lot of waste up there in the sunlight; but there is now waste in Sunlight Soap. Where Sunlight Soap is used by any of you, I find no leading refuse, no adulterations coming down to me in my home in the deep. Sunlight Soap reduces expense in the wear of clothes, and you don't waste money on loading mixtures, such as I have seen in common soap suds.

Please, dear Canadian women, don't send down any soap suds but those of Sunlight Soap. Have respect for your dear Canadian waters, and your purses, is the message of the Mermaid of the Canadian Lakes.

WITH A HEAD LIKE A HORSE

There were reports of a "sea serpent" with a head like a horse being seen to disport in the waters of Juan de Fuca Strait on the West Coast. In the following account it was spotted in Barkley Sound (as it is now spelled) in the waters of the Pacific Ocean.

This account is called "Saw a Sea Serpent" and appeared in *The Globe*, Toronto, 15 April 1903. The story was filed to newspapers across the land at the time when the Canadian Pacific Railway operated its own news service, just as later it operated its own private national radio network. Three decades later the "sea serpent" would acquire a name: Cadborosaurus, Caddy for short.

Saw a Sea Serpent
Off Bamfield Creek Pacific Cable Station
Story Vouched for by Officials of the Station
The Animal is 40 to 60 Feet Long,
With a Head like a Horse
(C.P.R. Press Despatch)

Victoria, B.C., April 14. — Officers of the cable stations at Bamfield Creek are sponsors for the story that a sea serpent from forty to sixty feet long and with a head like a horse has been seen off the station. The cable operators say in letters to local papers that the Indians had been telling of the existence of a sea serpent, but the stories are not credited. David Osborne, one of the officials, says that a week ago the animal was seen from the cable station to raise a big horse-like head and swim out from the mouth of Bamfield Creek into Barclay Sound. Mr. Godson of the cable staff says that when he first saw the animal it looked like a mass of seaweed, but presently he saw the head elevated and the big serpent moved off, its outline visible, toward the sea. Mr. Godson says it moved off with the speed of a torpedo boat. On April 10th an Indian saw the thing and was so frightened that he ran his canoe into the breakers, left it and fled along the beach to the cable station. The Indian said the thing had a head shaped like a horse and its body, ten feet of which was lifted, was the size of a barrel. The Indians in the neighborhood are terrified.

FIRE OR PHANTOM SHIP

W.F. Ganong (1864-1941), a native of the Maritimes, a botanist and a local historian of distinction, spent his most productive years teaching botany at Smith College, Northampton, Mass. But he returned to Nova Scotia and New Brunswick to enjoy his holidays and to conduct his research. He made signal contributions to natural science and the social customs of the region in the form of scholarly papers delivered before learned societies.

Ganong was drawn to the phenomenon of the fire ship and the phantom ship, the sight of which was frequently reported in Maritime waters, particularly in the Gulf of St. Lawrence, and notably in Bay Chaleur and Northumberland Strait. Ganong himself was not destined to witness the apparition or the effect itself, but he interviewed many men and women who did. He reported his findings in one of his academic papers, "The Fact Basis of the Fire (or Phantom) Ship of Bay Chaleur." It was published in the *Bulletins of the Natural History Society of New Brunswick*, Volume V: Bulletins XXI to XXV, 1903-1907 (Saint John, N.B., 1907). This paper, read before the Natural History Society on 4 April 1905, was revised, according to the author's note, in Jan. 1906.

Here in its entirety is that important paper on a natural phenomenon that has swirling around it the mists of myth and legend. Ganong's account may not be a memorate, that is, a eye-witness's account, but, as a description of the phenomenon of the flaming ship, it is dramatic, analytic, sympathetic, and definitive. The reader appreciates in every sentence Ganong's objectivity as well as the subjectivity of his informants.

The Fire or Phantom Ship of the Bay Chaleur

One cannot be long in the Bay Chaleur country, especially its eastern part, without hearing of the fire (or phantom) ship, said often to be seen on the bay. Until a short time ago I regarded the fire-ship as pure fiction, with no basis other than the proneness of humanity to see wonders where they are expected, or where others say they exist. But as a result of two visits to that country, during which I questioned many residents on the subject, I have had to change my opinion; and I now believe there is really some natural phenomenon in that region which manifests itself in such a way as to be imaginable as a vessel on fire.

First we note the literature of the subject. Naturally the imaginative writers who have visited Bay Chaleur have seized upon the story of the fire-ship as a rare treasure, and, adding to the wildest local tales sundry fanciful imaginings of their own, with embellishments of banshees, pirates or picturesque historical personages, have produced weird fantasies such as are preferred to truth even by grown-up persons. A type of such stories is found in Miss E.B. Chase's *Quest of the Quaint* (Philadelphia, 1902), which connects the ship with the voyages of the Cortereals, making it a vessel set on fire by one of them when attacked by the Indians. From such a treatment there is every gradation, through many newspaper, guide-book and other accounts up to serious descriptions of the phenomenon as something with probable fact basis. The best account of the latter type that I have seen, written apparently by Mr. A.M. Belding, appeared some years ago in the St. John *Sun*. It reads in part as follows: —

The extent to which a visitor may be impressed by the story of the phantom ship depends a good deal on the source of the information. Hon. Robert Young [of Caraquet] will tell you, for example, that frequently at night before a storm a large light may be seen on the surface of the bay. It may be seen in winter, when the ice has formed, as well as in summer, and it is not confined to any one portion of the bay. Sometimes it is much brighter than at other times and appears to dance along the surface. Joseph Poirier said he had seen it so bright that the reflection would appear on the houses at Grande Anse. Rev. Father Allard said he had seen it several times this season. In fact it appears to be quite a common phenomenon, though nobody is able to explain its cause....Those who decline to place full reliance in this interesting story [viz. the fanciful legend] nevertheless admit that sometimes the mysterious light emits rays that shoot into and athwart the gloom, and might by a particularly well nourished imagination be likened to the flame-lit rigging of a ship.

The information I have myself been able to collect from those who have seen the light is as follows. Of course I have sifted all testimony to the best of my ability, eliminating all exaggerations, whether these be due to the habit of a humanity to make a story as big and good as possible, or to the common tendency to gull an impressionable stranger, or to mere ignorance, superstition or mendacity.

Four years ago Captain Turner of Riverside, Albert County, a clear-headed sea captain, told me, in answer to my mention of the fire-ship as a freak of the imagination, that he had himself seen it and hence knew it to exist. Later, on my first visit to Caraquet, I was told by a lady, in whose word I have absolute confidence, that her attention was attracted one night by a light off Caraquet, which looked so much like a vessel afire that she supposed it to be one of her husband's schooners, and called him in alarm, only to find that it was the fire-ship. A prominent resident of Miscou, Mr. James Harper, told me he has seen it but once, in the winter on the ice off Clifton. It was seemingly some ten miles away and kept rising and falling, dying down to a very small scarcely visible flame, then rising slowly into a column "looking thirty feet high." It was not in the form of a ship, but a column, but people told him it was the fire-ship. He was told it preceded a storm, but he took notice and no storm followed. Mr. Robert Wilson of Miscou, who sails much on Bay Chaleur, tells me he has seen the fire-ship, (or as he calls it, the "burning ship"), several times. The time he was nearest it was about eleven years ago off Caraquet on a very dark night. The light appeared ahead, and finally he came near and passed within 100 yards to windward of it, so that he saw it with perfect clearness. It was somewhat the shape of a half-moon resting on the water, flat side down, or like a vessel on the water with a bowsprit but no masts etc., and "all glowing like a hot coal." He dared not run nearer and passed it, keeping his eyes upon it until far beyond. On other occasions he has seen it, at various distances, and has come to pay little attention to it. Sometimes it looked somewhat like a ship, sometimes not, and sometimes it vanished while he was watching it. Usually it is dancing or vibrating. Again he has seen it as one tall light which would settle down and rise again as three, which would again settle and so on. Recently I have been told by Dr. J. Orne Green of Boston, whose connection with Miscou is mentioned below, that Mr. Wilson reports seeing the light this (1905) autumn; it appeared ahead of his boat as he sailed up the bay, vanished as he neared it, and in a few minutes re-appeared astern. Mr. Andrew Wilson the other leading resident of Miscou, has also seen it when it resembled a whaleboat, not a ship, in form. Mr McConnell, keeper of the light at Miscou Gulley, tells me that he has seen the fire-ship, about two miles away but it did not look to him like a ship, but more like a big bonfire. Several others have told me that they have seen it, (the great majority of the residents in the region averring that they have seen it at one time or another), most of them agreeing that at times it looks like a ship on fire, but that at others more like a round light. All agree that it usually precedes a storm, and is seen over the ice in winter as well as over the water in summer. On the other hand, other trustworthy residents of Miscou, notably Mr. Jas. Bruno and Mr. Ed. Vibert, both of whom sail much on the bay, tell me they have never seen it, and do not believe in its existence.

So much for local testimony. But it receives confirmation from another source. For many years past Dr. J. Orne Green of Boston, a Professor in the Harvard Medical School, has spent several weeks on Miscou and has taken a great interest in all that relates to the region. He tells me that he has himself seen a light which he was told was the fire-ship. Many years ago when running at night towards Caraquet he saw a fire off in the bay and called the attention of his companions to it, but finally thought it must be a woods fire on the north side of the bay. Reaching Caraquet, however, he found the people excited, because they said the fire-ship was out in the bay. He told them of his belief that it was a woods fire, but they declared this could not be, because it had moved. The wind at the time was gentle, from the southwest, but it was followed the next day by a great northwester. His interest being thus aroused, Dr. Green, in later years, attempted to investigate the phenomenon. He found that it was reported not only in Bay Chaleur but also in the Gulf of St. Lawrence as far south as Northumberland Straits. He came to the conclusion that while the stories were mostly exaggerated and distorted there was nevertheless some basis for them in fact and that there does occur in this region some natural light of the general nature of "St. Elmo's Fire." This was exactly the conclusion to which I had come independently, as stated in this note when originally read before this Society.

Grouping together all the evidence it seems plain, — *first*, that a physical light is frequently seen over the waters of Bay Chaleur and vicinity; *second*, that it occurs at all seasons, or at least in winter as well as in summer; *third*, that it usually precedes a storm; *fourth*, that its usual form is roughly hemispherical with the flat side to the water, and that at times it simply glows without much change of form, but that at other times it rises into slender moving columns, giving rise to an appearance capable of interpretation as the flaming rigging of a ship, its vibrating and dancing movements increasing the illusion; *fifth*, its origin is probably electrical, and it is very likely a phase of the phenomenon known to sailors as *St. Elmo's Fire*.

I have, of course, made efforts to ascertain if any such phenomenon is known elsewhere in the world. Professor R. De C. Ward, Assistant Professor of Climatology in Harvard University, writes me that he knows of no record of a similar phenomenon, and no development of St. Elmo's Fire so great that it could be mistaken for a burning ship. Professor A.H. Pierce, my companion in my visit to this region last summer, has, however, called my attention to references to an allied subject in the Journal of the Society for Psychical Research, XXII, 1905, 108, and again in the Proceedings of the same Society, XIX, 1905, 80, where an account is given of lights claimed to have been seen around Tremadoc Bay in Wales; but the conclusion is reached that in all probability they have only a subjective basis, though the statement is also made that lights of unexplained origin were reported as common on the Welsh Coast over two hundred years ago. It is also of interest to note that Schmitt's newly-published *Monographie de l'Isle d'Anticosti* mentions manifestations of St. Elmo's Fire observed at that Island.

It is plain that in this phenomenon we have a subject which invites accurate investigation. It can best be studied by a scientifically-trained person, a physician or other student accustomed to scientific evidence, resident at Caraquet or Grande Anse.

THE PHANTOM SHIP OF ETOBICOKE

As a young sailor in 1910, Rowley W. Murphy experienced one of "the mysteries of the sea." Fifty years later, the veteran seaman and marine historian still cherished the memory of the sight of the strange steamer in Lake Ontario off Etobicoke in the West End of Toronto.

Was it a vision? A sighting? A spectre? According to his own account, written half a century after the initial encounter, Murphy remained of two minds about the nature of the "ghostly lake steamer."

Murphy's account is reprinted from "Ghosts of the Great Lakes," *Inland Seas*, Summer 1961.

My father, a cousin, and I were on a holiday cruise around the west end of Lake Ontario, and as we were late getting underway from Toronto Island, and were running before a light easterly, decided to spend the night in the quiet, sheltered and beautiful basin at the mouth of the creek, spelled "Etobicoke" — but always pronounced "Tobyco" by old timers. (This seems hard for present residents of that area to tolerate, as they insist on trying to pronounce each syllable.)

In 1910, the Tobyco Creek was really a small river which made an abrupt turn westward and widened into a small lake, with a good beach held by poplar trees, between this harbour and the Lake. There was perfect shelter in this excellent harbour from wind from any direction, though in a hard easterly, it was not easy to reach Lake Ontario through the narrow harbour entrance.

At the date of this cruise, there was one brick farm house to westward of the harbour entrance and no buildings at all among the walnuts and oaks on the lovely grassy banks of the creek, except one ancient landmark, known as "The Old House," from the veranda of which Lieutenant Governor Simcoe is said to have shot a deer in 1794. This house was in good condition, when a few years ago it was torn down to increase parking space for a supermarket! The whole area is now completely built up, but in 1910 the beautiful grassy plains contained no buildings from Lake Ontario to the Lakeshore Road, except the landmark mentioned.

Our cruising yawl, with a larger sister of the same rig and a still larger Mackinaw (one of several "fish boats" converted to cruising yachts with great success), were the only occupants of the harbour this perfect night. The crews of the three yachts numbered eleven in all, and as is generally the case, after dinner was over and dishes done, gathered on deck in the moonlight to engage in the best conversation known to man.

All hands turned in earlier than usual, there being no distractions ashore, and by midnight were deep in happy dreams, helped by the quiet ripple alongside. At what was about 1:30 a.m., the writer was wakened by four blasts on a steamer's whistle. After waiting for a repetition — to be sure it was not part of a dream — he put his head out of the companionway.

There, flooded by moonlight, was a steamer heading about WSW. — at about half speed, and approximately half a mile off shore. She had a good chime whistle but not much steam — like *Noronic* on that awful night of September 17, 1949, who also repeated her four blasts many times.

But who was she? On this amazingly beautiful night, with memory strained to the utmost, it was difficult to do more than think of who she was not! She was considerably smaller than the three famous Upper Lakers, *China*, *India*, and *Japan* (about this date under Canadian registry, known as *City of Montreal, City of Ottawa*, and *City* of *Hamilton*). She was not as small as *Lake Michigan*, but like her, did not appear to be of all wooden construction. However, there were many in the past, of quite related design and size. The vessel seen had white topsides and deckhouses, and appeared to be grey below her main deck, like the Welland Canal-sized freighters (at this date, the big wooden steamers of the Ogdensburg Line of the Rutland Transporation Company). *Persia* and *Ocean* were like her in size and arrangement, but were all white and came to known ends, and of course *Arabiana* was of iron, and was black.

In this appearance off "Toby Coke" (a variant of spelling), the starboard light, deck lights and some seen through cabin windows, had the quality of oil lamps; and her tall mast, with fitted topmast, carried gaff and brailed up hain-sail. Her smokestack was all black, and she had no hog beams — but appeared to have four white boats. Her chime whistle was a good one, but was reduced in volume as previously mentioned, and was sounded continuously for perhaps ten minutes. Very soon all hands now watching on the beach decided that something would be done. So a dinghy was quickly hauled over from the basin, and, with a crew of four made up from some of those aboard the three yachts, started to row out with all speed to the vessel in distress, to give her what assistance might be possible.

As the boys in the dinghy reached the area where something definite should have been seen, there was nothing there beyond clear and powerful moonlight, a few gulls wakened from sleep — but something else, impossible to ignore. This was a succession of long curving ripples in a more or less circular pattern, which just might have been the last appearance of those caused by the foundering of a steamer many years before on a night of similar beauty. In any case, the four in the dinghy returned in about an hour, reporting also small scraps of wreckage which were probably just old driftwood, seldom seen with any fresh breezes blowing.

But something more there was. This was the appearance to the visual and audible memory, which those on the beach and those afloat had seen and heard, of something which had occurred in the more or less distant past, and which had returned to the consciousness of living men after a long absence.

Whatever the cause, the experienced crews of the three yachts mentioned were of one mind as to what had been seen and heard. At least eleven lake sailors would be unlikely to agree on the character of this reappearance without good reason! And the reason was certainly not firewater working on the mass imagination, as no one of the three yachts had any aboard. So, reader, what is the answer?

FIRE-SHIP OF NORTHUMBERLAND STRAIT

Northumberland Strait is turbulent and it separates Nova Scotia and Prince Edward Island. Until it was spanned by the Confederation Bridge, it was the domain of ferry-boats and the stage-setting for spectacular appearances of the Fire-Ship.

It is known as the Burning Ship or the Fire-Ship of Northumberland Strait. Here is an account of its appearance told by Mrs. C.V., an informant from Halifax, N.S., who was living at the time of the sighting, about 1912, near Murray Harbour North, on the eastern end of Prince Edward Island.

The account originally appeared in Edward D. Ives's "The Burning Ship of the Northumberland Strait: Some Notes on that Apparition," *Northeast Folklore*, Vol. 2, 1959.

Now I will try to tell you just what I seen one afternoon the latter part of September. It was a beautiful day. There was not even a ripple on the water — no wind and the sun shining. I could see the shore of Cape Breton. I happened to look to my left and I seen a ship a long way away. It took about one-half hour as far as I could judge before I could see her good. When she came in full view I called my boy Fred (he was between seven and eight years) to come to me and see the vessel coming. Such a beautiful ship I never seen in my life. Something about her seemed different from other vessels. The sails seemed to be pure white and the ship seemed to be shining black. As it came nearer it seemed to lose speed, and as it came opposite our house it stopped still. I said to Fred, "Perhaps they are coming ashore." We got up on the banks to watch. There was no sign of anyone on board and no dory on tow.

I can't remember just how long it was, but I think about ten minutes after she stopped I seen smoke rising very slow all over the deck. Then it was only a few minutes I seen men that seemed to come up from below and they were running around the deck every way. Then as they were running around I seen a low flame all over the deck. When the flames started the men climbed up the masts of the vessel. When they was about halfway up the masts the sails caught. All the sails seemed to catch at the same time. I could not see the men any more as the flames hid my view. We watched it until the flames died and everything crumbled to the deck. There was nothing left but the hull on the water, and gradually it seemed to sink lower and finally disappeared as if it gradually filled with water and sunk.

I had forgotten that I had heard of the burning ship. My brother happened to come to see us just as the spars crumbled. When I seen him coming I ran to meet him all excited for I thought it was a real ship. He said, "Carrie, have you forgotten about the ghost ship?"

The story is that that ship burned years ago and the belief is that it is the souls of those that perished by fire. The story is they were drinking below or asleep. It does not appear every year and not always at the same time. At that time there was no gasoline boats. When the gasoline boats came to that shore they tried to get near to it, but the most of them were too afraid to go too near as they said the heat from it was intense....It seemed to me it was only half a mile off our shore....My father used to take his powerful field glasses and watch it. He seen just what I seen....Some fished there for years and never seen it.

PHANTOM SHIP OF THE BAY OF CHALEUR

The Phantom Ship of the Bay of Chaleur exists in story and song if not on the high seas. Catherine Jolicoeur began to collect ghost ship legends in 1960 and she eventually compiled over one thousand sightings from all over the world. "People who see the Phantom Ship are not just imagining things," she explained. "They certainly see something. One theory is that it's a kind of mirage; others think it's a marine phosphorescent manifestation."

She found a great many tales of a phantom ship that haunts the Bay of Chaleur, the turbulent body of water that lies between Quebec and New Brunswick. One of the most interesting features of some of the tales of phantom ships is the death motif: to behold it is to have a foretaste of death. Soon someone will die. That belief was sometimes attached to the *Teazer*; Helen Creighton heard one person say: "If you see the *Teazer* you will die before the year is out."

This account was related by Mrs. Joseph Comeau of Carleton, Gaspé, Quebec. It comes from unpublished research compiled by Edith Fowke which first appeared in John Robert Colombo's *Ghost Stories of Canada* (2000).

In June 1912, when I was twelve years old, after three or four rainy days ... one foggy morning near a sandy shoal called Larocque Shoal I had the sudden impression of seeing an enormous ship coming between two rocky capes and moving. I cried, "Papa, look at the ship run aground there near the shore, scarcely three hundred feet from us."

My father said to me after a long silence, "That, my child, is the fire-ship, look at it well." It was indeed the shape of an enormous vessel with dark grey sails flecked with white. You could distinguish the masts, the sails, large and small. I saw no rudder or bow, it was all a big mass. I didn't see any people but instead some black shadows overlapped each other; they resembled bodies or barrels. I was thown into confusion. It passed very quickly. After a good ten or fifteen minutes the famous ship advanced into the Bay of Chaleur with bigger waves, broke up, disintegrated, as though the hull, the sides, were eaten; finally it all disappeared from our sight, carried away by an enormous wave. My father seemed frightened by the apparition of the phantom ship.

We spoke of it at dinner. I recall that Papa spoke like this: "The first time that I saw it was the year that my father died; and another time, my brother died in the Klondike. This time I don't know what will happen within the year." In the month of October the same year, a little sister died....

July 1914, after a stormy night ... my brother and I saw a mass of black smoke, which seemed to have a long broad opening surface plunging into the most extensive of the two springs whose surface resembled a layer of water fifteen to thirty feet around. The rest of this mass was high, resembling a little mountain, taking different forms, swelling like sails. One would have said an animal whose sides moved in breathing. We were like jellyfish through fright, holding our breath. After quite a long time, at least half an hour, the black mass, as though satisfied, began to move, rocking, doubtless drawn by the sea, took the form of a great ship, releasing the sails, which we believed to be of smoke, and quietly launched itself into the sea between the two rocky capes....Concerning this sight of the phantom ship we weren't allowed to tell these stories of the abnormal sights we'd seen; we had to keep the secret lest we be taken for superstitious people.

CREATURES THAT ARE PROBABLY UNIQUE

Mermaids and mermen are creatures of fantasy. Such "merfolk" make their homes in fairy tales like Hans Christian Andersen's "The Little Mermaid."

Or do they? Perhaps they also exist in the real world. Perhaps they inhabit the world's seas. On record are sightings of mermaids in Canadian waters. They are described by practical-minded sailors and seamen.

Here is one such sighting. The intriguing item comes from the *Delbourne Progress*, Delbourne, Alta., 31 Aug. 1917.

Real Mermaids in Hamilton
Spaniard Possesses Two Most Curious Creatures, Half Human, Half Fish

J.E. Smith, a Spaniard residing in Hamilton, Ont., possesses two creatures that are probably unique. He considers them to be mermaids. Though these are described as "fabled" or "fictitious" creatures in the dictionaries, the creatures in Mr. Smith's hands have heads shaped like those of human beings and bodies that are distinctively fish-like. One is much larger than the other, and is considered to be the mother, and reckoned to be 300 years old. Both have fine hair like a human being, and a small moustache and beard. The head is attached to a human-like neck which merges into the fish-like body, and the arms are something like those of a monkey, only that the fingers are webbed. He has been offered $700 for his curios. It is said that the creatures were found in the wreck of a ship in the Arabian Sea.

THE DEVILFISH EPISODE

The author of the official report that is reproduced here is John W. Thompson, a sergeant in the Canadian Army. Although not a dramatic writer, Sergeant Thompson was a careful observer and had a dramatic incident to relate.

A Chinese internee at the William Head Quarantine Station was attacked by an octopus. The name of the Chinese man has not been recorded, nor were his injuries noted. He was one of many of the internees who were awaiting transport back to China at the end of World War I.

From 1913 to 1923, the Army was charged with the operation of the William Head Quarantine Station, located near Victoria, B.C. It is estimated that, in all, 88,000 Chinese passed through this one quarantine station.

Sergeant Thompson's report, written in the form of an official letter, was discovered in an old photographic album. It was first published by archivist J. Robert Davison as part of his article "Chinese at William Head" in *British Columbia Historical News*, Volume 16, No. 4. The article was drawn to my attention by Richard Thomas Wright, author of the scholarly study *In a Strange Land: A Pictorial Record of the Chinese in Canada 1788-1925* (1988).

Coolie Repatriation Camp
William Head
Victoria, B.C.
1st April, 1920

Lieutenant Heritage
William Head

Sir

In compliance with your request, I beg to submit the following description of the devilfish episode which occurred some months ago, when one of our Chinese charges was attacked by an octopus while engaged in gathering mussels, crabs, and other presumably edible material on the beach.

The incident occurred somewhere about three o'clock in the afternoon, the fatigue parties had just been disbanded for the day and I was making my final tour of inspection to ascertain if the work had been thoroughly carried out in accordance with my instructions, and I had just reached that part of the camp which abuts on the wharf when I observed a large number of coolies rushing over the rocky hill which forms the southern bastion of the compound and apparently running towards some common objective, or central point of interest, as they were all moving in one general direction. They appeared to be abnormally excited, as they were gesticulating frantically, and ejaculating vociferously, a circumstance which interested me to such an extent that I too joined the procession to ascertain the meaning of their unusual perturbation.

After pushing my way through the dense crowd who were congregated on the southern slope of the hill, and on all other points of observation adjacent to the sea, I observed a struggling crowd on the further rocky shore of the small bay which lies just back of the No. 3 latrine, who were evidently the cynosure of all eyes, and on pushing through the crowd to a better point of observation, I discovered that they had effected the capture of a very large octopus, measuring fully eight feet from tip to tip of the tentacles, and weighing approximately in the neighbourhood of one hundred and fifty pounds, which according to their statement had opened the offensive by wrapping its tentacles around the leg of an incautious chinaman whose contiguity to the water had rendered such an action possible, and attempted to pull him into the sea, an assertion which was substantiated by the fact that they were still engaged in disentangling its tentacles from his leg when I arrived, and I have very little doubt that if it had not been for the timely arrival of succor he would have been dragged under water.

I may say that Lance Corporal Wilson of the C.M.P. saw the remains of the monster a short time after on the ablution table where he could form a fair estimate of its size, although by that time the major portion of it had been expeditiously converted into "chow-chow" by the omnivorous Chinamen.

They appear to be very numerous as four others were subsequently captured here, one of which weighed in the vicinity of one hundred pounds.

I have Sir
    The honour to be
        Your obedient servant

    (sig.) John W. Thompson Sergt.

P.S. This incident was duly reported to Sergt. Major Scribbens at the time.

OGOPOGO AND THE LOCH NESS MONSTER

Ogopogo is routinely described as Canada's Loch Ness monster, but the reverse is true. Nessie, the monster of Loch Ness, should be described as Scotland's Ogopogo.

There are two reasons why this statement is true. The first reason has to do with the priority of sightings. Setting to one side native and Christian missionary legends, 20th-century reports of sightings of Ogo in British Columbia's Lake Okanagan predate by some years the reported appearances of Nessie in Loch Ness in Northern Scotland. The second reason has to do with the immediate causes of the sightings. Here we have to tread carefully — and on water.

As Mary Moon notes in *Ogopogo: The Okanagan Mystery* (1977), British Columbia's lake monster was christened with its palindromic name through a headline in the *Vancouver Daily Province*, August 24, 1926: "Ogopogo Now Official Name of the Famous Okanagan Sea Serpent." The news story covered a civic luncheon at Vernon, B.C., where the music-hall novelty song was sung, one verse of which goes like this:

I'm looking for the Ogopogo,
The bunny-hugging Ogopogo.
His mother was a mutton, his father was a whale.
I'm going to put a little bit of salt on his tail.
I'm looking for the Ogopogo.

The new name took over. Thereafter, Naitaka or N'ha-a-aitk, the Salish words for "snake" or "serpent," and Ook-ook mis-achie coupa lake, Chinook for "the wicked one in the lake," were shelved.

Legends about serpents that inhabit the depths of Scotland's largest loch were legion until modern times, but the words "Loch Ness Monster" were not used, in print at least, until they appeared in the *Inverness Courier*, April 14, 1933. The widely reproduced "Surgeon's Photo" of the elongated neck and mutton-like head of "Nessie" emerging from the choppy waters went a long way to establish the creature's credibility. Not until recent years was the photographic evidence itself debunked.

There is some evidence that goes beyond priority to establish the common ancestry of Ogo and Nessie. It seems that reports of Ogo are responsible for reports of Nessie; that both monsters were the creations of publicists; and that because of Ogo, Nessie sprang full-blown from the imagination of a firm of publicists in London, England. There is no direct proof of these assertions, but there is some evidence for them. Here it is.

Henry H. Bauer is Professor of Chemistry and Science Studies at Virginia Polytechnic Institute and State University, where he served for eight years as Dean of the College of Arts and Sciences. He is the author of *Beyond Velikovsky: The History of a Public Controversy* (1984) and *The Enigma of Loch Ness: Making Sense of a Mystery* (1986). Both books, published by the University of Illinois Press, are serious, scholarly studies of their subjects.

The first chapter of the latter book is titled "The Monster Is a Myth," and in its pages Bauer offers some evidence for the common ancestry of Ogo and Nessie plus the reason for the popularity of the reports in the first place. Chalk everything up to hoax or fraud or tourism publicity!

What appears below is an excerpt from that chapter, in which Bauer quotes from some personal correspondence. He does not immediately identify the correspondent; in fact, at first he deliberately withheld the identity of the letter-writer. But he did offer the careful reader a passel of clues as to the name of that informant. Bauer explained his reluctance to identify the correspondent in an end-note with these words: "The author, whom I shall call Lester Smith, asked me not to print his well-known *nom de plume*: 'When the book of mine you read appeared I was inundated with letters from all over the world. I don't want that to happen again.'"

A pleasant pastime for a literary scholar might have been the task of establishing the identity of the British author who was referred to as "Lester Smith," and then determining in which book the author made references to both Ogo and Nessie. But Bauer has saved his readers the trouble; the death of "Lester Smith" released Bauer from a obligation to protect his identity. The author turns out to be the English writer D.G. Gerahty who signed his books Stephen Lister (and also Robert Standish). As Lister, he wrote *Marise* (1950) which presents the claim about the twin genesis of Ogo-Nessie.

Ogopogo has never been lacking in critics, and some sixty years after it was taken, the celebrated "Surgeon's Photo" of Nessie, which started the craze for the Scottish "laird of the loch," was revealed to be a hoax. Nor has Ogo been lacking in backers, one of whom, the biologist Roy P. Mackal, after reading descriptions of Ogo's elongated profile, cautiously suggested it could be a surving zeuglodon, a serpent-like fossil whale now extinct.

Will revelations of the mundane origin of Ogo and Nessie affect the traffic of tourists and monster-hunters to Penticton, B.C., or Drumnadrochit, Scotland? Is the Pope Catholic? Is the world round? Is justice rewarded? Will wonders ever cease....

Humanity's knowledge of natural history was low in fact and high in fancy for so long that it is a daunting task now to separate the one from the other in legends and the older records....

When I began work on this book I recalled having read long ago in a semi-autobiographical novel that the Loch Ness Monster had been an invention of journalists. I wrote to ask the author of the book about the provenance of his story. Here is his reply:

Dear Mr. Bauer:

Your letter of July 8th has only just reached me.

Let me first tell you that ... [Lester Smith] writes fiction, although it may often appear otherwise. Truth with trimmings might describe it better. I am afraid I don't remember in which of my books the episode you quote may be found, but it was not necessarily the truth. The truth now follows.

In the early 1930s I, with two young partners, ran a publicity service in London. One of the partners was a native of Lossiemouth, Ramsay Macdonald's home, not far from Loch Ness. On returning from a holiday he brought us a small account. A group of hotels catering to tourists in that area wanted publicity and offered a fee of 50 pounds. We accepted....Around the same time we were offered a more important account by [a realtor] ... in the Okanagan Valley of British Columbia....We were told and I am inclined to believe that he invented the Ogopogo, a legendary creature inhabiting Lake Okanagan. This was

corn in Egypt. The Lossiemouth member of the firm then told us that for centuries a legendary creature was supposed to dwell in Loch Ness. We had never heard of it. At that time our "board room" was the saloon bar of a pub just off Trafalgar Square and over several pints of beer we became midwives of the reborn Loch Ness Monster. All we had to do was to arrange for the Monster to be sighted. This we did and the story snowballed. Thousands went north to see it and see it they did. It was, of course, pure hokum. The unwitting parent was the Ogopogo.

The technique is old and effective and has been used through the ages by organized religions. More recently did we not have soldiers wide-eyed on "seeing" the Angels of Mons!

I hope this helps you.

I could hardly believe that serendipity had thus brought me the explanation of the Loch Ness affair. Could Smith's recollection be trusted nearly fifty years after the event? Was it not implausible that he could not remember in which of his books he had told the story?

In point of fact I discovered that Smith had written under more than one pseudonym a total of more than forty books, as well as stories, articles, scripts, and so forth, so it was not implausible that he could not remember just where he had used a by-the-way reference to Loch Ness. Over the course of several years I reread Smith's books as I could find them (most were out of print and had never been published in the United States); several references to Okanagan were tantalizing. Finally I found the following, in an account published in 1950: " ... a great number of persons have sworn to having seen a creature called the Loch Ness Monster, and you may accept my assurance that the same Loch Ness Monster was born in my presence, during a conversation which took place in a London public house, under the shadow of the monument erected to the great Lord Nelson....The Loch Ness Monster ... was invented for a fee of 150 pounds by an ingenious publicity man employed by hotel-keepers." So Smith's recollection of the events had been the same in 1950 as in 1980, which makes his story all the more convincing — especially since my query to Smith had been based on a misrecollection of what I had read.

Apparently this publicity scheme of Smith and his colleagues — which doubtless involved the press, be it wittingly or unwittingly — proved to be very effective indeed. Loch Ness became the most popular destination in Britain for motorists: a patrolman for the Automobile Assocation recalled an occasion when 200 cars were drawn up by the side of the loch, and pandemonium would break out every time he pointed to something. Monster-hunting parties became fashionable, and all the hotels in the area were filled over the Christmas season of 1933. Inverness was flood-lit for the first time. On Boxing Day cars formed virtually a continuous line for the twenty miles from Inverness to Fort Augustus. In February 1934 the Inverness Town Council reduced its expenditure for advertising by one-third since the monsters was deemed sufficient publicity.

Smith's revelation helps greatly in elucidating the course of events. The Nessie sighting that spurred the flap of 1933 was reported in the *Inverness Courier* on May 2: an unnamed couple had seen a large creature disporting itself in Loch Ness. Rupert Gould's inquiries revealed that these people were, in point of fact, the lessees of the Drumnadrochit Hotel, near Urquhart Bay on the north side of the loch (the side on which the new road had been built). The report had been given to the *Inverness Courier* by a local correspondent, Alex Campbell, who was also the water bailiff at Fort Augustus.

Campbell himself subsequently saw the monster on a number of occasions....

All of the salient features of the Loch Ness phenomenon, then, can comfortably be explained by the stimulus of legend and of public relations acting on the gullible and expectant visitor, by human misperceptions made more likely by occasional combinations of mirage-like effects working on such natural objects as birds and tree trunks. Or can they?

CADBOROSAURUS

Cadborosaurus is the name of the sea serpent that is said to inhabit the waters of the West Coast. Although the range extends from Alaska to Oregon, it is most often seen to inhabit the inland waters around Vancouver Island and the northern Olympic Peninsula of the State of Washington. It has been nicknamed "Caddy."

Cadborosaurus is a portmanteau name which cleverly yokes together two words: Cadboro Bay (for Vancouver Island, where the creature was spotted early on) and *saurus* (for lizard, as in Brontosaurus). Coinage of the term is credited to Archie Willis, news editor and then managing editor of the *Daily Times* (Victoria) in the 1930s, who devoted numerous columns and articles to the cause of Caddy. He called the creature "the seafaring cousin of the Loch Ness Monster" and put sceptics in their place with the following, W.C. Fields-like declaration: "Any fool can disbelieve in sea serpents."

It should be noted that "sea serpents" are salt-water creatures that navigate the ocean's depths and disport in the shallower waters of its shores, whereas "lake monsters" are fresh-water creatures that find their habitat in the inland lakes and rivers that make up much of the country. If it is true that Canada has more rivers than any other country in the world, it stands to reason that it has more such hidden creatures to swim its lakes and rivers.

Here is an early description of Cadborosaurus from the report of F.W. Kemp, an officer of the Provincial Archives, Victoria, B.C. It was published in the *Daily Times* (Victoria, B.C.). Its immediate source is the interesting Internet website "Dragon Activity on Earth" *www.colba.net/7Etempest1/Earth_Activity/*.

It was this report, more than any other, that encouraged witnesses to feel free — or at somewhat free — to share with other people their accounts of their sightings of Caddy without the response of ridicule.

To recognize the seminal work of Archie Willis, marine scientists Paul H. Leblond and Edward L. Bousfield proposed that Caddy be recognized as "a new species representative of an unnamed subcategory of reptilia" and henceforth properly named: *Cadborosaurus willsi*.

On August 10, 1932, I was with my wife and son on Chatham Island in the Strait of Juan de Fuca. My wife called my attention to a mysterious something coming through the channel between Strong Tide Island and Chatham Island. Imagine my astonishment on observing a huge creature with head out of the water travelling about four miles per hour against the tide. Even at that speed a considerable wash was thrown on the rocks, which gave me the impression that it was more reptile than serpent to make so much displacement.

The channel at this point is about 500 yard wide. Swimming to the steep rocks of the Island opposite, the creature shot its head out of water on the rock, and moving its head from side to side, appeared to taking its bearings. Then fold after fold its body came to surface. Towards the tail it appeared serrated with something moving flail-like at the extreme end. The movements were like those of a crocodile. Around the head appeared a sort of mane, which drifted round the body like kelp.

The Thing's presence seemed to change the whole landscape, which make it difficult to describe my experiences. It did not seem to belong to the present scheme of things, but rather to the Long Ago when the world was young. The position it held on the rock was momentary. My wife and sixteen-year-old son ran to a point of land to get a clearer view. I think the sounds they made disturbed the animal. The sea being very calm, it seemed to slip back into deep water; there was a great commotion under the surface and it disappeared like a flash.

In my opinion, its speed must be terrific and it senses of smell, sight and hearing developed to a very high degree. It would be terribly hard to photograph, as its movements are different from anything I have ever seen or heard of. I should say its length to be not less than 80 feet. There were some logs on Strong Tide Island which gave me a good idea as to the size of monster as it passed them. I took a measurement of one the next day which was over 60 feet in length, and the creature overlapped it to a large extent at each end. I put a newspaper on the spot where it rested its head and took an observation from our previous point of vantage. The animal's was very much larger than the double sheet of newspaper. The body must have been at least 5 feet thick, and was of a bluish-green color which shone in the sun like aluminum. I could not determine the shape of the head, but it was much thicker than the body.

I did not report my strange adventure except to one or two trusted friends, for fear of ridicule and unbelief. About a year later, it fell to Major W.H. Langley's lot to see the same or at any rate, a similar monster in the vicinity also of Chatham island.

CADBOROSAURUS?

There is another description of the sea serpent subsequently known as Cadborosaurus swimming in the waters of Cadboro Bay, Victoria, B.C. The man who said he watched it as it cavorted in these waters in 1932 is the esteemed novelist Hubert Evans (1892-1986). Evans's recollections of that remarkable afternoon were taped almost fifty years after the episode occurred by Howard White, the editor and writer, who published his account of the conversation as "The Cadborosaurus Meets Hubert Evans" in *Raincoast Chronicles*, No. 16, 1983.

The conversation between the elderly novelist and the youthful editor took place in the front room of Evans's home at Roberts Creek, B.C. The two men were looking out across "the glassy calm" of the bay towards Nanaimo. On the radio they heard a news report about the Loch Ness monster. That triggered Evans's recollections. "When Hubert finished telling me this I was just as speechless as he must have been at the original event," White concluded.

White's estimation of Evans's veracity is apparent in his estimation of the man: "He is the sort of person who, if he tells you the Cadborosaurus exists, you suddenly discover you believe in Cadborosauruses. I would be hard put to say which is more remarkable."

"We had one here, you know."

"One what?"

"A sea serpent. Or some sort of sea creature quite similar to the way they describe that one over there."

"No!"

"Well, I've never told many people, but it's a fact," he said. "It was in 1932, right out there where you're looking. I was up on the back lot with Dick Reeve, our neighbour, working on the road — that same one you drove in on to get here. Bob Stephens, the old Scot from down the beach — he's dead these many years — came puffing up the hill and said, 'By God now, you've got to come down and see what you make of this. We've had the glass on it for half an hour. It's the damnedest thing.'

"It was late afternoon with the water dead calm just as it is now, and the sun was low so the water was just a sheet of gold. And here, out just beyond that deadhead, was a series of bumps breaking the water, all in dark silhouette and circled with ripples.

"'Sea lions,' I said. 'They run in a line like that sometimes.'

"'You just keep watching,' old Scotty said. And just a minute or so later, along at the end of this series of bumps, up out of the water comes a shaft — this was all in silhouette, so we couldn't see detail, although the outlines were very clear — up, up, up until it must have been six or eight feet out of the water. There was a spar buoy out on the reef then, which was about twelve inches through, and I could see this thing was about the same thickness — certainly no smaller.

"'You know, it could be a log,' I said. I'd seen a crooked log sometimes catch in the current and roll, so a limb comes up like that — when you see something you don't know what to make of, you keep trying to explain it by the things you know.

"But right there as we stood watching, none of us breathing a word, the top end of this shaft began to elongate horizontally, until we were presented with the profile of a head, very much like a horse's in general shape, with eye bumps, nostrils, and something in the way of ears or horns. The neighbour down the way said it had stuff hanging down like hair but I didn't see that. I tell you, it was a feeling, watching that head come round as if to look at us. It just put the hair up on the back of your neck.

A MYTH COME ALIVE

It is said that no one will understand the Inuit people without an appreciation of the power of Sedna, the goddess of the sea and the guardian of the seas. Sedna's deeds and fearsome features are celebrated in Eskimo and Inuit print, sculpture, story, and song. The creature is half-woman and-half fish and yet not a mermaid.

James Houston, the writer and artist who lived in the Eastern Arctic in the 1950s and introduced printmaking, has contributed an unexpected vignette about Sedna, and it appears in an unlikely place: the entry titled "Inuit Myth and Legend" that appears in Volume 2 of *The Canadian Encyclopedia* (1988). Here is an excerpt from that entry.

Among the most famous of the vast array of myths is the legend of the sea goddess who has various names (Sedna, Nuliayuk, Taluliyuk)....

Once, on south Baffin Island, I saw a myth come alive. Some young children were playing near a tidal ice barrier with many dangerous hidden cracks.

Their grandmother crept with great care down among the ice hummocks and from a hidden position called out, "Oohhwee, Oohhweee!"

The children ran back onto the land and said the sea goddess Taluliyuk had frightened them. Later, the grandmother said, "I told them about the woman who lives under the sea. Now she will keep them away from the dangerous places."

The grandmother was referring to the powerful sea goddess in this central Arctic song:

That woman down there beneath the sea,
She wants to hide the seals from us.
These hunters in the dance house,
They cannot mend matters.
They cannot mend matters.
Into the spirit world
Will go I,

Where no humans dwell.
Set matters right will I.
Set matters right will I.

The legend of the sea goddess, though known in various regions by different names, is one of the most widespread....

Many songs are sung to this powerful goddess. In new seasons, pieces of liver of the first-killed sea mammal are returned to the waters, imploring Sedna to release her bounty to the hunters so that they might feed their families.

THE STORY I USED TO HEAR

George W. Bauer worked as a counsellor for the Anglican Church and as a teacher for the Department of Indian and Northern Affairs among the Montagnais-Naskapi at the small Quebec community of Fort George on the east coast of James Bay. There he recorded many Cree narratives.

One of Bauer's informants was an elder named Sam Masti of Great Whale River. In 1966, speaking through a translator named Josie Sam, Masti told Bauer of the traditions of the powerful water creature named Mendo (male) or Mendoska (female). Communication with the captives of Mendo was possible through the medium of the Shaking Tent.

Bauer wrote, "Typically, Sam Masti scoffed at the relevance of Mendo for today's Indian. Sam, like many Indians, loves to talk, making his point the long way around."

Masti's account is reprinted from Bauer's *Cree Tales and Beliefs*, an issue of *Northeast Folklore*, Volume XII, 1971, printed by the University of Maine, Orono, Maine, U.S.A.

"It happened here at Great Whale long ago," he said. "There was two men in a canoe, and they saw a [*beluga*] whale coming humping along through the water. It came along and one [*of the men*] got the harpoon ready and the line, too, see. I made a mistake about that. There were two canoes in the water. So, they think that when they was close enough they can harpoon it. The one that sits in the front [*of the canoe*] gets the harppon ready. When he thought it was the right distance, he threw the harpoon, hitting the whale in the head. The whale made a big dive, and then came up again, and they saw this creature had a human head. Right away, they didn't know how to let the line go. It took them out, this creature did.

"These two men can see this island. There used to be an island in the middle of the river. Now, it's moved farther north. These men in the other canoe saw these men going so they chased after them to help, but they couldn't catch up. The other canoe is going very, very fast. They finally got out on the coast and they started to approach this island I told you about. These other two men [*those in the second canoe*] kept chasing after the two men that harpooned the whale. Finally, they [*the two in the first canoe*] got to the island they disappear

under the water. These other two men who tried to help, turn back and paddle home because there was nothing more they could do. As soon as they got back [*to the settlement*], they spread the sad news to all the people. The people decide they have to do something to find out what happened to the two men who went under water.

"There was an old man that used to perform the shaking tent. He built his shaking tent that evening and the shaking tent started to work. He sent his message out: 'What happened to the two men that disappeared under the water?' Two voices came back, 'There's nothing wrong with us, and we're not dead. We're living under the water with Mendo. The reason why we disappeared is because Mendo wanted us to marry his lovely daughters. We got everything here — all kinds of food that the Indians never seen. We visit the other group of people up at the rapids and have lots of fun. We use something that travels at tremendous speed to get there. You people that live on the dry land, you will always see death. To us, we will never see death until the end of the world. There's a lot of us here and at the other place up at the rapids, and we're all doing fine.'

"The old man performing the shaking tent asked another question: 'How about your children and your nice, good-looking wives back here?' The voices came back in answer, 'We cannot do anything to [*do for or accommodate*] our families. We can't go back [*to earth*] because we're just like people who are working steady. We're not allowed to go anywhere except the place we visit every night, you see. We visit the other group of people up to the rapids in the evenings. We use things that travel at great speed to get there which are not known in your world, and, also, you don't have the kind of food that we eat. Some foods we eat have strange colors and some food is white.' [*This incident, Sam explained to the translator at this point, had taken place long before the people of Great Whale River were familiar with such items as flour and sugar.*]

"The voices in the shaking tent continued to talk to the people on land: 'As we have already told you, we are married to the creature's daughters and when we raise families, we'll send the children to you. Someday, you'll find the kind of food we eat and our children will be living with you. All these things will come in the future. If you don't want to believe us, we will make a sign at the first rapids [*near the mouth of the Great Whale River*], and these people that are listening at the shaking tent can hear me say that.'

"The people listening at the shaking tent said, 'Let's go see if this is true or not.' The next day they went to the rapids and saw this big rock sitting at the foot of the rapids. The rock wasn't there before. They saw the mark on the rock, like a cross, one red mark and the other green. So they now call the place by this name Siniahmisinowit. That means 'the mark on the rock.' They still call it that to this day.

"The last the two men said was that they would never get old and we think they are still living. And, now, the day when the white man came to us, the Indians used to say that these are the children of the two men that were lost. The white man gave the Indians food that they did not know about, like in the story, and the Indians used to say that this was the food that the two men used to tell about in the shaking tent.

"Long after this happened, it was said, they perform another shaking tent just to find out if the two men are still there. A voice came back, 'They're still there living quite nicely. And they're still living in numbers in tthe two groups.'

"Yah. That's the story I used to hear the old men tell for true. Some story, isn't it?"

PHANTOM SHIP

The following memorate constitutes the greater part of a chapter in the booklet *The Phantom Ship of Northumberland Strait and Other Mysteries of the Sea* published by Lancelot Press of Hantsport, N.S., in 1975. The copy I have is the second edition, printed in 1989.

The delightful publication is the work of Roland H. Sherwood, photo-journalist for the *New Glasgow Evening News* and columnist or the *Pictou Advocate*. He is the author of a number of booklets of local lore. Here he describes one of his two experiences with the Phantom Ship or Ghost Ship or Fire Ship. Although Mr. Sherwood does not mention it, the sight of the Phantom Ship is said to be a forerunner of death. Would that he had described the second experience along with the first!

The Phantom Ship of Northumberland Strait

Because of the controversial nature of the subject of the existence of the so-called Phantom Ship of Northumberland Strait, and because of the many interviews I have had with those who claim to have seen the Ghost-Ship, and also because of the talks I've had with those who have never seen the spectre of the waters, and therefore do not believe a word of what has been told and written, I must add my own personal knowledge to the subject.

I, too, have seen the Phantom Ship. Not once but twice. But like many others, I make no effort to explain its appearance. If anyone wants to believe that it is only phosphorescence on the water, or gas rising from submarine coal beds, well, that's all right with me.

The first time I saw the Phantom Ship was when I was alone on the Caribou shore, and it looked just as others have reported. But at that time I had no witnesses to back up my statement of having seen the Fire-Ship.

The second time I was more fortunate. I had with me at the time a friend who was an out-and-out sceptic, not only about Phantom Ships, but about a number of other things as well ... my sceptic friend would not believe, and I knew of no way to convince him, since the Phantom Ship does not appear on call, or at any specific place or time. But this time I was fortunate.

We were returning from Wallace in Cumberland County, along the Sunrise Trail which skirts Northumberland Strait. It was after one o'clock on a dark morning in November. We were both tired, having worked all day and part of the night on telephone lines that had been disrupted in a recent storm. My friend was driving. I just sat and looked out over the dark water thinking of nothing in particular. Then I became aware of a light moving on the water, some miles out. I called this to my friend's attention. He said it was the lighthouse. I said nothing more at the time but continued to watch the light. I could see the lighthouse off to the right, and the dark outline of the land on the left, and between the two was a light that moved over the water. Finally I said, "That's a strange lighthouse. It's moving."

"You're seeing things," he said. "Go to sleep."

But I didn't. I still watched the strange light. Then suddenly I was seeing a vessel outlined in light that moved between the land and the lighthouse. "Hey," I yelled, "the Phantom Ship!"

We braked to a stop, jumped out of the car and rushed down to the water's edge. Sure enough, there it was. A vessel outlined in a glow, and most certainly moving over the water. As was his custom, my friend watched without comment. For some minutes we looked at the unusual sight. Then I had a bright idea. "Let's drive around the point," I said, "we'll get a better view."

So into the car once more, and in three minutes' time we were again down at the water's edge but in a different place. But the glowing ship was not there. The lighthouse was still visible; the dark outline of the land was there, but in the spot where the lighted vessel had been seen, there was nothing. Naturally, I was disappointed that we hadn't stayed where we were in the first place to see how and where the Phantom Ship disappeared. But we didn't and that couldn't be remedied. However, I couldn't refrain from saying to my sceptic friend, "You've seen the Phantom Ship." But, as on the other occasions when I had shown him something which he didn't believe, he said nothing.

Maybe he was the wise one. For, if one reports seeing the Phantom Ship, there are those who will laugh in one's face and inquire, "What were you drinking?"

Like many others, I have seen the Phantom Ship, but I don't ask anyone to believe our stories, because I know they won't. The Phantom Ship of Northumberland Strait is something you have to see to believe. And I warn you. If you ever do see the Phantom Ship, and believe that you have seen it, don't talk about it. Because no one will believe you.

OGOPOGO

I Saw Ogopogo is the title of a booklet written and produced with considerable charm. It is forty-eight pages in length, typewritten, mimeographed, and illustrated by an artist identified as Esther Noman. The booklet's author is identified as William Marks of Westbank, B.C. The printing company is identified: Peachland-Okanagan Review. The booklet itself is numbered: "Polka Dot Series," Vol. I, No. 1, 1971. The Metropolitan Toronto Reference Library, which possesses a copy of this publication, has no holdings for any subsequent titles in this series, if indeed any were issued.

Most of the booklet is devoted to the author's investigations of sightings of Ogopogo. Reprinted here is his personal account of a sighting of Ogopogo, Lake Okanagan's celebrated lake monster. "You may disagree as to it being the Ogopogo," he explained, "but I'm sure any thinking person will conclude that there is a *MONSTER* in Okanagan Lake."

I Saw Ogopogo

To get to my own experience of seeing Ogopogo, we will have to go back to the last day of Kelowna Regatta in 1958. To assure the readers that I am not a Regatta fan, and this is not written to boost the city of Kelowna, I have never attended one session of the famous Regatta. It has been said Ogopogo is generally sighted in the lake at Regatta time. This statement is generally accompanied with a smirk or wink. I have seen the parades, but am not interested in water sports. But on that particular day I drove my old car to the parking spot near the toll both, and walked across the bridge to get some small article. On my return the old car refused to go, so I left it and walked around the parking space, and in doing so took several glances out across Lake Okanagan. I saw what appeared to be, at the first glance, a number of small boats following each other, about halfway between the toll both and Casa Loma point! (Westside)

Suddenly I thought, "What would several little boats be doing out there following each other?" So I turned and took a real good look at the things, and saw a creature, or creatures, as illustrated below!

On the front, as illustrated, I saw 5 or 6 humps. These appeared to be about the size of a 200 lb. pig swimming in the water (if he could). In color they differed slightly from the hue of the lake, being more of a black or real dark blue. It could be plainly seen that the humps were NOT waves caused by the backwash of a boat. Beside that, the thing or things did not move.

Suddenly I realized that I was looking at the Ogopogo, or at the thing people called Ogopogo. I was also convinced that I was looking at two separate creatures, because there was a space of, I'd say, twenty feet between the last three humps shown and the five or six that appeared at the front.

The lake was calm that day, with hardly a ripple on its glassy surface. To me it seemed that Ogopogo must be sunning himself. Knowing the incredulity of those who, like myself, had never seen Ogy, I began to shout to attract someone's attention, so as to have a witness. A lady was standing outside a trailer parked on the Tsinycaptim reserve about 100 yards away, but she paid no attention. Either she was deaf, or thought I was just another drunk British Columbian. (I'm from Saskatchewan, Canada.) The toll collectors were, also, so engrossed in collecting their pound of flesh, so to speak, that they paid no attention either.

So I turned and stared for about five minutes, in amazed concentration at finally seeing the OGOPOGO!

"Now," I thought, "at last I've seen Ogopogo, or the thing they call Ogopogo." The arguments for it being Ogy are this — the humps stayed equidistant apart, in fact they DIDN'T move at all. If it had been a big school of say sturgeon, some of them would probably have moved apart. But no, they stayed in one position, and beside that, when the thing or things submerged, they all went down at once, as if something had frightened them. All I could see after was swirling water & foam apparently.

On the other hand to anyone that would theorize that the creatures were fish (sturgeon?) I would have to admit that I could see no tail or head. But, of course, it is possible that at that distance, there could have been both, and at that far away they would have been hard to see. My impression of the whole thing (really) was that I'd seen Ogopogo & his mate perhaps, and that they were sunning themselves.

WHAT I SAW IN THE REARVIEW MIRROR

Memphré is the name given the lake monster that is said to make its habitat in the waters of Lake Memphremagog in Quebec's Eastern Townships.

Leo Gervais is one of the four hundred or so residents and visitors who since 1813 (and presumably earlier) have reported seeing "something strange" in this beautiful lake. This is the ever-elusive Memphré. Gervais has contributed a remarkably clear, level-headed account of a sighting. When he is not vacationing in the area, he is the editor of *The Monitor*, a weekly paper that serves the interests of Montreal's west end community.

I received Gervais's account from Jacques Boisvert. A resident of the city of Magog, which is located on the shore of Lake Memphremagog, he is a founder of the La Société de dracontologie / International Dracontology Society, which celebrated its tenth anniversary on 19 June 1996 at the newly dedicated Place Memphré "Site d'observation de créatures lacustres non identifiées." Speeches on the occasion called Memphré the lake's "oldest resident." Here is a glimpse of him — or her — or it.

It was the summer of 1987. I was twenty-one, in my second year of university, and enjoying what was a wonderfully sunny July day. I had driven the 140 km or so from Montreal to my friend Andy Matthew's cottage on Lake Memphremagog, on the Knowlton side of the lake, near Knowlton's landing.

His cottage was on the lot right next to the Glenbrooke, a longtime bed'n'breakfast which, although not as fashionable as in its heyday back in the '40s and '50s, was still frequented by summer vacationers.

I rounded the last curve on the twisty gravel road approaching Andy's place. This turn dipped, then hairpinned to the left. On the right, as you turned, the lake was about fifty metres down a sloping hill. On this sunny, windless day the lake looked like it was covered with diamonds, reflecting the brightness on its watery surface like so many scattered jewels.

After making the hairpin, I looked in my rearview mirror, a reflex I suppose. I could see the road behind me and part of the lake in reflection, still shimmering in the bright of the day. In that brief moment that I looked in the mirror, I saw something else.

A dark, serpentine form moved in the lake about twenty metres from shore. I cannot say I saw a head, but the body had to be at least twenty feet long, since I watched it for a few seconds as it came above the surface and then disappeared, leaving a large ripple effect in the otherwise still lake.

I stopped the car and got out, surveying the spot where I had seen the snake-like form. The ripple was not caused by a fish — it was much too big for that.

I saw nothing else. After several anxious moments of hoping to get another look at what I'd seen, I continued on the last quarter-mile to Andy's cottage. Upon arrival, I told him what I'd seen and he, of course, laughed. But after detailing my sighting, he grudgingly acknowledged it may have been Memphré.

A MOVEMENT IN THE LAKE

Do strange creatures inhabit the loch-like lakes found in the interior of British Columbia?

The following letter suggests that they do. This letter originally appeared in the "Report from the Readers" column of the Dec. 1990 issue of *Fate* under the heading "Lake Monsters." It was contributed by Richard Medley, a vacationer to Lake Shuswap from Philomath, Oregon.

Lake Shuswap is part of B.C.'s Okanagan Valley where there are plenty of sightings of the legendary — but lively — Ogopogo.

I read with interest Dr. Karl Shuker's article ("Lesser-Known Lake Monsters," *Fate*, September 1990). His mention of the sightings in Lake Shuswap, British Columbia, confirm my own experience while vacationing there briefly in 1962.

I had been staying at some cabins in the woods on the south side of the lake, just behind the railroad tracks that run the length of the lake. On a clear August morning at about 6:30, I left my cabin to do some bank fishing. I walked down to the tracks and proceeded east along them into a short tunnel that took the tracks through a rocky headland.

Beyond the tunnel, the shore drops off steeply to a considerable depth and this is where I planned to do my fishing. As I emerged from the tunnel, however, I found that my intended fishing spot was taken by an empty houseboat that had apparently broken from its mooring somewhere on the lake and had grounded on some rocks near the shore. While I stood looking at the houseboat, a movement in the lake approximately 300 feet off shore caught my eye.

It was a glistening brown hump about two or three feet above the water level and about eight to ten feet long. In 1962 I had never heard of lake monsters, not even the Loch Ness phenomenon, and I stood totally perplexed as I watched the hump approach closer to shore.

I first thought that it was a log; but then I noticed that it was creating a wake and realized that it was moving under its own power. Then I proceeded to consider beaver, otter, moose and bear, but immediately knew that the object was too large for the former and that the latter would not swim with their heads underwater.

The hump continued moving toward shore until, within about 100 feet, it suddenly turned and proceeded west around the headland and out of sight, leaving me baffled as to what I had just seen.

Later, I stopped for a few days at Lake Okanagan, where stories of Ogopogo abound, and I realized that what I had seen was something very similar to the descriptions of that phenomenon.

My interest in lake monsters took a leap from there, and I'm glad to see *Fate* feature Dr. Shuker's article. I hope you continue to follow up on this fascinating subject; there really is something unknown to science out there in those deep lakes! — *Richard Medley, Philomath, OR*

OFF THE DEEP END

Here is an amusing account of a sighting of Memphré, the creature said to inhabit the depths of Lake Memphremagog, the focal point of Quebec's Eastern Townships. The lively account was written by Greg Duncan and posted in the summer of 1996 to "Log Cabin Chronicles," a homepage for prose and poetry about the district. The address of the interesting homepage is *jmahoney@tomifobia.com*.

You may think I've finally gone off the deep end of the wharf when I tell you what happened near the boathouses at Tompkin's Creek.

Like most people who have seen something unexplainable, I was hesitant to come forth with this.

About 3:00 p.m. on a Thursday, I was happily fishing away on the lake side of the creek. As usual, I was chatting with my fishing buddy for the day about everything under the sun. When he asked me if I believed in Memphré, our resident Lake Memphremagog monster, I replied that it would be great to see him (or it) someday.

Two or three perch had made their way up onto the concrete remnants of the old wharf that was our spot for the afternoon, when suddenly my partner started yelling and pointing south: "Do you see that? Do you see that?"

I thought he was trying to get me to see a surfacing fish. I couldn't seem to see what it was he was pointing at because I wasn't exactly expecting what was to come. About fifty yards away something very large was displacing a lot of water and leaving a wake behind. The sun's rays glittered off the waves as we watched whatever it was move along at slow speed. There just isn't any reasonable explanation of what we were seeing.

The water rolled off the top of the moving object, but its back never broke through the surface. The movement was similar to what a dark submarine might look like if it moved along just under the surface, or what happens when a whale or a porpoise swims alongside a boat. At any rate, we were amazed at what was happening, and as we watched, the wake stopped and the surface calmed.

Make no mistake — this was no subsurface school of smelt, and it was far too large to be an otter. At another time on another lake I had seen a large otter, and even one that measured six feet from head to tail could not displace that much water.

Although we never saw the creature in question surface, I believe that what we saw that day is what other people have seen and have also had a hard time explaining. It could be that my friend and I finally saw the legendary Lake Memphremagog monster — monstrously large perhaps but peaceful in its movement.

Memphré, I hope it was you because I can't get the incident out of my mind. Stay low and deep and continue to make us wonder. It's safer that way.

PART THREE
Creatures of Air

THEN appear the monsters of the Air: beings whose presences are otherwise known as apparitions, fantasies, ghosts, poltergeists, spectres, spirits, sprites, visions, or wraiths. Their names are legion.

They haunt our past, our present, and our future. They are desires and dreads, all the more potent and powerful for their immaterial nature. In Shakespeare's *The Tempest*, the magician Prospero delivers a magisterial speech in which he refers to the "all spirits" (including the human spirit) as "this insubstantial pageant faded...." There is a New Age homily that says we are not earthly beings with spiritual concerns, but spiritual beings with earthly concerns. The nursery rhyme that tells us what little boys and little girls are made of, but the physical and social sciences have yet to determine the composition of the inhabitants of the spirit world.

A creature of the air must be some form of energy, power, force, mana, personality, or essence that is known on this planet but yet is as insubstantial like mist, plasma, ether, or ectoplasm. Perhaps its energy is only "the power to cloud men's minds" (I am referring of course to the ability of radio's Lamont Cranston, alias The Shadow, who in the Mysterious East learned "the power to cloud men's minds"), but whatever its nature, it is with us to stay. There is a tendency, fostered by psychologists, to dismiss this "power" as abnormal or illusory. Yet in the long run it may prove to be the most enduring of human characteristics. Marshall McLuhan noted that "the most human thing about man is his technology." Perhaps the most basic thing about man is his immaterial nature.

We have a long history of interaction of human beings with immaterial forces, as these episodes show.

COMMUNICATION WITH THE DEVIL

Is there a Devil? Is it possible to communicate with Him, Her, or It?

These are some of the questions that were faced by the missionary Paul Le Jeune (1591-1664) who reported on the beliefs of the native people in the vicinity of modern-day Quebec City. He was the Superior of the Jesuit Missions in New France and he did so in his Relation or letter to Rome dated May 7, 1632. His description of what has since become known as the Rite of the Shaking Tent, the oracle of the Indians, offers an intriguing insight into Le Jeune's mind as he pits his training and thinking as a Jesuit against the unquestioned traditions and remarkable rites of "the Hiroquois" (otherwise known as the Iroquois) in his correspondence which appears in *The Jesuit Relations and Allied Documents* (1896-1901). The word *manitou* means "spirit" or "mystery." Some *manitous* are benevolent, some are malevolent; some combine good and evil, whereas others are simply indifferent to nature and to mankind.

There are some men among them who make a profession of consulting their Manitou. It seems to me that by this word "Manitou" they understand, as among us, an Angel or some powerful being. I believe they think that there are good and bad Manitous; I will speak of this with greater certainty some day.

The Son-in-law of our savage, wishing to go hunting, took counsel with him [the Manitou] near our house. He made a little wooden Cabin, shutting himself inside toward nightfall, singing, crying, and howling. The others were around him. I begged a Frenchman to fire a shot of the arquebus, to frighten them with the noise; but I am not sure that they heard it, so great was the uproar. The Manitou told him to go hunting in a certain direction, that he would find Moose there, and no Hiroquois. The Manitou was proved a liar; for the hunter returned almost starved, having found very little. As to the Hiroquois, he could not have run against any, because he kept at a great distance from them. I believe that the greater number of these consulters of the Manitou are only deceivers and charlatans. Notwithstanding this, when they advise anything it is carried out exactly. If one of them should tell the Savages that the Manitou wanted them to lie down naked in the snow, or to turn themselves in a certain place, he would be obeyed. And, after all, this Manitou, or Devil, does not talk to them any more than he does to me.

Nevertheless, I am inclined to think that there are some among them who really have communication with the Devil, if what the savages say is true; because some are seen to walk upon their huts, without breaking them down. They become furious and act as if possessed, striking blows hard enough to fell an ox, and yet the pain passes away very soon. Without any great injury, they cover themselves with blood, and are healed in a moment. They relate many other similar things; but, when I question them closely, they frankly admit that they have not seen him, but have only heard of him. One does not need to offer any very serious objections to their stories, to interrupt and confuse them.

THE GREAT TURTLE

Let us turn our attention to the turtle, the spirit of the Great Turtle, which, as the native peoples of North America maintain, is the foundation of the known world.

Travels and Adventures in Canada and the Indian Territories between the Years 1760 and 1776 (Boston, 1809) is a classic of travel and observation written by Alexander Henry (1739-1824). The writer is called Alexander Henry the Elder so that he may be distinguished from his nephew, Alexander Henry the Younger. Both the Henrys were fur traders who kept journals of their experiences in the Northwest.

Alexander Henry the Elder was especially knowledgeable about native ways. In 1764 he witnessed a performance of the rite of the Shaking Tent by the Ojibways in the vicinity of Sault Ste. Marie in present-day Ontario. The spirit of the Great Turtle, held in special awe by the Ojibway, was invoked by the shamans who operated the oracle. They interpreted the answers to the questions directed their way. Henry was impressed with its operation, for the oracle was able to answer two of his questions. They referred to the disposition of the troops under the command of the British leader Sir William Johnson in faraway Fort Niagara and also whether or not Henry would ever return to live among his own people. Apparently the answers were correctly given though Henry was not in a position to assess them at the time.

The earliest references to performances of the rite occur in the journal of Samuel de Champlain in 1604. The rite of the Shaking Tent has been remarkably influential to the present day in surprising ways. It is felt that the birchbark tent-form led directly to the draped "spirit cabinet" employed by professional spiritual-mediums during seances in the nineteenth century. Present-day performances of the rite are regularly held in connection with native healing ceremonies at Kenora, Ont.

Here are the words of Alexander Henry on the oracular turtle.

This was a project highly interesting to me, since it offered me the means of leaving the country. I intimated this to the chief of the village, and received his promise that I should accompany the deputation.

Very little time was proposed to be lost, in setting forward on the voyage; but, the occasion was of too much magnitude not to call for more than human knowledge and discretion; and preparations were accordingly made for solemnly invoking and consulting the GREAT TURTLE.

* * *

For invoking and consulting the GREAT TURTLE the first thing to be done was the building of a large house or wigwam, within which was placed a species of tent, for the use of the priest, and reception of the spirit. The tent was formed of moose-skins, hung over a frame-work of wood. Five poles, or rather pillars, of five different species of timber, about ten feet in height, and eight inches in diameter were set in a circle of about four feet in diameter. The holes made to receive them were about two feet deep; and the pillars being set, the holes were filled up again, with the earth which had been dug out. At top, the pillars were bound together by a circular hoop, or girder. Over the whole of this edifice were spread the moose-skins, covering it at top and round the sides, and made fast with thongs of the same; except that on one side a part was left unfastened to admit of the entrance of the priest.

The ceremonies did not commence but with the approach of night. To give light within the house, several fires were kindled round the tent. Nearly the whole village assembled in the house, and myself among the rest. It was not long before the priest appeared, almost in a state of nakedness. As he approached the tent the skins were lifted up, as much as was necessary to allow of his creeping under them, on his hands and knees. His head was scarcely within side, when the edifice, massy as it has been described, began to shake; and the skins were no sooner let fall, than the sounds of numerous voices were heard beneath them;

some yelling; some barking as dogs; some howling like wolves; and in this horrible concert were mingled screams and sobs, as of despair, anguish and the sharpest pain. Articulate speech was also uttered, as if from human lips: but in a tongue unknown to any of the audience.

After some time, these confused and frightful noises were succeeded by a perfect silence; and now a voice, not heard before, seemed to manifest the arrival of a new character in the tent. This was a low and feeble voice, resembling the cry of a young puppy. The sound was no sooner distinguished, than all the Indians clapped their hands for joy, exclaiming, that this was the Chief Spirit, the TURTLE, the spirit that never lied! Other voices, which they had discriminated from time to time, they had previously hissed, as recognising them to belong to evil and lying spirits, which deceive mankind.

New sounds came from the tent. During the space of half an hour, a succession of songs were heard, in which a diversity of voices met the ear. From his first entrance, till these songs were finished, we heard nothing in the proper voice of the priest; but, now, he addressed the multitude, declaring the presence of the GREAT TURTLE, and the spirit's readiness to answer such questions as should be proposed.

The questions were to come from the chief of the village, who was silent, however, till after he had put a large quantity of tobacco into the tent, introducing it to the aperture. This was a sacrifice, offered to the spirit; for spirits are supposed by the Indians to be as fond of tobacco as themselves. The tobacco accepted, he desired the priest to inquire, whether or not the English were preparing to make war upon the Indians? and, Whether or not there were at Fort Niagara a large number of English troops?

These questions having been put by the priest, the tent instantly shook; and for some seconds after, it continued to rock so violently, that I expected to see it levelled with the ground. All that was a prelude, as I supposed, to the answers to be given; but, a terrific cry announced, with sufficient intelligibility, the departure of the TURTLE.

A quarter of an hour elapsed in silence, and I waited impatiently to discover what was to be the next incident, in this scene of imposture. It consisted in the return of the spirit, whose voice was again heard, and who now delivered a continued speech. The language of the GREAT TURTLE, like that which we had heard before,

was wholly unintelligible to every ear, that of his priest excepted; and it was, therefore, that not till the latter gave us an interpretation, which did not commence before the spirit had finished, that we learned the purport of this extraordinary communication.

The spirit, as we were now informed by the priest, had, during his short absence, crossed Lake Huron, and even proceeded as far as Fort Niagara, which is at the head of Lake Ontario, and thence to Montréal. At Fort Niagara, he had seen no great number of soldiers; but, on descending the Saint Lawrence, as low as Montréal, he had found the river covered with boats, and the boats filled with soldiers, in number like the leaves of the trees. He had met them on their way up the river, coming to make war upon the Indians.

The chief had a third question to propose, and the spirit, without a fresh journey to Fort Niagara, was able to give it an instant and most favourable answer: "If," said the chief, "the Indians visit Sir William Johnson, will they be received as friends?"

"Sir William Johnson," said the spirit (and after the spirit, the priest), "Sir William Johnson will fill their canoes with presents; with blankets, kettles, guns, gunpowder and shot, and large barrels of rum, such as the stoutest of the Indians will not be able to lift; and every man will return in safety to his family."

At this, the transport was universal; and, amid the clapping of hands, a hundred voices exclaimed, "I will go, too! I will go, too!"

The questions of public interest being resolved, individuals were now permitted to seize the opportunity of inquiring into the condition of their absent friends, and the fate of such as were sick. I observed that the answers, given to these questions, allowed of much latitude of interpretation.

Amid this general inquisitiveness, I yielded to the solicitations of my own anxiety for the future; and having first, like the rest, made my offering of tobacco, I inquired, whether or not I should ever revisit my native country? The question being put by the priest, the tent shook as usual; after which I received this answer: "That I should take courage, and fear no danger, for that nothing would happen to hurt me; and that I should, in the end, reach my friends and country in safety." These assurances wrought so strongly on my gratitude, that I presented an additional and extra offering of tobacco.

The GREAT TURTLE continued to be consulted till near midnight, when all the crowd dispersed to their respective lodges. I was on the watch, through the scene

I have described, to detect the particular contrivances by which the fraud was carried on; but, such was the skill displayed in the performance, or such my deficiency of penetration, that I made no discoveries, but came away as I went, with no more than those general surmises which will naturally be entertained by every reader.

HORRORS

Henry Alline (1748-1784) was an itinerant preacher who evangelized throughout Nova Scotia and New Brunswick. His disciples were called "Allinites" and the religious revival that he sustained is now known as the "New Light" movement. Alline's mission was viewed with some alarm by the religious establishment of the day; today it is regarded with favour, especially by the Baptist Church.

The passage that follows originally appeared in *The Journal of Henry Alline* (1806). It is reprinted from the edition published by Lancelot Press in 1982 on behalf of the Acadia Divinity College and the Baptist Historical Committee.

The entries in Alline's journal are an excellent source for accounts of the psychological dimensions of "the conversion process." The episodes described are evangelical Christian in nature and emotionalistic in the extreme, as the psychologist William James noted in his classic study *The Varieties of Religious Experience* (1902).

O What Unspeakable Horrors

One evening as I was taking a walk of about two or three miles to spend the evening with some of my companions (as I had promised) being alone and pondering on my lost and undone condition, as I was at this time almost night and day, the evening was very dark, but all on a sudden I thought I was surrounded with an uncommon light; it seemed like a blaze of fire; I thought it out shone the sun at noon day: I was immediately plunged almost in keen despair. The first conception I had was that of the great day of judgment was come, and time at a period. O what unspeakable horrors broke forth immediately upon my soul: every power of my mind strained with terror and surprises. I thought the day of grace was now over, mercy abused, goodness rejected, time at a period, eternity commenced, the infinite judge approaching, conscience awake, and my soul burdened with almost an unsupportable load of guilt, darkness and tormenting fear, and a bottomless gulf beneath me. All this appeared as real as if it were actually so. I thought I saw thousands of devils and damned spirits, by whom I expected to be tormented. No friend, no Saviour, no Mediator! He that made me would have no mercy on me, and he that formed me would shew me no favour; and yet I clearly saw that his throne was just and wholly clear of my blood. I had nothing to lay to his charge, for I saw how I had wilfully refused his grace, and rejected his mercy: all times and opportunities of repentance were now at a period, and nothing but loss, loss, incessant loss, like a dagger shot through my poor distressed and almost despairing soul. Thus God shewed me in some degree for about three quarters of a minute, what it would be to meet that dreadful day in the condition I was then in, without a Saviour; and therefore informed me how exposed I was at every breath I drew, and what an awful day I must soon see, if I am found out of Christ; yea, methinks I saw more in that short time than I could express in one week. I stood all this time with my face towards the ground, trembling in body, and sinking in my mind, not having power to look, nor desire to ask for mercy, because I thought the case was really settled with me, and therefore it would be needless to ask for mercy, especially when I saw myself so justly condemned; and O too late I was convinced of my folly. My distress was so great that I believe it continued half an hour, as it would have separated my soul from my body, for my very flesh seemed to consume off of my bones with the weight; every thing conspired to load me with unspeakable distress.

O what a day! how will the wicked stand,
What scenes immortal open to their view?
All time deserted, mortal changes past,

And they awake before the awful Bar,
Where Grace and Hope to them are known no more.

The first thought I remember, exclusive of reviewing the shocking scene, was to look behind me and see how far the burning flood and sweeping deluge, which I imagined to be coming after me, was from me, that I might know how long I should be out of hell, or how long it would be, before my doom, should be finally settled. When I lifted up my eyes, I saw, to my unspeakable satisfaction, that it was not as I expected: the day was not really come, therefore I had an opportunity of repentance, and a possibility of escaping from that awful and eternal gulf. O how my heart seemed to leap for joy, and at the same time began to groan for mercy. I found the day of judgment was not come, nor the world in flames as I expected. There appeared, as I thought, a large blaze of light in the shape of a circle, with that side next to me open as though it yawned after me, and as it drew very night me, it closed up in a small compass, then broke out in small sparkles and vanished away. It is no matter whether the light which I saw with my bodily eyes, was one of the common phenomena of nature, such as exhaled vapours or nitre, that had gathered in the air; it was not the less alarming to me; for I believe it was really designed by God as an alarming means, as much as if it was a miracle sent to me in particular. We are very apt to evade the force of many alarming calls from God by such things as are not uncommon in nature.

When the light seemed to vanish, and the scene to withdraw, my whole soul seemed to be engaged to implore mercy and grace. O mercy, mercy, mercy, was every groan of my soul, and I began to make many promises, that I would never bear to sin as I had done, nor rest another day, unless I had found a Saviour for my poor soul. I thought very much of the Goodness of God to me in giving me one moment more for repentance, and that there appeared yet a possibility of my being saved.

THE WYNYARD APPARITION

There is much literature on the Wynyard Apparition, Canada's most famous crisis apparition. (A crisis apparition occurs when the spirit or apparition of a dying person appears to a relative or friend in another part of the world at the point of dying or great stress.) The account carried in these pages suggests that the apparition in question is little more than folklore (what today we might called an urban myth). Indeed, it seems to be a well-travelled tale; yet in its classic form it concerns Lieutenant (later General) Wynyard and Captain John C. Sherbrooke (later Lieutenant-Governor of Nova Scotia and still later Governor General of Canada) and it occurred on October 15, 1785, at approximately four o'clock in the afternoon, in the officers' quarters of the British garrison in Sydney, N.S. Here it is treated as a traditional ghost story, one that grows in the telling and moves around a lot. But it also appears in the standard biography of Governor General Sherbrooke written by A. Patchett Martin.

The incident is well documented and scary. It may be folklore or actual fact. For certain it is a memorate, a family story. "The Wynyard Apparition," this version, appeared in the *Montreal Herald*, November 6, 1822.

The Wynyard Apparition Supernatural Appearance

Sir John Sherbrooke and George Wynyard were as young men, officers in the same regiment, which was employed on foreign service. — They were connected by similarity of taste and studies, and spent together in literary occupation, much of that vacant time which was squandered by their brother officers in those excesses of the table, which some forty years ago, were considered among the necessary accomplishments of the military character. They were one afternoon sitting in Wynyard's apartment. It was perfect light, the hour was about four o'clock; they had dined but neither of them had drank wine, and they had retired from the mess to continue together the occupations of the day — I, ought to have said, that the apartment in which they were, had wo doors in it, the one opening into a passage, and the other opening into Wynyard's bedroom. There were no other means of entering the sitting room but from the passage, and no other egress from the bed-room but through the sitting room; so that any person passing into the bed-room must have remained there, unless he returned by the way he entered. This point is of consequence to the story. As these two young officers were pursuing their studies, Sherbrooke, whose eye happened accidentally to glance from the volume before him towards the door that opened in the passageway observed a tall youth, of about 20 years of age, whose appearance was that of extreme emaciation, standing behind him. Struck with the presence of a perfect stranger, he immediately turned to his friend, who was sitting near him, and directed his attention to the guest who had thus strangely broken in upon their studies. As soon as Wynyard's eyes were turned towards the mysterious visitor, his countenance became suddenly agitated. "I have heard," says Sir John Sherbrooke, "of a man's being as white as death, but I never saw a living face assume the appearance of a corpse, except Wynyard's at the moment. As they looked silently at the form before them — for Wynyard, who seemed to apprehend the import of the appearance, was deprived of the faculty of speech, and Sherbrooke, perceiving the agitation of his friend, felt no inclination to address it — as they looked silently upon the figure, it proceeded slowly into the adjoining apartment, and in the act of passing them, cast its eyes with an expression of somewhat melancholy affection on Wynyard. The oppression of this extraordinary presence was no sooner removed, than Wynyard, seizing his friend by the arm, and drawing a deep breath, as if recovering from the suffocation of intense astonishment and emotion, muttered in a low and almost inaudible tone of voice: "Good God! my brother!"

"Your brother," repeated Sherbrooke, "what can you mean, Wynyard? there must be some deception — follow me," and immediately taking his friend by the arm, he preceded him into the bed-room, which, as I before stated, was connected with the sitting room, and into which the strange visitor had evidently entered. I have already said that from this chamber there was no possibility of withdrawing but by the way of the apartment through which the figure had certainly passed, and as certainly never had returned. Wynyard's mind had received an impression at the first moment of his observing him, that the figure whom he had seen was the spirit of his brother. Sherbrooke still persevered in strenuously believing that some imposition had been practised. They took note of the day and hour in which the event had happened; but they resolved not to mention the occurrence in the regiment, and gradually they persuaded each other they had been imposed upon by some of their fellow officers, though they could neither account for the reason, or suspect the author, or conceive the means of its execution. They were content to imagine any thing possible rather than admit the possibility of a supernatural appearance. But though they had attempted these stratagems of self-delusion, Wynyard could not help expressing his solicitude with respect to the safety of the brother whose apparition he had either seen or imagined himself to have seen, and the anxiety which he exhibited for letters from England, and his frequent mention of his fears for his brother's health, at length awakened the curiosity of his comrades, and eventually betrayed him into a declaration of the circumstances which he had in vain determined to conceal. The story of the silent and unbidden visitor was no sooner bruited abroad, than the destiny of Wynyard's brother became an object of universal and painful interest to the officers of the regiment; there were few who did not inquire for Wynyard's letters before they made any demand after their own, and the packets that arrived from England were welcomed with more than usual eagerness, for they brought, not only remembrances from their friends at home, but promised to afford a clue to the mystery which had happened among themselves. By the first ship no intelligence relating to the story could have been received, for they had all departed from England previously to the appearance of the spirit. At length the long wished for vessels arrived; all the officers had letters except Wynyard. Still the secret was unexplained. They examined the several newspapers; they contained no mention of any death, or of any other circumstance connected with his family, that could account for the preternatural event. There was a solitary letter for Sherbrooke still unopened. The officers had received their letters in the mess room at the hour of supper. After Sherbrooke had broken the seal of his last packet, and cast a glance on its contents, he beckoned his friend a way from the company, and departed from the room. All were silent. The suspense of the interest was now at its climax; the impatience for the return of Sherbrooke was inexpressible. They doubted not but that letter had contained the long expected intelligence.

At the interval of one hour Sherbrooke joined them. No one dared be guilty of such rudeness as to enquire the nature of his correspondence; but they waited in mute attention, expecting that he would himself touch upon the subject. His mind was manifestly full of thoughts that pained, bewildered and oppressed him. He drew near the fire place, and leaning his head on the mantle piece, after a pause of some moments, said, in a low voice, to the person who was nearest to him, "Wynyard's brother is no more." The first line of Sher brooke's letter was, "Dear John, break to your friend Wynyard the death of his favourite brother." He had died on the way and at the very hour on which the friend had seen his spirit pass so mysteriously through the apartment.

It might have been imagined, that these events would have been sufficient to have impressed the mind of Sher brooke with the conviction of their truth; but so strong was his prepossession against the existence, or even the possibility, of any preternatural intercourse with the souls of the dead, that he still entertained a doubt of the report of his senses, supported as their testimony was by the coincidence of vision and event. Some years after, on his return from England, he was walking with two gentlemen in Piccadilly, when, on the opposite side of the way, he saw a person bearing the most striking resemblance to the figure which had been disclosed to Wynyard and himself. His companions were acquainted with the story; and he instantly directed their attention to the gentleman opposite, as the individual who had contrived to enter and depart from Wynyard's apartments without their being conscious of the means. Full of the impression, he immediately went over, and at once addressed the gentleman; he now fully expected to elucidate the mystery. He apologized for the interruption, but excused it by relating the occurrence which had induced to this solecism in manners. He had never been out of the country; but he was the twin brother of the youth whose spirit had been seen.

This story is related with several variations. It is sometimes told as having happened in Gibraltar, at others in England, at others in America. There are also differences with respect to the conclusion. Some say that gentleman who Sir John Sherbrooke afterwards met in London, and addressed, as the person whom he had previously seen in so mysterious a manner, was not another brother of General Wynyard, but a gentleman, who bore a strong resemblance to the family. But however the leading facts in every account are the same. Sir John Sherbrooke and General Wynyard, two gentlemen of veracity, were together present at the spiritual appearance of the brother of General Wynyard; the appearance took place at the moment of dissolution; and the countenance and form of the ghost's figure were so distinctly impressed upon the memory of Sir John Sherbrooke, to whom the living man had been unknown that on accidentally meeting with his likeness, he perceived and acknowledged the resemblance.

If this story be true, it silences the common objections, that ghosts always appear at night, and are never visible to two persons at the same time.

THE PHENOMENON OF 1819

Even the weather may produce monstrous effects.

A "dark day" is an eerie phenomenon that occurs from time to time. To the meteorologist such a day is a day during which daylight is replaced by darkness. The sky grows dark with heavy clouds so that noon resembles midnight. Many descriptions of the effect stress its freakish appearance as well as the fear and terror it occasions in the hearts and minds of those who live through it. There are natural causes at the root of the phenomenon, some of them simple, some of them complex, some of them known, some of them unknown. No two "dark days" are identical.

Montreal was the centre of a "dark day" that is known to meteorologists and historians as the Phenomenon of 1819. The difference between Montreal's "dark day" and many other such days is that the phenomenon in Montreal was accompanied by untypical electrical and luminous effects.

The account reproduced here, although an anonymous one, is based on personal experience. It appeared as "The Dark Day in Canada" in the 21 May 1881 issue of the *Scientific American*. It is reprinted from *Handbook of Unusual Natural Phenomena* (Glen Arm, Md.: The Sourcebook Project, 1978) compiled by William R. Corliss.

On the morning of Sunday, November 8, 1819, the sun rose upon a cloudy sky, which assumed as the light grew upon it, a strong greenish tint, varying in places to an inky blackness. After a short time the whole sky became terribly dark, dense black clouds filling the atmosphere, and there followed a heavy shower of rain, which appeared to be something of the nature of soapsuds, and was found to have deposited after settling a substance in all its qualities resembling soot. Late in the afternoon the sky cleared to its natural aspect, and the next day was fine and frosty. On the morning of Tuesday, the 10th, heavy clouds again covered the sky, and changed rapidly from a deep green to a pitchy black, and the sun, which occasionally seen through them, was sometimes of a dark brown or an unearthly yellow colour, and again bright orange, and even blood red. The clouds constantly deepened in colour and intensity, and later on a heavy vapour seemed to descend to the earth, and the day became almost as dark as night, the bloom increasing and diminishing most fitfully. At noon lights had to be burned in the courthouse, the banks, and public offices of that city. Everybody was more or less alarmed, and many were the conjectures as to the cause of the remarkable occurrence. The most sensible thought that immense woods or prairies were on fire somewhere to the west; others said that a great volcano must have broken out in the Province; still others asserted that our mountain was an extinct crater about to resume operations and to make of the city a second Pompeii; the superstitious quoted an old Indian prophecy that one day the Island of Montreal was to be destroyed by an earthquake, and some even cried that the world was about to come to an end.

About the middle of the afternoon a great body of clouds seemed to rush suddenly over the city, and the darkness became that of night. A pause and hush for a moment or two succeeded, and then one of the most glaring flashes of lightning ever beheld flamed over the country, accompanied by a clap of thunder which seemed to shake the city to its foundations. Another pause followed, and then came a light shower of rain of the same soapy and sooty nature as that of two days before. After that it appeared to grow brighter, but an hour later it was as dark as ever. Another rush of clouds came, and another vivid flash of lightning, which was seen to strike the spire of the old French parish church and to play curiously about the large iron cross at its summit before descending to the ground. A moment later came the climax of the day. Every bell in the city suddenly rang out the alarm of fire, and the affrighted citizens rushed out from their houses into the streets and made their way in the gloom toward the church, until Place d'Armes was crowded with people, their nerves all unstrung by the awful events of the day, gazing at, but scarcely daring to approach the strange sight before them. The sky above and around was as black as ink, but right in one spot in mid-air above them was the summit of the spire, with the lightning playing about it shining like a sun. Directly the great iron cross, together with the ball at its foot, fell to the ground with a crash, and was shivered to pieces. But the darkest hour comes just before the dawn. The glow above gradually subsided and died out, the people grew less fearful and returned to their homes, the real night came on, and when next morning dawned everything was bright and clear, and the world was as natural as before. The phenomenon was noticed in a greater or less degree from Quebec to Kingston, and far into the States, but Montreal seemed its centre. It has never yet been explained.

THE BALDOON MYSTERY

Poltergeists are "noisy ghosts," that is the outward signs of ghosts without their outward appearances. Ghostly effects — creaky doors, flickering lights, abrupt changes in temperature, eerie quasi-human sounds and other noises — are more widely reported than appearances of unknown ghosts in winding sheets or known spirits or "doubles" at the point of death.

What is now known as the Baldoon Mystery concerns poltergeist-like activities like these and more, many more, that took place on the McDonald farm near Baldoon, the Scottish farming community located northwest of Chatham, Ont. All manner of disturbances were reported by farmer John McDonald, members of his family, members of the farming community, and travellers and mediums during the three-year period from 1829 to 1831. The disturbances included a hail of bullets, stones, lead pellets, water, and sporadic fires. It is said that at one point the small wooden farmhouse heaved from its foundations. One night it was consumed in flames and burnt to the ground. These disturbances were never satisfactorily explained, though many fanciful tales were told about them, including the curse of a witch and the summoning of a witch-doctor.

There are a number of reasons for the continuing interest in this incident of poltergeistery. It is as complete an account of the haunting of a farmhouse by a poltergeist as anyone is likely to find in the annals of Canadian history. It quickly became associated with another local tradition, the legendary "witch-doctor" known as Doctor Troyer.

The details are described in dramatic detail in a widely available booklet titled *The Baldoon Mystery* (1871) which was issued by the local weekly newspaper, the *Wallaceburg News*, Wallaceburg, Ont., and is kept in print. The account here kept by William S. Fleury is but one of many that comes from that source. As well, the incident took place during a very special phase of the settlement of the southwestern part of the future Province of Ontario, which coincided with the arrival of Lord Selkirk's colony of Highland Scots. The settlement lasted but a few short years. Perhaps its longest-lasting legacy is this tale.

It was rumoured that there was a great mystery going on at McDonald's, and I, like a great many others, went to see for myself. I saw stones and brick bats coming through the doors and windows, making the hole whatever size the article was that came in. Parties would take these same things and throw them into the river, and in a few minutes they would come back again. I saw a child lying in a little cradle, when the cradle began to rock fearfully and no one was near it. They thought it would throw the child out, so two men undertook to stop it, but could not, still a third took hold, but stop it they could not. Some of the party said, "Let's test this," so they put a Bible in the cradle and it stopped instantly. They said that was a fair test.

The gun balls would come in through the windows and we would take them and throw them into the river, which is about thirty-six feet deep, and in a few minutes they would come back through the windows, so we were satisfied that the evil one was at the helm. I saw the house take fire upstairs in ten different places at once. There were plenty to watch the fires, as people came from all parts of the United States and Canada to see for themselves. No less than from twenty to fifty men were there all the time. The bedsteads would move from one side of the room to the other, and the chairs would move when someone was sitting on them and they could not get off. They thought the devil was going to take them, chair and all. I saw the pot, full of boiling water, come off the fireplace and sail about the room over our heads and never spill a drop, and then return to its starting place. I saw a large black dog sitting on the milk house while it was burning, and thinking it would burn we threw sticks at it, but it would not stir, but, all at once, he disappeared. I saw the mush pot chase the dog that happened to come with one of the neighbours, through a crowd, and the people thought the devil was in the pot. It chased the dog all over the house and out of doors, and mush stick would strike it first on one side and then on the other. The dog showed fight, and turning round caught hold of the ring in the stick, which swinging, would strike him first on one side of the face and then on the other. It finally let go of the dog's teeth and went back to the pot. I was acquainted with Mr. McDonald and knew him to be an upright man and in good standing in the Baptist Church.

This is my true statement of what I saw.

William S. Fleury

THE MACKENZIE RIVER GHOST

Here is the most famous true ghost story of the Northwest. It received its broadest readership through its appearance in *Lord Halifax's Ghost Book* (1936), an influential and widely read compilation of English ghost stories which was prepared for print by Lord Halifax, Viscount Charles Lindley.

The events themselves took place in the Great Northwest in 1853-54; a fur trader, accompanying a corpse by dog sled from Fort McPherson in the Mackenzie River District to Fort Simpson, heard the corpse utter the command "Marché!" at times that turned out to be critical to the survival of the group. It is told here in the words of Roderick MacFarlane (1835-1920), Fellow of the Royal Geographical Society, a fur trader in the Northwest Territories for over forty years. It was MacFarlane who established Fort Smith in 1874, and it was at his instigation that the first steamship for travel on the Mackenzie River was constructed in 1886.

MacFarlane was the principal witness of the eerie events and experiences recorded in this account. He recalled his experience at the request of a scholar at Oxford University in 1883. The full account appeared as "Ghost Story" in *The Beaver*, December 1986-January 1987. (That account is the original one and it is reproduced here.) It was given semi-factual, semi-fictional treatment by the British officer and explorer Sir W.F. Butler in *Good Words* (1877). It was retold by Ernest Thompson Seton in *Trail and Campfire Stories* (1940). Noted ghost-hunter R.S. Lambert, in *Exploring the Supernatural: The Weird in Canadian Folklore* (1955), recalling the story, called it "the most convincing of all Canadian apparitions."

The Mackenzie River Ghost

On the fifteenth day of March 1853, Augustus Richard Peers, a fur trader and post manager in the service of the Hudson's Bay Company, departed his life at Fort McPherson, Peel's River, in the Mackenzie River District, Arctic America. Although he had occasionally complained of ill health, his death after a few days' sickness at the comaparatively early age of thirty-three years was entirely unexpected. He was of Anglo-Irish origin, an able officer, much esteemed by his friends and popular among the Indians. During a residence of, I think, eleven years in that remote district, he had been stationed for two or three Outfit seasons at "Head-quarters," Fort Simpson, and afterwards at Forts Norman and McPherson. In 1849, Mr. Peers was married to the eldest daughter of the late Chief Trader John Bell of the Hudson's Bay Company. They had two children. In 1855 the widow remarried the late Alexander McKenzie, who succeeded Mr. Peers at Fort McPherson.

While a resident of both Norman and McPherson, the deceased had been heard to express a strong dislike, in the event of his death, that his bones should rest at either spot. Mr. Peers was thought to have made a holograph will some time previous to his demise; but if so, he must have mislaid or destroyed it, as no such document ever turned up.

Having entered the service of the Company in 1852, I was appointed to the Mackenzie River District the following year, and reached Fort Simpson five months after Mr. Peers's death, where I met his widow and infant children. In the autumn of 1859, at the urgent request of Mrs. McKenzie and her husband, it was decided that the long contemplated transfer of the remains of Mr. Peers from their place of interment at Peel's River to Fort Simpson on the Mackenzie, should be carried out that winter. Mr. Charles P. (now Chief Trader) Gaudet, then in charge of Fort McPherson, agreed to convey the body by dog train to my trade post at Fort Good Hope, a distance of three hundred miles, while I undertook to render it at its final destination, some five hundred miles further south.

Fort McPherson is situated about one degree north of the Arctic Circle. The soil in its neighbourhood is marshy, and frost is ever present at a shallow depth beneath the surface. On being exhumed by Mr. Gaudet, the body was found in much the same condition it had assumed shortly after its burial. It was then removed from the original coffin, and placed in a new and unnecessarily large coffin which, secured by a moose skin wrapper and lines on a Hudson's Bay dog sled or train, made it an extremely awkward and difficult load for men and dogs to haul and conduct over the rugged masses of tossed-up ice which annually occur at intervals along the mighty Mackenzie River, especially in the higher and more rapid portion of its course towards the northern ocean.

On the first day of March, 1860, Mr. Gaudet arrived at Good Hope and delivered up the body to my care, and I set out for Fort Simpson. The coffin was fixed on one team or train of three dogs conducted by an Iroquois Indian from Caughnawaga, near Montreal, named Michel Thomas (since deceased), while the second train carried our bedding, voyaging utensils and provisions. I myself led the march on snowshoes, and after seven days of very hard and trying labour, owing to the unusual depth of the snow and much rugged ice, the first two hundred miles of our journey to the nearest point (Fort Norman) from Good Hope, was successfully accomplished. At this place Mr. Nicol Taylor (now deceased) strongly pointed out that unless the coffin was removed, and the body properly secured on the train, it would be almost impossible to travel over the vast masses of tossed-up ice which were sure to be encountered at certain points between here and Fort Simpson. As I had previously gone twice over the ground in winter, and had already had some experience of *bourdions*, I acted on his advice, and we had subsequently good reason for congratulation on having done so.

After one day's rest at Norman, we started on the last and longest portion of the journey. There was no intervening station at that time, and we met few Indians. The Iroquois Thomas remained with the body train. The baggage train and man from Good Hope were exchanged at Norman for fresh animals and a new driver named Michel Iroquois. Mr. Taylor also assisted me in beating the track for the party, he having volunteered to accompany the remains of his former master and friend, Mr. Peers.

A full description of winter travelling in this country may be learned from the pages of Franklin, Back, Richardson and Butler. Here it may be briefly stated that we got under way by four o'clock in the morning; dined at some convenient spot about noon, and after an hour's rest, resumed our march until sunset, when we laid up for the night, generally in a pine bluff on the top or close to the immediate bank of the river. Clearing away the snow to the ground for a space of about ten feet square, cutting and carrying pine brush for carpeting the camp and collecting firewood for cooking and warming purposes, usually occupied us for about an hour. Another hour would see supper over and the dogs fed, and by the end of the next sixty or more minutes, most of the party would be sound asleep. Except on two occasions to be presently mentioned, the train carrying the body of the deceased was invariably hauled up and placed for the night in the immediate rear of our encampment, and except also on the first of the said occasions, our dogs never exhibited any desire to get at same, nor did they seem in the slightest degree affected by its presence in our midst.

About sunset on the fifteenth day of March, 1860, the

seventh anniversary of poor Peers's death, we were obliged to encamp at a short distance from *Roche qui trempe a l'eau*, the rock by the riverside of Sir Alexander Mackenzie, as there was no better place within reach. The banks here were high, rocky and steep, and we had to leave both trains on the ice; we experienced much difficulty in scrambling up the bank with our axes, snowshoes, bedding and provisions for supper and breakfast. The dogs were unharnessed and remained below, while the weather was calm and comparatively fine and mild. The bank rose about thirty feet to the summit where, on a shelving flat some thirty feet beyond, we selected a position for the night. All hands then set about making the camp, cutting and carrying the requisite supply of pine brush and firewood.

After being thus busily employed for ten or twelve minutes, the dogs began to bark and we at once concluded that Indians were approaching us, as this was a part of the river where a few were frequently met with. We, however, continued our work, the dogs still barking, though not so loudly or fiercely as they usually do under similar circumstances. Neither the dogs nor sleds were visible from the camp, but only from the summit of the river bank. While talking with Mr. Taylor about the expected Indians, we all distinctly heard the word "Marche" (I may remark that French terms are almost universally applied to hauling dogs and their work in the Northwest Territories of Canada.) It seemed to have been uttered by someone at the foot of the bank who wished to drive away the dogs in his path, and we all left off work in order to see who the stranger was; but as no one appeared in sight, Michel Thomas and myself proceeded to the aforesaid summit, where, to our astonishment, no man was visible, while the dogs were seen surrounding the body train at a distance of several feet, and still apparently excited at something. We had to call them repeatedly before they gave up barking, but after a few minutes they desisted and then somehow managed to ascend the bank to our encampment, where they remained perfectly quiet for the night, and thereafter continued as indifferent as before in respect to the deceased's body.

It struck me at the time I heard it that the word *marche* was enunciated in a clearer manner than I had ever before known an Indian to do so, as they seldom get beyond a *mashe* or *masse* pronunciation of the term.

On the eighteenth day of March we were compelled to travel two hours after dark in order to find a suitable encampment, and although we discovered a tolerably good place near the head of a large island on the Mackenzie, yet it was not an easy matter to ascend a perpendicular bank of some twelve feet in height. The baggage train being now rather light, by tying a line to the foremost dog, we managed to drag it and them to the top. The same plan answered with the dogs of the body train; but we considered it beyond our power to get it up, and we were therefore reluctantly obliged to leave it below. After cutting a trail through thick willows for about thirty or forty yards, we reached the edge of a dense forest of small spruce, where we camped. The customary operations were at once attended to, and when most of the work was over I turned up with some firewood from a distance where I had been collecting a lot for the night.

Mr. Taylor then asked me if I had heard a very loud call or yell twice repeated from the direction of the river.

I said, "No," as my cap ear protectors were closely tied down owing to the cold wind, and the thicket very dense.

The two Iroquois corroborated Mr. Taylor's statement, but to settle the matter and find out if any Indian had followed our tracks, we all proceeded to the bank, where nothing could be seen or heard, and we at once decided on having the body train hauled up by sheer force, and it proved a tough job to do so.

We remembered our experience of the fifteenth of March, and when we set out early next morning we had reason to congratulate ourselves on taking this trouble, as on reaching the spot from which we had removed the body train, we discovered that a *carcajou* or wolverine had been there during the night. To those who know the power of this destructive animal, I need not say that he would have played havoc with the aforesaid remains.

Fort Simpson was at length reached without a recurrence of anything of an unusual nature, in the forenoon of the twenty-first of March, and the body was duly buried in the adjacent graveyard on the twenty-third of that month. Shortly after my arrival, Mr. Taylor and I recounted everything to Chief Trader Bernard R. Ross (since deceased), the district manager, who had been an intimate friend and countryman of Mr. Peers. Mr. Ross was a good mimic and had an excellent memory. He was asked to utter the word *marche* in the voice of the deceased, and while I at once recognized the tone as similar to that heard by us at our encampment of the fifteenth of March, Mr. Taylor had no doubt whatever on the subject.

During my stay at Fort Simpson, I occupied a shakedown bed in the same room with Mr. Ross, and at a distance from his of some eight or ten feet. On the first or second night after retiring and extinguishing the candle light, while conversing on the subject of the rather remarkable occurrences narrated herein (including the supposed disappearance of his will) relating to the deceased, I became over poweringly conscious of what struck me then and since to have been the spiritual or supernatural presence of the late Mr. Peers. The feeling, however, came on so very suddenly and scaringly that I instantly covered my face with the blanket and remained speechless. After an interval of perhaps only a few seconds Mr. Ross (whose voice had also ceased) in a somewhat excited tone asked me if I had experienced a very peculiar sensation. I answered that I had and described the feeling, which he assured me agreed exactly with what he himself had just undergone. I know from experience what nightmare is; but while it is most unlikely that two individuals who were carrying on a conversation in which they felt a deep interest should be thus attacked simultaneously, it may be stated that neither of us had partaken of any wines, spirits or anything else which could have brought on a nightmare.

I leave it to others, if they can, to give a reasonable account or explanation of the facts I have here stated; but if it be assumed as an axiom that the spirits of some of the dead are occasionally permitted to revisit former scenes and to take more or less interest in their discarded bodies, then from what we have incidentally learned of the late Mr. Peers's sentiments in respect to the final disposition of his remains, what other or more natural course would the spirit of such a man be expected to take with the view of preventing any unnecessary desecration of them than that apparently adopted on the nights of the fifteenth and eighteenth of March, 1860?

From the position of our camp of the fifteenth of March, it may be taken for granted that it was almost impossible to have hauled the body train up such a steep and rugged rocky bank. Dogs are invariably hungry at the end of a long day's travel and, as the weather was fine that day, they may have scented the still fresh and perfect remains, and probably desired to get at them while their barking at and position around the sled would, on any other hypothesis, be at least equally strange and unaccountable. Of course, there was danger from wolves and wolverines, but it is presumed that spirits know more than mortals. On the night of March eighteen, however, although the bank was very difficult of ascent (to get up one had first to raise and push a man till he laid hold of the root of a stout willow by which he hoisted himself to the top, and then threw us a line which aided the rest) it was not insurmountable; and as a most vicious and destructive animal actually visited the spot where we intended leaving the body train for the night, but for the calls and yells referred to, I again ask what other course than that mentioned would any man or spirit possessed of future knowledge be likely to take? And as to the extraordinary feeling experienced by Mr. Ross and myself at the moment when we were talking about the deceased and his supposed will, if it be possible for spirits to communicate with mortals, might this not have arisen (as I actually felt at the time) from a desire on his part to convey some information to us who evinced so deep an interest in the matter but which, from losing our presence of mind, we missed the opportunity of ascertaining?

The foregoing facts made so indelible an impression on my mind that I firmly believe that my present account of them does not in any material point differ from what I communicated to Mr. Ross at the time, and repeatedly since to others. I also distinctly remember the occasion on which I gave similar details to General Sir William F. (then Captain) Butler, K.C.B. It was at Green Lake post, North-West Territory, in the month of February 1873. Captain Butler soon after proceeded to Ashanti, where he experienced a very severe attack of illness, and he, moreover, wrote me that he had taken poetical licence with my narrative, and this will naturally account for the discrepancies between the statements I have given in this paper and his story of same in *Good Words* for 1877.

A GHOST STORY

The following story is told in settlements of the Scots, a canny race of people with a sense of the uncanny. The story first appeared in the November 7, 1859, issue of the *Nova Scotian*, Halifax, N.S.

A Ghost Story

Mr. Hector M'Donald, of Canada, was recently on a visit to Boston. When he left home his family were enjoying good health, and he anticipated a pleasant journey. The second morning after his arrival in Boston, when leaving his bed to dress for breakfast, he saw reflected in a mirror the corpse of a woman lying in the bed from which he had just risen. Spell-bound, he gazed with intense feeling, and tried to recognize the features of the corpse, but in vain; he could not even move his eyelids; he felt deprived of action, for how long he knew not. He was at last startled by the ringing of the bell for breakfast, and sprang to the bed to satisfy himself if what he had seen reflected in the mirror was real or an illusion. He found the bed as he left it, he looked again into the mirror, but only saw the bed truly reflected. During the day he thought much upon the illusion, and determined next morning to rub his eyes and feel perfectly sure that he was wide awake before he left bed. But, notwithstanding these precautions, the vision was repeated with this addition, that he thought he recognized in the corpse some resemblance to the features of his wife.

In the course of the second day he received a letter from his wife, in which she stated that she was quite well, and hoped he was enjoying himself among his friends. As he was devotedly attached to her, and always anxious for her safety, he supposed that his morbid fears had conjured up the vision he had seen reflected in the glass; and went about his business as cheerfully as usual. — On the morning of the third day, after he had dressed, he found himself in thought in his own house, leaning over the coffin of his wife. His friends were assembled, the minister was performing the funeral services, his children wept — he was in the house of death. He followed the corpse to the grave; he heard the earth rumble upon the coffin, he saw the grave filled and the green sods covered over it; yet, by some strange power, he could see through the ground the entire form of his wife as she lay in her coffin.

He looked in the face of those around him, but no one seemed to notice him; he tried to weep, but the tears refused to flow, his very heart felt as hard as a rock. Enraged at his own want of feeling, he determined to throw himself upon the grave and lie there till his heart should break, when he was recalled to consciousness by a friend, who entered the room to inform him that breakfast was ready. He started as if awoke from a profound sleep, though he was standing before the mirror with a hair-brush in his hand.

After composing himself, he related to his friend what he had seen, and both concluded that a good breakfast only was wanting to dissipate his unpleasant impressions. A few days afterwards, however, he received the melancholy intelligence that his wife had died suddenly, and the time corresponded with the day he had been startled by the first vision in the mirror. When he returned home he described minutely all the details of the funeral he had seen in his vision, and they corresponded with the facts. This is probably one of the most vivid instances of clairvoyance on record. Mr. M'Donald knows nothing of modern spiritualism or clairvoyance, as most of his life has been passed upon a farm and among forests. It may not be amiss to state that his father, who was a Scotch Highlander, had the gift of "second sight." — *Boston Traveller*.

HE WAS NOT THERE

"The woods are full of creepy things."

So runs a line of a child's song. At least one of those "creepy things" is a sentinel spirit or guardian angel of some sort.

"My Ghostly Guide" is reprinted from the *Ottawa Free Press*, 15 Jan. 1891. It purports to be the words of an "assistant clerk in a large lumbering camp."

My Ghostly Guide
A Lumber Merchant's Story

In January 1853 I was engaged as assistant clerk in a large lumbering camp in the woods about a hundred miles north of the Ottawa river. Our main shanty, was by the side of an outlet of the Red Pine lake about two miles from the south side of the lake itself, a sheet of water of oblong shape, about a mile and a half wide and five miles long. There was a fairly good road from the edge of the lake to the shanty, and from the north or opposite side of the lake, a road had been made for some miles through the forest, to a point where a smaller camp had been established, and where a number of our men were engaged in making timber. From the main shanty to the smaller one was probably twenty miles. One day my chief, Mr. Simpson, sent me off with some instructions to the foreman in charge of what we called the Crooked Creek camp. I started with my snowshoes on my back and moccasins on my feet, at a brisk pace. It was a bright clear day. The road to the lake had been well worn by teams, and as there had been a thaw covered with frost, the ice on the lake was hard and smooth. The road from the lake to the Crooked Creek camp was rather rough and narrow, and a stranger might have difficulty in following it. However, I knew the route well, and arrived at my destination in good time, just as the men were returning from their work, with axes on their shoulders. I spent the night in the camp, being asked innumerable questions, and hearing all the petty gossip the men had to relate. It must be remembered that these shanty men go into the woods in October or November and excepting in rare instances hear nothing whatever from the outside world until they come out in the spring. Next morning I executed my commission and about ten o'clock started back for the main camp. I had not travelled more than half the distance when a snowstorm set in. In the woods the flakes fell down steadily, and I had no difficulty in keeping the road. It was about sun down when I reached the edge of the lake. The snow had reached the track across the ice and there was nothing to guide me to the entrance to the road to our main camp on the opposite shore. Out on the lake the storm was blinding, but I did not doubt my ability to reach the other side and find the road. So I started across the lake. When less than half a mile from the edge of the woods the snow was so thick that I could see neither shore. Moreover it was getting dark and exceedingly cold. If I should lose my way on the lake and have to spend the night there I would certainly perish. What was to be done? I turned in my tracks and managed to reach the North Shore again, stopping in the shelter of some bushes to recover my breath. Should I stay there all night? To tramp back to Crooked Lake camp was my first decision, but on reflection I remembered that any person travelling that road at night was liable to be attacked and eaten by wolves. Moreover I was hungry and fatigued. While I was thus communing with myself, jumping up and down and slapping my hands to keep myself warm, I saw a man dressed in a grey suit with a tuke on his head and a scarf around his waist, about 200 yards out on the lake, beckoning to me to follow him. I at once jumped to the conclusion that Mr. Simpson had sent one of the axe-men to meet me and guide me across the lake. So I ran with all my might towards him, calling to him at the same time. When I came close to the spot where he had stood, I looked around. He was not there, but a lull in the drift showed him some distance further on, still beckoning me to follow. No reply came to my calls to the man to wait for me, but every few moments he would appear some distance ahead beckoning me towards him. I could not tell what to make of the man's eccentric behaviour, but thought possible he was angry over being sent to look me up, and was taking this method of evincing his displeasure. At last I saw him on the shore, pointing towards the woods, and reaching the spot where he had been standing I found myself at the point where the road to our camp left the lake. The road was easy to follow, and I hurried forward, still somewhat puzzled over the refusal of my guide to wait for me; and wondering also why he had not brought a horse, and sled. I reached the camp just as the men had finished their supper, and everybody was surprised at my return. Mr. Simpson said he supposed that even if I had started from Crooked Creek camp in the morning I would have turned back when the snow storm came on. Somewhat bewildered I asked which of the men it was that guided me across the lake and pointed out the road to the camp. "Why did he not wait for me?" I asked in a rather injured tone. The men looked at one another in amazement. Not a man had been out of the camp that evening. Every man had returned from work at the usual time and remained in camp until my arrival. We were nearly seventy miles from the nearest settlement and there was no camp nearer than the one at Crooked Creek. Every person in the camp became restless and nervous. That man who guided me across the Red Pine lake was not a being of flesh and blood, was the general conclusion of the shanty men and my description of his disappearances and reappearances tended to strengthen their theory. The experience was such an inexplicable one that very few of the inmates of our camp slept that night. I was grateful for my rescue, and it was evidently that whoever my guide was it was not my destiny to be eaten by wolves or frozen to death in attempting to cross Red Pine lake in a snow storm.

THE BINSTEAD HAUNTING

The case of the Binstead Haunting was widely discussed in the late 19th century but was largely forgotten by the early 20th century. A detailed account of the haunting appeared in the prestigious *Journal* of the Society for Psychical Research in the section titled "On Recognised Apparitions Occurring More than a Year after Death" (SPR *Journal*, July 8, 1889). It is worth recalling that both the British and the American SPRs, far from being amateurish groups of people intent on proving "survival after death," were founded and run by the most eminent scientists of the day who conducted psychical research, studied mediumship, documented hallucinations, and investigated what was quaintly called "spirit-survival." The Societies were investigative agencies, not alliances for spiritualists.

The author of the account is identified, daintily, as "Mrs. Pennée, of St. Anne de Beaupré, Quebec, daughter of the late Mr. William Ward (a Conservative M.P. for London), and sister of the late Rev. A.B. Ward, of Cambridge." The calm of the estate, located outside East River, P.E.I., was compromised by events that took place in its past and that led to the appearance of "a woman with a baby" in one arm who stirred ashes in the fireplace with the other.

The text of the account printed here (with some additional comments by the SPR's editor) is based on the version that appeared in that journal rather than on the one that was published in the local newspaper. The newspaper's account was headed "A Real Ghost!" for its appearance in the columns of the *Daily Examiner* (Charlottetown, P.E.I.), November 28, 1889.

The newspaper account began with the following words: "The English Society for Psychical Research is still vigorously pursuing its investigations and is about to publish part XV. of its proceedings, containing articles on apparitions, duplex personality, seances with the celebrated medium, D.D. Home, &c." Minor variations in punctuation and spelling were noted, but the principle difference between the versions is that the newspaper story is shorter than the journal story. The newspaper story ends before the introduction of the second and third letters. So the full version appears here.

I will conclude my quoted cases with a somewhat painful and complex narrative, which ought, I think, to be considered when we are trying to form a conception as to the true significance of "haunting" sounds and sights.

XIV. — The following case, which we owe to the kindness Mr. Wilfrid Ward (and of Lord Tennyson, for whom it was first committed to writing some years ago), is sent by Mrs. Pennée, of St. Anne de Beaupré, Quebec, daughter of the late Mr. William Ward (a Conservative M.P. for London), and sister of the late Rev. A.B. Ward, of Cambridge.

Weston Manor, Freshwater, Isle of Wight.
1884.

It was in the year 1856 that my husband took me to live at a house called Binstead, about five miles from Charlottetown, P.E. Island. It was a good-sized house, and at the back had been considerably extended to allow of extra offices, since there were about 200 acres of farm land around it, necessitating several resident farming men. Although forming part of the house, these premises could only be entered through the inner kitchen, as no wall had ever been broken down to form a door or passage from upstairs. Thus the farming men's sleeping rooms were adjacent to those occupied by the family and visitors, although there was no communication through the upstairs corridor.

It was always in or near the sleeping apartment, immediately adjacent to the men's, that the apparition was seen, and as that was one of our spare bedrooms, it may have frequently been unperceived.

About 10 days after we had established ourselves at Binstead, we commenced hearing strange noises. For many weeks they were of very frequent occurrence, and were heard simultaneously in every part of the house, and always appeared to be in close proximity to each person. The noise was more like a rumbling which made the house vibrate, than like that produced by dragging a heavy body, of which one so often hears in ghost stories.

As spring came on we began to hear shrieks, which would grow fainter or louder, as if someone was being chased around the house, but always culminating in a volley of shrieks, sobs, moans, and half-uttered words, proceeding from beneath a tree that stood at a little distance from the dining-room window, and whose branches nearly touched the window of the bedroom I have mentioned.

It was in February (I think), 1857, that the firs apparition came under my notice. Two ladies wer sleeping in the bedroom. Of course, for that season o the year a fire had been lighted in the grate, and th fireplace really contained a grate and not an America substitute for one.

About 2 o'clock, Mrs. M. was awakened by a brigh light which pervaded the room. She saw a woma standing by the fireplace. On her left arm was a youn baby, and with her right hand she was stirring the ashes over which she was slightly stooping.

Mrs. M. pushed Miss C. to awaken her, and just the the figure turned her face towards them, disclosing th features of quite a young woman with a singularl anxious pleading look upon her face. They took notic of a little check shawl which was crossed over he bosom. Miss C. had previously heard some tale concerning the house being haunted (which neither Mrs M. nor I had ever heard), so jumping to the conclusio that she beheld a ghost, she screamed and pulled th bedclothes tightly over the heads of herself and he companion, so that the sequel of the ghost's proceedings is unknown.

The following spring I went home to England, and just before starting I had my own experience of seeing a ghost. I had temporarily established myself in the room, and one evening, finding my little daughter (now Mrs. Amyot) far from well, had her bed wheeled in beside mine that I might attend to her. About 12 o'clock I got up to give her some medicine, and was feeling for the matches when she called my attention to a brilliant light shining under the door. I exclaimed that it was her papa and threw open the door to admit him. I found myself face to face with a woman. She had a baby on her left arm, a check shawl crossed over her bosom, and all around her shone a bright pleasant light, whence emanating I could not say. Her look at me was one of entreaty — almost agonizing entreaty. She did not enter the room but moved across the staircase, vanishing into the opposite wall, exactly where the inner man-servant's room was situated.

Neither my daughter nor myself felt the slightest alarm; at the moment it appeared to be a matter of common occurrence. When Mr. Pennée came upstairs and I told him what we had seen, he examined the wall, the staircase, the passage, but found no traces of anything extraordinary. Nor did my dogs bark.

On my return from England in 1858 I was informed that "the creature had been carrying on," but it was the screams that had been the worst. However, Harry (a farm-servant) had had several visits but would tell no particulars. I never could get Harry to tell me much. He acknowledged that the woman had several times stood at the foot of his bed, but he would not tell me more. One night Harry had certainly been much disturbed in mind, and the other man heard voices and sobs. Nothing would ever induce Harry to let anyone share his room, and he was most careful to fasten his door before retiring. At the time, I attached no importance to "his ways," as we called them.

In the autumn of the following year, 1859, my connection with Binstead ceased, for we gave up the house and returned to Charlottetown.

I left Prince Edward Island in 1861, and went to Quebec. In 1877 I happened to return to the Island, and spent several months there. One day I was at the Bishop's residence, when the parish priest came in with a letter in his hand. He asked me about my residence at Binstead, and whether I could throw any light on the contents of his letter. It was from the wife of the then owner of Binstead, asking him to come out and try to deliver them from the ghost of a young woman with a baby in her arms, who had appeared several times.

After I went to live in Charlottetown, I became acquainted with the following facts, which seem to throw light on my ghost story.

The ground on which Binstead stood had been cleared, in about 1840, by a rich Englishman, who had built a very nice house. Getting tired of colonial life, he sold the property to a man whose name I forget, but whom I will call Pigott (that was like the name). He was a man of low tastes and immoral habits; but a capital farmer. It was he who added all the back wing of the house and made the necessary divisions, &c., for farming the land. He had two sisters in his service, the daughters of a labourer who lived in a regular hovel, about three miles nearer town. After a time each sister gave birth to a boy.

Very little can be learnt of the domestic arrangements, since Pigott bore so bad a name that the house was avoided by respectable people; but it is certain that one sister and one baby disappeared altogether, though when and how is a complete mystery.

When the other baby was between one and two years old, Pigott sold Binstead to an English gentleman named Fellowes, from whom we hired it, with the intention of eventually buying it. The other sister returned to her father's house, and leaving the baby with

Mrs. Newbury, her mother, went to the States, and has never returned. Before leaving she would reveal nothing, except that the boy was her sister's, her own being dead. It was this very Harry Newbury that we had unwittingly engaged as a farm-servant. He came to bid me farewell a few months after I left Binstead, saying he would never return there. In 1877, I inquired about him, and found that he had never been seen since in Prince Edward Island.

In another letter dated September 24th, 1887, Mrs. Pennée adds:—

Another fact has come to my notice. A young lady, then a child of from 5 to 10, remembers being afraid of sleeping alone when on a visit at Binstead on account of the screams she heard outside, and also the "woman with a baby," whom she saw passing through her room. Her experience goes back some 10 to 15 years before mine.

In a further letter, dated St. Anne de Beaupré, Quebec, January 23rd, 1889, Mrs. Pennée gives additional facts, as follows: —

(1) Mrs. Pennée interviewed Father Boudreault, the priest sent for by the C. family to exorcise the house. Father B., however, was on his death-bed; and although he remembered the fact that he had been sent for to Binstead for this purpose, he could not recollect what had been told him as to apparitions, &c.

(2) Mrs. M., who first saw the figure, has gone to England, and cannot now be traced. Mrs. Pennée adds: — "The lady in question told several people that she saw a woman with a baby in her arms when she slept at Binstead; and, like myself, she noticed a *frilled cap* on the woman. The woman whose ghost we imagine this to be was an Irish woman, and perhaps you have noticed their love of wide frills in their head-gear."

(3) Mrs. Pennée revisited Binstead in 1888, and says, "The tree whence the screams started is cut down; the room where all saw the ghost is totally uninhabited; and Mrs. C. would not let us stay in it, and entreated us to talk no further on the subject. From the man we got out a little, but she followed us up very closely. He says that since the priest blessed the house a woman has been seen (or *said* to have been seen, he corrected himself) round the front entrance, and once at an upper window."

The list of cases cited in this and the previous paper, while insufficient (as I have already said) to compel conviction, is striking enough to plead for serious attention to a subject which will never be properly threshed out unless the interest taken in it assumes a scientific rather than an emotional form.

BLUE DEVIL

The tribulations that Jehovah visited upon Job in the Old Testament are as naught alongside those visited by "a visible devil" on farmer Morley in Goderich, U.C.
    Might it be that Goderich abounds in devils or at least in deviltry? Perhaps not!
    The following article might be read as comic relief. It was written with tongue-in-cheek. "A Visible Devil at Goderich!" first appeared in the columns of the *Sarnia Observer* (Sarnia, U.C., today's Ontario), 9 Dec. 1859.

A Visible Devil at Goderich! — The *Signal* gives an account of the doings of a visible devil up in Goderich, which we reproduce for the benefit of our readers. As nothing is said about the color of the devil, we shall take it for granted that it is the "Blue Devil" which is referred to, as it is generally in that shade that his Satanic Majesty appears to his devotees now-a-days. The editor of the *Signal* proceeds: —

Our readers can form no adequate conception of that hellish disposition which can deliberately barricade a railway track in the dead hour of night, with the intention and in the hope of murdering and mangling a multitude of unknown fellow-beings, or, it may be, a number of friends. Our readers, we say, can have no correct idea of this hellish disposition, because they have not witnessed it, and it is not a part of human nature, but with some acts of the same disposition they are perhaps familiar.

Poor old Morley! Who has not heard of Morley and the visible Devil which for years past has been tormenting, and robbing, and seeking to murder him? Morley is the quietest, most inoffensive man in the township of Goderich, and though an old bachelor, is kind hearted and obliging. — He lives alone like a hermit and his farm is on the Maitland, near Disney's Sawmill, where he is respected, well spoken of, and even liked by all the neighborhood. Some years ago the visible Devil cast his eye on poor Morley, as he did on Job in days of yore, and after robbing his shanty of a large sum of money, burned it to the ground in Morley's absence. From that day to this, the visible devil has held poor Morley in his clutches, and has done all manner of evil and injury to him, except to kill him outright. His horses, cows, and cattle, his sheep and hogs, have been maimed, mangled, poisoned and drowned, and even forcibly driven over precipices and destroyed, not in ones or twos, but in half dozens, and not on a few occasions, but year after year, on every favorable opportunity, and we learn with regret and horror that this year has been among the worst. — We are informed that this same visible Devil has lately buried in his entrails about a dozen of Morley's best sheep; and the same authority assures us that first and last, the poor old must have lost property to the amount of at least *twelve hundred dollars*, by this malignant fiend. — Poor Morley has been waylaid and brutally maltreated on his own farm, in broad daylight, and with intent to take his life.

Now, we can barely be persuaded, that such deeds of darkness and malice can be the work of ordinary humanity, and though they be committed by human forces, we have long held the opinion, that such desperate wickedness must be wrought by the Devil in disguise, and that these human forms are incarnations of the arch Enemy.

With all that Science has done for man the great Arcana of Nature is still a sealed book. He knows little of Nature, little of himself beyond the simple phenomena that appeal to his senses — these senses are mystery, and the *How* and the *Why* are forever hid from his ken. Mind is united with matter, but what is mind and what is matter? How are they united and why do they affect each other? They are united in the dog as well as in the man, and what is the difference between the two unions? These and ten thousand questions simpler than these, cannot be answered; and in this universe of mysteries, may it not be, that the constitutionally wicked are produced by a mysterious union of Satan and humanity, just as simple as the union of mind and matter? We verily believe, that Morley's visible Devil is half Devil, half man, and we feel convinced that if some learned spiritualists, Judge

Edmunds or the Poughkeepsie Seer, were in the neighborhood, we would detect Morley's Devil in less than a week. Surely the neighbors should make a terrible effort to get quit of such a dangerous customer, more especially as others besides Morley are said to lose their sheep. Begin now.

VISIONS

Some commentators separate psychical matters from spiritual affairs, seeing the former as immersed in matter, the latter as immersed in spirit. The view of the present commentator is that the psychical and the spiritual are part and parcel of the same experience and, hence, such distinctions are without difference, being bereft of discernible difference. For this reason the present collection reproduces some passages that dramatize religious piety and sentimentality, sensations traditionally associated with Protestant fundamentalism. Instances of these are accounts of revival meetings, conversion experiences, and miraculous healings.

Nathan Bangs, an itinerant Methodist preacher, conducted religious revival services at camp meetings throughout Upper Canada. Visiting the village of York (now the City of Toronto) in 1801, he called it a "new little village, the settlers of which were as thoughtless and wicked as the Canaanites of old." His story is told by Abel Stevens in <i>Life and Times of Nathan Bangs, D.D.</i> (New York, 1863).

The effect of Bangs's evangelical enthusiasm is seen in light of emotional excess by the historian John Webster Grant in <i>A Profusion of Spires: Religion in Nineteenth-Century Ontario</i> (Toronto: University of Toronto Press, 1988). Grant noted that "it has customarily been argued that revival in Upper Canada was largely free of the abnormal psychic manifestations reported in the United States, but this judgment rests in large measure on exaggerated or one-sided accounts of happenings in Kentucky." He continued:

What relentless pressure such methods could impose on the unconverted becomes evident in Nathan Bangs's classic description of one of the first camp meetings to be held in Canada, a description especially revealing for its indications of constant interplay between the spontaneous and the carefully programmed....

In view of the intensity of feelings aroused, it is scarcely surprising that this pioneer period was recalled as one marked by signs and wonders of divine grace. Missions were frequently accompanied by warnings and portents. After a prosperous man had turned Bangs out of his house, "one untoward event after another occurred until he was a complete wreck, morally, mentally, socially, physically, as well as in his secular affairs. In time he was deserted by his wife, reduced to dependence on charity, and allowed no peace even on his deathbed."

An Unusual Sense of the Divine Presence

At five o'clock Saturday morning a prayer-meeting was held, and at ten o'clock a sermon was preached on the words, "My people are destroyed for lack of knowledge." At this time the congregation had increased to perhaps twenty-five hundred, and the people of God were seated together on logs near the stand, while a crowd were standing in a semicircle around them. During the sermon I felt an unusual sense of the divine presence, and I thought I could see a cloud of divine glory resting upon the congregation....

I ... descended from the stand among the hearers; the rest of the preachers spontaneously followed me, and we went among the people, exhorting the impenitent and comforting the distressed; for while Christians were filled with "joy unspeakable and full of glory," many a sinner was weeping and praying in the surrounding crowd. These we collected together in little groups, and exhorted God's people to join in prayer for them, and not to leave them until he should save their souls. O what a sense of tears and prayers was this! I suppose that not less than a dozen little praying circles were thus formed in the course of a few minutes. It was truly affecting to see parents, weeping over their children, neighbours exhorting their unconverted neighbours to repent, while all, old and young, were awe-struck. The wicked look on with silent amazement while they behold some of their companions struck down by the mighty power of God, and heard his people pray for them....

During this time some forty people were converted or sanctified.

WHAT IS TERMED A MIRAGE

This odd item, which originally appeared as "Singular Phenomenon" in the *Montreal Witness*, 13 Feb. 1862, describes, first-hand, the appearance of a mirage that formed above the far shore of a lake near the village of Barnston in Quebec's Eastern Townships. The air-borne mirage began with "a train of cars," presumably carriages of a train; continued with "an army of men"; and ended with "a ship." In turn, each image in turn collapsed into itself and turned perpendicular to the horizon.

Meteorologists talk about atmospheric inversions which turn the sky into something of a mirror. But where were to be found the cars, army, and ship that were being reflected and refracted?

Singular Phenomenon. — Mr. G.W. Kinney, of Barnston, communicates to the Stanstead *Journal* the following statement of an extraordinary appearance on the west side of a small lake in that Township. It was evidently what is termed a *mirage*, but the question is where was the army thus reflected? Were they British troops on their way from Halifax to Canada? — "Two weeks ago to-day in the morning, I discovered that the mountains on the west side of the lake looked very different from what they usually do. It came to my mind what I had heard had been seen a few days before this in the same place. I stopped and saw, apparently, a train of cars, four in number; presently they changed their position and came together, forming into one body, one side of which was perpendicular to a great height; and then another similar form made its appearance at a short distance, I then saw as it looked to me, an army of men advance towards each other and then disappear; it then passed away into some different position. I then saw a ship come in sight, turn broadside to the apparent army of men, and thus they appeared and disappeared for six hours, passing before my eyes like a splendid panorama. There were no clouds to be seen in the sky that day in that direction, or any fog. This is no idle dream or fancy, and I can substantiate it with the testimony of a very good number of people, who were with me in the morn-ing, and saw the same sight."

A TALL FIGURE CLOTHED IN WHITE

A facetious air is characteristic of the telling of this story. It appeared as "A Welland Avenue Sensation!" in the *St. Catharines Journal*, 15 May 1866. In it the reporter may have coined an expression new to spirit-hauntings and psychical research: "his ghost ship."

A Welland Avenue Sensation!
A Woman Sees a Ghost
Two Men Attempt to Capture It and Retire in a Fright

It will be recollected by our readers that some time ago, a German named Hoffman committed suicide in a house on Welland Avenue. Since that event the house has been unoccupied until yesterday, when a widow woman with two children moved into the premises. At night when she retired to bed, she was startled to see a tall figure clothed in white approach the bed, and motion to her to depart. In a terrible fright she arose and fled toward a neighboring domicile, where she related with fearful distinctness the size, weight and general appearance of the ghostly visitant. Two valiant Dutchmen, hearing the outcry, proceeded to the spot, and learning that a ghost was in the widow's house, armed themselves with heavy cudgels and proceeded to demolish the ghost. When they entered the door, they found his ghostship sitting on the bed enveloped in a white sheet. They stopped for a moment to consider how to approach it. But the halt was fatal for their pluck. Both made a simultaneous step forward, and then turned round and made a desperate plunge for the door, leaving the ghost to enjoy himself the best he knew how. What stories they told, or how much lager they consumed in recovering their courage remain untold, and perhaps will never be known. Whether the ghost is still in the house sitting on the bed, or whether it has departed to *Hades*, or some other mythical spot, we cannot tell, but no doubt time will develop all about it. In case it does we shall feel it our duty to put our readers in possession of all the ghostly and horrifying developments.

COMPLETELY CLAD IN WHITE

Here is a letter to the editor that describes, in a feverish fashion, the details of an apparition — or an actual person — who once walked the streets of St. Catharines, Ont. "A Strange Apparition" appeared in the *Evening Journal*, St. Catharines, Ont., August 17, 1866.

A Strange Apparition

To the Editor of the *Journal*: —

SIR, I would beg leave to call your attention to a very strange incident in connection with the fire the other night, which at the time made a strong impression on my mind; but believing that it was perhaps a mere hallucination of my own brain, induced by the sudden awakening at or near the hour of midnight, when the mind is most susceptible of supernatural influences, I did not give expression to my thoughts or the matter until I learned to-day that others beside myself witnessed the same startling phenomenon.

When awakened that night by the most startling of all cries — the cry of fire at midnight — I jumped out of bed, and dressing myself as hastily as possible, I ran down Queen street on the south side, and when I had reached that part of it situated between St. Paul and King streets, where the shade of the trees are deepest, I distinctly saw a figure moving on the other side to that on which I was going. Now, Sir, I think I am not superstitious, in fact I have always prided myself on my total want of faith in spiritual visitations, but there before my vision, and evidently with the consent of all my other senses, was a figure the first view of which brought me to a sudden halt and recalled lines long since impressed on my memory —

"For he reared at the sight of the lady in white,
   And he paused in his mad career.
She spoke and her words, when I heard them aright,
   They curdled my blood with fear."

The light from the burning building was just casting its lurid glare upon the dark and mazy atmosphere which prevailed at the time, and was bringing into view, in exaggerated proportions, every object within its influence. Whether it was this strange effect or my excited imagination I dare not say, but there, directly between me and the light of the conflagration, rose up a figure which I should judge was at least 10 or 12 feet in height and was from the knees upwards completely clad in white. Below the knees I thought I could discover a pair of legs and feet, which, considering the strides they were making, ought to have been enveloped in the seven league boots, which I remembered to have read of in my young days, but which were not, if my eyes were at all faithful to their trust, for they appeared to be as naked and bare, as if they were prepared for footing turf or searching for flag in a bog hole in the Emerald Isle. The head was surmounted with a cap, the climax of which, owing I suppose to the velocity with which the feet moved, stuck out behind to a great distance and left a trail which enabled me to follow its course for some time.

You may judge, Mr. Editor, what the effect of such an apparition was upon me at the moment, but as I watched it moving it suddenly disappeared before it reached the corner of King street and I saw no more of it. I am not, as I said before, superstitious, but I am certain there was something in it, and I would like to know what it was. I could not tell whether it was male or female, for I am not sure whether such distinctions exist in the spiritual world, but I am inclined to think it belonged to the latter gender. However this is not of material importance — but I would like to know from you whether you have had an intimation before this of such an apparition, or whether I am really the victim of my own imagination. I have thought that perhaps if followed up it might be made to account in some way for the origin of the fire; but this is a mere speculative hint, not worth much in itself. Do, Mr. Editor, try and unravel the mystery and you will confer a great favour on the community generally and myself particularly.

QUIS.
St. Catharines, August 16.

TWO FLAMING EYES

The correspondent (whose name has not been preserved) who wrote "Fearful Sight" for the *London Daily Advertiser*, July 8, 1870, manages to strike a supercilious tone but still keep the description within bounds, so as to successfully retain a sense of wonder about this appearance of the devil, or should one say this appearance of the Devil?

Fearful Sight
The Devil Looking in at Parkhill
through the Bar Room Window
[From a Correspondent]

Allow me a little space in the columns of your valuable paper to describe one of the most fearful sights that ever was seen in this village, as witnessed by six or seven persons.

On the night of Thursday, June 30th, at about eleven o'clock at night, the inmates of a certain hotel in Parkhill were apparently enjoying themselves carousing, singing sacred songs, and having a regular jollification, when suddenly appeared at the bar room window a most fearful-looking object taking a look at them through the window, and more particularly at Mr. Hastings, who generally is styled "The Deacon." The size of this unnatural object was about two feet in length, and not quite as broad, covering nearly two large panes of glass; its body was smooth, having four arms or legs extended with long, slender claws, and a fifth leg emanating from its body, upon which it turned backwards and forwards on the window. Its head was rather small, but therein were placed two fiery eyes, which stared like fiery globes at the inmates of the bar room. One would think that the age of such unnatural visions had long ago passed away. The consternation and awe of the beholders of this object cannot adequately be described, particularly that of Hasting's. To his horror he beheld two flaming eyes looking at him through the window. What to do in such a crisis he did not know, imagining that he was the object of pursuit, and feeling himself unprepared to accompany the old gentleman he took to his heels, and bound for the hall door, leading to the stairway; summoning all his strength and courage, the deacon with one or two such strides as he never before in his life had made, found himself at the top of a flight of stairs twenty feet long. But unfortunately for the deacon, he nearly lost his coat tail in his flight, it having come in contact with the railing. A dint of about an inch deep is said to have been left in the post.

The incident is all the talk in Parkhill; though there are those who profess to know that the object purposely placed at the window was much less formidable than the excited imagination of Hastings pictured it.

IMPENDING AND APPALLING DANGER

Here is a highly readable tale about a haunting in an unspecified location in a small frontier town in the Canadian West. "The Pedlar's Ghost Story" appeared in the *Toronto Telegram*, October 20, 1870.

The Pedlar's Ghost Story

Several years ago, I was engaged in the business of peddling among the frontier towns of Canada. The route over which I was accustomed to travel usually occupied me about six weeks; and so scattered were the settlements which I visited, that not infrequently I was obliged to encamp for the night in the woods. I carried my goods in a pack upon my back, and was accompanied in my journey back and forth by a huge hound mastiff — one of the most intelligent brutes I ever saw, and devotedly attached to me. Of course I was armed. In addition to a pair of good revolvers and a knife, I carried a cane, which I used as a staff in walking, but which I could, upon occasion, instantly convert into a most deadly weapon. It was charged with a heavy load of buckshot, and was quite as effective as a blunderbuss.

Much of my journey lay through a rough country just beginning to be broken up by the pioneers; and often for miles I had to travel through forests which none but the trapper, or men engaged in some business like my own had ever visited.

One afternoon I was seated on the bank of a little stream, resting from my walk; and being warm and tired, I proceeded to bathe my face. While thus engaged, I noticed a little path, which led from the water's edge up into the forest. I knew at a glance that it was made for deer and other animals coming down to drink; and, impelled by curiosity, I determined to follow it up for a short distance. I had passed less than a quarter of a mile, when I suddenly came upon an opening in the woods, of several acres, in the centre of which stood a good substantial log cabin. Going to the door, I pushed it open, and took a survey of the premises. There were but two rooms in the building — one on the ground, and a loft overhead, which was reached by a short ladder. At one end of the lower room was a huge fireplace, strewed with ashes and a few pieces of charred wood; while at the other, in one corner, a pile of fir boughs were flying, showing that some traveller had made it a shopping-place for the night; but it must have been long before, for the branches he had gathered for a couch were dried and dead.

Glancing at my watch, I saw that it was half-past five, and the sun was nearly down. Thinking myself fortunate in securing so good a camping-place, I proceeded to gather some dry sticks and kindle a fire. Dry wood there was in abundance, for directly in front of the cabin stood a pine tree, which the lightning had shivered, scattering splinters and boughs for rods in every direction, and I soon had a cheerful fire blazing and snapping on the hearth. Then, gathering a few armfuls of fir boughs for a bed, and extemporising a rough seat, my dog and I betook ourselves to supper. He seemed to be as well pleased with the situation as myself, and after eating the food I gave him, went and stretched in the doorway — for it was a pleasant spring evening — and composed himself for a nap, while I, filling my pipe, indulged in a smoke and a reverie.

For a long time after my pipe had gone out, I sat watching the fire creeping up the dried wood, now burning steadily, and now leaping with burning flame, as it caught at some part more combustible than the rest.

At length, tired with my day's journey, I nodded and fell asleep, but was soon awakened by the growling of my dog. Rising and rubbing my eyes, I went cautiously to the door, and looked about me. Everything was quite, and the full moon just peering over the tops of the forest trees, streaked the clearing here and there with patches of mellow light.

"What is it, Brave, old fellow, eh?" said I, speaking to the dog.

He wagged his tail, whined, and snuffed the air uneasily. Satisfied that something was wrong, I cocked a pistol and went out into the moonlight, closely followed by the dog. I went round the cabin; there was nothing to be seen. I peered into the shadows of the woods about me — all was still, save that the branches now and then swayed to and fro with the evening wind.

Satisfied that there was nothing within the opening, yet feeling a little uneasy, I entered the cabin, replenished the fire, and was about to close the door, when, as if in answer to a threatening growl from the dog, there came a quick, sharp blow against the side of the building, similar to that which could be produced by striking with a piece of board. With a short, savage bark, Brave sprang out of the open door, while I, with a pistol in readiness for instant use, followed. There was nothing to be seen, although I made a most careful search, and everything was as quiet as before; but there was something very strange about it, for the dog came to me with a half whine, half growl, his hair bristling, and he sniffling the air and looking uneasily overhead. A thought struck me. Had not some persons been in the cabin, and, seeing me coming, concealed themselves in the chimney, and were they not now, with some object in view, trying to frighten me? Impossible! for the smoke from the resinous pine I had burned would soon have driven them out, or suffocated them in their hiding-place.

"Brave," said I, "we are a couple of fools; there is no one here, and everything is all right; if it isn't we'll make it right in the morning."

As I spoke these words I reached the door, and was in the act of entering, when, without the least noise, with a motion silent as death itself, a huge bird, black as midnight, came swooping past so close that it almost brushed my face with its wings. On that instant the dog sprang, and though his motion was as swift as lightning itself, and I could swear that he grasped it in his jaws, yet I heard them clash together with a snap like a steel trap, while the bird, swooping upward, settled itself on a branch of the withered pine.

"Born in the woods, and scared by an owl." I repeated to myself; but looking at the dog, I saw that he had slunk into the cabin, and was shivering with fright.

Almost angry at his actions, I commanded him sharply to come to me, and he obeyed, though reluctantly.

"Now, Brave," said I, you are too wise and old a dog to be scared by a paltry owl, though he is a big one. He'll be giving us some of his precious music presently; and as I don't care about that kind of a serenade I'll drive him back into the woods."

So saying, I picked up a handful of stones and began trying to frighten away my unwelcome visitor. But the more I wanted him to leave, the more he wouldn't go; and though on several occasions I was sure I struck him, still he never altered his position or budged an inch. Now, when I begin to do a thing I like to carry it through; and so, without thinking what the consequences might be, I drew one of my pistols and fired at the strange bird. The report rang sharply out upon the night air, and went echoing through the forest and over the hills for miles and miles away. Half frightened at what I had done, and provoked that he did not stir, I fired again and again. How strange it was that I could not hit that bird! Did I miss my aim? I am a good shot — it was almost light as day, and he was not over twenty feet distant.

Going into the cabin, I reloaded my pistol, and being now fully aroused and provoked at my want of success, I determined that this time at least he should not escape me. I got my cane, adjusted it, took deliberate aim, and fired. The piece was heavily loaded, and the discharge almost deafened me; but when the smoke had cleared away and I looked upwards, the bird had gone.

"I thought I'd settle you that time," I muttered.

Gone! yes it was gone — but where? I looked into the air above me, on the ground around me; I peered into the tree to see if perchance it had lodged in any of the branches; I listened, that I might hear it flutter, if but wounded; but there was no sound save the wind moaning through the dead branches of the tree above me, that stood withered, scalped, and ghastly, like a thing accursed.

Partially satisfied in that the bird had disappeared, and musing on the strange occurrence, I took my way into the cabin, reloaded my piece, securely fastened the door, and calling my dog close to me, lay down on the branches to sleep, resolving that I would suffer no more mysterious sounds or strange birds to annoy me. With my faithful dog at hand, and my arms in readiness for use, a feeling of security came over me, and I fell into a sound slumber.

I must have slept for several hours, for when I woke the fire was burning but feebly, and its flickering, dying flames cast weird and grotesque shadows on the wall. But what was the strange presence in the room that made my flesh creep and the perspiration to stand in cold drops upon my brow? There was nothing that I could hear; yet a strange sense of impending and appalling danger almost paralyzed me. It came at length, as I knew it would — a wailing sound, at first faintly heard, but swelling louder and louder until it deepened in its hideous intensity to the pitch of an unearthly yell; then again all was still.

I sprung to my feet; there was nothing in the room but my dog, who stood with burning eyes and bristling hairs glaring at the opening in the loft overhead.

"By all the beings of earth and air!" I shouted, "I'll see this thing out, if it cost my life!" And kindling the fire to a roaring flame, I seized a blazing brand in one hand and a pistol in the other, and climbed to the loft above.

I searched in every nook and corner where even a mouse might hide. I went round it again and again; I descended to the open air and peered into places which I had examined a dozen times before. Nothing was changed. The old pine still stretched its long, gaunt arms in the moonlight, and the wind sighed and moaned like the wail of a wandering spirit through its shivered boughs.

I entered my cabin, took up my pack, and resolved to pass the remainder of the night beneath the open sky; but a feeling of pride prevented me; and closing the door once more, I flung myself upon my bed.

Suddenly, as I lay pondering on the mysterious manifestations, a livid gleam, like lightning, shot from the loft overhead; and that yell came once more — not as at first, slowly and indistinctly, but sharply and fearfully sudden; then it died away like a death groan. The fire, which was burning brightly, with a sudden hiss went out, and the room was left in utter darkness. Then a little vapory ball of light appeared at the opening in the lift; it grew brighter and brighter, till the room was as light as day; and from the centre of that vapory ball, a hand appeared — a hand! with moving fingers that seemed searching the air for something they found not. It moved towards me; at first the hand alone, but soon a wrist, and then an arm appeared, lengthening, lengthening, and slowly stretching out to grasp me. Great heaven! was there no end to that arm? My dog was crouched beside me, but not in fear now; his eyes were fixed with a steady glow upon the moving hand, and every nerve was braced for a deadly spring; and when at least it had reached so frightfully near that I might have reached it with my hand, and I might have touched it, and I shouted, "Take him, Brave!" the noble creature leaped, with panther spring, from the ground beside me. There was a growl, a crash, and a smothered fall, and then I was caught in a vice-like grasp. I struggled to free myself, but in vain; and when at last a pair of clammy arms were passed close to mine, I gave a shriek of terror and despair, and felt my senses leave me.

I knew no more till I woke up to find my faithful dog locking my face and whining piteously, and I lay on the bank of the stream where I had stopped to rest.

'Twas only a dream after all, but so frightfully real did it appear, that it was hours before I recovered my strength or composure of mind.

It was the last trip I ever made upon the route, for I never could shake off the impression left upon me by the dream. I believe it to have been a warning of danger ahead, and I shudder now, and ever shall, as I think of that afternoon nap in the woods of Canada.

EYES BURNING RED FLAMES

"A Ghost in Whitby" appeared in the *Sarnia Observer*, 15 Aug. 1873. Apparently the article was originally published by the *Whitby Chronicle*.

If the description of the "eyes burning red flames" seems unlikely, bear in mind that to this day the Court House in Whitby has the reputation of being a haunt.

A Ghost in Whitby
The Apparition Seen and Described

For some days past the ghost, which, it is asserted, has been seen in the neighbourhood of the Court House, has been the talk of Whitby. The apparition, according to report, is seen under various forms — that of a black dog, which suddenly assumes the shape of a rather tall man, and from whose eyes burning red flames seem to issue, being the most familiar. Others assert that the ghost has been seen leaning with both hands on a staff standing on the court house steps, or walking slowly between the steps and the entrance gate, at "the witching hour of night." Those who have had the temerity to approach the midnight intruder allege that on their approach it has all at once disappeared as in a flame of fire, sinking, as it were, into the ground. Others say that the most sorrowful moaning has been heard to proceed from where the ghost makes itself at first visible, and in fact all sorts of versions are given as to what has been seen and heard of what people persist in calling the "Court House Ghost." Last night a gathering assembled around the court house railings, and remained there until nearly twelve o'clock to ascertain what could be seen, but at that hour hurried home to bed, cold and disappointed at the non-appearance of his ghostship. After the departure of the crowd, however, it is stated that the apparition was again seen by respectable and creditable people, that it was a tall figure walking heavily with a cane, and frequently stopping to look up at the sky, and groan while making its round wearily through the grounds in front of the Court House. There are, as may be expected, all sorts of surmises as to what the trouble is, and a determination avowed by many parties to find out all about it, and if it be a trick, to expose those who would impose this latest ghost hoax upon a community. — *Whitby Chronicle.*

I AM DEAD NOW

Do the dead return? Are they able to communicate with the living?

Some answers to questions like these are seemingly offered by the writer of the article "A Nova Scotia Sensation" in the *Daily Evening News*, Saint John, N.B., December 16, 1873.

A Nova Scotia Sensation
A Dead Woman Appears to Her Friends

For some days past rumors have been in their circulation of spiritual manifestations witnessed by persons living in the vicinity of Tuft's Cove, which is some three miles outside of Dartmouth, N.S. The reports at last assumed such an importance that one of our reporters, whose faith in spirits of any kind is not very strong, decided to interview the people, and see what the story amounted to. The persons whom he interviewed appeared to be intelligent, and not over inclined to believe in ghosts. Their narrative is in substance as follows: About four months ago, "Agnes," wife of Briton McCabe, and daughter of a Mrs. Barnstead, died, and was, of course, buried. She and her husband lived some 12 miles from Dartmouth, on the Windsor Road, and before she died she was, at her own request, removed to her mother's house, at Tuft's Cove. There she died; was laid out by a Mrs. Gay, and was buried in the rural churchyard nearby. On Friday, the 12th inst., Mrs. Gay was sent for by Mrs. Barnstead, mother of the deceased woman; and upon going over she was somewhat startled at being informed that "Agnes had come back" — a statement which Mrs. B. proceeded to explain by stating that for some days previous herself and the other inmates of the house had heard mysterious rappings in different parts of the premises; that they attributed the noises to a mischievous young girl who lived with them; but that they had that morning been satisfied that such was not the cause, for she and the rest had distinctly heard the voice of her dead daughter Agnes. They were, the old lady said, all gathered in the room, when the mysterious rapping was heard, and afterwards the voice of Agnes was heard exclaiming in low tones, "Mother, Mother, Mother." Though all were startled, the mother answered he voice, asking what was wanted. The voice replied, "I am a spirit; I have been sent to warn you all. I was buried alive, and was awoke by hunger. I lived for two days after I awoke, and forced the end out of my coffin. I am come to invite you all to glory." Then the voice sang three verses from three different hymns, familiar to the family; and in reply to some questions again addressed them. They asked would they dig her up; the reply was "I am dead now, and my soul is full of glory." They asked what caused her death, and the voice made a reply which at present it would not be judicious, perhaps, to make public. (It may be stated that the doctors attributed the woman's death to a wasting of the system.) Some one then sent for a brother of the deceased woman, and he on coming heard the familiar voice. Upon the circumstances being stated to him, he said, "Agnes, do you want to see me?" and then he saw what appeared to him to be his sister's eyes, float past him, and felt a hand softly touch his shoulder. At this juncture Mrs. Gay was sent for, and she heard the voice address some of the members of the family by name, and heard a rapping on the floor beneath her feet. Then the voice said, "I am going now, and I will not come again until the last day; and that will be soon." After that the noises ceased; and since then there has been nothing seen nor heard. As before stated, the people from whom these particulars were obtained are intelligent, and do not appear to be at all superstitious. The suspected and mischievous girl was made to stand quietly by during the *seance*, with her hands folded, and was watched. So they have no doubt that she at least had no hand in the manifestation. The family do not appear at all alarmed; and not afraid of ghosts in ordinary; but have an abiding faith that the spirit of their departed friend and relative has been with them. They tell their story straightly, and express their willingness to testify under oath to all they have said. It is talked of to exhume the remains, but the husband of the deceased has not yet been communicated with; and until that is done it is not probable that any action will be taken in the matter. — *Halifax Express.*

THE GREAT AMHERST MYSTERY

A Canadian Tire Store stands at the corner of Princess Street and Church Street in downtown Amherst, N.S. There should be a plaque standing there to mark the location of the Cox family cottage which stood at 6 Princess Street. After all, in 1878-79, it was the site of the Great Amherst Mystery, one of the world's most widely reported hauntings.

I am not going to retell the fascinating story here because it would take too long. Besides I have told it elsewhere; it took me some four thousand words to summarize it in *Mysterious Canada*, one of innumerable accounts by many hands. Suffice it to say that a poltergeist was busy at the two-story, wooden cottage which was inhabited by eight members of the family including eighteen-year-old Esther Cox who was in poor health and unhappy in love. Esther had troubled dreams, her limbs would seem to swell to enormous size. Bed clothes would fly through the air. One night these words appeared on the bedroom wall in large characters: "Esther Cox, you are mine to kill." Then there were pounding sounds and loud retorts heard throughout the house.

Witnesses from the community heard these noises and attested to the fact that the house rocked on its foundation. Then small fires broke out in uninhabited rooms. Whenever Esther left the house the disturbances ceased. She finally left for good and later married, had children, and found peace. There is no doubt that she was the focus of the poltergeist disturbances but no one ever confronted her actually causing the manifestations.

So much for the Great Amherst Mystery, which might be seen to be an event or a misunderstanding that took place in the past and is of no later interest. Yet the events that happened at Amherst influenced events that took place a half-century later, halfway around the world. Intriguingly, many of the disturbances at the Cox family cottage in the 1870s were precisely recreated at Borley Rectory, Essex, England, in the 1930s, and there is evidence to show that the haunted house in

Amherst set the pattern for the events reported at Borley, "the most haunted house in England."

Rather than trace the threads in that pattern, I would prefer to share with readers an unfamiliar description of Esther Cox. It comes from an interview with the young woman that appeared in the *Daily Sun* (Saint John, N.B.), June 23, 1879. In poltergeist cases, a pubescent female is said to be the focus of the disturbances, their necessary if not their sole cause.

Miss Esther Cox, the spirit medium, commonly known as the "Amherst mystery," arrived here in care of friends on Friday afternoon last were done, and a detailed account of the manifestations and workings of "the mystery" were given in Ruddock's Hall on Friday evening and Saturday. Sunday evening, Miss Cox essayed to attend service at the Baptist Church, but during the first singing "the spirit," which had been quiet for some days, again manifested itself by rapping, apparently on the floor of the pew in front. When told to stop by Miss Cox it would cease the noise for a moment, but then break out worse than ever. Throughout the prayer it continued, and when the organ began for the second singing the noise became so distinct and disturbing that Miss Cox and party were forced to leave the church. Upon reaching the house on Wesley Street, where they were stopping, "the spirit" seemed to enter into Miss Cox, and she was sick and insensible until morning. Lying upon the bed she seemed for a time as though in great pain, her chest heaving as though in a rapid succession of hiccoughs — and the body and limbs being very much swollen. A medical gentleman of this town, who saw her at this time, states that the symptoms were as those of a functional heart disease, probably caused by nervous excitement. The heart was beating at an exceedingly rapid rate and the lungs seemed gorged with blood, so that a portion was forced into the stomach, causing the patient to vomit blood afterwards. A sound could be distinctly heard in the region of the heart, resembling the shaking of water in a muffled bottle, supposed to be caused by blood in a cavity being shaken by the violent jerking, hiccoughy motion of the body. As to the cause of the affection, that is the mystery.

Towards morning Miss Cox relapsed into a state of somnolence, and later in the day woke seemingly entirely recovered. She states, however, that on Monday afternoon, while sitting near the window of a room on the ground floor, a fan dropped out of the window, she went outside to recover it, and on returning, a chair from the opposite side of the room was found upside down near the door, as though it had attempted to follow her out of the room. No one else witnessed this occurrence. Again, while writing a letter, "the spirit" took possession of the pen and wrote in a different hand altogether, other and entirely different words from what were intended. In fact it wrote of itself, the young lady being able to look in another direction and not show the least interest in what the pen was writing. A gentleman who was present at the time asked "the spirit" its name, when it wrote in reply "Maggie Fisher," and stated that she had gone to "the red school-house on the hill in Upper Stewiacke" before Miss Cox did, but left when she went. Miss Cox did not know this Maggie Fisher, but it seems that one time she did attend the school indicated, and that a girl of that name, now dead, had attended previously.

Monday night Miss Cox was again attacked, and held under the power of "the spirit" much the same as the night previous.

A representative of the "Despatch" called on "the mystery" yesterday afternoon, but she not being "under the power" of course no "manifestations" could be seen. The young lady appeared quite pleasant and affable, and looked well. She considers her trouble to be a spirit, and is more perplexed with it than any one else. She says that she cannot tell by any premonitory symptoms when the manifestations are going to commence, is becoming rather frightened concerning "it," and is very easily annoyed and excited by any noise except that which she herself may cause.

If the spirit is willing and the flesh not too weak, Miss Cox will leave for Chatham by train today.

BRIGHT AND SHINING LIGHT

According to available records, a miraculous light played over a baptismal ceremony held by Mormons on the shore of the Thames River outside London, Ont. The ceremony, which took place on 29 Dec. 1875, is now a recognized part of the tradition and history of the Reorganized Church of Jesus Christ of Latter Day Saints (RLDs) in Canada.

The event was described by John J. Cornish, a Mormon elder, in his book *Into the Latter Day Light: An Autobiography* (Independence, Missouri: Herald House, 1929; reprinted with additions, 1957). Cornish titled it "A Notable Case of Divine Intervention."

Brighter than the Sun at Noonday

I must chronicle an event which occurred in 1875 in the city of London, Ontario, December 29, at a baptism in the River Thames, south branch, at which time two young ladies were baptized, viz: Mrs. Polly Taylor and Miss Sarah Lively. Of this Miss Lively wrote seven days later as follows:

"*London, Ontario*, January 5, 1876. — I have been in London the last three weeks visiting my sister where I first enjoyed listening to the true gospel as taught by the Latter Day Saints. I was converted under the preaching of Brother J.J. Cornish, and feel rejoiced that I can bear testimony to the truth of the work, fully convinced that this is the work of God; and ever shall I praise God that he has been pleased to lead me from the darkness into the light of the gospel. Although a constant attendant of the P.M.C., I was blind to much of the gospel truth until I was baptized and became a believer in the doctrine as taught by the Latter Day Saints; and I shall ever bless God for the hour that I submitted to bow in obedience to his commands. I shall never forget the glorious sight witnessed by myself and a number of my brothers and sisters in Christ at one. On entering the water to be baptized, I felt that God was with me and acknowledged me by shining a beautiful light down upon me from above. The heavens seemed lightened up with a bright and shining light, which continued to shine until I was immersed in the water and arose with the blessed assurance that my sins were washed away, and returned home rejoicing.

"As yet my parents know nothing of the change, and from my heart I pray God will lead them into the true light that I now rejoice in; and I hope they will very shortly join our number, as I know they were never opposed to the belief of the doctrine of the Saints, inasmuch as they ever heard. [Her parents and relatives were baptized later. — J.J.C.] Praying that we may all continue firm in the strength and power from God, I, too, am your sister in Christ. Sarah Lively." — *Saints' Herald*, Vol. 23, p. 54.

On account of working at daily labor this baptism was performed on Wednesday, late in the evening of December 29, 1875; an intensely dark night. After our prayer meeting Mrs. John Taylor and Miss Sarah Lively, who had, as stated in her letter, attended our meetings in the city, were baptized by me in the River Thames, when suddenly there came a very beautiful light from heaven, which rested upon all — both members and nonmembers — brighter than the sun at noonday. There were about thirty persons present, and I feel sure that none of them could forget that night. It came down with a sound like a mighty rushing wind. We could hear it far above in the distance, and as it reached the place where we stood we were enveloped in the brightest and most beautiful light I ever saw — the glory of the Lord. After making the covenant I took the hand of one of those dear sisters and led her into the water and baptized her in the name of the Father and of the Son and of the Holy Ghost, burying her in the water for the remission of sins; and while I stood in that water to thus baptize with my hand raised toward the heaven, I glanced upward, and how far it seemed I could see! And while administering the ordinances as I thought of the words I used, "Having been commissioned by Jesus Christ, I baptize you," etc., the Spirit thrilled through me as much to say, "Yes, you have been commissioned to thus act." It was an added testimony to me. Then the other sister was baptized after the same manner as the first, while we were thus walking in the light — the glorious light of God.

The light was round, straight up and down like a shaft from heaven to earth, and just as bright on the inside edge as it was in the center; and so far as we could see, it was just as dark on the outer edge as it was a mile away. Previous to our baptizing there had been a thaw; the ice had broken up, the great chunks and cakes of ice were floating down the river, which made it dangerous, especially in the dark. God not only gave us light to see, but also the power of the Holy Ghost to direct, and I could not notice one particle of ice the size of one's hand passing down until we had gone in and out twice and both had been baptized.

Among the number of people who witnessed the scene were John Taylor, the husband of Mrs. Taylor. He came from behind the crowd of people who were present, knelt down by my side with his arms around my body, and said: "Oh, Brother Cornish, pray for me. This is enough to convince anyone that this gospel is true. Pray for my father and mother in England, that they may hear this gospel, too. Oh, I know this is the true gospel, and I will obey it." He, as well as all that company who were not then baptized (about ten), afterwards came to the church for baptism.

No greater light did the Apostle Paul see when on his way to Damascus to persecute the saints. We were not struck blind as was the man Paul, for we were not on a mission to persecute the Saints as he was, but we did the will of God only.

While standing in the water by the side of the first candidate and having the hand raised, using the words, "Having been commissioned by Jesus Christ, I baptize you," etc., came the words to my mind with double assurance, "Yes, you have been commissioned to thus act," and at the same time an extra portion of the Holy Spirit came in confirmation. These two sisters now live in the State of Missouri at Independence. The Sister Lively of that day is now Sister May, the wife of Roderick May. Sister Taylor, having changed her name by marriage, is now Sister W.A. Bushnell, also of Independence.

One who had made fun about us and our work, viz., William Clow, was the only one of the whole company who did not fall on his knees in prayer to God at the time of baptism, and he alone heard the voice from heaven saying to him, "These are my people and you must not laugh at them."

As I came to the bank with the first candidate, I saw Brother Clow standing and looking up as one spellbound. On his right was Augustus Depper, kneeling on one knee with both hands clasped together, looking upward, tears running down his cheeks, praying, and the words I heard were: "We thank thee, O God, that thou hast acknowledged us in the presence of our opposers."

The newly baptized sister, upon reaching the bank, fell on her knees with the others; the other sister then arose and came forward, and as I took her by the hand I heard many voices: "Praise the Lord." "We thank thee, O God, for thy blessing," but not loud or confusing. While nearing the proper depth for baptism, this sister exclaimed, "Oh, Brother Johnnie, isn't this grand? Oh, I know this gospel is true." After baptism and dismissal the light did not go out, but gradually up until it vanished from our sight, leaving us in darkness as dense and impenetrable as before.

WRAPT IN MYSTERY

Throughout the Maritimes there are atmospheric descriptions of Grey Ladies who disconsolately wander littorals in search of their drowned children.

Here is a vivid account. It appeared as "Strange Occurrence" in the *Daily Patriot*, Charlottetown, P.E.I., 9 May 1878. It is identified as a reprint from the *St. John Telegraph*, Saint John, N.B.

Strange Occurrence. — A correspondent, who claims not to be unduly credulous, sends us the following: —

"On Monday afternoon, as a man, residing on the Black River road, was driving home from the city and when near the place where Mrs. Quinn was murdered, he came in sight of a woman a few rods ahead of him on the highway. The woman walked briskly ahead of him for about 150 yards, till she turned a curve in the road, when he lost view of her, and on his reaching the place she was nowhere to be seen, having disappeared as mysteriously as she came. The road here is on both sides lined with alder bushes, in which he supposes she must have concealed herself. From the imperfect view he had of her he is unable to give an accurate description of her features, but says she appeared to be deformed in the feet and wore a slate colored dress, plain hat, but neither shawl nor jacket of any description. From her movements it was clearly evident she desired to avoid recognition. The man lives but a short distance from the place, and is acquainted with all the residents of that locality, and is satisfied she was none of these. From her appearance it seemed most improbable that she had come any considerable distance. None of the people in the vicinity of the place have seen any strange woman answering to her description; and so far the whole matter is wrapt in mystery. Some are of the opinion that she must have been a relative of the murdered woman, who had been visiting the scene of the foul tragedy, the recollection of which had so unsettled her mind as to cause her to act in this eccentric manner. The truth of the story would certainly have been doubted had not the person who relates it been a man whose character for sincerity is proverbial in the neighborhood. — *St. John Telegraph.*

VANISHED IN A MOMENT

There is no shortage of ghost stories, but in short supply are stories that are as vividly told as this one is — with a Scots brogue, to add charm and flavour!
It first appeared as "Ghost Story," *Free Press*, Acton, Ont., March 6, 1879.

Ghost Story. — A stout Yorkshire farmer of the name of James Wreggit, having emigrated to Canada, settled himself and family on a good farm which he rented in one of the townships. He was considered fair-dealing and honour-able in all transactions with his neighbours, and in every respect bore a most excellent character. In the farmer's house was a first-floor sitting-room with a large fire-place. In this room the children slept, but from the first night evinced the greatest dislike to going to bed there, screaming with terror, and saying that a man was in the room with them. For a long time the parents paid no attention to their complaints. During harvest time a change was made, and the farmer himself slept in this room, as it was cooler and more convenient. The first night he slept there he was about to rise almost before the break of day, when, glancing towards the fire-place, he saw standing there a stranger of a dissipated drunken appearance. "Ha'lo! What's thee doing there?" was his very natural exclamation. Receiving no reply, "Won't thee speak? I'll make thee speak!" and picking up one of his heavy boots form the bedside he was preparing to throw it at the intruder, when the man, suddenly raising his arm as if to ward off the blow, vanished in a moment from before his eyes. Wreggit, unable to get this matter of our his head, brooded over it till the next day, when about noon he entered into conversation with a neighbour who was working with him, and asked him to describe the former tenant of the farm, who had died from excessive drinking. The description so entirely resembled the man he had seen in the room that he at once exclaimed, "I saw him last night!" Wreggit recounted this to some old friends near whom he had lived before taking the farm, and it is from the dictation of one of his auditors that I have written down this remarkable circumstance. At the time neither Wreggit nor his friend had the slightest belief in apparitions.

MARIAN VISION

"The Vision of Mary" might seem, at first glance, to describe what Catholics call a Marian vision, or what parapsychologists refer to as a BVM — a vision of the Blessed Virgin Mary. But on second glance it is apparent that the Mary in this account is not the Mary of the New Testament, but Mary Edward Melville, a talented young woman who died at the age of twenty-two in 1880 at Belleville, Ont. The account of this Mary's spectral or spiritual appearance was written by Flora McDonald for B.F. Austin's volume *What Converted Me to Spiritualism: One Hundred Testimonies* (1901).

Flora McDonald is the remarkable woman known today to a generation of feminists and others as Flora McDonald Denison (1867-1921). Flora — as she is also known — played an active role in the suffragette movement in Toronto in the 1910s. She was the person principally responsible for the dedication in 1919 of Gibraltar Rock in Bon Echo (then her property, now the Ontario provincial park) to the "democratic ideals" of Walt Whitman. She was the older sister of Mary Edwards Melville. She was, finally, as a highschool student in Belleville, a friend of B.F. Austin who was ordained a minister, was converted to the cause of spiritualism, and became the publisher of Flora's book — half-novel, half-memoir — titled *Mary Melville — The Psychic* (1900).

The Vision of Mary

We lose them not who pass away,
 For round our path they linger still
In ministry of love, and fill
 Our lives with sweetness day by day.
      — Austin.

I was still in my early teens. My school days had passed pleasantly with little care. I had taught school for a couple of years and disliked it very much, and now I began to realize that I must earn my own living, and teaching was the only vocation for which I was prepared. To keep on in the routine of a school-teacher's life was little more enticing to me than solitary confinement might have been. I decided to strike out in the world, and find something else to do. Much easier said than done. After striking out and endeavouring to find something to do I may have wished myself back in my little log school house, but to come to the night when I saw through different glasses.

I had undertaken a business at which I was a complete novice, and naturally made a failure of it. I had very little money and a bad cold had settled on my chest. It was shortly after supper and I was seriously contemplating the advisability of ending an earthly career that seemed so terribly discouraging. I went to a drug store and purchased something to relieve my cough, and then to my room and went to bed, though it was not yet seven o'clock. I was in a sitting position on the bed. The room was hardly dark. Hope and ambition seemed completely dead, and from the depths of a discouraged soul I asked the why of it all. To what end were we so unhappy here?

I looked up, being attracted by a light, apparently on the opposite wall, for on this side of the room there was no window or door. The light began to take form, and presently it was as bright as, and much resembled the round light thrown on a white sheet for stereoptican views. (Mary Melville was my sister and had been dead a few years.) Presently Mary appeared in the centre of the light. Her long, blonde hair was like scintillating threads of iridescent gold. Her face was beautifully happy, her eyes radiant, her form enveloped in a gauzy drapery that was exquisitely graceful. I was not at all nervous, and as I still looked she stepped down from the wall, glided, rather than walked, passed the foot of my bed, and came up nearer the head of it and stood beside me. I did not speak, and felt as though she were so ethereal I might have put my hand through her form. The light remained on the wall and she pointed to it. I looked, and a series of pictures passed along, all significant of scenes in our home life, and lastly I myself appeared — but so despondent, so discouraged, so crestfallen, that I hardly believed it was myself I was looking at. As I gazed the face began to brighten, the sinking attitude gave way to one of upright confidence. I saw ahead of me work and endeavour — but success. I felt strong and well as I looked, and the world, instead of being the hated habitation of a crushed life, became a vast field wherein to endeavour and accomplish — to learn — and finally to know, and as the picture faded I turned to Mary. She smiled, and instead of returning to the wall to disappear, faded where she stood. A quiet peace I had not known for many days took possession of me, but I got up, dressed, and went to tell of my experience.

The next day I thought of little else beside my experience and wishing to be alone that I might get another glimpse of encouragement and assurance. About five o'clock I wandered to a large creek that ran through a woods. There was a fallen tree which spanned the river, and about in the middle of the stream the branches formed a very comfortable seat. I sat down to reflect. I had now perfect confidence in the future, and that life, after all, proved worth living; but I still wondered. What could I do? Where or how to begin? I was looking in the still water when another series of pictures was presented to me. I shall not describe them

in detail, but will say they were prophetic of the future, and out of the half dozen pictures shown me four have already materialized in my life. And what did this do for me? It convinced me that Mary was still living, and under certain conditions, was able to make herself visible. It also proved to me that happenings can be prophesied years before. It also banished fear as to what might happen to me during this life or the life Mary was now living. It gave me confidence that all was well and the apparent evils were only burnishings to bring out the good.

This personal experience made me interested in Psychics and Psychic Phenomena, the study of which has not only proved most entertaining and instructive, but also taught me to master physical conditions in myself and others, and instead of being beaten by the material world I have been enabled to use it for my further psychic development as well as physical welfare.

> "Serene I hold my hands and wait,
>   Whate'er the cards of life may be;
> Faith guides me up to heaven's gates
>   And love shall bring my own to me."

THE MOST VIVID LIGHTNING

Celestial events are capable of striking terror in the hearts of men and women. Remember Comet Kohoutek which swept the heavens some decades ago? Then there are the falls of meteorites.

"A Ball of Fire" appeared in the *Daily Patriot*, Charlottetown, P.E.I., 2 Sept. 1880. It describes the crash of the meteorite, which took place around midnight, Saturday, 14 Aug. 1880.

A Ball of Fire
Twenty-five Feet in Diameter, Falls in Caledonia —
A Mass of Heated Metal Weighing Five Tons

Caledonia, Marion County, Aug. 19. — About midnight of Saturday our place was visited by a terrific thunder storm accompanied by hail and the most vivid lightning, flash following flash in quick succession. There had been a political meeting here that evening and the people from the neighboring villages and surrounding country were detained. Suddenly the sky appeared as bright as noonday, in fact fine print could easily have

been read, so great was the light, but strange to say the light was steady, not flash after flash as it would have been had the light been caused by lightning; a deafening roar was heard, continuing to become louder as the light became brighter. Gradually the roaring changed to a hissing sparkling sound. It is needless to say the people were frightened, and upon running into the street a ball of seeming fire came moving through the air from the north-east. The ball seemed to be at least twenty-five feet in diameter. As it neared the earth the heat could be plainly felt. The body struck just north of the village and buried over one-half of itself in the ground. Good judges estimate the weight at three to five tons, but the heat is yet so great that it is uncomfortable to go neare than thirty or forty. It looks like a mass of pig-iron. I was visited by hundreds yesterday. The gentleman who owns the land on which it fell has been offered $300 for it.

A STRANGE FLOATING MOTION

"A Ghastly Apparition" is reprinted from the *Toronto Mail*, 20 Nov. 1880. The last paragraph adds an unusual note. The reader is left to wonder what loot would "be serviceable" to a ghost.

A Ghastly Apparition
A Strange Spectre Haunting Niagara's Lone Places
Evidences of Nocturnal Appearances of an Extraordinary Nature

Niagara, Nov. 19. — The town is in a state of excitement over a ghastly apparition which has haunted the place of late. Tales of a blood-curdling nature are told by belated travellers. The appearance is differently described by those passed by the spectre, possibly owing to the unnerving nature of the occurrence, and these contradictions have given ground for contemptuous scoffing at the whole story by the incredulous. The experiences are nevertheless growing more numerous, and even men are chary of going abroad after dark. A farmer leaving town the other night about eleven o'clock, the moon being bright, avers that he saw the thing rise from among the tombs in the churchyard, and trail toward him. It had the semblance of a woman with long white garments and fair hair, apparently floating, or else with far more than the average length of limb. The farmer closed his eyes, and turning his horse drove back into town at a furious gallop, his animal seeming to share the fright. He never looked around until safely in the heart of the town. Another account states that at one of the lonely crossings in the outskirts of the place the woman was seen crouching beside a low fence. The spectators, two in number this time, did not at first recall the stories of the apparition, and went toward the thing under the impression that some vagrant was crouching there for shelter. As they went near, a peculiar sensation affected them both, and without speaking to each other or exactly knowing why, they stopped involuntarily and turned away. As they did so a shuddering thrill went through them, as they say, and they broke into a wild run for the nearest lights.

Other tales have contradictory points, but all agree that the apparition has the form of a woman, and possesses a strange floating motion. There is much speculation in the place over the matter.

Later. — Five successful burglaries have been accomplished, and three unsuccessful ones attempted, lately in the town, and the evil deeds are still going on. It is possible that the burglaries have been committed by the ghost, although there is nothing to show this positively. The people of the town argue that the spectre has not been guilty of the crimes, as nothing has been taken which would be serviceable to a ghost.

GRIM AND MYSTERIOUS

Here a vivid description of a derelict, drifter, lover, vagabond, vagrant, hobo ... call the wanderer what you will. In a settled community like that of Victoria in 1880, he stood out from the common crowd.

Although the name goes unmentioned in the text, Ahasuerus is the commonest name for the Wandering Jew. In Medieval Christian legend, Ahasuerus denied all knowledge of Jesus and was cursed by the Saviour on the way to Calvary to "tarry awhile" — to wander the face of the earth until the Day of Judgement. He is one of a class of "cursed immortals."

Perhaps the identity of this lone wanderer is that of Ahasuerus. "A Mysterious Personage" comes from the *Daily Colonist*, Victoria, B.C., December 9. 1880. The reference to "Mr. Price" is obscure (though it does bring to mind the expression "the price one has to pay").

A Mysterious Personage
Is He the Wandering Jew

Several persons who have had occasion to be out-of-doors at night recently report that they encountered a man of striking and mysterious mien — his figure tall, his head bowed upon his breast, silently stalking along the dark and silent streets of the suburbs. During the severest weather, when the thermometer scored 22 degrees of frost and the snow covered the land in heaps and drifts, this man was met long after midnight labouring through the drifts. When the change came and the rain poured down for two days and nights, when even dumb brutes sought shelter, still the stranger was met plodding his weary way through the mud and slush, his garments soaked with the moisture, his head still bent on his breast, pressing on in search of — Heaven only knows what. Newspaper carriers have met him on their routes — silent, grim and mysterious, stalking steadily on. Members of the Club wending their way home have been startled to observe him like an apparition rising, as it were, from the ground and hurrying away in the gloom. Two guests from the Pioneer dinner on last Saturday night met the stranger on Fort street, and tried to open a conversation with him. But he replied not to their salutation, nor raised his head nor quickened nor slackened his pace, but with the same measured, purposeless stride and dejected air turned off at Blanchard street and plunged into the darkness. Throughout the "silent watches of the night" the mysterious footfalls are heard on the sidewalks, but with daylight the man disappears and is seen no more until the sable mantle is again let down. Some imagine that the highwayman who asked Mr. Price to "stand and deliver" the other morning and this strange man are identical. Others associate him with the recent burglarious visitations; and others have ventured to think that he may be the Wandering Jew, who as a punishment for his brutality on a certain memorable occasion was condemned to "go on till the end of Time." Our own opinion is that the man's mind is distraught and that, following out an idiosyncrasy, he wanders in a purposeless manner through the city after dark and seeks his bed at daylight.

VEILED IN INKY GLOOM

What is called "daylight darkness" settled over the town of Goderich, a port on Lake Huron, Ont., on 5 Sept. 1881. It is well described in this account, which even refers in passing to the English prophetess Mother Shipton.

"Thick Darkness" appeared in the *Winnipeg Daily Times*, 15 Sept. 1881.

Thick Darkness
The Strange Occurrence of the 5th Inst.
Special Correspondent of the London Free Press

Goderich, Sept. 6. — Yesterday will be long remembered in Goderich. It was, in fact, the most remarkable day in its history. For several days past the atmosphere has been full of smoke, presumably from bush fires, although there have been no very large ones in the immediate vicinity; and the thermometer has mounted up among the nineties — something rather unusual in this cool lake town. Rain has been wonderfully scarce all summer, and of late the ground has become completely parched. There is no such thing as grass to be seen; pasture fields are dry and almost as dirty as the road bed. For a week or more —

> "All is hot and copper sky,
>   The bloody sun at noon
> Right above the earth did stand,
>   No bigger than the moon."

But yesterday afternoon it disappeared altogether, as effectually as though it had dropped out of the heavens. About noon clouds were observed gathering in the west and south. At one o'clock those who lunched at that hour found no little difficulty in distinguishing articles on the table; and shortly thereafter lamps had to be brought into requisition. From this out the gloom thickened; at two it was with great difficulty one could read large print out of doors. Three gave every appearance of midnight, and half an hour thereafter the entire town and surrounding country was veiled in inky gloom. "No sun, no moon, no stars, no noon; no proper time of day." The blackness of midnight reigned supreme. The hand held before the eyes within three inches of the face could not be seen. To lend awe and sublimity to the scene the intense blackness was ever and anon lit up by blinding flashes of lightning; and the reverberating thunder alone broke the painful stillness. In short, the scene was one never to be forgotten by those who saw it. The weak and the ignorant were of course terrified, and thought that at last of a certainty Mother Shipton's prophecy was about to be fulfilled to the letter. And others who would be insulted, and with reason, at being termed either ignorant or weak, were beginning to ask themselves and each other what it all meant. Little groups farther here and there about the square watched in wonder and awe for a termination of the phenom-enon, but it was a long time ere the darkness was sufficiently dissipated to see to move about outside the range of street lamps and shop windows. At last the darkness in the east gave place to a red gleam, as though from a huge fire, and the reflection from this somewhat relieved the gloom and enabled people to see as well as upon an ordinary moonless night — but no better. And there it remained through the remainder of the afternoon and night, and not till the following morning when Old Sol put in an appearance as usual and in his usual place were apprehensions entirely removed and the alarmed ones really convinced that all was, indeed, well. During the continuance of the darkness a small quantity of rain fell, but it was so combined with ashes, cinder and dirt that to expose one's self to it for a few minutes was to have the face and hands blackened. The next morning the whole country side was covered with a coating of dirt and filth — so much so that it was impossible to come in contact with a fence, tree, or, in fact, any exposed surface, without becoming soiled. The phenomenon is now of the past, but it is not forgotten, and is not likely to be for many a long year. And it is quite safe to say that every time the 5th of September rolls around the thought of the inhabitants of Goderich will revert back to the year eighty-one. Lake captains say the entire shores of Superior and Huron are in a blaze. The smoke from these and other fires are no doubt brought together by the wind, and floated over in dense masses, hemming us in on every side, and as completely shutting out the sunlight as though Old Sol had dropped entirely out of the sky. This is the first time night has ever set in here shortly after noon, and lasted until next morning. May it be the last.

I NEVER SAW ANYTHING LIKE IT

Most ghost stories are not really stories at all, but are "mood pieces" with indicative action plus sketchy accounts of sensations, impressions, suppositions, conjectures, and speculations. This account is an exception. It is the real thing, for there is nothing at all indicative or sketchy about it.

Few accounts of wraith-like visitors are as detailed as this one. It was contributed by the teacher P.A. O'Neill. "A Genuine Ghost Story" appeared in the columns of *The Irish Canadian*, 29 Nov. 1883.

A Genuine Ghost Story
How the Spirit was "Laid"

An article in the *Fortnightly Review*, entitled *Phantasms of the Living*, has induced me to relate here the circumstance of an apparition which I myself saw, and to the fact of seeing which I am prepared to make affidavit. I will premise by saying that I by no means belong to the superstitious class. On the contrary, I am strongly inclined to skepticism, and was at that time.

In 1877 I was engaged to teach in the third district of Ennismore, Peterboro' county, Ont. As was customary at that time, and is yet, the school teacher boarded round. But in this particular case a widow, possessor of a small farm, undertook the business of boarding the schoolmaster. After remaining with her for some time, she told me that she had concluded to rent or sell (I forget which) her small farm; consequently I should have to look out for another place to board. I was naturally a little perplexed, for upon the condition of boarding permanently with her during my engagement, I had accepted the situation.

However there was nothing for it but to acquiesce. So, next Sunday, I set out for mass to the one parish church of Ennismore. I knew there was a farmer living four miles distant, with a comparatively small family, who had a very large farm house. Originally it had been intended for a country tavern, with a row of horse stalls, large dance hall, etc., after the manner of the time. But through some cause, generally attributed to the dullness of the times, the house had fallen back to the rank of an ordinary farm house — a giant among its neighbors.

After mass it is a custom — especially an Irish custom — to assemble for some time and gossip in front of the church before driving home; and you may be sure that Ennismore marks no exception to the general rule. After the usual courtesies had been exchanged I broached the subject of board for the school teacher to my friend, Mr. — — (the only name which shall be held sacred in this relation). He said that, particularly for the sake of his two boys, nothing would suit him better than to board me; but he had no sleeping room for me. I naturally wondered at this, and frankly told him that a man living in the largest farm house in the township, with a comparatively small family, could not be hard pressed for sleeping room.

"Well," said he, "I don't own the farm; I merely lease it from the owner. But one-half of the house is entirely useless to me, except the lower half, which I use as a granary; for in the upper half is a very large room with a very fine bed in which no one will sleep."

Said I: "Did you ever try to sleep there yourself?"

"God forbid!" was the reply.

I was somewhat surprised at this remark, and begged to know the cause of the trouble, but all the information he would volunteer was that the room was haunted. It was the only available room he had in the house for a stranger, and he could scarcely offer hospitality to anyone in it, when nobody could sleep in it. The end of it was that I laughed down my worthy friend's superstition; occupied the next day the haunted room; congratulated myself upon having so large, cool and fine a room in hot July weather; ate generously of a most bounteously furnished table — nothing better in the world than in Ennismore; and, altogether rejoiced in my good luck in the change from the skrimpy widow's board to the generous farmer's cuisine; and enjoyed many a quiet laugh at the ghost's expense.

My first experience of her ghostship was while sitting on a rail fence in a warm August day at twilight, talking to a friend at a considerable elevation above the house. My friend, who seemed to know the room I occupied, suddenly, with an exclamation of surprise, turned to me and said:

"Look, Daly, there's some one in your room, and it's a woman, too."

I looked in the direction indicated, and sure enough there was a light in the room and a shadow upon the window curtains showed a woman moving to and fro. Of course I was somewhat nonplussed, but I accounted for the circumstance by thinking that some of the girls of the house were engaged in the room in the performance of the ordinary domestic duties. Still I thought this a little strange, knowing the abhorrence entertained by every member of the family of entering the so-called haunted room.

On returning that evening I congratulated the farmer's wife on her courage in once more throwing open the room. She stared at me with blank astonishment. She wouldn't, for all the world, having anything to do with the room. Why, did I suppose she had? I told her what I had seen. There had been nobody there, as far as she knew. I went up stairs; the door was locked, the lamp unlit, the wick as I had left it, no evidence in the world that anybody had been there since morning. I considered the whole thing an optical illusion, and went to sleep. My dreams were not disturbed.

Three or four nights after, however, operations began. I awoke about the witching hour of night — so my watch admonished me — feeling chilly. The covering was all off the bed. I jumped up and found that the bedclothes had been removed and placed on the floor in a heap below the foot-board. I replaced them deeming I had kicked them off, and thought no more about it. But the same thing occurred several successive nights, so that it became a worry to me; and at last I got worked up to such a nervous pitch that I could not sleep at all. Toward the middle of the night I distinctly felt the bed clothes begin to move downward. I clutched at them grimly, and quite an exciting struggle for their possession began. But my invisible antagonist proving the stronger I saw everything disappear slowly but surely through the open space between the foot-rail and the floor-board.

Meanwhile, I had turned on the light, and leaping from the bed exclaimed: "Now I've got you!" in no enviable frame of mind, either. I seized a stout cudgel and explored the foot of the bed, and everywhere in the room; found the door securely locked and bolted. Not a single vestige of my nocturnal visitant except the heap of bed clothing on the floor. To say the least, I was awed as well as puzzled; and not knowing what other deviltry might be forthcoming, I took care to keep the light burning the rest of the night.

I need not say I slept no more but lay awake thinking. What could it be? Nevertheless, a bright thought struck me. I was not going to be driven out of my comfortable quarters by any ghost who played such a shabby trick as this, for by this time I began to think it was a ghost after all. Still, if stealing bedclothes was all it could do it wasn't much of a terror; and I'd fix that. The next morning I procured a wide slat and nailed it securely across the open space at the foot of the bed. Several nights passed; no more annoyance from that source.

I had then, and still have, a habit of placing my boots at the side of the bed before retiring for the night. One night, at the usual hour, I was awakened by a sound as loud as a pistol shot succeeded by dead silence. I immediately jumped up, and, upon investigation found one of my boots missing. Looking around I espied it under the bed close to the wall, against which it had been thrown with such violence that it chipped off some of the plaster. Certainly my nocturnal visitant exhibited a strange inclination for working close to the ground.

By this time I was in a towering passion, and seizing the remaining boot I sent it flying with an oath accompanying it in the direction the other had apparently come from. I listened for a reply, but none coming, I got up on the bed. Scarcely had I lifted my legs from the floor when the boot was thrown back with such force that I felt the wind strike my leg as the missile passed it. Had it struck me it would surely have broken the limb. My investigations ceased for that night. I lay still and let the boots alone. Yet, after that, not wishing to undergo the same experience, I took the boots to bed with me, and nothing more of that kind occurring, I began to flatter myself on having laid the spirit. Besides, I was strengthened in my opinion by the congratulations of my neighbors, who looked upon me as a man of extraordinary moral courage, and, as my landlord had laughingly remarked, "undoubtedly ghost-proof." Of course I mentioned my experience to no one.

I feared ridicule, in fact, and really believed that I would solve the mystery, and prove the ghost theory to be all nonsense.

Nothing occurred for several weeks afterward. I enjoyed the old farmer's hospitality meanwhile, taught my school and made my mind easy. One night, however, I was rudely disturbed from this happy frame of mind. I awoke with a feeling of terror. My usual resource I at once turned on the light. Then I beheld a sight which filled me with mingled fear and amazement. There stood, evidently, my ghostly visitant, staring at me; — a woman, pale and wan, yet with traces of beauty on her face. She was dressed in an ordinary black dress, with a black ribbon around her throat. But the thing which riveted my attention most was the expression of dire sorrow and awful despair upon her countenance. I never saw anything like it, not even in the faces of those condemned to an ignominious death. Once or twice the lips parted as if to speak; then, I suppose, as the expression of horror upon my countenance increased, there was a slight frown. With a strange fascination I continued to gaze for what appeared to be a minute. Then I made a movement towards the woman, when she appeared to go through the doorway. I examined the door, however, but found it locked as usual, and bolted. I listened, but heard no footsteps or other sounds on the stairs.

Then, returning to my couch, I concluded, as I am now thoroughly convinced, that I had seen a spirit. I received, however, a severe nervous shock, which was plainly visible to my kind host at breakfast next morning. He questioned me, and I related to him the circumstances herein set forth. From him I ascertained the name of the owners of the farm, and when vacation occurred I hied me to Peterboro, where Mr. Sullivan lived, to get an explanation of the mystery. Of course I slept no more in the haunted room.

Mr. Sullivan was quite friendly in his manner. "Yes," he said; "that woman was my wife's sister. She died in that bed in that room of consumption. We did all we could for her in her last sickness. She had the priest with her, received the last sacraments, but, though suffering terribly from disease, seemed terribly unwilling to die. Yet, why she should not rest with the multitude who sleep in Christ, and rest in peace, we do not know. We did all we could to make her comfortable, and in return she has driven us from our farm. She appeared to my wife one night, shortly after death, and so terrified the woman that she came near joining her ghostly visitant in the other world. Nothing would ever induce my wife to sleep in the house again, so I had to move here, engage in another occupation and rent my farm. She has never troubled us here, but seems to confine her visits to the room where she died. To me the whole thing is unaccountable."

I assured him it was equally so to me, and took my departure.

Now, why was this spirit so spiteful against anybody sleeping in the bed she died on? Why did she visit the scene of her demise at all? Rev. Mr. Searless, in the *Catholic World*, says if the spirit of the friend appears to us and gives "reasonable proofs of his identity we may of course put faith in what he may tell us of his experience since his departure." But no such faith is needed in this essay, as the apparition will never be called upon for proofs of identity, or spoken to at all. The poor spirit may abandon hope. The scene is the heart of an exclusively Irish settlement, and there is not a man, woman or child who would dare to speak to it. It is graven upon the Irish mind, the superstition — coming, it is said, from druidical days — that he who speaks to a spirit shall surely die within a year.

The old house may sink and rot and pass away, and the day of judgement come, but in Ennismore it never will be known why this uneasy spirit revisits the "glimpses of the moon."

Perhaps, however, some adventurous stranger, bolder than I am, or rather with more presence of mind, may wish to undergo my experience and solve the mystery. The house is there yet; is easily accessible; the door of the room locked, and the room itself abandoned to its ghostly tenant.

A SPECTRAL-LOOKING FIGURE

In the past, the sight of an odd-looking person walking down the street of a Canadian city was a noteworthy event, not at all like today when the streets of any of the larger cities are thronged with peculiar-looking and oddly dressed men and women (though it is sometimes difficult to distinguish their differences at a glance).

"A White-Robed Figure" was printed in the *Brandon Mail*, 10 April 1884. The account was apparently reprinted from the *Toronto Mail* (Toronto, Ont.). It has been slightly edited for presentation here.

A White-Robed Figure. — Perhaps the most wonderful case of somnambulism that has been known in Toronto for years occurred recently at an early hour. Shortly after two o'clock a gentleman was proceeding homewards along King Street near Simcoe when he suddenly observed by the gas light a spectral-looking figure about one hundred yards in front of him on the opposite side of the street. The air was perfectly still so that ordinary footsteps on the sidewalk could be heard for some distance, but not a sound of any kind proceeded from the figure which moved towards him. When he first caught sight of it the figure was moving along in front of the Government House grounds, and, as it drew near the corner of Simcoe Street he perceived that it was clothed in white. The sight at first almost froze his blood with terror. He was on the point of resigning himself to belief in a supernatural agency when it occurred to him that he might as well face it out, and see where the apparition would go to. It kept its course silently and as if there was not a human being within a 1,000 miles of it, until it reached York Street, the gentleman followed stealthily on the other side of the street. At York Street there stood P.C. McFarlane. Both were at a loss to think what sort of a "ghost" it was making towards them. P.C. Davis approached it to stop when a sudden ejaculation of surprise and horror came in a man's voice. In a few moments the constable learned that the "mysterious apparition" was an unfortunate young man who was in a somnambulistic fit. When he had sufficiently regained his senses to realize where he was, he gave his name and address. As he was nearly dead with cold, the officers proceeded with him at once to his home. It appeared that he had leaped in his night-dress from his bedroom window, which is situated on the second floor of a house on Windsor Street. Strange enough, he was not awakened by the fall, but went to work and scaled a seven-foot fence and reached Wellington Street by means of a lane. He then walked along Wellington to John, up which he proceeded to King, and along King to York, where luckily he was noticed by the policemen. As he is a young man of very respectable connections, his name is suppressed.

"COME HERE!"

Warnings from a corpse are alarms to be heeded.

"A Ghost Story" comes from the columns of the *Canadian Statesman*, Bowmanville, Ont., February 23, 1887.

A Ghost Story. — This story was told by a Toronto doctor about an epoch in his very early career, when he was collecting bills for a subscription book publication firm, somewhere in the interior of the Province, and stopped to lodge in a house, where the only sleeping-place that could be provided for him was in the room with a corpse. He had been indiscreet enough in engaging his lodging to show his roll of bills. He heard suspicious movements about the house in the night; the entrance of some one by a back door and a whispered consultation somewhere. His candle had been taken out after he had got to bed. Presently there was a hoarse whisper from some one in the centre of the room where the corpse was laid out — "Come here!" His blood froze in his veins. "Come here!" the whisper repeated. Obeying an irresistible impulse, he crept, trembling, to the side of the dead. The corpse was sitting bolt upright upon the table where it had been laid. "Look out!" said the corpse; "they are after your money, and may murder you — they're capable of it." The young man took up a post by the window, which couldn't be opened, however. But he stayed there, and by-and-by, when some one crept stealthily into the room, and he heard the ghastly lunging of a knife into the bed clothes where he had lain, he leaped through the window, and took the sash with him as he went out. As the doctor began to tell his story, the wood fire on the hearth, which had been blazing brightly, flickered and burned low, as if cold, damp blasts had been blown over it. When he described the rasping accent with which the dead man uttered his call, "Come here!" the fire suddenly went out, leaving only the glimmering fringe of light around the edges of the lighted sticks. A current of cold rain came from some unknown quarter just at this moment. The "conditions were favourable" for the narrative. When it was over there were any number of questions. Was the dead man really alive? Did he revive for the moment only and sink back into unequivocal death when he had delivered his warning? Of course the doctor, who had not remained to discover the secret of the thing, could not answer these questions.

Plainly Seeing the Apparition

There is a lot of local colour in this account of the apparition of a black man. It comes complete with a quotation from Shakespeare's *Hamlet*, the source of which would have been obvious to readers in the 1880s, but a mere century later would need to be explained to the average newspaper reader.

"A Coloured Ghost" appeared in the *Daily Sun* (Saint John, N.B.), 28 Nov. 1889.

A Coloured Ghost
Seen by the Rev. H.A.S. Hartley, B.A.
In Mrs. Jackson's House in Lower Cove
Midnight Visit of Two Sun Reporters to the Haunted Cottage

The latest Lower Cove sensation is a coloured ghost. The Rev. Mr. Hartley reports that he has seen it.

Armed with this item from last evening's *Globe*, a *Sun* reporter sought out the Rev. Mr. Hartley. It took some time to find this busy evangelist, but once unearthed he talked freely. He said, in reply to a torrent of enquiries:

Last Friday about 2:30 p.m., I was in the cemetery attending to the duties of my ministry, when a messenger came to my house and left word with my wife to the effect that Mrs. Mary Jackson of Kentville, N.S., but who has been living in this city for over two years, had no rest or peace in her house, east end of Brittain Street, and had to leave it in consequence, saying that she had sent for the Rev. Mr. Lawson, pastor of Carmarethen Street Methodist Church, who had visited her house but who had failed to see any apparition as had been complained of.

Accordingly, at the close of my usual Friday night prayer meeting, I waited on Mrs. Jackson at Mrs. Mary Anderson's residence and told her I would meet her on Sunday at 1:00 p.m., after my morning services. At 1:05 p.m. on that day, I went to the house of Mrs. Jackson and there being a great many people, both white and coloured on the street, I asked several to go in with me, but none would enter the house, so, opening the door, I went in myself and closed the door tightly after me.

I saw nothing in the house as far as I had examined it, and was about walking out under the conviction that Mrs. Jackson was under the influence of liquor, but on reflection I decided to visit every room. I was then in the parlour and I walked straight into the bedroom and saw lying on the bed the shape and form of a man, covered with a white sheet, a white napkin fastened on the head and passing under the chin. I put out my hand to feel the object, but it was impervious to the sense of touch — that I will testify on oath.

Immediately I looked around and saw the form of a man dressed in black sitting in a chair about two yards from me, and as I approached the object and put my hand out to touch it, it was gone. Then I walked from the chamber to the parlour, and as I did the object appeared at my side and walked step by step with me into that part of the house. I looked at the object and could distinctly recognize the features. The complexion was of chocolate. The form I saw in the bed, the one sitting in the chair and the one which walked alongside of me was one and the same. The face was cleanly shaven, save a slight moustache and was apparently that of a man of about 40 years of age. The man was unquestionably a negro. On entering the parlor I opened a closet and the object walked into it. Then I opened my Bible and read the 23rd Psalm, "The Lord is my shepherd," plainly seeing the apparition standing before me at the time. I then read another psalm, in Latin, "Who shall ascend to the hill of the Lord," etc.

As soon as I finished reading this psalm, I knelt down, and with closed eyes prayed fervently, loud enough, I think, to be heard by those outside the building — concluding with the Lord's prayer. When I was done I immediately opened my eyes, and the object had disappeared. I then repeated the Exorcisms of the Roman Church, also in Latin, but saw nothing.

I came out of the house then and locked the door, but told the people outside nothing whatever concerning my experience inside the building, although I was asked several questions. Mrs. Jackson was standing on the corner and I told her I had seen an apparition three distinctive times.

I described the appearance, and she replied: "That is just what I told you and the Rev. Mr. Lawson. That is my husband, John Jackson."

This statement was also corroborated by Mrs. Mary Anderson, a neighbour, who said she had several times seen a man sitting in the house. I told her that as a Methodist minister I would not or could not encourage any superstitious belief, and thought that if she would lead a godly, sober, and religious life avoid strong drink and evil associations, go to church oftener than she did — in fact, become a converted woman — that she would not be troubled with such objects as those complained of.

I gave it as my opinion that as the house had been sanctified by prayer she would no longer see the ghost of her husband, provided she adhered to the injunction that I had given her.

On Monday about 12:30 p.m., while I was attending the Methodist preachers' meeting, my wife received a second message from Mrs. Jackson, to the effect that she had seen the apparition again, and that a young man who had been a school teacher in St. Kitts, W.I., named Edward Mussenden, had likewise seen it — and other persons also. On returning home I received the message and replied I could not come Monday as I had to attend a meeting of Hartley division S. of T. and Acadia Lodge No. 365. I.O.O.F. respectively, and on Tuesday had to attend a sacred concert in St. Phillips Church, but that I would be there at 11:00 a.m. Wednesday.

At that hour I went, in company with D.J. McIntyre of St. Phillips, Dr. Berryman, Ed. Mussenden who declared to me that he had seen a ghost on Monday, Mrs. N. Anderson who also had seen it, a Mr. Wilson and my wife Katherine. We went in different rooms but did not see anything. Dr. Berryman asked me if I thought the woman had been under the influence of drink, remarking that from his professional knowledge he knew Mrs. Jackson had one lung affected. I told him she was not intoxicated — at least on the day when I had seen the apparition, and was not so at present.

We then closed the door and left.

In reply to question as to his belief in ghosts, the Rev. Mr. Hartley said: "I never believed in ghost stories, and I have never before seen ghosts, and I am at a loss to account for what I saw. I, however, feel perfectly satisfied that Mrs. Jackson was not under the influence of liquor and that the facts are as I have stated."

"Well, do I understand, Mr. Hartley, that you really believe in spirits," said the reporter.

"As a theologian," said the Rev. gentleman, "I unhesitatingly express the opinion that the apparition of spirits is clearly taught in the Bible, and possibly when one's spiritual eye is opened he may see a disembodied spirit. I think there may be some philosophy, accuracy and truth in Shakespeare's ghost lore as taught in the plays of *Macbeth* and *Hamlet*."

* * *

Last evening, on invitation of the Rev. H.A.S. Hartley, B.A., two *Sun* reporters, D.J. McIntyre, a well-known tonsorial artist, a coloured gentleman who was a school teacher in St. Kitts, West Indies, and several other persons, visited the deserted house of Mrs. Jackson, shortly before midnight. A large number of persons were about the premises, but a police detachment in charge of Sergt. Kilpatrick kept the crowd back and enabled the reporters and Mr. Hartley's friends to enter.

The house stands some thirty or forty feet back from Brittain Street at the extreme east end. It is a small building, one storey in height, and is a neat little dwelling. The only entrance leads into the wood shed, and turning sharply to the left the visitor finds himself in the kitchen. This is a small room which consists of a cooking range, a table and several shelves. A number of cooking utensils decorate the walls. The kitchen is in the centre of the house, there being a bedroom on each side of it. The front room is beyond a doubt the best one. It is clean and completely furnished Its contents include a bed, table, trunk, and a kind of sideboard. Over the bed is a mantle on which a number of china and earthenware articles are arranged. There is a jug at each end, and a small satchel is suspended over the bed. The sideboard mentioned above is well supplied with glassware, and is really an attractive feature. The bedclothes seem to be clean, or rather those that could be seen were. There were only a few chairs in the house. The bedroom in the rear of the house was not nearly so elegantly furnished as the other one. It was evidently not the spare room. The house was, as stated above, clean and neat, considering that it has been visited by almost every coloured individual in town who is inquisitive enough to see the haunted house.

The visitors being all in, the door was locked, and under escort of the Rev. Mr. Hartley and Mr. McIntyre, *The Sun* reporters made a thorough search of the house, and failed to find disembodied spirits. It was then suggested that the room in which the ghost was last seen should be entered and the light extinguished. That was agreed to and all hands proceeded to Mrs. Jackson's chamber. At 12:00 o'clock,

The witching time of night;
When churchyards yawn, and hell itself breathes out
Contagion to the world

the Rev. Mr. Hartley made an extempore prayer with special fitness to the occasion, concluding with the Lord's prayer, in which all the visitors joined. No ghost appearing, the company sang the hymn, "All Hail the Power of Jesus's Name," and "The Sweet Bye and Bye." This was followed by a short period of silent prayer, the singing of "Shall We Gather at the River" following. No ghost putting in an appearance, it was decided to retire to the adjoining room and leave three or four men to watch the bed.

After some five minutes waiting in the outer room, Messrs. McIntyre, Mussenden and two others called to the Rev. Mr. Hartley and others to come in and bring the light. Mr. Mussenden declared he had heard footsteps and that the bed clothing had been disturbed. The bed clothing, when the Rev. Mr. Hartley and visitors entered the room, was considerably tossed about, and all who were in the room declared that the bed clothing had been disturbed.

This means of finding that a ghost had charge of the house was enacted two or three times and each time the men who were in the bedroom were quite positive of the appearance of an invisible object which disturbed the bed clothing. At each of these tests of the presence of a ghost, four or more coloured men were in the room, in all of whom the Rev. Mr. Hartley has the utmost confidence, and is quite satisfied that what they tell is true.

The number of persons who sought admission to the house was entirely too large, and owing to this fact the Rev. Mr. Hartley did not have an opportunity of proving to those whom he invited that this particular ghost really had an existence in St. John.

COLD, FORBIDDING, AND SINISTER

Here is a terrifying tale of a man who fears for his life in a country inn in Western Canada. It first appeared in a newspaper in time for the Christmas season, as it was a tradition at this time of year for entire families in households in the New World (and perhaps in the Old World as well) to sit before the fireplace and listen to ghost stories being recited or read.

This tale of terror could have been written by Algernon Blackwood, that master of the macabre, author of such stories as "The Willows" and "The Wendigo." (He lived in the Toronto area in the early 1880s.) Instead, we have no clue as to the identity of the writer of this story, "That Moment of Horror," which appeared in the pages of the *Canadian Statesman*, 24 December 1889.

That Moment of Horror
A Thrilling Adventure A Pedlar's Startling Experience
at a Backwoods Tavern in the Early Days of Ontario

In all my travels, over thousands of miles of country, I was never really terrified but once; and then I confess I had a fright which I did not recover from for weeks, and which I still never recall without a secret shudder. My life might be said to have hung on a bare thread; and nothing but heaven's kind providence, interposed in a most miraculous manner, saved me from the awful doom.

In the regular pursuit of my vocation, I was travelling through Western Canada, when, towards evening of one hot, sultry, summer day, I found myself passing through a long stretch of swampy woodland, along what might much better have been denominated a horse-path than a road. I had taken a rather obscure by-way, in the hopes, if I found few customers, to find those who would pay well; but I had made a serious mistake, in that I had discovered none at all. In a walk of eight tedious miles, I had seen only three dwellings, and these miserable shanties, one of which was unoccupied, and the other two with ragged families who had no money for trade. At the last house, I inquired the distance to the next, and I was informed that four miles further on I would come to a main road, where there was an inn for travellers; and towards this I was now making my way, with the intention of putting up there for the night.

I came in sight of the road and the inn just as the sun was setting behind a drift of clouds, that seemed to betoken the gathering of a storm. Tired and hungry as I was, with night setting in upon me in such a lonely country, I was very glad to come in sight of a place of rest, and went forward in comparatively good spirits.

The inn was a brown stone building, two stories in height, and quite respectable looking for that region of country. As I came up to it, however, I fancied it had a certain air of gloom, which had a rather depressing effect upon my spirits; but then this, I thought, might be caused by the absence of sparkling lights and bustle, and seeing it at the hour of twilight. No one met me at the door; nor did I perceive a human being in or about it till I had entered the unlighted bar room, where a man, who was sitting in a corner, rose and came forward, with a slight nod of salutation.

"Are you the landlord?" I inquired.

"I am," was the answer.

"I suppose I can put up with you for the night?" I said.

"Certainly," he answered, glancing at my trunks. "Shall I take care of them for you?"

"I will merely set them behind your bar till I retire for the night, and then I will take them to my room. I suppose you can give me a single apartment to myself."

"Oh, yes, easy enough — my house is large, and will not be crowded to-night."

"Have you any other guests?" I inquired, feeling, from some cause for which I could not account, strangely ill at ease.

"There is no one here yet," he replied; "and it is getting rather late for the drovers, who often stop with me."

It was a relief to think that drovers were in the habit of putting up at the house, for that implied a certain honesty in the landlord, and a consequent security for onely travellers; and I really needed this reflection to counterbalance a strange sense of something wrong, if not absolutely wicked and dangerous.

I informed the host that I was very tired and hungry, and wished a good supper and a good bed, and he assured me that I should be provided with the best he had. He went out of the room, as he said, to give the necessary directions and get a light. He was gone some ten minutes, and returned with a candle in his hand, which he placed on the bar. I had taken a seat during his absence, and, being a little back in the shade, I now had a chance to scrutinize his features closely without being perceived in the act.

I did not like the appearance of his countenance. His face was long and angular, with black eyes and bushy brows, and the whole expression was cold, forbidding, and sinister.

He remarked that the night was very warm and sultry, and that it was likely to be showery, and then inquired if I had come far that day, and which direction? I informed him of my tedious walk over the by-road, and unguardedly added that I did not think my day's experience would encline me to travel through that region again in a hurry. He asked me where I was from, if I had seen many persons that day, if I was an entire stranger in that part of the country, and so forth, and so on — to all of which I gave correct answers.

Thus we conversed till a little bell announced supper, when he ushered me into a good-sized dining room, and did the honours of the table, trying to make himself very agreeable. That there was somebody else in the house I had good reason to believe — for I heard steps and the rattling of dishes in an adjoining room — but the landlord himself was the only person I saw during the evening, if I except a glance at a disappearing female dress as he was in the act of lighting me to my room.

My bedroom was small, but looked clean and neat, and contained an inviting bed, curtains of chintz at the single window, a chest of drawers, a looking-glass, a wash stand, a couple of chairs, and was really quite as well furnished as many an apartment in hotels of far greater pretension. With all this I was pleased, of course; and judging by the appearance that there was nothing wrong about an inn so properly conducted, I bolted my door, raised the window for a little fresh air, looked out and discovered the night was intensely dark, undressed, blew out my light, jumped into bed, and almost immediately fell asleep.

I was awakened by a crash of thunder, that was rolling over and shaking the house to its foundation at the moment my senses returned to me; and being rather timid about lightning, and remembering to have heard that the electric fluid would follow a current of air, and also recollecting that I had left my window open, I sprang up hastily to close it. As I did so, my head barely touched some soft substance, just above me; but the fact produced no impression upon my excited mind at the moment. I reached the window, and for an instant stood and looked out to get a view of the approaching storm; but, as before, I could not see anything at all — all was as black as the darkness of a pit — and as before, too, the air was perfectly still — so much so, that I fancied I felt a stifling sensation. I was the more surprised at this that I thought I heard the roar of the wind, and the falling of rain; and certainly there was another clap of thunder, whose preceding flash of lighting I had not perceived.

Awed by the mystery, I hastily let down the sash, and returned to the bed in a state of some trepidation; but, as I put out my hand to feel my way in, it came into contact with a mattress nearly as high as my neck from the floor. Now really terrified by a sense of some unknown danger, and half believing that the room was haunted, I clutched the mattress convulsively, and felt over and under it, and found it was separate from the bed on which I had been sleeping, and was slowly descending!

Gracious heaven! how shall I attempt to describe that moment of horror, when I first got a comprehension of the whole diabolical plot! a plot to murder me in my sleep! I was walled up in a room prepared with machinery for the express purpose of murdering the unsuspecting traveller, and had been saved from the awful fate by the report of heaven's thunder. The window of course was only a blind to deceive, placed inside of a blank wall, which accounted for my seeing nothing from it and getting no current of air when the sash was raised; and the mattress I had hold of was arranged to be lowered by pulleys, and held down by weights upon the sleeping traveller till life should be smothered out of him. All this I comprehended as by a sudden flash of thought and as I stood trembling and almost paralyzed, there came a quick rattling of cords and pulleys, and the upper bed dropped down with a force that denoted the heavy weights placed upon it.

But though left out from under it — alive as it were, by a miracle — what was I now to do to preserve my life? As yet, all was dark, and no one appeared; but I now heard voices speaking in low, hushed tones and knew that soon the truth would be discovered, and in all probability my life attempted in some other way. What was I to do? how defend myself from the midnight murderers? I had no weapon but an ordinary clash-knife, and what would this avail against two or more? Still, I was determined not to yield my life tamely; and as in all probability every avenue of escape was barred against me, I resolved to crawl under the bed and take my chance there. Mechanically, while considering, I had felt for my clothes and drawn on my pantaloons; and now cautiously trying the door, and finding it, as I had expected, fastened on the outside, I stealthily glided under the bed, and placed myself far back, close against the wall. I had barely gained this position, when a light shone into the room from above; and looking up between the bed and the wall, I saw an opening in the ceiling, about five feet by eight, through which I suppose the upper mattress had descended; and, standing on the edge of this opening, looking down, was the landlord of the inn, and beside him a tall, thin, sinister virago, who looked wicked enough to be his wife, as undoubtedly she was.

"All right, Meg.," he said, at length: "he is quiet enough now; and if not, I can soon finish him;" — and with this he took the candle from her hand, and leapt down upon the bed, and then sprang off upon the floor. "Now hoist away," he continued, "and let us go through with this job as quick as possible."

Again I heard the noise of ropes and pulleys, and knew the upper bed was being raised, which in another moment would disclose to the human monster the fact that my dead body was not under it. What then?

Merciful heaven! it must be a struggle of life and death between him and me! — and I was already nerving myself for the dreadful encounter, when I experienced a kind of transitory sensation of a crash and a shock.

The next thing I remember, was finding myself exposed to the fury of the tempest — the wind howling past me, the rain beating upon me, the lightning flashing, and the thunder roaring. I was still in my room, but it was all open on one side of me, and it took my bewildered sense some time to comprehend the awful fate of heaven's peculiar providence.

The lightning had struck the portion of building I was in, and had thus given me life and freedom!

As soon as I fairly comprehended this, I leapt to the ground outside, escaping injury, and ran for my life. took the main road, and ran on through the storm, as if pursued by a thousand fiends, as I sometimes fancied was. I ran thus till daylight, when I met a stage-coach full of passengers, hailed the driver, and told him my wonderful story. He thought me mad, but persuaded me to mount his box and go back with him. On arriving at the inn, he found a confirmation of my fearful tale.

The house had not only been struck, but, strange to relate, both the landlord and his wife had been killed by the bolt of heaven, and were found dead among the ruins!

I subsequently had to appear before a magistrate acting as coroner, and depose to the facts and the jury returned a verdict in accordance therewith.

I got away from that fearful region as soon as I could, but to this day I have never fully recovered from the effects of that night of horror at the inn!

THE DAGG POLTERGEIST

The Dagg Poltergeist is the case of a "an invisible inhabitant of the woodshed" on the Dagg family farm, outside Shawville, Que., in September, October, and November of 1889.

This account has at least two interesting features. The first feature is that the effects of the poltergeist-like voice were observed taking place by so many members of the community in the Ottawa Valley, and that they swore oaths that the effect that the manifestations occurred precisely as described. The second feature is the intermittent presence of the man who described them, the reporter Percy Woodcock, who offered readers of the Brockville *Recorder and Times* exclusive, eye-witness accounts of events and experiences on the farm, before giving them exposure in newspapers North America. The Dagg Poltergeist was a big story in its day, a seven-day wonder.

The poltergeist in question brings to mind the celebrated case of "Gef the Talking Mongoose" which was investigated on a farm on the Isle of Man by

British ghosthunter Harry Price and broadcaster R.S. Lambert. They wrote about their experiences in *The Haunting of Cashen's Gap: A Modern "Miracle" Investigated* (1936). But in many respects the doings of the Dagg poltergeist are much more exciting than those of the elusive Gef, as Lambert would admit when he came to discuss the latter account in *Exploring the Supernatural* (1955), his study of "the weird" in Canadian folklore.

This relatively complete account of the whole affair is titled "Dagg's Demon" and is reprinted from the columns of the *Evening Journal* (Ottawa), Nov. 25, 1889. The multiple headlines given by the Ottawa editors to the news story just about say it all.

What became of little Dinah, the focus of the poltergeist-like effects, is unknown.

Dagg's Demon
The Doings and Sayings of the Pontiac Spook
What Mr. Percy Woodcock, R.C.A., Experienced
A Statement Signed by Seventeen Residents of the Neighbourhood
Is it a Devil from Below or an Angel from Above?
Cock and Bull Yarns

The Brockville *Times* of Saturday publishes five columns regarding the Clarendon Front spook in Pontiac county, apropos of a visit paid to the scene by Mr. Percy Woodcock, the sculptor and member of the Royal Canadian Academy of Art.

For two months past there has been a lot of excitement around Shawville and Portage du Fort n the subject of the spook. On the 15th of September last, the family of George Dagg, a farmer living in the township of Clarendon, in the county of Pontiac, seven miles from Shawville, on the Pontiac & Pacific railroad, began to be troubled by some strange spirit of mischief that played havoc with their peaceful home and drove them nearly distracted. The family consisted of George Dagg, aged about 35 years, his wife Susan, little Mary Dagg, aged five years, little Johnny Dagg, aged two years, and Dinah Burden McLean, aged 11 years. The little girl Dinah was sent out from Scotland by Mr. Quarrier, and was adopted from the Belleville Home by Mr. Dagg five years ago.

Alleged Occurrences

The county papers have been full of recitals of the alleged strange occureences in the Daggs' home. Strange voices are said to have been heard in the house; fire is said to have suddenly broken out in many places; filth was strewn about the house by unseen hands; window panes were smashed, stones thrown through the open door, the children's hair was mysteriously cut, etc. It was noticed that when the little girl Dinah was away from the house the manifestations ceased, so she was closely watched, but nothing could be discovered, and the people came to the conclusion that spirits were at work.

Mr. Woodcock to the Fore

Mr. Woodcock, who is well known as an artist in Ottawa, heard of the matter at his home in Brockville, and as he has a leaning towards spiritualism, he decided to investigate for himself. On Thursday, Nov. 14, he accordingly started for Clarendon. He spent Friday, Saturday and Sunday with the Daggs, made careful enquiries among the neighbours about the occurrences previous to his arrival, and made careful and copious notes during his visit. From these the Brockville *Times* furnishes its lengthy account. Mr. Woodcock *heard* many strange things, and had long talks with the alleged spirit, but he *saw* nothing strange during his three days' visit except, as he claims, a lead pencil writing of its own accord. With this preliminary, the following account is given just as published in the *Brockville Times*:

Mr. Woodcock's Story

Mr. Woodcock arrived in Shawville on Thursday

evening, 14th inst., and the next morning procured a rig and drove to the Dagg farm house. He found it in a common rural district surrounded for the most part with ordinarily well-to-do farmers. The house where the phenomena occurred was found to be a small log house, of one story and an attic with an open board shed at the rear, recently erected, but not yet shingled. He found the Daggs to be a very decent, respectable, honest family, of good average intelligence. Mr. Woodcock was received by them on his arrival as an ordinary curiosity seeker, of whom they had already had an abundance, but after some conversation, Mr. Dagg said they expected to have a quiet day, as they had sent Dinah, the little girl, over to Dagg's father's house, about two miles away, and when she was gone the manifestations ceased.

Mr. Woodcock, however, was not to be put off with this, and finally succeeded in so far securing their confidence as to induce them to promise to send for the little girl the following day.

On Saturday morning when he arrived at the house, he was met by the children outside, and being introduced to Dinah, asked her if she had seen anything since she had come back home. She replied that she had, a few minutes before while coming from the well, back of the house. She and Mr. Woodcock went around to the open shed, back of the house. Dinah said: "Are you there, mister?" To Mr. Woodcock's intense astonishment a deep, gruff voice, as of an old man, seemingly within four or five feet from him, instantly replied in language that cannot be repeated here. Mr. Woodcock, recovering from his astonishment, said: "Who are you?" "I am the Devil; I'll have you in my clutches; get out of this or I'll break your neck." And further expressions of enmity came out of the air to the ears of the astounded listeners. Mr. Woodcock replied that that sort of thing might frighten the people there and the children, but it did not scare him at all, and he further told the voice or whatever it was that he ought to be ashmed to use such filthy language before the children. The voice retaliated by calling Mr. Woodcock a derisive name.

Talking for Five Hours

A conversation then ensued between Mr. Woodcock, the voice and Mr. George Dagg, who afterwards joined them, lasting for five hours without a break. Mr. Woodcock took the position that he had to deal with an invisible personality, as real as though there in the flesh and on this basis endeavoured to shame him into bette behaviour and stop persecuting the Daggs who had admittedly done him (the voice) no harm. On the othe hand the voice resisted for a long time, but finally seemed to yield to the expostulations of Mr. Woodcoc and Mr. Dagg and agreed to cease the use of obscene language and finally admitted that it had been actuated solely by a spirit of mischief, of having fun, as it termed it, and had no ill will against any body excep Woodcock and the little girl Dinah, to whom he seemed to have a decided antipathy. He asked to be forgiven by Mr. Dagg, Mrs. Dagg, Mr. Arthur Smart, and others about whom he had said hard things.

To satisfy himself that there was no collusion on the part of any person who might be practising ventriloquism or some other art, Mr. Woodcock made a thorough investigation of the premises, and found that it was utterly impossible that there could be anything o the kind. He carefully watched Dinah, who was the only one present with him at the opening of the conversation and was perfectly satisfied that the voice did not emanate from her, and further the voice was very gruff and coarse, entirely different to hers which is delicate and very effeminate. To make assurance doubly sure he asked Dinah to fill her mouth with water which she did and the conversation continued the same as before.

A Lively Lead Pencil

The shed in which the conversation began was a bare open building with no floor, nor any place in which it was possible that any person could have been concealed. The house is a log one, not plastered, no closets, and only ordinary thin board partitions dividing it into three rooms, used for a kitchen and two bed rooms. The family having told Mr. Woodcock of writings having been found about the house, he asked the voice to be kind enough to write something that he might be able to show to his friends. This took place in the morning while in the shed. At first the voice refused to do so, but after a good deal of coaxing consented. Mr. Woodcock, in the meantime, having laid on a bench in the shed a piece of paper and a lead pencil, immediately on the voice consenting, he observed the pencil to stand up and proceed to write. So soon as the pencil dropped, Mr. Woodcock stepped over, and examining the paper said: "I asked you to write something decent." To this the voice replied, in an angry tone, "I'll steal you a lead pencil," and immediately the pencil rose and was thrown violently across the room.

More Talk

Immediately after this Mr. Woodcock went into the hosue and the voice was heard there. The following conversation then took place:

Mr. Woodcock — What are your reasons for thus persecuting the Dagg family?

Answer — Mrs. Wallace sends me. (Mrs. Wallace is a resident with whom the Daggs are not on good terms.)

Mr. W. — Will your engagement with Mrs. Wallace soon cease?

Answer — Won't tell you. Shut up; you meddle with the Black Art. I will break your neck, for I'm the Devil, the son of the Blessed!

Mr. W. — No you won't, nor am I afraid of you. Answer me civilly, I am not your enemy.

Answer — (The reply to this was so obscene as to be unfit for publication.)

Mr. W. — Now, spirit, be a decent fellow and use better language, please.

Answer — I will, but you keep me here talking all the time. I'm tired. Go to Mrs. Wallace and make her confess her sins. She's trying and she's waiting for you, she and the other two.

Mr. W. — I will soon go.

Answer — No you won't. You say you will but you won't.

The voice then cried out, "George" (referring to Mr. Dagg), "I like you. I'll talk to you, not to him."

Turns Angel

After some further cross-examination by Mr. Woodcock and others, the voice expressed some repentance for the trouble caused the Daggs and promised Mr. Woodcock that it would say good-bye on the following night (Sunday) at midnight and would not bother them any more. On being asked why he did not leave immediately he replied that the next day lots of people would be there, and he wanted to convince the unbelievers. Mr. Woodcock then, about 2 a.m., went home with Mr. Arthur Smart, and remained the balance of the night, returning to Dagg's with Mr. Smart and some of his family on Sunday at an early hour. All day on Sunday the house was crowded with visitors from all parts of the surrounding country.

From early morning the voice, which apparently was on its good behaviour, as had been promised, answered the questions of everybody and made comments on different persons as they entered the room. Some of his remarks were very amusing, and displayed an intimate knowledge of the private affairs of many of his questioners.

During the forenoon some person spoke to the voice and remarked on his not using any obscene language as on former occasions. The reply came. "I am not that person who used the dirty language, I am an angel from heaven, sent by God to drive away that fellow," and this character he assumed throughout the day.

What Seventeen People Say

During the evening Mr. Woodcock drew up a brief report of the occurrences before and during his presence there which he read to those assembled. This report was signed by seventeen respectable and responsible citizens of the neighbourhood and from a distance, which report is found below, with the names and addresses of the signers. Mr. Woodcock said he could have procured fifty signatures to this, but when he got the seventeenth name concluded it was enough.

Report

To Whom It May Concern:

We, the undersigned, solemnly declare that the following curious proceedings, which began on the 15th day of September 1889 and are still gong on this 17th day of November, 1889, in the home of Mr. George Dagg, a farmer living seven miles from Shawville, Clarendon Township, Pontiac County, Province of Quebec, actually occurred as below described.

1st That fires have broken out spontaneously throughout the house, as many as eight occurring on one day, six being in the house and two outside; that the window curtains were burned whilst on the windows, this happening in broad daylight, whilst the family and neighbours were in the house.

2nd The stones were thrown by invisible hands through the windows, and as many as eight panes of glass being broken; that articles such as a water jug, milk pitcher, a wash basin, cream tub, butter tub and other articles were thronw about the house by the same invisible agency, a jar of water being thrown in the face of Mrs. John Dagg, also one in the face of Mrs. George

Dagg, whilst they were busy about their household duties, Mrs. Dagg being alone in the house at the time it was thrown in her face; that a large dining table was thrown down; a mouth organ, which was lying on a small shelf, was heard distinctly to be played, and was soon to move across the room on to the floor; immediately after, a rocking chair began rocking furiously; that a wash board was sent flying down the stairs from the garret, no one being in the garret at the time; that when the child Dinah is present a deep, gruff voice like that of an aged man has been hear at various times, both in the house and out doors, and when asked questions answered so as to be distinctly heard, showing that he is cognizant of all that has taken place, not only in Mr. Dagg's family, but also in the families in the surrounding neighbourhood; that he claims to be a disincarnated being, who died twenty years ago, aged eight years, that he gave his name to Mr. George Dagg and Mr. Willie Dagg, forbidding them to tell it; that this intelligence is able to make himself visible to Dinah, little Mary and Johnnie, who have seen him under different forms at different times, at one time as a tall thin man with a cow's head, horns, tail and cloven foot, at another time as a big black dog, and finally as a man with a beautiful face and long white hair, dressed in white, wearing a crown with stars in it.

Signed,

John Dagg, Portage du Fort, P.Q.

George Dagg, Portage du Fort, P.Q.

William Eddes, Radsford, P.Q.

William H. Dagg, Portage du Fort, P.Q.

Arthur Smart, Portage du Fort, P.Q.

Charles A. Dagg, Portage du Fort, P.Q.

Bruno Morrow, Portage du Fort, P.Q.

Benjamin Smart, Shawville, P.Q.

William J. Dagg, Shawville, P.Q.

Robert J. Peever, Cobden, Ont.

R.H. Lockhart, Portage du Fort, P.Q.

John Fulford, Portage du Fort, P.Q.

George G. Hodgins, Shawville, P.Q.

Richard E. Dagg, Shawville, P.Q.

George Blackwell, Haley's, Ont.

William Smart, Portague du Fort, P.Q.

John J. Dagg, Portage du Fort, P.Q.

Mr. Woodcock left the house about 12:30 Sunday night and the occurrences after he left are given on the authority of the Daggs, Miss Mary Smart, Alex. and Benjamin Smart and others of the neighbours, as a very large crowd stayed there till morning.

Rev. Mr. Bell's Troubles

The voice asked that two clergymen, Rev. Mr. Duclo and Rev. Mr. Naylor, one a Presbyterian, the othe English church, and the editor of the Pontiac *Advance* Portage du Fort, be sent for; that these men wer unbelievers, and thought the Dagg family were doing al these things themselves, that they might get talke about, and that he wanted them to come and he woul convince them that they were mistaken. Thes gentlemen being so far away were not sent for, but th Rev. Mr. Bell, a Baptist clergyman, having preache that evening in the neighbourhood it was suggested b some one that he be sent for, which was done. Mr. Bel at first was averse to coming, but finally consented t do so, and arrived shortly after 11 o'clock. As soon a he entered the door his name was called aloud by th voice, but Mr. Bell paid no attention. The voice agai called him by name, when Mr. Bell said to som persons standing near that he would have nothing to d with evil spirits. The voice then called him a coward and said he was all words, that he had better d something else than preach, that he was better than th preacher, and that he (the preacher) was not genuine Mr. Bell, who was visibly agitated, proposed that the have prayers. A chapter from the Bible was read b him, the voice accompanying him through it an occasionally going in advance of the clergyman. Whe they knelt to pray the voice responded. Mr. Bell praye for the family whom he said had brought the troubl upon themselves by trampling the Bible underfoot, o words to that effect, and finally exorcised the spirit commanding him in the name of the Saviour to depart whereupon the spirit laughed and said it was all words that Mr. Bell had better stick to photography. Mr. Bel left the house without directly speaking to the voice a any time.

An Extraordinary Scene

After Mr. Bell had gone and while the house was full of people the voice cried out, "You don't believe that I am an angel because my voice is coarse; I will show you that I don't lie, but always tell the truth," when instantly the voice changed to one of exquisite sweetness. When asked afterwards why he did not change his voice before, he replied that he was afraid if he did they would think it was Dinah. He then sang the following rhymes which he dictated afterwards and they were copied by Dinah and by William Dagg:

I am waiting, I am waiting,
To call you dear sinner,
Come to the Saviour, come to Him now,
Won't you receive Him just now, right now?
Oh! list now, he is calling to-day,
He is calling you to Jesus,
Move! Come to Him now;
Come to Him, dear brothers and sisters,
Come to Him now.
   *

Trust in the Lord and He will save,
He is calling to save us just now,
He will save you,
Come, come to Jesus, come away,
He is willing, He will trust you,
Come to Jesus,
Come to Jesus, Come away,
Come, come to Jesus, come away.

These were beautifully sung by the voice, at his request Miss Mary Smart accompanying him where she could.

Those present unite in saying that though Miss Smart is considered a very fine singer, her voice was coarse compared to that of the spirit. This singing was kept up until the whole crowd was in a state of violent agitation, many of the women crying heartily. One o'clock was the hour fixed for his departure, but at that time the people had become so interested they begged of him to stay and he consented to remain another hour which he did. At the end of that hour they again urged him to stay until three o'clock which he consented to do. At three o'clock he bade them good-bye except Dinah, saying he would return at eleven o'clock next evening and show himself to her, little Mary and Johnny.

For Mr. Woodcock's Benefit

Mr. Woodcock returned to Dagg's house on Monday morning to say good-bye to them before leaving for home, and spent the forenoon arranging his notes and comparing them with the recollections of the Daggs and other neighbours, including Mr. Smart and some of the members of the family. It will be remembered that the voice had promised the previous night to return on Monday and say good-bye to the children. Mr. Woodcock relates that as he sat talking to the different persons in the room, the three children who had been out the door came rushing into the house wide-eyed and fearfully excited, little Mary crying out, "Oh! mamma, the beautiful man, he took little Johnny and me in his arms, and oh, mamma, I played on the music and he went to heaven and was all red." They rushed to the door but nothing unusual was to be seen. On questioning the girls they both told the same story. Their accounts said a beautiful man, dressed in white with ribbons and "pretty things" all over his clothes, with gold things on his head and stars in it. They said he had a lovely face and long white hair, that he stooped down and took little Mary and the baby (Johnny) in his arms, and said Johnny was a fine little fellow, and that Mary played on the music thing he had with him. Dinah said she distinctly saw him stoop and lift Mary and Johnny in his arms and heard him speak to Johnny. Dinah said he spoke to her and said that man Woodcock thought he was not angel but he would show that he was, and then she said he went up to heaven.

With this final transformation scene disappeared according to promise the mysterious disturber of this formerly peaceful home. Whether this visitation has ceased for good remains to be seen but on re-appearance Mr. Dagg agreed to at once notify Mr. Woodcock when the little girl Dinah will be brought here (Brockville), and taken into Mr. Woodcock's family. So far no word has reached here of any further disturbance.

GHOST'S HOLLOW

Why is that that ghost stories are so highly readable? Are they such a pleasure to read because they themselves are "ghostly," that is, because they produce in the reader the symptoms of fear (goose pimples, hair on end, increased muscular tension?) that the witnesses in the tales are said to experience?

Whether or not this is so, here is a highly readable ghost story. "Warned of Danger by a Ghost" appeared in the columns of the *Regina Leader Post*, March 11, 1890. It was published in time for Easter reading.

Warned of Danger by a Ghost
The Meeting on the Road and the Specter's Words of Guidance
The Shade Was "Not Wrapped Up for Driving"
and Refused the Invitation to Ride, as "Walking Was Warmer"

Such a glorious night! The snow sparkled like diamond dust, and the sleigh runners squeaked as they passed over it, with frosty sound so dear to the heart of the true Canadian.

The moon had risen, and it was as bright as day. The horse's breath seemed to fill the air with clouds, and his coat already began to sparkle with frost. Oh, it was good to be home again! "Canada for the Canadians." Is it any wonder we love our beautiful country with such passionate devotion?

From these high and patriotic thoughts I was aroused by coming to a turn in the road, a fork. Now there were two roads to the village from this point, one leading down a long, steep hill, at the bottom of which an aboideau, or primitive bridge, built of fire trees and brush, with alternate layers of earth and stones — a sort of earthwork, in fact — spanned a deep treacherous little creek, in which the ice piled in huge blocks in winter, and, as it was an estuary of the river, it was a dangerous spot when the tide was high. Taking this road would cut off more than half a mile of my journey, so I decided to try it, despite a curious reluctance on the part of my horse. The road certainly did not look as if it was traveled much, but just at the turn the snow had drifted off, leaving it nearly bare. So I forced the unwilling nag into the roadway and jogged on cautiously.

The spot bore an unpleasant name, and a still more unpleasant reputation. It was called "Ghost's Hollow."

Fifty years ago, in the old days when the province was thinly settled and a weekly stage coach was the only means of communication between the different towns, the horses of a heavily laden coach had taken

fright at the top of the hill, and dashing down at mad speed gone over the aboideau. The tide was full in at the time and the creek filled with great floating blocks of ice. There were none to help in that lonely spot, so every one had been drowned, and the superstitious country people insisted that on wild winter nights any one standing at the top of the hill and listening intently could hear the muffled sound of sleigh bells, the shouts and the splashing and struggling of the horses. Certain it was that, when the tide was very low and the wind high, the water rushing through the sluices under the aboideau made an eerie, gurgling sound that was not by any means cheerful. I could hear it now with painful distinctiveness, though there was no wind. And my thoughts travelled back to my boyhood and to old Angus McDonald, a queer old Scotch farmer, with whom I had been a favorite, who had taught me how to make fox traps and to shoot rabbits, to believe in omens and to be frightened in dreams.

He was a superstitious old fellow, who declared that he had the gift of second sight, and who had always insisted that to hear the sound of the groans and struggles in "Ghost's Hollow," was a sure forerunner of coming misfortune to the one hearing them.

I smiled to myself as I remembered it, and made a mental note that I would tell Angus the first time I saw him, and ask him what he made of the omen now.

The horse stopped so suddenly that I nearly fell over the dashboard! And directly in front of the sleigh I saw a man plodding slowly along through the snow. I could have sworn that he was not there half a minute before, and yet he could not have come out of the woods without my seeing him. "Holloa!" I called. He turned slowly, and I saw that it was old Angus himself.

"Why, Angus, old fellow," I said, "what in the world are you doing in this lonely spot? Jump in and I'll drive you home. I was just thinking about you."

"Many thanks, Walter, for yer offer and yer thoughts, too; but it's a cold night, and I'm not that wrapped up for driving; walking's warmer," he answered.

"But what brings you out here on such a night, Angus?" I persisted. "Your rheumatism must be better than it was, or you would not run such risks."

"Ay, the rheumatism's a not that bad, I was seein' to the fox traps, an' then I heard the bells an' knew some one was going down the hill, so I came out to warn them. The 'bito's' all down, Walter, an' you'd get an ugly fall amongst those ice cakes if ye went over; turn back, boy, an' go the long way."

"But, Angus," I cried, "I don't like to have you here."

"I'll do well enough, lad; I'm going home now, good night."

"Good night," I answered reluctantly, "I'll see you to-morrow."

He made no answer and I turned the trembling horse, who pranced and snorted and tried to bolt until he realized that he was going the other way. When I looked back Angus was gone.

Once on the main road again we went like the wind, and soon the lights of home shone out, and in a few minutes more I was in the hall being shaken hands with, and kissed and questioned, passed around from one to the other like a sort of cordial, exclaimed over and commiserated because I had not any tea, and reading a welcome in Maggie's sweet eyes that was more "truly sustaining," as the old ladies say, than all the tears in the world.

"Walter, dear," said Maggie, "you have not been taking care of yourself. You look terribly worn and pale."

"Never mind, Maggie," I answered, "I am going to rest and get strong again now."

The boys were both home for the day.

Jack was in the civil service and Will was in a bank, both younger than I, and already winning their own way in the world I thought with a sigh.

Then mother came in to tell me my supper was ready, and every one came into the dining room to see that I was taken care of. Maggie poured out hastily made coffee, and if I could only have shaken off a curious feeling of languor that would creep over me, I should have felt as if I were in Paradise, after my long months of solitude.

"By the way, Walter," said Jack suddenly. "How did you happen to come the marsh road, as of course you did, or you would not be here — you know you always take the old coaching road because it was a little shorter. Was it by chance, or did they tell you at the hotel that the aboideau was down?"

"I believe they did tell me, I answered. "At least the hostler called after me, but I did not hear him. So I took the coach road, and if it had not been for poor old Angus McDonald I should be floundering among the ice cakes now instead of sitting here. I met him before I had more than started down the hill, and he told me about the 'bito,' as he called it."

For a full minute after I spoke there was a dead silence. Then Jack opened his mouth to speak, but was checked instantly by a look from father. Maggie grew very pale, and then flushed uneasily, and mother said something hurriedly about my having missed the train, and how disappointed the girls had been.

Something had evidently happened, for every one seemed constrained, but made nervous efforts to talk, so I was glad when the meal, which had begun so merrily, came to a close.

I went back to the parlor with the girls and tried to feel as I did when I first came in, but it was of no use, and, hearing Jack's footstep crossing the hall, I slipped out and stopped him.

"Look here, Jack," I began, "did I say anything out of the way at supper?" "No! Oh, no," said Jack, uneasily; he had evidently received private instructions to hold his tongue, and he found the task a hard one.

"Very well," I answered shortly; "if you don't choose to tell me, I'll go out in the kitchen and ask the servants. They will tell me fast enough. Now what was there in my saying I had seen old Angus to startle any one so?"

"Well, if you will have it, there was a good deal. Angus died six weeks ago. I can't imagine how we forgot to write you about it — Walter!!!"

I can't tell much about what happened after that, for the reason that I don't know. Jack says I just staggered and fell, as if I had received a blow. And when I was able to take any interest in what was passing around me it was nearly the last of January, and I had lost count of time for many weeks.

A MONSTER EAGLE

This newspaper account of an encounter with "a monster eagle" in rural Quebec appeared in *The Gazette* (Fort Macleod, Alta.), Nov. 3, 1892. The researcher W. Ritchie Benedict referred to this event in his article "Thunderbirds in Canada," *Fate*, June 2002. "What are we to make of this?" he asked. "According to the *Guinness Book of World Records*, the largest wingspan for a bird is considered to be the albatross, and they are about 11 feet from wing tip to wing tip at maximum. But this thing seems to be some sort of genetic aberration with a taste for mutton. The monkey-like face does not make sense for a bird. A pterodactyl would be described as more alligator-like. Joliette is is located just north of Montreal, and one would think that the shooting of such a creature would cause quite a stir."

Yet Ritchie, an intrepid researcher, could find no other reference to this weird winged creature in Montreal-area newspapers for the year 1892. The account retains some of the charm of folklore.

A Winged Monstrosity Said to Have Been Shot Near Joliette, Quebec

The following tough yarn comes from Joliette. Last week, Joseph Lasalle of the little village of Ste. Emelie de l'Energie, a big young fellow, went in search of a supposed bear that was nightly visiting the sheep-folds and carrying off the finest lambs. Some five miles back in the woods from the village, he was startled by hearing a loud croaking cry, and looking upwards he saw, circling high up in the air, an immense creature that he first took to be a monster eagle. The bird, or whatever it was, was rapidly descending, and Lasalle, who is a track marksman, took careful aim and fired.

The monster was struck and badly wounded by the heavy rifle bullet, and screaming with pain and rage, it came tumbling to the earth. As it landed he gave it the other barrel of the rifle, and still thinking it was an eagle, rushed on to it with his clubbed gun. A terrible battle ensued, lasting for several moments; then the victory was with the man and the monster lay dead at his feet. It had two great wings measuring fifteen feet from tip to tip. The head, which was fifteen inches in circumference, resembled that of a large monkey. The body was five feet long, and the back part was covered with a fur or coarse hair. The feet or claws resembled the legs of a wolf, and under the tail feathers was a long appendage with a tuft at the end that looked like the tail of a large calf.

Lying with wings extended on the ground, the monster looked as big as a horse, and when weighed was found to turn the scale at 300 pounds. A team had to be sent for to bring it back to the village. Then it was seen by Mr. Alderie Charland, a councillor of the town of Joliette, who was going through the country purchasing produce. He bought the monster probably for exhibition purposes from the Lasalles, and Friday last it was brought by train to his place of business in Joliette, where it is now in process of preparation to prevent decay, after which it will be shipped to this city for scientific examination. — *Montreal Exchange*

THE BEAST AT THE DOOR

The "beast" in this account may or may not be an animal. What we have here is a haunted farmhouse in Kent County, Ont. It is not a ghost *per se* that is doing the haunting, but a "noisy spirit," an invisible poltergeist.

"Uncanny Doings" was published in the *Daily Sun*, Saint John, N.B., October 4, 1894.

Uncanny Doings
At the House of Joseph McDowell, Kent Co., Ontario
Mysterious Rappings, and Stones Fired by Unseen Hands
The Bushes Full of Grinning Skeleton Faces —
A Terrible beast Appears to a Little Girl
(Special Cor. Toronto Globe)

Chatham, Sept. 26. — Having heard rumors of mysterious and uncanny happenings at the home of Mr. Joseph McDowell, on the 15th concession of Raleigh, a reporter drove out yesterday morning to ascertain whether or not the reports had any foundation in fact, and, if so, to get all possible particulars, and, if possible, to solve the mystery which surrounds the place.

Arriving at Mr. McDowell's, the scene of operations, we found Mrs. McDowell alone in the house, with little 13-year-old Lettie, an adopted daughter, who has been with her upwards of six years. Mr. McDowell, who was ploughing, was sent for, and, while awaiting his arrival, his wife told the following:

"I was standing outside, near the door, Saturday morning, after we had milked and had breakfast, working my butter. Lettie was just behind me washing the dish-pans. The rain-barrel was at the corner of the house, about ten or twelve feet away, and in plain sight of both of us, when a stone the size of a small goose-egg fell upon a board which was over the top of the barrel; but, though I looked up, I paid no further attention to it and thought nothing more of it until afterwards. I continued to work my butter, when showers of gravel came from under the house, where there was an opening barely large enough to let a cat through, and, flying to a considerable height in the air, fell on our heads, quite a bit of it getting into the butter I was working. I then kept watch, to see where the gravel came from, when the same thing occurred a second and third time, in rapid succession, and, though we could plainly see it go, we could not see anything throwing it. I took my butter and went into the cook-house, and, even after I was in there, a lot more gravel flew in the open door at me, and more stones went into my butter. I could see Lettie as she was standing at the door of the cook-house, and I know that she had no hand in it, and, besides, Lettie would not do such a thing. I told her to open the screen-door, so that I could take my butter in the kitchen. She tried to do so, but the door was swollen so that she could not. I set my butter down in the cook-house, and found the screen-door very hard to open. I then went back to get my butter, and just as I reached it a lot more stones came into it. I told Lettie to run down to the field and tell her father about it and tell him to come up to the house at once; which he did. In the kitchen I picked the stones out of the butter and put it in a crock, and started mixing bread. After I had been at that a little while large stones began to come through the window, breaking four panes of glass, and after them came nearly a bushel of gravel. When Lettie returned without Mr. McDowell, the stones were still coming in, and I myself went to fetch him, as the former run had made the girl feel sick. Cautioning Lettie to remain in the house, I left, and, during my absence, some animal, about three feet long, with a head like a cat and the same kind of whiskers as that animal, came to the screen-door and tore it with its claws. Lettie told it to go away, whereupon it growled at her, terrifying the poor child so that she dropped a stick of wood which she had picked up to defend herself, and ran, screaming, into the adjoining room. When I returned she was so upset with what she had seen that I could scarcely pacify her."

Mr. McDowell, who had left his ploughing to give what information he could, arrived at this juncture and took up the narrative:

"When Mrs. McDowell came running for me in the field and told me what had happened, I came up as soon as possible, and, seeing the pile of gravel and stones which had come in the window, told her not to touch it until I came back. I then went out and brought in one of my neighbors, Ed. Murdock, and we took out of the house over a bushel of the dirt, and sand and gravel were piled up on the window-casing, on the outside, to the height of the bottom of the glass. This I scraped off with my hand."

When asked as to previous occurrences, Mr. McDowell said: "Some months ago tobacco worms seemed to be gathering around the house from all quarters and made their way everywhere. One day my wife was washing in the cook-house when many of the disgusting things fell from the roof on her back and all over her. These worms, which came by hundreds, never touched anyone but my wife, and, after a visit of nearly a month, left as they had arrived, going in a body down the road.

"Soon afterwards myriads of red ants came up the concession, and, arriving at the house, came in and made an extended stay. These also would bite my wife most unmercifully, and not touch either myself or Lettie. I took her away for a while, and during the time she was away she was not bitten, but the moment she came home the ants met her at the gate. I then took her to a doctor, but he could make nothing of her case and could do nothing for her. After the ants had gone away up the concession in a body, crickets came in most unusual numbers, and they, like the others, appeared to have special liking for my wife. A couple of weeks ago there were mysterious rappings all about the house, but we paid no attention to them; but on Friday night last the main trouble commenced and since then I have not slept a wink. I started to go to the station and had got to the railway, which passes about 40 rods in front of the house, when I heard something pounding. It sounded as though it was here, and I wondered what my wife was doing, but thought no more of it until on my return I learned that she and Lettie were sitting in the room when a great pounding and moaning were heard under the house, followed almost immediately by the same noise on the roof. Then came a rap like a man's knock on the front door, beside which Mrs. McDowell was seated. My wife says the knock was undoubtedly upon one of the panels of the door, and, as the wire fly-screen was shut and hooked, this startled her so that she would not open the door, but peeked out of the window, where, though it was a bright moonlight night, nothing was to be seen. Just after this an animal, similar to the one seen by Lettie on Saturday, was heard and seen by the latter sitting upon its haunches on the window sill, with its forepaws against the top of the second pane from the bottom, looking in. And every day since then, with the exception of yesterday and today, stones and gravel were thrown in and peculiar noises heard. On Sunday, my wife, with her sister, Mrs. Michael Broadbent, were in the cook-house, when stones were thrown in on them. Mrs. Broadbent went to the barn for her husband, who was there with quite a number of men, including myself. He went to the house with her, and he also saw the stones coming in.

"Nothing of this kind has occurred when I was present, and never yet when there is a crowd of folk around."

Upon being questioned as to what she saw, Lettie said: "The animal which came to the screen and tore it was the most terrible looking thing I ever saw. It was over two feet and a half long, with rough, shaggy brown fur, a face somewhat like that of a man, but entirely covered with hair; it had long whiskers and ears like those of a cat. A short, bushy tail completed the picture. When mother went to get father I was reading aloud, when I heard the beast at the door, and when I looked up it had its head through a hole it had ripped in the screen.

"It growled at me, and I threw a stick of wood at it and ran into the other room. While there I thought I heard it in the room, but cannot be sure, as I kept the door shut until mother came back. Monday night, while Mr. McDowell was at the station, I saw the same animal sitting at the window, with its feet upon the pane. I also saw the stones coming into the house. The most of them came right up the side of the house from under the back doorstep, and when on a level with the window turned right off sharply and went in. After I had shut myself in the room on Saturday I looked out of the front window and saw the beast jump the fences and go away towards the bush. It did not run, but jumped, all the time taking over half the width of the road in a leap."

Daniel Broadbent, upon being questioned, said: "Night before last (Monday), between dusk and darkness, I went with my brother, Albert Broadbent, to Joseph McDowell's farm, to see for myself what there was, and whether or not there was any truth in the many incredible reports which were being circulated concerning the mystery surrounding the place. I took my double-barrelled shotgun with me. Upon arriving at the farm, I sat on a log a few feet away from the cook-house. Mr. McDowell asked me to come in and have tea with him; but, having had supper just before going, I thanked him, and said I would stay where I was. I had not been there fifteen minutes when a considerable quantity of gravel, amongst which were several stones about the size of a hen's egg, fell in a perfect shower on the top of the cook-house and upon us. It appeared to be coming straight down, and landed with great force. A few minutes later it fell again, whereupon I got up, went to the door and told Joe I had seen enough to satisfy me. I stayed until nearly 9 o'clock, but neither heard nor saw anything more. Before taking up my position on the log on which I was sitting, Albert and I thoroughly searched every nook and cranny which could possibly afford a place of concealment for any practical joker, and I know the missiles were not thrown by human hands, though where they came from is, and must remain, a mystery."

An old resident, who stands high in the estimation of all — his name will be withheld for the present — in reply to the reporter's question as to the cause of the supernatural visitations, said: "It is nearly half a century since I came to these parts, having come here when I was but a young man, and at that time there stood in the bush just about where Joe McDowell's little house now stands, a small deserted and tumble-down log hut, which, even at that early date, no one would pass after night. A little bit after I came here — I was in my prime then and proud of my unusual strength — I heard tell of the 'haunted hut,' as folks called it, and openly made fun of those who refused to pass. I never thought of trying it myself until one day one of the young men remarked that they noticed, with all my brave talk, I myself never travelled that path. It was immediately arranged that I was to make the trip that same evening at dusk, leaving half the party at one end of the path and meeting the rest of them about half a mile past the hut. I started in the best of spirits and took with me a good pistol with which I was a first-rate shot. When I arrived near the hut the very atmosphere seemed stifling and peculiarly oppressive, and yet I was not afraid, but pushed on until I arrived just about where the present haunted house now stands. What happened then I never knew further than that I met a man dressed in plain, badly worn clothes going the opposite direction. When I was nearly up to him I said: 'I thought I was the only one around here not afraid to pass the — ghost, but I see I am not,' and I put out my hand to shake hands with him and congratulate him on his pluck. He took my hand in his, when to my horror I discovered I held the hand of a skeleton, and then I saw that the head of the one whose hand I held was only a fleshless skull, the stare of whose empty sockets seemed to fairly freeze the very marrow in my bones. At the very moment I took its hand the bush on every side seemed full of grinning skeleton-faces, which glared at me from behind every tree, and filled the air with hideous, discordant laughter. Then fine gravel began to rain down upon me, after which came stones of increasing size, which bent me to the ground insensible. When I recovered consciousness I was lying on a lounge in my own house. They told me they had found me lying on the cow-path through the bush. I never told the story to anyone till today. Nor did I ever go near that spot again after nightfall."

A SOMETHING IN THE SKY

Around the turn of the century, the subject of aviation was much in the news, if not in the air. But it was not until 1903 that powered flight in a craft heavier-than-air was achieved at Kitty Hawk, North Carolina.

This account suggests that the achievement was realized six years earlier by a Canadian inventor, but that he "came to grief in the wilds north of Lake Superior."

"The What Is It" appeared in the *Daily Colonist* (Victoria, B.C.), 7 Oct. 1897. The article is apparently reprinted from the *Canadian Engineer*.

The What Is It
A Learned Publication Deals with the Aerial Mystery

The *Canadian Engineer* says:

"On the 13th of August, at Vancouver, an object was seen in the sky travelling eastward, which had all the appearance of an airship, and what was said to be a balloon was reported at two or three different points in Manitoba and the Territories.

At 12:40 on the morning of the 16th, C.W. Spencer, superintendent of the Eastern division of the C.P.R., was sitting with Thos. Hay, his assistant, in the observation car of the train which had left Port Arthur for Sudbury, and as they were approaching Gravel River, and sat admiring the clear starlit heavens, they saw, in the words of Coleridge, "a something in the sky." There was a large white light, and at an angle above it on the left a red light and at a like angle on the right a white light. The object appeared to be about half a mile above the earth, and when first seen was at an angle of 30 to 40 degrees above the horizon. It seemed to be moving with the wind about 30 miles an hour, as the train was running at 45 miles an hour, and the object appeared to all in their wake. When they had watched it about three minutes the train turned inland from the shore at Lake Superior, and before it was hidden behind the bluffs it tilted and turned inland, apparently following them up the valley. As it turned the red light became blue, and there was disclosed in line with the main headlight a row of four lights terminated by a circle or ellipse of a dozen lights, in the midst of which was the dark body of an air ship. The light had the steady clearness of electric or acetylene light, and Mr Spencer and Mr. Hay could form no other opinion than that it was an airship, and if the object seen at Vancouver was the same, it must have travelled to this point, 2,100 miles, at the rate of about 700 miles a day. It is quite possible that some inventor has set to work quietly and unostentatiously, and thus put his theories into practice before announcing his discoveries to the world; and if he has not since come to grief in the wilds north of Lake Superior, we should soon know that air navigation was first accomplished on Canadian territory."

A Stranger by My Side

Prospectors live by hope and often by superstition.

Here is a story of a mysterious stranger whose appearance in the Cassiar Mountains of British Columbia in the 1870s haunted an old miner a quarter-century later.

"Colonel Reagan's Ghost" comes from the columns of the *Ottawa Free Press*, February 28, 1900. The story is apparently reprinted from the *Dawson Weekly News*.

Colonel Reagan's Ghost
Incident in the Life of an Old Cassiar Miner in the Winter of '72

The *Dawson Weekly News* of Jan. 26 has the following:

J. Reagan is a typical old-time prospector. He has followed the fortunes of many mining camps since the early '50s in California and now that he has reached the ripe old age of 75 winters with hardly a friend to lend him a helping-hand his lot in life seems gloomy and despair has helped to break his once robust frame and subdue his once indomitable spirit. He came to Dawson in the rush of 1898 from the Cassiar mining district, but in the hurly-burly rush for desirable ground he was pushed aside and lost in the scramble. The old-time method of prospecting and then recording was not the way of the Klondike to make a success and so his funds have run short, and he now depends upon a few old-time friends to give him shelter and provisions. He has been living in a little cabin on the hillside but his wood becoming exhausted and his provisions about gone he has found a temporary shelter at the Flannery hotel.

In the early '70s, when the Cassiar mining district was in its heyday of prosperity, Colonel Reagan was well-to-do, having a rich paying claim on Tibbett creek. In those days of frontier hospitality no man came to Reagan's cabin without receiving food or shelter. He was known all over the diggings as an eccentric character, devout in the observance of his religious duties and lavish in his gifts when called upon to help a fellow miner. He was held in considerable reverence by the Indians as a great medicine man, having cured several of the tribe of their prevailing sicknesses.

He was a good talker, and the story he tells of meeting a ghost during the last years of his life in the Cassiar mining district is interesting. He never tires of telling it, for he says that that experience has taught him that this manifestation of the unknown in the spirit world proves to him the existence of a hereafter and the truth of the immortality of the soul. He is a very little man — about 5 feet 4 inches in height, attenuated in form, with a large head covered with gray straggling locks and bright eyes that mark him as a man of an iron resolution ready to battle with the vicissitudes of life as long as he had a breath in his body. As he narrated, at the Flannery hotel last night, the story of meeting with the stranger in the lone cabin, the fire of zealous belief kindled in his eyes and seemed to bring back the scene of 28 years ago. He said:

"It was a cold and bitter night in the winter of 1872 when I crossed over the ridge and came to Dick Willoughby's cabin at Buck's Bar, on the Cassiar river. It was full of miners and they directed me to an empty cabin across the stream which was said to be haunted. I pulled my sled over to the shelter and entered, finding two rooms, one of them containing a fireplace which had not been used for some time. I started a fire and fried a little bacon and made some tea. As I was eating I looked up and found a stranger by my side. I did not hear him come through the doorway and was naturally surprised. He was an Englishman, smartly dressed and wore no coat. He had his arms folded across his breast and gazed upon me. His eyes seemed to look through me and I felt very uncomfortable.

"Finally I addressed him and asked him if he owned the cabin. He shook his head and said no. I asked him where he came from and he pointed to a number of graves standing white on the hillside. I had now become thoroughly alarmed and asked him if he was going to stay for the night.

"He pointed to the graves and beckoned me to follow him. As he was dressed in a strangely fashioned suit foreign to our miner's clothes I was puzzled and began to believe that he was a supernatural being, a genuine ghost. I finally pulled myself together and offered him some of my bacon, bread and tea, but he silently left the room without a sound of footsteps. When he had disappeared the fire blazed up into a flame and roared up the chimney, my frying pan rattled and banged on the floor and finally balanced in the flames while the bacon turned to a deep blood red hue. I almost swooned with fright. When all of a sudden the fire subsided and I was alone with my thoughts. I looked at the bacon and it had still the blood-red hue and to this day I could never solve the mystery."

THE DEVIL-GOD

Here is a tale that tells about the contest between the superstitions of the old shamans and the beliefs of the new Christians — or is it the beliefs of the new shamans and the superstitions of the old Christians? The spirit of the Indians is challenged by a black-suited missionary priest. In this account — indeed, in all such accounts on record — superstitions succumb to Christianity.

"How the Devil-God Lost His Head" appeared in the *Morning Leader* (Regina), 9 Jan. 1907. The legend was contributed by J. Theo. Wilson. I have regularized the spellings of "devil-god" and of the spirit "Wanka."

How the Devil-God Lost His Head. — When silhouetted against the azure of a sunset sky, seen through a rift in the Rockies, the massive column at the apex of Devil's mountain is a source of momentary fear seized upon all beholders. The approach to the tabooed valley of the Blackfeet Indians from the west is well worthy of the old, uncanny legends about it. Lake Minnewanka, Devil's lake, is one of the glories of the Canadian national park. Its waters are almost black, of an unfathomable depth, and, surrounded on all sides by preciptious mountains, it appears suitable for the western confine of the valley of Wanka, the Indian's evil spirit.

And when the lake, that follows in course a parallel of latitude, is traversed, entrance is at once given to the pass made sacred by a thousand years' traditions in the eyes of all orthodox Blackfeet. A narrow beach of shingle, stretching in a graceful curve for a couple of hundred yards, affords a good hauling place for the canoe. The beach is backed by a clump of mighty firs and hemlock. There are traces of old trails, passable by only one at a time, and one is chosen lending opportunity towards the mountain at the head of the pass. The path is traversed for about a quarter of a mile, when it stops abruptly in front of an enormous mass of granite. It is only after much scrambling over fallen logs and matted underbrush that a detour is made successfully, and when the other side is reached it is found that the obstruction is a mighty boulder. Circular in shape, with a diameter of at least fifty feet, its truck can be traced far up the valley. This mass is the head of Wanka, the devil-god of the Blackfeet. Now comes the story of how the devil lost his head.

The valley is a place of sudden storms; of mighty thunder claps that go reverberating with innumerable echoes among its craggy fastnesses. When the lightning flashes it seems to lick at the hillsides and gather fresh power as it rives, a monarch of the forest. Such is the place to which the Blackfeet went every spring to worship Wanka. No member of the tribe dared hunt within the valley. The medicine man told that an arrow fired within its confines meant death to the sender. It was the hunting ground of Wanka, and of Wanka alone.

And so it was from time immemorial, but the white men began to invade the Blackfeet territory. First came the hardy Scotchmen and French Canadian couriers du bois, the advance guard of "King George men," pioneers of the Hudson's Bay Company. But they did not stop. Their eyes were turned towards the west and on, on on they went, searching for furs. Most passed to the north, through easier valleys, and though word was sent that at Jasper House and that named after the Rocky Moun-tains the pelts of beaver, mink, marten and fox would be bought and paid for no stoppage was made near the pass of Wanka.

But soon a visitor of a very different kind arrived. He did not hurry west, but stayed among the Blackfeet. His talk was not of furs, nor of horses, nor of cattle. It was of a new spirit, the Lord of all the others, of One whose mighty power embraced the earth and heavens, both time and eternity. And the visitor was of a different aspect to all the others. His coat was long and black. There was nothing of the hunter about him. On his head was a large wide-brimmed hat, not the sombrero that had even then strayed up from the plains of Mexico, but like his coat of deepest black. Round his waist was something strange. From a long string of beads an image was suspended, nailed to a cross. This aroused the curiosity of the Blackfeet. Well they knew the Sun dance, the order through which a youth must pass before he became a brave. They knew the circling round the pole, where brave young breasts were torn. They knew how the barb was passed through the tender flesh, and attached to rawhide thongs connected with the summit of the sacred mast. Many of them had felt the

agony themselves as hair's breadth by hair's breadth th flesh was blown away, in some cases the barb bein; forced free on the outside. But this Man on the cros had torture worse than that. What did it mean? Th priest answered, "Peace, peace and goodwill."

Could this untold agony mean peace? And then th priest gave answer, "Peace, not to himself, but to all th world." Gradually in the minds of the more susceptibl Indians a glimmering grew of what this now, strang story meant. It was each not for himself and his tribe but every other tribe also. Some one has truly said tha in every heart there is a spark of this divine, and thi spark became enkindled under the influence of the gentle father. Round the camp fires in the winter he tol his curious story of peace, goodwill towards all men And then he asked who would follow, who woul embrace the new faith.

The murmurings of the medicine men grew loud; the wise women of the tribe huddled together and, i whispered converse debated how they should comba the rising influence of the long frocked man in black Yet still he continued his teaching and, as the middle o the winter arrived, a dozen of the younger braves gave their word to accept the new faith, and be baptise according to its ritual with the advent of the coming spring. It was time for the leaders of the old faith to be up and doing — to show the tribe the old gods were the mightiest. Many consultations were held and at last challenge was hurled at the apostle of the new religion Would he dare to invade and carry out the ceremonie of this strange belief in the valley sacred to the devil god's name? The father answered, "Yes, we are in His hands everywhere." And so it befell.

Traversing the Bow river and then turning in a half circle the tribe reached Devil's lake. The canoes quickly took them across it and landed all on the shingled beach. It was the Monday before Easter. While the rest of the tribe waited on the shore in sullen silence the little band of converts, headed by the man in black, struck a short distance into the forest. Only a quarter of a mile had to be passed when a comparatively open space was reached and in this spot, where a short grove of trees formed a natural cathedral, preparations were made to erect the rude altar. The enormous boulder was not there then as it rested on the mighty column that now rises majestically from the summit of Devil's mountain.

The few days passed peacefully to the little party. Teaching, prayer and meditation occupied the time after the altar was erected. All things were ready and the priest and his dozen converts arose on Easter morn, the latter anxious to receive and the former willing to bestow the outward symbols of accepting the new faith. It was a gracious, golden morning. Two were sent to tell the tribe that all was ready for the test. Yet a few dared to witness the impious invasion of the devil-god's chosen domain; some sought refuge on the sombre bosom of the lake. Still, a half dozen of the hardier braves remained to see the downfall of the new religion, concealing themselves in the trees and bushes to witness the wrath of Wanka.

Slowly the ceremony progressed. The gentle father drew from within his cassock the little vial of water blessed by his archbishop away east in Montreal. He had carried it with infinite care during his long, long journey across the mountain and prairie and now the time for use had arrived. He was to baptise his first converts, the pioneers of their race to accept the story of the cross. With outstretched hands he stood in front of the altar, a blessing on his lips.

Suddenly the very earth seemed to tremble. The unbelievers threw aside their concealment and staggered through the bush towards the lake. It was as if the foundations of the globe were allied with Wanka for the defeat of the teachings of peace. The mountains on the north appeared to bow to the crags on the south — there was the uprooting of monarchs of the forest that had stood unscathed through a thousand years. The converts fell to the ground in a paroxysm of fear. With faces buried in the earth yet with hands uplifted to the altar they awaited their fate. In an instant a new terror became visible. From far up at the head of the valley there came the sound of a mighty crash. All looked instinctively. What was this? The head of Wanka had disappeared; the gigantic circular mass at the summit of

his columnar neck was bounding down the mountain side like a thing of life. It bowed its way through timber and underbrush crashing fir and hemlock, whatever their girth, like matchwood.

The surface of the lake became like a raging ocean. Frail canoes were upset, their occupants hurled into the seething waters. Some struggled for the shore, some expired of fright. And down, down the valley came the fallen head of the god. Only one man stood erect facing whatever might befall. Bare headed, holding aloft the crucifix, his pale lips moving in prayer, the teacher of the gospel of peace implored the Almighty even yet to spare his flock. With cries and yells of fear, the medicine men and wise women called on Wanka to complete his revenge, to continue in his might and crush out those who sought to undermine his power. It was all over in five minutes. The head of Wanka slackened up in its career. Slowly and more slowly it came, though none present realized it. Paralyzed with fear they could not move. They had no thought but one of terror; the Christians looked with new-found faith towards their God; the believers in the old religion realised the wondrous power of Wanka. But the career of Wanka's head was over. Within a foot of the Christian altar it came to rest — never more to be moved. Then up rose the converts and joining with trembling voices to that of their beloved teacher they sang "Gloria in Excelsis, Deo."

All that now remains in support of this old-time legend is the enormous boulder near the head of Devil's lake and the signs of its avalanche-like course down the valley. A nearby tree is marked with the sign of the cross. Yet ancient squaws, even in the twentieth century, tell the papooses when gathered in the tepee at night, the story of how the devil lost his head.

THE SINGULAR VISITATION

Do the spirits of the dead return? Do they communicate with the living?

This account assumes that they do return from the land of the dead and that they do communicate with grief-stricken relatives in the land of the living.

"His Spirit Rose in Mystic Light" appeared in the *News Telegram* (Calgary, Alta.), 15 Dec. 1908.

His Spirit Rose in Mystic Light
New Brunswick Girl's Disquieting Vision in Her Bed Room

Montreal, Dec. 14. — A very remarkable revelation of the statements of apparently trustworthy witnesses are accepted of a supernormal kind has just been had to a family in New Brunswick who died within the past fortnight near Englehart, on the Montreal River, in Northern Ontario, and whose remains, after disinterment, passed through Bonaventure Station today on their way to Salisbury in the Eastern Provinces.

According to the statement of Jane and Robert McIlwraith, who are accompanying the body to the old home of the deceased, Miss McIlwraith had either a very remarkable vision, in which her brother Joseph appeared to her on the night of Tuesday, Nov. 24, or, as she believes, his ghostly body appeared before her in her room and asked her if she did not know that he was dead. The brother had been away from home two years, at work in the silver region of Cobalt.

She had been in bed for some time and on awakening, as she thought, she saw a light in the room that could not be accounted for by lamp, candle or the moon. "Instantly," she said, "I saw my brother appear before me in a brownish suit of clothes that I had never seen him wear before. He suddenly seemed to start up from nowhere and he asked in a perfectly natural voice, 'Don't you know I am dead?' Having said that he receded back, presumably through the wall. The light also disappeared very shortly.

"I did not seem to be afraid until the light vanished and then I became so frightened, thinking about the appearance of my brother and the message, that I aroused my brother Robert, as well as mother, to whom I communicated the terrible experience."

The family was fearfully agitated, but living some distance away from a telegraph station, they did not take steps for several days after the occurrence to communicate with Joseph. They had not heard from him for about six weeks and he was then preparing for work for the winter or his claim on the Montreal River, which he was to develop with money he had saved at Cobalt. On the Friday they telegraphed and got an answer the following day that Joe McIlwraith had died of pneumonia a few days before, and had been buried. The telegram also stated that he had left fifteen hundred dollars behind.

It was decided that the remains should be disinterred and brought east in order that the deceased might be buried where he spent his early life. His brother went to bring them along, and today was met here by the sister who had the extraordinary experience. They all went east by the I.C.R., Robert and the body having come east over the Ontario Government Railway and the Grand Trunk.

Miss McIlwraith seemed to be a woman of some refinement and exceedingly modest and sensitive-looking, but extraordinary pale — a fact which she attributed to the shock she had received from the singular visitation and the startling confirmation given to the message. The brother found no difficulty in getting the money belonging to the deceased.

From the inquiries that Robert was able to make, his brother died on the day before the sister had the remarkable experience narrated.

THE SHAKING TENT

Here is a description of the rite of the Shaking Tent which is remarkable for its sense of high drama and its range of unusual details.

This account was written by Chief Buffalo Child Long Lance and is reprinted from his highly readable book of memories titled *Long Lance* (New York, 1928). It is difficult to determine how much of Long Lance's description is remembered and how much of it is imagined. If the writer is describing the traditional manner in which the rite was practised by the Blackfoot Indians of Alberta in the early years of this century, it must be borne in mind that he was not there to observe the ceremony. As scholar and biographer Donald B. Smith has determined, Long Lance was an imposter and as such had much in common with the conservationist Grey Owl. Neither man was an Indian, yet both men were outstandingly successful in addressing issues of conservation and ecology to native and white alike.

Sylvestre Long (1890-1932) was an American of mixed Indian, white, and possibly black ancestry, who escaped segregation by "going native." He was adopted by the Blood as Buffalo Child in Alberta in 1922. He took his own life when his origins became common knowledge.

But the most weird and interesting part of the medicine-man's practices were the sensational rites which he would carry out when "getting in touch with the spirits." Whenever he wanted to get a forecast of the future, get the outcome of some future event or cure some sick person who was lying at the point of death, he would hold this rite in the big medicine-teepee, and the entire tribe would be allowed to witness it. I often watched this as a youngster, and to this day I marvel over what I saw. I have never seen any old Indian who could explain it.

An hour or so preceeding one of these medicine lodges the camp crier would go through the camp crying out the news that the "medicine-man was preparing to talk with the spirits." This caused great excitement in camp. The entire tribe would go early to the medicine lodge in order to get seats; for only about one hundred could get inside the lodge, and the rest had to stay outside and listen to the weird ceremony. Our mother owuld take us children with her and bundle us close to her on the women's side of the lodge.

As we sat and looked on with eyes agape, the medicine-man's assistant would erect four poles in the centre of the big lodge and tie them together at the top in tripod fashion. Under these poles there was an area about twelve feet across. In this area the assistant, with the help of four men, would drive into the ground a series of sharp pegs, placing them at intervals of about an inch apart until the entire area was covered. These pegs were so sharp at the top that they would go through a man's foot if stepped upon. In the centre of the twelve-foot area a little square was left clear, a place just large enough for a man to stand in. The only way one could reach this area over the sharp pegs was to jump into it, and that seemingly would mean serious injury or death.

The medicine-man would now enter with four men. These men would undress him, leaving only his breech-cloth on his body, and then lay him down on his back. They would place his two hands together, palm to palm, and with a strong rawhide thong they would bind his two thumbs together so tightly that they would sometimes bleed. They would place each pair of fingers together and bind them together in the same way. Then they would go down to his feet and tie his two big toes together, pulling with all their strength to bind them as tightly as they could.

Now they would take a hide about the size of a blanket, and roll it tightly around him head to foot, like a cigar wrapper. Around this wrapper they would twine him up from neck to ankles with a stout rawhide thong, winding it tightly around and around his body at intervals of each inch down the length of his form until he was securely bound. And still another hide was wrapped around him, and another rawhide thong was wound tightly around his motionless form. Now, as he lay helpless on the ground, he reembled a long brown cigar. Literally, he could not move a finger.

The assistants would now raise the medicine-man to a standing position and carefully balance him on the soles of his bare feet. He would stand there for a while like a post. Then gradually he would begin slightly to bend his knees and draw them up again, and after a while each bend of the knees would take the form of a short jump. These jumps would keep increasing in length until finally he would be leaping around and around the four poles with startling speed, resembling some ghostly post bobbing up and down through the air so fast that the eye could hardly follow them.

Then, suddenly, with a huge leap, so quickly executed that no one could see how he made it, he would dart through space and land with a thud in the one-foot clearing in the centre of the area of sharp pegs. He had leaped six feet over the dangerous spikes and landed safely in the little clearing, which was just big enough to hold his two feet — truly a remarkable exploit in itself.

But he has not yet started the really thrilling part of the ceremony.

As he stands there in the centre under the poles, still bound securely, he commences to sing his medicine song, accompanied by the throbbing boom of the big medicine-drum in the hands of his assistant.

What I am going to describe now may seem strange; it is strange, but it is exactly what happens. Now and why, no one knows.

Presently, as the medicine-man stands there singing his weird chant to the spirits, voices from above are heard; voices which seem to emanate from the opening away up at the top of the big medicine-teepee. As everyone can see, there is nothing up there but the night air and the stars above. Where these voices come from no Indian has ever been able to explain. But, according to the medicine-man, they are the voices of the spirits — the spirits with whom he is trying to get in touch. The mystery of it is that no one has ever been able to prove that they were anything else.

These voices speak in a language which we cannot understand. Even the medicine-man cannot understand most of them. All he can say is that they are speaking in foreign tongues, and that they are not the spirits that he wants. There are only four spirits whom our medicine-man White Dog could understand. I remember the name of only one of them, and that was "First White Man." And that name had been with our medicine-men for years before our tribe knew that there was a white man on this earth.

As these voices kept chattering down into the lodge, the medicine-man rejects them one by one, and continues to ask for one of the four spirits whom he can understand. Sometimes it takes him many minutes to do this. I remember one or two times when he could not get hold of one of them at all, and he had to end the ceremony without accomplishing his aim.

But when he did get hold of the spirit whom he was seeking he would become excited and talk away so fast that he could hardly hear what he was saying. It seemed that he had to hurry to get in what he wanted to say before the spirit departed. If it was a cure he was after, the dying patient laying there in the medicine lodge would also become excited; and we have seen them get up and walk. If it was information the medicine-man was seeking, he would make his inquiries in short parables of his own, and he would be answered by the spirits in these same unintelligible parables, which later had to be explained to us. It was our language, but it was phrased in a way that we could not understand. And, furthermore, it was the ancient method of speaking our language — the way it was spoken a long time ago — and only our oldest men could understand some of the phraseology and old words.

But the part of the ceremony which made us youngsters afraid came at the conclusion of the medicine-man's interview with the spirits.

These interviews ended in many exciting ways, bu always the final scene was accompanied by a howlin wind, which would start to roar across the top of th lodge as the spirits ceased talking. The big medicine teepee would rock and quiver under the strain of thi wind, as it screeched through the poles at the top of th teepee and caused us to shake with fright. It was startling climax. A chaotic medley of noise would com down to us from above — from the round opening at th top of the lodge where the teepee poles jutted out int the night air. Strange voices shrieking in weir pandemonium above the wailing of the winds; th clanking and jingling of unknown objects, and then sudden jerk of the entire lodge, a flicker of flames, terrifying yell from the medicine-man, and then —

He would disappear right in front of our eyes. But i the same instant we would hear him yelling for help And looking up in the direction of his voice, we woul see him hanging precariously by one foot at the top o the lodge, stipped as naked as the day he was born. Th only thing that held him from falling and breaking hi neck was his foot, which seemed to be caught i between the skin covering of the teepee and one of th slanting poles which supported it.

"*Kokenaytuksishpewow!* — Hurry!" he would yel frantically.

And the men would rush for long poles with which t remove him from his dangerous, dangling perch at th roof of the lodge, lets he should fall and break his neck

How he got there, no one knows; but he said that th spirits left him there on their way out. But the greates puzzle to us youngsters as how he got stripped of thos stout bindings!

I have seen some miraculous things done by the old time medicine-men, who have practically passed out o existence and taken all of their uncanny knowledge wit them. I have seen them send messages for a distance o many miles merely by going into their teepee and sittin down, "thinking the message" to the other camp. Ther were quite a few old Indians who could "receive" thes messages. I have seen them curing dying people, and have seen them to foretell with accuracy the outcome o future events.

I AWAKENED IN TERROR

The Rocky Mountains are an awesome sight and attract visitors and tourists from around the world. Banff and Lake Louise are fabled for their scenery. Skiers come to ski the slopes, not to see the ghosts.

Wayne MacDonald had ghosts in mind. A reporter for *The Calgary Albertan*, he wrote an account of a night he spent in Halfway House in Banff National Park and published it in that newspaper on 3 Feb. 1962. The account was so popular that he wrote a second account of an experience at Lake Louise which was published two days later.

Perhaps it is safe to assume that there is more on those slopes than snow!

HALFWAY HOUSE, Banff National Park – Dozens of skiers have fled from this country ski lodge late at night.

They believe it is haunted. I wanted to run on the first night of my visit here to check their stories. Not that I believe in ghost stories, but strange things happen in Halfway.

Frightening things happen, especially at night, but despite my imagination, they can all be explained — so far — by using common sense.

That's the hardest thing up here — common sense.

I skied into Halfway with guide-companion Glenn Cowan late Wednesday afternoon. The cabin itself is one-roomed, log, and situated high on a knoll in a wind-swept valley. Immediately to the east the blank cliffs of Redoubt Mountain tower high in the frosty air.

To the south, Mt. Temple reaches for the gods and beyond that the Valley of the Ten Peaks nestles on the horizon.

The cabin has two bunk beds, a steel one and a wooden one. It has two stoves, one which doesn't work.

There's a wooden table, a wooden bench, a wash stand, some cookware and plates, and that's all.

Glenn and I arrived in time for supper. After bacon, eggs and fried bread, he left.

The sun was lowering behind the peaks as he started; the evening was still.

My mind was working overtime. I heard new noises — creaks and groans. The crackling fire startled me, and I imagined a broom in the corner had moved.

I told myself that ghosts don't exist.

As night came on, it worried me that the sky was black. There were no stars; the moon was hidden.

A wind was starting to wheeze in the pines and even this sound was unfriendly.

I tried to read. I placed three candles on the table and huddled close to the book. Each new sound jerked me from the pages. I found myself stepping to the window, fighting the reflection of the candles in the glass, peering into the blackness.

I finally admitted that no matter what, I was in Halfway for the night. I could never find the trail to Temple chalet without moonlight.

I returned to my reading. Suddenly, without warning, two candles blew out.

I lit them again and sat, almost fearing to move. When I did I found an eight-inch crack in the log by the window. The wind has extinguished the candles.

I decided, shortly after 7:00 p.m., that the best place would be bed. The fire was burning low; I had been warned not to burn too many candles. I felt sleep would drown my fears.

In bed the noises magnified. I heard a low creaking and something banging on the door, but I had been warned of this. The wind often rocks an overhead sign on the cabin.

The fire was now dead, save for final glowing embers. I fell asleep. An hour later, I awakened in terror. Bright shadows were leaping across the room. My immediate reaction was that the moon had risen. But this light was too bright.

I silently reached for my glasses. The fire was raging.

A full, orange blaze was crackling in the stove, hot and bright and loud.

I was terrified.

After ageless minutes I rationalized. There must have been an unburned log in the stove. It must have caught fire after I fell asleep.

The night went without further event. I wakened in the morning to a cry of "anybody home!" A park warden stepped in, tripping on the bench I had placed against the door. He was on his way to Skoki and stopped to check how I was.

How was I?

Oh, Halfway's fine — in daylight.

LAKE LOUISE – A grey-haired man turned to me in the coffee shop of the Post Hotel. "So you spent two nights in Halfway House?" he asked.

I replied I had.

"Son," he said, "you're mighty lucky to be alive."

The man was Ray LeGace, manager of the hotel and a twenty-year veteran of the Rockies. He's like most residents of Lake Louise; he honestly believes there are ghosts in Halfway House.

"I'd never stay there alone," he said. "In fact, I don't think I'd stay there at all. Especially at night."

Ray believes the tiny skiers' cabin halfway between Lake Louise and Skoki Lodge is occupied by the ghost of a Calgary painter who died there several years ago.

The painter and his dog lived in Halfway for several months. He refused to come out in even the bitterest weather because he was waiting for a perfect mountain sunset.

He wanted to see a "perfect" sun dip behind Redoubt Mountain — but it never happened. The painter was never satisfied with the colours of the sky.

He starved to death in the lonely lodge.

Others in Lake Louise believe the ghost to be a woman, an attractive girl killed in an avalanche. Or two brothers buried in snow in the '30s. Or a mountain-born skier killed on Mount Ptarmigan.

Everyone you talk to has a different tale to tell. Only a handful will say there's no ghost.

My second night in Halfway was much like the first. An over-imaginative mind was my greatest foe.

I had busied myself during the day, melting snow, washing dishes, writing, preparing food. There were no fears in daylight, but as darkness fell, uneasiness returned.

The loneliness was hardest; the knowledge that no matter what, I couldn't get out. I had never skied before my journey in, and I could never find my way to Temple Chalet without a guide.

The darkness on the second night brought with it a storm. It snowed heavily, and the wind came up, whistling through the pines, pounding on the lodge, banging at the windows, sniffing at the candles.

But at the same time, it was melting.

Water dripped throughout the night from the roof, splattering on the snow around the cabin. The dripping sounded — in my mind — like footsteps in the snow.

Drip, drip, drip. Step, step, step.

Was someone out there?

I buried my head in my pillow and tried to sleep.

The wind again banged the sign above the cabin door. It crashed against the logs, fell back, crashed, fell back, crashed.

The sign is suspended from three links of chain. The chain, when the sign wasn't banging, grated against the metal hook, creaking and groaning. It was a horrible sound.

And the crackling of the fire bothered me. I started every time a chunk of wood "popped" in the heat. It would seem the fire was finally dead, and suddenly "Crack."

But the ghost — or ghosts — didn't come.

I wakened in the morning to a voice — a distant yodel. By the time I dressed, Glenn Cowan was at the door to guide me back to Temple.

He seemed partly disappointed, partly relieved, that the ghost who visited him hadn't visited me. When he stayed at Halfway a fortnight ago, he was startled when his fire suddenly went out. He turned to see a plate on the middle of the table move to the edge and crash to the floor. A cup in its saucer on the table tipped.

As he hurried to get his skies on to escape the "thing," he suddenly smelled a woman's perfume. "It was as if I was helping a woman on with her coat," he said, "and I suddenly smelled the perfume in her hair."

Is there a ghost in Halfway? A ghost that has haunted Cowan and skiers by the score? A ghost that keeps Ray LeGace away

I don't know.

The people who have fled Halfway cannot be swayed. They're convinced the ghost is there.

On the other hand, skiers have stayed in the cabin for weeks, for months, and more. One stayed throughout a winter.

I doubt the ghost is there — but can I say? A prime minister of Canada believed in them, and writers have told of them through the years.

We scoff at their beliefs, but who can tell?

SOMETHING EVIL ABROAD

Was the long-time residence of Healey Willan haunted by two spirits whose footsteps were heard time and time again? His daughter thinks so....

The one-time home of Healey Willan and family on Inglewood Drive in Toronto was believed to be haunted from 1920 to 1968. Mary Mason, actress and writer, who described her experiences to on 24 June 1999, is the daughter of the late Healey Willan, composer and choirmaster of St. Mary Magdelene Church. From her birth in 1921 to her marriage in 1943 she lived in the Willan Residence at 139 Inglewood Drive. The family sold the three-storey house following Dr. Willan's death in 1968. In an interview in 1994, Mary Mason recalled how the spirits of the house affected her and the rest of the family.

So often people feel they're in control of their lives, but it seems as though there is something evil abroad that we cannot control because of our reliance on something called "science," which is really another name for knowledge, and nothing else seems to count. There is a loss of spiritual cognizance. It is a tremendous loss.

I first realized there was a "presence" in the house when I was five. It happened one day in 1926. I had had scarlet fever and was in isolation in my bedroom on the second floor. I was awfully bored. The window of my room was closed so the door of my room was open all night. I distinctly heard footsteps descending the stairs from the third floor. I sat up in bed. I had a narrow view of the hall but I could see nothing there. I thought it's my youngest brother who was then in the cadet band at Upper Canada College. He was coming to visit me before early practice and I would have someone to talk to. The footsteps continued coming down the stairs and along the hall and approached my room where they stopped. That was it. There was no one there. It was very odd. This happened a number of times. The door was no barrier. There was a nasty feeling. I felt awful and frightened.

My mother and father had both heard the phantom footsteps on other occasions. "Don't tell anyone," mother cautioned me, "we may want to sell the house!" Sometimes I woke rigid with fear; I felt a disembodied presence beside me. I couldn't see anyone in the room with me, yet there was someone there. Mother spoke to Father Hiscocks, the rector of St. Mary Magdalene, because she knew I was disturbed. He came and had tea with us and then spoke to me privately. "Let me tell you about the the time I was the vicar of the little Anglican church at Cannes. It had been part of a Catholic monastery years before. Every Sunday evening the people came for vespers and sometimes we saw a little monk coming up the centre aisle. He floated up the aisle and seemed to be searching for something. He disturbed the service and I had to do something. So I addressed the congregation. 'We all know someone else is here, a little monk looking for something. Let's all pray that he finds whatever it is he seeks.' So we bowed our heads and prayed in silence. We didn't see him again. So try to pray for this soul who is troubling you." What Father Hiscocks said helped a lot.

One time my eldest brother had a party and one of the entertainers was a psychic. When it came time to have supper, everyone went downstairs to the dining room. So I asked her if she had been offered anything to eat. When she said no, I took her a tray of food. We began to chat and she said, "I see you lying flat on your back in bed and you are frightened. You know someone is in the bedroom with you. That someone is troubling your brother too. Don't worry. Your Grandfather is looking out for him. Grandmother is looking out for you. They are guarding you. Don't worry." I found what she said comforting. Both my grandparents had died before I was born.

It was not limited to family members. The cleaning woman once told me, "Mary, someone is walking about in the house upstairs when nobody else is here." I suggested it might be the dog but she would have none of it.

Once, when I was fourteen or fifteen, everyone went to a concert and I was left alone in the house with our dog, Nicky, a collie. I heard footsteps descending from the second to the first floor. The footsteps were heavy, as if someone were carrying something. Our dog leapt up on the sofa beside me, every hair on his body sticking straight out. He stared at something, eyes wide, watching something coming down the stairs. It was horrifying.

One Sunday afternoon I was in one of the third-floor rooms studying for exams. Downstairs, afternoon tea was being served. The door of the room was closed. I heard footsteps coming right up to the closed door. They were light-footed steps. I thought it was my young nephew. There was nobody there.

They surprised you when you had no thought of them in your head. I felt they were mean-spirited. Our house was the original house in the area. It had been a farming area. Perhaps one or more of the early occupants of the house had committed a crime. Maybe the heavy-footed one and the soft-footed one were compelled to repeat their actions. It might be what purgatory or hell or damnation is. I think there's a retribution there somewhere.

I left the house when I married in 1943. I have three brothers. After the Second World War, my middle brother returned from England with his war bride.

Sheila is Irish and she sensed there were spirits in the house. Mother called Father Brain, the rector of St Mary Magdalene. He exorcised the house, going in a procession around the outside, praying. What the neighbours thought of the "bell, book, and candle" routine I do not know! The rite helped but did not put the spirits to rest completely.

Basically the family ignored the disturbances. We never gave the spirits names. You don't want to assign them personalities.

After my father died in 1968, the house was sold. The new owners gutted and renovated it. I wonder what happened to the spirits. If people want to say I'm crazy, that's their privilege. Mother and dad and my brothers were well aware of the haunting but we were all philosophical about it. If anybody tries to tell me that once the body stops breathing the spirit dies, I disagree. It is obvious to me that such a person has not had these experiences. For those of us who have, it is not a laughing matter.

THE GREY LADY

When I was researching the book that appeared as *Haunted Toronto*, I realized I needed some photographs of the interior and exterior of the Church of St. Mary Magdalene. The church, which is located near Harbord and Bathurst Streets in Toronto, has a notable musical tradition as well as a notable ghostly tradition, and both of these involve one man: Healey Willan.

Members of the congregation cherish the memory of Dr. Willan, who was for much of his professional life the resident organist and choral conductor. Lovers of serious music across Canada respect his work and legacy as a leading composer and musician. It is no secret that Dr. Willan said that on a number of occasions he was astonished to behold "the grey lady" in the church when he knew no one was there!

My need for photographs led me to Tom Hyland, a long-time member of the gallery choir of the church and a close friend of Dr. Willan. Tom is a character in his own right. Until his retirement he was employed in the photography department at Eaton's downtown store. A skilled photographer, he showed me his sensitive black-and-white portraits of Dr. Willan and also a number of fine atmospheric shots of the church's interior. He allowed me to reproduce a group of these in the entries on the church and its organist in *Haunted Toronto*. We established rapport and Tom shared with me the suspicion that he too had seen the ghost. At my request he prepared a narrative account of his experiences and sent it to me on 13 Nov. 1997. I am very happy to be able to include that account here in his own inimitable style.

Tom is now dead, but he took immense efforts to write and correct the printout of "A Fable Turned Fact." He regarded it as very important. I do too. Thank you, Tom.

A Fable Turned Fact

At this time of writing, I've lived almost seven years beyond my allotted three-score-and-ten. My rather mature age, combined with the problem that I write of an incident close to fifty years old, makes this narrative exercise a most taxing effort. But yet it affords me the nostalgic pleasure of reliving some precious moments of the past.

There seems to be an indignant consensus among young people — especially hard-rock enthusiasts, aspiring computer analysts, and other adolescent ignoramuses — that older persons lose their memories. Or, as they playfully put it, "marbles." This, of course, is completely false! After all, we've lived longer, have a great deal more to remember and, if we didn't discard the trivia, we'd burst our memory banks! Therefore we are inclined to remember the importance of the personal; treat the impersonal as excess; embrace the fact, but dismiss the inexplicable as coincidence. Thus, in order to put to rest any concern as to my mental stability, and to bolster your belief in the validity of this tale, I must meander through some of my personal history that has a direct bearing on your assessment of myself and my sanity.

I began singing, as a boy soprano, in the Anglican choir of Christ Church, Belleville, before my eleventh birthday. I soon became lead boy and soprano soloist. Then, with the onset of manhood, successively graduated through the choral ranks of alto, tenor, to bass. Also, for several years, I served as choir librarian for that parish choir. (You might say — with all that training and responsibility — I knew every piece of music from the top to the bottom and the correct alphabetical sequence of our complete repertoire!) The duties of that post gave me free access to the church, day and night. Quite often, I laid out Sunday morning's music in the choir stalls the Saturday night before, and became accustomed to being mortally alone in the building. The loneliness of those occasions gave birth to my lifelong addiction to test the acoustics of the empty church by the sound of my own voice.

In September, 1945 (my wife and I having moved to Toronto from our native Belleville in the summer of '44), I had the extremely good fortune to be accepted as a bass member in the gallery choir of the Church of St. Mary Magdalene by its eminent director and precentor, the late Dr. Healey Willan. The gallery choir consisted of sixteen voices in those golden days of liturgical music, and Willan left no stone unturned to achieve choral perfection. Time seemed to be expendable. Within ten days, preceding and including Easter Sunday, we sang two full-length rehearsals, several short rehearsals, attended and sang eight services! *Nothing* was left to chance — not even the simplest of hymns — and, from our busy schedule of rehearsals, services, recitals, it was easily imagined the average choir becoming so totally exhausted they'd "throw-in-the-towel" and *quit!*

At the beginning of my lengthy tenure of service in the choir, I was a fledgling photographer. When I became familiar with Anglo-Catholic rites, the fluent beauty of properly sung plainsong, and the precision with which all rites, rituals, masses, motets, processions, etc., were performed, I fell madly in love with the music and the uniqueness of the church: The austere solemnity of its architecture; the inviting refuge of its colourful appointments.

There was a mystical aura about the place that defies adequate description. I can only suppose it was generated by the dramatic differences in its contrasts. The entire interior of the nave was bare and grey — walls; pillars; arches ... cold as death! Whereas the chancel and side chapels were *alive* with warmth. In the Chapel of St. Joseph, a children's altar: pink in motif; portrait of child in field of wildflowers, butterflies, and birds. In the Chapel of Our Lady: heavenly serenity; blue, vaulted ceiling; Virgin Mother and Child looking down lovingly, forgivingly on all who came and all who passed by. In the chancel, sanctuary: aptly named high altar; massive canopy, seasonal trappings; candles; ever-present Host, and magnificent gold cross — resplendent — infinite — commanding reverence in the brilliance of its shining. And the huge rood suspended high above the entrance from the main, broad arch with its Christ seemingly saying, "This is the House of God." "Here is the Gate of Heaven." They all gave one a strange sense of feeling a part of antiquity, without being old, and a part of the present, without being blatantly modern.

Here, indeed, was ample opportunity for me to pursue the art, capture the mood, and make memorable photographs with permanent appeal. There were *so* many things and atmospheres in that building crying out to be recorded on film that I started toting my camera along with me.

Eventually, by trial and error, by investment in equipment and the sacrifice of persistence, my skill became quite effectual. The results of my painstaking efforts were soon rewarded by the friendship and confidence of the clergy, and I found myself in the enviable position of coming and going as I pleased at any reasonable hour of the day or night to photograph whatever I wished. Thereafter, I spent innumerable hours by daylight or incandescent light (and, sometimes, the near lack of either!) to satisfy my desire that the church, in its varied aspects of sanctity, should be visually preserved as a special environment for Christian worship. And I'm forever grateful that some of those prints have found their places in books, on record jackets and music covers, and in the homes of many individuals whose love of that church and its music was equal to mine.

The gallery choir never donned the conventional choir robes. To some, that may seem sacrilegious. But, if anything, it was the opposite, as well as unnecessary. Being seated high above the back of the nave, we were out of sight and hidden from the view of the congregation. The absence of those robes had three distinct advantages. First, it was economical, saving us the expense of upkeep and the wasted time of dressing and undressing before and after each service. Second, it was convenient, should we have to silently slip down the gallery stairs during the sermon and rush, via an exterior route, to the basement lavatory. Third — and perhaps *most* important — it saved us the emotional distress of feeling "holier than thou" along with the damnations of women's mortarboards and makeup!

Healey was kind and considerate to all people of good intent — especially the members of his choirs (there were two). But that did not deter his stern demand for their sincere devotion to *both* the music *and* the words. I can still hear his most oft-uttered critical precaution: "*Any* fool can sing *notes!*"

Our weekly rehearsals were held Friday nights between the hours of eight and ten, *precisely*, with a ten-minute "smoke and gossip" break approximately halfway through. The ritual choir (the other choir and an exceptionally capable group of men and cantor who sang [traditionally robed] in the chancel and responsible for all plainchant) held their rehearsal the same night, prior to ours, from seven to eight, and *again*, precisely. When we arrived, the two choirs joined forces to practise all music in which we had mutual or overlapping parts (hymns, responses, canticles, etc.)

that was required for the following Sunday's services. They then departed and we continued with our rehearsal.

The rehearsal room was in the basement of the church, directly below the chancel and sanctuary. It was adequately large but had the advantage of "flat" acoustics which prevented echoes from masking errors. The outside entrance to that room and the basement was through a street-level doorway on the southeast side of the church and a landing for stairs that went up to the vestry, chancel, and nave, and down to our rehearsal room. When the members of the ritual choir made their exit, the last one out tripped the latch on that door, and any gallery member who dared to arrive later — without Healey's permission — would have to knock, be let in; come down those stairs and ... face the music!

There were two petty annoyances that plagued the choirs, clergy, and congregation in those days, even though they were confined to frigid temperatures. That door to the basement, when opened, ushered in an arctic blast of air that came rushing down the stairs, flooding our rehearsal room with chilly discomfort. The other annoyance was caused by the heating system in the church. There were radiators spaced along the perimeter walls at floor level that made their presence known by their noisy expansions and contractions. One of those convenience eyesores, in particular, had the habit of infusing its off-key harmony right smack-in-the-middle of our motet, or punctuating a solemn, sermon sentence with a loud "ssss" and a "bang"! Also, the supply pipes for those radiators ran beneath the floorboards of the chancel and chapels, leaving those boards *so* dry they "squeaked" at the least of foot pressures. In short, we were *all* thankful for warmer weather!

But I remember it *was* in the cold of winter when this disturbing incident occurred, for there were overcoats, hats, and parkas hanging along the walls on hooks and hangers — one of the few necessities in our rehearsal room. The others being a piano, a music cupboard, an assortment of wooden chairs; a washbasin, one-seater toilet, and a table on which Healey placed his music; sat upon with one leg up and one leg down to conduct, or lecture us for our (thankfully few!) *faux-pas* and occasionally emphasize, by illustration, the proper pronunciation of ecclesiastical Latin ... usually followed by a relevant witticism quoted from one source or another.

One Friday night, during our break, Healey called me aside: "Tommy, old man, be a good chap; run up to the gallery and fetch me my copy of....You'll find it...." (I honestly can't remember the title of the organ score, nor where I should find it.) Giving me his key for the gallery door, he explained his need of it the following day and expressed his frustration for not having had time to go get it himself. So off I went.

There were two flights of stairs from the basement to the main body of the church. The one on the south side, which I've already described, and another on the north with a passageway at its top, running parallel with the chancel to a doorway for entry to the nave. I opted to take those stairs for they were nearer to the gallery stairway in the northwest corner of the church. In the passageway, there was a single light bulb in a pull-chain socket hanging from the ceiling. This I pulled on, opened the door, propped it open, and made my way to the opposite end of the church.

Healey and I had become close friends. So much so that I welcomed the opportunity, and pleasure, to stay behind after mass or evensong, lock up the gallery, and accompany him down to the basement where a large pot of hot tea was waiting to lubricate the vocal chords of choir members ... courtesy of a very kindly lady and parishioner, Mrs. Bailey. (I do hope I've spelled "Bailey" correctly. She justly deserves proper recognition.) On those journeys he might ask, "What did you think of the Kyrie this morning, old man?" or discuss a problem with the tempo in a certain hymn. (And you have *no* idea how vainly proud *I* felt at being asked for *my* personal opinion — sometimes advice! — from such a renowned musician as Healey.)

The path we travelled on those intimate occasions was the same as I followed in this instance, and so familiar I probably could have traversed it fully with my eyes closed, as in the unconscious sight of sleep. But the dim light from the open doorway partially lifted the eerie shroud of darkness from the unlit aisle and prevented me from bumping into a pew or two.

There was a high, spacious vestibule the full length of the west wall of the church for coats and hats and more silent and draft-free entry to the nave. It had three sets of double doors with the gallery stairway in the north corner. I opened one of the nearest set, switched on the vestibule light, and mounted the gallery stairs. At the top, I switched on the two lights in the gallery, unlocked the door, and went in. Unfortunately, the empty church proved too tempting for me to resist my youthful addiction, and I started humming, quite loudly, with a few bass "booms" thrown in to more enjoy the echo.

Having found the requested score, I was about to leave the gallery when I noticed the effect of those gallery lights fading into the darkness of the sanctuary.

Always on the lookout for a different angle, different highlight, different shadow, I paused to analyze the photographic possibilities. I was standing near the back wall, and from that position could barely see the front row of pews in the nave as the gallery railing was table-top high and heavily draped to block the view of any obnoxious gawker from below. So I moved closer until I could scan the entire nave. Still humming, I looked down and caught sight of something so *totally* unexpected that I nearly fell over the railing in cardiac arrest!

There, below me, kneeling in a pew part way up the south side of the nave, was a woman on whom I'd never laid eyes before! I was *so* startled that my lungs forgot to breathe — my vocal chords ceased to function — and my eyes became fixed like a lifeless statue's! Her faded, grey apparel appeared to be more suitable for warm weather than for the frigid temperature outside, and, oddly enough, no protective outerwear was anywhere visible. I was so *petrified* by surprise and so mortified with embarrassment, my wits became *so* befuddled that I *could* not *think* straight, and could *not* determine whether to attempt a pleading apology for intruding on the privacy of prayer, or to vacate the premises as quickly and quietly as possible. But as she was an absolute stranger to me, and I, probably to her, I thought I'd better *leave* it that way and chose the latter option.

As I locked the door, switched off the gallery lights, descended the stairs, switched off the vestibule light, and retraced my steps to the passageway door, I kept thinking it also *very* odd that my considerable vocalizing seemed not to have disturbed her! I did not look back. There was little point to staring at the blackness of the nave. But as I closed that door, pulled off the light, and descended the stairs to our rehearsal room, I felt an immense sense of relief at leaving her and the church to the darkness in which I'd found them.

When I entered the room, Healey was poised to conduct the second half of our practice. So I took my seat, after laying the copy on his table, and my common sense suggested that I shouldn't report the unbelievable lest I be deemed a loony — if not *called* one! But through the remainder of that rehearsal, I kept one ear cocked for the sound of a squeaky board overhead, and one foot firmly on the floor for the feel of a cold draft ... but I neither heard nor felt, either.

(There was a *third* oddity about that woman's appearance — a haunting enigma that's eluded my comprehension ever since that night. But now, in the poignant remembering of so *many* personal and related truths of the past, I've finally solved the mystery of her presence. *And* the motivation that's prompted my telling of this tale.)

I write this on the 10th day of November, 1997. Comes the 27th day of this month, my wife and I will celebrate our fifty-fourth wedding anniversary — God willing. On that Saturday date, 1943, we came to Toronto for our honeymoon. The following day, Sunday, the 28th, we attended High Mass at St. Mary Magdalene. The music of the Mass and motet that morning was exquisitely beautiful, and sung so clearly and devoutly by the gallery choir that I actually wept. (That, I think, is the greatest compliment that can be paid for a sterling, sincere performance.)

Shortly after I'd joined the choir, I learned of a particular area in the nave where the gallery choir could best be heard. A place almost in isolation with angels. It so happened, on that glorious Sunday morning of our honeymoon, my wife and I — by accident and because of its availability — sat, knelt, and prayed in that same area — perhaps in the very same pew where this grey-clad lady knelt!

The vivid recollection of that most precious time; that special place — that *separate* beatitude of beauty — had finally solved the riddle of the third oddity: It was her location! ... As if in anticipation, she occupied the exact spot, chosen by many an astute listener as the ideal ambience to fully experience the ecstasy of sound floating from that loft in an *a cappella* halo of faultless harmony — veritably enveloping *all* within our resonant House of God in a polyphonous paradise of immaculate adoration!

Healey used to tell of a ghost, dubbed "the grey lady," who interrupted his private organ practice in the church by her visual presence. Frankly, I never knew whether to doubt his sober sincerity or marvel at his clairvoyant sensitivity ... whether we had a female phantom in our midst, or a figure evolved in a spasm of indigestion! But, after putting all the facts of two and two (or twenty and twenty) together: the dark, unlit church; the late hour; the long-locked doors; the squeaky boards; the frigid temperature; the cold draft; her lack of outer clothing; her undisturbed composure; and the pew she occupied, I'm thoroughly convinced there really *was* a "grey lady," and I — most *surely* — had seen her!

Now this anecdote would still be a latent episode locked for life in my own mind — straddling the fence of indecision with its facts, doubts, and possibilities — had it not been for a request from our local author, John Colombo, to supply prints of the church and Healey. These were gladly given and faithfully reproduced in two articles of his excellent book *Haunted Toronto* published last year (1996) by Dundurn Press. Obviously, I've read those entries *and* the book itself, and would urge all those interested in the subject of "ghosts" — however remotely — to do also.

Colombo's request and that reading had revived my lazy memory, and my ostentatious ego suggested I could write of "ghosts" as well as *he*! And since I had witnessed a *bona-fide* visit of an apparition, I've given it a shot. And there it is ... faults and all ... and *that's that!*

Tom Hyland
The [yet] City of Scarborough
November 10, 1997

THUNDERBIRDS

Native traditions speak of powerful thunderbirds, giant bird-like spirits of the air, the guardians of the weather. The sight of these birds of power flying low overhead has been reported within living memory in the region of Shoal Lake, Lake of the Woods, Man. The following account, in which an unnamed informant recalls both Indian traditions and his own memories of such a sighting in 1971, appeared as "Promise of the Thunderbird," *Native Press*, Feb. 2, 1974.

It is worth noting that the thunderbird has been dubbed a species of UFO — "Unidentified Feathered Object" — by anomalies researcher W. Ritchie Benedict.

At Manitou's meeting in the beginning the thunderbirds promised they would do everything they could to help develop the world, to make it a good place to live in. They solemnly promised God that they would do this. The spirit-gods of wind and rain were to blow softly and fall lightonly on the lands of the Indian people. if the Anishinabek smoked their pipes and said their sacred words, as the thunderbirds were flying by, they would hear the Indians' pleas.

To the Ojibway, the thunderbird is one of the most powerful spirits. These winged creatures obtained their power from Manitou to look after everything in the world. Their power is formidable. When a thunderstorm is coming up you can not see anything moving, no snakes or animals. They hide in the presence of the thunderbirds; even the fish stay still until the thunderbird goes by. I have seen whitetail deer in a storm; they lie down, heads close to the ground. Fish, in a storm, will not take a bait until the storm goes over and the great birds have passed.

The thunderbirds reside at sacred places upon the earth. There are three great thunderbird nests near Shoal Lake. Great big rocks and boulders are piled up on each other, making a round place. My family used to live about four miles from one place and at night we could see the red lightning flashing around the nest. We went down there once and there was a big animal skull, great big bones, skeletons, and feathers lying in the nest. Where did they get those bones? Those animals cannot be found around here. Only the moose and the deer are located around the Lake of the Woods, and these were not moose or deer bones. They were bison or some other kind of animal. At the other two nests, they used to find those great animal heads also. Where did the thunderbirds get those heads?

In the moon of berries, when the young thunderbirds go by, they cause destruction because they don't know any better. They are like children and this is the fault of the young birds, not the parents. When they go by in August and September, they are pretty rough on the Ojibways. They knock down trees with lightning from their beaks. Houses are struck and smashed also. The older thunderbirds try to correct these foolish young birds, but they do not learn because they are so young.

In the olden days the people used to say: "When the thunderbirds are too low, get a shotgun and shoot into the air and it will make them go up." I saw my dad do this one time. He got the muzzle loader and fired into the air, to scare them up. Boy! It was lightning and raining. Coming down! Coming down! They were so low, you could almost hear their wings flapping; they were too low. No! Nothing. It did not work. So he said, "I'll try shooting up again a little later."

Then he loaded up his gun the second time and shot it into the air again. You know, the storm died right away; it went off into the east.

We saw a thunderbird a few summers ago. Ho! A huge bird it was — a lot bigger than the planes that you see go by today. Many of the people at Shoal Lake saw it go by. It didn't flap its wings, not even once. It was white on the under side and black on the top. Ho! A big, big bird. There were some great big thunder clouds making up a storm and out of the clouds came this big bird.

MACKENZIE KING'S GHOST

It might seem strange to regard the ghost of Mackenzie King as a "monster." Yet it would be monstrous indeed if the spirits of the deceased Prime Ministers of Canada returned from the dead and entered into colloquies with their successors, their friends, and their colleagues. I am aware that two Prime Ministers are said to have returned from the dead to address the living (and they are Sir John A. Macdonald and W.L. Mackenzie King).

The witness for the return of Mackenzie King is Percy J. Philip (1880-1956), former war correspondent and Ottawa correspondent for *The New York Times*, who created quite a commotion when he broadcast a talk on CBC Radio about his conversation with the late Prime Minister, and subsequently wrote up an account of his experiences and then an article of the reception of his revelation. The latter contribution gives the reader some sense of the reaction of the public and even of friends when witnesses "come out of the closet."

The account itself appeared as "I Talked with Mackenzie King's Ghost," *Fate Magazine*, Dec. 1955. It is followed by Philip's article on the subject, which appeared as "My Conversation with Mackenzie King's Ghost," *Liberty*, January 1955.

I Talked with Mackenzie King's Ghost
By Percy J. Philip

On a June evening in 1954 I had a long conversation with the former Canadian Prime Minister William L. Mackenzie King as we sat on a bench in the grounds of his old summer home at Kingsmere, 12 miles from Ottawa. It seemed to me an entirely normal thing although I knew perfectly well that Mr. King had been dead for four years.

Of course, when I returned to Ottawa and told my story nobody quite believed me. I myself became just the least bit uncertain as to whether it really had happened, or at least as to how it had happened. Did I fall asleep and dream? Was this due to paranormal circumstances which cannot be explained?

Of one thing I am sure. Mr. King himself would believe me. He once held similar conversations — almost daily in some cases — with persons who had left this world. He talked with his father and mother regularly and with great men and women of the past. His diary, in which he recorded his spiritual experiences, as well as his political activities and contacts, gives detailed accounts of these conversations. Unfortunately it is not likely to be published in full because his will provided that certain parts should be destroyed. His literary executors feel bound to carry out these instructions.

It was not until after his death that the Canadian people learned that their bachelor, liberal Prime Minister communed with the dead both directly and, occasionally, through mediums. When it did become known — in a rather sensational way — it shocked many.

Yet the Prime Minister made no secret of his beliefs and practices. To friends who had lost dear ones he wrote in this manner: "I know how you feel. It seems as though you cannot bear to go on without that wonderful companionship and affection. But let me assure you that love still exists. A bond as strong as that is not broken by death or anything else. Your father is still near you. If you can be still and listen and feel, you will realize he is close to you all your life. I know that because it is so

with my mother and me."

That quotation is from one of the many hundreds of letters of condolence which Mr. King wrote with his own hand for he was punctilious in such matters. At funerals he always spoke similar words of comfort to those bereaved. Otherwise, although he made no secret of his beliefs, he did not parade them.

Once, at Government House, about Christmas time in 1945, he told the Governor General, the Earl of Athlone, that he had spoken with President Roosevelt the previous night. "President Truman, you mean," said the Governor. The Earl saw that some of his staff were making signs from behind Mr. King's back, evidently trying to convey some message. He was puzzled but being a good constitutional Governor Gneeral, he kept quiet and did not again correct the Prime Minister when he repeated, "Oh, no, I mean the late President Roosevelt."

The occasion of the incident was the showing of the Noel Coward film, "Blythe Spirit," which Mr. King found "most interesting."

"It is difficult to imagine the life after death," he said chatting gaily. "Probably the best thing to do is to regard it as a continuation of the one we know with the same processes of growth and change until, eventually we forget our life and associations on this earth, just as old people tend to forget their childhood experiences."

His Excellency who was a brother of the late Queen Mary and a soldier by profession muttered, "Yes, yes probably." He obviously was shaken. He had been chosen by Mr. King to be Governor General of Canada and it made him nervous to learn that his Prime Minister was receiving advice from extra-mundane sources.

"Good God," he exclaimed when his staff explained why they had tried to shush him, "is that where the man gets his policies?"

Having an open mind about the occult and being inquisitive by nature, I later managed to turn several conversations with Mr. King to this subject. Once, especially, when we were crossing the Atlantic to Europe, he talked freely about his beliefs and experiences as we walked the deck.

"If one believes in God and a life after death," he said, "it is inevitable that one must believe that the spirits of those who have gone take an interest in the people and places they loved during their lives on earth. It is the matter of communication that is difficult. For myself I have found that the method of solitary, direct, communion is best. After my father and mother died I felt terribly alone. But I also felt that they were near me. Almost accidentally I established contact by talking to them as if they were present and soon I began to get replies."

These and other things that the Prime Minister said to me at different times came back to my mind as, on that June evening, I drove up the Kingsmere road and was reminded by a sign that the estate of Moorside, which Mr. King had left to the Canadian people in his will, lay just ahead.

It is a beautiful place. There are 550 acres of woodland and clearings, through most of which everyone is free to wander at will. A little stream with a waterfall flows through it down to the valley below. Mr. King accumulated it almost acre by acre, adding steadily in his methodical way, to the original lot he had bought when he first came to Ottawa at the beginning of the century. His quick temper seldom flashed more hotly than when he discovered that some neighbor had sold a parcel of land without giving him a chance to buy. Adding to his estate became a passion with the future Prime Minister. There he loved to receive visitors and also to be alone.

In buying the land Mr. King showed his Scottish shrewdness. But the building of the "ruins" was a perfect example of that romantic daftness that sometimes bewitches the supposedly hard-headed Scot. The direction sign now set up for tourists calls them "ruins" but the uninformed must wonder what they once were. There were doorways and windows, a fireplace, a row of columns, which Mr. King called the cloisters, coats of arms carved in stone, bits and pieces of the old Parliament Buildings, the mint, banks and private houses all built into an artistic enough a wholly whimsical suggestion of a ruined castle. Somehow, perhaps because the surroundings with outcrop rock and pine are so fitting, they escape being silly.

On that evening there were no other visitors. The air was clear and cool. I sat down on a bench beside the ruins and thought about the strange little man who loved his hill-top home so dlearly. I suppose I was in what I called a receptive mood. Although I had not then read it I was following the instructions in that letter from which I already have quoted, to "be still and listen and feel."

I became conscious that I was not alone. Someone sat on the park bench beside me.

There were no sighs, groans and lightning flashes such as mark a spirit's arrival on the Shakespearian stage. There was, if anything, a deeper peace. Through a fold in the hills I could see stretch of the broad Ottawa Valley. I tried to concentrate on it and keep contact with the normal but the presence on the bench would not be denied.

Without turning my head, for somehow I feared to look, I said as naturally as I could, "Good evening, Mr. King."

In that warm tone which always marked his conversation the voice of Mr. King replied, "Good evening, Philip. I am so glad you spoke to me."

That surprised me. "I was thinking of you," I muttered.

"Oh, yes," he replied. "I knew that. But one of the rules which govern our conduct on this side is that we are like the children and must not speak unless we are spoken to. I suppose it is a good rule because it would be very disturbing if we went around talking to people. The sad thing is that so few of them ever talk to us."

Here I think I should say that the reader must decide for himself whether or not he believes this story. It puzzles me greatly.

"I suppose," I said, or I think I said, resuming the conversation, "that we are just a bit scared. You know how hard it is to speak into a dark, empty room."

"That certainly is a difficulty for many people," Mr. King said. "But the room is never really empty. It is often filled with lonely ones who would like to be spoken to. They must, however, be called by name, confidently, affectionately, now challenged to declare themselves."

"Your name," I said, "must often be so mentioned in this lovely place you bequeathed to the Canadian people."

"Oh, yes, mentioned," he said. I glanced at him and seemed to see his eyes sparkle as they did in life, for he had a great deal of puckish humor. "But between being mentioned and being addressed by name, as you addressed me, there is a great deal of difference. I have heard things about my character, motives, political actions and even my personal appearance and habits that have made me laugh so loudly I thought I must break the sound barrier. And I have heard things about myself, too, that have made me shrink."

In the evening silence I had the sensation of being suspended in time and space as the quiet voice went on. "There are things that I said and did that I could regret but, on this side, we soon learn to have no regrets. Life would be meaningless if we did not all make mistakes, and eternity intolerable if we spent it regretting them."

He paused and I thought he looked at me quizzically. "By the way," he said, "Do you still write for the *New York Times?*"

When I said that I had retired he chuckled. "But still," he said, "I think I had better not give indiscreet answers to your questions."

I asked several but he answered with the same skill as marked his replies to questions in the House of Commons and at meetings with the press, divulging nothing. It was I who was the interviewed. He was eager for news and it surprised me then, as it does now, that he seemed not to know fully what was happening in the world. The dead, I discovered, are not omniscient. Or perhaps what we think important is not important to them.

We talked of the development of Canada, of housing and new enterprises like the St. Lawrence Seaway. "My successor has been lucky," Mr. King said. That was as far as he went in any personal reference. "Canada has been very prosperous. I hope it will continue to be so. But you cannot expect good times always. It is adversity that proves the real value of men and nations."

The conversation drifted to the international scene, to philosophic discussion of forms of government, of the balance between Liberty and Authority, the growth and decay of nations and of systems. I cannot tell how long it lasted but I noticed that the sickle moon was getting brighter. I mentioned the time, fumbling for my watch.

"Time," said Mr. King, "I had almost forgotten about time. I suppose I spend a great deal of time up here. There is so much beauty and peace. I gave it to the Canadian people but in a way I have preserved it for myself. It is good to have some familiar, well-loved place to spend 'time' in, until one gets used to eternity."

We both rose from the bench — or at least I did. When I looked at him, as I then did for the first time directly, he seemed just as I had known him in life, just as when I had talked with him once at this very spot.

"I think you told me once that you are Scottish bor[n] and a wee bit 'fey,'" he said. "It's a good thing to b[e]. We have two worlds. Those people who think thei[r] world is the only one, and who take it and themselve[s] too seriously, have a very dull time. Do come back an[d] talk with me again."

I muttered words of thanks and then, following th[e] habit of a lifetime, stretched out my hand to bi[d] goodbye. He was not there.

My Conversation with Mackenzie King's Ghost

So many people have asked me to tell them "the rea[l] truth" about my recent "interview" with the late Prim[e] Minister Mackenzie King on the park bench a[t] Kingsmere, Que., that I am glad to have the opportunit[y] offered me by *Liberty*, to fill in the background an[d] correct some misunderstandings, of the "ghost story" which I told over the CBC network last September 24[.]

Perhaps I should begin by saying that in Scotland where I was born, we believe in ghosts. My father, wh[o] was a minister of the Church of Scotland, told me ho[w] his father had come to him in dreams, and on the edg[e] of sleep, so vividly he could not afterwards believe tha[t] it was not real. Even more oddly, though he died at th[e] age of 86 when I was three years old, my gaunt ol[d] grandfather, wrapped in his homespun plaid, has pai[d] me several visits. afterwards, I could not say definitel[y] whether I had been asleep or awake. But the whol[e] conversation, even to the old man's sligh[t] Aberdeenshire accident, was so vivid that I was positiv[e] it had actually taken place.

And that is how it was in my conversation with M[r] King on the park bench among the ruins at Kingsmer[e] last June.

What the explanation may be of such phenomena I d[o] not claim to understand. They may be due to psychi[c] influence, to a stimulated imagination, or to tha[t] subconscious working of the mind which happens i[n] dreams.

Yet there is no incompatibility between being [a] Christian and church-goer, as Mr. King was, and bein[g] a searcher into the mystery of the hereafter. During hi[s] life, we had several discussions on the fascinatin[g] subject, and it came to me as a surprise when, after hi[s] death, it was "revealed" in a magazine article that h[e] had been a practising spiritualist. I thought everybod[y] knew about it.

Like many others of his friends, I resented this, perhaps unintentional, exposure of Mr. King to ridicule. Perhaps I should have been warned not to touch such a sensitive subject. There may be no witches in Canada, but there are witch-hunters.

Still I have been a reporter all my life, and I could not resist trying to write an account of that strange experience at Kingsmere. I did it with the greatest care.

I offered what I had written to a national Canadian magazine — not *Liberty* — but it was courteously rejected. I was told later it had gone to the fiction department and had not been regarded as very good fiction.

So I redrafted it for broadcasting. I thought that my Scottish voice might convey my meaning with more subtlety than the cold printed word. I stress its unusual character, I called the talk *Fantasio*. As I would have a much wider audience on the air, I strengthened the warnings that it should not be taken too literally, writing that I was not sure that I believed my story myself, and prefacing my account of the "facts" with the conditional phrase — "If in the mystery of life and the hereafter, there are such things as facts."

That, it seemed to me, provided the key to the story. It was a mystery, and a pleasant one.

The CBC editors, to whom the script was submitted, read it understandingly, and accepted it for broadcasting.

Listeners from one end of the country to another seem also to have understood. Two of Mr. King's literary executors, who have had access to all his private papers, and a former member of his cabinet, were enthusiastic about the portrait I had drawn of their old leader.

But when we come to the treatment of the story by the press, that is another matter.

It perhaps ill becomes one who has been a newspaper reporter all his life, and has undoubtedly made his full measure of mistakes of interpretation and even of fact, to be critical of his colleagues who may fall into error.

I find, however, that some account of how my broadcast was handled by the press is necessary for the proper understanding of the Legend of the Bench at Kingsmere.

That legend has already travelled far beyond Canada. It has brought more than 200 letters, from every province and from many states of the American Union. Every weekend, and even during the week, hundreds of visitors have been flocking up to Moorside and arguing hostly whether or not the "ghost" really appeared. The delegates of the Colombo Plan conference in Ottawa have carried the story to the ends of the earth. Political commentators have seized on it as a peg on which to hang pontifical articles. Collins, in the Montreal *Gazette*, lifted it to a high point of humor with his cartoon of Prime Minister St. Laurent sitting on the bench among the ruins, looking pensively upward and asking: "Have you anything to say to *me*?"

But the condensed version of the talk circulated by The Canadian Press was not so well inspired. Probably it was the first time that that news agency had ever put a ghost story on its wires. Certainly it was the fist time a CP staff member, in the Ottawa bureua, had ever been asked to provide one.

It was no excuse that the poor fellow had not heard the broadcast. The first thing to do, of course, was to secure the text. There was none available at the CBC studios, as the broadcast had been recorded. I live at Aylmer, Ont., 10 miles from Ottawa, and apparently the CP Ottawa bureau is not equipped to send an intelligent reporter so far to get a story.

I soon found it was impossible to get the facts, nuances, qualifications, suggestions, anecdotes and imponderables into position by telephone. After a struggle, I consented to drive in myself with the text. I might, I thought, be able to keep the story from running wild.

My efforts were wasted. The CP had asked for a ghost story, and the more I insisted that the subject was delicate and the treatment whimsical, the more certain I became that the ghost story I had told over the CBC network, and the one that would be printed, would have little resemblance.

What a fool I had been. I had thought that my broadcast might stir some interest, but I had definitely under-estimated its impact on the ghost-hungry newspaper mind. It made the front pages all across Canada, pushing aside the argument then in progress between Mr. St. Laurent and Quebec Premier Maurice Duplessis.

There were odd little changes. Whereas I had said Mr. King talked to me, the headlines ran that I had talked with Mr. King. The title word, *Fantasio*, became "Fantastic," which is quite different. Sentences were transposed and others, which had seemed so important to me, were entirely omitted.

Not a single newspaper published the text of the talk. Even those, to which a copy had been sent in advance, preferred to publish the CBC version, rather than go to the trouble of writing their own.

The telephone began ringing. Was it true? Argument was warm.

Editors began telegraphing their Ottawa correspondents: Had Philip gone "crackers"? One wit, of sorts, telephoned to ask what brand of whisky I drank.

At 8:30 a.m., on the following Sunday, one of the msot enterprising and joyous of my colleagues burst into my cottage, shouting gaily: "The question is — is it true, or is it not true?"

There were others who did not bother even to telephone but began writing freely, interviewing parsons, chauffeurs, CBC officials and residents of Kingsmere.

In the press, the skeptics certainly outnumbered the believers, but the latter were much more industrious in writing private letters. Two spiritualists told of recent conversations with Mr. King who, they said, had confirmed my story. I shall not call them witnesses.

THE HAUNTING OF MACKENZIE HOUSE

Mackenzie House is one of the most historic homes in Toronto. Since 1960 it has been maintained as a museum by the Toronto Historical Board. Despite the fact that Mackenzie House has been called the most haunted house in Toronto — and perhaps the most haunted house in all of Canada — it was the policy of the Board to maintain that Mackenzie House is not haunted. Guides dressed in period costume who escort visitors through its halls and rooms, which are furnished to recall the period of the 1860s, make no mention of reports of ghosts or poltergeists or mysterious happenings.

The residence bears the proud name of William Lyon Mackenzie (1795-1861). Mackenzie was the energetic publisher of the *Colonial Advocate*, first Mayor of the City of Toronto in 1834, the promoter of Responsible Government, and the leader of the Rebellion of 1837 in Upper Canada. When the rebellions were suppressed, Mackenzie fled (dressed as a woman) and found refuge in New York State. There he continued his agitation. With the amnesty he returned to Toronto in triumph. He is known to this day as "the firebrand."

The three-story brick residence at 82 Bond Street, erected in the 1850s, was acquired and presented to him by grateful friends in recognition of public service. He lived in the house from 1859 until his death in the second-floor bedroom on 28 Aug. 1861. Isabel Grace King, his youngest daughter, also lived and died in the residence. She was the wife of the lawyer John King and the mother of William Lyon Mackenzie King.

William Lyon Mackenzie King (1874-1950), the grandson of William Lyon Mackenzie, was born at "Woodside" in Berlin (now Kitchener), Ont. The grandson took great pride in the grandfather's commitment to responsible government. He studied law and went on to became Canada's tenth Prime Minister and the country's most curious and long-lasting leader. It is now known that throughout his life Mackenzie King was fascinated with spiritualism and with the question of human survival after death. Indeed, one of his friends, the correspondent Percy J. Philip, claimed that in 1954 the ghost of Mackenzie King joined him and conversed with him for some time on a park bench at Kingsmere, Mackenzie King's country estate in the Gatineau region of Quebec. While Mackenzie King's spiritualistic beliefs and practices are well documented, the views of his grandfather, William Lyon Mackenzie, go unrecorded. Yet it is hard to believe that the grandfather, who was Scottish-born, was unfamiliar with the subject.

There are no reports of any psychical occurrences in Mackenzie House prior to 1956; there are none of substance later than 1966. The earliest accounts come from a responsible couple, Mrs. and Mrs. Charles Edmunds. They were the house's first live-in, caretaking couple. They occupied Mackenzie House from 13 Aug. 1956 to April 1960 and only left because of the disturbances. They were followed by Mr. and Mrs. Alex Dobban who arrived in April 1960. The Dobbans, complaining of the same disturbances as the Edmunds, left that June. Archdeacon John Frank of Holy Trinity Anglican Church was called to conduct an exorcism in the parlour, which he did in the presence of reporters on 2 July 1960. Since that time the house's caretakers have lived off the premises, but workmen on the premises and visitors have intermittently complained of disturbances.

The most intelligent discussion — and debunking — of the ghostly happenings at Mackenzie House was conducted by investigator Joe Nickell in his book *Secrets of the Supernatural: Investigating the World's Occult Mysteries* (Buffalo: Prometheus Books, 1988). Nickell is a both a professional stage magician and a licensed private investigator. He has both prosaic and highly imaginative explanations for all the disturbances. Although he writes well, the story he has to tell is simply not as gripping as the stories that were told by members of the Edmunds family!

Mr. and Mrs. Charles Edmunds, the first caretaking couple, lived in the house for four years. Their reports are included here, as are the shorter reports of their son Robert and his wife Minnie who were guests in the house. The four reports first appeared in the *Toronto Telegram* on 28 June 1960 as part of a series of articles titled "The Ghosts that Live in Toronto" written by the paper's enterprising reporter Andrew MacFarlane. The series appeared following the refusal of the Dobbans to remain in the house. MacFarlane secured sworn affidavits from all four member of the Edmunds family. They are reproduced here in a slightly edited form.

1. Mrs. Charles Edmunds

From the first day my husband and I went to stay at the Mackenzie Homestead, we could hear footsteps on the stairs when there was nobody in the house but us.

The first day, when I was alone in the house, I could hear someone clearly, walking up the stairs from the second floor to the top. Nearly every day there were footsteps at times when there was no one there to make them.

One night I woke up at midnight. I couldn't sleep, although I am normally a good sleeper. I saw a Lady standing over my bed. She wasn't at the side, but at the head of the bed, leaning over me. There is no room for anyone to stand where she was. The bed is pushed up against the wall.

She was hanging down, like a shadow, but I could see her clearly. Something seemed to touch me on the shoulder to wake me up. She had long hair hanging down in front of her shoulders, not black or gray or white, but dark brown, I think. She had a long narrow face. Then it was gone.

Two years ago, early in March, I saw the Lady again. It was the same — except this time she reached out and hit me. When I woke up, my left eye was purple and bloodshot.

I also saw the man at night, a little bald man in a frock coat. I would just see him for a few seconds, and then he would vanish.

I often saw one or the other standing in the room — at least eight or nine times.

A year ago last April, I told my husband: "I have to get out of here." I had to get out of that house. If I didn't get out, I knew I'd be carried out in a box.

I think it was the strain all the time that made me feel this way. I went from 130 pounds to 90½ pounds. I wasn't frightened, but it was getting my nerves down.

It was just like knowing there was someone watching you from behind all the time, from just over your shoulder.

Sometimes we'd sit watching the television. My husband might look up all of a sudden at the doorway. I knew what it was. You felt that someone had just come in.

My son and his wife heard the piano playing at night when they were staying with us. When my husband and my son went to look — it stopped.

We could feel the homestead shaking with a rumbling noise some nights. It must have been the press in the basement. We thought at first it might be the subway. But we were too far from the subway ....

I did not believe in ghosts when I went to stay at the

Mackenzie Homestead. But I do now. It's the only explanation I can think of.

I wish to say that I would not say anything against the Mackenzies. They were hard-working people and so are we. They were not hard on us ... it's just that the house was a strain on the nerves.

2. Mr. Charles Edmunds

Certain happenings during the three years and eight months my wife and I served as caretakers of the Mackenzie Homestead have convinced me that there is something peculiar about the place.

On one occasion my wife and I were sleeping in the upstairs bedroom. She woke me up in the middle of the night and said that she had seen a man standing beside her bed.

My wife, to my certain knowledge, knew nothing of Mackenzie or his history. All of the pictures in the homestead show Mackenzie as a man with hair on his head. The man my wife saw and described to me was completely bald with side whiskers. I had read about Mackenzie. And I know that the man she described to me was Mackenzie. He wore a wig to cover his baldness. But she did not know this.

On another occasion, just after we moved in, my two grandchildren, Susan (then aged 4) and Ronnie (then aged 3) went from the upstairs bedroom down to the second-floor bathroom at night.

A few minutes later there were terrific screams. I went down and they were both huddled in the bathroom, terrified. They said there was a Lady in the bathroom. I asked where she was now and they said she just disappeared.

On another night my wife woke up screaming. She said: "There was a small man standing over my bed." She described Mackenzie.

Another night, a woman came up to the bed and looked at my missus. She was a little woman, about my wife's height. My wife said: "Dad — there was a woman here." I told her she was dreaming.

Another night my wife woke up and woke me. She was upset. She said the Lady had hit her. There were three red welts on the left side of her face. They were like finger marks. The next day her eye was bloodshot. Then it turned black and blue. Something hit her. It wasn't me. And I don't think she could have done it herself. And there wasn't anyone else in the house.

On another occasion something peculiar happened with some flowers we had in pots on a window ledg inside the house. This was in winter and we had th geraniums inside. We watered the plants twice a wee on Sundays and Wednesdays.

On a Saturday morning we found that they had al been watered, although we hadn't done it. There wa water spilled all over the plants and the saucers the were standing in were full. There was mud on th curtains, and holes in the earth as someone had poke their fingers in the earth. There was water on th dressing table. Neither of us had watered the plants, an neither had anyone else.

We often heard footsteps on the stairs. Thumpin footsteps like someone with heavy boots on. Thi happened frequently when there was no one in th house but us, when we were sitting together upstairs.

The whole house used to shake with a rumblin sound sometimes. My wife is convinced that this wa Mackenzie's press.

I am not an imaginative man, and I do not believe i ghosts. But the fact is that the house was strange enoug so that we had to leave.

We would have stayed if it had not been for thes happenings. But my wife could not stand it any longer

3. Robert Edmunds

One night my wife woke me up. She said she heard th piano playing downstairs. I heard it, too. I canno remember what the music was like, but it was the pian downstairs playing.

Dad and I went downstairs. When we got to the las landing before the bottom, the piano stopped.

It was similar with the printing press in the basement My wife heard it first and wakened me. I heard it, too I identified the sound because it was the same as ol presses I'd seen in movies and on television. A rumbling, clanking noise — not like modern presses When Dad and I went downstairs to see about it, i stopped when we reached the same landing.

We heard the piano three or four times, the press jus once.

I was not walking in my sleep. I heard them. I don' know what the explanation is. I am not prepared to say I saw any ghosts or apparitions. But I can say that dreamt more in that house than I ever have before o since.

I do not believe in ghosts. But I find it hard to explain what we heard.

4. Mrs. Minnie Edmunds

When my husband and I were staying at Mackenzie Homestead I heard the piano playing downstairs at night three or four times.

We discovered that there was no one downstairs to play it these times, and yet I heard it distinctly. Each time, I woke my husband, and when he and his father went downstairs to investigate it, it stopped.

On one other occasion I heard the printing press running in the basement. I woke my husband, and he and his father went to investigate it. It stopped.

It is not possible to operate the press, because it is locked, and on the occasions when I heard the piano, there was no one downstairs to play it. I can find no natural explanation for these occurrences.

A MYSTERIOUS BALL

Catharine Côté lives in a charming house in a small community north of Toronto. It was while living in a friend's isolated country home that she and others saw a number of strange sights. She wrote about them in this detailed memoir which I received on 23 Nov. 1992.

Here, with minimal editing, is her account of these odd experiences. She refers in passing to the abductee investigator Budd Hopkins. The reader is left to make of Catharine Côté's experiences with the mystery lights and "the Floaty Ball" what he or she will.

My two youngest children and I had moved temporarily into the home of a friend, so we had the good fortune to live in the country in the heart of a dairy farming district, with corn and wheat growing up everywhere.

My children are LeeAnne and Katie. We were assigned the largest bedroom in the house. This made it possible for the three of us to sleep in the same huge, well-lit room. The room was located over the double garage. I felt that this location was going to be my spiritual therapy, as we had faced several crises the previous year.

Smoking was not allowed in the house, so it became my habit to smoke while walking the spacious grounds and drinking in the tranquillity of nature. It was also my habit to go out every night for one last cigarette just before I went to bed. Not even rain storms prevented me from doing this.

One night, after we had been living in the house for about a week, the children and I were driving home up the long country road. The kids noticed a low-level, slow-moving light coming from the east across the field. I slowed the car down in order to get a better look. I could not believe how low the light was, as I was under the impression that it was the light of an airplane. But when it flew over the road just ahead of us, it did not continue to go west. Instead, it made a brief pause, and began going up the road just ahead of it. I felt that the only thing we could do was follow it.

The light moved ahead slowly, as did we. When we got to the driveway of the house and turned in, the light turned west over the field just north of the property. We leapt out of the car and ran round the side of the house to watch it. It made absolutely no sound. There was a casual, lilting bounce to its movement. We watched it till it was out of sight. We found we didn't really have very much to say about it.

About a week later, at about nine o'clock, I was standing at the end of the driveway. I was having my usual cigarette, thinking about nothing more important than the peaceful darkness. My children were in bed and the house was otherwise unoccupied. I found myself looking down the road. A few cars were approaching from the distance, so I thought nothing of the light that I saw until it was about three hundred feet away. I suddenly realized that this single light was not on the level of the road. It was at tree-top level, and it was lighting up the tops of the trees as it approached. I turned and ran for the house without looking back.

I cannot say what it was, but I was later to learn something of interest from my friend's son. About a year earlier, he and others had been driving from the same direction as this light came, and as he slowed the car to approach the driveway, the light paced them at ground-level in the field on the east side of the road. When they stopped to take a look, the light also stopped, then took off at an angle at a fast rate of speed.

Perhaps the light I was seeing was the same light the friend's son had seen.

A few weeks later, as I was speaking with my friend's daughter out front of the house at about 10:00 p.m., I saw a light approaching from the east. As we watched it, it moved noiselessly over us, with that familiar lilting bounce. We decided to call it the Floaty Ball, as if naming it would somehow help us to understand it and deal with it.

It was about this time that the teenage son of my friend told me of what he had experienced with the mysterious light. The previous summer, he had decided to ride his bicycle north on the country road to accompany a friend home. While they were biking, a light came into view just over them. They were too terrified to move, so they stood in the darkness and watched it. After a while, it moved on at an unbelievable rate of speed. The son of my friend said that they both felt that whatever it was that they were watching, it knew they were there.

At the beginning of November, we were entering the third month of our stay at my friend's country house. One night, as usual, at about 11:30 p.m., I went out for my smoke. I stood at the end of the driveway and drank in the peace of the surroundings. Eventually I went inside the house and saw that the bedroom light was still on. I knew that my eight-year-old was probably still awake, reading. The rest of the house was in darkness. I made my way to the room. My little one was closing her book and I walked past the window to turn off the light. I gave a quick glance outside. I could not believe what I was seeing.

A beautiful, soft, glowing light, pinkish-orange in colour, was sitting above the ground. I could see the soft edges of the furrows of the frozen field beneath it. I could see all around it, and I could see nothing else at all. No people. What was the most surprising aspect of what I saw was the knowledge that I had just been out there, probably no farther then from thirty to fifty feet from the point where this light was now positioned. I had just come in, and no more than five minutes had passed. I was left to ponder the implications of the fact that it had been out there. Maybe it had been watching me.

I needed another opinion. I called LeeAnne over, and casually asked her, "Do you see anything unusual out there?"

She immediately said, "Mommy, what's the light doing out there in the field?"

I turned out the light in the room and we watched. The sight was so beautiful; it had a certain tranquillity. The only thing of which we were aware was of Katie's peaceful breathing in the dark. After about twenty minutes, the light just disappeared. We waited to see if it would reappear. After a few minutes, a white light appeared in the field a fair distance away. It was halfway up a bank of pine trees. We spent quite a long time watching as this bright white light glowed and increased and decreased in size for quite some time. In time it winked out and we were left peering into the darkness. A few minutes later, however, a fast-moving, wildly spinning light went from left to right in our view. The next morning I was able to determine, using as reference points the window, that the light had been spinning at the height of the hydro lines corridor.

At this point, LeeAnne made an interesting point. She said it was if they were putting on a show for us. This comment became increasingly significant for us as we had one more visual treat in store. When the spinning light disappeared, we waited. Suddenly, a bright light appeared high above the horizon. It glowed and grew so huge so quickly that both LeeAnne and I instinctively dropped to our knees behind the windowsill. It seemed that my daughter felt as I did that something was coming to us, closing the distance between us. Nothing further happened that night. Then I realized that it was after 2:00 a.m. LeeAnne and I went to bed. I was more than a little ashamed of myself that I had not wakened Katie. To this day I cannot explain why I did not. I would have been more in my personality to have shared the experience with my children, particularly an experience so weird and wonderful.

I could not wait until the next afternoon to share this unusual story with my friend's son. We had become quite close, as he too had had an experience with the light. When he returned, about 4:00 p.m. the next day, I stopped him. I just had to tell him about the weird thing that had happened to LeeAnne and me the previous night. But he was more excited than I was.

He begged to tell what had happened to him the same night. He had been in the back of the darkened house, looking out the kitchen window, when he heard me return after smoking my cigarette. He didn't say anything to me because he was planning to go to bed. His little pet kitten Smokey was in its usual place, perched lovingly on its master's shoulder. He said that after he had heard me come in, he was suddenly gripped with a terror for which he had no name or explanation.

His vision was diminished. He could still see, but there was a general darkness, as if a filter had been put over his entire field of vision. He stated that he was paralyzed, and when he tried to move he was unable to move a muscle. He could not say how long he was in this state, but he did add that the kitten was also unable to move and sat motionless on his shoulder. He said that when he was released from this force and was finally able to move, so too was the kitten.

Little did he know what LeeAnne and I were going through. He said that when he was finally able to move, he ran down to his basement bedroom and locked the door. He and the kitten stayed under the covers all night long. Due to this nameless fear, he was unable to sleep. He felt that it was interesting that the kitten did not move during the night, as the kitten usually kept everyone up. It was a little terror with its all-night scampering.

It was about a year later, when I was writing up this account of the experiences, that Lee Anne's remark about something putting on a show for us to see took on a deeper meaning. Could it have been that something wanted the only other people who were awake that night to be kept busy? We were enthralled for two hours, and we did not even do what would have been a normal thing, that is, wake up other members of the household. This was odd, as Katie was sleeping only five feet away. Needless to say, I am even more puzzled today than I was a year or so ago.

This leads me to relate the most unusual experience that I have ever had in my life. It occurred around the middle of the month of November. I had my late-night cigarette as usual, and the children and I went to bed. I cannot say when this experience began, but it must have been after 12:00 midnight and before 2:00 a.m. I was awakened out of my sleep by the incessant meowing of one of the numerous family cats. The cat would not let up. I finally got up and began to search for the rude kitty in the dark. After seeing its form dimly in the darkness, I basically told it to shut up before it succeeded in waking everyone up. Then I returned to bed, slightly annoyed, hoping to resume my sleep.

I have never in my adult life had a fear of the dark. Suddenly I became utterly terrified. It was as if the very hairs on my back were standing on end. I have never known such a nameless, unprovoked terror in my entire life. What I said to myself was that I knew that if were to roll over at that moment, I would see something. And the thought chilled me to the bone. Never before had I

had such a feeling in my life. Then I had an even more scary realization. I tried to move my body but I could not. My eyes were wide open and I could not close them. I attempted to move the most easily moved part of my body, one of my fingers, but I could not budge it. Now I was really frightened. I knew something was right behind me.

What happened next is completely unbelievable, but it happened the way I am going to describe it. I felt what seemed like an arm slip under my shoulder, and another slip under my leg. I was still lying on my side and I still could not move. It seemed I was screaming in my mind, "What are you doing?" and I was stunned when an answer came back directly. I was told, "Don't worry, we won't hurt you."

With that, I watched my visual perspective change, as I began to rise in the air. It was wild, because everything that I could see was changing in my view, the way the view changes when I rise from a chair. Before long I could see the bedroom window, and I was slowly heading towards it. There was the most beautiful glow of light on the other side of the sheer curtains. As I seemed to float towards the window, I screamed out in my mind, "Please, I cannot go through a window. It's not possible. Please, let me pass out."

And that was the last thing I remembered until I was back on my bed. I still had the feeling of paralysis, and I still could not move a muscle. But now I was totally vexed on a beautiful white ball of light that was hanging suspended in the air on the other side of my bed. It was about five feet in height. I said, in my mind I assume, "What just happened here?" I was told that there was something about my mind that amazed them. And then they said something to me that was very personal, a message that only this year acquired a deeper significance.

With that, the beautiful light began slowly to shrink in size, and then it just winked out. With the light gone, my body was released and I could move. My body and its movements felt bizarre. I looked at the clock. It was just after 2:00 a.m. I have no idea how long this thing went on. After puzzling it out for a while, I was finally able to go back to sleep.

When I awoke the next morning, my children knew that there was something wrong with me. I told them that I had had a rough night. They had to get themselves ready for school, as I was physically quite out of it. During the course of the day, I alternated between feeling "wow" and "I think I must be losing my mind."

But something else was about to happen. It occurred when the children returned home from school. It put a whole new complection on what had happened the night before. When the school bus brought Katie home, she told me something that gave me the chills. She said that one of her school friends, who lived on a farm property about a mile down the road from us, had been at school that day, telling the teacher that she and her mom had witnessed a UFO appear over their back field. This had occurred the very night that I had had the experience. I later learned from my daughter LeeAnne that she had heard the cat meowing repeatedly that same night. She had heard me instruct the cat to shut up. She remembers nothing else happening that night.

There is one more part to the story. Approximately two weeks after the last incident, the children and I moved. But just before we moved out, my children and my friend's children watched across the field to the east, and on more than one occasion we saw fast-moving lights travelling at low levels across the field with apparent disregard for wire fences and other things that were in the way. In one sense, I was happy that we were moving. I was not sure how much more of this we could take. In another sense, I was a little disappointed as I had an understandable fascination with all of it.

But that was not the end of it. The night we moved into our new house, I looked out and saw once again the Floaty Ball. And since we have been living in our new house, I have seen it two more times. Last March, I contacted Budd Hopkins. I was having problems that I had never had before: unable to sleep, bad nerves, extremely emotional, low self-esteem. In addition, I was not handling it very well.

I have recently been in touch with a researcher in Montreal. He is going to arrange for hypnosis sessions so I can begin to piece together what has probably happened to me and to my children.

"BETTY LOUTY"

George Gamester, a lively columnist with the *Toronto Star*, has an odd range of enthusiasms. From time to time he invites his readers to contribute to a series of "theme" columns.

"Tell Us Your Eerie Tales" was the theme of one of his series of columns. Here is how Gamester began the series on 16 June 1989:

Forget it, Rod Serling. Get lost, Vincent Price. Dry up, Edgar Allan Poe. We have all the spooky stories we need right here — thanks to *Star* readers' incredible response to our invitation to:

Tell us your eerie tales.

So who needs fantasy?

As we learn from our first $50 winner, Jo Atkins of North York, real life is strange enough ....

Here is Jo Atkins, a writer in Willowdale, Ont., telling the amazing story of "Betty Louty."

When Elizabeth was small, "Betty Louty" appeared as an imaginary playmate. She came every afternoon for a friendly visit. We arranged the coffee table for Betty's visit: lace tea cloth, tiny cups and saucers, cream and sugar, and the inevitable cookies were part of the ritual. Elizabeth held her one-sided, polite, somewhat-comforting conversations with her unseen guest and played the sympathetic friend. Before my older child was due home, Betty Louty would depart.

"Where does Betty live?" I asked.

"A long way away," was the only answer I ever got.

No one in our family knew anyone by that name. It was unusual and we often wondered what had prompted Elizabeth to invent it. We put it down to the vivid imagination of a creative high-strung child who had suddenly found herself without her closest friend and ally ... her sister.

A few years later we all went to Jamaica for a holiday. In Kingston, a visit to the famous straw market was mandatory, as they each wanted a doll dressed colourfully in the traditional costume, balancing a basket of fruit on its head.

Our older girl chose a doll from the first stall in the market. But not Elizabeth. She moved from stall to stall but did not find a doll she wanted. No! No! was all we heard. We became a little fractious: She became more determined.

"I want that one," Elizabeth said finally, pointing most definitely in the direction of the farthest corner of the stop row of dolls.

"Take one from the bottom row," I said. "They're all the same." The heat in the market and the intractability of my daughter were getting to me.

"I want that one," she insisted, still pointing.

The old lady moved her pole along the row, first to one doll then the next. She turned to look at me.

"They are not all the same. Each one is signed by the person who made it," she said reproachfully.

"That's her!" said Elizabeth suddenly, eyes alight.

With a great deal of patience the old lady hooked the doll down for her. She patted the child on her head.

"This one is made just for you, darlin'. This lady is not makin' dolls any more. This is the last one she made. She's been waitin' here for you."

"I know she's special. I'll look after her," said Elizabeth as she hugged the doll tightly and covered her with kisses.

Throughout our holiday, that doll never left Elizabeth's side. She slept, ate, walked with her, and would prop her gently on the sand before going into the water.

"She would like to swim too, but she's afraid of the currents in the water," said our young one.

"Currants are in cake," I said jokingly. How could she possibly have known about ocean currents since she was so young and not familiar with the seashore?

It was so quiet in Elizabeth's room, I thought she must have fallen asleep, but when I peeped in I found the doll had been carefully undressed by my little girl. She had taken off all the clothes and had only the bare rag doll in her hands, cradling it gently as if it were a new-born child.

"Your bath's ready but you can't put your doll in with you. She'll get too wet," I said.

"She's afraid of water. She told me so," said Elizabeth very defensively. This game was getting to be too much for me!

"Well, let's pick up her clothes anyway," I said. "After your bath you can put her clothes back on."

As I picked up the clothes, I remembered the old lady in the Kingston market. I could not see the signature of the maker. Good saleswoman, I thought!

"I wonder who made this doll," I said.

"Betty. It's writing; I can't read it," said Elizabeth as she handed me the doll's apron.

There, on the inside band, was the maker's name ... "Betty Louty."

The imaginary playmate never appeared after that holiday in Jamaica. My daughter has her own home now but she still has the doll. For all these years she has treasured her.

It seems that "Betty Louty" finally came home.

BLUE BOY

October signals the fullness of the Fall season. It also warns of the advent of Halloween.

To prepare for the thirty-first of the month, with all its winds and whispers of witches and warlocks, Barbara Neyedly and the other editors of *Midtown Voice*, Toronto's lively inner-city monthly tabloid, asked those readers who had experienced the unexplained to send in their best true-life ghost stories. Then they asked me, as a regular columnist, to rank them and publish the eeriest. Here is one of the scariest that appeared in the Oct. 1991 issue. It was contributed by a regular reader, Neal Landon.

As for the identity of the Blue Boy....

Whenever I hear people use the expression "looked as though he'd seen a ghost," it is usually to describe a look of blind terror, witlessness, and a wearer who seems capable of doing little more than retreating into shock. But having actually seen a ghost and compared my reactions, I conclude that the phrase is not particularly apt.

In the final years of my marriage, my wife and I lived

in Scarborough, interred by our financial situation in an ugly cinder block of a structure that provided every one of its sixteen floors with bugs, rodents, cold rusty water from every tap, and a basement generator as dependable as the postal system. I never brought up the fact there was a ghost in my dwelling at tenant meetings or mentioned it to my wife.

The ghost looked to me to be that of a small boy, perhaps six to eight years old. He had unruly, medium-length hair and there was always a quick and merry look in his eyes. He smiled whenever he was spied upon playing his hide-and-seek games. Then he would vanish. He had Caucasian features although his skin was blue. His clothes and, for that matter, everything about him was enveloped in a fluorescent turquoise aura. He never uttered a word or stayed more than a few seconds in one place.

I wrote off the first four visits as inventions of fatigue, a hallucination caused by a faulty bulb blinking, or the passing headlights from a car outside. Those times he just raced past me, a blue blur on the periphery of my vision, vaguely identifiable but nothing to lose sleep over.

One night the glow caught my eye for the fifth time. I turned suddenly and there he was, exactly as I have described him. Right before my eyes he ran away from me, growing smaller and smaller, like a figure receding into the horizon until he was gone. It was too small an apartment. His actions had been confined to the same spot where he had been standing. It reminded me of a television set being turned off. Was I scared? I was more relieved than anything. I finally had a clear picture of what had been disturbing me, I thought, as I remembered the earlier instances.

Now, it's hard to rationalize a ghost, but compared to other creatures of the night, or rats, or bugs, a ghost is not difficult to accept. Over the next half year, he showed himself to me a total of three more times. Those visits went along the same lines as the fifth, so there's not much point in going into them now. One thing: I' crouch to his level.

One night I was in the bathroom with the door open when I heard my wife in the kitchen say, in a sweetl admonishing voice, "What are you doing here?" I knew she wasn't talking to our son because from where I wa I would have seen his bedroom door open. He had bee asleep for an hour. Hearing a sudden rush of air into m wife's lungs gave me a better idea of whom she wa addressing. I saw her go charging through the apartmer wearing an expression Clint Eastwood would have bee comfortable with.

We checked in on the kid's room and, satisfied tha everything was safe, returned to the kitchen. I assure her I had seen no movement of any kind around tha door. When I pressed her for details, she shut right u and viewed me with suspicion. I confessed to seein weird sights but would give her no details of my own Her interest aroused, we agreed to a trade. Withou saying a word we would write down a description of ou visions and read each other's.

As it turned out, that had been her fourth and fina sighting of the ghost. We talked about seeing him, abou what it meant, what could be causing it, and what w could do about it until, after ten minutes, we exhauste our capacity to converse without repeating what w already knew, which amounted to very little. We simpl never mentioned it again.

It wasn't like we wanted to go out of our way lookin, for trouble. We had enough problems with the rea world as it was.

A year later the wife and I broke up. It wasn't th fault of the ghost. I never even saw him again an haven't thought much about the whole experience in th interim. Naw, what happened with me and the wife was well, actually I'm rather hard-pressed to come up wit a cut-and-dried explanation for you.

So what else is new, eh?

THE STICKY MAN

Donna Schillaci, a mother who lives in Oakville, Ont., saw a letter from me in a local newspaper, inviting readers to send me their true-life "ghost stories."

Ms. Schillaci had a scary experience to relate, one that involved not only herself but also her young son Adam. She sent me one account of "the sticky man" on 5 June 1900 and then, on 22 June 1900, a second, fuller account. It is the second account that is being reproduced here.

One cannot help but wonder: Is there a "sticky man" in the basement of her house? Is the spirit there still, biding time until the appropriate moment when it will reappear ...?

June 22, 1990

Dear Mr. Colombo:

As I'm writing this letter to you I can't help but wonder if anyone could possibly understand or even believe what both my small son Adam and I experienced. But I guess that's what you want to hear about.

About a year and a half ago, when Adam was almost two years old, we moved into an older house. I think the house was between eighty and ninety years old. I never felt anything unusual about the house when we first moved in, but as time went on I felt a heaviness about the walls. I ignored the feeling.

Then one day, while in the basement, I felt the heaviness again. It was stronger this time. I noticed the furnace room door was more open than usual. Perhaps in vacuuming I had bumped into it. I couldn't remember.

And then I saw it — its form transparent so I could see the bricks of the wall through it. What caught my eye most of all was the figure's face. It was male. His eyes were leering and devilishly playful. He seemed to be challenging me — and in a frightening way.

I ran back upstairs as fast as I could. I tried to pretend I had imagined it all. It was hard. The bathroom, the shower, the tub were all down there in the basement, and when I went down there, I had to feel comfortable.

Thereafter, as best as possible, I tried to keep the furnace room door closed. Some days I felt something in there, other days nothing. Gradually I began to forget about it all.

Then one day, while I was showering in the basement, Adam screamed from outside the shower curtains. It was a horrible scream, one I had never heard from him before. I shakingly opened the curtain and asked him what was wrong. He screamed, "Mommie, a sticky man on the wall!"

I quickly climbed out of the tub, looked around, and tried as best as I could to see something where he pointed with his tiny finger. There was nothing there. He kept saying, "Sticky man, sticky man!" Instead of asking Adam too many questions, I knelt beside him and told him it was all pretend. He calmed down.

The first time this happened my explanation was enough. Yet it happened two more times. And always it was a "sticky man" he saw. Early one evening Adam was dancing in the kitchen. He got strangely delirious with joy and laughter. With both arms waving to the music he loudly cried out, "Sticky man is coming upstairs!"

Frightened, I yelled out powerfully for the "sticky man" to go back downstairs and to leave us alone. I ranted, raged, and repeatedly stamped my feet at the edge of the basement steps. I stated it wasn't fair. He was frightening a little child. I never let on he was scaring the skin off my face, too.

From that evening on, we were no longer bothered by his appearances. And if I did "feel" him around, I bravely and confidently spoke out. My commands were simple. Go away. Sometimes my tone would soften and I would pray for this poor soul to find its way back to God because I instinctively sensed he was lost. But I always made it very clear — I didn't want him around.

I try not to talk to Adam about his experiences. I have to admit I'd love to know how much he does remember. Six months ago he asked if Mommy remembered the "sticky man." A jolt of panic sped up my spine. I looked sadly into his clear hazel eyes, quickly nodded "yes," and changed the subject. I don't want him to be afraid of life, and I don't want him believing in ghosts. I'm firm about that. Yet it's too late. He's constantly zapping ghosts with an imaginary gun. Maybe he's lucky: He hasn't associated "sticky man" with ghosts. I really don't know.

As for myself, I still feel my stomach turn whenever I talk about it. No matter how much courage I mustered up in facing it, there was always fear not far behind. But I have to admit I'm stronger for having stood up to a .. can I say it? ... a ghost!

Sincerely
Donna Schillac

THREE NIGHTS OF HELL

"Three Nights of Hell" is a riveting, first-person account of a haunting. It was first published as part of "Ghost Stories" in *The Hamilton Spectator* on 29 July 1995. It bears the signature "Linda W."

The account was prepared for publication by the journalist John Mentek who kindly extended to me permission to reproduce it here. I also have the permission of "Linda W.," the former private duty nurse who recalled these scary three nights. The house where all this occurred is located in the vicinity of Hamilton, Ont.

About fifteen years ago, I was on private duty, nursing an old woman. She lived by herself in this old house. It's still out there. My husband and I drove by it this summer. It's been fixed up now, but it's still old and its brick is covered with ivy. The house is set way back from the road. It has those Amityville eyes on top, two kinds of rounded windows.

When I drove up, I got this overwhelming feeling that I didn't want to be there. I was almost sick to my stomach. But at the time I never thought about ghosts. I went in and met the old woman. She wasn't the nicest person, but it was a job. She was very old and sick.

That night, the weirdest things started happening. The tap turned on by itself. The doorbell would ring and nobody was there. Doors would open by themselves. I thought, "It's just an old house. It's got ... problems."

As I was getting ready for bed that night, she told me to put a chair under each window and leave the windows open an inch. The whole front of the house was windows. She said in the morning all the chairs would be moved and the windows would be closed.

I thought, "She's trying to scare me." But I did as she said, got her into bed, and went up to my room. I was upstairs, she was downstairs. The house had never been fixed up. It still had the old feather mattresses and everything. I went to sleep.

In the middle of the night I heard footsteps and heavy breathing, like moans and sighs, coming up the stairs. I'd left the hall lights on in case I had to get down the stairs to her in a hurry. The lights were out, and I thought, "Gee, she's up and is trying to scare me." I was always trying to find a way to explain it, you know.

So I got up and put the hall lights on and I looked around, but I didn't see anything. I went downstairs to check on her, and she was sound asleep, so I figured she had been up and had got back into bed. In the morning, all the chairs were moved and the windows closed, just as she had predicted.

Later that morning I went home and didn't want to go back. I called the agency, but they didn't have anyone to replace me. Later I found out that nobody wanted to go to this house. I went back the next night, and it was a little worse. There was a door in the kitchen that led to the basement. Every time I went near it, I thought I was going to throw up, the vibes were so bad.

So that night I got her to sleep, and I went through the same routine, leaving the hall light on. In the middle of the night, it was the same deal again, the heavy breathing, moaning, the footsteps up the stairs and the light going off. I thought, "Geez, this is really stupid," so I put on the light in my room, and then I went to the bathroom.

The bathroom is right at the top of the stairs. I just sat in there and could hear something coming up the stairs. But I looked and looked and didn't see anything. So I started talking, saying, "I can't get out of the assignment now, but I'll try in the morning." All of a sudden, downstairs, one of those big brass serving trays crashed to the floor and started to spin around like a coin. I went down and checked her. She was sound asleep. I sat up the rest of the night.

The third night, it was all I could do to get myself back into the house. It was a hundred times worse. The doorbells were ringing every five minutes. The grandfather clock was going bong, bong, bong, not even on the hour. Doors were opening, and the tap was running by itself.

"She doesn't seem to notice," I thought. So I got her into bed and told her, "Now, don't get up in the night. If you need me, just call." I was still looking for a logical explanation. I thought it was just tricks she was playing.

After I put her to bed, I put the hall light on and went up to my room. When I turned on the light in my room, the whole room was covered in moths. Thousands of moths, just covering the ceiling. The closet door was open a crack, so I figured they had come out of the closet. I wasn't too happy, but I went to bed.

I woke up later that night with an awful charley-horse in my leg, and that's the only way I know one-hundred percent that what happened next is for real. As the charley-horse settled down, I heard a scratching sound coming from a three-drawer dresser under one of the eye-shaped windows. I thought, "Oh great, I've got a mouse in there."

I got up — the moths were gone by then — and kicked the dresser, thinking to scare the mouse away. A drawer flew out at me, the light went out, and I heard, "Oooooooooohhhhhhhh," and footsteps rushing up the stairs.

I grabbed my clothes and ran into the bathroom. The door was open and I was sitting in there, when this thing, this presence, just charged at me. And I started talking aloud, saying, "I will not be back after tonight. Don't worry, I'm leaving."

Coming down the stairs, I felt something breathing on the back of my neck. I checked the woman, always the loyal nurse, and she was sound asleep, totally conked out. I went into the kitchen and called my Mom. It was four in the morning, but I said, "Mom, you've got to come and get me out of here. I can't take this."

Later my Mom said she actually heard moaning and breathing behind me over the phone, and her hair stood on end when she heard it. She said she couldn't come till daylight. So I talked to her for five minutes and then said, "Okay, I'm going to sit in the living-room until you come." I got dressed in the kitchen, went into the living-room, and sat with my back to the wall.

I piled a bunch of books around me to throw at it. There were footsteps pacing up and down the living-room, heavy breathing, and the grandfather clock was going bong, bong, like crazy. I pleaded with it, "I will not be back, I will not be back. Don't hurt me."

I was sitting against the wall and a couch to my left lifted up and turned around. There were two hours of this. It was awful. I had all the lights on and just sat there till morning.

The housekeeper came before my Mom got there, and she told me all kinds of strange stuff had always gone on in the house. Apparently even the old lady was terrified living in the house, and that's what the business was with the chairs under the windows. She always thought spirits or whatever were trying to come in through the windows, and she was trying to block them.

When I got home, I called the agency and told them I had a cold. I never went back.

THE SPIRIT OF THE HANGING JUDGE

The Hanging Judge is the moniker by which the public recalls Sir Matthew Begbie (1819-1894), the pioneer law-giver of the Cariboo, who was known far and wide for his harsh but generally fair judicial decisions. It is said that Sir Matthew knew more about human nature than he did the law.

I first learned that the spirit of British Columbia's Hanging Judge may still dwell among us from Robin Skelton. A widely admired poet, an industrious scholar, Robin was also a practising witch. In the latter years of his life he formed an alliance with Jean Kozocari, a well-respected medium and practitioner of wicca. Robin and Jean would visit haunted sites and exorcise them.

In response to my query about Sir Matthew, Jean sent me an audio cassette in which she recounted the details of her encounter with the spirit of the Hanging Judge. Here is the text of that cassette.

In 1980 we were invited to investigate a haunted house. We found the house to be a Fifties bungalow built on the side of a hill in Saanich, which is just outside Victoria, B.C. It was a comfortable house, a very beautiful one. The people as newlyweds had drawn up a plan for their dream house, and this house fit every criterion they had. Years later they found and bought it. They owned it for more than three years. And although they were paying two mortgages, they were never able to live there in comfort.

Strange things happened. Workmen made commitments and never showed up. There were floods although the house was built on top of a hill. There were plagues of rats, and when the rats died in the building, there were plagues of flies. No matter what they did, always something came up to make the house unliveable. The woman suffered severe personality changes there. The man found that an incredible lethargy came over him whenever he tried to do work on the hill.

We arrived on Father's Day, and on the way out, the two mediums whom I took with me, although best of friends and always pleasant and congenial, fought constantly all the way out. When we arrived at the house, we went in, walked through it, and investigated it. There were several places that were very uncomfortable, including one room in the basement that had been built over a large protruding rock so that the rock became part of the room. Over the three years that we investigated the house, this rock frequently oozed a very strange, oily substance that had the consistency of thick motor oil that was shiny and aluminum-looking. We would find it on clothing, on dowsing instruments, all over us, all over the people who came in and out of the house.

The haunting resisted exorcism. We had all sorts of meetings. We had dowsers come in to see if there were water deposits under the earth. One afternoon my eight-year-old son was having tea with us in the living-room of the house. As he was sitting there, drinking tea, a beautiful glass picture-frame lifted up off the bookshelf, did a complete somersault in the air, and landed in his lap! There was absolutely no way that it could have fallen — four feet high! — into the air, and in a complete circle, before it landed into his sister's lap. He's now twenty, and we were talking about it last night. It is one of the lasting memories of his childhood, much outweighing Christmas and Halloween.

One of the unexplained phenomena was that the owners of the house had fastened glass mirrors to the wall and then built bookshelves in front of them. Slowly over the weeks the letter M appeared. It was scratched into the silvering on the back of the mirror in a place where no one could have got at it. At the time we didn't see any great significance to the letter M.

All our efforts failed in the house. All we were able to do was clean it up temporarily, then something else would happen. We began a research on the property. The house was reasonably modern, but in researching it back to its first owner, we found that the property had been the property of Sir Matthew Begbie, the Hanging Judge. We found that, although he had never lived there, built a shed, built a building, or did anything else on the land, he used to ride out on his horse, taking his lunch with him. He was seen from the distance sitting on the large rock (the one that now protruded through the basement) and meditating. He would spend hours just staring off into space.

This made a lot of sense to us because for some reason or other ropes accumulated in the basement of the house. The lean-to shed where they put their car had the modified shape of a gallows. But of course until we had the clue that this was Sir Matthew Begbie's property, we were never able to contact Sir Matthew Begbie.

At this time the owners were offered an enormous sum of money for the house. They sold it and threatened me: "Please, don't tell anyone that the house is haunted!" They were terrified that the deal would not go through.

On the last day they were in the house, I went there with a photographer who sometimes has the ability to photograph "extras" — shapes, sizes, or ghosts. We used an old-fashioned Polaroid camera, the kind with the pictures that separate. You have a negative and a positive with a gummy substance on it. She put the filmpack into the camera and walked around, taking pictures of the house. However, we were unable to get a photograph of the corner of the house that extends over the rock. That corresponded to the dining-room. It was always missing from the picture. If we took it in the middle of the pictures, the rest of the picture would be fine, but there would be a white column down the middle. If we took it from the side, that part of the house never photographed. We went to two drugstores and got two different packs of film, thinking that perhaps there was a problem with the film. The packs were not labelled consecutively, so we knew they were from different batches. However, we were unable to ake pictures of the dining-room. Everything else — the front of the house, the back of the house, the trees, the rock garden, the pond — were fine. It was only the one part of the house that refused to be photographed.

As we were driving away, the owners were standing, waving to us, and the photographer had one more negative. So she put the camera out the window and took a quick picture. As we drove down the driveway, she pulled out the film and held it for the proper time, then pulled it apart. The image turned out to be badly underexposed. We placed the negative, which was sticky, on the dashboard of the car and promptly forgot about it. (That sounds awful, but I am a slob about my car!)

One evening several weeks later we were sitting talking, and someone said, "Well, the negative is out in the car." So someone went out and got it and placed it on the table. On the negative was a picture of Sir Matthew Begbie. All of us had seen the photographs of him that appear in books and articles. In these he wears a broad-brimmed, cowboyish hat, he has a dark beard and looks very elegant. So we were able to recognize him immediately, despite the fact that in our picture he had no hat on and his beard and hair were white and curly. It was not until three years later that I found a picture of him in his older years. Indeed, his beard and hair were white the curly. The Polaroid photogrpah is very old now. I put a strip of plastic across it to preserve it as much as I could. But for anyone who has ever seen a picture of St. Matthew Begbie, it is quite obvious that Sir Matthew was there with the owners of the house saying goodbye to us — obviously quite relieved that we were leaving him and his property in peace.

One of the awkward things about investigating ghosts and haunted houses is that you can't, really, ten years later, go back and knock on the door and say, "Hello, I was here ten years ago, and this house was haunted. Do you still have a ghost?" Somehow, if I were a little bit pushier, maybe I could do that. But, at present, it's just not part of my reality."

That is Sir Matthew's story. While he is certainly not the offending ghost, it is obvious that his very strong presence at the house made it possible for other and later things to manifest. And we did find out in researching that practically everybody who had lived in the house had had problems with it. The previous owners had been a Navy gentleman and his wife. he had retired early and decided to become a minister. He studied there, rehearsing and memorizing passages from the Bible and hymns and prayers and so on. His wife, on the other hand, was totally devoted to the Maharishi Mahesh Yogi. She was deeply into meditation and her mantras. So perhaps all this mental, spiritual activity added to the already overpowering presence of Sir Matthew Begbie, made this haunting indeed most violent.

AN EARLY MORNING VISITOR

This is a creepy tale about something "that seemed to drip evil."

It recalls an event that occurred almost fifty years earlier. It originally appeared as "An Early Morning Visitor to the Abandoned Hotel" on a page reserved for true-life ghost stories published in the *Edmonton Journal*, 30 Oct. 1988. The writer is F.D. Blackley, Professor Emeritus of History, University of Alberta, Edmonton.

The narrative recalls a scary episode in the life of the author while still a student in Southern Ontario in 1939. It conveys some of the enthusiasm of youth!

In the summer before the outbreak of the Second World War, my girlfriend had a summer job in a small town on Lake Ontario.

One afternoon I hitchhiked from Toronto to see her. We had a pleasant evening, including a walk along the beach. I noticed an abandoned building, presumably an old hotel, a little distance from the water, in a grove of trees. Eventually, I parted with the young lady and had to decide what I should do for the night, as it was now dark.

A university student, I had very little money. I considered the town hotel but it was very close to the chiming town clock, which I knew would bother me. I recalled the abandoned building and thought that I might find a dry spot there on which to curl up until morning.

I went back to the beach and had no problem entering the building. I went to the second floor. This had a long, central hall with many rooms opening from it on either side. I took a room at the far end of the hall with a window that overlooked the roof of a porch. I lay down on a raincoat that I had brought with me.

About 4:00 a.m., while it was still dark, I awakened with a jump. It was as if I had been startled by a loud noise, although I am convinced that this had not been so. I stood up and looked down the hall, lit by a bit of moonlight from a window over the stair. Coming towards me was an indistinct figure with a softly burning lantern.

It was entering each room in turn as if it was looking for someone, or something. As it neared my end of the hall, I saw its face, a horrible one that seemed to drip

evil. Worse, perhaps, I could see some of the details o the hall through its body. I did not wait for the lantern carrier to enter my room. I went out the window onte the porch roof. As I jumped to the ground, I could se the lantern flashing in my "bedroom."

I went uptown and found an all-night truck stop where I had coffee to calm my nerves, and som breakfast. The cafe wasn't very busy and I was able t ask the proprietor about the abandoned building by th beach. It had been a hotel, he said, but it had not bee successful. Some locals, he added, said that it wa haunted by an old man with a lantern! He didn't believ the story. I did not tell him that I did.

SOMETHING TOUCHED ME

Every year thousands of people visit the Stephen Leacock Memorial Home on Old Brewery Bay outside Orillia, Ont. The site is one of the country's leading "literary shrines," perhaps second only in attendance and importance to Green Gables, L.M. Montgomery's site in Cavendish, P.E.I.

At Old Brewery Bay, the knowledgeable tour guide leads visitors through the fine old house, drawing attention to its peculiarities and to the foibles of its long-time owner, Stephen Leacock. In his time he was Canada's best-known humourist. Even today, fifty years after his death, he has more books in print than any other Canadian author. Leacock was a Professor of Economics at McGill University in Montreal so he was able to spent only the summer months on Old Brewery Bay. Here he completed many of his articles and essays, as well as his classic collection of linked stories *Sunshine Sketches of a Little Town.*

As far as I know, Leacock held no views on the subject of the afterlife, though in a number of sketches he spoofed the pretensions of spiritualists. In one essay he asked the rhetorical question, "What lies 'back of beyond'?"

On a number of occasions I have joined the guided tour of the Memorial Home, and each time I learned something new about the man and about human nature. On each visit I sensed the presence of Leacock's spirit, the good spirit of *bonhommie* and mischief, but never that of a malicious sprite.

Could it be that the malicious sprite is the legacy of the humourist's sole child, young Stephen Lushington Leacock.

"The Possession" was written by Kathryn Newman, a Toronto journalist, for the Halloween issue of *Midtown Voice*, Oct. 1994. It was declared one of the winning entries.

Stephen Leacock's home in Orillia is a fine sprawling old mansion stocked with memorabilia from Leacock's life.

In the Spring a group of writers met to learn more about Leacock, the humourist, and to bask in the literary inspiration that oozes from the grand old house.

I had no idea that the house was haunted. However, when I first appeared on that fateful morning, I had a

strange sense something was awry.

I stood outside the house and peered up at the bedroom windows. I felt I was being watched.

The moment I stepped across the threshold, I knew my instincts were right on. This house was haunted, and whoever, or whatever, was interested in me.

I was led through to the rear of the house where the kitchen is situated.

Luckily for me, I was standing next to a writer who just happened to be psychic.

I began to feel dizzy, and the whole room began swirling. The floor was moving right under my feet. "You have to protect yourself. Build an imaginary wall of mirrors," she said.

I was aware of someone, or something, intensely evil watching me.

Something touched me. It was cold, unhuman, and the hairs on the back of my neck stood up straight. I wanted to run from the house, but I am a writer, and I just had to find out what this thing was.

I was determined to get to the bottom of this ghostly mystery.

The main hall felt cold, and I felt those unseen eyes on me once again.

I walked into Stephen Leacock Jr.'s bedroom, and I froze. A fine mist hovered over the bed. Staff had reported footsteps on the stairs ... doors opening, and closing, and many other unusual happenings. But I had never heard anything about mists.

It seems that Stephen Leacock Jr. was a person of small stature. He was known to have a rather nasty disposition, and stories tell of how he took pleasure in butchering goats on the pool table and the kitchen table.

I felt that the spirit was that of Stephen Jr., and he was angry, and haunting the bedrooms and halls of the house.

I should have left well enough alone. I should have made my very quick exit and left while I still had time.

The moment I crossed the threshold I felt a grey mass envelop me. I could not breathe. I was paralyzed. It seemed the ghost was waiting for me.

I don't remember coming down the stairs. But I was told later that I was leaping down three steps at a time. I ran out of the house and pointed an accusatory finger at my psychic companion.

"Hey you, look at me," I screeched. I was definitely not myself.

I returned to another building on the grounds where the seminar was underway. The psychic sat next to me. She was watching me all the time.

"All right," she whispered under her breath. She grabbed hold of my hand very tightly. Then she began to drive the spirit out of me.

It was a most unusual experience.

I felt the mass of evil being pushed down through my body, and a light coming in through my head.

At one point I remember an intense light entering into my body and driving the spirit out through the ground.

The psychic was mentally chasing the spirit back into the house. He was intensely angry, cursing up a storm. I felt much better after my experience. However, I was still very shaken.

I returned to the house once more that day to use the washroom before I left for the journey back to Toronto. The floor and walls began to move and to ooze a greenish substance. I ran from the house vowing never to step into Stephen Leacock's house again unless an exorcism was performed.

I was so unnerved by my experience that I slept with the light on in my room for a week.

Until recently I could not bring myself to talk or write about this incident. I felt that the ghost of Stephen Leacock Jr. might still be listening in to my thoughts and listening in on my conversation. Is he?

THE GHOST IN THE HEALTH CLUB

The following account comes from the October 2000 issue of the emailed monthly newsletter of the Toronto Ghosts and Hauntings Research Society. The TGHRS is headed by a very resourceful and personable computer specialist named Matthew Didier who is a fan of the supernatural.

Fans of the supernatural are of recent origin. In the past we had spiritualists and mediums, psychical researchers and parapsychologists. Now we have a generation of fans who enjoy the world of ghosts and spirits. For them ether and ectoplasm are as intriguing as nanotechnologies and recombinant DNA.

For a lot of fun, visit the Society's website: *http://www.torontoghosts.org*

I admit that I'm a little ... okay, a LOT plump. I've recently been working out and looking into local gyms to hopefully start the fight against my spare tire. (I often joke that some men have abs like a six pack, I have a keg!)

I went to a rather famous downtown gym and was chatting it up with one of the managers of it and on my second visit, he remarked that he had seen me on a local Toronto television show and as such, wanted to discuss his own "ghost story" with me. I listened to him and we were even joined by another employee who also had experiences in the gym. After a bit, I asked if I could use it. Sadly, the club owners do NOT want the story out and about and after a bit of good old fashioned horse trading, he agreed to send me the story via e-mail to use here AS LONG AS I didn't mention his name, the name of the gym or it's location. Not great for our website but good for here ... It's an interesting story.

Needless to say, it's been edited rather heavily....

Hi Matthew....

I started working at the gym over seven years ago and have done almost every job you can do here. We've trained athletes of all types and some have gone on to great champions of their chosen sports and some were already established and have come in to hone their skills. It's a great job.

My second week there, I was asked to help closing the gym (we close VERY late at night), and I started collecting loose equipment and generally tidying up.

On my way out of one of the rooms, I switched off the lights. Seconds later, as I was just closing the door, the lights went back on by themselves. I reached in and shut them off again, started closing the door and CLICK! They went on again.

I figured that the switch was just sticking or something so I went back in the room and switched the light off hard and held it down for a while. I removed my hand and the lights stayed off and after a few minutes, I felt that the lights were off for good.

I walked to the door and as it was swinging shut, CLICK! The lights went on again!

Needless to say, I didn't think it was anything paranormal and yelled out "Shoot!" [Editor's note: This was not what the author shouted but it is a PG newsletter.]

The person helping me close up came over and said "What's wrong?"

I explained to him the problems I was having with the lights. He went.... "Oh! That's just George. We'll have to ask him if we can turn out the lights. GEORGE! WE'R CLOSING UP NOW AND HAVE TO TURN OUT THE LIGHTS SORRY!"

He walked into the room and turned off the light with no problem. He came back to me at the door an closed the door and the lights stayed off this time.

I didn't believe it. I had to know who or what George was. He told me that many years before, a boxer name George was training when all of a sudden, he just fe over dead after a sparring round in the gym. There wa no reason for this as George was a healthy man. Thi guy said he thinks he heard George had a stroke of sort but wasn't sure. He said that since then, George haunt the gym and occasionally causes problems.

I didn't believe this ... well, not really. I just sort c accepted the story and we left the gym for a bee together where he shared more stories about George George played with lights, took equipment out c lockers, opened and closed doors and occasionally wa seen (maybe) in the showers.

The staff all accepted George as he never di anything mean or really harmful.

The story was a good one and after that, anything tha went wrong, everyone would just say, "Oh, it's jus George!"

About a year later, I was working very late alone an had to lock up myself. I had earlier lost my watch in th locker rooms and wasted a lot of time looking for it an so had to work late to catch up on some paperwork.

I got up from my desk in the office, and (as wa everyone's custom who worked there) I said in a lou voice, "Thanks George. I'm going home now and hav to lock up! I'll see you tomorrow!"

With that, I did the rounds, turned off the lights an was leaving through the main doors when I hear something make a metallic sounding "thunk" noise i the middle of our ring.

I went over to investigate and there, in the middle o the ring, was my watch.

All afternoon, people had been sparring and using th ring and no one had noticed my watch? What could do, I was happy so I said, "Thanks, George!" and locke up and went home.

Customers and staff have seen doors open and clos by themselves and staff members are very fond of ou ghost. George is as much a fixture in the gym as an piece of equipment.

There are many more stories of George's antics. On time, he turned on every light in the place at three in th morning which lead to the local police to come and investigate. The owner had to come in and say, "Don't worry, it's nothing," but didn't tell them about George.

Once, in the middle of a busy Saturday afternoon, George turned out all the lights in the place. All the electronic equipment was on but all the lights went out! I remember that you [Matthew] mentioned that was weird because we use a mix of fluorescent and incandescent light bulbs. That was the only time George ever scared me. Not only did the lights all go out but the temperature in the gym dropped to freezing! After a few seconds, it all came back to normal. I wonder what bothered George that day?

Like I said, George has even been seen. I can't tell you who but once, we stayed open very late for a famous athlete to work out alone. He wanted privacy and must have paid the owner a ton of money. I got stuck waiting for him to finish to lock up.

After he finished, he went to the showers and in a few minutes, I heard him yell, "Hey!"

I thought he'd run out of hot water or something but that wasn't it. He came out and was very shaken. He said he'd seen man in boxing gear sitting just outside the showers. He yelled because he was upset to see someone else in the gym besides himself and me and was going to yell at the man for being there.

Just as he was going to get out of the shower to grab the man, he vanished.

I told him all about George and he seemed to be very upset. What's cool is that after I told him about George, he and I sat down and he told me all about a ghost in a house he lived at in Georgia when he was playing for another team. He told me that he likes looking for ghosts but didn't like running into one at a gym and especially while he was showering!

Well, that's my story. Please make sure you keep my name and the gym's name out of it as the owner is not as happy with George as we are. He's even threatened an exorcism!

[Editor's note: An exorcism at a gym ... HAHAHA-HAHA!]

This gym is VERY busy in the early evenings and I find it weird that the three staff I've spoken to (at different times) all know and seem to love George!

George seems very happy in his gym and I guess he may really like the concept of spending eternity working out and sparring at his leisure with only those annoying "live" people cramping his workout!

I hope that the only exorcise that George gets is his rope jumping. (Unless, of course, one day he makes it clear that he wants to leave!)

THE LADY WITH THE LAMP

A few days before Christmas 2001, I received an unusual Christmas gift. It was a letter with an enclosure, and it was sent to me by William Thornton-Trump, a resident of Surrey, B.C. The correspondent, a gentleman unknown to me, was familiar with my work as a collector of accounts of supernatural and paranormal experiences.

In his letter dated 15 Dec. 2001, he explained that he was writing to me on behalf of his brother, Sandy. Here is what he wrote:

I enclose a story by my brother, Alexander Thornton-Trump. A friend suggested that you might find this story interesting.

As my brother has little remaining eyesight, I have edited and formatted the story, but it is his story.

I hope that you might find it to be of interest and perhaps suitable for publication. In any case, please let me know. You can contact me either at the above address or at the e-mail address at the end of this letter.

Needless to say I read the enclosed story and marvelled at the experience and the telling. I replied by email requesting a few particulars. Mr. Thornton-Thump replied by email on Dec. 28, 2001:

Thank you for your kind remarks about my brother's story.

He and I have been working on this together, but since he lives in Winnipeg and I am near Vancouver, there is a certain time lag. I can tell you that he is delighted, though, to know that it will be published. In a recent e-mail he said:

"I think it is wonderful that the little Ukrainian-Canadian town of Senkiw (now comprising one Ukrainian Orthodox Church with onion dome and seating for at least a dozen people), one small community hall with Senkiw painted on a board in an arc over the door, and two outhouses, shall finally have one of its catastrophes noticed."

You asked: "In the meantime, could you send me some particulars about your brother, such as his age at the time of the occurrence, the place where it occurred, and any other relevant details."

My brother, Alexander Thornton-Trump, has taught Engineering at the University of Manitoba for many years. Since he mentions in the narrative that the incident took place in 1980, and since he is now 61, he would have been around 40 at the time.

I had never heard of Senkiw before reading his story (and the above description explains why!) but I assume that it is near Winnipeg, since I know that my brother has some land around there.

In any case, he would be able to answer any specific questions much better than I. You can contact him directly by e-mail.

While his actual name is Alexander, he is known to everybody as Sandy.

Finally, as you requested, I am attaching the story to this e-mail in Word Document format.

So I am in the debt of the two Thornton-Trumps for the chance to read this account and for the opportunity to share "The Lady with the Lamp" with my readers. I like it because it is a rattling good story, and a true one at that. I find it to be convincing because of its origin, and because it fits to a T the pattern of so many rural hauntings.

It was a wonderful Christmas gift!

N.B. It was followed by a New Year's gift, which arrived on 31 Dec. 2001. The gift took the form of another email from Sandy's brother:

Dear Mr. Colombo,

Today I received an e-mail from my brother Sandy containing the information that I copy below. I thought you might like to see it:

I met the Lady with the Lamp when I was 39, the year after I had purchased the five acres on which the first school house for the town of Senkiw had been built. The town had been founded by a group of Ukrainian immigrants who migrated to Canada in 1911. The homestead land was very poor since it was not in the Red River Valley, but up on a sandy bench left behind when Lake Agassiz drained. The land had only a few inches of top soil and had been covered in Manitoba bush, a combination of small poplar trees, bush oak and a variety of wild plum, saskatoon and other low bushes. Senkiw is located to the east of the Red River approximately seventy kilometers south of Winnipeg.

While the town of Senkiw no longer exists as a town, the church and the town hall are still in use for special events of the people who still form, in their own minds, the spirit of Senkiw. The school house was moved in the 1920s to a location near the town hall, then abandoned sometime in the late '40s.

The language of the community is still substantially Ukrainian, but the newest generation seems to be losing that. The Lady with the Lamp spoke to me in Ukrainian, was rather well-dressed considering the lack of wealth of the community, and wearing what was possibly a beaver coat. Beavers are always damming the creek and flooding my 160 acres of woods. In the story I did not do justice to her panic and near hysteria.

As my brother has told you, I teach Engineering at the University of Manitoba and continue to do so. At the time of the meeting of the Lady, we were building a garage on the property next to the old wagon track that connected Senkiw to the small town of Rosa. We keep the trail open out of a sense of historical duty, as do the neighbours on their portion. Across the township road there is an Ukrainian house of the traditional mud wattle and white plaster construction, built in 1917 and Mr. Andrushko helped us build our garage. He was the last of that family line to live in the house.

Will Trump
Surrey, B.C.
Canada

We had a cloth-top camper trailer back in 1980 and had gone out to the farm to clear the young poplar shoots from the area where I wished to build a garage in which to keep the machinery I was accumulating for my experiments in silvaculture.

It was mid October, a beautiful Indian summer day of soft winds, warm sun, blue skies, and green grass. The air smelled sweet with the ancient grasses of the prairie that still grow in my bit of wild woods and glades. That evening we made dinner on the campfire and listened to the whippoorwill calling as dusk turned to dark. Under a black clear sky, the stars shining in their millions from the Milky Way, we put the kids to bed, and they slept deeply as we talked a bit, then turned in ourselves.

The camper was parked on a small, flat-topped mound that had once served as the base for a schoolmaster's house. We had purchased the five-acre block that was the old Senkiw school site. The school on this site had been built in 1912, then moved to a new location about a mile away around 1918. So, in this historical setting we went to bed and I zipped up the canvas flap and we went to sleep.

The tapping on the metal was insistent. I awoke slowly, aware of the wind whistling around the camper and the continued tapping. I got up and unzipped the tent flap and was startled by a white face, large dark eyes, and beautiful dark hair. The young woman carried a hurricane lantern of unusual construction, and she was dressed in a heavy coat, scarf, and fur hat. She was obviously very upset and frantically asking or pleading with me for something. I put on my heavy, fleece-lined coat, my heavy boots, and climbed out of the camper to follow her.

The transformation of the surroundings was startling. Heavy snow was swirling down, an accumulation of about ten inches beginning to drift heavily in the exposed areas. We set off on the Rosa to Senkiw trail that ran through my woods, crossed a field, and entered another wooded area.

Here I found a horse with a two-wheeled carriage that was stuck, the wheels off the road in a drift of snow.

The woman mounted the carriage and encouraged the horse to try again. I put my back against a wheel, grasped the rough spoke of the large wheel, and heaved, and the carriage moved.

I watched the light retreat with the carriage, but the light went from one side of the trail to the other, as if the woman were hunting for something. She called out something in a Slavic language, a little like the Russian which I had heard in my youth. I trudged back to the camper and climbed in, cleaning off my boots and shaking the snow off my coat, then went back to bed.

In the morning I woke up to silence and was pleased the wind had stopped, but knew I would have trouble getting the car out and home in all the snow. I unzipped the flap and was stunned. There was no snow. The grass was green and the sun was filtering through the bare branches of the poplars from a perfect blue sky. A heavy dew sparkled on the field.

But the dream was such a reality!

George, a neighbour, invited us over for lunch with some of the local farmers, all of Ukrainian ancestry. At one point Bill Smook said, "It was just like this the day before the great storm. The lady with the lamp will be out looking for her son."

"What do you mean? I asked.

"Back in 1912 it started to snow heavily at noon in mid-October. The schoolmaster sent all the children home so they could get there safely before the storm got really bad and the snow plugged the road. Late that day the mother of one of the small boys showed up at the schoolmaster's house and asked for her son, but he had left with the other children. She left the schoolmaster, saying she would keep looking and asked him to get help. The weather turned cold right after the snow, and neither she nor the boy was ever seen again. But sometimes, at this time of year, people claim they see her walking up the old road with her lamp, looking for her son. She is the local ghost."

"I know," I said. "I met her last night." And in the shocked silence around the table, I told them my story and watched the colour drain from their faces.

Well, I own much of that old trail today, and in certain places I could swear I feel the fear and panic of that woman. I feel her grief and her pain and her love.

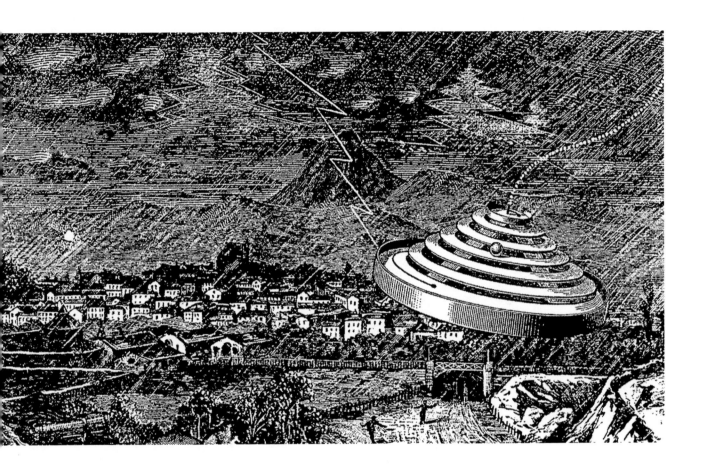

PART FOUR

Creatures of Fire

WE speak of the existence of four elements, not three and not five, but this is conventional usage. Physicists and chemists acknowledge the existence of close to 100 naturally recurring elements. Currently 118 elements are recognized or hypothesized. Some of the natural elements are extremely hazardous, uranium for instance, but the most universally feared of the four traditional elements is that of fire.

And for good reason. Chemically, its heat and its flames are the enemy of all forms of matter. At the same time, alchemically at least, fire's properties or "intelligences" are said to transform base matter into spiritual substances.

Fire is the sole element that is lethal to life as we known it. Salamanders and other spirits may be said to thrive in flames, but human beings are not among their kind. Yet life as we know it would be impossible without the heat, heat from kindled fires, from controlled combustion, and from the rays of the sun.

Associated with flames, blazes, and conflagrations are poltergeists or "noisy spirits." Such spirits are unseen, but they are known by their works — they are heard, sensed, and smelled. They are incendiary spirits, known to start fires. If they are not themselves offshoots of the spirits of fire, they command the movements of such spirits.

In the nineteenth century, poltergeists were forces to be feared. Most houses in small towns were cottages built of wood and thus highly flammable. Entire towns were gutted by fires.

So this section, devoted as it is to the element of fire, begins with accounts of "fire-starters," adolescent girls who were feared in their day as the loci of "fire-setting" associated with haunted houses. Fire-starters are with us today. Remember *Carrie*, the Stephen King novel and the Brian DePalma movie based on it? Carrie White was a fictional character, but her attitude and behaviour might well have been modelled on series of real-life Carries, some of whom lived in early Canada.

But this section is not limited to "fire-starters." (The subject would be too hot to handle, too scorching to read!) I have reinterpreted the notion of fire to include accounts of alien beings. You might want to ask why this should be so. Here is why.

The Ancients believed that the stars that studded the heavens were "fires" that lit up the night sky. Rocketry is the science of propulsion and the propulsive power is a form of fire. In this section there are reports called "sightings" of alien craft from other planets in our solar system or from extra-solar planets that revolve around suns so distant that we describe their appearance in the night skies as stars. Some of the alien craft are "unmanned," if that is the appropriate term, but others are "piloted" by alien beings intent on exploratory missions of Earth and its inhabitants. Such beings would travel to Earth by means of interplanetary or interstellar craft that would need to be driven at speeds approaching that of light, fired by "furnaces" that employ nuclear or some para-nuclear power, a form of "heat" that derives from fire.

Human beings have ever raised their eyes to the sky to discern what lies "up there," in effect, what engulfs us on all sides. As a species we wonder about the sun and the clouds by day and the moon and the stars by night. From the earliest of times we have yearned to sprout wings and fly upwards to claim the lower and the upper atmospheres and to cross the vacuum of space to alight on the nearby planets and then the faraway worlds that populate the distant constellations. As the eyes of man have searched upwards, it is possible that the orbs of creatures not at all human have scrutinized us from across the void of space. Who does not thrill to the sentiments expressed in these lines?

Yet, across the gulf of space, minds that are to our minds as ours are to those of the beasts that perish, intellects vast and cool and unsympathetic, regarded this earth with envious eyes, and slowly and surely drew their plans against us. And early in the twentieth century came the great disillusionment.

The two sentences come from H.G. Wells's influential novel *The War of the Worlds* (1898), which set the pace for literary works of the imagination about interplanetary battle — and menace.

In Wells's novel the Martian invaders land near the town of Ipswich, Suffolk, England. In Orson Welles's radio adaptation of the novel for his Mercury Theatre production in 1938, they land near Grovers Mills, an actual location (like Ipswich) not far from the Princeton, N.J. In the 1953 movie version, their landing site is the imaginary town of Linda Rosa in southern California. It does not matter where the Martians land as long as they touch down in some populated part of the planet Earth. Their mission is to eradicate Earth of Earthlings. Yet things always turn out other than planned....

So much for a works of fiction. Encounters with real-life alien beings follow.

Keep watching the sky!

THUNDER POWER

Here is a traditional tale of belief (and disbelief) in the awesome spirit of the Thunderbird. The tale was told by an Ojibwa woman Marjorie St. Germain, a resident of the Rama Reserve, near Orillia, Ont. In 1921, she told the story to Colonel G.E. Laidlaw, a local collector, who published the text in the *Ontario Sessional Papers* issued by the Provincial Government.

This version of the text appears in John Robert Colombo's *Voices of Rama: Traditional Ojibwa Tales from the Rama Reserve, Lake Couchiching, Ontario* (1994).

A long time ago, the Indians lived on their own settlement. They all believed in Thunderbirds, except for one man who did not quite believe in them. He listened to the white-man preacher who said, "Quit worshipping idols!" The preacher just imagined that they were idols, but the Indians said to the preacher that they were not worshipping idols. If the Thunderbirds were just idols, they would not have the power to kill serpents. Every time it thunders, the serpents go underground. The Thunderbirds go after them like fish, the way Indians like to go fishing. Of course, the preacher would not believe it. (Lots of people nowadays say there are no such things as Thunderbirds.)

One day this Indian, as above-mentioned, thought he would go hunting. After climbing over the high rocks, he saw a pretty scene in the distance. It was a circle of nice greenish colour. He went closer to investigate. The pretty scene seemed to vanish away before his eyes. It began to spread out longer. To his surprise, it turned into a serpent and a big white bird about the size of an eagle.

The serpent spoke to the man, saying, "Shoot the enemy, it's going to kill me."

The bird said, "No, don't shoot me with your bow and arrow, shoot the serpent."

The man got so bewildered that he did not know which to shoot at.

The serpent said, "If you shoot the enemy, I will give you power to kill any wild game you wish."

The bird again spoke. "I perhaps have a better power than the serpent. Anything you wish will happen and will aid you all along."

So the Indian shot the serpent.

The scene vanished, gradually, and then a big thunderstorm and lightning came on. The man noticed a big white feather, about so long. He picked it up and wished for the storm to cease, and it did. He went home, glad to tell of his fortune.

So again the white-man preacher came along to preach a sermon to the Indians. This Indian went and had a chat with the preacher about his "feather fortune." The preacher told the man, "Wish a big storm, just to see if it will come one." He did it, and the most awful storm that anyone had seen came on, and it ceased in a little while.

Everything went well in the village. The minister never thought of idols any more. That is the end of the story.

THE MAN FROM THE SKY

The appearance of "the Skyman" is a traditional tale told by Jonas George, a Chippewa who lived on the Rama Reserve, Lake Couchiching. In 1917, he related the tale to the collector Colonel G.E. Laidlaw who printed the text in the *Ontario Sessional Papers* issued by the Provincial Government. The present text is reprinted from John Robert Colombo's *Voices of Rama: Traditional Ojibwa Tales from the Rama Reserve, Lake Couchiching, Ontario* (1994).

At first glance this radiant tale may seem to be a description of the tradition of an encounter with an "ancient astronaut," *à la* the Swiss theorist Erich von Däniken. Yet it should be borne in mind that when this tale was collected by Colonel G.E. Laidlaw in the mid-1910s, the skies were full of airships. There were balloons and dirigibles aplenty. Pilots barnstormed from cleared farmers' fields. There was exhibition flying in August 1909 at Scarborough Beach in the east end of Toronto where, in 1915, the Curtiss School was established to train pilots for the war effort. Eyes were focussed on the skies as never before.

At the same time, not all aerial phenomena are so easily explained. Awe and wonder was elicited by the procession of meteors that streaked across the skies of North America on the evening of 9 February 1913. Today the display is known as Chant's Meteors after C.A. Chant, Professor of Astronomy at the University of Toronto, who published the two definitive scientific papers on the subject. Between November 1896 and April 1897, there were sightings across North America of "mystery airships," as noted by Daniel Cohen in *The Great Airship Mystery* (1981).

Perhaps the Ojibwa informant Jonas George, whose myths and legends are "vague and mysterious, and have a local colouring to suit the expressions of the times," according to Colonel Laidlaw, had in mind "ancient astronauts" and what would later be called UFOs; then again, perhaps not.

About four hundred years ago there were five or six hundred Indians living together somewhere south of Barrie on what is now called Pine Plains. These Indians had a big time at that place.

Two Indians walked up and looked around those plains. They went a little ways and saw somebody sitting on the grass. This was a man, so they went to see. The man put up his hand to keep them back, so they stopped and looked. After a while the man spoke and said, "I don't belong to this land, I dropped down from above, yesterday, so I am here now."

Those two men wanted him to go with them down home. "Yes," he said, "you go home and clean the place where I will stay, and come back again, then I will go with you for a few days."

The two men went home and told the people about it. They began to clean the place where they were to keep the Skyman for two days. Then they went to get him.

Skyman was a nice-looking man, clean and shining bright. Just at sundown, he looked up, just like he was watching. He spoke sometimes in a clear voice. Just after dark he spoke. He said, "Stay for two days. I'll go up, something will come down and get me to go up."

This wise man said that he was running from where he came. There was an open place and he could not stop running, so he got in and dropped. The next day he said, "It's a nice country where we live, everything good. Tomorrow noon, I am going up, I will leave you, and you people all be good. Every Indian must be home tomorrow to see me go up."

Just after noon the next day, he looked up and said, "It's coming." Everybody looked up but could see nothing for a long time. The man that kept Skyman at his home could see good and saw something like a bright star shining away up. The other people did not see anything till it came near the ground. This thing was the nicest thing ever seen in this world. Two men got hold of it and pulled down heavy, then Skyman got in and said, "All right," and away he went up happy.

I guess he is living there yet.

FLEET OF SHIPS

Fear was certainly felt by the observers of this curious sight observed in the sky above New Minas, a community near Minas Basin on the northwest shore of the Bay of Fundy, N.S. The aerial feature, based on reported accounts, was described by the colonial judge Simeon Perkins (1735-1812), a prosperous resident of Liverpool, N.S. This account appears in his diary for Oct. 12, 1796. It is reprinted from the third volume of *The Diary of Simeon Perkins* (Toronto: Champlain Society, 1849-1961).

It is often said that these "15 Ships" constitute the first recorded sighting of a UFO (Unidentified Flying Object) over the skies of North America.

A Strange Story is going that Fleet of Ships have been Seen in the Air in Some part of the Bay of Fundy. Mr. Darrow is lately from there by Land. I enquired of him. He Says they were Said to be Seen in New Minas, at one Mr. Ratchford's, by a Girl, about Sunrise, & that the Girl being frightened, Called out, & two men that were in the House went out & Saw the Same Sight, being 15 Ships and a Man forward of them with his hand Stretched out. The Ships made to the Eastward. They were So Near that the people Saw their Sides & ports. The Story did not obtain universal Credit, but Some people believed it. My Own Opinion is that it was only an Imagination, as the Cloud at Sunrise might Make Some Such appearance, which being Improved by Imagination, might be all they Saw. Exceeding pleasant day & Evening.

ALIEN VISITOR

John Meares (1756-1809) was a lieutenant in the Royal Navy who resigned in 1771 to establish a fur-trading enterprise on the Northwest Coast of America. He served as sea captain of three voyages which took him from China to Nootka Sound. Meares was a fine observer of the beliefs and practices of the Nootka Indians in the late 18th century. The account of his travels, *Voyages Made in the Years 1788 and 1789, from China to the North West Coast of America ...* (London, 1790), preserves a number of the traditions of the Nootka people. Today, there is a Mearnes Island in Clayoquot Sound to recall the industrious and impressionistic merchant seaman.

Among these traditions is the archetype or memory of "the extraordinary stranger ... from the sky" who one day arrived among the native people and gave them instruction (moral advice) and instructions (practical tips). The man of old and his mission are recalled in "the images in their houses," which might be a roundabout reference to totemic images, even poles, which recall the semblances of this man who "came from the sky," possibly an ancient astronaut. Meares's informant was "the son of Hanapa, a boy of very uncommon sagacity for a native Nootka...."

The Man from the Sky

This discovery arose from our enquiries of a subject of a very different nature. — On expressing our wish to be informed of what means they became acquainted with copper, and why it was such a peculiar object of their admiration, — this intelligent young man told us all he knew, and as we believe all that is known by this nation on the subject. Where words were wanting, or not intelligible, which frequently happened in the course of his narration, he supplied the deficiency by those expressive actions which nature or necessity seems to have communicated to people whose language is confined; and the young Nootkan discovered so much skill in conveying his ideas by signs and symbols, as to render his discourse perfectly intelligible whenever he found it necessary to have resource to them. He related his story in the following manner: —

He first placed a certain number of sticks on the ground, at small distances from each other, to which he gave separate names. Thus he called the first his father and the next his grandfather: he then took what remained, and threw them all into confusion together; as much as to say that they were the general heap of his ancestors, whom he could not individually reckon. He then, pointing to this bundle, said that when they lived, an old man entered the Sound in a copper canoe, with copper paddles, and every thing else in his possession of the same metal: — That he paddled along the shore, on which all the people were assembled, to contemplate so strange a sight; and that, having thrown one of his copper paddles on shore, he himself landed. The extraordinary stranger then told the natives, that he came from the sky, — to which the boy pointed with his hand, — that their country would one day be destroyed, when they would all be killed, and rise again to live in the place from whence he came. Our young interpreter explained this circumstance of his narrative by lying

down as if he were dead; and then, rising up suddenly he imitated the action of soaring through the air.

He continued to inform us that the people killed the old man, and took his canoe; and that from this event they derived their fondness for copper. He also gave us to understand that the images in their houses were intended to represent the form, and perpetuate the mission of the old man who came from the sky.

Such was the imperfect tradition which we received of what may be called the sacred history of this country and on which the inhabitants rested the common hope of the human mind in every state and form of our nature, — that there will be an existence hereafter beyond the reach of sublunary sorrow.

Thus have we given such an account of this people country, and the customs of it, as occurred to our observations. We had not time, even if we had possessed the ability, to have pursued the track of the philosopher and the naturalist. We had other objects before us; and all the knowledge we had obtained was as it were, accidentally acquired in the pursuit of them Of the country we had no reason to complain, and we left Nootka Sound with no small share of esteem for the inhabitants of it.

THE MEN IN THE AIR

Charles Cooper, a farmer, observed something strange crossing the sky in the middle of the afternoon on Tuesday, October 3, 1843. At the time of the sighting he was working in his field outside Warwick, a small farming community located between Strathroy and Sarnia, Canada West, today's Ontario. Cooper claimed that he saw "a cloud of very remarkable appearance" but also "the appearance of three men, perfectly white, sailing through the air." Two labourers in an adjoining field said they observed the cloud but not the men. Other witnesses in the community admitted that they saw "the cloud and persons."

These testimonies are included in the millennialist tract that is titled *Wonderful Phenomena: Wonders of the Age ... Carefully Compiled by Eli Curtis, Proprietor and Publisher, New York, 1850.*

Warwick, C.W., Nov. 1, 1843

On the 3rd day of October, as I was labouring in the field, I saw a remarkable rainbow, after a slight shower of rain. Soon after, the bow passed away and the sky became clear, and I heard a distant rumbling sound resembling thunder. I laid by my work, and looked towards the west from whence the sound proceeded, but seeing nothing returned to my labour. The sound continued to increase until it became ery heavy, and seemed to approach nearer. I again laid by my work,

and looking towards the west once more, to ascertain its cause, I beheld a cloud of very remarkable appearance approaching, and underneath it, the appearance of three men, perfectly white, sailing through the air, one following the other, the foremost one appearing a little the latest. My surprise was great, and concluding that I was deceived, I watched them carefully. They still approached me underneath the cloud, and came directly over my head, little higher up than the tops of the trees, so that I could view every feature as perfectly as one standing directly before me. I could see nothing but a milk-white body, with extended arms, destitute of motion, while they continued to utter doleful moans, which, I found as they approached, to be the distant roar that first attracted my attention. These moans sounded much like Wo — Wo — Wo! I watched them until they passed out of sight. The effect can be better imagined than described. Two men were labouring at a distance, to whom I called to see the men in the air; but they say they did not see them. I never believed in such an appearance until that time.

COMPLETELY CLAD IN WHITE

This is an account of an apparition that was ten or twelve feet in height and "completely clad in white." The account appeared under the heading "A Strange Apparition" in the correspondence column of the St. Catharines *Evening Journal*, Aug. 17, 1866.

It was signed "QUIS.," which is the Latin word for "who" or "what." The identity of "QUIS." has yet to be determined. No other letter about this strange apparition or similar disturbances connected with the fire appeared in the *Evening Journal*.

To the Editor of the Journal: —

SIR, — I would beg leave to call your attention to a very strange incident in connection with the fire the other night, which at the time made a strong impression on my mind; but believing that it was a merely hallucination of my own brain, induced by the sudden awakening at or near the hour of midnight, when the mind is most susceptible of supernatural influences, I did not give expression to my thoughts or the matter until I learned to-day that others beside myself witnessed the same startling phenomenon.

When awakened that night by the most startling of all cries — the cry of fire at midnight — I jumped out of bed, and dressing myself as hastily as possible, I ran down Queen street on the south side, and when I had reached that part of it situated between St. Paul and King streets, where the shade of the trees are deepest, I distinctly saw a figure moving on the other side to that on which I was going. Now, Sir, I think I am not superstitious, in fact, I have always prided myself on my total want of faith in spiritual visitations, but there before my vision, and evidently with the consent of all my other senses, was a figure the first view of which brought me to a sudden halt and recalled lines long since impressed on my memory —

"For he reared at the sight of the lady in white,
  And he paused in his mad career.
She spoke and her words, when I heard them aright,
  They curdled my blood with fear."

The light from the burning building was just casting its lurid glare upon the dark and mazy atmosphere which prevailed at the time, and was bringing into view, in exaggerated proportions, every object within its influence. Whether it was this strange effect or my excited imagination I dare not say, but there, directly between me and the light of the conflagration, rose up a figure which I should judge was at least 10 or 12 feet in height and was from the knees upwards completely clad in white. Below the knees I thought I could discover a pair of legs and feet, which, considering the strides they were making, ought to have been enveloped in the seven league boots, which I remembered to have read of in my young days, but which were not, if my eyes were at all faithful to their trust, for they appeared to be as naked and bare, as if they were prepared for footing turf or searching for flax in a bog hole in the Emerald Isle. The head was surmounted with a cap, the climax of which, owing I suppose to the velocity with which the feet moved, stuck out behind to a great distance and left a trail which enabled me to follow its course for some time.

You may judge, Mr. Editor, what the effect of such an apparition was upon me at the moment, but as I watched it moving it suddenly disappeared before it reached the corner of King street and I saw no more of it. I am not, as I said before, superstitious, but I am certain there was something in it, and I would like to know what it was. I could not tell whether it was male or female, for I am not sure whether such distinctions exist in the spiritual world, but I am inclined to think it belonged to the latter gender. However this is not of material importance — but I would like to know from you whether you have had any intimation before this of such an apparition, or whether I am really the victim of my own imagination. I have thought that perhaps if followed up it might be made to account in some way

for the origin of the fire; but this is a mere speculative hint, not worth much in itself. Do, Mr. Editor, try and unravel the mystery and you will confer a great favour on the community generally and myself particularly.

QUIS

St. Catharines, August 16.

THE FIERY BODY

Here is a vivid description of a meteor plunging into Lake Ontario. It is based on an interview with an eye-witness, the captain of a vessel in the vicinity of the fall. What is remarkable about the account is the profound effect of the event on Captain Turner of the *Algerine* and his great fear for the safety of his ship and crew. The spectacle was observed late Wednesday evening, Sept. 4, 1867.

"A Meteor Falls into Lake Ontario" appeared in the *Observer* (Sarnia, Ont.), Sept. 6, 1867.

Meteor Falls into Lake Ontario

Captain Turner, of the schooner *Algerine*, who arrived in this city this morning, reports having witnessed, at about the hour of 11 o'clock, Wednesday night, a terrific and splendid phenomenon in the descent of an immense meteor into Lake Ontario, which struck the water not more than three hundred yards from his vessel. The Captain states that a few moments previous to the appearance he had come up from his cabin on deck, and was standing on the main hatch. The vessel was on the starboard tack, sailing along finely with a light southwest breeze, for Port Dalhousie, and about twelve miles off the Niagara lighthouse, bearing S.S.W. Presently his attention was attracted by a sudden illumination from the northwest, which almost instantly increased to a dazzling brilliancy. On turning he beheld a large body of fire in the heavens, which seemed to be approaching at the descent of about thirty degrees, and growing rapidly larger as it came nearer, the observation of time being as brief as hardly to admit of computation in seconds. The momentary impression of Captain Turner was, that certain and complete destruction awaited his vessel and all on board, as the terrific missile seemed to be directed to strike the vessel broadside. The time for reflection, however, was brief, and the light emitted was so blinding in its effect, that the man at the wheel and another of the crew on deck, fell prostrate, and remained for some time completely stupified with terror. The Captain himself, as he states,

remained transfixed, and saw the fiery body enter the water some three hundred yards ahead of his vessel, about two points to the windward. A loud explosion attended the contact with the water, which was sharp and deafening, equal to a thunderbolt close at hand, and a large volume of steam and spray ascended into the air, which was noticed for some moments afterwards. In the confusion of the moment Captain Turner was unable to comprehend what had occurred, and the crew were inclined to believe that the phenomenon was an explosion of lightning, the sky being perfectly cloudless at the time. The Captain estimates, as well as he was enabled to judge from the brief time for observation afforded, that the meteor was a body of about twenty feet in diameter. A long tail of flame of the most intense brilliancy was noticed as it struck the water. As Captain Turner describes his sensation, his faculties for the moment were all compressed in the sense of sight, so overwhelming was the light from the fiery object, but he believes he was sensible to a terrific whizzing, howling noise, similar to that made by the steam issuing from the escape pipe of a steamer, which attended the meteor previous to its grand explosion on striking the water. Capt. Turner arrived at Port Dalhousie, on Wed'y morning. He assures us that his nervous sytem did not recover from the shock experienced for many hours afterwards. — *Hamilton Times*.

Dazzling Flash

The following description of the passage and descent of a meteor might not be monstrous but it bears a sense of menace and magnificence that is decidedly unearthly! The sighting was "only five or six seconds in duration" yet what an impression it created on its witnesses. Note also the psychologically charged vocabulary: sudden, fearful, startled, burst, descended, spectacle, fiery, whirring, terrible, boiling, noise, terrifying, sudden, etc. This was an event to be associated with the end of days.

"A Remarkable Meteor" appeared in the *Daily Colonist* (Victoria, B.C.), Oct. 2, 1887. It refers to the meteorological event that took place in the night sky over Barrington, N.S., the evening of Sept. 15, 1887.

A Remarkable Meteor
Brilliant Spectacle Witnessed by Nova Scotians
Wonderful Phenomenon

Halifax, N.S., Sept. 16. — A special from Barrington says a wonderful phenomenon occurred there last night, about 8:20 o'clock. A luminous body, looking as large as an elephant, with a long tail attached, suddenly appeared in the southwestern sky and shot out of sight in a southerly direction. The night was cloudless and without moon, but the stars were out and a strange soft blue and white light lit up the whole firmament as bright as day. The light was only five or six seconds in duration, when all became suddenly dark again. No matter in what part of the city no one could help noticing the sudden illumination. To a person at the south end it appeared like a frightful explosion in the vicinity of the northwest end, in which direction the light was brightest, but the noise supposed to accompany most explosions was absent. A reporter was crossing the north end of the common when he was startled by a sudden burst of fire lighting up the whole neighbourhood. The meteor descended like a shot out of the misty air. It looked like a large electric light, and a long tail of sparks trailed behind, the whole presenting a beautiful spectacle. To the reporters the fiery visitor seemed to strike the ground a short distance away. Afterwards a low shirring sound was heard in the direction where it had disappeared. The sound kept increasing in volume till the power was terrible. It seemed as if the bed of the ocean was a huge pot of water boiling over. The noise, which was terrifying, lasted fully a minute and a half. What was doubtless the same meteor was seen in Halifax last night, but the time was 9 o'clock. Its fall was accompanied by a most vivid illumination of the entire city. There was a sudden and almost dazzling flash, then all was over.

FIRE SPOOK AT MILLVILLE

The annals of the Maritimes offer many reports of the dreaded "fire spooks" or "fire-starters."

Here is one such account, "Fire Spook at Millville," which appeared in the columns of the *Daily Sun*, Saint John, N.B., June 7, 1888. Apparently it was reprinted from the *Fredericton Gleaner*.

Winter fires were quite common in isolated farmhouses, and so were reports of "fire spooks" and other poltergeist-like outbreaks. Millville is a village located northwest of Fredericton, N.B.

Fire Spook at Millville
Forty-seven Fires in Forty-eight Hours
Mysterious Fires Break Up a Quiet Country Home
(Fredericton Gleaner)

The fire spook is again at large. This time it is carrying on its work of devastation in a hitherto quiet home at Howland Ridge near Millville.

On Friday and Saturday of last week it was currently reported about town that mysterious fires, similar to the Woodstock fire mystery, had broken out in the house of Duncan Good near Millville, and was destroying his property and peace and happiness. The report, however, was not credited at the time, but has since been confirmed by eye witnesses of the mystery. The report is true enough — too true for Mr. Good's liking. It is the talk of the whole country round about and hundreds have gone to visit the scene of desolation. Mr. Estey, merchant at Millville, was among those who visited Good's place at the time the fire spook was doing its work.

He states that while he was there and examining the different places where the fire had broken out, an almanac hanging from a peg on the side of the wall suddenly caught fire, and in an instant the almanac was enveloped in flames. He stood aghast. He was informed that that was the 47th fire that had thus mysteriously occurred during the 48 hours previous to his visit. Curtains, bed clothing, cushions, carpets, books, articles of clothing, had alike been visited by the fire spook. The fires, however, occurred only in the daytime, and when they were least expected.

Not only were the mysterious fires confined to the house, but the barns and outbuildings were also haunted by the strange visitant, one of the barns being totally consumed by the fire spook.

Mr. Pinder, of Nackawick, was also an eye witness of one of the unaccountable fires and has many remarkable stories to tell about its work. During Wednesday of last week the fire fiend proved the most destructive, fire breaking out in nearly every hour of the day; first in the house, then in the barns or some of the outbuildings.

Our Millville correspondent writes under date of June 1st:

At last we have a thorough sensation, all our own, which looks as if it might have the effect of giving us a world-wide celebrity. On Howland or Beckwith Ridge, some two miles east of this village, live a family named Good, who have for years been working and living along the same as the rest of us poor mortals, with nothing pointing to the great celebrity they are now enjoying. This sylvan quietness was broken suddenly last Monday by the appearance of fire in their dwelling, which was easily extinguished, but this forerunner was followed on the following day by the breaking out of fires, very mysteriously, in different parts of their dwelling, consuming clothing, bedding, papers, etc., in fact of whatever appeared to be of an inflammatory nature. This continued all through Tuesday and Wednesday, until the family were compelled to remove from the dwelling. One of the odd phases of the affair is that the fire does not catch at night, or while anyone is looking for it.

On Thursday, about one o'clock, their barn caught and was consumed, with some farming implements and about six tons of hay.

Mr. Good, in describing the fire in the barn to your

correspondent, said it appeared to flame up instantly, and in an inconceivably short time the flames burst from every quarter. The fire resembles very much the burning which caused so much excitement in Woodstock about a year ago.

The inhabitants, for miles around, have visited the scene, and it is rather amusing to listen to the different causes assigned for this. It may well be styled mysterious fire, witchcraft, visitants from the world of spirits, judgements for sins, &c. It appears to have brought to the surface all the latent superstition natural to the natural man. The most sensible reason, according to my mind, and I have minutely examined the premises, is put forth by Mr. Earle, railway agent here, who claims it is caused by the escape of natural gases only inflammable when coming in contact with certain gases contained in the atmosphere we breathe. Let the cause be what it may, it is certainly to us mysterious.

Your correspondent would very much like to see the matter thoroughly investigated by scientists, and a preventive found.

Mr. Good's loss will be quite a serious one to him, and take years of patient toil and frugality to replace.

JENNIE BRAMWELL

Canada's equivalent of Carrie White, Stephen King's "fire-starter," is the real-life adolescent girl named Jennie Bramwell. The fires that she set are legendary in Maritime life and lore. In an earlier age, the secular and religious authorities would have dealt with her as a witch. Today she would be placed in custody or considered a candidate for Prozac. Hers is a classic case of what is called "fire-setting" poltergeistery.

Two accounts of her doings were published in the *Toronto World*. The first account appeared in the issue of 7 Nov. 1891. Beaverton is located in Thorah Township on the east coast of Lake Simcoe, northeast of Sutton, Ont.

Spooks, or What Mysterious Doings in a Torah Farmer's House
An Incorporeal Firebug Cats Take Fire, Towels Burn up and Wood Disappears
Queer Pranks in Broad Daylight
A Young Girl's Name Connected with the Mystery
Over Fifty Years in the House in One Day
The Ghost's Queer Pranks Astonishing All the Neighbors,
Who Are Visiting the Scene by Hundreds What the Inmates Say
These Strange Phenomena Have Now Been Going on for Over a Week.

Beaverton, Ont., Nov. 6. — The residents of the sleepy township of Thorah have been for the past week considerably excited by the reports of curious antics rumored to be performed by supernatural means, in a house owned and occupied by Robert Dawson, a reputable farmer on the first concession of Thorah, about three miles from this village. The story, told by neighbors arriving here, was that an adopted daughter of Mr. and Mrs. Dawson had been seriously ill with brain fever; that about a week ago she went into a trance and on awakening suddenly jumped up, exclaiming, "Look at that!" and pointing with her finger towards the ceiling of the house. The rest of the members on looking towards the point indicated by the girl were surprised to see the ceiling on fire. They immediately extinguished the fire and nothing more was thought of the matter until the following day, when the girl again startled the family with the same exclamation and the interior of the house broke out in flames. This performance, according to the rumor, was continued every day thereafter.

From an investigation by The World's Ghost Exterminator, it is evident that the ghost sleeps just at present, but for a time it was fully as persistent as the one detailed for Banquo's special benefit.

The house is situated about one hundred yards from the road on lot 17, con. 1, Thorah — about seven miles from Cannington and three from Beaverton. It is a small and rather an ancient structure and is built of logs There is a window in the front of the house, but no door; entrance to it being by a door in the rear through an old summer kitchen.

On arriving at the house Mrs. Dawson, the wife of the farmer, introduced the girl, whose name had been mentioned in connection with these mysteries. She was engaged in washing dishes. The girl was adopted by Mr. and Mrs. Dawson from an immigrant home in Belleville some time ago. She was originally from England, where she was known as Jennie B. Bramwell, but since coming to her present home she has adopted the name of Jennie B. Dawson. Miss Bramwell, or Miss Dawson, is a bright intelligent girl of about 14 years of age. She is well educated and an excellent conversationalist.

After being shown over the premises, both up stairs and down, Mrs. Dawson tells this story of the girl's illness and the mysterious fires:

On Monday afternoon, Oct. 25, she and her husband went to a neighbor's to spend a few hours, and on returning home in the evening Jennie informed them that the house had been on fire and pointed out the place — near the chimney. Mr. Dawson, thinking that there might still be some fire around the chimney, remained up all night to watch it, but nothing occurred during the night. After breakfast on Tuesday morning Mr. Dawson went out to the barn to load some grain to take to market, and Mrs. Dawson also went out into the yard. They had scarcely left the house when the girl, Jennie, came out shouting the house was again on fire. On entering the house they found that the west gable end was on fire. With the aid of water the fire upstairs was extinguished, but no sooner had that been accomplished than the fire broke out in several places on the wall in the room in the lower flat, and while extinguishing it there it again broke out on the wall in another room in the east end — there being no visible connection between any of the fires. They finally succeeded, with the assistance of some neighbors, in getting the fire extinguished. The next day the fire again broke out, and as on the former day, when it was extinguished in one place it would suddenly break out in some other place, several feet away.

On one occasion, while the fire was burning at the extreme west end of the house, a picture hanging on the wall at the opposite end of the house suddenly took fire and was consumed before their eyes. On examination it was found there was no fire near it. The family had now

become thoroughly aroused, and after succeeding in extinguishing the fire, they removed the stove from the house as they had an idea that the fire was caused by it. But the removal of the stove had no effect, as on the following day — Thursday — the fire again broke out. While sitting looking at the wall fire would suddenly break out on it; a stick of wood lying in the old summer kitchen suddenly took fire and was partly consumed; a piece of paper pulled from the wall and thrown on the floor would immediately take fire and burn up. A towel which Mrs. Dawson had been using to wipe a table with on being thrown onto another table suddenly took fire and would have been consumed had not water been thrown over it, and a basket hanging in the woodshed also took fire.

The dress of the girl Jennie took fire and she narrowly escaped being burned to death. Mrs. Dawson also had her right hand burned while helping to extinguish the fire. Wherever the fire appeared it would char into the wood over half an inch in a second, and the other side of the board or log would instantly become so hot that a person could not place their hand on it. A peculiar thing connected with these fires was that as soon as any of the burning lumber, paper, cloth or wood (no matter how furiously they were burning in the house) was thrown outside the fire would immediately die out. After all the fires had been extinguished Mrs. Dawson pulled a piece of paper from the wall and rolled it up in a piece of old muslin dress and roped it on the centre of the floor and, accompanied by Mr. Dawson and the rest of the family, stepped outside to see the result. No sooner had they stepped out of the door than the muslin and the paper became ignited and burned furiously. Friday was no exception — in fact the fire was ten times as bad, there being nearly 50 fires in different parts of the house that day. But the climax was reached on Saturday when a kitten, which was lying in the centre of the floor of one of the rooms, became enwrapped in flames and rushed out into the orchard, where the flames, like that on the wood, paper, etc., immediately died out. On the kitten being examined it was found that the hair on its back was badly singed. The fires in the house also broke out twice that day.

Mrs. Dawson, to prove what she said, showed the towel, basket, kitten, etc., which had so mysteriously taken fire, and everything was as she had stated. The kitten, which was examined closely, was badly singed. Mr. John Shier, brother of Mrs. Dawson, was also present and corroborated what his sister had told, as did also the girl Jennie. Mr. Shier also added, "That when he was first told of the fires he just laughed, and so lightly did he treat it that he did not visit the place until Wednesday and saw the mysterious fires himself." He was there when the cat took fire and when the linen and towel were burned, but neither he nor Mrs. Dawson or any other of the members of the family could in any way account for the origin of these fires. Neither can any of the neighbors who were at the fires.

On asking if it was true that the girl Jennie was ill or subject to fits, Mrs. Dawson said: "The girl was taken ill some weeks ago with whooping cough, but when she was recovering from that she was taken down with brain fever, but was now all right again. During the girl's illness the doctor in attendance injected into her arm morphine, and immediately after the girl went into convulsions and for some time after was subject to them. However, she could in no wise connect the girl's illness with the fires.

The house is still standing, but all the partitions have been removed from the top story, and the furniture has been taken to a neighbor's. A peculiar feature was that no fires occurred at night — all being in daylight, and they appeared to be more numerous during the two days when the stove was outside.

Chemist Smith Thompson and Editor Robinson of The Cannington Gleaner have visited the scene and are unable to explain the phenomena. Everything has been suggested that reasoning minds could imagine as a natural cause for the phenomena, but they have in turn been rejected. Human agency and electricity have been mentioned, but at every fresh suggestion of cause the apparently angry author of the mysterious fires repelled the insinuation by blazing out in a new place and destroying all topographical calculations. If it be human agency the one who constructed the machinery must be an expert and a model of ingenuity. If it be electricity the house must be charged more powerfully than any building yet tested.

There is a great stir in the neighborhood and the house is daily visited by scores. All are politely received and given every facility for inspecting the rooms, charred articles, etc. Both the girl and Mrs. Dawson tell their story in a plain, unvarnished manner, devoid of exaggeration and seemingly with a firm faith in the supernatural character of the manifestations. Mr. and Mrs. Dawson have lived on the place for a number of years and are well-to-do, kind and highly respected people. The neighbors speak in the highest terms of them and also of the girl Jennie. The neighbors are all deeply impressed with both what they saw and what they were told.

The second account of Jennie Bramwell's fiery work appeared in the same newspaper on 12 Nov. 1891. At the time, newspaper reporters were often careless or took liberties with the spellings of personal names. The reporter who wrote up this account is no exception. Here Jennie's surname is mistakenly spelled "Bromwell" rather than "Bramwell." I have left it as it appeared in print.

That Ghostly Firebrand
An Investigator Who Failed to Investigate — The Case Still a Mystery

Brockville, Nov. 11. — The young girl Lillie Bromwell, whose name was mentioned in connection with the mysterious fires in the house of Farmer Dawson near Beaverton, has been returned to Fairknowe Home here. Mr. Burges told a Recorder reporter very emphatically that the statement made by The Globe that the girl has a knowledge of chemistry is all nonsense, that she possesses no such knowledge, and with this emphatic statement The Globe reporter's theory falls to the ground and he will have to begin over again. Mr. Burges states that the Dawsons had got the girl from the orphans' home when she was about five years of age, some nine years ago, and so far as he is concerned he is not inclined to believe that the girl had anything to do with the manifestations.

The Globe reporter after fully questioning the girl's adopted parents admits that the fire could not have been started with matches, and then proceeds to show that the girl had a knowledge of the rudiments of chemistry, and that she procured phosphorus and thus the mysterious fires are accounted for. No one is forthcoming who sold the girl phosphorus, so the reporter concludes that she must have stolen it from a neighboring drug store, and then admits that "it is difficult to see how she applied it." We should think it is. If the reporter knows anything about phosphorus he must know that no mere novice in chemistry could have produced the effects, or could have handled it without danger of burning themselves, so that theory is untenable.

FIRE-SPOOK OF CALEDONIA MILLS

Students of Canadian mysteries are familiar with what has been called the Fire-Spook of Caledonia Mills. Between 1899 and 1922, the MacDonald Homestead at Caledonia Mills, a small community of the Highland Scottish located south of Antigonish, N.S., was subjected to terrific, poltergeist-like effects. There were strange lights, peculiar noises, mysterious fires, unexplained movements of animals and household articles, etc.

During the winter of 1922 these effects were studied by the well-known Maritime detective P.O. (Peachy) Carroll from Pictou and Dr. Walter Franklin Prince, principal research officer of the American Society for Psychical Research. Prince's expenses from New York were borne by the Halifax *Herald* in exchange for exclusive coverage of the investigation. Carroll and Prince, working independently, came to the conclusion that the cause of the manifestations was Mary Ellen MacDonald, the MacDonald's adopted daughter, who had no knowledge that she was the agency through which the effects were made manifest. In the parlance of psychical research, she was the "focus" of the poltergeist effects.

Here is an account of a visit to the site of the famous mystery written by N. Carroll Macintyre, a native of Antigonish, and it comes from his fine publication, *The Fire-Spook of Caledonia Mills* (Antigonish: N.S.: Sundown Publications, 1985).

Growing up in the Town of Antigonish, most people were always interested in the stories about the Spook Farm. It was in the fall of 1961 that I had my first opportunity to visit the MacDonald homestead. A friend of mine, Art Farrell from Glencoe (across the woods from Caledonia), promised me a trip to the historic site. In preparation for the occasion, I asked questions and read any material that was available in order that I might fortify myself for the adventure.

On a sunny Saturday afternoon, I was formally escorted to the Spook Farm by Art Farrell, Ed MacDonald from Salmon River, and our driver from Roman Valley who was also to be our tour guide. Since Roman Valley is the next community to Caledonia Mills, we were assured that our guide was well familiar with the area. We boarded his old Jeep and made the trip through the woods to the homesite. As we drew near the location we were warned just to look about and not touch anything or take any souvenirs. He told us several stories about the farm, some of which I knew to be true, while others had the distinct flavour of local folklore. Being a "townie," I was subjected to more jibs and jabs than the others.

Upon arriving at the location of the farm, I was immediately disappointed. There was no haunted house, no barns — they had all fallen down years ago. There were just indentations in the ground where they once stood. As I wandered about the area, I tried to reconstruct the strange occurrences of the winter of 1922. I did not experience anything "eerie" (which I was well prepared for); it just appeared to be another old deserted plot of land that could be found in any rural area of Antigonish Country.

We were told by our guide, "Don't touch nothing." Having ventured to the area of mystery, it was my decision not to leave the old homestead without a souvenir, no matter how minuscule it might be. When no one was looking, I stuffed a piece of burnt shingle which I had dug up from around the foundation, into my back pocket. We finally completed our investigation of the area and boarded the Jeep for the trip back to the main road.

As we approached the half-way point in our journey to the main road, our guide stopped the Jeep and asked if anyone had taken anything from the farm. Not wanting to give up my souvenir and hoping that it was just a whim on his part, I immediately answered no. We then proceeded. As we drew nearer to the main road, the Jeep was once again stopped, and the same question was asked. Our guide was not satisfied with the answer of no, and refused to move. Without warning, he turned towards me and said, "Macintyre, you took something." Of course I remembered the shingle in my back pocket and produced it. The Jeep was turned around, and we returned to the farm, where I was asked to replace it, which I did.

Many would pass this off as normal, but to me it was a touch of the abnormal. I was pleased with the experience; at least I had something to tell about when I returned home. It was several years later, when I mentioned the occurrence to the noted folklorist C.I.N.MacLeod, that he stated some people had the "Celtic feeling," and when certain people visited such a location, they were able to draw out of the area a type of extrasensory perception. It appeared that our man from Roman Valley had that feeling and caused the return of my souvenir.

Evidently I did not learn my lesson....

*   *   *

It was probably the poltergeistic aspect of the Fire-Spook of Caledonia Mills, always in the back of my mind, that prompted me to chronicle the events that took place on the MacDonald homestead from 1899 to 1922. That aspect had to do with my last visit to the farm, the first week of May, 1971.

I was asked by one of the senior members of the Casket Printing and Publishing Company Ltd., Eileen Henry, to give her a tour of the Spook Farm. As it was ten years since I had visited the site, I was only too glad to oblige. Of course I wanted to see for myself the changes that had taken place in the area during the past decade.

On a sunny, Saturday afternoon, we parked the car at the end of the lane heading up to the farm. It was considerably more difficult to find the actual site as it had grown over. However, after some misses, we arrived at the precise location where the house once stood. I gave Mrs. Henry an impromptu tour of the area and reconstructed some of the events that had taken place some fifty years previous. Of course, I added a few stories that were well-laced with local folklore. I remember Eileen distinctly hanging on to my arm all the way back to the car.

I could not resist the temptation to dig about a bit in the area of the old foundation. To my surprise I came across an old-fashioned, hand-painted egg cup that had resisted the test of years underneath a board.

I should have learned from my experience years earlier — the shingle episode — and left well enough alone, but for me the temptation was too great. I placed the egg cup carefully in my pocket, and took it away from the homesite of Alexander "Black John" MacDonald. That evening, after returning to Antigonish, I drove down to our summer farmhouse at Frog Hollow. When I arrived I realized that I still had the egg cup in my pocket. I decided that a small shelf in the kitchen would be the proper resting place for my new-found treasure. I knew that it would be a good conversation piece, and on many occasions late at night would lend itself to a good ghost story. However, this was not to be.

On the Victoria Day weekend, a few Saturdays later, I held the first gathering of the summer season at the farmhouse. The Saturday night affair was enlivened by the addition of the egg cup. The result was that numerous stories were told of Mary Ellen the Spook. Of course, as the evening wore on (as well as the refreshments), the stories got better and spookier. It seemed that the egg cup was the centre of attraction that evening.

Around 1:30 a.m., my guests began to leave, and by 2:00 a.m. there remained myself and two friends to help clean up. It would have been about 2:45 a.m. when we finished — dishes were done, ashtrays emptied, fires put out, *et al*. A suggestion was made by Dubie that rather than go back to town we stay the night at the house, as it was quite late (early) and we were all well "under the weather." I remember that I was quite adamant about the fact that the beds would be damp and we would "catch our death" if we stayed the night. As I had the only transportation back to town, my friends had to concede and return to town with me. Was it some premonition on my part that we did not stay in the house that night, or was it that I was just plain scared that we would "catch our death"?

Three and a half hours later, at 6:15 a.m., I returned to Frog Hollow, as Antigonish Harbour was popularly known. The only thing left standing of the once-lovely old farmhouse was the chimney. It had burnt to the ground! Would we have "caught our death" if we had stayed the night?

INCIDENT AT ONION LAKE

This account is quite disturbing.

It was sent to me in 1990 in response to my request, carried by *The Thunder Bay Chronicle-Journal* and other weekly papers across the country, for first-person accounts of "extraordinary experiences."

Its author, whom I have identified as W.A., is a resident of Thunder Bay, Ont. It is not pleasant reading.

In 1966, June 30th, my husband aged 55, my son aged 13, and I myself aged 45, went fishing 20 miles from home at Onion Lake — a very remote lake with a gravel pit which is kind of hard to get to because of a poor road. We had a reliable truck, a half-ton, with a camper on back — a 1940 truck. My son was smart, excellent student, with a winning personality — high I.Q. and a perfect person.

The sky was clear as we started out at 11:00 p.m., hoping to sleep in the camper and then spend the morning fishing. The sky was clear all the way. We arrived at the spot and we decided to spend the night in the gravel pit. No one else was there — we had the whole lake to ourselves. We were just about to climb into the back camper when we were engulfed in a total, complete darkness and stillness. Not a tree rustled — nothing except a grinding noise that ws intermittent. I was scared stiff — I had never had such an experience. There was a strange smell like that of carborundum rubbing on steel — I had never smelled that before or since. Then all of a sudden my son completely disappeared — no sound of him walking away. I called and called and tried to look and my husband did the same, but everything was so black — couldn't even see any sky at all — just like we were in a bowl of blackness. It seemed like years but I guess it was about 15 minutes — all of a sudden my son appeared as if out of nowhere again — very agitated. He said he had seen a plane, saucer-shaped with red-and-blue lights, and went over toward it, and doesn't remember anything else. We tried to start the truck and there was no spark — the first time the battery was ever dead inall the ten years e had owned it and there was no reason for it to be dead, because we didn't have a radio, hearter or lights on.

But my son was never the same — he had lost hi mind!

He has been in a mental hospital ever since and i still there — so ill that even with the mass exodus of patients from mental hospitals during the last year he has to remain. He has a round mark on his left leg nea his ankle about the size of a dime like a vaccinatio mark which came that night and the scar is still there.

My son had all the great potential of being prim minister or someone great because he was well read very obedient, very intelligent. Now he's a complete vegetable, unable to speak or hear. My sorrow has bee great, as people blame me — I won't go near Onio Lake again.

I feel that you will tell me if you know of anyone els who has had similar sad experiences. I've cried and cried for 23 years. My son is now 36 years old. Hi whole life is ruined, and mine and my husband's also I can't tell this story to anyone but you and it's so true What an expensive fishing trip.

THE FALCON LAKE ENCOUNTER

The Falcon Lake Encounter is the name given to the sighting of two unidentified flying objects from Manitoba's Falcon Lake Provincial Park on May 20, 1967. More information is available on this incident than on any other UFO sighting reported in Canada. There is also about the episode the suggestion of lingering menace.

The sole observer of the two UFOs was Stephen Michalak, a fifty-one-year-old Polish Canadian. Later that year Michalak offered the following account of himself: "In 1949 I came to Canada, and some years later, settled in Winnipeg, Manitoba. I live with my wife, two sons and a daughter in a modest home. I have a steady income from my job as a mechanic at the Inland Cement Company. Two of my children attend the University of Manitoba. We live a happy, satisfied life of average Canadians, fully enjoying all the blessings this country is offering us."

It was Michalak's passion for amateur prospecting that took him that weekend to Falcon Lake. What he saw that Saturday is open to interpretation. What is laudable and sincere is his desire to tell others what he witnessed and what he felt about the experience. His account appeared in a privately printed, forty-page booklet titled *My Encounter with the UFO* (1967). Michalak wrote about his experiences in Polish; the manuscript was translated and printed for private distribution by his friend Paul Pihichyn.

There were unexpected consequences from the sighting. The encounter left Michalak, as he wrote, "desperately in need of medical attention." He suffered nausea and first-degree burns on his chest. He was admitted to the Misericordia Hospital in Winnipeg, his first hospital treatment for recurring, sighting-related health problems. This did not deter him from leading investigators to the exact spot where the sighting had taken place. "Landing traces" were found there. Earth analysis showed "some radiation but not enough to be dangerous."

The case was widely reported by the media. There were investigations by the RCMP and the RCAF, by representatives of the National Research Council and the Atomic Energy Commission, as well as by the Aerial Phenomena Research Organization. A question about the government's silence connected with the case was asked in the House of Commons by Ed Schreyer, then a Member of Parliament, not yet the Governor General. The Minister of National Defence replied, "It is not the intention of the Department of National Defence to make public the report of the alleged sighting."

The full story of the Falcon Lake Encounter will not be known until Chris Rutkowski, the Winnipeg-based UFO researcher and investigator, publishes his study of the episode. Even then there will be aspects of the story that will never be explained to everybody's satisfaction.

It was 5:30 a.m. when I left the motel and started out on my geological trek. I took with me a hammer, a map, a compass, paper and pencil and a little food to see me through the day, — wearing a light jacket against the morning chill.

The day was bright, sunny — not a cloud in the sky. It seemed like just another ordinary day, but events which were to take place within the next six hours were to change my entire life more than anyone could ever imagine. I will never forget May 20, 1967.

Crossing the Trans-Canada Highway from the motel on the south side, I made my way into the bush and the pine forest on the north side. After travelling some distance I got out my map and compass and orientated myself.

By 9 o'clock I had found an area that particularly fascinated me because of the rock formation near a bog along a stream flowing in the southward direction. I was searching for some specimens that I had found on my earlier expedition.

My approach had startled a flock of geese, but before long they became accustomed to my presence, quieted down and went about their business.

At 11 o'clock I began to feel the effects of the breakfast I did not eat that morning. I sat down and took out the lunch I had brought with me. Following a simple meal of smoked sausage, cheese and bread, an apple and two oranges washed down with a couple of cups of coffee, and after a short rest, I returned to the quartz vein I was examining. It was 12:15, the sun was high in the sky and a few clouds were gathering in the west.

While chopping at quartz I was startled by the most uncanny cackle of the geese that were still in the area. Something had obviously frightened them far more than my presence earlier in the morning when they gave out with a mild protest.

Then I saw it. Two cigar-shaped objects with humps on them about half-way down from the sky. They appeared to be descending and glowing with an intense scarlet glare. As these "objects" came closer to the earth they became more oval-shaped.

They came down at the same speed keeping a constant distance between them, appearing to be as one inseparable unit, yet each one completely separate from the other.

Suddenly the farthest of the two objects — farthest from my point of vision — stopped dead in the air while its companion slipped down closer and closer to the ground and landed squarely on the flat top of a rock about 159 feet away from me.

The "object" that had remained in the air hovered approximately fifteen feet above me for about three minutes, then lifted up skyward again.

As it ascended its colour began to change from bright red to an orange shade, then to a grey tone. Finally, when it was just about to disappear behind the gathering clouds, it again turned bright orange.

The "craft," if I may be allowed to call it a craft, had appeared and disappeared in such a short time that it was impossible to estimate the length of the time it remained visible. My astonishment at and fear of [the] unusual sight that I had just witnessed dulled my senses and made me lose all realization of time.

I cannot describe or estimate the speed of the ascent because I have seen nothing in the world that moved so swiftly, noiselessly, without a sound.

Then my attention was drawn back to the craft that had landed on the rock. It too was changing in colour, turning from red to grey-red to light grey and then to the colour of hot stainless steel, with a golden glow around it.

I realized that I was still kneeling on the rock with my small pick hammer in my hand. I was still wearing goggles which I used to protect my eyes from the rock chips.

After recovering my composure and regaining my senses to some degree I began watching the craft intently, ready to record in my mind everything that happened.

I noticed an opening near the top of the craft and a brilliant purple light pouring out of [the] aperture. The light was so intense that it hurt my eyes when I looked at it directly. Gripped with fear and excitement, I was unable to move from the rock. I decided to wait and watch.

Soon I became aware of wafts of warm air that seemed to come out in waves from the craft, accompanied by [the] pungent smell of sulphur. I heard a soft murmur, like the whirl of a tiny electric motor running very fast. I also heard a hissing sound as if the air had been sucked into the interior of the craft.

It was now that I wanted a camera more than anything else, but, of course, there is no need for one on a geological expedition. Then I remembered the paper and pencil that I had brought with me. I made a sketch of what I saw.

By now some of the initial fear had left me and I managed to gather enough courage to get closer to the craft and to investigate. I fully expected someone to get out at any moment and survey the landing site.

Because I had never seen anything like this before, I thought it may have been an American space project of some sort. I checked for the markings of the United States Air Force on the hull of the craft, but found nothing.

I was most interested in the flood of lights that poured out of the upper reaches of the craft. The light, distinctly purple, also cast out various other shades. In spite of the bright midday sun in the sky, the light cast a purple hue on the ground and eclipsed the sunlight in the immediate area.

I was forced to continually turn my eyes from the light which made red dots to appear before my eyes every time I looked away.

I approached the object closer, coming to within 60 feet of the glowing mass of material. Then I heard voices. They sounded like humans, although somewhat muffled by the sounds of the motor and the rush of air that was continuously coming out from somewhere inside. I was able to make out two distinct voices, one with a higher pitch than the other.

This latest discovery added to my excitement and I was sure that the craft was of an earthly origin. I came even closer and beckoned to those inside:

"Okey, Yankee boys, having trouble? Come on out and we'll see what we can do about it."

There was no answer and no sign from within. I had prepared myself for some response and was taken aback when none came. I was at a loss, perplexed. I didn't know what to do next.

But then, more to encourage myself than anything else, I addressed the voices in Russian, asking them if they spoke Russian. No answer. I tried again in German, Italian, French and Ukrainian. Still no answer.

Then I spoke again in English and walked closer to the craft.

By now I found myself directly in front of it and decided to take a look inside. However, standing within the beam of light was too much for my eyes to bear. I was forced to turn away. Then, placing green lenses over my goggles, I stuck my head inside the opening.

The inside was a maze of lights. Direct beams running in horizontal and diagonal paths and a series of flashing lights, it seemed to me, were working in a random fashion, with no particular order or sequence.

Again I stepped back and awaited some reaction from the craft. As I did this I took note of the thickness of the walls of the craft. They were about 20 inches thick at the cross-section.

Then came the first sign of motion since the craft touched down.

Two panels slid over the opening and a third piece dropped over them from above. This completely closed off the opening in the side of the craft.

Then I noticed a small screen pattern on the side of the craft. It seemed to be some sort of ventilation system. The screen openings appeared to be about 3/16 of an inch in diameter.

I approached the craft one again and touched its side. It was hot to the touch. It appeared to be made of a stainless steel-like substance. There were no signs of welding or joints to be seen anywhere. The outer surface was highly polished and looked like coloured glass with light reflecting off it. It formed a spectrum with a silver background as the sunlight hit the sides.

I noticed that I had burned my glove I was wearing at the time, when I touched the side of the craft.

These most recent events occurred in less time than it takes to describe them.

All of a sudden the craft tilted slightly leftward. I turned and felt a scorching pain around my chest; my shirt and my undershirt were afire. A sharp beam of heat had shot from the craft.

I tore off my short and undershirt and threw them to the ground. My chest was severely burned.

When I looked back at the ship I felt a sudden rush of air around me. The craft was rising above the treetops. It began to change colour and shape, following much the same pattern as its sister ship when it had returned to the sky. Soon the craft had disappeared, gone without a trace.

UFO MIND TRANSPLANT

Winifred G. Barton attracted newspaper headlines in the 1960s and 1970s when she travelled across the country conducting metaphysical workshops and collecting accounts of the paranormal. She edited a collection of "extraordinary experiences" called *Psychic Phenomena in Canada* (Ottawa: Psi-Science Productions Ltd., 1967). The appearance of her book predated the well-heralded advent of the so-called New Age; newspaper editors had not yet turned their editorial attention to spiritual and metaphysical adventures.

Mrs. Barton dropped out of the headlines and many people assumed that she had left for greener pastures or gone beyond the veil or passed into the great beyond or entered into a nunnery of some sort or other. But the writer Michael Poulton discovered her — through a classified advertisement in the "National Personals" of *The Globe and Mail!*

It turns out that what happened to Mrs. Barton is much more exciting than any of the statements above. It seems that she had a "close encounter" with alien intelligences and that she was abducted by alien beings and taken aboard one of their star ships. As she explained in a letter to the present editor, dated 25 April 1991:

I was abducted on September 26, 1973, and was taken "through the mirror." The next 17 years were spent in getting an intensive education. I was caught between dimensions, locked into a scenario over which I had no control. My psyche alternated between experiencing the heights of heaven and the depths of hell. It was like dying. Only now that I am fully "processed" as Biological Mutant can I come back to tell about it.

At one time Mrs. Barton ran the Institute of Applied Metaphysics (I AM). Generally addressed as Dr. Barton, she currently lives near Frankford, Ont., where she serves as public-relations officer for the Golden Triangle UFO Club for Ontario.

I Had a Mind Transplant on a UFO

Against my will, and without any anaesthetic, I had a mind reversal on a UFO. It happened during and in the period following an abduction on the evening of September 26, 1973, at the Lester B. Pearson Peace Park, at Actinolite, Ontario.

It had been a glorious autumn day. I was with a group of friends who had gathered from many parts of Canada and the U.S.A. to enjoy the end of the summer season. We were using the old Madoc Art School which sits at the foot of the hill next to the Peace Park.

The Peace Pagoda was a favourite place for our evening meetings, but on this particular night a sudden heavy mist seemed to envelop the area. The mist did not seem like a normal mist; it seemed to have a silvery glow as if there was a light behind it. I went to investigate and as I walked up the hill, pieces of the mist seemed to break away from the mass and coagulate into the forms of beings.

Nothing touched me but I felt a powerful magnetic attraction to continue towards the central glow. As I got closer I saw in it the outline of a Starship. I could hear some of my friends calling out to one another as they too were drawn towards the celestial car.

My will to resist was completely paralyzed. The hatch was down and I went into the foyer where I vaguely saw some of my friends being led to different rooms or parts of the ship. I was taken to a large circular room — a translucent aqua colour — with two transparent doors set approximately opposite each other. Through these I could see that there was an outer walkway which seemed to go right around the room. I coud see a woman sitting at a communications desk through one of these windows.

In the beginning I was alone in the room. I felt no sense of fear, only curiosity. There was a large circular lazy-susan type table in the centre of the room with chairs around it. I sat on one of these. There was a bowl of fruit — small berry-type fruit on the table. I was tempted to eat some but decided it was best not to.

A man came into the room from the opposite door to where the woman was sitting. (I guessed she was keeping an eye on me through the door.) The man barely glanced in my direction but walked straight across the room to what seemed like a circular shower stall, where he dropped off his dirty overalls and stepped into the stall which lit up. He emerged a few moments later and put on clean clothes.

Books I have written clearly record how since infancy I was trained in telepathic communication. So though no words were spoken, I had no difficulty in communicating with this Space Being. He offered some of the fruit. This time I took it and ate. It was like mango.

I could sense this man was trying to override my free will. At first I firmly resisted. Then they changed my electro-magnetic circuit from Alternating to Direct Current. I emerged as a circuit in a *Gigantic Robot* known as "Hal." I was wide awake but completely paralyzed during the proceedings. There were about thirty other persons beside me.

Now everything looks transparent. Form and finity is meaningless. It was as if my bony skull was replaced and my head put into a glass bubble. As a circuit in this *Giant Robot* I was powerless to escape over a fifteen-year period. If I struggled they prodded my neurons here and there with electrical sticks....

When I returned, just before noon on the morning of September 27th, 1973, I was no longer "Winifred." I was "Sasoleah," a citizen of Sumeria who had reincarnated in the 20th century through my physical instrument.

The same thing had happened to at least twenty of the other abductees. All had undergone some sort of a transmutation technique and mind transplant. All were trapped in the world of Robotics. Each had been given a silent mission. Each brain had been joined to an ancient personality. Each one was under total mind control and forced to keep the intruding ancient soul a secret.

Over the next decade the abductees got to talking about their "inductees" and how we found that "aliens" were actually ancient peoples who had completed a Universal cycle and were coming back to claim the modern world. They had left overwhelming mounds of evidence to prove this point ... "That the sower and the reaper may rejoice together in the New Heaven and the New Earth on the completion of the life cycle Genesis I — from chaos to cosmos via Robotics."

One of my fellow abductees was a man from Ottawa named Marcel Lafleur whom I had known for some years. After the operation we watched the whole scenery around us being torn down like a ragged canvas. The colours behind the canvas were brilliant. We understood that it is only the light energy of the real world shining through the web of matter that makes the holograph on our mirror world of the illusion tick.

Lafleur drove me home. We were both in a state approaching incoherence. He drove into the driveway of my home at 3045 Otterson Drive, in Ottawa, but I did not recognize the house. When I got in the house, I felt exactly like a stranger walking in for the first time. I could feel Sasoleah tapping Winifred's computer to find her way around. Sa was in total domination at this time.

About now I realized something else. "I" was neither of these two. I was an observer watching two actors using my mind. I watched them interacting, arguing points of logic, as they began to make an harmonic convergence in my mind. I understood the principle of the left- and right-hand sides of the brain being kept in perfect balance. One living in the finite now, the other accessing infinity. One bent on "rendering unto Caesar that which is Caesar's," the other committed to "and to God that which is God's."

But I am neither ... *I AM* ... My Divine Will is the Umpire between the two. I have watched Sasoleah writing "*I Am, The Book of Life,* using Winifred's professional skills. I look in one direction and see that Winifred has been held like a bond slave to serve the cause of Sasoleah and the Space People for eighteen years. In return, Winifred has been in an advanced interdimensional classroom wherein she received the full and complete knowledge of The Gods.

Winifred mostly ruled the daytime consciousness (Hadit). Sasoleah could flit all over the Universe at will and usually took over when the sun went down (Nuit). Sasoleah could work miracles with ease. For example, some fellow abductees took us on a fully paid, two-week trip to Egypt to celebrate the Equinox of The Gods. I knew nothing whatsoever about these people, nor they of me. That's what their instructions were and that's what they did. That's how the "COSMIC WAY COMMUNITY" operates. It's called spiritual humility.

Today the three of us are one. The actor and the observer function as an integrated unit. In physics this reads $(+ 1) + (- 1) = 0$ or $E = mc3$ — all of which is detailed with extensive diagrams in the *Cosmic Cube*.

Today, if I speak a word that is not the Triple Truth, I feel a tremendous weight on my heart and mind. I get rewarded with an inrush of light energy when I please "The Master's Will."

On the lowest end of the dimensional scale in some ways I am no more than a meticulously accurate translation device though my human emotions are still locked deep inside me. There are many more of us who have been stripped of our flesh-and-blood kinship connections and locked into the ETI system of the "Mighty Ones" which makes us "Walk-ins" or "Superbeings." It means we have 20/20 vision of the reality both above and below the abyss.

Earth Governments have maintained silence about this matter though they knew full well what was going on. They agreed to let us be used in a potentially diabolical experiment in return for hi-tec data. However, the "Time Bomb" is about to explode and the story is due to climax in a wonderful state of Millennium for the whole Earth Starship as She slips out of the time warp to regain her rightful place in the Cosmic Fleet.

Yes, there is a Cosmic Conspiracy — yes, there has been a deliberate conspiracy of silence on the part of global governments everywhere. Yes, there is a flip to Millennium. Yes, there is a Cosmic Changeover for the whole earth system. Yes, the ultimate outcome is GOOD!

CONTACT

Oscar Magocsi (1928-2002) was born in Hungary, came to Canada in 1957, and worked as an electronics technician. As a youngster he was interested in flying saucers (the term in the 1940s for what came to be called in the 1950s unidentified flying objects or UFOs). He claimed that he was contacted by alien beings in 1975, when he was taken aboard one of their flying saucers after it landed in Muskoka, Ont. Then he was taken for a visit to the aliens' home planet "Argona" in the "Omm-Onn system, a member of the Psychean Federation Worlds." Magocsi's account of his travels appeared in his breathlessly written, 146-page memoir titled *My Space Odyssey in UFOs* (Toronto: Quest Group Publications, 1st ed., 1979; 2nd ed., 1980; 3rd ed., 1985). "Contact," the title of Chapter Three of that publication, is reproduced here.

What effect did the experience have on the contactee? A note attached to the publication explains it was all to the good: "Due to my experiences with the aliens and their effect on me, I became more spiritually oriented and psychically more aware, strongly life-affirming and as a result—better balanced, happier and luckier."

A discussion of Magocsi's contribution to contactee literature appears in my book *UFOs over Canada* (1991).

That summer of '75 I arranged to take two weeks' vacation starting with the end of July. I planned to spend most of that time at my Muskoka lot, in the hope of some revealing UFO encounters. Therefore, right after a friend's wedding, later Sunday afternoon, July 27, I was on my way driving towards Huntsville.

I arrived at my lot by sunset, when most cottagers for the weekend only had already left for Toronto. There was enough time left before darkness to unload my camping gear and to gather enough firewood for the night vigil. I was quite determined to be up all night till the "wee" hours of the morning. Then I could still sleep

until noon, and go to some nearby beach if the day became too hot. It was good to be back in nature after a long winter and with half summer already gone. Somehow I never got around to come up here since last Fall, except for one short and uneventful trip in May.

It was already dark and the stars were shining brightly, when I finally lit up my campfire. The night was dry, but not too warm. I had to wear my long-sleeved sweater as I sat on the stool by the fire, at the pile of wood, stacked within arm's reach. Mentally, I recalled the whole chain of strange events that led me up to this point, making me trust a stranger's word for some UFO experiences about to come. I still wondered about it. I hadn't seen Quentin, or Steve, since. I hadn't had any new dramatic encounters either, not even dreams or hunches. The last few months this whole UFO topic had faded into insignificance, as if it was unreal somehow.

Nevertheless, I still enjoyed sitting out by the fire, the same way I had done it many times before. Around 02:30 hours though, I felt tiredness creeping up more and more on me. Since there were no UFOs about, not even a hint of a sensation, I decided to turn in for the night.

Next day, after sunset I walked up to the ridge to my "eerie" twilight magic spot. Barely five minutes after I got there, a wave of excitement hit me all of a sudden. I just knew positively that I would have a UFO experience that night!

I am at total loss to explain how this strong conviction came to me. One second I still felt pleasantly blank, the next second I knew "they" were on their way to transit into this dimension, and some time that night I'd be visited by a UFO. There wasn't even a pulsating glow in my mind, yet I knew they were coming and that there were only a few more hours left before actual show-up time.

I walked back slowly to my lot and lit the campfire. The vigil part ended, it was just a matter of some waiting.

It was shortly after midnight, when I began to feel that the UFO already was very close. Few minutes later, I thought I saw a faint pulsating orange glow briefly. Whether I saw it in the sky or in my mind, I wasn't sure. But I was sure that this signal was directed at me, as a form of making me aware. A strange notion struck me: if this was their first deliberate signal, then how did I know hours earlier about their coming? Was it possible that I became more sensitive, no more passive telepathic subject any longer, but an activated mind "sniffing" way ahead? Or had my "eerie" twilight spot something to do with it, like triggering my knowing somehow? It was all very intriguing, especially with this new angle added to it.

I stopped feeding the campfire, and backed away from it to probe the vast expanse of the sky overhead. Soon enough I perceived the approach pattern of some blinking orange light on a zig-zag course. It didn't behave like an aircraft, besides there was no engine noise. It kept disappearing, but kept converging on my hill. For a full two minutes it was blinked out of sight;

then it got magically materialized out of nowhere, less than a few hundred feet away from me and close to the tree-top level, glowing orange, a disc-like shape.

I got on top of my observation deck, well away from the slowly dying campfire. From this vantage point I had an unobstructed view across the valley. Also, I was fully engulfed by the darkness, which made me invisible to nay observer farther than a few feet away. Then I raised both my arms and waved towards the motionless distant glowing of the disc.

The glow blinked twice, as if to acknowledge my signal of being aware of it. Although I half expected the blinking response, it still surprised me that the UFO could see me in the darkness from that distance.

Now the UFO started to pulsate in a slow manner, and I sensed that I was being probed to the core of my mind. This went on for about ten minutes, while the cycling pulsations nearly put me into a pleasant drowsiness of some hypnotic trance. To check if my conscious will was still functioning, I climbed down to the smouldering campfire momentarily, then climbed back on the platform. Well, it worked, but I don't know if it really proved anything.

Soon after my exercise, the disc stopped its pulsations, changed its colour into steady greenish and started moving in my general direction. Rising up higher, it swam slowly past me almost overhead with a faint purring sound, heading somewhere beyond the ridge towards "no man's land"! My eyes kept following it, trying to make out its detail. But all I could see was just a hazy glow of an oval shape that became circular when passing overhead. I couldn't detect its source of illumination: the whole disc was just one big blob of yellow-green luminous glow. Only the centre core of its underbelly, like a hole in a doughnut, pulsated with some blue light.

After the disc went out of sight beyond the ridge, I stayed another few minutes in the dark, in case it came back again. But somehow I knew it wouldn't, for it just must have landed in "no man's land," possibly waiting there for my move. Even though I became aware of a gentle pull in that direction as if telepathically induced, I was quite ready to go and see on my own, too.

I put the dying fire out, grabbed my flashlight and took off on foot for the logging road that led into "no man's land." The night was quiet, the few cottages this side of the turn-off were dark. No one seemed to be up. Other than me, perhaps no one even saw the UFO.

It took me a good minute's walk to reach the general

area where the UFO might have landed. At a familiar turn of the logging road, I came up on a big clearing, close to my "power" magic spot.

And there it was! What a dramatic moment! Not more than about sixty feet fro me, a realy flying saucer was moving in the air just a few feet above the ground. I guessed its size for roughly thirty feet in diameter and ten feet in "thickness." It was bathed in a diffused, greenish-blush and soft-glowing luminosity that was radiating from its entire surface rather than coming from points of light. There were two porthole-like, dark oval spots resembling a pair of eyes. On its top there was a bubble-dome-like turret, on its underside there were some ball-like bulges that suggested a landing gear.

There I stood frozen in my tracks, by a clump of trees in the darkness. I was very much excited, but also very nervous with unknown fears. What a magnificently thrilling sight I beheld! This was the living proof of intelligent, extraterrestrial life. For I had no doubt that this flying saucer was from outer space. Possibly even from another dimension, as Quentin claimed, but certainly not of Earthly origin.

At this moment, as if trying to prove the point, the saucer started to fade away without moving its position. Then "presto!" and it was gone with a peculiar sighing sound as if the air moved into its place. I shone my flashlight through the spot, but found nothing. The saucer went totally invisible....

Then, within a few moments, a very faint glow came from the same empty space, solidfying slowly back into the flying saucer again. It was very dramatic! After all, it was quite true about fading out of this dimension and fading back again.

This time the saucer gently lowered itself to the ground, into a real landed position. Then it stood there motionless, soundless — just like I stood farther away, frozen and breathless. No one came out of the sucer; it just sat there patiently, as if waiting for me. Somehow I knew that it actually was waiting for me, but I just oculd not make myself move. I was simply terrified to go near, that's all. Recalling a few speculations I read of sinister alien motives, my mind was working overtime. I guessed if the saucer wanted to, it could have attempted to draw me hypnotically towards itself. But there were no such indications; it seemed my move had to be made entirely of my own free will. For without my moving, there was no other way to learn more. It was as simple as that.

Finally, I decided to take the risk: with cold swea breaking out all over me, I walked up to the saucer!

After some hesitation, I poked at its hull with my rubberized flashlight. The hull felt more like fiberglas than metal, yet emanating some heat like the hood of a car in hot summer. Next, I pressed my cigarette pape back to the pull for a second to guess at the surface temperature. My pack just got warmer, but did not ge burned; yet I didn't feel like touching it with my bare hand.

I found the saucer's actual size to be about thirty-five feet in diameter, ten feet high from top to bottom, plus another two feet perhaps for the upper dome. I guessed its true colour for light grey. I walked around it a few times, looking for some door, or some indication of an opening. There were none. Equally set apart around the circumference, there were three oval-shaped portholes. I couldn't peek through them, for they were above my eye-level, as the saucer squatted on three ball-like protrusions that raised its bottom about three feet from the rocky ground. There would be no marks left by the landing gear on that rock; so far I didn't detect any burn marks, either. Yet there was the definite smell of ozone, as if some high-voltage corona discharge was being produced by the saucer's hull. Maybe it was wise not to touch.

By now I was considerably calmer, although still on the jittery side. Satisfied with my close-up survey of the exterior, I backed away thirty feet or so, wondering about further developments — if any.

Less than a minute, there came the new development and a rather dramatic one at that! A three-foot-long horizontal crack appeared and widened into a closed mouth-like slot, well under the line of portholes and between two of them. Then the slot started to widen vertically, as if a gigantic mouth was opening up. Finally, it formed itself into a man-sized open doorway, while a short walk-up ramp got lowered from it to the ground. Soft yellow light spilled out from the interior invitingly.

I nearly took to my feet in a momentary panic. Then I took a grip on myself, and decided facing the aliens to come out of the saucer. Or else I'd never see one. This venture wasn't exactly for faint hearts, I thought. So braced myself for my first alien encounter, and waited....

Finally, I realized that there would be no aliens coming out. There were no telepathic proddings or hint coming, either. The saucer was just sitting there blankly. Were the occupants incapacitated? Or were they some immobile life-form? Somebody had to be here inside; otherwise who did all the signalling, the telepathic probing earlier, not mentioning the piloting of the craft itself, the fade-out, the door-opening? I felt rather confused.

I edged up near the doorway for a peek inside. But this didn't give me a clue, for a partition behind the door prevented my looking into the interior. obviously, I had to take another risk, and a tremendous risk this time: Since no one was coming out, I should go in and see for myself. Yet, only heaven knew what manner of alien monsters could be waiting in there! Besides, what about radiation, toxic air, or other harmful substances? Well, there was only one way to find it out....

I summoned up my courage, and with a deep breath, I went up the ramp. Then I stepped onto the inner platform within the doorway, finding that there was no partition at all. It was only a curtain of yellow light, which had created the illusion of a wall from the ground at that angle. The square of the platform was illuminated, but the interior was shrouded in darkness. I tried my flashlight — it didn't work.

I hesitated for a moment, then took a couple of steps into the unlit area. My weight on the floor must have activated built-in sensors, for some blue-green glow sprang up all around me, illuminating most of the interior.

At first glance everything looked incomprehensibly alien. But I had no time to look more, for a subtle noise behind made me turn around fast. It was the doorway closing down. Sudden panic seized me, it was a wonder I didn't have a heart attack! Good heavens, I was captive. The closing crack sealed itself into one seamless wall, making me stare paralyzed at it.

Then I tried to calm down. Perhaps this was just another automatic piece of function — once the occupant was inside, the door just got shut by itself. I stepped back on the paltform and waited. Nothing. Meanwhile, I noticed one shaft of white light shooting down vertically from the ceiling, slightly to the left. I had a hunch this could be the door-opening activator. So I stuck my insulated rubber flashlight through the beam, and it did the trick — the door started to open up.

Just to make sure, I stepped out momentarily into the night, then back again, making the door close. I repeated the procedure to put my mind at ease. Then I started to look for some manual back-up system for the door-opener, in case something went wrong with the light. I never trusted a fully automatic gadget, and felt safer if I found some manual override. Slightly to the right where the door should have been, I found a fist-sized indentation in the wall. I poked my flashlight into it, which made the door open again. It had to be similar to a spring-loaded activator, which was the next best thing to a manual crank. I just wondered who or what made the door open in the first place, while I still had been outside, for I had the feeling that the saucer was devoid of any creatures.

Feeling much calmer now, I turned back to the interior for a close examination. My eyes were first attracted to a three-foot diameter globe hanging at eye-level. It was suspended in the saucer's centre, inside a transparent vertical tubing that connected the domed porthole in the ceiling to an identically shaped porthole in the floor.

The synthetic material of the floor was pearl-greyish and honeycomb patterned, as if a conglomeration of battery cells. Three curved sections of benches that resembled soap-stone Eskimo sculptures were ringing the vertical tube. There was a circular railing of bone-like material that girdled the tube, convenient to grip if one was seated on the bench. Very handy in a turbulent flight for humanoids, or even for any creature with arm-like appendages. At least the saucer's interior walls were designed for transporting some manner of creatures. This seemed a reassuring thought, even if there was nobody home momentarily. Or maybe the occupants were just out on some business, liable to return soon; though somehow this line of thought did not make sense in view of the events that got me inside here.

All this left only one possibility — the saucer was a robot vehicle, an unmanned probe, or rather "manned" by some kind of a programmed computer — or remote-controlled by some unseen intelligence, perhaps through a built-in computerized system.

I found nothing, though, that would even vaguely resemble some computer system. Unless if it was built in a completely alien manner, inconceivable to my earthly framework of possible technologies. There was no electronic gear or other gadgetry in sight. Therefore, it had to be a vastly different type of technology behind all this — if it was technology at all!

That thought gave me a shiver, as I was scrutinizing the "suspended" huge ball in a vertical plastic tubing. Inside the globe itself, there were myriads of flickering lights in swirling patches of multi-coloured mists, as if some artist's conception to show a three-dimensional visual model of a supermind's functioning. Of which I had no doubt it was — either a living intelligence, or the strangest computer.

I tried to poke my flashlight through the plastic tubing-like shaft of light. I met a soft, but firm resistance of a flexible shield, which would yield only so far. Apparently, it was a force-field that acted like a protective tubing. And inside it, perhaps the shaft of light was what held the globe suspended at my eye level. I noticed some very faint vertical *"flow lines,"* or traces of energy flow taking place within the shaft. As I turned away, my left hand accidentally bumped into the force-field. Much to my relief, there was no adverse effect, just a touch of silky but firm resistance.

I looked up on the gently domed ceiling — there was a wall-to-wall spiral that centered on the tubing like a gigantic heating element, made of shiny gold-looking material. Another energy device, I guessed, perhaps in conjunction with the vertical tube that centred on the globe. Or vice-versa. Who knows?

I turned my attention to the circular wall. The blank space for the sealed doorway was flanked on both sides by huge, semi-curved bulges from floor to ceiling — perhaps some storage tanks or cabinets that I could see no doors for. Each bulge was followed by one porthole, with the third porthole being on the opposite wall section. They were equally spaced apart, slightly oval and about three feet in diameter. Then there were two towering *"instrument"* slabs jutting out from blank wall spaces — one to my left and one to my right, each flanked by a gigantic 6 x 4 foot screen with some sofa under them. And that brought my survey around the wall to its completion....

Matter of fact, that completed my first preliminary survey of the whole interior, for the time being. All of a sudden, I felt the exhaustion, caused by my nervous tension weighing down on me. I wondered if I should get into a much more detailed scrutiny, or just....

At that moment, the ceiling spiral glowed up to an intense orange hue, and started to pulsate slowly. Panic seized me again — I felt a drastic change to come in the *"status quo,"* which I wasn't sure I wanted to face. Now, the shaft had energized, too — there was a strong downward flow of some currents taking place in it.

Maybe I'd better beat it, I thought, before this darned thing takes off with me, or brainwashes me, or disintegrates me, or who knows what. Fear won over the spirit of adventure — in a hurry, I activated the door opener — and it worked! I scrambled down the ramp, retreating to the edge of the clearing like a frightened deer. Or rather like a dumb bunny — but I just couldn't help my reaction. I thought it would be wildly humorous, if a hidden onlooker now took me for a scary alien out to eat him, or something.

But there was nothing out there (or ran away and dropped dead since), except the darkness and the bush. I stopped and turned around.

The saucer glowed orange pulsatingly for a short while. Then it retracted the ramp and sealed its door. Now it changed its light into a steady greenish-blue, and started to lift off the ground. It rose slowly up and up, to a few hundred feet. I wondered what could be its driving force. Some kind of anti-gravity device? For I did not detect flame exhaust, compressed air, not even sound except a faint whirring noise.

Now the saucer blinked twice and flew away rapidly into a rising arc, soon going out of sight.

It seemed that my encounter was over. Yet, I stood there for quite a while in the completely dark woods, filled with awe and wonder, relief and regret, pride over my bold adventure, but shame over my cowardly running away. And also, I felt terribly tired, drained.

Time to turn in, I thought. So I slowly walked back through the woods to my lot....

A GIANT LIZARD WITH WINGS

"So now with thanks also to Prince George radio station CJCI for its taped interview with one of the men (referred to as X) in the highway incident, and to Adrienne Radford for serving as a helpful contact person, we carry the story of these remarkable northern sightings, realizing there almost certainly will be more."

So wrote former Ottawa newspaper correspondent John Magor in *Canadian UFO Report*, Summer 1977, about this so-called highway incident. This is a reference to a specific sighting amid a series of sightings of UFOs reported in the Summer of 1976 from the vicinity of Prince George, B.C.

Magor went on to reproduce the transcript of the station's interview with the driver of the truck who reported this strange encounter with an alien vehicle and its occupant. The experience even involves a loss of consciousness over a measurable period — a syndrome that has come to be known as "missing time."

The driver is identified as X. In a subsequent issue of *Canadian UFO Report*, Winter-Spring 1978, Magor, with permission, identified the informant as supermarket employee Kirk Alore. The episode occurred on Highway 16 between Prince George and Vanderhoof as Alore was *en route* to Fort St. James, early on the morning of July 5.

I am reproducing here, with slight editing, the transcript of the interview, followed by the substance of Magor's subsequent interview with Alore.

X: About a mile before it happened I looked at my watch and it was about ten past four. I was coming on to this straight stretch, and I noticed this red light in the sky, and I noticed this car coming towards me. Our cars were about three hundred yards apart when this red light dropped right out of the sky and started coming towards me. In panic I swerved and almost immediately this light was right on me and lit up the interior of my truck. My motor went dead and my radio went dead and I passed out. About four-thirty a guy was shaking me and said, "Are you all right?" I said, "Yes." Then he said, "A strange thing happened. I woke up outside my car." "Then what am I doing here?" I was on the passenger side of my truck and our cars were no more than two feet apart and there were no skid marks. And he said he passed out, too, and his motor died and his motor went all crazy.

Q: Could you describe the object you saw?

X: To me it looked like a giant lizard with wings, and it was a little over one and a half times the size of the road width.

Q: Did the object look foreign or like something we could build here on earth?

X: I don't think it was ike anything we could build. That's how strange it looked and that's what scared me. It didn't look like anything I had seen before, except maybe the lizard part. That's about the only thing I could relate it to.

Q: Did it have wings?

X: Yes, it did. They looked like frog legs spread out, with that gap in them.

Q: Do you remember seeing engines?

X: I don't remember anything like that but maybe on the back there was something. It was a round thing.

Q: What shape was the body?

X: It was oblong, and the outer surface reminded me of alligator skin. It was rough looking. On top there was a dome and that's where the light was coming from.

Q: Do you have a record of passing out?

X: No. I've never fainted before in my life.

Q: What sort of feeling did you have when you passed out in the car?

X: I felt as if there were a bunch of pins in me, and then I sort of went into nothing. The last thing I remember was my motor dying, my radio going funny and seeing this guy not more than a hundred yards away and heading straight for me. I was doing at least seventy miles per hour. I remember putting my foot on the brake but there were no skid marks.

Q: Had you been drinking?

X: No, not a bit. I had even pulled over to the side of the road farther south and had two or three hours sleep, so I was wide awake and had the radio on full blast.

Q: Do you believe in UFOs?

X: I do now. I didn't before but I do now.

* * *

I came up around a corner on the way from Prince George and noticed a red light about a mile away, to my right above some hydro towers. I just kept driving on and looking at it, and then I saw a car coming. He was about half a mile away. Then I noticed this red light move. I kept staring at it and it just sort of shot right over the top of the oncoming car.

I just stared at it in amazement. Then it shot towards me, when the oncoming car was about 300 yards away, and it was huge! It took up about two highway widths, and at that instant the red light lit up the interior of my cab and I got strange sensations, like my arms fell asleep and my legs fell asleep and they felt like pins and needles. Then I swerved and missed this thing because it was coming right towards me.

It all happened so fast I just don't remember anything after. I sort of blacked out, I guess. According to our watches it was 15 minutes later or so (making it about 4:30 a.m.) and this guy was opening my door and shaking me. He was asking if I was all right. I said, "Yes, I'm o.k., I guess." But I was sort of sick at the moment and was aching all over. My arms and everything were sore. Our cars were about two feet apart.

He said, "A strange thing happened to me. I was outside my car when I came to." We could find no skid marks and I was doing at least 70 miles an hour when I swerved into his lane.

We went to the hospital in Vanderhoof, both of us, and they checked us over and there was apparently just shock. That's all it was. I never did get the other guy's name.

Asked for a description of the object, Kirk replied:

It was oblong, the outer shell looked more or less like alligator skin. It had little protruding wings, except they were rounded. Underneath between the wings it had a circular thing, like an electric razor. You know, the discs? That's what it had underneath, one turning slowly inside the other, which was turning the other way. It had a dome on top with different coloured lights inside — green, red, yellow, blue, all like little dots. Then it had just one straight beam of red light when it shone the red light in my truck....

I could see everything in great detail.

THE "TWILIGHT ZONE" TRUCK STOP

"Visit to the 'Twilight Zone' Truck Stop" is the title of this account of an eerie experience. In this instance the "monster" is the atmosphere and the surroundings, the trip back in time and perhaps also in place, perhaps into another dimension, the truck stop that should not have been there at all. The experience itself evokes a sense of the decade of the 1960s and it does so in such detail that the event might well have been an episode of Rod Serling's long-running *Twilight Zone* television series. The reader visualizes it.

Yet whatever it was that sparked this shared experience, it occurred not in the 1960s but in the year 1978. It happened to Phyllis and Don Griffiths. Mrs. Griffiths sent me this account after she heard me talk about "extraordinary experiences" on CFAX Radio in Victoria, B.C.

"I have a story that you may wish to add to your files of strange experiences," she explained in her letter of 17 March 1989. "My husband and I refer to this as our 'twilight zone' visit. If it was a hallucination, then it is one that we both shared. The story is enclosed with this letter."

I first published Mrs. Griffiths' account in my book *Mysterious Encounters* (1990). Here it is again.

Sky Chief indeed!

In March of 1978, we were returning to our home in Lethbridge, Alberta, after spending Easter Week visiting relatives on Vancouver Island. This was a trip that the family had taken many times before, and the route we usually followed was first along Highway 1, the northern route, and then south from Calgary. This time, we decided, just for a change of pace, that we would take Highway 3. We had not taken this southern highway before when returning from Vancouver Island.

As usual with return trips, this one was to be driven

straight through. But the route was unfamiliar to us, and the southern route was taking much longer than the familiar, northern route. Our two young sons slept cuddled up to their dog in the back seat of the family station wagon. My husband and I drove through the night and into the ealry hours of the next day without a rest.

At two-thirty in the morning we drove into the town of Creston, B.C. The only place open at that early hour was a tiny service station, where we stopped to refuel the car. Tired as we were, we had no choice but to drive on. There was no money for a motel room, nor were there camp-grounds in the area.

Relief was found about half way between Creston and Cranbrook. It took the form of an old Texaco Truck Stop which we were approaching. It was on the north side of the highway, Highway 3, but it was located in the middle of nowhere. It was a totally unexpected sight, but a very welcome one.

The Texaco Truck Stop had an unusual location, but it also had an unusual appearance. The large old Texaco sign was a solid sign lit by spotlights mounted on top and focused on the painted surface. The gas pumps were also old-fashioned looking, and they dispensed good old Fire Chief and Sky Chief gasoline. There was a diesel pump at the side, but no pumps for unleaded gas were in sight.

The station itself looked as if it had not changed one bit since the year 1960. Even the semi-trailer unit, idling in the truck lot to one side, was of an early Sixties vintage. Everything looked strange indeed. Was this a scene from Rod Serling's *Twilight Zone*?

Nevertheless, my husband and I, tired and thirsty as we were, drove in, pulled up under the pump lights, got out of the car, and locked it. We left our two children asleep in the back seat of the car.

The inside of the restaurant matched the outside to such a degree that everything felt spooky. The interior was frozen in time in the year 1960, yet the decor showed none of the wear and tear that would be found after nearly twenty years of use. We could see nothing that was out of place. There was nothing new or modern about the appointments or the personnel. The waitress was dressed in period clothes, as was the driver of the

semi parked in the yard.

The price of the coffee was all of a dime a cup, and a placard advertised the price of a piece of pie as a quarter. The music blaring from the radio dated from the late Fifties, and the d.j. introduced the songs without once referring to the period or to any item of news. No calendar was in sight. But the coffee was good and was appreciated. We felt uneasy in the place, so we were not unhappy to be out and on the road for home once more.

We had driven this stretch of Highway 3 on previous occasions, but it had always been in daylight and heading in the other direction. We had never taken it at night or while returning from Vancouver Island. We had memorized the location of every truck stop on Highway 3, and we thought we knew the location of all the truck stops that were open twenty-four hours a day on this highway as well. But never before had we seen this one. Nor did we ever see it again.

The visit left us with an eerie feeling. Try as we might, we could not shake it off. We asked those of our friends and relatives who occasionally travelled that stretch of Highway 3 if they were familiar with the old Texaco Truck Stop. No one knew anything about it. Everyone was of the opinion that there was no such establishment between Lethbridge, Alta., and Hope, B.C.

The only thing that we could do was re-drive that stretch of highway in broad daylight and watch out for it to see for ourselves whether or not the place really existed. Some months later we did just that. We re-travelled Highway 3. Mid-way between Cranbrook and Creston, on the north side of the road, we found the place where we had stopped that eerie night.

The building had long been boarded over. The presence of the pumps was marked only by their cement bases. The same was true of the Texaco signpost. The yard where the semi had sat was overgrown with bush and with aspen poplars which were twenty or more feet in height. It had been many years since that particular service station had pumped gas or served coffee at a dime a cup. But my husband and I know that the old Truck Stop had been open for business that lonely March night in 1978, when a weary family had stopped — in need of a cup of coffee and a bit of rest.

ALIEN ABDUCTION

Ufology entered a new and dramatic phase in the 1980s when it was revealed to the public that there was a motive for and a method behind the UFO experience: Apparently alien beings were intent on abducting men and women at will and subjecting them to bizarre gynaecological examinations and procedures. This was the burden of books written by investigators like Budd Hopkins, Whitley Strieber, David Jacobs, and John Mack, which offered first-person accounts and arguments that everything could be explained by the knowledge that behind the seemingly random sightings of alien craft and contacts and abductions with alien beings was the production of "a new race." There were to be hybrid creatures, half-human, half-alien ... monsters if ever they existed.

Sceptics like Philip J. Klass would have none of it. In his analysis *UFO Abductions: A Dangerous Game* (Buffalo: Prometheus Books, 1989), Klass argued that the hypothesis was wrong and that there was no credible evidence that any of it had occurred. He noted that not one of the self-styled abductees bothered to report his or her "kidnapping" to the FBI, so he offered the sum of $10,000 as a reward to any victim of an abduction "providing the alleged abduction is reported to the Federal Bureau of Investigation and FBI investigation confirms that the kidnapping really occurred." Klass attached the following warning to his offer: "Anyone who knowingly reports a spurious kidnapping to the FBI is vulnerable to a $10,000 fine and up to five years in prison." To date Klass's reward has gone unclaimed.

In *UFO Aductions*, Klass described the appearance of two women who identified themselves as abductees on the *Oprah Winfrey Show* on May 22, 1987. One of the women was Constance Morgan, an aspiring New York actress; the other was Dorothy Wallis, a middle-aged woman from St. Catharines, Ont. Ms. Wallis was identified as one of the people who sought out Budd Hopkins for help and who subsequently made an appearance with Roy Bonisteel on CBC-TV's *Man Alive*. Ms. Wallis described a series of three abductions and the presence of a mysterious "implant" in her nostril. There was a third guest on the show that day and that was Klass himself. He represented the sceptical point of view. Here, in dialogue form, is the substance of the remarks made on that occasion by the Canadian abductee.

Winfrey asked Wallis if she had a number of alien abduction experiences or just one.

Wallis: "Yes — I've had a number of experiences. My first was when I was eight years old. I woke up about ll:00 p.m. with this compulsion to go down to a nearby field.... When I went out of the house, the clock said ll:00. So I went down, and in this field was a very bright light, obviously shining out of a doorway. And there was this huge craft behind it — I would guess 30 feet across — and there was this little being in the doorway — very much as she [Constance Morgan] described it. Three-and-a-half to four feet tall, with huge compelling eyes, and he communicated that he wanted me to come in."

Winfrey: "How did he communicate that, and how do you know it was a 'he'?"

Wallis: "I don't know. I had a feeling of a man."

Winfrey asked if the alien's skin was black.

Wallis: "I would call it more than a tannish gray....The door closed behind me, and he asked me — there were two other beings, maybe three inches taller — and they wanted me to get up on the table....They asked me to get up on this table."

Winfrey: "How did they ask you?"

Wallis: "When I argued, they just put their hands on my arms and I was flat on my back on the table. I was absolutely unable to move. I could move my head, but the rest of my body was just paralyzed. They proceeded to take this scraping off the arm."

Wallis reported that the aliens inserted an instrument "with a 2 c.m. metallic burr up into the nostril. And they just sort of generally examined me all over."

Winfrey asked about subsequent abductions.

Wallis replied that the second had occurred when she

was fourteen. She and her brother were returning home from school at about 2:30 in the afternoon when they saw a flying saucer, about half a mile from where the earlier incident allegedly had occurred. She described this UFO as having "a slightly different shape from the first one. And there was one being on the outside who was wearing a sort of coverall ... and he was digging away on the other side."

Wallis continued: "The same fellow who met me at the door the first time was at the door again and he told me I would have to wait until the other one had finished what he was doing, because he could not breathe our air and that's why he was wearing a hood...."

Wallis said the aliens "examined me again....They checked the thing in the nostril."

Winfrey asked if she could feel the "thing" that had been implanted there seven years earlier.

Wallis: "No, I could not. They inserted a long — it looked like a knitting needle — a long probe inside the navel ... rather painful. And he told me they were taking ova — I was 15....They said they were going to see if they could create a hybrid. *And that really upset me!*"

Winfrey asked if she had ever seen her offspring or pictures of her offspring.

Wallis: "It horrifies me. I've had dreams where I'm holding a malformed child."

Winfrey asked how she knew it was not simply a dream.

Wallis: "Well, if you're using five senses, you're usually awake. And I could hear. I could see. I could feel. I could smell, and whatever the other one is."

Winfrey added the fifth sense, "taste."

Wallis: "They gave me a kind of blue thick stuff to drink at one point. When I left the craft when I was eight, he told me I couldn't remember and my thought was, 'I will if I damn well want to.' I have two-thirds recall from that strong effort."

Winfrey asked if she had told anyone about her UFO abductions as a child.

Wallis: "No. My father was of a religious persuasion. My experience had a lot of demons in it, so I wasn't about to put myself in that."

Winfrey asked what such an experience "does to your life." "If you know it's not a dream, do you spend the rest of your days wondering if they're coming back, or why you were chosen?"

Wallis: "Yes, you always have a sense that — they did say they would be back, that there would be things that I would be expected to do."

Winfrey asked if the aliens had told Wallis why they had come.

Wallis: "Well, they wanted the ova."

Wallis went on to say that under hypnosis she recalled that the aliens had shown her a sort of "movie" that gave her a "horrendous feeling of cataclysms on the earth, with people dying all over the place....Under hypnosis I hardly looked at it. It was horrifying to me."

And on that note the interview ended.

A CREATURE SORT OF WHITISH IN COLOUR

Do children experience the mysterious? Are the memories of childhood as recalled in adulthood the material of alien encounters?

This account of alien visitation comes in the form of a letter addressed to Bonnie Wheeler, who for a good many years was the prime mover of the Cambridge UFO Research Group, one of the few Canadian UFO groups that undertook to research and release its findings in its own quarterly bulletins which Wheeler edited.

The letter was written by C.B., a middle-aged woman who at the time was living somewhere in the Maritimes. As a child she lived in Quebec where she had an unusual encounter. She wrote about it in this letter addressed to Wheeler. The letter is dated 4 Sept. 1992.

The contents of the letter are reproduced here with the kind permission of C.B., who wishes to remain anonymous, and with thanks to Wheeler who first drew the letter to my attention and then arranged for me to communicate with C.B.

It is a psychological fact that children sometimes fantasize about "imaginary playmates." Fantasy may be a way of dismissing this lucid recollection; yet, if it is fantasy, it is an incredibly detailed one.

September 04, 1992

Cambridge UFO Research Group
170 Strathcona Street
Cambridge, Ontario
N3C 1R4

Attention: Bonnie Wheeler

Dear Bonnie:

I must state before I commence that I am indeed extremely apprehensive and nervous about this letter but, at the same time, very compelled to send this information to you.

As I stated to you on the phone, I am 32 years old. The events that I am about to recount happened to me at the ages of 8, 9, or 10 in the years 1968, 1969, or 1970 respectively.

During the period from 1965 to Sept. 1970, I lived in Lachine, Quebec. Across the street I played with a girl two years older than myself whose name was J. We became great friends. Both of J.'s parents worked. She had 3 much older siblings ... K. (a boy), H. (a girl), and D. (a boy). Her older brother K., along with the help of his Dad, built a cottage on Lac Lebeau some time prior to my moving to Lachine.

E. and M. (J.'s parents) used to invite me to the cottage almost every weekend in the summer. I was a playmate for J. I enjoyed going there very much and looked forward to the weekends. As young girls, our favourite pastime was swimming, canoeing, boating, water skiing, and swinging on the one swing overlooking the water. To get to the cottage, we had to cross by the boat that belonged to J.'s Dad. The cottage, to my recollection, was partly built on rocks. It was red and white in colour, with miles and miles of wooded area behind it. At that time there were not very many cottages on the lake, and they were sparsely placed. I recall only 3 bedrooms in the cottage. J. and I slept in bunk beds. Her parents had a double bed in the same room. Her older sister and K., one of her brothers, were married and usually occupied the other rooms.

One particular night I woke up to find myself floating out the bedroom cottage window. (I cannot remember if I was sleeping on the lower or upper bunk that particular evening ... J. and I usually took turns.) I was very astonished. In particular, I thought, "Wow, what a neat dream I am having!" My head was turned to the left side. I remember turning it to the right. To my horror and utter amazement, I remember seeing a creature sort of whitish in colour with big, big, black eyes. I was initially scared, and even more so when I slowly floated down toward this creature, facing him eye to eye. I believe, at this particular time, I fell unconscious. The next thing I can consciously recall is that I had a terrible pain in my right ear. So intense was this pain that it caused me to have an excruciating, pounding headache. I felt like my head was going to burst open. I begged God to stop it, but then I thought that this was silly, God would not hurt me. The pain did stop, and I thought, "Oh, thank you." To my surprise, a voice replied, "That was nice." (I will state here that the particular conversation to follow was done through thoughts only. I did not speak out loud, or at least I don't believe I did.) I do not recall the sequence of the conversation and I cannot even be sure of the exactness of this conversation.

"What was nice? You mean ... saying 'thank you'?"
"Yes."
"My parents always taught me to be polite."
"Are you God?"
"No."
"Then you must be Jesus?"
"No. I can see you are disappointed that I am not these particular people. I am from another planet, far, far away from here past the Milky Way.
"Another planet ... oh? What is your name?"
I recall him mentioning his name several times to me, but I could not grasp how to pronounce it. I think it was rather long.
"You will find it hard to pronounce. We do not have an alphabet like you."
I believe he was referring to our phonetic alphabet.
"May I see what you look like? Can I open my eyes?"
"You would only think I am ugly. I would scare you and I do not want you to be scared."
"Then what do you look like?"
"I am rather thin, no hair on my head, pale in colour, very white, large black eyes.
"No hair, pale in colour. You'd better sit out in the sun and get a suntan. How come you have no hair?"
"We are born with no hair. We cannot go out in the sun. It is very bad for our body type. You should not stay in the sun very long either."
"Oh, but I love the sun and suntanning. It is good for the body. I love the water too. You should not say you are ugly ... it's not what you look like that counts but what is in your heart."
Then I sensed another presence in the room. This "voice" seemed to turn away from me, as though he was

communicating with someone else. I heard no conversation.

"Who is with you? Is there someone else here?"

"Yes. My friend, who would be considered a doctor on your planet, and I am a scientist. We are, however, much more advanced than your doctors or scientists. Your heart is only an organ. It is not what is in your heart but your head that makes you feel."

I became confused as this was not what we were taught as children and adults. I changed the subject.

"I do not need a doctor, I am not sick."

"The doctor is examining you."

I remember this conversation continuing. I can recall that he mentioned that I was healthy, both externally and internally, except for one internal part of me that was not correctly placed, but that they would fix it when the time came. (I do not want to mention what I believe they may have fixed.)

I recall him expressing his desire to become very close to me, as close as I was with J. I was edgy and nervous about this and informed him that he could not become as close as J. was with me. He stated the reason why he wanted to become close to me. (I do not wish and cannot now bring myself to recount this reason to you at this point in time.)

He informed me that he had been watching me from the woods that particular day. Maybe it was in the afternoon; it had been a sunny day. (I become confused here. I knew that the sun bothered their skin, because he told me so.) He was fascinated by the ease in which I swam on top of the water, and in particular how I dove underwater and popped up in different locations. It amused him too.

Then I recalled diving under the water and surfacing. I was scaring J. who was lying on a flotation device. I was just having some fun with J., who would laugh and scream with delight every time we played this game.

"Can you swim?"

"No."

"Then I will teach you. I can swim very well."

"I would love to learn how, but we cannot go in water."

"How sad. That is too bad."

"I will be content just to watch you."

I recall him wanting to know what the water felt like on my skin. However, I do not recall having the words or the intelligence to really explain how water feels on the skin. I might have mentioned that the sensation was "so beautiful."

I know at one point that I informed him that I was left-handed and that the majority of people were right-handed. I asked him which hand he used. He stated that they can use both hands equally, that one hand is not better than the other, and that their brains are not divided like ours. I sensed that he meant there was no division.

I recall that he inquired if I ever took walks in the woods. I replied no because I was afraid of bears. They would eat me. I think he asked what bears are, though I am not sure about this. He said that he hadn't seen any bears and that it was beautiful in the woods. He asked if it would be all right if he came and got me from time to time to take me to his home in the woods. (He informed me that his home was not like ours, that it moved and had long rectangular windows to see out of.) I "thought" sure, since he promised me that no bears would hurt me.

I know he liked our woods and thought they were beautiful. I gathered that their planet must be somewhat barren. At this point I believe he took my earring from my right ear as a souvenir. I have pierced ears. He then told me to go back to sleep, at which time I informed him that I did not want to go back to sleep. He insisted that I go back to sleep, and with much reluctance I did.

I know I woke up again, looking at that window, wondering what had happened to me and whether or not it had been a dream. That morning I told M. (I am using his first name, but as a child I used Mr.) about my experience, about floating out the window, seeing the creature with the black eyes, etc. He then laughed and laughed. I became very angry. I don't recall ever being angry with him before. He knew I was angry and inquired about my dream. I said, "You will only laugh. Why do you want to know any more?" He stated that he wanted to know more because he had had a similar dream, except that there were bright lights and that every time he had this dream he felt sick. He inquired if there were any bright lights in my dream. I told him I did not remember bright lights. He told me it felt like he was on a table with bright lights and could see some figures but not their eyes. He could not see the figures clearly.

I told him that his dream was not the same as mine. (I was a child of nine or ten at the time. I did not know what UFOs were; I had no idea that there could possibly be life on other planets. I cannot recall if I had ever heard about flying saucers.)

M. expressed the desire to know more. He asked me to tell him if I ever had any more dreams with creatures in them. I believe there may have been another dream, though I know I never mentioned it to him or to anyone else.

Some weeks later, M. expressed the desire to go walking in the woods. So E., M., J., and I went. (I do not recall liking the idea very much, being nervous about bears that might eat me.) We walked for some time. I would look up through the trees, quite fascinated by the sun's rays as they were reflected by the leaves and the ground.

Eventually we came upon a rather large, burnt area. To my recollection, the area was circular (disk-like) in form. Outside the circular pattern, none of the other trees had been burnt. There was no débris, no signs of trees that were burnt in this particular patch. It was just scorched black. M. became very excited about what he saw, and started discussing this particular burnt patch with his wife. J. went down into the burnt area. M., seeing his daughter in the area, screamed at her to get out of there and stay away from there. I didn't understand why he became so upset with her.

There is one more event that I must mention that also frightened me. One afternoon I was swinging on the swing overlooking the water. I stopped the swing to look at the ground. I believe I was singing or daydreaming. I looked up into the woods and saw a form. It was quite thin. I was not sure about its size, but it seemed to be wearing a dark blue suit that covered its head and went all the way down to its feet. Upon realizing that I had noticed him, this thing quickly hid behind a tree. I stared into the woods just waiting for it to reappear. It did not. I then called out, "Hello." No response. "Hello." No response. "I saw you." No response. I then became frightened. My thoughts were that this thing was going to steal me.

At that time no one else was outside. I ran inside the cottage. E. inquired, "Who were you talking to?" I explained to her what I thought I had seen. I believe she doubted me. M. asked me again to describe what I had seen. I explained again. He asked me if the mask looked like a stocking. I said no, it was like a suit that covered his whole body. They then told me not to go outside.

Later I did go onto the balcony. E. asked M. to check before I could venture down to the swing again. (The swing was not far from the cottage.) I told M. which tree that I believed I saw this particular form near. He looked behind it. There was nothing there. He told me everything was okay. I was still scared. M., upon realizing this, called out into the woods, "You see this little girl. If you touch her I will come after you and if I catch you I will kill you! Do you hear me? I will kill you!"

I was very upset by his tone and turned to M. and asked, "You will kill him?"

"I'll kill him," was his response.

This is all I can remember. If it is truly only a dream, then it is the most unusual dream that I have ever had. In fact, I never remembered a dream in so much detail. This is the only one. I have no explanation, but I remembered this event for some time after, then forgot it for a long period of time. I know it is quite unusual for someone to remember this much after, say, 23 years. I have no explanation to offer you as to why I remember this much. I can understand it if you find these events unbelievable.

These events were very real to me, and I have had great difficulty just passing them off as an extraordinary, unusual nightmare. Their reality is what I think compelled me to recount these events to you. In some way doing so makes me feel better.

Sincerely,
C.B.

Bibliography

THE purpose of this bibliography is to draw the attention of the general reader to previously published books and to articles in magazines and journals devoted in whole or in part to accounts of monsters in Canada. Some representation is given to those giants who act as twin pillars: the Gog of imaginative literature and the Magog of folklore studies. Yet the book's burden lies between them, being memorates, "told-as-true" personal accounts of actual experiences.

The reader who has a special interest in this subject may wish to consult the detailed bibliographies that appear in my "supernatural trilogy," which is comprised of *Mysterious Canada* (1988), *Mysteries of Ontario* (1999), and *Haunted Toronto* (1996), along with the compiler's other contributions to this field of interest, which are accorded a separate listing here.

GENERAL

Atwood, Margaret. "Canadian Monsters: Some Aspects of the Supernatural in Canadian Fiction," *The Canadian Imagination: Dimensions of a Literary Culture*. Cambridge: Harvard University Press, 1977) edited by David Staines.

Atwood, Margaret. *Strange Things: The Malevolent North in Canadian Literature*. Oxford: Clarendon Press / Oxford University Press, 1995.

Bradley, Michael. *More than a Myth: The Search for the Monster of Muskrat Lake*. Toronto: Hounslow Press, 1989.

Casgrain, Henri-Raymond. *Légends canadiens*. Québec: Impr. A. Coté & Cie., 1876.

Clark, Ella Elizabeth. *Indian Legends of Canada*. Toronto: McClelland & Stewart, 1960.

Cohen, Daniel. *Encyclopedia of Monsters*. New York: Dodd, Mead, 1984.

Creighton, Helen. *Bluenose Ghosts*. Toronto: The Ryerson Press, 1957.

Corrales, Scott. "High Strangeness in the High Arctic," *Fate*, January 2003.

Dahinden, René, and Don Hunter. *Sasquatch*. Toronto: McClelland & Stewart, 1973.

Davies, Robertson. *High Spirits*. Penguin Books of Canada, 1982.

Fowke, Edith. *Folklore of Canada*. Toronto: McClelland & Stewart, 1976.

Fowke, Edith. *Folk Tales of French Canada*. Toronto: NC Press, 1981.

Fowke, Edith. *Tales Told in Canada*. Toronto: Doubleday Canada, 1986.

Fowke, Edith. *Legends Told in Canada*. Toronto: Royal Ontario Museum, 1994.

Gaal, Arlene B. *Beneath the Depths*. Okanagan Valley: Valley Review Publishing Ltd., 1976.

Garner, Betty Sanders. *Canada's Monsters*. Hamilton: Potlatch Publications, 1976.

Green, John. *Sasquatch: The Apes Among Us*. Saanichton, B.C.: Hancock House, 1978.

Guiley, Rosemary Ellen. *The Encyclopedia of Ghosts and Spirits*. New York: Facts on File, 1995.

Halpin, Marjorie, and Michael M. Ames, editors. *Manlike Monsters on Trial: Early Records and Modern Evidence*. Vancouver: University of British Columbia Press, 1980. 336 pp.

Heuvelmans, Bernard. *On the Track of Unknown Animals*. London: Hart-Davis, 1958.

Heuvelmans, Bernard. *In the Wake of the Sea Serpents*. Translated from the French by Richard Garnett. London: Rupert Hart-Davis, 1968.

Joseph, Frank. *Sacred Sites: A Guidebook to Sacred Centers and Mysterious Places in the United States*. St. Paul, Minn.: Llewellyn Publications, 1992.

Kirk, John. *In the Domain of the Lake Monsters*. Toronto: Key Porter Books, 1998.

Lambert, R.S. *Exploring the Supernatural: The Weird in Canadian Folklore*. Toronto: McCelland & Stewart, 1955.

LeBlond, Paul H., and Edward L. Bousfield. *Cadborosaurus: Survivor from the Deep*. Victoria: Horsdal and Schubart, 1995.

Mestern, Pat. *Ontario's Only Self-Guided Ghost Tour*. Fergus: Fergus and District Chamber of Commerce, 1994.

Meurger, Michel, and Claude Gagnon. *Monstres des lacs du Québec: Mythes et troublantes réalités*. Montréal: Stanké, 1982.

Meurger, Michel, and Claude Gagnon. *Lake Monster Traditions: A Cross-Cultural Analysis*. London: Fortean Tomes, 1988.

Moon, May. *Ogopogo: The Okanagan Mystery*.

Vancouver: J.J. Douglas Ltd., 1977.

Northey, Margot. *The Haunted Wilderness: The Gothic and Grotesque in Canadian Fiction.* Toronto: University of Toronto Press, 1973.

Owen, A.R.G. *Psychic Mysteries of Canada: Discoveries from the Maritime Provinces and Beyond.* New York: Harper & Row, 1975.

Perkowski, Jan. L. *Vampires, Dwarves, and Witches among the Ontario Kashubs.* Ottawa: National Museum of Man, Canadian Centre for Folk Culture Studies, Mercury Series, July 1972.

Sherwood, Roland H. *Maritime Mysteries: Haunting Tales from Atlantic Canada.* Windsor, N.S.: Lancelot Press, 1976.

Trueman, Stuart. *Tall Tales and True Tales from Down East.* Toronto: McClelland & Stewart, 1979.

JOHN ROBERT COLOMBO

Close Encounters of the Canadian Kind. Toronto: Colombo & Company, 1994.

Closer than You Think. Toronto: Colombo & Company, 1998.

Colombo's Book of Marvels. Toronto: NC Press, 1979.

Dark Visions: Personal Accounts of the Mysterious in Canada. Toronto: Hounslow Press, 1992.

Extraordinary Experiences: Personal Accounts of the Paranormal in Canada. Toronto: Hounslow Press, 1989.

Ghost Stories of Ontario. Toronto: Hounslow Press, 1995.

Ghost Stories of Canada. Toronto: Hounslow Press, 2000.

Ghosts Galore! Personal Accounts of Hauntings in Canada: Toronto: Colombo & Company, 1994.

Ghosts in Our Past: 60 True Ghost Stories from 19th-Century Canadian Newspapers. Toronto: Colombo & Company, 1999.

Haunted Toronto. Toronto: Hounslow Press, 1996.

The Little Blue Book of UFOs. Vancouver: Pulp Press 1992.

Mackenzie King's Ghost and Other Personal Accounts of Canadian Hauntings. Toronto: Hounslow Press 1991.

Many Mysteries. Toronto: Colombo & Company, 2001

Marvellous Stories. Toronto: Colombo & Company 1998.

The Midnight Hour: Canadian Accounts of Eerie Experiences. Toronto: Hounslow Press, 2004.

Mysteries of Ontario. Toronto: Hounslow Press, 1999.

Mysterious Canada: Strange Sights, Extraordinary Events, and Peculiar Places. Toronto: Doubleday Canada Limited, 1988.

Mysterious Encounters: Personal Accounts of the Super-natural in Canada. Toronto: Hounslow Press, 1990.

The Mystery of the Shaking Tent. Toronto: Hounslow Press, 1993.

Singular Stories: Tales of Wonder from 19th-Century Canadian Newspapers. Toronto: Colombo & Company, 1994.

Strange Stories: Weird and Wonderful Events and Experiences from Canada's Past. Toronto: Colombo & Company, 1994.

Three Mysteries of Nova Scotia. Toronto: Colombo & Company, 1999.

True Canadian Ghost Stories. Toronto: Prospero / Key Porter Books, 2003.

True Canadian UFO Stories. Toronto: Prospero / Key Porter Books, 2004.

The UFO Quote Book. Toronto: Colombo & Company 1999.

UFOs over Canada. Toronto: Hounslow Press, 1991.

Voices of Rama. Toronto: Colombo & Company, 1994

Weird Stories from 19th–Century Canadian Newspapers. Toronto: Colombo & Company, 2000.

Windigo: An Anthology of Fact and Fantastic Fiction. Saskatoon: Western Producer Prairie Books, 1992.

Index

Most general references and many specific references that appear in the text are represented in the index. To keep the index of manageable length and of interest to the general reader, important and interesting descriptions are featured. In an entry usually only the first appearance of a name, word, or phrase has been noted. Spellings have been standardized and variations minimized.